Local Officials and the Struggle to Transform Cities

Local Officials and the Struggle to Transform Cities

A view from post-apartheid South Africa

Edited by Claire Bénit-Gbaffou

UCL PRESS

First published in 2024 by
UCL Press
University College London
Gower Street
London WC1E 6BT

Available to download free: www.uclpress.co.uk

A CIP catalogue record for this book is available from The British Library.

ISBN: 978-1-80008-548-0 (Hbk.)
ISBN: 978-1-80008-547-3 (Pbk.)
ISBN: 978-1-80008-546-6 (PDF)
ISBN: 978-1-80008-549-7 (epub)
DOI: https://doi.org/10.14324/111.9781800085466

Contents

List of figures vii
List of tables viii
List of contributors ix
List of abbreviations xiii

1 Introduction: seeing like a City 1
Claire Bénit-Gbaffou

Part I: Seeing the local state through City officials' practices

2 'Welcome to Alcatraz': a reflection on three years in a City bureaucracy 27
Philip Harrison

3 Activists in the State: City officials working behind the scenes for change in post-apartheid Johannesburg 49
Claire Bénit-Gbaffou

4 Bureaucratic activism for inclusionary development in the City of Johannesburg 81
Margot Rubin

5 Entering the state as a community activist: the Operation Khanyisa Movement in Johannesburg City Council 105
Nicolette Pingo and Claire Bénit-Gbaffou

Part II: Seeing the local state from its margins

6 Acting like the state? Leaders' participation in street trade management in Gauteng municipalities 135
Mamokete Modiba

7 Crafting a xenophobic bureaucratic order after the May 2008 pogroms in Cape Town 161
Rodolphe Demeestère

8 The politics of formulating policy on housing evictions in post-apartheid Johannesburg 197
Neil Klug

Part III: Seeing the local state through its policy instruments

9 Identifying learners in Johannesburg's schools: how state rationalities converge to construct institutional xenophobia 233
Jeanne Bouyat

10 Seeing and unseeing: housing, poverty and privilege on Johannesburg's Corridors of Freedom 265
Sarah Charlton

11 Deceptive lenses: officials' and activists' visions of water issues in eThekwini 291
Mary Galvin

12 Lost in translation: the elusive equity objective in Johannesburg's water policy 325
Darlington Mushongera

13 'Doing things right' or 'doing the right thing'? Limits to evaluative thinking in Johannesburg 361
Laila Smith

Part IV: International perspectives on the art of progressive city government

14 Is there a 'left art' of city government? A view from post-apartheid South Africa 387
Claire Bénit-Gbaffou

15 Preserving the progressive City: a North American perspective 419
Pierre Clavel

16 Porous bureaucracies, land and urban inclusion: a perspective from Indian cities 429
Varun Patil and Solomon Benjamin

17 Blurred boundaries and institutional activism: reflections from Brazil 455
Rebecca Neaera Abers

Index 471

List of figures

3.1 Matt's area of intervention: Norwood and the Corridor of Freedom project in Johannesburg 59
5.1 Location of Thembelihle informal settlement 113
6.1 Location of the case study areas in the Gauteng-City region 140
7.1 Eviction letter from the Zanokhanyo Retailers Association in Khayelitsha, 22 August 2008 169
7.2 Letter signed by a representative of the Khayelitsha Somali Retailers Association (KSRA), 28 October 2008 174
7.3 Khayelitsha General Agreement, signed under the supervision of the South African Police Services, 27 November 2008 175
7.4 The Look-Out Hill communiqué, 28 March 2012 183
8.1 Timeline for the formulation of the housing eviction policy 208
10.1 'Notice to vacate' issued to Diane 266
10.2 Small subdivided living space, Louis Botha Avenue 271
10.3 Extract from *Corridors of Freedom: Re-stitching our City to Create a New Future* 274
10.4 Typical retail and residential building along Louis Botha Avenue 277
11.1 Governing the City? eThekwini Municipality and Ingonyama Trust land 294
11.2 Expected versus actual alignment of interests and positions of water stakeholders 317
12.1 Main actants and the respective intermediaries 327
12.2 Environment and Infrastructure Services Department (EISD) – organogram 329
13.1 City of Johannesburg Group Heads administrative structure 373
13.2 City of Johannesburg line functions reporting to the City manager and relevant political portfolios 378
16.1 The squatter settlement at Uru on Gowmala land 435
16.2 The title deed of a squatter in Uru 437
16.3 Regularising informal settlements through a variety of land statuses – Uru and its surroundings 438
16.4 'Electrified tenures' shape urban landscapes 448

List of tables

5.1 Local Government Group: the Operation Khaniysa Movement leadership structure 116
9.1 Three State rationalities underpinning identification at school 243
11.1 Water consumption and payment in eThekwini, 2010 299
11.2 Interest, image and ideology: factors behind the deceptive lenses, for officials and activists 309
12.1 Water service standards in the City of Johannesburg 2015 Integrated Development Plan 340
12.2 City scorecard on specific Integrated Development Plan (IDP) programmes related to water 341
12.3 Oversight bodies for water in the City of Johannesburg 344
12.4 Compared Key Performance Areas for various senior City officials in charge of water (2017–18) 348
12.5 Elements of water service regulation in the City of Johannesburg 352
12.6 Assessing progress in water delivery to Johannesburg's informal settlements 354
16.1 The various state institutions mobilised by residents to produce the Uru settlement over the years (Bangalore) 440
16.2 Varied electrical loads as land tenures schemes for 'unplanned' activities in Delhi 446

List of contributors

Rebecca Neaera Abers, PhD in Urban Planning, is Professor at the Institute of Political Science of the University of Brasília, Brazil. Her research has focused on the politics of institutional change, participatory decision-making, the relations between social movements and the state, and activism inside the policy process. She is the author or editor of four books, including *Inventing Local Democracy: Grassroots politics in Brazil* (Lynne Rienner 2000), and, with Margaret E. Keck, *Practical Authority: Agency and institutional change in Brazilian water Politics* (Oxford 2013). Her recent research explores social movement responses to the pandemic in Brazil.

Claire Bénit-Gbaffou, PhD in Urban Geography and former fellow of Ecole Normale Supérieure (Ulm), is an Associate Professor, Planning in the Department of Geography, Planning, Environment and Development, Aix Marseille University. She is a researcher at MESOPOLHIS (Aix-en Provence), and Visiting Scholar in the School of Architecture and Planning, University of the Witwatersrand, Johannesburg (where she was previously an Associate Professor). Her research focuses on urban governance and spatial justice in large cities, with a particular interest in the governance of public spaces in urban contexts marked by strong inequalities.

Solomon Benjamin is Professor at the Humanities and Social Science Department of the Indian Institute of Technology Madras, India. An urbanist, he explores the situated histories of land tenure as a basis to think about settlement processes. His current interest is the social practices connected to smartphone refurbishing, where small traders connect 'China Bazaars' in Indian cities to Shenzhen. Benjamin is part of the International Critical Geography Association and has been on the editorial board of *Antipode*. He has engaged in critical art practice with various groups.

Jeanne Bouyat, PhD in Political Science (IEP Paris), is a post-doctoral fellow at the University of Johannesburg, Centre for Education Rights and Transformation and previously at University of Oxford, Department of Politics and International Relations. She is a fellow at the Institut Convergences Migrations (CNRS) and at Sciences Po (Paris), Centre for International Studies. Her research looks at xenophobia, nationhood and citizenship in South African schools, with a focus on public administration, political attitudes, pedagogy and activism.

Sarah Charlton, PhD in Planning (University of Sheffield), is Associate Professor in CUBES in the School of Architecture and Planning at the University of the Witwatersrand, Johannesburg and a Research Associate of the Southern Centre for Inequality Studies. After a period working in local government and in the non-profit sector she moved into teaching and research, where her current work focuses on housing policy and practice, state interventions in development, and people's lived experiences of cities. She serves on the boards of the journals *African Studies, International Development Planning Review, and the International Journal on Homelessness.*

Pierre Clavel is Professor Emeritus in the Department of City and Regional Planning, Cornell University. He worked in the field at Blair and Stein Associates doing plans in Cranston, RI, Cape Cod, MA and Binghamton, NY, then did a PhD at Cornell. He taught at the University of Puerto Rico in 1965–67; then at Cornell in 1967–2010. At Cornell, he was director of the Progressive Planning Summer Program (1978–83) and department chair (2001–04). He wrote *The Progressive City* in 1986 and several other books: *Opposition Planning in Wales and Appalachia* (1983); *Harold Washington and the Neighborhoods* (1991 with Wim Wiewel); *Reinventing Cities: Equity planners tell their stories* (1994 with Norman Krumholz); and *Activists in City Hall* (2010).

Rodolphe Demeestère is a doctoral candidate in Political Science, University of Paris I Panthéon-Sorbonne (Centre Européen de Sociologie et de Science Politique – CESSP) and a Teaching Assistant, University of Lille (Centre d'Études et de Recherches Administratives, Politiques et Sociales – CERAPS). His research focuses on the government of urban margins, through the regulation of small trading activities led by diasporic groups in South African cities. Focusing on processes of political contention, social exclusion and economic dispossession, his work analyses the dynamics of institutionalisation of xenophobia in contemporary South Africa.

Mary Galvin, PhD in Political Science (University of California Berkely), is an Associate Professor, Department of Anthropology and Development Studies, University of Johannesburg. She has worked in South Africa's water and sanitation sector since 1994 as a development practitioner, social justice activist and researcher. Her work focuses on local hydropolitics, its impact on universal access to water, and scope for systemic change.

Philip Harrison, PhD in Planning, is the South African Research Chair in Spatial Analysis and City Planning in the School of Architecture and Planning, University of the Witwatersrand, Johannesburg. He was Executive Director in Development Planning and Urban Management at the City of Johannesburg from 2006–10. Prior to that, he held academic positions at the Universities of the Witwatersrand and Natal. He also served as a member of the National Planning Commission from 2010–15, participating in the formulation of the National Development Plan. His current work focuses on urban governance, spatial transformation, and large-scale project investment in African cities.

Neil Klug, PhD in Planning, is a Senior Lecturer and Planner, School of Architecture and Planning, University of the Witwatersrand, Johannesburg. He has also run an urban planning consultancy since 1999. As a practitioner he has covered a wide range of projects from plan preparations, policy formulation and evaluations, project implementation and training mainly related to low-income housing. His current research focuses are on urban governance, specifically around low-income housing policy and implementation.

Mamokete Modiba, PhD in Planning, is a Senior Researcher, Gauteng City Region Observatory, University of the Witwatersrand, Johannesburg. Her PhD investigated the role and influence of street trader leaders in urban governance in three South African metropolitan cities with reflections from Ahmedabad, India. With a background in urban planning, her research spans across a variety of areas including inclusive economies, informal and township economies, urban governance, poverty, inequality and social mobility and spatial change.

Darlington Mushongera, PhD in Planning, is a Senior Researcher, Gauteng City Region Observatory (GCRO). With a background in economics and urban planning, Darlington's research interests span across a number of areas including poverty and inequality, governance, policy planning, and methods of measuring development. His PhD thesis titled 'Who Governs Johannesburg Water? An actor-network reading of water services governance in the City of Johannesburg (2000–18)' explores the mazes of bureaucracy with respect to water service delivery in the City.

Varun Patil is a Sociologist having completed his master's and MPhil in Sociology at the University of Delhi, currently engaged as a PhD researcher at Max Weber Kolleg, University of Erfurt, Germany. He has worked on several research projects looking at the impact of urban renewal schemes and urban governance reforms both at the local community and state level in Bangalore, Jalandhar-Punjab, and Mumbai. As a filmmaker, he is also involved in visual documentation of city transformations in contemporary India.

Nicolette Pingo is a Programme Manager: Inclusive Cities, at the South African Cities Network, South Africa. She was formerly a Development Facilitation Manager at Johannesburg Development Agency, City of Johannesburg, and is a former Master's student at the University of Witwatersrand, School of Architecture and Planning. Her work focuses on participatory approaches to spatial justice for more equitable Cities.

Margot Rubin, PhD in Planning, is a Lecturer in Spatial Planning, School of Geography and Planning, University of Cardiff and is a visiting lecturer at the School of Architecture and Planning, University of the Witwatersrand, Johannesburg, where she was formerly an Associate Professor, South African Research Chair in Spatial Analysis and City Planning. She is also a Research Associate in the Gauteng City-Region Observatory. Currently, she is engaged in research on urban governance in African cities, issues of housing and elite engagement with space in the Global South.

Laila Smith, PhD in Urban Geography, is a Senior Policy Analyst, Climate Change, Policy and Partnerships in the Strategic Policy Branch, Ministry of Agriculture and Agri-Food Canada. She is the former Director of CLEAR-AA, Centre for Learning on Evaluation and Results, Anglophone Africa, School of Governance, University of the Witwatersrand, Johannesburg, South Africa. Laila worked previously as a Johannesburg City official, when she was appointed the Director of Evaluation and Research for the Contract Management Unit within the City Manager's Office of the City of Johannesburg: the unit monitoring the relationship between the City of Johannesburg and its utility entities (such as Johannesburg Water, City Power, etc).

List of abbreviations

ACC	African Centre for Cities
AEC	Anti-Eviction Campaign
AFD	Agence Française de Développement
ANC	African National Congress
ANT	Actor-Network Theory
APF	Anti-Privatisation Forum
ARP	Alexandra Renewal Project
AVCC	Alexandra Vukuzenzele Crisis Committee
BDA	Bangalore Development Authority
BEC	Branch Executive Committee
BPP	Better Buildings programme
BRT	Bus Rapid Transit
CALS	Centre for Applied Legal Studies
CAPEX	Capital Expenditure
CCF	Concerned Citizen's Forum
CCL	Centre for Child Law
CCS	Centre for Civil Society
CDC	Community Development Corporation
CJP	Central Johannesburg Partnership
CLEAR-AA	Centre for Learning on Evaluation and Results for Anglophone Africa
CMU	Contracts Management Unit
COGTA	Cooperative Governance and Traditional Affairs
COHRE	Centre on Housing Rights and Evictions
CoJ	City of Johannesburg
CSU	Corporate Strategy Unit
CUBES	Centre for Urbanism and the Built Environment Studies
DA	Delhi Administration
DA	Democratic Alliance
DBE	Department of Basic Education

DED	Department of Economic Development
DESU	Delhi Electrical Supply Undertaking
DFU	Development Facilitation Unit
DHA	Department of Home Affairs
DLF	Democratic Left Front
DPME	Department of Monitoring and Evaluation
DPSA	Department of Public Service and Administration
DPUM	Development Planning and Urban Management
DSBD	Department of Small Business Development
DSS	Dalit Sangharsh Samiti
DTI	Department of Trade and Industry
DWS	Department of Water and Sanitation, then Water Affairs
ECDOE	Eastern Cape Department of Education
ED	Executive Director
EFF	Economic Freedom Fighters
EHP	Emergency Housing Programme
EISD	Environment, Infrastructure and Service Delivery Department
EMG	Environmental Monitoring Group
EMS	Emergency Management Services
EMT	Executive Management Committee
EWS	eThekwini Water Services
FBW	Free Basic Water
GBF	Gugulethu Business Forum
GCR	Gauteng City-Region
GCRO	Gauteng City-Region Observatory
GEAR	Growth, Employment and Redistribution
GEMTRAP	Germiston Traders Partnership
GDE	Gauteng Department of Education
GDS	Growth and Development Strategy
GJMC	Greater Johannesburg Metropolitan Council
GSPCR	Group Strategy, Policy Coordination and Relations
GWM&E	Government-wide Monitoring and Evaluation
HoDs	Heads of Department
ICHIP	Inner City Housing Implementation Plan
ICPS	Inner City Property Scheme
ID	Identification Document
IDP	Integrated Development Plan
IEC	Independent Electoral Commission
IFP	Inkatha Freedom Party

IHB	Inclusionary Housing Bill
ISD	Infrastructure and Services Department
JCPZ	Johannesburg City Parks and Zoo
JDA	Johannesburg Development Agency
JMPD	Johannesburg Metropolitan Police Department
JOC	Joint Operation Committee
JOSHCO	Johannesburg Social Housing Committee
JPC	Johannesburg Property Company
JRA	Johannesburg Roads Agency
JSIP	Johannesburg Strategic Infrastructure Platform
JW	Johannesburg Water
KIADB	Karnataka Industrial Areas Development Board
KPA	Key Performance Area
KPIs	Key Performance Indicators
KSRA	Khayelitsha Somali Retailers Association
KZNDOE	KwaZulu Natal Department of Education
LED	Local Economic Development
LG	Local Government
LHR	Lawyers for Human Rights
MCD	Municipal Corporation of Delhi
MD	Managing Director
MES	Metropolitan Evangelical Services
MFMA	Municipal Financial Management Act
MLA	Member of Legislative Assembly
MMC	Member of the Mayoral Committee
MoE	Municipally Owned Entities
M&E	Monitoring and Evaluation
MTC	Metropolitan Trading company
NAF	Neighbourhood as Factory
NAFCOC	National African Federated Chamber of Commerce and Industry
NIBDS	National Informal Business Development Strategy
NORA	Norwood Residents Association
NPM	New Public Management
NUSP	National Upgrading Support Programme
OKM	Operation Khaniysa Movement
PFMA	Public Finance Management Act
PPPs	Public-Private Partnerships
PR	Proportional Representative
PSUG	Practices of the State in Urban Governance
PT	Partidos dos Trabalhadores

RD	Regional Director
RDP	Reconstruction and Development Programme
SAPOA	South African Property Owners Association
SAPS	South African Police Service
SASAMS	South African School Administration and Management System
SAWC	South African Water Caucus
SDA	Service Delivery Agreement
SDBIP	Service Delivery Budget Implementation Plan
SDF	Spatial Development Framework
SDS	Students for a Democratic Society
SEEC	Soweto Electricity Crisis Committee
SERI	Socio-Economic Rights Institute
SHRA	Social Housing Regulatory Agency
SLO	Stakeholders Liaison Officer
SMME	Small, Medium and Micro Enterprise
SPLUMA	Spatial Planning Land Use Management Act
SPRE	Special Process for the Relocation of Evictees
TCC	Thembelihle Crisis Committee
TEA	Temporary Emergency Accommodation
TEAP	Temporary Emergency Accommodation Provision Policy
TITRC	Tshwane Informal Trading Committee
TOD	Transit-Oriented Development
TNPD	Tshwane Metro Police Department
TRA	Transitional Residential Accommodation
UDF	Urban Development Framework
UNHCR	United Nations High-Commissioner for Refugees
VN	Viswas Nagar
WFRA	Westcliff Flats Residents' Association
WR&B	Water Resources and Biodiversity
WSR&PD	Water Services Regulation and Policy Development
ZEIS	Zones of Special Public Interest
ZRA	Zanokhanyo Retailers Association

1 Introduction: seeing like a City

Claire Bénit-Gbaffou

At the source of this book

This book was born from three encounters.

The first was with a book: *Reinventing Cities: Equity Planners Tell Their Stories* (Krumholz and Clavel 1994); followed by stimulating engagements with one of its authors, Pierre Clavel, to whom this book is dedicated. *Reinventing Cities*, a collection of constructed and focused testimonies of municipal planners working from inside the state to make cities more socially and spatially just, in the context of post-civil rights movements in North American cities, was possibly the most inspiring planning book I have ever read, and I use it regularly to teach my students. I discovered the book laying inconspicuously on a shelf of the University of the Witwatersrand's library, where I was starting to teach planning students – many of whom would become City, Provincial and State[1] officials trying to rebuild, restructure and transform South African spaces and societies.

Krumholz and Clavel's book was one of its kind: not a developmental nor technical planning manual, not a theoretical nor a normative planning essay with only a remote link to the realities of planning practice (Harrison 2014), and not a critical social sciences text unpacking public policies from their (outside) effects on urban societies. Rather, it engaged with the nitty-gritty of what planning meant for those who initiate it from within a bureaucracy, when driven by a strong objective, a sense of a mission, a cause. It placed the specificities of planning interventions (on affordable housing, collective transport, public space and urban regeneration) into the complex world of administrative rules and processes, fluid politics, shifting media sympathy, uneven social pressure and mobilisation, and the messiness of urban societies. More than any other text I had read, it provided a realistic, rich and deep basis from which to prepare my students for public office and urban intervention, and to reflect on what it means to conduct urban change 'from within the state'.

The second encounter that triggered this book came from my experience, shared with colleagues at Wits University,[2] of action-research with street trader organisations attempting to reform City policy, institutions and practices, towards a more progressive approach to street trading in Johannesburg. This experience, carried out in various degrees from 2010–21, crystallised in the aftermath of the 2013 Operation Clean Sweep in Johannesburg, where the City brutally chased thousands of street traders out of the inner city intervention that was eventually condemned by the South African Constitutional Court as 'inhumane'.

The research team that I coordinated was approached to support street trader organisations with research evidence and ideas so that alternative street trading governance models could be brought to the negotiation table by street trader organisations. We ended up accompanying street trader leadership in many engagements with different parts of the state. Together with traders, we engaged with officials in various City and Provincial departments, senior and junior bureaucrats as well as politicians. In parallel, Wits School of Architecture and Planning was asked by the City to suggest ways forward to govern urban informal economies, a context in which we were able to present and debate some ideas with other municipal officials, and to actively contribute to the policy-making process. This multi-pronged experience highlighted how little we understood of City politics, processes and practices. Public intervention was an arcana in highly fragmented and shifting institutional and political spaces. Policy decisions were 'black boxes' where it was difficult to locate key actors as well as identify key stumbling blocks (Bénit-Gbaffou 2018a). The experience also reflected the limitations of studying social movement, participation processes and the dynamics from the outer borders of the state, to fully understand the actual governance of cities. It revealed the polarisation of academic literature on city government leading to a double shortcoming. On the one hand, radical critique of state local interventions tend to conceptualise 'the state' in unified terms: for the purpose of presenting some of its devastating effects on urban livelihoods and spaces, or analysing urban policy and states as not only inefficient, inconsistent or corrupt, but merely irrelevant, especially in cities of the global South (Amin and Thrift 2016). On the other hand, normative and developmental discourses may have more disaggregated vision of 'the state', but often from a distance and a quite institutional perspective, and are sometimes as ill-equipped as the former approach to make sense of the realities, constraints and actual policy instruments faced by even well-intentioned officials to drive urban change (Mosse 2004).

As a third encounter at the origin of this book, there is the 'post-apartheid moment' in South African Cities and in Johannesburg in particular. It is no coincidence that Krumholz and Clavel (1994) developed ideas on what constitute 'progressive cities', through testimonies of municipal planners, in a particular moment of North American urban history: after the civil rights movement had transmuted into a wave of electoral successes, with Black mayors endorsing hopes for change in several large metropolises. This was a short but intense moment, soon to be curtailed by president Reagan's financial cuts in public spending. It was during Lula's then Rousseff's presidencies that Brazilian scholarship (Abers 2019; Dowbor and Houtzager 2014) explored an original direction in social studies movements under the concept of 'institutional activism' – when social movements' activists won local, regional and national elections, entering government with the explicit mandate, and internal sense of a mission, to change society in particular for the more marginalised. Likewise, the transition out of the apartheid regime, the end of which is more difficult to date (as the African National Congress – ANC is still in power, marred by feuds and scandals and no longer holding its capacity and commitment towards social justice), opened a moment where anti-apartheid activists (and later a younger generation of 'born-free') entered 'the state' as elected officials or as bureaucrats. They did so with the clear mandate, partly self-determined and internalised, of transforming society towards what they saw as social redress and spatial justice. It is the reality of these people, intensely working from local public institutions to 'make a difference' in cities, that this book aims at understanding.

In this context, not only were discourses of social change and redistribution exceptionally explicit, but policy instruments were debated, invented and set up towards this aim. Scholars were largely invited to contribute, intellectually and practically, to urban policy and social reform, in dialogue with activists-turned-officials or officials-with-activism. Some scholars became officials, some officials conducted academic studies, many students trained in universities joined the local state apparatus, sometimes keeping in touch with their former lecturers. All of this contributed to blurring an often rigid boundary and to opening original spaces for debates. Moreover, in this book, many of the contributors have had experience as officials in local government – either as a moment in their academic career, or as movement out of local government towards academia. This inside, experiential knowledge turned into academic knowledge (Bénit-Gbaffou and Williams 2022), also gives the book a specific and original value.

This context as well as the original making of this book induced, and relied on, a position of sympathy with the (few) parts of the state that would open themselves to an academic gaze, implying research methods ranging from critical ethnography to action research; from applied consultancy or activism to more abstract theorisation. This position, close to the people and the realities of the government of post-apartheid urban change, made it difficult for us to align with, but interesting to borrow from, the literature demonising the state on the one hand and the literature celebrating its developmental capacities on the other. Such proximity of academia to urban policy reform and local state practices departs from usual critical social sciences, but capacitates researchers to observe what is otherwise not accessible to their scrutiny (Aguilera 2018; Dubois 2017). Although this positioning always run the risk of blurring academic critical distance and requires constant caution and debate (Moodley 2022), and while this moment was short-lived and exceptional in the hopes, mobilisation, debates and resources unleashed, both elements provide a unique glimpse into (local) 'states at work' that are so difficult to apprehend in usual circumstances (Bierschenk and Olivier de Sardan 2014). Hence, this book largely centred on South African cities, is not written primarily as a monograph, but offers an original look into state practices as they shape cities, echoing other experiences in numerous cities in the world. Testimony to this relevance are the ongoing conversations, threaded in the book, with Indian and Brazilian contexts in particular.

The focus of the book: what municipal governments do to cities, especially when aiming at progressive change

This book interrogates not so much *who* governs the city (Dahl 1961) but *what* in the city is governed (Stone 1995, 2013; Borraz and Le Galès 2010) in contemporary contexts, and, in these sections or portions of the city that are governed or are less governed, *how* government, regulation or management of urban spaces are performed and effected, interrogating the role municipal officials play therein.

It is indeed the role that local public officials (municipal bureaucrats mainly, elected local councillors sometimes) play in urban governance that is at the core of the book. A contested, fragmented, inconsistent, incomplete and messy governance; a role they play not in isolation from the rest of society; but that they built through conflict and compromises, adaptation and iteration – enmeshed as they are in various types of interactions with their own administration, City politics, and social dynamics. But a role in which they have nevertheless a degree of agency, and whose specific actions, practices, tactics and strategies largely fall outside the radar of academic research.

The book interrogates what municipal officials do in the city with a normative question in mind: to what extent is it possible for them to initiate, to support or to drive urban policies committed to social and spatial justice? If there is 'a left art of government' (Ferguson 2011), what does it mean in practice? How is it explored, sought and constructed? This normative question does not only stem from the Johannesburg post-apartheid moment, where the drive towards 'reconstruction' and 'transformation' constituted an explicit thread in public, academic and social debates.[3] It participates in the contemporary quest for 'spaces of hope' using Harvey's term (Harvey 2000), in global and local contexts where global environmental change and the multi-dimensional crises it generates, the rise of violent or non-democratic forces and regimes, the increase of inequalities and social polarisation in an era of continued neoliberalisation, lead to deep pessimism and multiple anxieties. These dark forces are not ignored here, but they are not the book's central object, nor treated as an essential and irredeemable feature of the state and its practices. They are taken as elements of context, constraining, shaping state progressive actions.

Indeed, in the Johannesburg moment, many people working in the municipality have committed their time, energies, sometimes their souls, to try and make cities better places. We do not assess so much in this book whether they succeeded or not. Stories of failures abound: the book tells stories of small victories and half successes, looking at minute rather than structural policy and urban change. It was written at a time where this post-apartheid parenthesis is closed, where South African cities and state are in dire straits. It is a book about officials' explorations, their attempts, half-cooked strategies and fragile tactics. It is about the things that constrain or support their progressive attempts and what their attempts reveal of how Cities work more generally.

This book joins Ferguson (2011) in departing from the necessary but sometimes sterile radical critique of the state; in making neoliberalism or post-colonialism less of an essential feature of the state, its structural core, than an element of context and structure that shape officials' actions without necessarily determining them. It adopts the pragmatic position that state internal practices need to be understood as an instrument rather than *only* as an obstacle to social justice; that power can and should be examined not only as oppressive but also as a creative force. Where so many forces coalesce towards progressive change, in very short-lived moments such as the post-apartheid, or post-World War in Europe, post-civil rights in the US and the Lula government in Brazil, it is relevant to examine in this perspective what and how state institutions work – taking seriously Ferguson's question around what a 'left art of government' might mean.

I use the term 'progressive' in the sense proposed by Clavel (2010) – both simple and powerful: a City, or rather an urban policy that puts forward and pushes both redistribution and democratic participation as its core objectives – two values that generally run counter to market forces (Stone 1995). I chose this term in spite of all its imperfections, the unfortunate echoes with obsolete teleologic or positivist visions of history, confidently equating technical with social progress. Alternative concepts or terms abound, but none has the clarity of Clavel's definition. Analyses in terms of 'Just cities' (Fainstein 2011) or 'justice in cities' (Gervais-Lambony et al. 2014) are interesting contributions, but focus on (difficult-to-define) state of justice to be achieved in different urban and national contexts, rather than on processes actually trying to build more just cities. 'Transformative', 'alternative' policies or 'alterpolicies' (Béal and Rousseau 2014) invoke radical, anti-capitalist or revolutionary visions, often embedded in citizen-led initiatives, democratic experiments, identity or environment-based movements. Both bodies of work build conceptual or practical urban utopias that are very necessary in these times of political disenchantment, but sometimes underplay the importance of class inequality and redistributive policy instruments. None look at internal processes of building 'just' or 'alternative' policies from the inside – from the apparatus of local government.

For this normative enquiry, however, the book does *not* adopt a normative analysis. It observes and, to some extent, accompanies local officials' actual practices: not departing from observing what officials actually do, without slipping towards what they ought to do nor confining our analyses to what they would like to do. It relates their practices to the meaning they build in their actions, without disconnecting these practices and meanings from an analysis of the broader institutional, political, social and urban context in which they inscribe their interventions.

Theoretical and methodological positions: urban governance, state practices, the City and the city

Placing our endeavour in a broader interrogation on urban governance of contemporary cities, we wish to present now what we mean in this book by looking at officials' *practices*, sketch what we understand by *the state* and why we think it is useful to see the *City as a (local) state*. We then stress one originality of this book: the grounding of the policy and institutional analyses in the urban, local space and the materiality of its change.

Lost in translation: urban governance, and the actual government of cities

'Governance' is used in contrast to 'government' since the 1990s, stating that the act of governing is not restricted to public institutions alone, but grounded in the conflict, negotiations, interplays between a much wider range of actors in society. The concept allows for not only expanding the gaze towards non-state actors such as mobilised business or civil society groups, but also opening analyses to a much broader and heterogeneous set of public or para-public institutions. Public institutions are no longer seen as able to drive social change in the city space on their own – even less so in developing societies where poverty is massive, resources are scarce and informal territorial organisations abound in response to state remote presence (Lund 2006). The concept of 'governance' also interrogates public institutions in their own heterogeneity, both internal and between different, sometimes competing or overlapping, state institutions – within a vision of the state whose imagined unity no longer holds.

However, while the institution or set of institutions called 'government' is no longer the only relevant site of observation to understand 'who governs' cities (Dahl 1961), the act of governing cities still requires a specific conceptualisation – which is often, arguably, lost in the translation to 'governance' (Bénit-Gbaffou 2018a). The concept of government in the sense of 'capacity to govern' cities, to steer (Peters 1997), to give a direction that otherwise would not have prevailed in shaping urban spaces and social practices, that is not the direction shaped by unhinged market forces (Stone 1995), seems to have disappeared from academic interrogations on the city. Most governance studies pay more attention to the complex and shifting power network, alliances and *coups*, rather than to what these networks actually do to cities, to urban spaces, to urban lives.

This distraction of energies away from goal-setting, towards alliance and resource-building, is not the prerogative of researchers alone. In an era of expanded social needs and insufficient public resources directed at them, it is also the curse of public officials. They spend a lot of their time looking for resources and partners while overcoming obstacles and responding to emergencies, compiling reports and application to grants for projects that are not their own, and muddling through, rather than elaborating on long- or medium-term strategies to respond to locally-grounded, specific and wicked urban problems (Rittel and Webel 1973) – even if these visions (or preferences) are obviously also shaped by existing and potential resources and alliances (Stone 1993).

This loss in translation could also be explained by the theoretical impossibility of conceptualising a clear policy objective in a multi-levelled governance era, or in the analytical framework of 'governance'. If the processes of decision-making and policy design are fluid and multi-layered, influenced by a diversity of state and non-state actors with differing interests, visions and goals, through iterative, multiple, and entangled processes, policies become political compromises or inconsistent patchworks of various agents' interests, rather than a declaration of public intent, let alone a choice between conflicting values and options (Bénit-Gbaffou 2018a).

This complexification of governance (both in practice and in the research lens) and the difficulty of conceptualising the state's capacity to steer in that context, is reflected in the debates around policy design (Linder and Peters 1987), policy implementation (Winter 2006), development studies (Mosse 2004), and ethnographies of the state (Das and Poole 2004; Bierschenk and Olivier de Sardan 2004; Gupta 2012). It becomes virtually impossible, when reading dominant academic literature, to believe that any policy can be successfully implemented and achieve intended effects. Gupta (2012), for instance, in his bottom-up study of bureaucratic practices in the Indian developmental state, concludes that in spite of good intentions (the welfare and development of the poor), Indian state's policies are intrinsically arbitrary in their outcomes, caught in the web of complex administration, difficult contexts and centrifugal official agencies. Or, if states or development agencies are able to claim 'success' in their policies, it is because they frame the evaluation of their own practices in ways that make policy outcomes look as if they were intended in the first place – actually building narratives on policy objectives from practices, rather than the other way round (Mosse 2004).

We follow Le Galès and Lorrain (2003), Bezès and Pierru (2012), in refusing this position, that is limiting our ability to question and research public policy choices in their relation to social realities. Following Stone, we do not want to give up studying policy goal-setting and political steering as key to the act of governing:

> Governing is active policy making, it is about neither what is settled, nor about broad changes taking shape outside the intentions of policy makers. Governing consists of deliberate efforts to bring about or actively prevent policy changes. It is selective in what is addressed, both in substantive terms (addressing 'this' while not addressing 'that') and in scope (falling in each instance somewhere in a range from tinkering with narrow particulars to efforts to remake large slices of city life) (Stone 2013, 4).

What is illuminating in Stone's view is that the ability for the state (and other agents) to steer cities in particular directions is not conceptualised as a characteristic of 'the state' or 'Cities' as a whole. Stone alerts us to the fact that it might be more useful to look at parts of the state, sectors or areas of the City, at specific moments or under specific urban regimes, to interrogate the capacity to govern. This idea is also explicitly raised by Borraz and Le Galès:

> Do governments always govern? What do they govern, and how? What is not governed? ... Some activities of government take place routinely, such as raising taxes, planning and caring for specific groups. However, most government activities are not continuous. What is governed is a key question and it may change over time. ... Some sectors are heavily governed with dense public policies and laws. By contrast, other sectors are not governed at all or weakly governed (Borraz and Le Galès 2010, 2–3).

It is useful to reframe the question of the government of city, away from a categorisation of a city as a whole (where specific cities would be more governed, or more ungovernable, than others), and away from an assessment of the state as an object (where certain states would be 'failed' and others more successful). The government of cities is rather to be approached through the study of defined sectors of intervention, specific areas in cities, or bounded sections of the state, at particular moments in time, and with various degrees of 'government' (steering) effort, focus and capacity.

It is also helpful to differentiate officials' practices according to the degree of government of their area of intervention. An urban sector or area may be 'fully governed': steered with a policy objective, a direction, with the resources, pressure and oversight that are attached to this level of political prioritisation. It may be rather 'regulated': coordinated, with an attention to mitigate or counter structural disruptive forces (including the excesses of market dynamics). Or it could be only 'managed': a routine and minimal form of daily intervention aimed at avoiding disorder, alternating moments of tolerance or *laissez-faire* and moments of episodic, sometimes brutal, social and spatial ordering.

Investigating officials' practices: paying attention to what municipal officials do and how they work in the City and in the city

This book is interested in what officials (bureaucrats mainly, elected representatives to some extent) *do*, in conjunction or in confrontation with other actors (internal and external to the state), in local contexts and situations, that has a bearing on the way city space works. As highlighted by Dubois (2014) reflecting on Bourdieu's interest for understanding 'the state' through its actions, or by Bezès and Pierru (2012) on the contemporary relevance of studying the state 'through its interventions', this entry allows for going beyond classic, disciplinary and conceptual divisions between state-building and state-formation, state structure and public policies, state and society, administrative and political dimensions of the state. Practically, following Forester et al. (2005) investigating planners' practices, we are more interested in 'what they do', than in 'what they think', 'would like to do', 'are expected to do' or 'say they ought to do', although of course their specific worldviews, imagination, professional training and social norms are encapsulated in their actions. The point is to make use of the particular access we have been able to secure, in different ways, to different parts of the local state,[4] to go beyond studies of public discourses and public policy documents (Bénit-Gbaffou 2018a) on the one hand, and beyond an external observation of state agents as they interact with the public, on the other.

Observing officials' practices reveals institutions, processes and legislations not by the book, but how they actually play out, and are sometimes played by officials. This means following officials in the way they strategise and navigate constraints and opportunities (Krumholz and Clavel 1994) of the triple front of City administration, party politics and society at large. It requires understanding the various policy instruments they use, and how these instruments are constructed, are implemented or side-lined, reformed and contested (Lascoumes and Le Gales 2007). It means identifying patterns and regularities in practices, in order to excavate different types of norms often conflicting with one another. This means only contrasting what officials are expected to do with what they actually do (Olivier de Sardan 2015), but also understanding the many layers of the state that officials need to respond to, and the ways in which they engage with various social groups, and how they are positioned in relation to these (Bourdieu 1993; Dubois 2014), to produce and implement their interventions on the city – at times opening spaces of informality within the state (Bénit-Gbaffou 2018b).

The point is to keep 'the city' in mind when we observe and analyse how bureaucrats work – arguing that both the materiality of urban spaces and their shifting local social dynamics cannot be forgotten at this scale of the state (Magnusson 1985), and that local officials' practices and urban policy change cannot be understood solely in terms of organisational or even field logics (Bourdieu and Christin 1990). In this respect, it is important to stress that, while some chapters analyse street-level bureaucrats regularly interfacing with residents and local spaces (Part 2 of this book), many chapters look at middle-level bureaucrats (and some, more senior bureaucrats), more seldom the subject of academic research due to difficulties of access, and whose link with urban spaces and with residents might be blurred, distant or indirect.

Most of the bureaucrats we have researched in this book are indeed in an intermediary position: understanding the rules of the political and administrative apparatus, but also connected to lower-rank bureaucrats and their difficulties on the ground. Much of the existing anthropological literature focusing on opposition between front-stage and back-stage in bureaucracies is therefore partly ill-adapted (Hahonou and Martin 2019). This intermediary level of bureaucracy is said to be vested with more potential to drive change (Barrier et al. 2015); whether this power is real (Clavel 2010) or illusory (Bourdieu 1991; Jeannot and Goodchild 2011; Laurens 2008); whether the multiplicity of the demands and norms they are entangled in offers them a capacity to negotiate, or puts them in unbearable and constant double-binds leading to either paralysis or schizophrenia. Deepening knowledge on intermediary municipal bureaucrats, we hope to build upon but also complement the interesting anthropology of the state often focusing on bureaucracies at street- or interface-level (Olivier de Sardan 2014; Dubois 2014).

Seeing the City as (local) state, rather than (only) opposed to the State

The term 'the state', for this book, refers to all public institutions considered not as homogeneous or unified, but sharing at least two broad common features, different from any other institution: the mandate to deliver public goods and services, and a form of accountability to the public.

As clearly put by Olivier de Sardan (2014), the state, whatever the political regime and level of development, is expected to deliver public and collective goods and services – a 'delivering state', which is not equivalent to the classic 'developmental state' conceptualised at national level. The nature of these public and collective goods and services varies in space and shifts over time (from territorial, collective and individual security to the wellbeing of the population, as argued by Foucault for modern Europe). In most contemporary cities, it is at the municipal level that access to basic services (water, sanitation, electricity, roads – the list differing depending on national contexts and their level of decentralisation) are generally expected to be delivered, through the production, maintenance, and expansion, of urban infrastructures and networks. 'The state' is therefore, for this book, not synonymous with the national, central state, as opposed to decentralised local authorities. Rather, local governments municipalities are considered part of 'the state' – and this local level of 'the state' is actually the level of the state this book mostly focuses on.

It is to be noted that the dominant political science tradition opposes 'the State' to 'local authorities' and in particular urban municipalities (Le Galès 2020), starting from Weber (1966) who defines 'the City', at least its European medieval incarnation, as framed in an essential confrontation, opposition, rebellion or subversion of national States' emerging sovereignty. More recent work on globalising cities (Brenner 2004) also give central space to this opposition, even if arguing that Cities have become the terrain and the scale of reconfigured State action in a neoliberalising era. This opposition, that possibly conflates national State institutions with the concept of 'the state', is also central for researchers who attempt to 'see[ing] like a city', in reference to Scott's book *Seeing Like a State* (1998). Magnusson (2011), Valverde (2011), Amin and Thrift (2016), who all title their work *Seeing like a city*, argue for a different way of understanding who governs cities, departing from the political notion of 'the state' by which they understand, in a shortcut that we precisely aim at unpacking in this book, an ideal, consistent and unified, national sovereignty.

Of course, there is no doubt that local authorities and central States are in tension when it comes to defining their respective prerogatives, mandates and resources; and that municipalities are not the reproduction at a local scale of central States, as their reduction or their projection – they have their own polity. But we chose in this book not to focus on the City-State relations, as it is only one element, among many, of what officials do when partaking in urban governance. What is more, given the richness of research on 'the state' and its internal workings that have precisely questioned its consistency, unity, ability to govern, and historicised as well as politicised the question of sovereignty as a construct, we find it more useful for our purpose to explore how this blossoming reflection and literature on 'the state' is also relevant to understand 'the City'. We explore what it means to see Cities like (local) states, rather than building from the essential opposition between local authorities and national States. Said differently, we offer to 'see like a City', with a capital C. Unlike Magnusson (2011), who argues that 'seeing like a city' (with a small c) entails looking at all local institutions, public or not, that take the city as their object (that he calls the 'local state' in previous work: 1985). Unlike Amin and Thrift (2016, quoted in Le Galès 2020), for whom 'seeing like a city' means looking at every urban institution except for municipal ones, considered meaningless to understand how cities are actually shaped. They might well be, but it depends on what one seeks to understand in and about cities.

Few authors actually explicitly assume seeing Cities like (local) states. Most do so implicitly (Boudreau 2019), slipping from interrogating state to Cities' interventions (Robinson and Attuyer 2021). Others subsume regional or local government under what they call 'the subnational state' (Parnell and Pieterse 2010; Heller 2019). In this book, we explore what seeing the City as (local) state may mean, and what this opens to, based on a conception of the 'state' as multi-layered, multi-scaled, marked by stark inconsistencies and contradictions or even centrifugal movement, but also by constant efforts, endeavours, attempts, to bring about degrees of consistency and reach.

Coming back to the work of Olivier de Sardan on the state, the specificity of this institution is not only that it embodies citizens' expectations of delivery of collective goods and services. Contrary to Bierschenk and Olivier de Sardan's assumption (2019) that state bureaucracies are organisations like others, state bureaucracies in general, and local state bureaucracies in particular, are submitted to specific sets of norms, over and above those governing conducts in other organisations' bureaucracies. Not only are state bureaucrats part of an administrative hierarchy to whom they need to be responsive and accountable, they are also subjected to pressing political demands that create their own, often informal but nonetheless essential, norms: the need to avoid the discontent not only of administrative managers but also of various political bosses, sensitive to a degree to citizens' claims (Laurens 2008).

Directly or indirectly (depending on their position in the bureaucratic hierarchy), state officials' practices are therefore shaped broadly by a degree of responsiveness to political pressures and social mobilisations that regularly emerge in societies. The dual nature of public authorities (political and administrative), does create specific sets of norms within the state. It is possibly even more the case at the local scale given the proximity of the represented, at least in democratic countries, and the direct visibility of social disorder to local authorities. In democratic countries such as the ones we are engaging with in this book (as imperfect and fragile these democratic regimes may be), this has been framed as two different and essential demands placed on local government, pulling in often different directions (Pierre 1999): a demand for democracy (responsiveness to, interaction with social demands; ability to peacefully resolve social conflicts and distribution of resources) and a demand for efficiency (the ability to deliver public and collective goods and services with a degree of continuity and quality). These are the two essential elements that urban governments are to respond to and to balance differently depending on cities, times and spaces.

Within the truly proliferating and multi-disciplinary literature on the state, and while each book contributor borrowed from different schools of thoughts, we share a double positioning. The first one is a distance towards two equally normative, and polarised, understandings of the state. The state is often depicted as malevolent, manipulative, oppressive, in much of the neo-Marxist and the post-structuralist traditions, radically critiquing its capitalistic (or, now, neoliberal) essence, or its modernist and imperialist (or, now, post-colonial) nature. On the other side of the spectrum, the state is seen, perhaps as a misreading of a Weberian approach, as the driver of development, the grantor of public good, a somehow neutral instrument that needs to be fixed to produce social development: in much of the grey, developmental literature but also in the recent reflections on the developmental state. Our analyses of state practices are located in between these two ideal-types, with an obvious interest for testing the idea of 'the developmental state'[5] at the local level (Parnell and Pieterse 2010), quite prominent in the post-apartheid context, but with the overall awareness, theoretically and empirically-grounded, that both oppressive and developmental rationalities exist simultaneously within the state. Practically, our collective position is also to pay particular attention to the productive dimension of the exercise of power at the city scale, whether its effects are socially progressive or regressive (Ferguson 2011).

A second common position within the book is taking stock of the state's heterogeneity, but not ending there. This heterogeneity of the state has been amply theorised (Das and Poole 2004), in its illusionary nature (Abrams 1988), its elusiveness (Mitchell 2011), its contradictions and messiness (Gupta 2012; de Herdt and Olivier de Sardan 2015), and its multiple limits and incapacities (Murray Li 1985; Gupta 2012). This conceptual deconstruction is paralleled by the actual transformations of the state at the end of the twentieth century, through a double movement, seeking increased efficiency on the one hand and democratisation on the other. Globally circulating (even if locally variegated) neoliberal reforms have largely reshaped the state under the principles of New Public Management, in the name of efficiency and alignment to business logics: multiplying agencies, contractors, delegations to non-state agents to operate and deliver what used to be or was conceived as public services, while the state would be confined to a role of strategic direction and oversight over execution (Hibou 2012). Almost simultaneously, and not always disjointed (even if with opposite ideological inspirations), pressures for democratisation, decentralisation and citizen participation (Heller 2001) have led to a second type of proliferation of state institutions: the emergence or consolidation of other scales of the state and political arenas where public intervention is debated, negotiated or disputed.

In developing countries, this double shift is accompanied by (as much as it also reshapes) another key feature of existing states – their bifurcated nature (Mamdani 1996), inherited from colonial legacies and reproduced in post-colonial societies marked by stark socio-economic contrasts, where heterogeneous systems and modes of government are being framed and reframed for different spaces and different social groups (Fourchard 2018). Attempts at state reform, in particular through international aid, seem to rather expand such bifurcations by creating 'islands of efficiency' (Bierschenk 2014), 'pockets of effectiveness' (Roll 2014) within disempowered bureaucracies, or at least resourced and temporary arms of the state (Dasgupta and Williams 2022), that are partly disconnected from both the rest of the administration, and sometimes from the societies they are supposed to serve (Mosse 2004; Murray Li 2007; Tendler 1997).

To sum up, theoretical shifts outlining the essential heterogeneity of the state are paralleled by empirical trends where state institutions multiply, spread out and take a vast variety of forms that may both expand the state's realm and reach over society, by 'governing by discharge', governing at a distance (Hibou 1999), but also rendering the state far more opaque, disjointed and untraceable.

Despite this literature being key to deconstructing abstract ideas of the state, and enriching the way it can be understood and analysed; stating this heterogeneity and messiness today is not sufficient to define the contemporary state. This statement has even become disempowering for both analysis and political action, invisibilising actual policy choices, erasing ideas of individual and collective agency, let alone democratic accountability; dissolving what remains a very specific object into an overall vision of society marked by complexity and diversity. Sets of heterogeneous state departments and agencies might not, indeed, constitute a consistent 'system'. Even if they do – and it is not to be underestimated, in the gaze of its officials and the citizens defined by its interventions, as well as a myth necessary for social movements and legal action to unfold (Abrams 1988) – they are nevertheless marked by constant and recurrent attempts by political and bureaucratic leadership to reassert authority, control and unity upon them. Hence, the state could be better understood as the permanent and repeated tension between the centrifugal forces of a complex set of departments and state agencies developing autonomy, and repeated attempts from official leadership to (re)assert control and consistency. This chronic (internal) struggle doubles and parallels the (external) struggle of governing societies, in their attempt to escape being governed (Kooiman 2008), particularly where societies are marked by a high level of poverty and informality (Chatterjee 2004; Fourchard 2018), and where state formation is highly conflictual.

Beyond the chronic rivalry between the political and administrative arms of local government (Lodge and Wegrich 2012), a classic focus in public administration literature, the heterogeneity between different departments within a City, with their specific mandates, officials' skills and professional training, appears less theorised. Jones (1995) asserts, for instance, that it is hardly surprising if legal, finance or economic departments are focused on attracting investment and promoting business-friendly policies, while community services, welfare or housing departments are pushing for redistributive policies. Bourdieu offers the metaphor of the 'right' and the 'left hand' of the state (1993), similarly opposing 'regalian' to 'welfare' functions of the state, but complexifying this opposition by adding a vertical dimension, an increasing rift between low and high state nobility; the lower-level bureaucrats anchored in social interactions and sensitive to 'the misery of the world', versus higher-level technocrats disconnected from social needs. For Bourdieu (1993), in a neoliberalising era, the left hand of the state is becoming powerless, increasingly delegitimised and disempowered, and compelled to service the right hand. For Jones (1995), this dichotomy is less contextual, more essential to the state: unity in state intervention is to be constructed by political leadership at the top municipal level, which can mitigate professional, technical and functional rationalities of each department and create consistency to drive municipal interventions. Beyond individual leadership though, specific historical junctures may also provide narratives powerful enough to become common ground throughout state administrations and agencies – the civil rights revolution in the North American cities of the 1970s, the post-apartheid redistributive and transformative ideal in the late 1990s and early 2000s, the participatory and workers democratic moment in Brazil in the 2000s, the contemporary municipalist moment in some European countries (Béal and Rousseau 2014).

Seeing the State in the city, seeing the State from the city, the urban, the local

A specificity of this book is to look at state practices at and from the local scale (rather than the national scale as most ethnographies of the state do), and also, through and around the materiality of the urban spaces they affect. This location of our research at local government level is not arbitrary, nor innocuous.

The local level of government is firstly a space in the state where policy conception and implementation collide – where local councillors and bureaucrats directly feel the impact and social effects of their policy interventions, planning regulation, project development, that their government (at local but also regional and national levels) is driving. Local officials (bureaucrats and politicians) are policy-makers who are also implementers; they are executioners who also have an understanding and often a say on policy and regulations, narrowing the (in)famous 'policy-implementation gap' that is sometimes a misleading shortcut to explain policy failure (Bénit-Gbaffou 2018a). Although the issue of restricted local resources and mandates might curtail their ability to act, the proximity and immediacy of the social effects of public action is theirs to deal with. While this does not necessarily lead to more 'horizontality' and democracy (Magnusson 2011), it gives a particular flavour to their practices in the city, its spaces and its inhabitants. They might be able to directly witness the results of their collective and sometimes individual action, at a scale that also seems within human reach, and therefore adapt or reform it. This gives a sense of possibility and opportunity to officials' practice, in the midst of many constraints and obstacles to effective public action.

The second interest in observing the state from the local scale, and in particular the urban municipal (or metropolitan) scale, is that unlike national or regional scales of public action, the city is the locus of intervention of multiple levels of the state (local, regional and national, sometimes supranational institutions) – where they intersect, coalesce, compete or conflict. The local (and the city) is the space where, more than elsewhere, the complex interface 'on the ground' of different, contradictory or at least heterogeneous public interventions can be seen stemming from different levels, departments and agencies of the state, with uneven attempts or success at coordinating these interventions. For officials in the local state, this may bring both a form of political pragmatism and a variety of avenues for action, that render the study of their practices particularly insightful. It can be argued that the urban context we focus upon, and in particular the metropolitan context, may multiply the resources available, both economically and socially; it may enhance the ability to play within the heterogeneous state, politically use its contradictions, garner political and budgetary support. It raises the potential to rely on a diversified civil society and build a variety of networks, for mobilisation and expertise, in order to pressurise or to support multiple political constituencies at various scales.

Beyond the question of the local scale or level of observation, this book seeks to interrogate state practices in their grounding in, interactions with and effects on a material space, and more particularly urban spaces, at the metropolitan and neighbourhood levels. It shares its grounding in space materiality with other planners and political geographers (Boudreau 2019), yet seeks to keep focusing on the 'black box' of the local state – investigating how it is that municipal officials act upon urban space, and adjust their interventions to the messy and contested implementation of their visions: keeping a view from 'the inside' of the state.

It is an endeavour to taking city spaces as the core object upon which policies, practices and projects act in order to change society. Indeed, it is easy to slip into debates and analyses that lose sight of the materiality of urban spaces and the contextual nature of the practices and policies studied. Such an oblivion is common in state and policy studies, where the complexities of policy processes, institutional apparatus and power networks often result in the leaving aside of the particular spaces and societies upon which they are acting. This endeavour, constantly reminded to authors and brought back in earlier versions of this book, implies first a selectivity in the urban policies and practices observed. With only a few exceptions, most chapters either start with a particular space on which public intervention focuses, or highlight the contextual and spatially-anchored dimensions of the practices and policies analysed. It implies, secondly, to spatialise the analysis of officials' practices, and attempt to ground them in particular spaces and scales, at times in the very materiality of urban landscapes, to understand how the specificities of contexts shape practices, from policy to implementation. What this spatialisation produces is often a nuanced understanding of policies, far from broad-brushed discourses on neoliberal policies or inclusive grand projects; but also of officials' practices, their making and their effects, away from abstract understanding of officials' choices. Officials' practices are linked in fact to very specific, local, contextualised situations which they need to confront and respond to: 'porous bureaucracies' (Benjamin 2004) are also locally-grounded ones, finding echoes and entering in resonance with public discourses displayed at other scales of the state.

A collective experience

This book practically results from a collective research programme, 'Practices of the State in Urban Governance' (PSUG), that I coordinated from 2014–18, supported by the South African National Research Foundation.[6] Based at the Wits School of Architecture and Planning, in the Centre for Urbanism and the Built Environment Studies (CUBES), it brought together about 15 researchers and doctoral students, mostly from the planning discipline but also political studies, in South Africa and in France. The programme's results were built across the years and regularly presented and debated with researchers from France, South Africa, Brazil and India.

One element of this programme worth stressing is that it deliberately invited participants who had worked in South African municipalities, and in particular sought and supported PhD candidates with professional experience in local government, planning agencies or NGOs working therewith. This specificity, with the support of a PhD exchange programme between the Universities of Wits and Sheffield (UK),[7] led to specific reflexions on the articulation between experiential and academic knowledge (central to the planning discipline, but not limited to it), and the specific mentoring that building the latter based on the former required (Bénit-Gbaffou and Williams 2022). While this epistemological analysis is not central to the book, dialogue between the two types of knowledge is reflected therein, with several contributions from former planners-turned-scholars (Klug, Charlton), and from academics with an experience in local government (Harrison, Smith). It also features numerous chapters written by PhD candidates or early career researchers, who framed their thesis topic around the specific focus of the programme – aiming at understanding local officials' practices and visions of the city in order to transform it.

Structure of the book – three combined approaches

The book combines three approaches that structure the book.

The first focuses on officials' agency in local government, observed directly or through their own reflexions, and what this agency reveals of City structure. Such agency is, implicitly or not, studied through the prism of 'institutional activism' (Abers 2019), where officials proactively pursuing a cause and a project (and in so doing, pushing the boundaries of public institutions), reveal through their practice the way governmental institutions work, by navigating its constraints and constructing its opportunities. These officials, mostly belonging to middle and high ranks of the municipal bureaucracy (let alone the case of local councillors, the focus of Chapter 5), are straddling policy and implementation, strategic and operational, political and administrative, realms of intervention – making their experience particularly valuable in understanding how cities are governed.

The second approach interrogates the porosity of the state at City level, and through the crafting of locally specific policy instruments to govern cities, unpacks processes of formalisation of society and informalisation of the state. While it builds on a classic view of the 'state from its margins' (Das and Poole 2004), it is not confined to the lower, street level of bureaucracy, rather following policy circulations between local and national levels of the state. The section excavates how these iterative movements, mutual influences and rescaling processes contribute to state-formation ('a historical process whose outcome is a largely unconscious and contradictory process of conflicts, negotiations and compromises between diverse groups'), but also state-building (a 'conscious effort at creating an apparatus of control') (Berman and

Lonsdale 1992, 5). Its anchoring at the local scale of analysis emphasises the role of situated contexts, to frame (bottom-up) policies and explain the specific echoes (top-down) policies may have in a locality.

The third section analyses state intervention in the city through the internal politics of policy instruments (Uitermark 2005; Lascoumes and Le Gales 2007): deciphering state rationalities and political dynamics through the multi-pronged and contested definition of instruments to intervene on specific urban issues. As New Public Management tends to deprive the state of directly operating in the city, focusing its interventions on delegating and monitoring what agencies, contractors, or other institutions do on their behalf (Hibou 2012), the section reflects more precisely on the construction of knowledge and ignorance in local government, as an increasing part of officials' daily activities seem to be focusing on framing, capturing, monitoring and circulating various data sets, while they lose direct operational capacity, experience and capacity to adjust to local situations. By analysing state rationalities and its politics of knowledge, the section analyses officials' practical capacity to govern cities.

Notes

1 Throughout this book, we refer to 'the State' (capital S) to refer to the national, central institution of the state. 'The state' (small s) refers to the concept. Likewise, 'the City' (capital C) indicates the municipal or metropolitan institution, while 'the city' (small c) refers to the urban area.

2 Available at: https://www.wits.ac.za/cubes/projects/street-trading--urban-governance/. Accessed 23 June 2023.

3 The dominant term for a post-apartheid urbanism was initially 'reconstruction', in reference to the 1994 ANC Reconstruction and Development Programme (RDP), a national policy aiming at constructing public housing and infrastructures in under-resourced and under-equipped segregated areas. Soon, however, and as reference to RDP became scarcer after the national 'neoliberal turn' at the end of the 1990s, the dominant term became the 'transformation' of society and cities – referring to the redistribution of resources from the rich to the poor, but also and perhaps primarily, to the racial change in power, institutions, bureaucracies, political and economic leadership.

4 This question of access obviously introduces a bias, but the multiplicity of types of access to different sections of the state limits to some extent this bias upon which each different contributor was able to reflect. A more general and cross-cutting methodological and epistemological reflection is still to be developed, beyond the scope of this book.

5 In the broader sense (not restricted to the Asian model and its authoritarian state figure) of 'the state' being a key player, although not disconnected from society, in framing and driving developmental objectives.

6 Available at: https://www.wits.ac.za/cubes/projects/practices-of-the-state-in-urban-governance/. Accessed 24 June 2023.

7 The programme, supported by RCUK Newton Fund/NRF South Africa, was titled 'Developing Research Capacity for Inclusive Urban Governance: A Sheffield-Witwatersrand PhD training partnership' (Award Number: ES/N013816/1), and ran from November 2015–April 2019.

References

Abers, R. 2019. 'Bureaucratic activism: Pursuing environmentalism inside the Brazilian State', *Latin American Politics and Society,* 61(2): 21–44.

Abrams, P. 1988. 'Notes on the difficulty of studying the state', *Journal of Historical Sociology* 1(1): 58–89.

Aguilera, T. 2018. 'Gouvernance urbaine et critique dans les métropoles européennes: Une posture méthodologique pour étudier les effets des mouvements sociaux sur les politiques publiques', *Métropoles*. Available at: https://doi.org/10.4000/metropoles.5789. Accessed 23 June 2023.

Amin, A. and Thrift, N. 2016. *Seeing Like a City*. Cambridge: Polity Press.

Barrier, J., Pillon, J.M. and Quéré, O. 2015. 'Les cadres intermédiaires de la fonction publique: Travail administratif et recompositions managériales de l'État', *Gouvernement et Action Publique* 4(4): 9–32.

Béal, V. and Rousseau, M. 2014. 'Alterpolitiques! Politiques urbaines alternatives (1)', *Métropoles* 15. Available at: https://doi.org/10.4000/metropoles.4948. Accessed 23 June 2023.

Bénit-Gbaffou, C. 2018a. 'Beyond the policy-implementation gap: How the City of Johannesburg manufactured the ungovernability of street trading', *The Journal of Development Studies* 54(12): 2149–67.

Bénit-Gbaffou, C. 2018b. 'Unpacking state practices in city-making, in conversations with Ananya Roy', *Journal of Development Studies* 54(12): 2139–48.

Bénit-Gbaffou, C. and Williams, G. 2022. 'Producing doctoral planning knowledge: How professional PhD candidates bridge research – practice divides', *Urban Forum*. Available at: https://doi.org/10.1007/s12132-022-09472-w. Accessed 23 June 2023.

Benjamin, S. 2004. 'Urban land transformation for pro-poor economies', *Geoforum* 35: 177–87.

Berman, B. and Lonsdale, J. 1992. *Unhappy Valley: Conflict in Kenya and Africa*. London: James Currey.

Bezès, P. and Pierru, F. 2012. 'État, administration et politiques publiques: Les dé-liaisons dangereuses: La France au miroir des sciences sociales nord-américaines', *Gouvernement et Action Publique* 2(2): 41–87.

Bierschenk, T. 2014. 'Sedimentation, fragmentation and normative double-bind in (West) African public services'. In *States at Work: Dynamics of African bureaucracies*, edited by T. Bierschenk and J-P. Olivier de Sardan, 221–45. Leiden: Brill.

Bierschenk, T. and Olivier de Sardan, J-P. (eds). 2014. *States at Work: Dynamics of African bureaucracies*. Leiden: Brill.

Bierschenk, T. and Olivier de Sardan, J-P. 2019. 'How to study bureaucracies ethnographically?', *Critique of Anthropology* 39(2): 243–57.

Borraz, O. and Le Galès, P. 2010. 'Urban governance in Europe: The government of what?' *Métropoles* 7: 1–14. Available at: https://doi.org/10.4000/metropoles.4297. Accessed 23 June 2023.

Boudreau, J.A. 2019. 'State theory from the street altar: The muscles, the saint, and the Amparo', *International Journal of Urban and Regional Research 43(3): 405–22.*

Bourdieu, P. 1991. 'Une mission impossible: Entretien avec Pascale Raymon, chef de projet dans le Nord de la France', *Actes de la Recherche en Sciences Sociales* 90: 84–94.

Bourdieu, P. 1993. 'La démission de l'Etat'. In *La Misère du Monde*, edited by P. Bourdieu, 219–32. Paris: Le Seuil.

Bourdieu, P. and Christin, R. 1990. 'La construction du marché: Le champ administratif et la production de la "politique du logement"', *Actes de la Recherche en Sciences Sociales* 81–82: 65–85.

Brenner, N. 2004. 'Urban governance and the production of new state spaces in western Europe, 1960–2000', *Review of International Political Economy* 11(3): 447–88.

Chatterjee, P. 2004. *The Politics of the Governed: Reflections on popular politics in most of the world*. New York: Columbia University Press.

Clavel, P. 2010. *Activists in City Hall: The progressive response to the Reagan era in Boston and Chicago*. New York: University of Cornell Press.

Dahl, R. 1961. *Who Governs? Democracy and power in an American city*. New Haven: Yale University Press.

Das, V. and Poole, D. (eds). 2004. *Anthropology in the Margins of the State*. London: James Currey.
Dasgupta, D. and Williams, G. 2022. 'The creation and withdrawal of spaces for participatory governance: The case of village development committees in West Bengal, India', *Politics and Society*. Available at: https://doi.org/10.1177/00323292221102133. Accessed 24 June 2023.
Dowbor, M. and Houtzager, P.P. 2014. 'The role of professionals in policy reform: Cases from the city level, São Paulo', *Latin American Politics and Society* 56(3): 141–62.
Dubois, V. 2014. 'L'Etat, l'action publique et la sociologie des champs', *Revue Suisse de Science Politique* 20(1): 25–30.
Dubois, V. 2017. 'Policy ethnography as a combat sport. Analysing the Welfare State against the grain'. In *If Truth be Told: The politics of public ethnography*, edited by D. Fassin, 184–202. Durham: Duke University Press.
Fainstein, S. 2011. *The Just City*. New York: Cornell University Press.
Ferguson, J. 2011. 'Toward a left art of government: From "Foucauldian critique" to Foucauldian politics', *History of the Human Sciences* 24(4): 61–68.
Forester, J., Peters, S. and Hittleman, M. 2005. *Profile of practitioners: Practice stories from the field*. Cornell University. Available at: https://courses2.cit.cornell.edu/fit117/index.htm. Accessed 23 June 2023.
Fourchard, L. 2018. *Trier, exclure et policer: Vies urbaines en Afrique du Sud et au Nigéria*. Paris: Les Presses de Sciences Po.
Gervais-Lambony, P. Bénit-Gbaffou, C., Piermay, J-L., Musset, A. and Planel, S. 2014. *La Justice Spatiale et la Ville*. Regards du Sud. Paris: Karthala.
Gupta, A. 2012. *Red Tape: Bureaucracy, structural violence, and poverty in India*. Durham: Duke University Press.
Hahonou, E. and Martin, T. 2019. 'Immersion in the bureaucratic field: Methodological pathways', *Critique in Anthropology* 39(2): 122–38.
Harrison, P. 2014. 'Making planning theory real', *Planning Theory* 13(1): 65–81.
Harvey, D. 2000. *Spaces of Hope*. Edinburgh: Edinburgh University Press.
Heller, P. 2019. 'Divergent trajectories of democratic deepening: Comparing Brazil, India and South Africa', *Theory and Society* 48(3): 351–82.
Heller, P. 2001. 'Moving the State: The politics of democratic decentralisation in Kerala, South Africa, and Porto Alegre', *Politics and Society* 29(1): 131–63.
de Herdt, T. and J-P. Olivier de Sardan (eds). 2015. *Real Governance and Practical Norms in Sub-Saharan Africa: The game of the rules*. Abingdon: Routledge.
Hibou, B. 1999. 'La "décharge", nouvel interventionnisme', *Politique Africaine* 1(73): 6–15.
Hibou, B. 2015 [2012]. *The Bureaucratisation of the World in the Neoliberal Era: An international and comparative perspective*. New York: Palgrave Macmillan.
Jeannot, G. and Goodchild, B. 2011. 'Fuzzy jobs in local partnerships: Case studies of urban and rural regeneration in France and England', *Public Administration* 89(3): 1110–27.
Jones, B. 1995. 'Bureaucrats and urban politics: Who controls? Who benefits?' In *Theories of Urban Politics*, edited by D. Judge, G. Stoker and H. Wolman, 72–95. London: Sage.
Kooiman, J. 2008. 'Exploring the concept of governability', *Journal of Comparative Policy Analysis: Research and Practice* 10: 171–90.
Krumholz, N. and Clavel, P. 1994. *Reinventing Cities: Equity planners tell their stories*. Philadelphia: Temple University Press.
Lascoumes, P. and Le Galès, P. 2007. 'Understanding public policy through its Instruments: From the nature of instruments to the sociology of public policy instrumentation', *Governance* 20(1): 1–21.
Laurens, S. 2008. 'Les agents de l'État face à leur propre pouvoir: Éléments pour une micro-analyse des mots griffonnés en marge des décisions officielles', *Genèses* 3(72): 26–41.
Le Galès, P. 2020. 'A la recherche du politique dans les villes', *Raisons Politiques* 79(3): 11–40.
Le Galès, P. and Lorrain, D. 2003. 'Gouverner les très grandes métropoles?', *Revue Française D'administration Publique* 3: 305–17.
Linder, H. and Peters, B.G. 1987. 'A design perspective on policy implementation: The fallacies of misplaced prescription', *Policy Studies Review* 6: 459–75.
Lodge, M. and Wegrich, K. 2012. 'Public administration and executive politics: Perennial questions in changing contexts', *Public Policy and Administration* 27: 212–29.
Lund, C. 2006. 'Twilight institutions: Public authority and local politics in Africa', *Development and Change* 37(4): 685–705.

Magnusson, W. 1985. 'Urban politics and the local state', *Studies in Political Economy* 16(1): 111–42. Magnusson, W. 2011. *Politics of Urbanism: Seeing like a city*. London and New York: Routledge.
Mamdani, M. 1996. *Citizen and subject: Contemporary Africa and the legacy of late colonialism*. Princeton: Princeton University Press.
Mitchell, T. 2011. 'The limits of the state: Beyond statist approaches and their critics', *The American Political Science Review* 85(1): 77–96.
Moodley, S. 2022. 'Navigating proximity and distance in researching the local state: An insider–outsider perspective', *Urban Forum*. Available at: https://doi.org/10.1007/s12132-022-09474-8. Accessed 23 June 2023.
Mosse, D. 2004. 'Is good policy unimplementable? Reflections on the ethnography of aid policy and practice', *Development and Change* 35(4): 639–71.
Murray Li, T. 1985. 'Beyond "the State" and failed schemes', *American Anthropologist* 107(3): 383–94.
Murray Li, T. 2007. *The Will To Improve: Governmentality, development, and the practice of politics*. Durham: Duke University Press.
Olivier de Sardan, J-P. 2014. 'The delivery state in Africa: Interface bureaucrats, professional: Cultures and the bureaucratic mode of governance'. In *States at Work: Dynamics of African bureaucracies*, edited by T. Bierschenk and J-P. Olivier de Sardan, 399–429. Leiden: Brill.
Olivier de Sardan, J-P. 2015. 'Practical norms: Informal regulations within public bureaucracies (in Africa and beyond)'. In *Real Governance and Practical Norms in Sub-Saharan Africa: The game of the rules*, edited by T. de Herdt and J-P. Olivier de Sardan, 365–98. Abingdon: Routledge.
Parnell, S. and Pieterse, E. 2010. 'The "Right to the City": Institutional imperatives of a developmental state', *International Journal of Urban and Regional Research* 34(1): 146–62.
Peters, B.G. 1997. 'Shouldn't row, can't steer: What's a government to do?', *Public Policy and Administration* 12(2): 51–61.
Pierre, J. 1999. 'Models of urban governance. The institutional dimension of urban politics', *Urban Affairs Review* 34(3): 372–96.
Rittel, H. and Webber, M. 1973. 'Dilemmas in a general theory of planning', *Policy Sciences* 4(2): 155–69.
Robinson, J. and Attuyer, K. 2021. 'Extracting value, London style: Revisiting the role of the State in urban development', *International Journal of Urban and Regional Research* 45(2): 303–31.
Roll, M. 2014. 'The State that works: A 'pockets of effectiveness' perspective on Nigeria and beyond'. In *States at Work: Dynamics of African bureaucracies*, edited by T. Bierschenk and J-P. Olivier de Sardan, 365–98. Leiden: Brill.
Scott, J.C. 1998. *Seeing Like a State: How certain schemes to improve the human condition have failed*. New Haven: Yale University Press.
Stone, C. 1993. 'Urban regimes and the capacity to govern: A political economy approach', *Journal of Urban Affairs* 15(1): 1–28.
Stone, C. 1995. 'Political leadership in urban politics'. In *Theories of Urban Politics*, edited by D. Judge, G. Stoker and H. Wolman, 96–116. London: Sage.
Stone, C. 2013. 'The Empowerment Puzzle: In Pursuit of a New Dimension in Governing the City'. Paper presented at the American Political Science Association Annual meeting, Chicago.
Tendler, J. 1997. *Good Governance in the Tropics*. Baltimore: John Hopkins University Press.
Uitermark, J. 2005. 'The genesis and evolution of urban policy: A confrontation of regulationist and governmentality approaches', *Political Geography* 24: 137–63.
Valverde, M. 2011. 'Seeing like a city: The dialectic of modern and premodern ways of seeing in urban governance', *Law and Society Review* 45(2): 277–312.
Weber, M. 1966. *The City*. New York and London: The Free Press.
Winter, S. 2006. 'Implementation'. In *Handbook of Public Policy*, edited by B.G. Peters and J. Pierre, 151–66. London: Sage.

Part I

Seeing the local state through City officials' practices

2

'Welcome to Alcatraz': a reflection on three years in a City bureaucracy

Philip Harrison

Introduction

I was walking anxiously down the long corridor to the City Manager's office to report for duty on my first day of work when I passed an old acquaintance walking in the opposite direction. 'Welcome to Alcatraz,' he quipped. I was of course glad to see a familiar face but his salutation hardly settled my nerves. This was the start of a short but intense period of my life – around three-and-a-half-years – as a senior official in the City of Johannesburg, with the designation, Executive Director of Development Planning and Urban Management (DPUM).

I had moved in mid-2006 from an academic position as Professor of Urban Planning to the City administration. I had no thought of carrying out 'ethnography of the state' and produced only occasional and sketchy scribbled notes of my experience. I had come to the City of Johannesburg to do a job; to bring what I rather naively imagined were the insights of scholarship to the task of governing a large, complex metropolitan agglomeration that was the economic heart of South Africa but also listed in official rankings as the most unequal city in the world. When I returned to the university at the beginning of 2010, I did not write of my experiences. I needed professional and emotional distance (and a period of recovery).

Implicitly, however, I have drawn continually on my experiences in City administration in further work. My time 'served in Alcatraz' was life-changing, and my preoccupations as an academic shifted towards a better understanding of the materiality of the city I had acted on as a City planner and to addressing questions of governance. A critical question for me remains 'how to make things actually happen' and this has drawn me, for example, to concerns with 'state capability'.

At the same time, however, I have become aware that my slowly fading memories of daily life as a bureaucrat may in fact be a helpful practical and intellectual resource. I am an accidental (or unpremeditated) ethnographer, with my reflections emerging retrospectively from a faulty memory aided partly by a few private notes and some official documents. I learned after leaving the City bureaucracy that, 'states can be anthropologically examined' (Sharma and Gupta 2006, 27). One of the approaches to institutional ethnography is indeed 'spending time on the inside'. This differs from the more commonly deployed 'getting at the inside' using techniques including interviews with organisational actors and textual analysis (Billo and Mountz 2016). In most cases, however, the process is deliberate, with researchers located within institutions as participant observers. In South Africa, this has included the work of the Mistra Urban Futures Programme at the African Centre for Cities (ACC) at the University of Cape Town where researchers have been placed in government offices for agreed periods of time (Lawhon et al. 2012). In this book, Darlington Mushongera writes of the time he spent in the City of Johannesburg for his doctoral research.

In this chapter, I am engaging in a form of retrospective *auto*-ethnography (see also the reflections of Sogen Moodley in this book on his time as an official in eThekwini Municipality). Apart from challenges of memory (and therefore of validation), auto-ethnography raises the following questions:

- what to include (and leave out) in a short account
- how to deal responsibly towards others who appear in the narrative
- how to avoid the temptation to retrofit the past
- how to balance the personal element with explanation and context (Denshire 2014).

Auto-ethnography remains a largely unexplored area of methodological application, and is necessarily experimental.

This account may contribute to an understanding of the City bureaucracy during the period that I was an official. The tricky question, however, is whether it is possible to extract from a personalised narrative of contextually embedded experience meaningful guidance for action by others elsewhere. Purposeful bureaucrats must deploy their 'tactical repertoires' (Ennis 1987) in a complex 'field of action' which includes the intentions and actions of others but also the political apparatus, organisational hierarchy, budgets, managerial prescriptions, regulatory requirements and, less tangibly, the norms, cultures and accepted practices of their institution. In doing so, they draw on a range of resources in the act of practical deliberation including their own stock of knowledge and experience but also the guidance of others, and *perhaps* their knowledge of the experience of others. The value of narratives about other people acting in other places and times remains an open question.

This chapter offers a necessarily limited account of some aspects of my experience in the City bureaucracy. I focus here largely on my work relating to 'inner city regeneration' and 'informal settlement upgrading' as these areas of work raise for me many of the challenges of personal ethical deliberation within the constraining context of a complicated, and, sometimes conflicted, bureaucracy. They also reveal the difficulties of 'making things happen' within such a structure. However, to understand these two areas of work, context is needed, and this is where I begin.

Contexts

The City of Johannesburg

When I arrived in the City of Johannesburg mid-2006, I was impressed with its energy and drive. Preparations for the 2010 FIFA World Cup were gathering momentum: Africa's first Bus Rapid Transit (BRT) system was being implemented as the key legacy project of the games; Soweto was undergoing an impressive facelift; the Alexandra Renewal Project (ARP) was making visible changes in Johannesburg's second township; climate change was being taken seriously; the rate of public housing delivery was around 20,000 units per years; there was the rollout of a package of free basic services for indigent households; and there was a serious initiative to tackle the HIV/Aids epidemic.

This was happening in an administration that was only five years old, having been created at the end of 2000 with the amalgamation of four transitional metropolitan local councils and the previous metropolitan council.

I knew, however, that there was another side to the administration, and I took up my position with some apprehension. The creation of the new metropolitan government had been vigorously contested by labour unions and an alliance of organisations in civil society, mainly because of corporatisation of service delivery. Also the world class aspirations of the *Jo'burg 2030* strategy,[1] launched in early 2002, seemed somewhat incongruous in a city struggling to provide basic livelihoods for the majority of its citizens. Most worrying, however, was the City's inner city regeneration programme which, driven by a desire to bring order to the apparent chaos produced during a tumultuous transition, had resulted in large-scale evictions of the occupants of so-called 'bad buildings'. In July 2006, shortly after I arrived in the City of Johannesburg, the administration was shaken when Judge Jajbhay dismissed the City of Johannesburg's application for an eviction order for the 400 or so residents of the dilapidated San Jose apartment block in Berea. He ruled that evictions without alternative accommodation was a violation of human rights and that the City had failed in its constitutional obligations to proactively address the housing needs of residents in the inner city.[2] This added to my discomfort.

In terms of policy, however, there was progress. A progressively-framed Growth and Development Strategy (GDS) prepared by the Central Strategy Unit in the Mayor's office had been approved by Council, and preparations were underway to bring a negotiated Inner City Charter to a public summit. The first half of the new mayoral term was in fact one of good progress, and of organisational consolidation, but a series of institutional shocks from early 2008 placed pressure on the administration.

In May 2008, there was an outburst of xenophobic violence starting in Johannesburg with a death toll of around 60. The administration, including my own department, was diverted from its core programmes to set up and manage emergency camps for thousands of displaced and traumatised transnational migrants. Although the mayor took a stand against xenophobia, I learned that society and bureaucracy are inter-penetrated, and that the attitudes and tensions of the wider society permeate the bureaucracy.

In September 2008, the Zuma-led African National Congress (ANC) forced the resignation of President Thabo Mbeki, creating a period of political uncertainty and factionalism within the City of Johannesburg. Mayor Masondo survived, although narrowly, but the levels of cohesion and trust which had marked the City administration since 2000 declined sharply.

The collapse of Lehman Brothers in the USA, also in September 2008, went seemingly unnoticed within the administration, and yet it was to have huge consequences for the City. Following Mbeki's instruction at a 'Presidential Imbizo' (general public meeting) in April 2007, the City of Johannesburg had adopted a 9 per cent annual economic growth target but, by 2009, South Africa was in recession. The finance of the city deteriorated at a time when spending on the World Cup stadia was ballooning.[3] The situation was exacerbated by a chaotic billings system with revenue collection rates in the city dropping from almost 98 per cent at the beginning of 2008 to around 86 per cent at the end of the same year.[4] The crisis did much to annihilate the image of Masondo within the mainstream media and among the (mainly White) middle class. As his tenure as mayor came to an end in 2010, Stephen Grootes wrote in the *Daily Maverick* that 'Masondo's really a bit of a dinosaur'.[5] It was an irony that a mayor who had exercised such an impressive hold over his administration and had achieved so much in terms of delivery ended his term in these circumstances.

To understand the context of the administration I inhabited in the period 2006–9, it is necessary to appreciate the personality of Amos Masondo, and the apparent contradictions that surrounded him. Masondo was the product of a brave struggle against apartheid, having spent six years in prison on Robben Island in the late 1970s and a further two stints in detention in the late 1980s. He was known and respected for his work in setting up underground structures of *Umkhonto we Sizwe,* the ANC's armed wing, and establishing and leading civic and trade union movements. As a veteran of the struggle, Masondo had the moral authority to lead a complex administration.

However, he was not a strategic or sophisticated thinker (in the way that his Finance Member of the Mayoral Committee (MMC), and successor as mayor, Parks Tau, was). As mayor, his overwhelming focus was on producing order in the city but this had anti-poor outcomes and led to mounting criticism. Masondo's simple demand for order resonated through the administration in ways that the more sophisticated GDS, for example, could not. The source of Masondo's preoccupation had seemingly something to do with an old-school fear of 'anarchy' (a term Masondo used on various occasions), an aspiration for a post-apartheid city to be recognised for global excellence, and a robust sense of 'human dignity'. The conditions of people living in 'bad buildings', for example, apparently affronting the sensibilities of a man who had framed his struggle against apartheid as a struggle against the indignities of apartheid.

Although Masondo was a forceful presence in the administration, the actions of the City of Johannesburg cannot, of course, be reduced to the influence of a single person. There was, for example, the strategic mind Parks Tau; the progressive influence of the MMC for Planning, Ruby Mathang; the passionate commitment to public transport of MMC Rehana Moosajee; and the technocratic and brusque efficiency of the City Manager, Mavela Dlamini. Perhaps, more important than the personalities involved, were the unavoidable imperatives of governance, some of which were conflicted, creating innate tension within the administration. One imperative was indeed that of 'normalising' the city after a prolonged and traumatic transition. The other was of ensuring financial stability, with the 1997 fiscal crisis in Johannesburg still casting a dark shadow over the administration. Protecting the local tax base meant that a post-apartheid administration paid close attention to the anxieties of the White middle class. Although capital budgets were restructured towards historically Black African townships, the still mainly White suburbs continued to receive disproportionate attention in terms of operational support.

However, there was also an imperative towards meeting the demands of the electorally dominant urban poor, and to visibly responding to apartheid legacies. The 'pro-poor' policies of the city included:

- the nearly universal extension of basic services such as water, sanitation, electricity and refuse removal
- the introduction of a social support package targeted at 250,000 households
- the local rollout of the government's housing programme
- the installation of public transport
- the programme to address the HIV/Aids epidemic.

This mix of imperatives and actions makes glib labelling of the nature of the administration unhelpful. I learned that the City of Johannesburg had to be understood in its complexity, and that the most I could expect in relation to the administration I served was an uncomfortable ambivalence.

The department

I was Executive Director of the DPUM and shared a suite of offices with MCC Ruby Mathang.[6] The relationship between the administrative head of department (the Executive Director) and the political head (the MMC) was in fact never adequately defined, and a source of considerable complexity, and occasional dysfunctionality, within the bureaucracy. Although the Executive Director was formally responsible for administrative matters, serving as the accounting officer for the department, and the MMC was officially there to provide political direction, 'role perception' is another matter (Carboni 2010). The Executive Directors and MMCs in the City of Johannesburg interfaced ambiguously, often crossing the weakly delineated boundaries, with different practices across departments. While the Weberian model may be that the politician decides and the bureaucrat implements, reality is far more complicated, with varying forms and degrees of political-bureaucratic entanglement (Carboni 2010). I was fortunate with the MMCs I worked with and was generally able to negotiate working arrangements.

The bulk of the DPUM was taken up with the administration of development applications (townships, rezoning, building control and outdoor advertising). At one level, this was a highly technical function, but this is a function of enormous importance to the practice of planning, as this is the real interface between planning and the shaping of the city. The system of development management rested on formal, constitutionally protected, property rights but did not accommodate the claims of those who had to access land, accommodation and livelihoods in the city in extra-legal ways.

The first event in the department I attended was a workshop on the enforcement of planning and building control. I was unsettled by an entry into planning through this lens although I came to understand over time that a large proportion of Johannesburg citizenry, across race and class, demanded the regularities that a well-enforced planning system could provide. I shuddered every morning when I opened my email box, knowing that it would be filled with angry emails about contraventions of the planning scheme and building regulations. I tried with limited legal resources to respond. The profound challenge of course was that many individuals, with means to comply, willfully contravened the regulations, but enforcement also affected the lives of many who simply could not comply. Following Brazil's use of Zones of Special Public Interest (ZEIS), we tried to create 'zones of exception' where residents were exempted from full compliance but had to meet basic standards of health and safety. This acceptance of differentiation was, I think, an important step but the inherent tensions remained deep.

The DPUM inherited the separate apartheid-era town planning schemes of 13 previous local authorities. The process of amalgamation started when I was Executive Director around 2006 but it took until early 2019 to complete, largely because the process had to take legal account of pre-existing property and land use rights. Importantly, in this protracted process, there was an attempt to align the strategic objectives of city planning with the technicalities of the scheme. The promulgated scheme included provision for a modest increase in urban densities in the suburbs, a requirement for affordable (or inclusionary) housing, and regulatory reforms making it easier to run a home business. The scheme was met with an outcry with a coalition of resident associations taking legal action against the City (*The Star,* 23 September 2019), but I digress.

There was a much smaller section in planning dealing with strategic spatial planning. When the metropolitan City was established in 2000, it had no overall spatial plan, despite the fact that there were huge pressures for sprawl and spatial fragmentation. The few planners engaged in the task worked energetically and successfully to put a system of strategic spatial planning in place, and to align to it the City of Johannesburg's capital budgeting processes. Importantly, the implementation of new transportation systems – the BRT and Gautrain rapid rail – provided the opportunity for transit-oriented development.

While the general trajectory of strategic spatial planning was well established when I arrived, due to the agency of adept and committed officials led by previous Midrand-planner Herman Pienaar there were remaining challenges. In particular, after years of a sustained real estate boom, there was severe strain on the bulk infrastructure of the city. In my first week of work, I accepted an invitation to an evening meeting in Craigavon on the northern edge of Johannesburg, and here I was held near-hostage until midnight by a crowd of White middle-class residents led by a well-known Democratic Alliance (DA) Member of Parliament who were fuming at continued rapid (mainly townhouse-style) development in an area of extreme road congestion which lacked necessary services such as schools. It was an uncomfortable but formative experience that directed my thoughts towards infrastructure and growth management. When President Mbeki visited Johannesburg in May 2007, and demanded that it accelerate economic growth to 9 per cent per annum, we felt near desperation. We were failing to meet the infrastructural requirements in the growth band of 4–6 per cent per annum, and a doubling was a fearful prospect. However, from this dilemma emerged a Growth Management Strategy that targeted infrastructure investment more efficiently in relation to growth trends, while still addressing the deficiencies of infrastructure in the historically neglected townships and informal settlements. It was a difficult balance. The global financial crisis from the end of 2008 brought the property boom to an end, relieving the growth pressures but also making it more difficult to achieve plans for shaping new growth, especially transit-oriented development.

One contribution I tried to make was to strengthen the deliberative, relational and participatory component of planning. There were already difficulties in this area with a well-intentioned initiative to allow individual communities to prepare their own plans arguably producing further spatial inequality, as it was almost only the wealthier communities that had the resources to do so. I tried to set up forums for ongoing engagement between the DPUM and other departments in the City administration, as well as with provincial government, neighbouring municipalities, civil society organisations, the organised real estate sector, and planning consultants. Here I learned salutary lessons.

Within the administrations, relationships were uneven. The Department of Housing, for example, was tasked with accelerating the pace of housing delivery for the urban poor using subsidies allocated by Provincial government, and this clashed at times with the mandate of our department to achieve a more functional and equitable urban form. We squabbled, for example, over the application of the Urban Development Boundary, a provision in the Spatial Development Framework (SDF) which made it difficult for the Housing department to access cheap land on the urban periphery where housing units could be provided at scale. There were similar challenges around our relationship with the Department of Economic Development which was tasked with facilitating rapid growth, and which was frustrated by the planning frameworks and regulations. The Johannesburg Property Company (JPC) tried to maximise returns on land, chafed at planning's direction on the use of land. It was easier, however, with the Departments of Transport, Environment and Infrastructure, and with the Central Strategy Unit in the Mayor's office, as our objectives and interests largely corresponded.

Relationships with Provincial government in the planning field were complicated by a high-profile court battle challenging the constitutionality of the Development Facilitation Act 1995, which allowed Provincial government to establish planning tribunals to adjudicate development applications. This parallel system of decision-making created enormous complications in achieving the spatial objectives we were pursuing, but taking another sphere of government (one controlled by the same political party as in the City of Johannesburg) to court was an unusual and risky step. Provincial government had its own, more generous, urban development boundary and this also created difficulties, while its Department of Housing was dedicated to the eradication of informal settlements and was clearly suspicious of our initiative to regularise these settlements. The contests were less obvious with neighbouring municipalities but we battled to achieve any meaningful coordination across municipal boundaries. With civil society (that is, built environment NGOs) the problem was a lack of sustained capacity to engage with the City of Johannesburg and our collaborative initiative faltered. The only sustained engagements were with the real estate sector and planning consultants, reflecting perhaps the immediate concern and interest that these players have in the regulatory actions of local government.

As an individual, I was less comfortable with the 'urban management' function of the department than with planning. Urban management was the responsibility of regional directors (RDs) who were located in decentralised administrative offices of the seven (sub-city) regions. In 2000, the regions had been set up as powerful entities performing a range of functions including housing, sports and recreation, community development, and councillor and community liaison. In 2006, however, the regions and their RDs had been effectively demoted.[7] Now, the RDs were reporting to me and the only remaining function was one of 'urban management'. There was a simmering, but understandable, resentment among some RDs at this turn of events, and I was uneasy with the 'passive aggression' that I encountered.

In 2006, urban management was in fact an ill-defined function in the City, relating mainly to the coordination of law enforcement functions (such as the Johannesburg Metropolitan Police Department – JMPD, or municipal police, environmental health, and planning and building control) and monitoring of the performance of the corporatised service delivery entities (including City Power, Jo'burg Water, City Parks, Pikitup and the Jo'burg Roads Agency). Performing these functions required complex relational engagements within the extended City administration. The favoured instrument of coordination was 'the blitz' which brought enforcement officers together in *ad hoc* operations. I was troubled at some of the actions taken during these operations and at the lack of sustainability of sporadic activity like this. However, when I attempted to revise the targets performance scorecards away from the number of blitz-style operations towards outcomes-based measurement of sustained urban quality, I met concerted resistance. For a critical discussion of the use of the 'blitz' by the City of Johannesburg, see McMichael (2015). Regrettably, I was a poor fit for urban management and I required far more than three and-a-half years to make the changes I hoped for.

The DPUM was also responsible for the oversight of area-based initiatives in the city, such as the Alexandra Renewal Project (ARP), Cosmo City and Inner City Regeneration, and special projects such as informal settlement upgrading. Significantly, Soweto, a clear priority for the city, was largely excluded from our coordinating role. Soweto's politics were complex and sensitive, and murky to an outsider such as me. There was, I was told, a base of political opposition to the mayor in Soweto, and this was accommodated by giving Soweto a separate council committee (to which I was never invited). The MMC Mathang was, however, a veteran Soweto politician and gave us the political cover we needed, which included engaging with the Soweto icon, Winnie

Madikizela-Mandela. The ARP was an iconic presidential project led politically by a formidable alliance of politicians, of which Alexandra-born Paul Mashatile was the most powerful. The day-to-day operations of the ARP, however, reported to the City of Johannesburg through the DPUM. The ARP was fraught with contest, with many lines of conflict bedeviling the initiative, but the ARP's Director, Julian Baskin, managed the project 'on his feet' with extraordinary dexterity. Cosmo City was a mixed-income turnkey housing project which represented for me the tensions of creating an ordered environment while also providing opportunities for local livelihoods and income.

The two programmes I wish to detail in a little more are inner city regeneration, and informal settlement regularisation and upgrading. I had a nearly daily involvement with these programmes and they represent for me both the challenges of ethical deliberation and of making things happen in a contested environment.

Inner city regeneration

As explained before, the inner city was a key priority of the executive mayor, and also a site of underlying tension within the administration. For me, it was a source of personal stress and moral dilemma.

By mid-2006, the hard-line positions on the inner city had, in fact, been moderated by the legal action against the city brought to court by the Centre for Applied Legal Studies (CALS), and by negotiations leading to the adoption of the Inner City Charter. Evictions, for example, had slowed as the City was required to provide alternative accommodation, and to negotiate with residents in 'bad buildings'. Nevertheless, the official positions in the Charter and the GDS were often conflicted by the statements of the political leadership in the city. The official position that the inner city would develop in a balanced way to accommodate residents of all social classes (City of Johannesburg 2007) was contradicted at times by Masondo's insistence that the 'inner city is for business'.[8]

Individuals pushed periodically for extreme action, including calling in the army to restore order and using mass evacuation orders. The MMC for Public Safety argued that 'we should go in with the heavy fist' and at one meeting of the Mayoral Committee, the Emergency Management Services (EMS) brought a document to the Mayoral Committee entitled 'Inner City Unsafe Buildings' Evacuation Plan' which argued that the fire chief had the power to order a mass evacuation of the inner city on the grounds of potential fire-related fatalities. When the Mayoral Committee leaned towards supporting such action, MMC

Mathang provided political cover as we argued for a reprieve, asking the political leadership to give an urban management strategy a chance. I worked day and night for two weeks or so with sympathetic colleagues putting together an urban management plan, dividing the inner city into quadrants, and each quadrant into blocks. I worried about what such a rigorous management plan might mean for those who found their livelihood and residence in unregulated spaces but at the time it seemed like the lesser of two evils. I comforted myself also with the Inner City Charter which balanced urban management with interventions in support of inner city housing, job creation, social services including migrant support, and public environment upgrades. Over R2 billion was in fact set aside over a five-year period for upgrading the public environment in the inner city,[9] raised mainly by imposing a special surcharge on ratepayers.

The challenge in practice, however, was that the Charter, approved towards the end of 2007, was implemented extremely unevenly with urban management constantly scoring the highest points in independent evaluations, with housing and economic development doing consistently badly, and community services also lagging behind. The newly appointed RD for the inner city, Nathi Mthethwa, performed his task with precision, setting up inter-agency service delivery teams for each quadrant, and joining with the South African Police Services and National Crime Intelligence in taking action against slumlords and building hijackers. I soon realised that Mayor Masondo had a direct line to the RD, and that many activities in the inner city were outside my purview as Executive Director.

I did, however, chair an early morning weekly meeting of the 'Inner City Discussion and Monitoring Forum Meeting' on behalf of the City Manager in the so-called War Room. This was an inter-departmental forum that attempted to coordinate activities across departments and agencies. For me, it was an opportunity to mediate and balance actions in the inner city, supporting interventions such as an inner city housing action plan, the public environmental upgrade, transitional housing facilities, and child and youth sanctuaries. But, the limited progress we were making with such initiatives was periodically interrupted by hard-line actions such as building and trader evictions, the demolition of informal settlements in the inner city, and large-scale arrests of transnational migrants on loitering charges.

There are at least two occasions seared in my memory. One was the instruction that the mayor gave on a visit organised by the DPUM to demolish an informal settlement that had developed largely hidden from view under electricity pylons on the edge of the inner city. The other was the collapse of a carefully negotiated agreement with Bishop Paul Verryn to relocate Zimbabwean refugees from the increasingly pressurised Central Methodist Church to a new and hopefully better-managed facility. The negotiations had been supported by high profile individuals such as George Bizos and Mary Metcalfe and the logistical arrangement had been made by an inter-governmental committee with the support of the Pretoria-based offices of the United Nations High-Commissioner for Refugees (UNHCR). The rapport with Bishop Verryn was not universally supported in the City of Johannesburg, but it was still a distasteful surprise when the JMPD arrested hundreds of migrants for 'loitering' on the eve of the planned move causing an intractable breakdown in discussions with the church. For an account of what happened, see Kuljian (2013). In both cases, I felt dejected and compromised by not taking a (career-ending) public stand. The ethics of inner city involvement had become increasing fraught for me. I had no doubt of the immorality of these repressive actions, with the ethical question essentially being 'what should I do?'

But, there were many other areas of inner city interventions where I at least felt ambivalence. This included the sort of urban management that the Region F office was involved with, which was clearly improving the visible quality of the inner city but may have been closing down opportunities for livelihood and accommodation. There was also the question for me of what the consequence was of the public environment upgrade programme. The Johannesburg Development Agency (JDA) argued convincingly that the modest investment in public upgrades by the City was leveraging in massive investments by the private sector.[10] This was impressive but with the City's continued failure to put in place a viable inner city housing plan for the urban poor, this real-estate–led regeneration threatened to be displacing and exclusionary.

The inner city remained a source of anguish for me through my time in the City of Johannesburg. It was hard to avoid the conclusion that an administration that was progressive in many respects was failing the poor with its obsessive concern with order in the inner city,[11] even though this concern came at least part from a desire to protect human dignity.

Informal settlements

It is easier for me to write of the informal settlement and upgrading programme, as this was an initiative that represented progressive intentions in the City supported, even championed, by the executive mayor. The bitter pill is that the programme never took root, beaten by opposition – or rather, feigned compliance – from within the bureaucracy.

I came to the City of Johannesburg with the hope of influencing the administration towards the upgrading of informal settlements, but I found that Mayor Masondo had already been urging the administration to give attention to this. For him, granting some form of recognition to households in an informal settlement, even a residential address, was a matter of human dignity. He had been influenced by a reading of Hernando de Soto's *The Mystery of Capital* which argued that with tenure recognition, poor households could leverage their modest assets. Masondo was self-consciously taking a different line from that of the provincial housing MEC, Nomvula Mokonyane, who insisted that the goal should be the complete eradication of informal settlements. However, there was one point on which Masondo was adamant – there was to be no informal settlement in the inner city.

Although the City's political leadership was open to the idea of regularising informal settlements, there was no understanding of how this could be achieved. In 2007, the City of Johannesburg supported my participation in an academic conference in Rio de Janeiro, Brazil, but required me to report to the Mayoral Committee on its value to the City of Johannesburg. The conference was marked by high levels of theoretical abstraction but I used the opportunity to advise the political leadership on the suite of progressive instruments that Brazil had introduced through the Statute of the City 2002, and on the measures that leading cities were introducing to give recognition to their informal settlements, the *favelas*. There was an enthusiastic reception and senior politicians and officials joined me in a subsequent trip to Brazil, early in 2008, to explore approaches to informal settlements more carefully.

On our return, I put together a proposal for the upgrading and regularisation of informal settlement, with technical support from the Urban LandMark Programme. The idea was that by 2014, no informal settlement in Johannesburg would be without legal status, with the Brazilian ZEIS adapted to South African circumstances through the use of amendments to the town planning scheme to give settlements legal recognition and appropriate regulations. I shepherded the proposal through the Mayoral Committee and Section 79 Committee (the multi-party council sub-committee) and to a full meeting of Council where it was unanimously adopted in April 2008. In the opening speech at the Summit on Human Settlements in 2009, Masondo elaborated in detail on the informal settlement programme speaking of regularisation and upgrading as 'part of a bigger programme of restoring the dignity of the people'.[12]

So far, so good, but support from the mayor was not sufficient. Many ward councillors were anxious that informal settlement upgrading was a potential alternative to the provision of RDP housing, and were worried that their constituents would reject the programme. The main opposition, however, came from within the bureaucracy, although all departments and senior officials were ostensibly in support.

I chaired a multi-departmental steering committee on informal settlement regularisation and upgrading to coordinate the implementation of the programme. The committee included a representative of the Provincial Housing Department who was overtly hostile, insisting, for example, that no regularisation should happen in the north of the city, as Provincial government intended to relocate the residents of all informal settlements in this sector to a large new formal development at Lion Park. The City's Department of Housing lent its formal support but made it clear that 109 of the 180 identified informal settlements in the city could not be brought into the programme. The department had other plans for these settlements, mainly involving relocation to new formal housing estates such as Lehae, Lufhereng and Pennyville. This left 71 mainly small and peripheral settlements as targets of regularisation.[13] About 23 of them were apparent candidates for regularisation but little was known about the others, requiring a series of feasibility studies to investigate issues such as land ownership (regularisation of settlement on privately owned land being a tricky matter) and the underlying geology (with dolomite being a particular concern). The steering committee met regularly but there was a continual squabbling over the settlement lists, and departmental responsibilities. The Department of Housing had allies among the RDs who saw their task as containing the growth of informal settlements (they had teams dedicated for this purpose), and who feared that the promise of regularisation would draw in new residents. There were even colleagues in Planning who were ambivalent towards the programme as many informal settlements were peripheral to the city, and their upgrading would hardly assist in creating a more compact urban form. The Infrastructure services and Health Departments, however, welcomed the prospect of regularisation as it would enable them to spend their budgets in informal settlements, which they were then precluded from doing by the illegal status of the settlements.

The programme had a troubled passage through the administration, with some officials and politicians white-anting the programme, even as they gave it their ostensible support. A serious blow came, however, through the budgeting process. With the high-profile support given by the Mayor, I was expecting a substantial budgetary allocation to the programme, but the budget panel was skeptical, especially when housing needs could be met by provincially allocated subsidies without drawing on City's increasingly pressurised resources. A paltry R3 million was provided for the programme in the 2009/10 budget, allowing us only to establish a small unit to coordinate regularisation and undertake a few feasibility studies. We could do little more than experiment with regularisation and upgrading in a few small settlements such as Happy Valley, a previous transit camp where around 30 households still lived in prefabricated housing.

I left the City of Johannesburg at the end of 2009, and was later informed that responsibility for the programme was transferred to the Department of Housing. This was the death knell of the programme. With the Mayor's position weakened and his attention on the FIFA World Cup, there was also no champion for the programme. The collapse of the informal settlement regularisation and upgrading programme was a personal disappointment to me, but a salutary case of how the bureaucracy works. I will never know of course if I could have saved the programme if I had stayed in the City of Johannesburg.

The 'field of action'

The many initiatives and programmes I encountered over a fairly short period left me with many questions around what it takes to achieve success through bureaucratic action. I tried to be a purposeful official trying to do more than simply reacting to the instructions of politicians and the bureaucratic hierarchy. However, real success was often elusive, and working in the City bureaucracy was taking a personal toll. The stress came from at least two sources. First, there were the moral dilemmas I have referred to in the case of inner city regeneration, and secondly there were the bureaucratic struggles I have illustrated through the case of informal settlement upgrading.

The two key elements of the 'field of action' within which I was operating was 'the political' and 'the bureaucratic' (although these were highly interpenetrated). My encounter with the political apparatus was challenging but bracing. By entering the bureaucracy, I had accepted that my actions would be subordinate to democratic processes and outcomes, as represented by the political leadership of the City. But, I was not prepared for the intricacy of the interface between the political and the administrative, and the constant negotiation, adaptation and deliberation required in negotiating this. The simple model of bureaucrats advising politicians on appropriate policy and action, and receiving and implementing political instruction, hardly pertains in the South African context where the interface is ambiguously drawn and where boundaries are porous, roles are negotiated, and personalities count.

I was mainly fortunate in this area but I became aware of many cases of bureaucratic failure stemming from dysfunctional relations at the administrative–political interface.[14] As a bureaucrat, I had to:

- navigate the differences within the political apparatus (discerning the 'will of the people' can be a confusing task)
- confront the whims, quirks, inconsistencies and self-interest of individual politicians
- relate long-term planning to short-term agendas structured by political cycles
- deal with moral dilemmas when political instructions impinged on personal conscience.

I can only write from the perspective of a previous bureaucrat but I am aware of course that the frustrations work both ways, and that the political leadership perceived itself at times to be dealing with a recalcitrant and undermining bureaucracy.

The administrative hierarchy is the second key element of the structure but it is hardly separate from the political. In the South African case many political battles are played out within the bureaucracy and this was the case in Johannesburg although Mayor Masondo did his best to insulate the bureaucracy from direct political involvement in financial allocations, tendering, and decision-making (around development applications). We were fortunate also to have had a City Manager who acted with technocratic proficiently, without pursuing an evident political agenda. However, closer inspection revealed the porous boundary and there were rumours, for example, that ineffectual or bungling bureaucrats were retained in their position because they had political cover from influential politicians.

The administrative hierarchy in the City of Johannesburg was certainly functional, sustained by factors including an elaborate system of performance management with its built-in financial incentives; the efficiency of the City Manager; and a culture of compliance driven in part by fear and blame avoidance. The system operated through the downward transmission of pressure, with the executive mayor placing huge pressures on the City Manager, who relayed this to the executive directors who did the same to their directors, although with different management styles.

However, the operation of the bureaucracy cannot be reduced to the functioning of the hierarchy. It was much more subtle and complex as bureaucracies are also complex networks of real people with personal attachments, antagonisms, obligations, jealousies, resentments, prejudice, egos, ambitions, and more. As Bernstein and Mertz (2011) put it, the bureaucracy 'has an everyday life of its own'. To be an outsider is both an advantage and disadvantage. Initially, I acted somewhat naively of these networks, but having the benefit of not being entangled within them. This, however, changed over time. To act effectively within a bureaucracy requires sensitivity to the 'personal', as much as it requires an ability to manoeuvre within formal structures.

It is impossible to give an adequate account here of the multiple other elements that constrained and enabled individual action. It is necessary, however, to mention the role of budgets, performance management, and tendering and human resource processes. These elements provide stability and a degree of accountability to the bureaucracy but also constrain capabilities for adaptation. Financial processes are tightly regulated through the Municipal Financial Management Act 2003 (MFMA) and monitored by the auditor general. The regulations have no doubt helped in containing creeping corruption but they severely inhibit institutional innovation and adaptive responses. Any new initiative must be budgeted for and this is a complex matter often requiring intense lobbying of the budget panel, and long lead-in times as the draft budgets wend their way through a nearly year-long process. Once budgets are approved, it is difficult to make adjustments.

Performance management offers a similar process. There is a degree of flexibility at the beginning as senior managers negotiate scorecards with the City Manager and the Performance Management and Remuneration Panel, but once indicators and targets have been agreed on, deviations are rarely granted. Although performance management is an important management tool, motivating bureaucrats through incentive to implement the objectives of the administration, it also has perverse effects. Some officials work to the letter of the scorecard rather than responding sensitively to a changing environment. To my annoyance, I had to award 100 per cent on the scorecard to direct reports who I knew were playing the system, and having limited real impact in their work, and far lower scores to those who I knew were working creatively as real problem solvers. Tendering processes was the other challenge. Achieving targets for capital spending, for example, requires careful attention to timing, or various forms of creative manipulation, as tendering processes for a project may take six to eight months, leaving a short period at the end of a financial year for actual expenditure. It is almost impossible to establish innovative partnerships with non-state agents, or even with other spheres of government, given the tight regulatory framework.

Institutional structures and HR processes are also tough constraints. There is a short window after a local government election for institutional reform, but once this is closed there is little space for manoeuvre. I had an unwieldy department to manage with 15 direct reports (a reasonable load may be 4–6) and I knew that this was a serious limitation on my effectiveness. I found a degree of empathy from colleagues, the city managers and politicians, but apparently nothing could be done.[15] Functions of the department changed somewhat over time as new programmes were introduced but it was difficult to adapt institutions due to the difficulties and time-consuming nature of changing organisational structures, post grading and job descriptions, and then advertising and appointing to positions. In the case of the informal settlement programme, we were given ambitious targets for the first year, but a tiny budget for setting up a coordinating unit, with the bureaucratic requirements for doing so requiring at least a year.

The purpose of this discussion is not to extend the Alcatraz metaphor. To be sure, on a bad day, I felt that I was in a cruel prison. But the bureaucracy is not an iron cage and bureaucrats are not helpless prisoners incapable of agency. It is continually morphing in response to multiple internal and external pressures, and bureaucrats are exercising agency in multiple ways. Understanding this agency – including the 'tactical repertoires' of officials – is important if political leadership, for example, is to use the bureaucracy to achieve its objectives.

I found Christopher Hood's book, *The Blame Game: Spin, bureaucracy, and self-preservation in government*, resonant of my experience in the City of Johannesburg (Hood 2010). Hood argues that bureaucrats are continually engaged in a process of blame avoidance, with finger-pointing, buck-passing, risk avoidance, and spinning one's way out of trouble, constant tactics. Elsewhere, Hood writes of the 'creative compliance' of officials. They give ostensible support to directives but white-ant at the same time using tactics such as cheating on scorecards, holding back critical information, direct lobbying of politicians outside the framework of the bureaucratic hierarchy, sowing divisions, and the use of strategic delays (Hood 2002). Importantly, Hood did not write to criticise bureaucrats, making the point only that we need to understand the way bureaucrats operate if we are to be successful with institutional reform. And, of course, there were officials I worked with who acted differently, taking responsibility for their actions, and showing genuine concern for the consequences of their work.

Conclusion

The complexities of action, inaction, success and failure in the bureaucracy are immense and no ethnography or individual experience can illuminate more than a tiny fragment of the bureaucracy during a slice in time. It is difficult to derive helpful generalities, but it is possible perhaps to use narrative and experience to develop critical sensitivities.

I experienced a bureaucracy that was both impressive for its energy, motivation, leadership and progressive policies but disheartening for its inconsistencies, lapses, and regressive actions. I learned that governance in large and complex cities defy simplistic attempts at glib labelling (such as, for example, 'pro-poor' or 'anti-poor'). The City of Johannesburg was, for me, continually mediating diverse imperatives, and was doing so in the context of highly complex entanglements of personal, political and organisational intentions, orientations, and capabilities. In the process there were constant tensions.

The City bureaucracy is not, however, an unknowable morass. Although much remains hidden to observers, and even participants, the bureaucracy has structure, formally and informally, and critical investigation does bring insights.

My time in the City bureaucracy, limited to a few years within a very particular context, has left me with rich experience and enduring scars. It produced within me a kind of cognitive dissonance, even trauma, although my experiences of the bureaucracy were far less distressing, for example, than those recounted by Crispian Olver in his book, *How to Steal a City: The battle for Nelson Mandela Bay, an inside account* (Olver 2017). Importantly, however, it continues to direct my attention to how to make things happen. At the very general level, I know, for example, that much needs to be done to clarify the relationships between the administrative and political spheres; build into the system incentives for innovation and problem solving rather than only for compliance; prod inwardly-focused bureaucracies towards openness and external orientation; reconsider strictures of financial regulation, performance management and tendering; collect and use internally embedded information far more effectively; and so on.

At the level of the individual bureaucrat, however, I know that a translation of the insights gleaned from anthropologies of the state is far more difficult. Contexts, personalities, commitments, and experiential meaning, vary immensely. There is often little alternative but to 'muddle through' as intelligently and strategically as possible, and to go, individually, through the anguish of situated ethical deliberation. However, a body of work of situated narratives, of how individuals have navigated the bureaucracy, may help officials develop the sensitivities and sensibilities that they need to be effective actors in the complex world they inhabit.

Notes

1 Joburg 2030 strategy is a strategic planning document produced by the City of Johannesburg, that has, for its critics, reflected or marked a neoliberal turn of the City of Johannesburg's vision and policies.
2 City of Johannesburg v. Rand Properties (Pty), Residents of ERF 381, Berea Township and Ors (referred to as the Rand Properties case), 2006.
3 The capital budget dropped from R6.4 billion in 2008/09 to a mere R2.5 billion in 2010/11, with annual deficits in excess of R500 million.
4 The dysfunctionality had to do with a complex process of integrating the IT system of previous municipalities that went badly wrong. In 2009, the City of Johannesburg cancelled its contract with Masana Technologies, the company undertaking the task, but the damage to the processes and reputation of the City administration was serious.
5 Grootes, S. 2010. 'Johannesburg deserves better than Mayor Amos Masondo', *Daily Maverick*, 12 March.
6 The Mayoral Committee consists of 10 MMCs, elected councillors selected by the mayor to support its executive team. Each MMC holds a (thematic) portfolio and heads the administrative department attached to this portfolio.
7 The reason for the reshuffle is that the RDs had become politically threatening to the centre with their powers, prompting the mayor to centralise most functions within newly created core departments.
8 Recorded in personal notes.
9 The work was to be undertaken mainly by the Johannesburg Development Agency (JDA).
10 The JDA claimed that there was R8.665 billion planned investment by the private sector between 2007 and 2011, and that this could be directly linked to the R2 billion public environment upgrades.
11 See Rubin's and Klug's chapters in this book (Chapters 4 and 8).
12 Speech by the Executive Mayor of Johannesburg, Councillor Amos Masondo, on the occasion of the Summit on Human Settlements, Nasrec Expo Centre, 25 November 2009, Johannesburg.
13 The labelling of many of these as 'informal settlements' was, in fact, questionable as a number were in fact created by the City or Province as emergency camps or transitional settlements, or were very small clusters of shacks or semi-formal accommodation on scattered sites.
14 In general, relationships worked best when politicians provided political guidance and cover and did not interfere unduly in operational matters, and when officials had no direct political ambition and position.
15 It was only after the local government election in 2011, that the 'urban management' function was separated from 'planning' and the department was restructured to a manageable form. By that time, of course, I had left the City.

References

Bernstein, A. and Mertz E. 2011. 'Introduction: Bureaucracy: Ethnography of the State in everyday life', *Polar: Political and Legal Anthropology Review* 34(1): 6–10. Available at: https://doi.org/10.1111/j.1555-2934.2011.01135.x. Accessed 3 July 2023.

Billo, E. and Mountz, A. 2016. 'For institutional ethnography: Geographical approaches to institutions and the everyday', *Progress in Human Geography* 40(2): 199–220. Available at: https://doi.org/10.1177/0309132515572269. Accessed 3 July 2023.

Carboni, N. 2010. 'Changing relationships between politicians and bureaucrats in contemporary democracies: An empirical analysis of the Italian experience', *International Public Management Review* 11(1): 90–109. Available at: https://ipmr.net/index.php/ipmr/article/view/77. Accessed 14 July 2023.

City of Johannesburg. 2007. *City of Johannesburg Inner City Regeneration Charter.* Available online at https://www.gpma.co.za/files/inner_city_regeneration_charter.pdf.

Denshire, S. 2014. 'On auto-ethnography', *Current Sociology Review* 62(6): 831–50. Available at: https://doi.org/10.1177/0011392114533339. Accessed 3 July 2023.

Ennis, J.G. 1987. 'Fields of action: Structure in movements' tactical repertoires', *Sociological Forum* 2(3): 520–33. Available at: http://www.jstor.org/stable/684672.

Hood, C. 2002. 'Control, bargains, and cheating: The politics of public-service reform', *Journal of Public Administration Research and Theory* 12(3): 309–32. Available at: https://doi.org/10.1093/oxfordjournals.jpart.a003536. Accessed 3 July 2023.

Hood, C. 2010. *The Blame Game: Spin, bureaucracy, and self-preservation.* New Jersey: Princeton University Press.

Kuljian, C. 2013. *Sanctuary: How an inner-city church spilled onto a sidewalk.* Pretoria: Jacana.

Lawhon, M., Taylor, A. and Patel, Z. 2012. 'Co-producing knowledge on urban sustainability through local government-university interactions: A case study of Mistra Urban Futures in Cape Town'. Cape Town: ICLEI State of African Cities Report.

McMichael, C. 2015. 'Urban pacification and "blitzes" in contemporary Johannesburg', *Antipode* 47(5): 1261–78. Available at: https://doi.org/10.1111/anti.12160. Accessed 3 July 2023.

Olver, C. 2017. *How to Steal a City: The battle for Nelson Mandela Bay, an inside account.* Cape Town: Jonathan Ball Publishers.

Sharma, A. and Gupta, A. 2006. 'Introduction: Thinking theories of the State in an age of globalisation'. In *An Anthropology of the State: A reader,* edited by A. Gupta and A. Sharma, 1–42. Oxford: Blackwell Publishing.

3

Activists in the State: City officials working behind the scenes for change in post-apartheid Johannesburg

Claire Bénit-Gbaffou

Introduction

One day, I used the term 'activist in the state' in a conversation with a former student: a young Black man born in a poor family, having defended his master's thesis in urban studies on issues of spatial justice, and who had just found a job in the Western Cape provincial administration, ruled by the Democratic Alliance (DA).[1] When I suggested he had become an 'activist in the state', his eyes brightened and a large smile illuminated his face: surprise, relief, a whole world opening. He said, 'This actually exists? So ... it means I can tell my friends that I am not a sell-out!'

The academic field of social movement studies, but also popular discourse, tend to see working for the state as compromising: being coopted, yielding to power, betraying or losing sight of one's cause. Not without reason, as accusations abound that liberation movement activists have turned into self-enriching elites, and as state-provided job opportunities (direct or indirect) have become one main avenue for economic upliftment (von Holdt 2013), especially in a time of neoliberalisation where contracting out if not outright privatisation has become one dominant mode of service delivery (Miraftab 2004), and even of resource redistribution (Chipkin et al. 2014).

Social movement scientists have theorised why entry of activists into state institutions has been seen with such suspicion. Michels (1911) warns against the 'cruel game' in which institutionalisation leads to the formation of a professional elite that divides the movement and leads to its de-radicalisation. Barker (2001) further links this suspicion to an essential, possibly misled, criticism against individual agency and leadership, in a world of social movement studies celebrating the collective in mass mobilisation. This dominant literature, combined with large and increasing distrust against institutions and the realm of 'politics', have arguably contained and limited research on activism in the realm of state institutions – in spite of some ventures, reemerging today, around the notion of 'institutional activism'. It is this arena that I wish to enter in this chapter, where I propose the exploratory concept of 'activism in the state', as a way to shift our disciplinary gaze away from some of the normative framings of the social movement literature. This concept and this shift are inspired by the grounded realities of 'activism in the state' observed in the post-apartheid City of Johannesburg, that I illustrate by three portraits in practice.

Institutional activism, inside activism, activism in city hall – framing 'activism in the state' in the study of urban governance

Some authors interested in what social movements actually achieve in terms of social and political change (Giugni 1998) started questioning the social movement-state divide (Goldstone 2003), and how 'entering the state' might be part of a long-term strategy for social movement to increase their ability to open up public imagination towards more systemic interventions in terms of policies and public resources redistribution aligned to their cause (Domhoff 2011). Some developed the notion of 'institutional activism' (Santoro and McGuire 1997; Pettinicchio 2012; Abers and Tatagiba 2015), 'inside' or 'insider activism' (Banaszak 2010; Hysing and Olsson 2017), to account for social movement activists who continue to act from a government position:

> An inside activist is an individual who is engaged in civil society networks and organisations, who holds a formal position within public administration, and who acts strategically from inside public administration to change government policy and action in line with personal value commitment (Hysing and Olsson 2017, 6).

One key defining element of institutional or inside activism was the link existing between the activist and social movements or looser civil society networks. This literature documents the complex reframing of the relationship between the activist official and the social movement they belonged to (Abers and Tatagiba 2015), the cultural adjustment activists undergo when they work for the state (Blatrix 2001; Goldstone 2003; Neveu 2011), and the gaps opening between the two types of activists. Abers and Tatagiba (2015), for instance, narrate how one feminist activist working under the Lula administration develops a set of strategies based on her understanding of the internal challenges of passing a progressive legislation and how these strategies are misunderstood and ultimately defeated by social movements' external actions. The interrogation is framed around issues of loyalty to the cause, accountability to the social movement, as well as how the activist-turned-official is able to 'push' the cause, but also needs to reframe it, entering in a world of compromises, possibly compromising the cause in the process.

The activists I am looking at in this paper do not formally belong to such networks: they can be said to be active citizens with strong personal values, but have not necessarily been socialised as activists outside or prior to the opportunity provided by their government job, even if they do have social networks built in particular in universities. This configuration has been analysed some time ago by two specific threads in social movement research, feminist studies (Staggenborg 1988; Katzenstein 1998, 2012; Banaszak 2010; Revillard 2011; Bereni and Revillard 2012) and environmental studies (Boucher and Villalba 1990; van der Heijden 1997; Seippel 2001). This body of work demonstrates how feminist and environmental ideas, policies and institutions were developed thanks to officials who had no particular link to social movements, and who even started developing awareness to the cause when in an official position to act upon it. Institutional activists with limited links to civil society networks are the focus of recent analyses, leading authors to coin other terms differentiating this phenomenon from 'institutional activism': some propose 'bureaucratic activism' (Niez and Krishnamurthy 2013; Abers 2019), others talk of 'governmental activism' (Verhoeven and Duyvendak 2017).

Broadening the definition of 'inside activists' to individuals who do not have strong links to existing civil society networks, severing the conceptualisation of activists from social movements, however, raises a question: how do you define activism, if commitment to a cause is no longer materialised and objectified by collective commitment and networks with a social group? Any public official with a vision for change and some degree of initiative may then be characterised as, or might claim to be, an 'activist'. Rebecca Abers (2019, 23) proposes a useful definition of bureaucratic activism in this perspective, as the 'proactive pursuit of opportunities to defend contentious causes' by workers inside bureaucracies, further defining a cause as:

> a particular kind of idea, one that, from the perspective of believers, needs to be defended against powerful forces of either stability or change. … Being a cause is not an inherent quality of the idea itself (Abers 2019, 24).

This definition illuminates another implicit normative dimension in social movement literature – that social movements and contentious politics are generally assumed to be 'progressive', aligned to broad goals of social justice. Taking away this assumed normative dimension does open other questions: in particular, does it include as 'activists in the state' those who actively drive change from within the state, in the name of exclusionary or identity politics that they see as causes to fight for? Does it mean an activist in the state might include officials actively constructing the neoliberalisation of the state, that they see as triggering progress in service delivery efficiency, and that many do construe as 'progressive' and perhaps even 'contentious', given the level of in-fighting against bureaucratic inertia driving this reform entails? Of course, one might consider that various identity politics or new public management have now become the dominant norm in contemporary societies – so they are not contentious issues anymore; and this is what renders such sweeping reforms of institutions possible. But, could this not be said of what leftists consider progressive reform as well? This doubt cautions against entirely relying on actors' descriptions of their own actions. It requires researchers to still define what constitutes a contentious cause, and identify against which dominant power structures they are fought. In this respect, Clarence Stone (1995), possibly bringing back a degree of normativity, considers that urban leadership (equated to a form of activism in the state in specific positions) consists for a mayor in developing interventions *going against the flow of market forces* – constructing policy instruments that broadly counter, amend or regulate dominant dynamics, those of the market. Contemporary social challenges might, however, call for a finer characterisation of what constitutes dominant forces and contentious causes, in an age of complex neoliberal, populist and identity politics.

Intersecting these interrogations on institutional and bureaucratic activism, urban politics and planning studies have also engaged with this object. It has other, perhaps more explicit, normative assumptions, at least in the field of the planning discipline which explicitly questions 'what should be done', in particular for planners appointed in government positions, who want to, and often are trained to, drive change for social justice. Clavel's 'activists in City Hall' (2010) and his research network on 'progressive cities', Krumholz and Clavel's 'equity planners' (1994), Stone's reflection on urban 'leadership' (1995), Forester's collection of stories of 'deliberative practitioners' (1999) contribute to this reflexion – even if they struggle to be incorporated in broader planning theories that remain poorly informed by the actual challenges of practice (Harrison 2013). These activists are not only part of a 'guerilla in the bureaucracy' (Needleman and Needleman 1974), confronting their hierarchy overtly or covertly to reform state practices, or to more collectively subvert public interventions by appealing to civil society support, pressure and resources. They are actively part of the state apparatus, can work with a degree of support of the institution and are sometimes purposefully appointed for their activist skills, values and ideas to champion reform in newly elected local governments. The articulation between different types of activism (with or against the grain), how one may shift from one to the other, what they have in common and how they differ, remains to be thought. Here, we are considering mostly institutional activists working openly for progressive reform, in (generally short) moments of grace: what could be called 'progressive moments', to nuance Clavel's quest for 'progressive cities', that are indeed difficult to find as they do not subsist for long (Shrock 2015).

Clavel (1986) defines 'progressive cities' (and Shrock defines 'progressive urban policies') as those committed to pursuing both redistribution and participation in their policies, the balance between the two varying according to contexts – opportunities, sector and nature of intervention, identity and skills of the leading activist. This definition complexifies the link between activist officials and civil society networks, beyond deployment or entryism. Often, the civil society networks that institutional activists might call for support are constructed by and through their interventions, rather than pre-existing such action. To some degree, these links with civil society networks are instrumental in supporting policy change (putting pressure on councillors and politicians, through street or electoral politics), rather than essentially providing guiding ideas and values on what ought to be done. Without this mobilisation, Clavel argues, progressive reforms are short-lived (2010), and politicians tend to abandon what are often difficult political moves (a 'difficult dive', as per Stone's metaphor (1995). This is also what scholars argue about the health sector reform in Brazil (Dowbor and Houtzager 2014) they explain politicians' retreat from health reform programmes when seeking their second mandate by the disconnect between the broader, mass and grassroots *sanitarista* movement, and the small groups of professionals and officials actively leading the health system reform within the state. This conceptualisation of civil society mobilisation seen as an instrument to support reform for insider activists assists in further understanding how social movement and state actions are co-constructed. It goes further than what Verhoeven and Duyvendak (2017, 570) construe as a 'division of oppositional labour in which each player [government activist and social movement] focuses on what it knows and does best, and on what is seen by a broader public as a legitimate form of action by that player'. Each player and its resources are not that clearly defined, and co-construct in situated and relational ways their own mandate and the resources they mobilise.

Then, why did I use a new term, 'activism in the state'? This formulation refers to Katzenstein's attention to the *location* of where activism is deployed and what it implies for its *form* (Katzenstein 1998) without assuming that its development 'within the state' necessarily affects its *content* (by de-radicalising it). Secondly, it assists in shifting our gaze from the activists' links to civil society, towards the state apparatus, as central to understand *what it is that activists in the state do*. In this respect, Verhoeven and Duyvendak (2017) call for 'breaking down the state' for better understanding of 'governmental activism'. Yet, it is not enough to only see the state as a set of multiple, heterogenous and centrifugal entities – it would not exist without repeated and iterative attempts at regulating these dynamics and building internal unity and control. The heterogeneous nature of the state is therefore constantly challenged and tempered by a hierarchised bureaucracy animated by political leadership.

Building on this reflection, the emerging field that is being constructed currently globally – quite productively today in Brazilian academia (Abers and Tatagiba 2015; Abers 2019; Clavel 2010; Dagnino and Tatagiba 2010; Dowbor and Houtzager 2014; Rubin 2021), offers three promising directions. Firstly, an interrogation on activists in the state's specific values, actual practices, and strategies, following social movements' concepts of resources, repertoires, and framings (McAdam et al. 1996). Secondly, an exploration of the effects of these practices on policy change (discourses and norms, projects, plans, policies, institutions), a less developed and more arduous analysis (Giugni 1998). Thirdly, a line of research around what activists' practices reveal of (and also how they potentially reshape) state structures, normative constraints and opportunities for change. In this respect, it is useful to ask directly, using Verhoeven and Duyvendak's expression (2017): what is it that activists in the state 'know and do best'? Rather than assuming it is a given, I would like to keep this as a driving question – including the consideration that officials also learn to navigate state institutions and to build a strategic balance with civil society networks, mostly through trial and errors, as in any political game.

I find it productive to borrow from the literature on policy instrumentation, and the work developed by Lascoumes and Le Galès (2007) on 'governing through instruments', inspired by Foucault. They posit policy instrument as political constructions whose genealogy is important to study, both to understand the conflicted rationalities that they brought together (in the state and outside the state), and to analyse what it is they do in society – encapsulating not only their 'impact' (planned and unforeseen material effects), but also what vision of society and social relations they naturalise. I argue, in this chapter, that a major difference between activists in the state and activists outside the state is the former's focus on building policy instruments aligning to the cause they have chosen to defend or to drive from their institutional position. They actually do so more often in reaction to the opportunity opened by such a position, than from a long-standing expertise or sector-specific ideological drive (or perhaps, in the encounter between the two). Social movements' activists will gauge their success in their ability to mobilise large sections of society (direct constituencies and the public at large); to influence public debate and transform a social issue into a 'public problem' or reframe an existing 'public problem'; to get public visibility to the point governments are compelled to engage, to backtrack, if not to change their policy. Activists in the state will focus their effort primarily in altering or crafting policy instruments, as this is how government works – both as an opportunity and a constraint. They will attempt to change dominant policy and bureaucratic norms, institutions, categorisation and discourses; construct projects, plans, frameworks, policies and find ways of having them adopted, budgeted and implemented, in line with the cause they are driving – be it affordable housing and desegregation, inclusive public space, extension of public services to the most marginal urban areas. Paying particular attention to the politics of the framing of instruments, in their technical and narrow details, assists in illuminating what activists in the state actually do.

Furthermore, as argued in previous work (Bénit-Gbaffou 2018a), it is not one single policy instrument that one needs to look at, but a set of instruments working together towards changing a whole sector of intervention in the city. The work of an activist in the state does not stop at passing a policy and its by-law – it also involves finding a budget, partners and resources; inscribing the new policy direction in the diverse departments that are involved in its implementation; and developing the practical tools for each of these departments to actualise this new direction. Actually developing these other instruments might be a requirement for passing new City policies. That echoes with Katzenstein's definition of 'institutionalisation' (1998): creating new norms within the complex, heterogeneous, fragmented state institution. This leads to another point I wish to make in this chapter, about which 'activists in the state' I am interested in – a dimension we lose by shifting from 'city hall' to 'the state' in naming these activists: that is the city, and the value of the 'local' as the locus of immediate confrontation between policy and its implementation, and where the interventions of several levels of the state (national, regional, local) are intertwined and made visible.

What made this research possible

This chapter relies on individual portraits and narratives of officials working in the City in post-apartheid Johannesburg. These officials were all in intermediary positions – neither street-level bureaucrats nor senior officials, a position that is arguably key for imagining and practically conducting change in organisations (Chiha 2006). I engaged a conversation with these officials about one key initiative, project or goal they had been working towards while working in the City administration.

The narratives took the form of recorded and transcribed interviews but also informal conversations, in the context of long-standing engagement mixing focused research (in particular, on issues of public space, and parks' management) and personal relationships (some of these officials being former students in the Wits School of Architecture and Planning). The interviews and conversations were further contextualised and complemented through the use of three other methods.

Firstly, complementary research was conducted, partly through coordinating students' research around the projects mentioned by activists (Bosaka 2015; Daniel and Foto 2016; Memela and Nyanda 2016; Molema 2016; Laures 2017; Mogkere 2018). Complementary sources were gathered to give background to the projects narrated by the interviewees.

Secondly, before proceeding to the interview, I involved myself in parts of the project mentioned by the activist interviewed: workshopping research results, strategically framing these results for different platforms around specific stakes, debating and jointly framing content, together with the activist in the state (in various degrees, depending on opportunity and need: high with Ayanda, medium with Matt, low with Nikki). This research-action process – jointly strategising with the activist I was portraying – has been illuminating: learning by doing some of the 'tricks of the trade', the ways things can be done or actually work but also better understanding the context, the challenges and fault-lines in institutions, and learning how to handle them through trial and error.

Thirdly, I engaged in a process of peer-review of the stories, by the three actors I am portraying but also by colleagues familiar with Johannesburg's politics and environment.

Finally, there is the issue of confidentiality, not dissimilar to the 'black box' on internal strategies in social movements: publicising a political strategy while it is current might jeopardise it. Two elements limit the risk. The first is this chapter has been read and debated with each of the activists portrayed, and the second is that time has elapsed between the collection of these stories (2016) and their publication time (2023).

Story 1: Building support for a homeless shelter in the suburb, outside and inside the state

The main character

Matt Jackson is a former student of Wits Planning Programme. As long as I have known him, he has been in awe of entrepreneurship, with a desire for action, efficacy and pragmatism, mixed with a longing for social justice. This was the streak of activism, that he first developed when working with the Central Johannesburg Partnership, a coalition of property developers and private companies interested in the inner-city revitalisation, and instrumental in crafting the provincial legislation on City Improvement Districts (CID). He expanded this passion when he was appointed to the City of Johannesburg Development Agency (JDA) in 2015, in charge of facilitating the development of the mayoral flagship project: Corridors of Freedom,[2] in the northern suburbs, around the Louis Botha Corridor.

While engaging with White middle-class residents, mostly adverse to the project of densification and social mix that the Corridors of Freedom entailed (Applebaum 2017), Matt focused on making the project understood and accepted through a process of education and bargaining. That is where he developed his awareness on issues of homelessness in the suburbs, and worked towards convincing local suburban associations to support a homeless shelter as part of a neighborhood plan of revitalisation of public space. This is the project this story is focusing on. Having left the City in 2017, Matt involved himself in social entrepreneurship to construct a national network, with churches, NGOs, officials, and researchers, around the issue of homelessness.

The context: trading the inclusion of homeless people for public investment in public space

The JDA Facilitation Unit, where Matt used to be positioned, is a relatively free environment, a small mobile unit within a resourced and partly autonomous, powerful municipal-owned entity.[3] This unit within the JDA was set up by a visionary JDA senior official, frustrated by how often their interventions to regenerate the city were blocked by social protests, which she linked to the absence of engagement with citizens. Her proposed unit happened to respond to the practical need for the City to have a large project like the Corridors of Freedom run smoothly.

The Corridors of Freedom (constructing urban density along public rapid transport lines, linking townships, inner city and suburban centers) was a flagship project under Parks Tau's African National Congress (ANC) mayorship (2011–17). It had backing from the mayor and the overall City administration: financial resources, political visibility and legitimacy, directed towards the neighborhoods that the bus line affected. This focused and fast-tracked public investment opened possibilities for bargaining and for innovative state practices beyond the usual departmental silos. Even though literature focusing on large projects (Flyvbjerg 2014) emphasise their democratic limitations and their limited governability, in the case of Matt, in charge of development around one specific corridor (Louis Botha Avenue), the project was small scale, focused, powerful, and manageable at a neighbourbood level. A pragmatic take (avoiding large projects being derailed by social protests), had opened a space for democratic possibilities, processes taking community participation seriously, at least in terms of resources committed to the process.

The area of intervention, the middle-class suburb of Norwood, is marked by strong and visible public interventions: the construction of the Bus rapid transit line and station on Louis Botha Avenue, and the project of building social housing units in a section of Paterson Park in Norwood.

Norwood resident associations were up in arms against the social housing project (not led by JDA, but by another municipal owned entity: Johannesburg Property Company – JPC), multiplying objections and threatening litigation (Applebaum 2017). As a way to calm the situation,

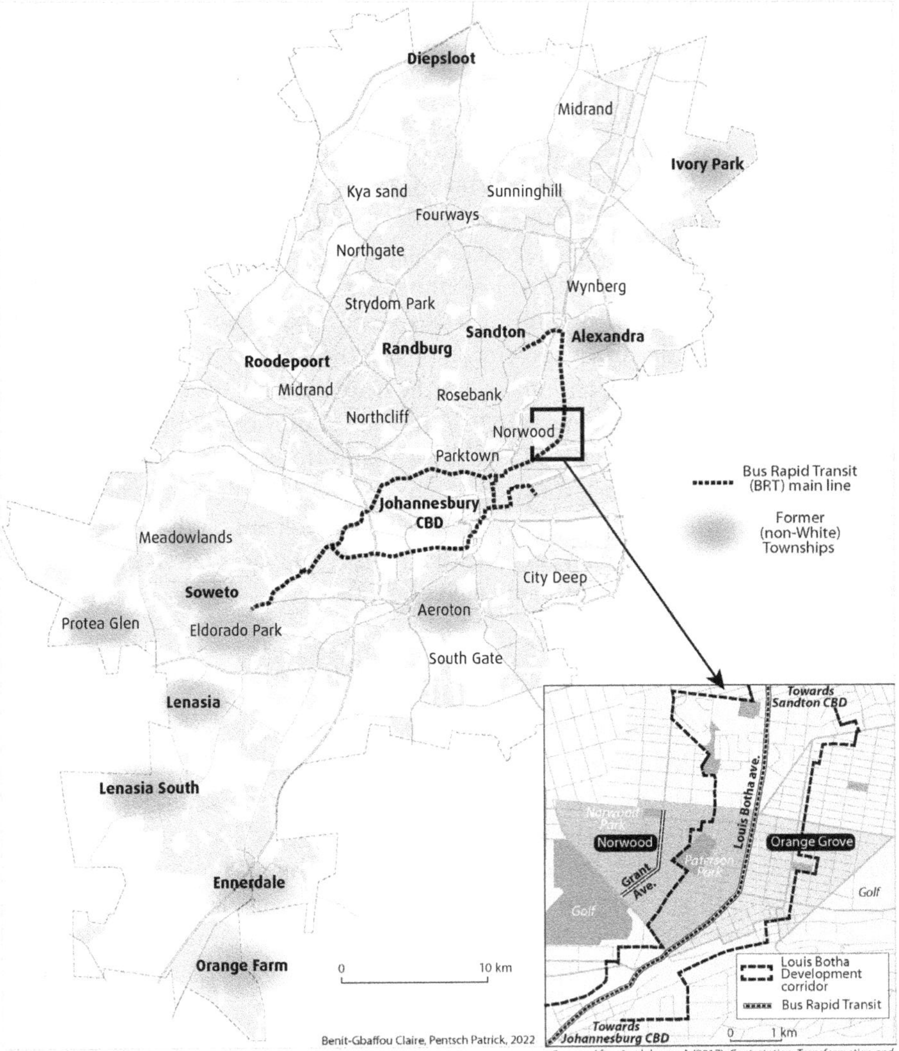

Source: After Applebaum A (2017). *Contestation, Transformation and Competing Visions: A Study of Orange Grove and Norwood.* SA&CP, University of the Witwatersrand, Johannesburg.

Figure 3.1 Matt's area of intervention: Norwood and the Corridor of Freedom project in Johannesburg. Matt broadened the City's area of intervention beyond the official area earmarked for the Corridors of Freedom. This allowed him to intervene on broader issues of public space in Norwood, and construct multiple sites of engagement with the local community, beyond the conflict around Patterson's social housing project.
Map: © Claire Bénit-Gbaffou and Patrick Pentsch, with thanks to Aix Marseille University 2022

the JDA developed a plan to revamp Norwood's high street – in spite of the fact it fell outside the strict perimeter of the Corridor (**Figure 3.1**), hence requiring a specific action by Matt to expand the scope of public intervention. Problems that were identified by business people and residents included the large number of beggars and informal car guards (some with substance abuse issues), that the residents felt were contributing to crime and grime. The car guards and beggars were living in Norwood's park, together with a number of informal recyclers using the park as their depot and living space (Laures 2017). The Paterson park housing project had the unplanned effect of displacing the homeless people living there, towards Norwood's park, where their visibility increased due to their aggregation, and the fact that the (smaller) park in Norwood is also more central to the neighourhood than Paterson's park.

Matt's project was to gain the buy-in of Norwood residents to the whole Corridor of Freedom project, and through engagement around public space along Norwood's high street (that borders Norwood's park), to convince residents and businesses to contribute to the integration of the homeless locally, in exchange for City support and investment. The project went far, but was stalled ultimately.

Matt's intervention – becoming an advocate for the homeless

Matt put most of his efforts into building support in the Norwood community, in a context of vocal discontent and opposition to the JPC project and the idea of densification in the first place. Playing on the fragmentation of the state, he embodied the 'good cop' from the JDA in contrast to JPC's contentious social housing project, successfully separating platforms of engagement: 'the City is diverse, I am here to engage about your high street regeneration, do you wish to talk about that?' Not necessarily as a cynical intention, but as a definite effect, Matt was able to build a constructive relationship between Norwood's residents and businesses, and the City, from which he was able, incrementally, to bring into the debate a better understanding of the benefit of densification and integration. He likes to tell the story, heard in a public meeting, of the diverse profiles of people needing affordable accommodation in the area: a single Jewish mother, a trendy young gay couple, a cashier working in a local shop and a waiter in a local restaurant, reminding us of Krumholz and Clavel's stories of planners' strategies to demystify social housing in conservative American neighbourhoods (1994).

These public meetings did not succeed immediately though. Matt had to first engage with each stakeholder group and key local figures, hear their concerns and get to know them (their interests and characters). An example of this was the Business Forum's leader who supported a homeless person sitting on his business' doorstep by putting him through rehabilitation, providing him with accommodation and a job in security in the area. This businessman was not translating his practice into any general discourse on homelessness. Matt's initiative allowed this translation to occur to a certain extent. Another element in Matt's approach was to reason concretely and pragmatically, rather than starting with normative discourses on integration and social mix: 'the street is not managed, the City does not have the resources, the homeless are not going to go away. Why not set up a management mechanism?' Another tactic was to use as a bargaining tool public funding (investment in the park revamp and high street regeneration) and resources (the possibility of establishing paid parking on the street, and delegate the fee collection to a local community body). But he maintained a strong line – public resources could be invested only if some public good would result, contributing to uplifting the poor in the area: the homeless people.

This pragmatic discourse (realistic management and bargaining) was held with multiple stakeholders and in a number of fragmented community forums. Then the issue was to try and overcome local fragmentation, between the residents' association on the one hand (focusing on the park, already raising funds to pay for a gardener, since municipal management was insufficient), and the business forum on the other (interested in the high street where businesses are concentrated). Matt attempted to construct a sustainable instrument for community-led public space management, inspired by his experience with City Improvement Districts in the Central Johannesburg Partnership. His key idea was to negotiate the delegation to a community body of parking fee collection in the high street (a form of privatisation), which would provide the revenue for the community body to hire cleaners and security and contribute to the management of a homeless shelter.[4]

Simultaneously, Matt multiplied initiatives to try and make the plan real. He started connecting with churches, NGOs and advocacy groups engaging with the homeless; commissioned research on existing local support structures (a dense but uncoordinated network of local churches: Laures 2017) that could potentially run the homeless shelter. He identified a potential building, together with an official from the Department of Social Development. He gained the institutional support of the City's Planning Department that informally committed funding to the initiative, not initially ear-marked since Norwood was outside the Corridor's official boundary. This was sufficient to both revamp the park and purchase and regenerate the shelter. This was the 'carrot' proposed to Norwood's residents, presented as two intertwined, and not to be separated, budgets. Matt also worked on convincing his own hierarchy in JDA (beyond his unit), of the potentialities of the project, by inviting his hierarchy in public meetings where he presented the park revamp-cum-homeless shelter project to the residents.

Interestingly enough, Matt was not initially the champion of the homeless. Although sensitive to inequality and a supporter of micro-entreprise as a way out of poverty, his awareness grew incrementally, one crystallising moment being a Wits report on the Corridor of Freedom. The report had been contracted by the City explicitly to support the Planning Department in running the Corridor Project (Harrison et al. 2019). The report expressed robust criticism of the exclusionary effects of the Corridor's interventions ('you are actually chasing the poor out of the suburbs'), especially around the Louis Botha Corridor (Applebaum 2017). This was not only a critical moment for Matt; it was also a moment of shock for the Planning Department, partly explaining its later backing of Matt's project around the shelter in Norwood.

However, at the last minute, the project collapsed. It did so in the conjunction with three elements. When the project was about to take off, the Department of Social Development (under-resourced and under-staffed: hence Matt's imagined NGO structure, paid by parking fees, to manage the shelter) refused to sign support for the City's investment in the shelter and purchase of the building. The official who Matt had worked with had not done his internal work, and Matt had not followed protocol in engaging the Department of Social Development's hierarchy early and formally enough. This blocked the project. Secondly, with the change of leadership in the City and DA Mayor Herman Mashaba elected, the Corridor of Freedom project was marginalised and underwent drastic budget cuts. The funds earmarked by the Planning Department for the Norwood shelter were redeployed by the JDA to cover its committed projects. No one in the JDA's executive defended the project nor considered the funding to be 'committed' in Norwood, in spite of two years of intense community engagement driven by Matt. The JDA's withdrawal echoed and amplified some of the comments his intervention had attracted earlier from the JDA executive: 'spending public funding for a bunch of White privileged residents is not [politically] sustainable'. Matt took it as a strong personal setback, a betrayal by his institution, and a lack of recognition of his action – in the (White) suburbs indeed, but towards the crucial inclusion of the (Black) poor in these suburbs.

What Matt's story tells us about institutional activism

The process required a set of specific skills: strategic facilitation, advocacy, leadership and mobilisation, together with the local (fragmented) community and with the City's internal apparatus (legislations, departmental protocols and egos, political rhetoric). Matt spent most of his time on the former (engaging in external politics), and possibly not enough on the latter (building internal support).

The joint management instrument Matt attempted at building (community-led management of public space; raising parking fees as income; contributing to an NGO running the homeless shelter; possible employment of homeless people for the cleaning and monitoring of the street) is a sophisticated and complex one. It reveals the absence, or under-capacity, of the City departments in urban management (in charge with the streets), city parks, and social development (in charge of homeless shelters). It does mobilise additional resources (a local tax on parking, residents and business's time to collect, manage and coordinate the revenue), using a model similar to the City Improvement District, but tailored locally and with strong and explicit social objectives. This is a way of responding to scarce public resources, to create a social service contributing to the public realm: the usual discard of City Improvement Districts as neoliberal tools might not be relevant here (Joshi and Moore 2004). Its complexity and the difficulty in formalising it might make it a fragile instrument (Ferguson 2010), difficult to sustain over time, far more than it would be for functional state departments. It is also more complex than straightforward privatisation, with limited strings attached and a simple exchange, service against public payment (Stone 2006). But it is certainly an innovative way to produce a managed and not (too) exclusive public realm that should be recognised as such.

The ultimate failure, and the lack of institutional and political backing of Matt's intervention, casts a light on dominant representations of citizenship, participation, poverty and race – not only in Johannesburg as an emblematic post-apartheid city, but also in the global contemporary city. The reluctance to engage with White urban citizens and their suburbs as a legitimate part of the urban fabric ('why are you spending all your time convincing these rich White guys?') is partly a legitimate concern given the scarcity of public resources. But how to address the structure of inequalities without also changing 'the rich?'[5] This reluctance reveals the invisibility of suburban poverty (Charlton, Chapter 10 in this book) – as illustrated by Matt's failed attempt to convince the ANC and the Economic Freedom Fighters (EFF),[6] consolidating a pro-poor discourse especially under DA rule, that it was a cause worth supporting.[7] By not constructing politically the social acceptability of the poor in middle-class suburbs, and their material access to these spaces, however, the battle against urban inequality and segregation remains limited. This simplistic reading of space in static racial terms, in fighting around transportation across urban areas identified as 'White', is not unique to Johannesburg: complex mobility patterns do not translate well into (clear-cut) political discourses. Matt's action has prepared the ground for legitimising a place for the (Black) homeless and the poor, for shelter and affordable housing, in a suburb that was up in arms against it. While some might say it is a huge amount of energy spent for a small result, it might be crucial to shift public discourses and dominant representations around the 'inclusive city' and the place of the poor in middle-class suburbs.

Story 2: moving institutions to render community engagement relevant in City Parks

The main character

Ayanda Roji has been the General Manager of the Corporate Research, Policy and Knowledge Management unit in Johannesburg City Parks and Zoo (JCPZ, hereafter City Parks) since 2013. The JCPZ is a municipal-owned entity in charge of green open spaces in Johannesburg. Ayanda was raised in a family involved in the anti-apartheid struggle and in the ANC and she defines herself as a pan-Africanist and a feminist. She is committed to having parks recognised as public spaces which also need to cater for the poorer and more marginalised residents – recognition for which she uses research partnerships (the core of her official mandate) to both deconstruct dominant representations of what a park is (focused on issues of biodiversity, City Parks being conceived as a 'grass-cutting' department), and seek alternative ways in which parks could be developed and managed. Her specific goal narrated below was to transform City Parks' internal structure, to enable it to more meaningfully engage with user communities, make parks more responsive to a diversity of needs, particularly in the decayed Johannesburg inner city where homelessness and informal activities in parks are constantly criminalised.

The context: recognising parks as social objects

Since 2013, City Parks has claimed its intention to better engage with what it calls 'stakeholders', with a dedicated stakeholders engagement department, but also a number of programmes for environmental education (directed towards disadvantaged schools), job creation in parks through contracts to emerging small Black companies, and strategic efforts to better frame joint management of parks with local user groups. The framing of such engagement can be seen as neoliberal, responding to City Parks' chronic under-funding and obvious inability to manage Johannesburg's own 2,000 green open spaces. Yet City Parks is also marked by a sense of its transformative mandate in post-apartheid Johannesburg, where access to green space has been a privilege of the White and the rich, and the spatial distribution of parks is biased towards the northern suburbs (previously the White only spaces), 'leafy suburbs' contrasting with the 'dusty townships' (Bénit-Gbaffou 2018b). In a post-apartheid and racialised context, City Parks is more than elsewhere aware of the dangers of privatisation, and attempting to assert its mandate even when it delegates most of the daily management of the park: opening a space for possible, actual co-production.

What is missing, however, for such co-production, is a set of dedicated and resourced City Parks officials to regularly meet with existing user groups (in the suburbs), and to consolidate user groups in the more disadvantaged urban spaces – in townships where open spaces were not developed parks for a long time,[8] or in the inner city where urban decay, impoverishment combined with lack of park management have made them risk-prone areas. In theory, (and as stated in the organogram), it is the Stakeholders Liaison Officers (SLOs) who are in charge with engaging with communities in parks (Bénit-Gbaffou 2018b). However, there are only four of them for the entire metropolitan area and they are unable to regularly engage with the park user groups (whose list they do not even have), let alone encourage the creation of new ones. Some of these officials have political and community facilitation skills, but cannot exert it properly. Most have given up and invest little in their practice, seeing communities as a nuisance. It is park managers, who are actually 'on the ground' on a regular basis, who end up playing the role of interface between users and the state. Trained as horticulturists, their mandate is to make sure grass is cut and trees are pruned and park equipment is maintained. But some have developed *ad hoc* community engagement skills, as social issues are central in their ability to fulfill their restricted mandate.[9] However, they too are too few to engage regularly with user groups. For the inner city, there is one single park manager, with 58 inner city parks under his responsibility. Some of these parks are tiny playgrounds; other are regional parks. All are characterised by heavy and complex social issues, reflecting their difficult urban environment marked by poverty, informality, lack of public space, homelessness, and substance abuse, violent crime and insecurity. Beyond their number which is too low (but still higher than the number of SLOs, and capacitates them to have a degree of knowledge of each park and some of their users), park managers are not mandated to engage with users nor facilitate continued engagements or partnerships. But they have been identified, both by research and some officials in City Parks, as the best placed to do so.

Ayanda's intervention: institutionalising community participation in park management

Ayanda's objective is to have parks recognised as public spaces, and to encourage community and user participation in park management. The concrete instrument to do so is an institutional restructuring of City Parks, that redefine park managers' mandate (and training, status, salaries) to include community engagement, that some of them already do in practice. The definition and advancement of this vision involved several steps.

First, Ayanda initiated a research partnership with Wits School of Planning and Architecture to conduct research on park management and community participation. Wits' case studies, initially grounded in middle-class White suburbs, were not necessarily audible in the Johannesburg political context, as illustrated in Matt's story. But these case studies allowed for the identification of the structural powerlessness of park managers facing the (legitimate) discontent of (structurally) powerful user groups. The research highlighted the importance for City Parks transformation objectives to not simply delegate park management to private and privileged groups but to be in a position to facilitate the joint management of parks. It showed the key difference a strategic and skilled park manager can make, and the institutional and structural limitation of partnerships in the absence of a mandated and resourced park representative (Bénit-Gbaffou 2018a).

Ayanda started a pilot project in an inner-city park (End Street North), in partnership with the JDA and City Safety – through a network based on three powerful and committed female officials driving the project together, resourced by external institutions (UN Habitat, GIZ, and a local NGO facilitating community meetings). The pilot showed the benefits of community engagement for local problem solving. The residents, for instance, succeeded in lobbying the Johannesburg Roads Agency (JRA) to build a speed hump in the street bordering the park that had been identified as a major security issue for the park, but on which City Park had no mandate and no capacity to act (Mogkere 2018). Once aware of how the City worked and that the JRA was the agency in charge of roads and streets, residents organised a sit-in at the JRA, and lobbied the JRA through street politics, in ways that City Parks had been unable to do through internal bargaining. But the pilot also illustrated the unsustainability of community mobilisation without a dedicated facilitator. When the pilot ended, the engagement collapsed, and it was unreasonable to expect a community champion to emerge and sustain action, especially in impoverished and fragmented inner-city communities. Reporting on the pilot thus became strategic in Ayanda's attempt to change institutions and practices, not only to demonstrate the value of community engagement, but also to call for dedicated and grounded officials facilitating it.

Backed by this pilot and the research, Ayanda and her City partners developed an inner city open space safety strategy (JCPZ 2017). This tapped into the mayor's interest for regenerating the inner city, and a political context possibly opening a space for institutional change, where the mayor had been critical of his predecessors' externalisation of municipal entities (for example, City Parks, the JDA, etc), calling for their reintegration into the City administration. The strategy emphasises the need for resourcing City Park in the inner city; for clustered park management; for empowered and resourced park managers for these clusters. It constructs parks as social objects, whose value is not only measured in terms of biodiversity but also in terms of 'social cohesion'.

To have this strategy adopted and become a City official document, the path was not obvious. As a strategy that cuts across departments and entities, it was to be reported to several departments and their political heads. The JDA was responding to the Department of Development Planning, JCPZ was reporting to City Community Development and City Safety Department was a third department. As a document concerning the inner city, it also needed to go through the Inner-City Office, another City unit. This proliferation of authorities diluted the protocol and perhaps opened up a space for advocacy, instead of trying to first have the strategy approved by City Parks itself. As a matter of fact, convincing City Parks' executive came very late in the process, as its leadership was uncertain, changing, and not likely to be sympathetic to the document unless it had strong political backing.

A chance encounter of the political head of the Department of Development Planning, who was also chairing the Inner-City office, meant that Ayanda was invited to present the strategy to the Mayor directly. In the meeting, he showed interest for the strategy, thanks to Ayanda's charisma, drive and strategic thinking, even committing to allocate significant resources. Instead of R900,000 per annum for managing the 58 inner-city parks, Ayanda advocated for R900,000 per month, and this was heard.

Through Ayanda's position as organiser of public events around parks, she was in a position to meet and gain the trust of the political head of the Department of Community Development (to which City Parks is accountable administratively). However, this strategy still needed to be formally adopted by the Community Development Section 79 Committee, the group of elected councillors (from different political parties) appointed to that portfolio in an oversight capacity. Not only was Ayanda not well prepared by her own institution (which did not disclose to her what the presentation she had to make to the committee was about), but the whole committee rejected her report with derogatory comments. Ayanda learnt later on that the committee had decided to reject all reports submitted to its oversight, as a way to challenge the political head who was not taking the committee seriously. Her choice not to follow protocol and start from gaining mayoral support might have backlashed, but she did not have a real choice: following protocol by obtaining endorsement first from City Parks, then the Community Development Committee, then mayoral level, given these institutions' petty politics, rivalries and lack of strategic visioning, would have killed the project from the start.

Building support from within the institution, but from below City Parks executive (seen as a likely stumbling block), was equally crucial, especially with park and regional managers with whom Ayanda has a good working relation. At the time of writing, she was starting to debate ideas about institutional restructuring through research dissemination workshops and weekly regional managers' meetings. From the research workshop debates I was part of, many stakes were at play. It was about redefining overlapping functions, as the new function of park managers would compete with the role of SLOs. It was about redistributing resources (new park managers would need a status and salary upgrade, besides higher numbers). Would resources come from a higher subsidy from the City, or the internal reshuffling of an institution whose top is too heavy? And it was also about defining City Parks' mandate, where some officials sympathised with informal and poor users of the parks, while others saw their role in protecting biodiversity and classic uses of the park, even if it meant allying with conservative users in chasing away people defined as 'undesirable'. From these internal debates at the middle range managerial level, Ayanda then hoped to have the strategy adopted by the City Parks' board (an array of business people and civil society representatives whose mandate is to guide the municipal entity) – and from then only lobby the city Section 79 Committee and City Parks' management to have the strategy adopted, budgeted and implemented.

What Ayanda's story teaches us about institutional activism

What does this story show us about the interplay between agency and structure? Ayanda's drive and goal were crucial, her frustration with existing practices, institutions and policies, and her desire for change. But she also did not set her action in opposition to existing directions, rather opening, actually shaping a space of opportunity using the gaps she could identify. This relates to Dahl's vision of leadership as resource creators (1961), and Krumholz and Clavel's illustration of how the bringing together of various limited networks and resources can end up causing significant shifts (1994). Ayanda used her seemingly innocuous research and knowledge management position to try and reform institutions and practices. The pilot in End Street North, catalysing partnerships (with funders, internal city allies and a web of researchers and NGOs), provided the project with funding, legitimacy, and knowledge, each dimension reinforcing the other. It was ultimately translated into a political instrument (the strategy document, as well as the narrative around the pilot as a marketing tool). This pilot crystallised cooperation across City departments, escaping City Parks' narrow identity, leadership and mandate (marked by the perennial battle between environmentalist and socially-oriented officials). It demonstrated in practice that parks are not only about grass cutting; strategically choosing the inner city (of high strategic stakes for the mayor) to make the point to him, and reaching out to get his support. Not that all of this was planned in advance. Some of it is luck, some of it is personal charisma and networking skills, and some of it is just the effect of bringing resources together at the right time.

Ayanda's actions show in retrospect what the City's spaces of opportunity are, and how to bring them together to create potential change – agency informs about structures, testing their boundaries and learning, by trial and error, how to navigate them. Three structural elements assisted in opening such a space. First, City Parks' acute need for partnerships and community engagement, as it has no actual capacity to manage parks on its own in post-apartheid Johannesburg. This instrumental quest for community engagement arguably opens a space for negotiation between state and society. Secondly, street-level officials (park and regional managers) have a practical understanding of parks as social objects, requiring multi-departmental and stakeholders' intervention. City Parks did offer space for them to voice their challenges, as their daily task is to manage scorecards and scarce personnel, rather than think strategically. But, as City parks is under the threat of institutional restructuring, possible re-integration in the City, and undergoes changes in its executive leadership, a space opens where conversations are potentially impactful. For an activist in the state, it is a moment to build on the gap, use a space to consolidate these voices, and create support from the bottom for an institutional change that reflects her vision. Thirdly, the mayor has clearly indicated his commitment to regenerate the inner city, to invest and attract investors, to fight crime and grime. His vision is not particularly a socially-inclusive one; but bringing forth a new strategy for the inner city, framed in the language of increased safety and efficient urban management, could have been a winning gamble.

Identifying and building a network of fellow activists in various parts of the local state and outside the state was equally crucial to find the confidence and resources to drive the pilot and transform it into a legitimate and credible policy document proposal (the safety strategy). This network, however, was not a given: the collective was constructed through the project, and one of the officials involved, initially reluctant to move beyond a legalistic approach, shifted to a more socially-oriented one.

Ayanda multiplied arenas of mobilisation. She did not, as Matt did, rely on social mobilisation and external constituency. There are indeed no social movements focusing on parks and public spaces in Johannesburg. The voices of civil society around parks are muted in the inner city, disconnected in the townships (parks are not a key area of mobilisation), and delegitimised in the suburbs (Bénit-Gbaffou 2018b). Ayanda and some other officials contemplated mobilising the latter – and thought of using the Centre for Urbanism and the Built Environment Studies (CUBES) research and facilitation to launch a forum of park user groups (that would have been dominated by suburban White middle classes) in which to start engagement. Although possibly talking to DA constituencies, such engagement was not politically correct, and could have easily backlashed, as it was also a difficult engagement: City Parks could have been under attack by this group rather than being supported in its reform agenda.

Therefore, Ayanda focused on navigating the inner complexities of local government apparatus. Seizing an opportunity, she sidelined protocol to make things move by achieving support from the top. In a context of lukewarm support from City Parks' leadership, the backing of the mayor was in retrospect the only way to effect change. But her navigation of protocol is not only through sidelining obstacles by running to the top. It is also about informally discussing issues with leadership, coining the right terms that can be heard by each; doing the round of involved stakeholders; using different strategies to respond to challenges tackled one after the other in an unconventional order (political head of of the Department of Development Planning and Inner-City Office, then the mayor, then the political head of the Department of Community Development, then the City Parks' Board to move back to the City Parks' executive, her direct hierarchy). Her other concomitant tactic is equally crucial. This involved building bottom-up support within the institution, opening a space for awareness and mobilisation of park and regional managers, low- to middle-rank officials, including SLOs, whose position might be threatened by such a shift, so that the idea of the reform penetrates the thickness of the apparatus rather than being a policy veneer, easy to wash away if it is not known, understood and supported by the core City Parks' bureaucracy.

Story 3: going beyond community meetings: the hard work of circulating claims and building policy instruments through the internal intricacies of the state

Main character

Nicolette (Nikki) Pingo, like Matt Jackson, is an official in the Johannesburg Development Agency (JDA)'s Development Facilitation Unit (DFU). Prior to joining the City in 2015, she worked with an NGO committed to community participation, after having been trained in educational applied drama – street theatre and development planning at the University of the Witwatersrand. One of her first tasks in her position at the DFU was to create a five-year strategic plan – Urban Development Framework (UDF) – for the eastern section of the inner city (the Eastern Gateway), comprising low-income residential, derelict and squatted industrial areas, migrant hostels, and pockets of rapid gentrification. In this endeavour, Nicolette was part of several community meetings in the area to discuss the plan. She was struck by the urgent claim for affordable and decent housing which is something that the UDF generally does not deal with, and is neither the mandate of the JDA, nor directly the competency of the Department of Planning for whom the JDA was developing the plan. Nicolette endeavoured to construct a set of policy instruments to address that need.

Nikki's action – taking the public production of inner-city affordable housing seriously

She first developed the housing component of the UDF, in more detail than usually done for this type of planning instrument. Rather than stating broad intentions ('there is a need for affordable housing in the sector'), she included maps identifying sites where affordable housing could be developed locally, indicating densities and number of units that could be developed for each. She admits having made a mistake there: she prioritised state-owned sites (including City-owned ones), assuming that these would be easier to access for affordable housing development. However, she soon realised that the reverse was true: privately-owned land was in fact far easier to access (and not expensive given the area's urban decay), while discussion with other branches of the state, and even with the agency holding the City's land asset, the Johannesburg Property Company (JPC), reached a dead end.

Nikki then initiated networks with social housing and state institutions, to devise funding mechanisms to construct affordable housing; identifying private buildings that could be purchased and redeveloped as social housing in the Eastern Gateway. In particular, a partnership with the Social Housing Regulatory Agency (SHRA) at national level, seemed to be yielding results: budget was set aside, a number of private buildings were identified, social housing institutions were approached that could be given the grant and develop and manage affordable housing on this basis.

As a JDA official working on the inner city, Nikki was, together with other activists in the state and former fellow students from Wits Planning School, part of a policy process on housing, the Inner City Housing Implementation Plan (ICHIP) – developed in response to a number of Constitutional Court judgements.[10] There, she developed several types of affordable housing provision programmes she had started imagining with potential partners in the making of the Eastern Gateway UDF that would be piloted in the Eastern Gateway, based on the UDF she had constructed. An office was to be created by the JDA to drive the implementation of the plan which would of course assist in piloting the projects in the area as well as consolidate the policy itself.

However, no affordable housing intervention had taken place three years after the UDF was completed, and a number of initiatives did not materialise. The CEO of the JDA, initially supportive of the JDA taking charge of the implementation of ICHIP (in collaboration with the Johannesburg Housing Department), changed his views on the matter after an ANC caucus. Nicolette explains that this change occurred because he thought the plan was too complex to be implemented and would lead the JDA to failure; or because he was told to leave ICHIP to the (notoriously inefficient and possibly corrupt) Housing Department. Its management, with attributions of tenders and inner-city buildings to be redeveloped, was seen as being too strategic an instrument to be left to the JDA. The JDA then lost its ability to drive the plan's implementation. The ICHIP was ultimately passed in Council with great difficulty, having been deprived of many of its core elements, and seems today to be put aside, and considered 'too complex to implement' by the Housing Department.

Many local initiatives that Nikki had identified, with funding and institutions to develop and manage affordable housing, are stuck because of one stumbling block – the purchase of urban land. The institution officially in charge of purchasing urban land for the City, the JPC, is structurally driven by the need to raise revenue, and not easily convinced to purchase or sell land for (unprofitable) affordable housing. The high financial stakes (and possibly some kickbacks attached to transactions) on urban land, and the multiplicity of fragmented state agencies involved in the process (the JDA developing projects and land for City departments, working mostly with the City's Planning Department, Housing Department; and the JPC, another municipal agency) render interventions complicated.

Finally, the newly elected mayor, the DA Herman Mashaba, has limited sympathy or enthusiasm for the development of affordable housing in the inner city, rather focusing on attracting private developers with no strings attached. Out of 13 existing buildings that the JDA had identified to be transferred to social housing institutions in the Eastern Gateway, most have now been sold to the private sector for 'redevelopment' by the Department of Housing, under direct instruction from the mayor and in contradiction with prior discussions with the JDA.

Reflecting on the disappointing results of her three years of efforts, Nicolette wonders if she was not wrong to 'put all her eggs in the same basket', namely the development of affordable housing in the eastern section of the inner city. She felt very close to a breakthrough, but the space for pushing affordable housing in the inner city closed down under the new mayor. She is now considering working less with other City agencies or departments, using the JDA's degree of autonomy to work on smaller-scale projects, and possibly in more peripheral parts of the city, attracting less attention from private developers and the other City departments.

What Nicolette's story tells us about institutional activism

There is something risky, but simultaneously necessary, in 'putting one's eggs in the same baskets' as an activist – it is about focus, grounded knowledge and cumulative engagements that multiplies areas of opportunities. In the process of engaging around the UDF, Nicolette did not only hear the local needs (for affordable housing in particular), she also identified local resources, partners and opportunities, as well as the gap in policy instruments. She was able to scale up, from understanding the nature of local needs, towards pushing the boundaries of the usual local planning tools (the UDF), to making inputs into a municipal policy process (ICHIP), that it seemed the JDA could pilot in the very same area. This straddling of multiple scales of intervention, construction of networks within the City and outside (with housing associations and central housing institutions), open spaces to imagine and to craft new instruments for intervention.

To some extent this seemed to work under the previous mayor. But with a change of leadership and party in power, this direction no longer works with the grain, and the magnitude of the policy instrument innovation cannot hold without political backing, let alone if it is in opposition to political leadership. The urban land question is possibly the most relevant and powerful tool for redistribution in the city – yet it has not, even under ANC leadership, been attributed to an institution with a clear redistribution mandate. Instead, it is fragmented, between the JPC (the only agency entitled to purchase and keep land in the name of the City but works on a revenue-raising model that is not questioned); the notoriously inefficient Housing Department, whose leadership is perpetually contested and possibly corrupted; the Department of Economic Development which is in charge of specific programmes using inner-city buildings as an asset to kick-start Black economic empowerment,[11] and marginally, the more progressive department which may be able to play on zoning regulations but has limited say on these matters. This fragmentation contributes to opacifying political stakes, and to blocking attempts at reforming or challenging the inner-city growth machine. Here the agency of individual officials cannot do much, especially in the absence of either a vocal constituency (such as an inner-city wide social movement), or strong political backing. In this context, the strategy of the activist in the state is shifting towards keeping a low profile and becoming rather a 'resistant' in the state – another, different, form of activism.

Concluding remarks

The commonality between these cases is first that each of these state activists has had to straddle three fields of mobilisation: the City administration itself (and its hierarchical but also fragmented institutions), City political leadership (where political support is key), and civil society. Three interconnected fields, where political backing could help overcome administrative resistance, civil society pressure could convince politicians of policy gains, administrative support could multiply the chances of legitimation and feasibility. Each of the three activists has worked out a different balance between these three fields (administrative, political and social), through a process of trial and error. Matt has overinvested the mobilisation of civil society, at the expense of consolidating administrative and political support. Ayanda and Nicolette were focused on internal mobilisation with higher-level political investment for Ayanda, using her ANC networks and managerial position; and a deeper local grounding of Nicolette engaged in participatory planning processes. Such choices depend on personalities, skills and preexisting dispositions. It also depends on position within the bureaucracy (a higher position opening up the field of political leadership). One might hypothesise that it also depends on the costs of building and sustaining social mobilisation that does not exist (absence of an inner-city tenant's constituency), or that is ambiguous in its political effects – White suburban middle class engaged around parks turned out to be a politically complicated ally in a post-apartheid era.

A second commonality was a strong focus on building policy instruments as key to achieving change. In all three cases, this was about building a set of instruments (not just one), to ensure budgeting, implementation, follow up and deep institutionalisation: that is, the meaning of 'all eggs in the same basket':

- For Nicolette, this meant stretching the UDF planning tool to incorporate housing; identifying land and buildings, budget and financial strategy and the construction of the ICHIP policy and its implementation.
- For Matt, this meant the Norwood Park and High Street revitalisation plan, budgeting, identification of buildings and the construction of a management vehicle.
- For Ayanda, this meant building strategic research partnerships as a tool to foster debate within City Parks' administration; starting a pilot project in an inner city park; developing a strategic document and lobbying for budget and institutional restructuring to make it work.

The activists' efforts could not be targeted at crafting policy documents only and their main battles were actually around the City's fragmented institutions and their rivalry on roles and functions.

A third commonality is the relative failure of these initiatives, the fragility of these strategies, and time running short in unstable social and political environments. In this respect, one may contrast Matt's short-term mandate as a City official (within the frame of a quite specific and bounded project), with Ayanda and Nicolette's longer standing in administration, allowing a better reach and understanding of the internal administrative and political logics of the state. Nevertheless, it is important to say that they all undertook their jobs with incredible intensity and an often-felt feeling of being burnt-out, especially in the face of the many battles that were lost in a continued drive towards achieving their progressive objective. We may remind ourselves that policy reform has always been a long-term battle (Domhoff 2011; Giugni 1998), and in this respect, building external constituencies may be key in providing a buffer to these unstable politics, reminding politicians of pressing urban agendas. But building civil society mobilisation is too big a task for officials, and a serious limit to their action might be linked to the thinness of their collective networks outside the state.

Finally, what do the stories of these activites reveal about the role of the state in governing cities? Their practices reveal 'the state's' high level of fragmentation, even at the City's internal level. This is sometimes an opportunity (if one has an overview and can play one to sideline another, as was partly the case for Ayanda), but more often a challenge in the capacity to act (Matt's and Nicolette's final disappointment in these institutional battles). The permanence of strong land-based elite interests in the city blocking progressive change, together with mayoral and strategic departments that have remained market-oriented (Department of Economic Development and the JPC), severely restricts progressive action and reveals the limits of the post-apartheid transformative discourse. For activists in City Hall, this might mean resorting to more covert, modest and discrete interventions from within the state – finding solace in the fact that change takes time and holding an official's position might expose them to future opportunities. Or it might mean driving change from outside the state as the brief, post-apartheid window of opportunity for change seems to be closing.

Acknowledgements

This chapter was debated with many colleagues, whom I want to thank here: Rebecca Abers, Sarah Charlton, Vanille Laborde, Sogen Moodley, Margot Rubin, Aude Signoles, Jérome Tadié, and many others whose remarks, questions and comments assisted in the finalisation of this chapter.

Notes

1 The main opposition party to the ANC.
2 Corridors of Freedom is a transit-oriented development project, aiming at interconnecting different areas of the sprawling city through bus rapid transit, and densifying the urban fabric (Harrison et al. 2019).
3 The JDA is the development arm of the city, works closely with the Department of Development Planning, peopled by activists with a strong sense of the urgency of post-apartheid transformation of the city (Rubin, Chapter 4, this book).
4 The formalisation of the agreement in legal terms, the negotiation around the creation of parking fees on the street and the delegation of their collection to a community body were, however, left pending – they were in process when Matt's project collapsed.
5 Using broad-brushed categories, Norwood can be defined as middle class, not high bourgeoisie.
6 The ANC is the liberation party in power at national level since 1994, but starting to lose the main metropolitan municipalities (such as Johannesburg in 2017), to the DA, main opposition party (liberal). The EFF, a splinter group from the ANC, led by a charismatic leader, professes radical positions in terms of Black economic empowerment and land redistribution.
7 One could have expected the DA to protect the middle-class residents of Norwood as their core constituency, but the discard of the Corridors of Freedom by the new (DA) mayor was not conducive to it.
8 They are often wetlands with a mix of informal uses (cattle grazing, car washing, religious worshipping, criminal activities, dumping zones, informal settlements) occasionally leisure activities in a green open environment.
9 How to have grass cut, if the park has developed into a dumping zone, or has become home to the homeless? Beyond blaming and evicting, some park managers have adopted a pragmatic and social approach to what they understand as a structural issue one cannot find a quick fix for (Bénit-Gbaffou 2018b).
10 See Rubin's Chapter 4 and Klug's Chapter 8, this book.
11 Seeing the buildings' asset value for Black private developers, rather than their use value for low-income (Black) residents.

References

Abers, R. 2019. 'Bureaucratic activism: Pursuing environmentalism inside the Brazilian State', *Latin American Politics and Society* 61(2): 22–44.

Abers, R. and Tatagiba, L. 2015. 'Institutional activism: Mobilizing for women's health from inside the Brazilian bureaucracy'. In *Social movements in Latin America: New theoretical trends and lessons from a mobilised regions*, edited by F.M. Rossi and M. von Bülow, 73–104. London: Ashgate.

Applebaum, A. 2017. *Contestation, transformation and competing visions: A study of Orange Grove and Norwood.* Spatial Transformation through Transit-Oriented Development Series 7. Johannesburg: University of the Witwatersrand.

Banaszak, L.A. 2010. *The Women's Movement Inside and Outside the State*. New York: Cambridge University Press.

Barker, C. 2001. 'Robert Michels and the cruel game'. In *Leadership and Social Movements,* edited by C. Barker, A. Johnson and M. Lavallette, 24–43. Manchester: Manchester University Press.

Bénit-Gbaffou, C. 2018a. 'Beyond the policy-implementation gap: How the City of Johannesburg manufactured the ungovernability of street trading', *Journal of Development Studies* 54(12): 2149–67.

Bénit-Gbaffou, C. 2018b. 'Why is co-management of parks not working in Johannesburg? The difficult reframing of state mandate and practices in the post-apartheid era', *International Development Policy* 10: 101–36.

Bereni, L. and Revillard A. 2012. 'A Paradigmatic Social Movement? Women's movements and the definition of contentious politics', *Sociétés Contemporaines* 1(85): 17–41.

Blatrix, C. 2002. 'Devoir débattre. Les effets de l'institutionnalisation de la participation sur les formes de l'action collective', *Politix* 15(57): 79–102.

Bosaka, P. 2015. 'Changing Practices of the State: Johannesburg City Parks and Zoo officials' Views on Opportunities and Challenges of Community Engagement'. Honours research report, School of Architecture and Planning. Johannesburg: University of the Witwatersrand.

Boucher, Y. and Villalba, B. 1990. 'Le militant, la compétence et l'éthique. Les conditions de l'investiture chez les Verts', *Politix* 3(9): 37–43.

Chiha, J. 2006. 'Les cadres intermédiaires, leviers du changement radical', *La Revue des Sciences de Gestion, Direction et Gestion* 220–1: 177–82.

Chipkin, I., Tshimomola, G. and Meny-Gibert, S. 2014. *The Contract State: Outsourcing and Decentralisation in Contemporary South Africa*. Research report for the Public Affairs Research Institute. Johannesburg: PARI.

Clavel, P. 1986. *The Progressive City: Planning and participation, 1969–1984*. New Jersey: Rutgers University Press.

Clavel, P. 2010. *Activists in City Hall: The progressive response to the Reagan era in Boston and Chicago*. New York: Cornell University Press.

Dagnino and Tatagiba, 2010. 'Mouvements sociaux et participation institutionnelle: répertoires d'action collective et dynamiques culturelles dans la difficile construction de la démocratie brésilienne'. *Revue Internationale e Politique Comparée* 2(17): 167–85.

Dahl, R. 1961. *Who Governs? Democracy and power in the American city*. New Haven: Yale University Press.

Daniel, M. and Foto, T. 2016. 'Profile of Nicolette Pingo'. In *Facilitating Community Participation in Divided Society*, edited by C. Bénit-Gbaffou. Johannesburg: Wits School of Architecture and Planning, Master class report.

Domhoff, G. 2011. 'Why San Francisco is (or used to be) different: Progressive activists and neighborhoods had a big impact', *Who rules America?* Available at: http://www2.ucsc.edu/whorulesamerica/local/san_francisco.html. Accessed 4 July 2023.

Dowbor, M. and Houtzager, P. 2014. 'The role of professionals in policy reform: Cases from the city level, São Paulo', *Latin American Politics and Society* 56(3): 141–62.

Ferguson, J. 2010. 'The uses of neoliberalism', *Antipode* 41(S1): 166–84.

Flyvbjerg, B. 2014. 'What you should know about megaprojects and why: An overview', *Project Management Journal* 45(2): 6–19.

Forester, J. 1999. *The Deliberative Practitioner: Encouraging participatory planning processes*. Cambridge: MIT Press.

Giugni, M. 1998. 'Was it worth the effort? The outcomes and consequences of social movements', *Annual Review of Sociology* 24: 371–93.

Goldstone, J. 2003. 'Introduction: Bridging institutionalised and non-institutionalised politics'. In *States, Parties and Social Movements: Pushing the boundaries of institutional change*, edited by J. Goldstone, 1–26. New York: Cambridge University Press.

Harrison, P. 2013. 'Making planning theory real', *Planning Theory* 13(1): 65–81.

Harrison, P., Rubin, M., Appelbaum, A. and Dittgen, R. 2019. 'Corridors of Freedom: Analyzing Johannesburg's ambitious inclusionary transit-oriented development', *Journal of Planning Education and Research* 39(4): 1–13.

Hysing, E. and Olsson, J. 2017. *Green Inside Activism for Sustainable Development: Political agency and institutional change*. Switzerland: Palgrave McMillan.

Joshi, A. and Moore, M. 2004. 'Institutionalised coproduction: Unorthodox public service delivery in challenging environments', *Journal of Development Studies* 40(4): 31–49.

Katzenstein, M. 1998. 'Stepsisters: Feminist movement activism in different institutional spaces'. In *The Social Movement Society: Contentious politics for a new century,* edited by D.S. Meyer and S. Tarrow, 195–216. Lanham, MD: Rowman and Littlefield.

Katzenstein, M. 2012. 'Quand la contestation se déploie dans les institutions', *Société Contemporaine* 85(1): 11–131.

Krumholz, N. and Clavel, P. 1994. *Reinventing Cities: Equity planners tell their stories.* Philadelphia: Temple University Press.

Lascoumes, P. and Le Galès, P. 2007. 'Introduction: Understanding public policy through its instruments – from the nature of instruments to the sociology of public policy instrumentation', *Governance* 20(1): 1–21.

Laures, A. 2017. 'The Management of Homelessness in Norwood Park, Johannesburg'. Unpublished Masters report in Development Studies. Paris: University of Paris I – Sorbonne.

McAdam, D., McCarthy, J. and Zald, M. (eds). 1996. *Comparative Perspectives on Social Movements.* New York: Cambridge University Press.

Memela, W. and Nyanda, N. 2016. 'Profile of Matt Jackson'. In *Facilitating Community Participation in Divided Society,* edited by C. Bénit-Gbaffou. Johannesburg: Wits School of Architecture and Planning, Master class report.

Michels, R. 1965 [1911]. *Political Parties: A sociological study of the oligarchical tendencies of modern democracy.* New York: Routledge.

Miraftab, F. 2004. 'Making neo-liberal governance: The disempowering work of empowerment', *International Planning Studies* 9: 239–59.

Mogkere, T. 2018. *Formalising partnerships between park users and City Park in inner city Johannesburg.* Unpublished Masters report in Urban Studies. Johannesburg: Wits University.

Molema, L. 2016. 'Exploring City officials' Practices of Community Engagement. The Case of Johannesburg Development Agency, Johannesburg'. Unpublished Honours report. Johannesburg: Wits University, School of Architecture and Planning.

Needleman, M. and Needleman, C. 1974. *Guerrillas in the Bureaucracy: The community planning experiment in the United States.* New York: Wiley.

Neveu, C. 2011. 'Démocratie participative et mouvements sociaux: Entre domestication et ensauvagement?', *Participations* 1(1): 186–209.

Niez, T. and Krishnamurthy, R. 2013. 'Bureaucratic activism and radical school change in Tamil Nadu, India', *Journal of Educational Change* 14: 29–35.

Pettinicchio, D. 2012. 'Institutional activism: Reconsidering the insider/outsider dichotomy', *Sociology Compass* 6(6): 499–510.

Revillard, A. 2011. 'Le féminisme dans l'Etat', *Revue Francaise de Science Politique* 61(5): 956–9.

Rubin, M. 2021. 'Local government as the stage for resistance: Strategies and tactics of opposing mega projects in the City of Johannesburg'. In *Refractions of the National, the Popular, and the Global in African Cities,* edited by S. Bekker, G. Therborn and S Croese, 71–84. Pretoria: HSRC Press.

Santoro, W.A. and McGuire, G.M. 1997. 'Social movement insiders: The impact of institutional activists on affirmative action and comparable worth policies', *Social Issues* 44(4): 503–19.

Seippel, Ø. 2001. 'From mobilization to institutionalization? The case of Norwegian environmentalism', *Acta Sociologica* 44(2): 123–37.

Shrock, G. 2015. 'Remains of the progressive city? First source hiring in Portland and Chicago', *Urban Affairs Review* 51(5): 649–75.

Staggenborg, S. 1988. 'The consequences of professionalisation and formalisation in the Pro-choice Movement', *American Sociological Review* 53(4): 585–605.

Stone, C. 1995. 'Political leadership in urban politics'. In *Theories of Urban Politics,* edited by D. Judge, G. Stoker and H. Wolman, 96–116. London: Sage.

Stone, C. 2006. 'Power, reform, and urban regime analysis', *City and Community* 5(1): 23–38.

van der Heijden, H. 1997. 'Political opportunity structure and the institutionalisation of the environmental movement', *Environmental Politics* 6(4): 25–50.

Verhoeven, I. and Duyvendak, J.W. 2017. 'Understanding governmental activism', *Social Movement Studies,* 16(5): 564–77.

von Holdt, K. 2013. 'South Africa: The transition to violent democracy', *Review of African Political Economy* 40(1): 589–604.

Official documents

City of Johannesburg. 2017. *Inner City Housing Implementation Plan* (ICHIP).

City of Johannesburg. 2014. *Corridors of Freedom: Re-stitching our city to create new futures.* Available at: https://www.joburg.org.za/Campaigns/Documents/2014%20Documents/corridors%20of%20freedom_s.pdf . Accessed 22 August 2023.

Johannesburg City Park and Zoo (JPCZ). 2019. *Transforming Public Parks into Safe and Inclusive Community Space: Lessons on collaboration and participation from the City of Joburg.* Available at: https://www.saferspaces.org.za/uploads/files/WEB_CoJ_Lessons_Learnt_public_spaces.pdf . Accessed 22 August 2023.

Johannesburg City Park and Zoo (JCPZ). 2017. *Inner City Regeneration: Strategy for safe community parks.* Available at: https://www.africanpublicspaces.org/wp-content/uploads/2022/10/Johannesburg-inner-city-Strategy-for-safe-community-parks.pdf. Accessed 11 August 2023.

Johannesburg City Park and Zoo (JCPZ). 2013. *Corporate Strategic Plan, 2013–18.*

4

Bureaucratic activism for inclusionary development in the City of Johannesburg

Margot Rubin

Introduction

In February 2018, the City of Johannesburg's City Transformation Unit in the Planning Department, sent out notification of a document that 'outlines the requirements, incentives, regulations and mechanisms for implementing inclusionary housing in the City of Johannesburg' (CoJ 2018) for public comment. The document defined inclusionary housing as:

> A housing programme that requires private developers to dedicate a certain percentage of new housing developments to low-income and low middle-income households at affordable housing cost. This document includes only rental housing as inclusionary housing (CoJ 2018, 2).

It proposed that inclusionary housing would now be mandatory for all new projects with 10 units or more, and would have to be set aside for a rental capped at R2,100 a month, excluding utilities. The document also announced that the units would have to meet certain basic requirements, size, design and amenity and that they would have to stay as rental units to the affordable housing sector in perpetuity.

The proposal of new mechanisms, incentives and regulations came as quite a shock to housing practitioners and policy advisors, largely because (as will be demonstrated below) there was originally little support from the provincial or national government and ambivalence from the private sector, who expressed both outright antagonism and grudging acceptance. Furthermore, it had not worked before when the City of Johannesburg attempted it over a decade ago. It is within this context that the City of Johannesburg launched this document for public comment, inspiring a host of questions from observers of the state, not least of which was: what on earth is going on? Where does this come from? What is motivating such a course of action? And how, given the context, did this document ever get this far?

It is to these questions that this chapter responds: looking initially at the City of Johannesburg's City Transformation Unit's proposal and how surprising it was within the larger context of indifference and outright hostility. It also looks at what the directorate was attempting to achieve with this document and policy approach. The second part of this chapter examines some of the tactics and strategies that the City Transformation Unit utilised in order to achieve its short- and long-term goals; and the last part of this chapter attempts to delve into the question of what motivated these actions and how they can be understood within the wider rubric of bureaucratic activism.

The contribution of this chapter is manifold: to extend and enhance existing research and to attempt to fill in a few gaps. There has been a recognition of the importance of studying 'the state', complexifying and challenging our sense of what it is and how it should act; the task has only been undertaken by a few people within the South African academy. Within studies of the South African state, much attention has been paid to judicial activism (Wilson and Dugard 2013; Brinks and Gauri 2014), the state's interaction with the public and social movements (Hoag 2010; 2014) and the response and engagement to protest (von Holdt et al. 2010; Pernegger 2021) with few paying attention to other actors within the state (Heller 2012; Bénit-Gbaffou 2012; von Holdt 2010, and more recently the work undertaken by the Public Affairs Research Institute). However, despite these important interventions, to many, South African bureaucrats and their day-to-day activities are still lumped together into popular memes: lazy, corrupt, politically captured or incompetent. The press treats readers to a cacophony of stories relating to corruption charges and financial mismanagement on a regular basis. Headlines scream 'Bribery tops list of corrupt activities in SA'[1] and one which speaks to a trifecta of faults: 'A comradely brew of incompetence, greed and narcissism.'[2] However, the lesser-known stories of the many dedicated, active and sincere people who work in the state is then lost, as are the narratives and accounts of just how these people work to make change and what drives their actions. Thus, aside from a few key studies (von Holdt 2010; Chipkin 2011; Bénit-Gbaffou 2011), South African bureaucrats remain almost invisible (as was described in Brazil by Dowbor and Houtzager 2014).

In the context of urban South Africa, leaving out these narratives misses a key way in understanding how cities are constructed and some of the most important actors who are shaping contemporary city environments. Positioning bureaucrats in stereotypical polemics does not help us to understand the nature of current power relations and how actions, inactions and daily practices influence, effect and construct our cities. Thus, this chapter resonates with Dowbor and Houtzager who write:

> All polities periodically produce opportunities for institutional reform, and reformist professionals, more often than is acknowledged in recent social science or international development policy circles, have played a critical role in defining the content of such reforms and seeing that they redefine how public institutions operate and to whose welfare they contribute (Dowbor and Houtzager 2014, 158).

In order to respond to this line of thinking, I conducted a set of six interviews with City officials who were directly or indirectly responsible for the development of the public document, and the inclusionary housing clauses in the City's Spatial Development Framework (SDF), as well as one interview with a consultant who had worked on national and provincial inclusionary housing policy. I also attended a series of workshops throughout 2017 and 2018 on the topic. Using these engagements, this chapter seeks to interrogate the attempted promulgation of inclusionary housing and its associated documents as lens and an access point to begin to understand the 'work' that officials can do, and the normative worlds that inform and drive their actions. The respondents were candid and open with me as a researcher, largely owing, I assume, to our long-standing relationships, some of whom were old friends and colleagues and ex-students that I had taught or people I had studied with. The relationships of trust and reciprocity had been built over a number of years and allowed for this honest and insightful exchange. I also shared the final paper with them and asked for comments out of respect for our relationships and to make sure that they were comfortable with the narrative I had produced.

I position these officials as bureaucratic activists seen as a combination of Krumholz and Clavel's (1994, 1) 'equity planners' who make conscious attempts towards redistributive policies and practices from within the state and 'institutional activists' seen as 'individuals who affect change (from changing organisational norms to policy reform) from within organisations and institutions' (Pettinicchio 2012, 501), as well as a third idea taken from political studies which forefronts the question of agency and embeddedness in institutions, but importantly notes: 'Embedding structures do not simply generate constraints on agency but, instead, provide a platform for the unfolding of entrepreneurial activities.' According to this view, actors are knowledgeable agents with a capacity to reflect and act in ways other than those prescribed by accepted social rules and technological artifacts (Garud et al. 2007, 961).

The combination is necessary since none of the definitional accounts are sufficient; all have necessary components but are slightly problematic. The notion of equity planners insists on thinking of equity planners as planners, who aside from policy work seek to push the modes of participation, which I would argue is not necessary for all bureaucratic activists, but usefully provide insights into the modes of activation and mobilisation within the state. Institutional activists are generally seen as 'insiders working on outsider causes' (Santoro and McGuire 1997; Pettinicchio 2012, 502) and see a strong relationship between social movements and the state, which, as will be demonstrated below, is not necessarily the case. However, the important and under-investigated insight that 'institutional activists may act as issue entrepreneurs because of personal histories and experiences with an issue or constituency, biographical characteristics, ideology, and career ambitions' (Pettinicchio 2012, 502) is a point that I return to later in the chapter. But institutional activists are seen to ultimately restructure and construct new institutions for the ends that they want to achieve and are thus defined by their success.

Thus, I consider the actions of a small group of public officials who utilise their position within a state institution, leverage their position and their access to resources, to produce and drive their own self-devised progressive agenda. They were not aligned with a social movement, a political party, or any other external constituency, nor were they seeking to overhaul the institution in which they operated. It is this modest, but important form of progressive advocacy that I would term 'bureaucratic activism'. How and why this unfolded will be explored in the following sections of this chapter.

Contextualising inclusionary housing

The announcement of an inclusionary housing policy or set of regulations hardly remains unprecedented within the realms of contemporary urbanism (Calavita and Mallach 2010). Nearly 200 North American cities (Thaden and Wang 2017), Canadian cities, as well as a host of European centres, have incorporated some form of inclusionary development into their regulations and buildings requirements. The literature is filled with debates around the ability of inclusionary housing to achieve its stated ends (Padilla 1995; Mukhija et al. 2010) and the best mechanisms through which some form of spatial inclusion of demographic groups integration and improved access to housing or urban amenities can be achieved (Basolo 2011; Brunick 2004; Lerman 2006). What is surprising is that the push towards inclusionary housing in Johannesburg was an initiative of a unit within the City's Planning Department, not their Housing Department. The further surprise to those of us keeping an eye on housing and urban developments in the City comes from knowing that an inclusionary housing policy had been attempted in the City in 2008 but had been shelved soon after it was initiated, and there was some caution about re-visiting the idea. It had faced a series of challenges including litigation and a deep-seated refusal by property owners and their representatives such as the South African Property Owners Association (SAPOA), as well as a number of legislative difficulties around its implementation (Klug et al. 2013).

At the provincial level, the Gauteng Department of Human Settlements also began to investigate an inclusionary housing policy at about the same time but that too was never passed and was put on hold for a number of years. In 2016, private consultants and teams were once again tasked by Provincial government with investigating the implementability of the 2008 Draft Inclusionary Housing Bill (IHB) (private consultant, personal communication 2018). In particular, consultants were asked to conduct 'a review of the inclusionary housing cost benefit assessment' using a set of scenarios in four settlements, including Steyn City and the Waterfall Estate, two very high-income private developments, to see if inclusionary housing could be built into these settlement typologies in the future.[3] The question was asked of a Inclusive Housing Bill that was already eight years out of date and the team concluded that: 'The implementation of the Inclusive Housing Bill in exclusive residential developments [was] not feasible. It appear[ed] to have a negative impact on the expected returns of large-scale residential projects.'[4] In informal conversations with provincial officials, they signaled that these findings would not be looked upon favourably by some of those in more powerful political and official positions.[5] It was speculated that inclusionary principles were desirable because of the potential to mix poorer households, who were presumably African National Congress (ANC) supporters, into wealthier areas. It would also help to dilute the voting patterns of middle-income households, who are largely Democratic Alliance voters, and thus give the ANC back the majority vote and lessen threats in forthcoming elections of the opposition parties taking control of the metros again (private consultant, personal communication 2018).

The national Department of Human Settlements, has over time expressed a desire for inclusionary housing principles, such as mixed-income, mixed-use sustainable human settlements.[6] In 2007, the department was involved in the development of a Framework for an Inclusionary Housing Policy (IHP) in South Africa; however, it seems to have retreated from the idea of inclusionary development. By the mid-2010s, inclusionary housing was apparently 'a swear word' in national government circles (private consultant, personal communication 2018). Unwilling to support the very idea of inclusionary housing, afraid of further litigation, the national Department of Human Settlements argued that, relative to the expenses that would be incurred to make inclusionary housing work, there would be little 'benefit' to a department that was primarily judged on the number of houses that it produces (private consultant, personal communication 2018).

The private sector as a large and diverse group has had an ambivalent relationship with the idea of inclusionary housing. They had been the ones to litigate against the original inclusionary housing policy but in their public pronouncements were more supportive: 'In principle [SAPOA] supports the need for IHP in South Africa and encourages the development of an inclusionary housing policy that is both incentivised and voluntary, and promotes effective public–private partnerships (PPPs).'[7] In the more recent process, a set of joint workshops were held in 2016 and 2017. At the ones that I attended, most private developers harshly critiqued the idea and there were only a few voices of support. In practice, there has also been resistance to inclusionary projects; the key example has been that of the City of Johannesburg's transit-oriented development named the 'Corridors of Freedom', where they had attempted to put mixed-income housing into a middle-income neighbourhood, Patterson Park. The proposed project had been met with middle-class rage, a large number of objections and had taken up an enormous amount of the City's time and capacity, resulting in what was eventually a very compromised and diluted version (Appelbaum 2019).

However, the City of Johannesburg officials interviewed argued that despite these prevailing conditions, they saw that the time was right to try and pursue inclusionary housing: the National Development Plan, although a few years old referred to the idea of spatial inclusion. But, more particularly, the national fire power was seen to be coming through the 2016 Integrated Urban Development Framework, which explicitly notes the need and desire for inclusionary housing and a supportive national policy.[8] More importantly, the 2013 Spatial Planning and Land Use Management Act has as one of its objectives 'to provide for the inclusive, developmental, equitable and efficient spatial planning at the different spheres of government' and notes that a municipal Spatial Development Framework (SDF), must 'i. identify the designated areas where a national or provincial inclusionary housing policy may be applicable'[9] and that provinces needed to find the mechanisms of support for the implementation of inclusionary residences. As a requirement of the 2013 Spatial Planning and Land Use Management Act,[10] all three spheres of government are required to develop SDFs to assist with spatial transformation. The SDFs detail the ways in which each municipality intends to achieve spatial transformation and forms part of city's Integrated Development Plans. In the case of Johannesburg's SDF, Spatial Development Framework 2040, inclusionary housing was included as a city-wide strategy and the SDF was approved by the Mayor and Council and sits as official City policy in 2016.

Inclusionary housing: intended outcomes

It was in this context, with on the one hand, indifference from the national Department of Human Settlements, questionable motives from Province and outright antagonism from the private sector, and on the other a supportive national planning and policy environment, that the idea of inclusionary housing was once again raised in the City of Johannesburg. The bureaucrats who initially put inclusionary housing into the SDF and later drafted the document for public comment seem to have been motivated by some shared concerns and were largely in agreement about what inclusionary housing could achieve. Much of this was framed around the idea of spatial transformation and thinking through the levers and instruments that were available. The main tool of transformation since 2013 was supposed to be the Corridors of Freedom, a Transit Oriented Development (ToD) project running through the centre of Johannesburg, but some officials wondered what else could be used 'because I think one provocative question that was once asked, on the ToD session that we had, was: if transport wasn't the backbone of achieving spatial transformation, how else would you be able to achieve it?' (CoJ, Planning official 1, personal communication 2018). In developing the SDF, the City was also engaged in thinking through its spatial plan and with help from Un-Habitat and the Urban Morphology Institute, they came up with the compact polycentric model, which would enhance the current nodes and build and connect new ones. Another official feared that:

> to concentrate on [specific areas] where we want investment to go, could make those areas unaffordable and that could drive people out of those spaces. So we could cause gentrification in that process. So how do we prevent that from happening? (CoJ, Planning official 2, personal communication 2018).

Existing policies and programmes were also not seen as assisting in spatial transformation. One official politely mentioned that 'some previous policies like give away houses[11] [and] those kinds of things aren't really working as well as they should be working' (CoJ, Planning official 1, personal communication, 2018). Others were more direct about the problem: 'The public [housing] sector remained the biggest culprit in terms of continuing that [apartheid] spatial planning and legacy' (CoJ, Planning senior official 1, personal communication 2018) referring to the predilection of state housing to be located on the urban periphery far from livelihood opportunities and facilities and contributing to the continued sprawl of the city (Bradlow et al. 2011).

Inclusionary housing was then proposed as an option that would possibly address a number of existing and future problems. It was hoped that inclusionary housing 'could [try] to match [address] the live and the work [mismatch]' (CoJ, Planning official 2, personal communication 2018) and that despite it being only 'a drop in the ocean, it could assist the spatial transformation that we seek to have' (CoJ, Planning official 2, personal communication 2018) and would be a useful 'additional mechanism to actually be providing affordable housing'; it would 'lead to more integration and begin to bridge certain class gaps' (CoJ, Planning official 2, personal communication 2018). The idea was that through inclusionary housing, in future the impact of development and investment would not be for areas to become Sandton and Rosebank (high-income retail and financial centres in Johannesburg), where 'the middle-income households can't even afford those areas' (CoJ, Planning official 2, personal communication 2018). Inclusionary housing was thus seen as a potential tool that could play a part in redress, access and mediating various forms of exclusion while assisting in achieving the desired outcome of spatial transformation. It offered a solution to the question of 'how does this plan [the SDF] actually translate into all these nice principles of spatial justice, inclusivity' (CoJ, Planning official 2, personal communication 2018).

The Unit also led the process of defining and pushing an inclusionary housing agenda, despite the legislative injunction in SPLUMA that says 'Province must put in regulations for inclusionary housing' (senior CoJ official 2, personal communication 2018). 'But we think that's backwards because SPLUMA says obviously that land use is a municipal function and inclusionary housing fundamentally is a land use tool. It's not a housing tool.' Thus, there was a larger set of claims that were going on, which was to reclaim municipal planning as a site, obviously for planners, but more particularly for municipal planners and should not be left or allowed to be controlled by other spheres of government. There was also a reinforcement of the idea that Johannesburg was a leading municipality in the country:

> So hopefully that will even affect the national debate and the provincial debate if needed. And national policy should learn from ours the successes and the mistakes. And if there are changes to make us better then that will be great, but we have sort of just taken a decision to try and lead the thing (senior CoJ official 2, personal communication 2018).

The other hope was that 'when our policy comes out, they must take it seriously and incorporate it into theirs'.

The City Transformation Unit thus saw inclusionary housing as a potential tool not only for integration, spatial transformation and potentially the ability to address future gentrification, but also as a way of inscribing their authority and jurisdiction on land use planning within the City Council. According to van Wyk:

> The *Constitution* determines that the legislative and executive powers regarding 'regional planning and development', 'urban and rural development', 'provincial planning' and 'municipal planning' are divided among the three spheres of government (van Wyk 2012, no page).

The confusion as to exactly which specific sphere of government has been responsible for which specific functional element of planning has historically led to much contention between the City and national and provincial government and eventually to a Constitutional Court case. The Constitutional Court judgement reinforced municipalities' authority over planning within their boundaries (van Wyk 2012). However, despite the judgement, this issue has reappeared more recently as a contestation between national and local government in the case of the proposed mega-projects. While national government is insisting on the development of new, large-scale 'catalytic' human settlements on the peripheries of cities, most of the cities' policies drive towards compaction and densification (Rubin 2021). Thus, introducing and getting buy-in into the idea of inclusionary housing and its regulations was fraught with cross-currents of support and inter-governmental politics. The following section of this chapter offers an account of just how the team managed and negotiated these and managed to push through their agenda.

Doing the work, making it work: tactics and strategies, an entangled web

The following section engages with the question of 'how' exactly the team was able to make inclusionary housing happen. What was the work they did? This is resonant with other studies in a variety of contexts, especially Krumholz and Clavel's 1994 seminal study, which Bénit-Gbaffou (2018, 8) describes as 'testimonies [that] showcase in a high level of details the work of building coalitions, framing internal and external alliances, navigating Council politics, sidelining hostile or obstructive departments, institutionalising instruments or adopting informal practices in the pursuit of specific policy goals'. Similarly, the following section looks at these actions. However, what is also important in this case is that this is not the subtle workings of officials in relatively weaker positions trying to fend off an imposition from above (Rubin 2021) or a social movement with a specific agenda of change, nor were the officials highly politicised. This is a case of what was at the time a unit with a significant power and legitimacy, skill, political connections and agency. This team, although constrained by the institutional setting, were still able to act according to what they thought was best and had the freedom and capacity to do so. The strategies and tactics used in such a case vary considerably from situations of less powerful units and officials.

Where less powerful officials are concerned, there is a need to protect their identities and ensure that responsibility cannot be assigned to any one person (Hoag 2011; Hull 2003), as well as their long-term careers as bureaucrats within the civil service (von Holdt 2010) and so less confrontational tactics, understood as the subtle and subversive manipulations of the subaltern, are used (de Certeau 1984). In terms of actions, these may be seen as the 'weapons of the weak', which Scott (1985) sees as the 'subtle but powerful forms of "every day resistance"', not the grand gestures of coups and rebellion but the small ways in which the less powerful respond to and contest domination. I would argue in the case that is presented here, what can be seen is an intertwined set of tactics and strategies, seen as the use of codified and ruled space using, maps, laws, regulations, and grids to control space (Jessop 2013). The bureaucrats, in this case, actively move between subtle tactics and overt presentations of power to get the job done, sometimes with the very same protagonists in order to achieve their ends. They are clever and creative in the ways in which they use their power over different groups and the resources that they control (Allen 2008). The following section describes the sheer range of what they did and then assists in classifying and understanding these actions.

Issues of power

The Planning Unit needed to get a number of other departments and units onboard before the SDF was passed and in order to get inclusionary housing included into the agenda. They did this by carefully deploying their various forms of power – creatively using their power over certain groups where possible, which forced consensus, while in other moments they had to be more creative and subtle (Allen 2008). As mentioned earlier, some of the worst perpetrators of maintaining the city's spatial patterns were the public housing departments. Two units in particular were seen as being slightly recalcitrant, Johannesburg Social Housing Committee (JOSHCO), the municipally-owned social housing institution, and the Provincial Department of Human Settlements, both of whom seemed determined to continue with their plans irrespective of the drive towards compaction and spatial change. This was largely due to the fact that like all state housing agencies in South Africa, their performance is measured by how much housing they produce and whether they achieve their Key Performance Indicators (KPIs). Since the focus is still on the number of housing units that they produce and their targets being met, projects, policies and programmes that do not contribute to their 'performance' are often ignored or sidelined.

As a consequence, planning basically pushed them in the 'required' direction to rethink their plans by utilising two of the very powerful tools at their disposal: budget and planning permission. A senior official (1), described how 'we first literally informed JOSHCO that we were aware of their project plans but of course ... we wouldn't necessarily allocate capital budget to them in the next two or three years unless they start engaging with us on what they're actually planning to do there'. Acknowledging that such actions would not go uncontested, they then also had a contingency plan. 'You [JOSHCO] know that you still have a good two [or] three, years before you're ready to break ground. We can make it much longer if you don't start talking to us because we think you should do something different.' Thus, through exerting their power through two of their key tools, the City Transformation Unit was able to force discussions, drive JOSHCO to redraft their strategic direction and support the approach encapsulated in the SDF. These were strategies that were intentionally deployed, which recognised that although they [the City Transformation Unit] 'don't control the entire budget, we have enough influence and they have enough projects to take us seriously'. In this case, the officials were referring to the Johannesburg Strategic Infrastructure Platform (JSIP), which is the City's capital investment prioritisation model and which at the time, the City Transformation Unit controlled. Given that the Unit had such power, they were quite clear that their position meant opponents have to carefully 'count [their] risks when [they] have to fight someone' (senior official 1, personal communication 2018).

The Unit also utilised two other instruments to demonstrate their power and embed their authority on these proceedings: the first is that they simply changed the framing of the debate, noting that inclusionary housing as a policy was simply not up for debate, it had legislative support in SPLUMA, legal standing as part of the City's approved SDF and thus 'it [was] not a question of whether we must do it, it's a question of the how to do it' (senior CoJ official, personal communication 2018). So in many ways, once the SDF had been approved, the City Transformation Unit and their supporters could confidently state that the approach was a *fait accompli* and only the details could be discussed and negotiated. This was a creative use of their power (Allen 2008). However, there were also circumstances in which the Unit was not in the dominant position and had to creatively rejig their strategies; in these cases they tried to be useful to those in positions of power. A very senior member of the executive team mentioned that in these cases 'my view with these things if they hold the power and you need them, you have to be useful to them first before you start getting stuff out of them' (personal communication 2018). The Provincial Department of Human Settlements has been tasked with constructing fully integrated, sustainable human settlements, for which they need to put in place educational and healthcare facilities; however, the responsibility for these lies outside of the Department of Human Settlements. So 'after [a] session with Housing, we're like, yeah, maybe the way around this is to help them land bank for schools'. Thus, utilising municipal land planning and zoning tools, they could potentially help to reserve land for these purposes within new settlements, so that when the various departments finally did have the money to build hospitals or schools in these settlements, then land would be available. All departments could then achieve their mandates and score well on their KPIs against which their performance is measured. If the City of Johannesburg Planning Department was able to do this, then they could get the Provincial Housing officials onboard around inclusionary housing, as a kind of reciprocation, a bureaucratic tit-for-tat.

However, outright demonstrations of their power were not the only way that they were able to experiment and creatively build coalitions. They also used more subtle means such as gaining political support; utilising formal and informal channels; offering exchanges and simply changing the terms of the debate.

The officials recognised that they needed to bolster their position within all spheres of government and that their new direction meant a 'change [in] the different policies across the City not just in the Planning Department. So it was meant to be a whole City intervention' (senior CoJ official, personal communication 2018). Thus, when they started the SDF and inclusionary housing programme, they asked: 'Okay. Who's going [to] support this thing?' (CoJ official 1) and the official remembers that they 'scrambled around, looked for contact details throughout the City Support Programme [in National Treasury]. Emailed national [and asked them]: "What do you think of this? Would you support it?" Saved all the emails because we need a background. Emailed Province [and asked them]: "What do you think of this?"' They then held a series of discussions, with Provincial officials, and with other departments within the City of Johannesburg, using the formal inter-governmental platforms. A senior official described their actions:

> We tried to make sure that everyone who [is] processing this is aware of this thing. We engaged with various sector departments like our bulk contribution guys to find out what would happen. We spoke to Land Use to try and understand as well the historical

> context and what people do and knowledge [they] share. And I guess that's how we tried to push it internally so it was very much at the forefront and [in] people's faces (personal communication 2018).

Thus, the team used a broad-based approach to garner support and to get as much feedback as possible in both the vertical and horizontal structures of the state.

Discussions, dialogues and debates

They were able to achieve some internal success: the Rates and Revenue Department Ratings Unit, and Public Infrastructure all came onboard with minor words of caution about not giving away too much with incentives. They were apparently a little concerned that what might be gained in terms of value capture would be lost by the City making too many concessions. However, not all engagements worked: the City Transformation Unit attempted to make it a joint Housing and Planning departmental approach, co-designed and co-owned, so they 'tried really hard and even the team that I was doing this stuff with would try to make sure that it was both Planning and Housing with the view that the Housing people would take the lead. But I don't think they ever saw this as their product'. The result of all these meetings was that Housing continued to focus on producing Reconstruction and Development Programme (RDP) units, which meant that in principle 'they supported it, but they didn't champion it' (senior official, personal communication 2018).

They also found that they needed a range of internal approaches. Very often the discussions were with more senior officials, leaving many of the more junior or 'street-level' bureaucrats to hear about the policies and approaches through rumours or have only part of the idea communicated to them. This resulted in some misunderstandings, anxiety and as a consequence some resistance. One of the officials related that there was a 'disjointed understanding' and 'the professionals who work[ed] with an application every day felt a bit frustrated at times because they [didn't] fully understand, what is inclusionary housing. They thought of it as almost a kind of constraint, you know that I earn R15,000, does it mean that I can't go buy a property anywhere else and I'm now forced to buy into inclusionary housing?'(official 1, personal communication 2018). As a result, some of the Planning officials started to have informal conversations to combat these misinterpretations – literally chats in the hallways, or when they ran into each other in lifts and the like. They also began to invite some of the more operational officials into meetings in which these matters were discussed. It seemed to have some effect and lowered resistance and brought some people into the fold.

Externally, the City Transformation Unit used the same set of tactics and with the South African Property Owner (SAPOA), co-organised a series of panel discussions, with private sector developers, to 'get the dialogue going' (official 1, personal communication 2018), engage in a public debate, air some of the concerns and test what may and may not work. As it turned out, the strategy was only partially effective. In response to the launch of the public document, SAPOA responded by saying that it 'does not believe that the draft policy is a workable solution and may, in its current form, possibly deter the private sector from developing residential units'.[12] They then went on to propose four recommendations that they believed were 'essential to the inclusionary housing policy envisioned by the property industry'.[13] However, as hoped, the public conversation became one regarding the feasibility of the details rather than whether inclusionary housing should or should not happen. At the University of the Witwatersrand, a meeting was held regarding inclusionary housing in March 2018 and a further meeting was held at the Trust for Urban Housing Finance a few days later. The general sentiment from the banking sector and the developers was that they certainly did not like inclusionary housing but if it was a policy then they would accept it and negotiate to find a way to make it work.

The team also used any and all opportunities to bring up, garner support and make the technical changes that they needed in order to get inclusionary housing accepted. For example, the respondents remembered that they used discussions about rates rebates for social housing as an opening to push their agenda. 'So sometimes it was using something else that we're dealing with as a trigger to say that this is an approach and how would this follow through?' (senior executive official, personal communication 2018). Thus, there were moments when the agenda was camouflaged within other issues to make it more subtle and palatable for the other departments.

Taking advantage of context

All of this was taking place in a context in which the team had strong mayoral support, from two subsequent mayors. In the case of the first, Mayor Tau (2011–16), from the ANC, the Planning Unit recollected that they were in a strange position where the mayor wanted them to run faster with the idea than they were technically able. There was also a personal and long-standing connection between the City Transformation Unit and the mayor. The following anecdote demonstrates how deeply this relationship ran:

> [senior officials] were presenting our business plan and what we were focusing on in that year, and he [Mayor Parks Tau] said something to the effect that clearly the Planning Department is committed to maintaining the apartheid city form. And so, Parks and I are friends, right? We play golf together ... [I said] 'I can't believe you said that. I would think you of all people know what I'm about but for you to sit where I can't take you on, because you're the mayor, and say something like that, I think that's ... I would think you know me! but never mind anything else.' He was like, 'No way'. So when we got back to the mayoral committee then he said, 'You know perhaps I was a little bit harsh, blah, blah, and I apologise because besides anything else I risk losing a friendship' (personal communication 2018).

When they presented the SDF and inclusionary housing approach to Herman Mashaba, the subsequent Democratic Alliance mayor (2016–19), he apparently said: 'I've been waiting for this for a very long time. I'm glad that it's finally here' (CoJ, official 1 2018). At the same meeting, he suggested that between the Planning Unit and the Mayor, they pen an opinion editorial for one of the local papers, going on record and publicising his support (senior CoJ official).[14]

The support of the mayors meant that when the approach was contested internally, the team already had the ear of the mayor and was further able to brief the mayor on its legislative standing, and its general benefits and so fend off their objections and go ahead. In the one case, Mayor Tau was able to defend them against accusations that the Planning Unit had 'gone rogue' and was 'going to kill development' (senior executive official, personal communication 2018). Later on, Mayor Mashaba, who understood that the inclusionary housing was already in SPLUMA and the SDF, told councillors who were objecting: 'What policy is not there? What you want people to live far away? No! No! No! It's not going happen. We will help the developer but the poor people will live here. So we just sat back and [laughed]' (senior executive official, personal communication 2018).

The more recent coalition-led Council has also proven to be an advantage to the Planning Unit. At the time, the mayor was from the

Democratic Alliance, which had secured a coalition with the far more left-leaning Economic Freedom Fighters (EFF) against the long-standing ANC. When presenting the approach to the relevant Council committees, the EFF took the position: 'Oh, 20 per cent is not enough, we must do 60 per cent.' Pushing the percentages for inclusionary housing to 'the ridiculous' and then 'the only solution [was] ... for the DA to move to the reasonable' at which point, 'the DA [had] no choice but to choose a reasonable 20 per cent', which is exactly the figure that the Planning Unit was hoping for in their policy (senior executive official, personal communication 2018).

The previous sections have noted the policy intentions that motivated the official's behaviour and also the array of tactics and strategies that the various officials deployed. Everything from overt demonstrations of power, which put on full display the position of authority that the City Transformation Unit had, all the way through to carefully thought through acts of reciprocation, negotiation and subtly camouflaging the intent of some actions. A few things are clear. The first is that enormous agency, skill and effort were utilised. These officials consistently stepped out of the defined channels and modes of engagement and were innovative and creative in how they interacted. They were bold and active. They also pushed and manipulated when they needed to and took advantage of the political opportunities in which they operated – all of which takes high levels of institutional skill, dedication and adds an element of risk. Considering that none of these elements are required by the officials' job descriptions, and they will not be rewarded for it personally, professionally or politically, it does beg the question: why would people behave in this manner?

Neither angels nor demons

Recent literature has cautioned analyses that simplify or stereotype the behaviour and actions of officials, demanding that we pay attention to their 'humanity' and that we neither demonise nor canonise their behaviour (Drivdal 2014). However, more needs to be understood about why certain units, officials and departments do what they do. There is a need to step away from historical constructions of bureaucratic identity, which:

> ... puts forward a theory of African bureaucracy by examining its historical construction during the colonial and postcolonial period, contrasted with the rise of bureaucratic states in Europe. [...]

> Whereas the figure of the bureaucrat in Europe is one who applies a rule with excessive rigidity, in Africa the bureaucrat is more often seen as capricious and abusive (de Sardan 2007 in Hoag and Hull 2017,17).

Current explanations about political patronage (Blundo 2015), looking up (von Holdt 2010) are useful but once again limited. Following the advice of Hoag and Hull (2017) that 'anthropologists would therefore be wise not to presume that bureaucrats are robotic' – an advice that all students of the state should contemplate, the following section looks into the particular and specific reasons that these people do what they do.

Few studies (Murray Li 2007) have focused on the deep-seated sets of beliefs that officials hold and which drive them. For the most part, this has been contextualised within the social movement literature, noting how normative views have been institutionalised (Niesz and Krishnamurthy 2013). This case offers something slightly different. Many of the planners hold a deeply held set of beliefs that has led them to work as officials in this unit. When asked about why they do what they do, many of the respondents said that they joined this specific unit (the City Transformation Unit) in the City as it resonates with their personal ethical positions and view of their lives and their world. For most officials there was a sense that this unit should 'lead' and that it was a unit dedicated to transforming the status quo rather than letting things continue as they had been. As such, it was a unit that attracted largely university-educated planning professionals who had been steeped in social justice theory, not just the practicalities and technicalities of land use planning. One of the respondents described the situation as:

> Whereas the Strategic Department [attracted] a lot more university graduates, and for the Land Use Department it was a lot more sort of technical graduates. I think that does play a big role so almost everyone on this floor has been trained not in technical planning, but, like, how can we critique the system, and look at what the problems are with the system to make it better (senior CoJ official 2, personal communication 2018).

Almost all of the respondents articulated the view that they promoted inclusionary housing as it formed part of a larger worldview and project, driven by race and social position. When I asked respondents why they do what they do and why they carry on when it becomes difficult, the responses were small variations on the same theme:

> If you don't do these hard things, what do you do? Wake up in the morning every day to sign leave forms? No, I think it would be squandering an opportunity to not do that, because government has to work for the good of society. The injustice of what you see every day will not correct itself. And it's an obligation of those who are in government in particular to do something about it and to kind of force the system to work slightly differently (senior executive official, personal communication 2018).

One of the other respondents echoed this sentiment: 'Well I suppose the reason I do planning in the first place, is to try and make a bit of a difference in society' (senior CoJ official, personal communication 2018). Another claimed: 'We are concerned with the public interest' (CoJ official 2, personal communication 2018).

Part of this mobilisation was also the way they understood their own racialised identity in the current context. One of the senior executive officials argued that affirmative action is not just about redress and redistribution but has a further role in the state:

> It [affirmative action policies in government] is so that the bureaucracy starts to see things as the majority of the people experience them. I said to them, when I drive around on a Sunday the things that hit me are different to the things that hit a middle- or high-income White person. And I mean no disrespect to my White colleagues, but do you think [they] see that and think, 'Hmm that's worth doing something about'. And that's why there's affirmative action. Not so that you the individual can benefit. It's so that you start to change how the system interacts with society (senior executive official, CoJ, personnal communication 2018).

When asked the same question about why they do what they do, another official replied, 'I almost said [because] I'm Black, and want to advocate for Black people in space based on my social upbringing, I guess my race as well, and our history, the injustices of the past' (CoJ official 2, personal communication 2018).

One of the White senior members of staff also saw race and history contributing to their decisions and actions: 'For me, as someone who comes from a privileged background and who this society has privileged hugely, I see it as sort of giving back, you know.' The sentiments expressed above are clearly deeply felt, and the earlier incident described when the mayor accused the planning team of perpetuating existing spatial patterns left the senior executive official in tears, and ready to strike back. I asked why the mayor's comments had affected them so deeply: 'You know, I felt it as an unfair statement and ignored how hard people were working to affect change.'

Conclusion

I defined bureaucratic activists as those who utilise their position within a state institution, who leverage their position and their access to resources, to produce and drive their own self-devised progressive agenda – who in effect have agency. As the case demonstrates, the officials in question were not in their positions to simply collect pay checks, or to stamp documents and eke out the days until their retirement, but felt that they had an ethical obligation to make a change for good. Inclusionary housing as a policy approach is simply a material manifestation of a deep-seated set of beliefs about the world and their role in it – which is to make a difference. Given their skill set and professional abilities, this then is manifest in urban policy. However, such beliefs and their passion may also explain the lengths that they went to in order to get this policy approach passed. The meetings, dialogues, thinking through, reciprocation, camouflage, informal discussion and the willingness to utilise the levers of power at their disposal all make sense if seen as ways of making a set of beliefs into a material reality. This aspect of bureaucracy should not be ignored: the connection between belief, and policy development. The case also illustrates that the power of this group is not consistent and there were moments when they could use the instruments within their grasp to leverage and push their own agenda but other moments when they were not as powerful as other players and so had to be far more surreptitious, subtle and make deals to get what they wanted (Allen 2008).

Thus, despite a generally highly adverse external environment, but with some national policy support, the Unit pushed through a public document for comment, utilising the various strategies and tactics mentioned above, but also the place of time and history should not be ignored (Allen 2008). Dowbor and Houtzager note the importance of context and history arguing:

> The role of the *sanitaristas* and economists in the two programs examined here was therefore embedded in particular historical trajectories – that of a democratic transition after 21 years of

> military rule; that of the professions themselves under authoritarian rule; and a broader international zeitgeist from the 1980s on that favored citizen participation, new forms of social policy, and new forms of provisioning public services (Dowbor and Houtzager 2014, 157).

So too in this case are specificities important. In post-apartheid South Africa, context and the specificity of this historical trajectory should not be ignored: individuals with particular history and identity (mostly university educated and educated by a group of people with a strong sense of social justice), enabled by two mayoral terms to construct an institutional position, within a broader zeitgeist of social justice, spatial justice, language of inclusivity, all finding a department with the requisite power and institutional levers. These elements altogether construct an ideal environment in which this particular brand of social justice-led bureaucratic activism can flourish. The case demonstrates what can happen when a group of skilled, able, and passionate individuals, with deep-seated conviction, are facilitated and how urban changes may result.

Notes

1 Gous, N. 2018. 'Bribery tops list of corrupt activities in SA', *Timeslive*, 8 August 2018. Available at: https://www.timeslive.co.za/news/south-africa/2018-08-08-bribery-tops-list-of-corrupt-activities-in-sa/. Accessed 11 July 2023.

2 Herbst, E. 2018. A comradely brew of incompetence, greed and narcissism, *BizNews*, 30 July 2018.

3 KPMG. 2016. *Housing Affordability in Gauteng: A review of the inclusionary housing bill cost benefit assessment*, Johannesburg, 30 March 2016.

4 KPMG. 2016. *Housing Affordability in Gauteng: A review of the inclusionary housing bill cost benefit assessment*, Johannesburg, 30 March 2016.

5 Unfortunately, the officials in question did not want to be quoted and there is a need to remain vague in order to ensure their anonymity.

6 Republic of South Africa. 2004. *Breaking New Ground policy. A comprehensive plan for the development of integrated settlements*. Pretoria.

7 Property24. 2007. 'SAPOA: all for inclusionary housing', 12 April 2007. Available at: https://www.property24.com/articles/sapoa-all-for-inclusionary-housing/5081. Accessed 11 July 2023.

8 COGTA. 2016. *Integrated Urban Development Framework: A new deal for South African cities and towns*. Pretoria.

9 Republic of South Africa. 2013. SPLUMA, *Government Gazette*, 13. See Republic of South Africa. 2013, 32.

10 Republic of South Africa. 2013, Spatial Planning and Land Use Management Act 16 of 2013. Pretoria.

11 Referring to the South African state's provision of free housing to households earning less than R3,500 a month.

12 Cited in Slabbert, A. 2018. 'Blanket inclusionary housing policy 'unworkable' Sapoa opposes Joburg's mandatory scheme'. Moneyweb, 24 April 2018. Available at: https://www.moneyweb.co.za/news/south-africa/blanket-inclusionary-housing-policy-unworkable/. Accessed 12 July 2023.

13 SAPOA. 2018. 'SAPOA Comments on the City of Johannesburg Draft Inclusionary Policy', 23 April 2018, SAPOA News. Available at: http://www.sapoa.org.za/media/press-releases/sapoa-comments-on-the-city-of-johannesburgs-draft-inclusionary-housing-policy/. Accessed 12 July 2023.

14 The opinion editorial was published at: https://www.news24.com/Columnists/GuestColumn/joburgs-plans-to-foster-economic-and-racial-integration-20180423. Accessed 12 July 2023.

References

Allen, J. 2008. 'Pragmatism and power, or the power to make a difference in a radically contingent world', *Geoforum* 39(4): 1613–24.

Appelbaum, A. 2019. 'The micro-politics of state-led spatial transformation: The suburban middle class in a municipal tribunal'. In *Reversing Urban Inequality? Debating spatial transformation in globalising Johannesburg*, edited by M. Myambo, 13–23. London: Routledge.

Basolo, V. 2011. 'Inclusionary housing: The controversy continues', *The Town Planning Review* 82(2): i–vi.

Bénit-Gbaffou, C. 2011. ' "Up close and personal". How does local democracy help the poor access the state? Stories of accountability and clientelism in Johannesburg', *Journal of Asian and African Studies* 46(5): 453–64.

Bénit-Gbaffou, C. 2012. 'Party politics, civil society and local democracy: Reflections from Johannesburg', *Geoforum* 43(2): 178–89.

Bénit-Gbaffou, C. 2018. 'Beyond the policy-implementation gap. How the City of Johannesburg manufactured the ungovernability of street trading', *Journal of Development Studies* 54(12): 2149–67.

Blundo, G. 2015. 'The king is not a kinsman: Multiple accountabilities and practical norms in West African bureaucracies'. In *Real Governance and Practical Norms in Sub-Saharan Africa*, edited by R. de Hedt and J-P. Olivier de Sardan, 152–69. London and New York: Routledge.

Bradlow, B., Bolnick, J. and Shearing, C. 2011. 'Housing, institutions, money: The failures and promise of human settlements policy and practice in South Africa', *Environment and Urbanisation* 23(1): 267–75.

Brinks, D.M. and Gauri, V. 2014. 'The law's majestic equality? The distributive impact of judicialising social and economic rights', *Perspectives on Politics* 12(2): 375–93.

Brunick, N. 2004. 'The inclusionary housing debate: The effectiveness of mandatory programs over voluntary', *Zoning Practice* 21(9): 1–7.

Calavita, N. and Mallach, A. (eds). 2010. *Inclusionary Housing in International Perspective: Affordable housing social inclusion and land value recapture.* Cambridge: Lincoln Institute of Land Policy.

Chipkin, I. 2011. 'Transcending bureaucracy: State transformation in the age of the manager', *Transformation: Critical Perspectives on Southern Africa* 77(1): 31–51.

City of Johannesburg. 2018. *City of Johannesburg, Inclusionary Housing Policy, Incentives, Regulations and Mechanisms.*

de Certeau, M. 1984. *The Practice of Everyday Life.* Berkeley: University of California Press.

Dowbor, M. and Houtzager, P.P. 2014. 'The role of professionals in policy reform: Cases from the city level, São Paulo', *Latin American Politics and Society* 56(3): 141–62.

Drivdal, J. 2014. 'The Politics of Leadership Organising in Informal Settlements: Ambiguities of speaking publicly and mediating conflicting institutional logics'. Unpublished PhD thesis, Centre of Criminology, University of Cape Town.

Garud, R., Hardy C. and Maguire, S. 2007. 'Institutional entrepreneurship as embedded agency: An introduction to the special issue', *Organisation Studies* 28(7): 957–69.

Heller, P. 2012. 'Democracy, participatory politics and development: Some comparative lessons from Brazil, India and South Africa', *Polity* 44(4): 643–65.

Hoag, C. 2010. 'The magic of the populace: An ethnography of illegibility in the South African immigration bureaucracy', *Political and Legal Anthropology Review* 33(1): 6–25.
Hoag, C. 2011. 'Assembling partial perspectives: Thoughts on the anthropology of bureaucracy', *Political and Legal Anthropology Review* 34(1): 81–94.
Hoag, C. 2014. 'Dereliction at the South African Department of Home Affairs: Time for the anthropology of bureaucracy', *Critique of Anthropology* 34(4): 410–28.
Hoag, C. and Hull, M. 2017. 'A Review of the Anthropological Literature on the Civil Service'. Policy Research Working Paper No. 8081. Washington DC: World Bank.
von Holdt, K. 2010. 'Nationalism, bureaucracy and the developmental state: The South African case', *South African Review of Sociology* 41(1): 4–27.
Hull, M. 2003. 'The file: Agency, authority, and autography in an Islamabad bureaucracy', *Language and Communication* 23: 287–314.
Jessop, B. 2013. 'The governance of complexity and the complexity of governance: Preliminary remarks on some problems and limits of economic guidance'. In *Beyond Markets and Hierarchy: Interactive governance and social complexity*, edited by A. Amin and J. Hausner, 111–47. Cheltenham: Edward Elgar.
Klug, N., Rubin, M. and Todes, A. 2013. 'Inclusionary housing policy: A tool for re-shaping South Africa's spatial legacy?', *Journal of Housing and the Built Environment* 28(4): 667–78.
Krumholz, N. and Clavel, P. 1994. *Reinventing Cities: Equity planners tell their stories.* Philadelphia: Temple University Press.
Lerman, B. 2006. 'Mandatory inclusionary zoning: The answer to affordable housing problem', *Boston College Environmental Affairs Law Review* 33(2): 383–416.
Mukhija, V., Regus, L., Slovin, S. and Das, A. 2010. 'Can inclusionary zoning be an effective and efficient housing policy? Evidence from Los Angeles and Orange Counties', *Journal of Urban Affairs* 32(2): 229–52.
Murray Li, T. 2007. *The Will to Improve: Governmentality, development, and the practice of politics.* Durham: Duke University Press.
Niesz, T. and Krishnamurthy, R. 2013. 'Bureaucratic activism and radical school change in Tamil Nadu, India', *Journal of Educational Change* 14(1): 29–50.
Padilla, L.M. 1995. *Reflections on Inclusionary Housing and a Renewed Look at its Viability.* Cambridge: Lincoln Institute on Land Policy.
Pernegger, L. 2021. 'Effects of the state's informal practices on organisational capability and social inclusion: Three cases of city governance in Johannesburg', *Urban Studies* 58(6): 1193–1210.
Pettinicchio, D. 2012. 'Institutional activism: Reconsidering the insider/outsider dichotomy', *Sociology Compass* 6(6): 499–510.
Rubin, M. 2021. 'Local government as the stage for resistance: Strategies and tactics of opposing mega projects in the city of Johannesburg'. In *Refractions of the National, the Popular, and the Global in African cities*, edited by S. Bekker and S. Croese, 69–84. Cape Town: African Minds Publishers.
Santoro, W.A. and McGuire, G.M. 1997. 'Social movement insiders: The impact of institutional activists on affirmative action and comparable worth policies', *Social Issues* 44(4): 503–19.
Scott, J. 1985. *Weapons of the weak. Everyday forms of peasant resistance.* New Haven and London: Yale University Press.
Thaden, E. and Wang, R. 2017. *Inclusionary Housing in the United States: Prevalence, impact, and practices.* Cambridge: Lincoln Institute of Land Policy.
van Wyk, J. 2012. 'Planning in all its (dis)guises: Spheres of government, functional areas and authority', *PER: Potchefstroomse Elektroniese Regsblad* 15(5): 287–318.
Wilson, S. and Dugard, J. 2013. 'Constitutional jurisprudence'. In *Socio-Economic Rights in South Africa: Symbols or substance?*, edited by M. Langford, N. Cousins, J. Dugard and T. Malindlozi, 35–62. New York: Cambridge University Press.

5

Entering the state as a community activist: the Operation Khanyisa Movement in Johannesburg City Council

Nicolette Pingo and Claire Bénit-Gbaffou

Introduction

In post-apartheid South African cities, there is a wide political and academic interest in the interface between civil society and the state, as a key anchor to study the transformation of citizenship in a democratising society. Scholars have questioned the nature of this interface, through various observation sites: social movements (Ballard et al. 2006; Alexander 2010; Dawson and Sinwell 2012); local government agents and structures (*Transformation* 2008); the multiple sites of engagement between residents and the state (Oldfield and Stokke 2006; *Journal of Asian and African Studies* 2011). They have highlighted this interface's blurriness, in particular through the key role of party politics within both the state and residents' organisations (von Holdt et al. 2011; *Geoforum* 2012; Dawson 2014). Party politics have been analysed as a key channel of communication and responsiveness between residents and the state; a form of control of residents' organisations and claims, and also a site of competition for positions and resources often determinant for social movements' internal dynamics. The complex positioning of movements' leadership, often tempted to sacrifice the loyalty to their bases in favour of recognition within the state or party, has started to be explored (Bénit-Gbaffou and Katsaura 2014). Taking this approach a step further, this paper examines an original case in the Johannesburg political landscape: the participation of a social movement in local elections, through the setting up of an electoral front, and the election of a local councillor in the City of Johannesburg.

This participation of a social movement, which is often understood theoretically and practically as radically opposed to the state and the formal system of participation, in local government, is analysed using the concept of *institutionalisation*, in the two meanings we found useful for the purpose of this chapter. Firstly, the term refers to social movements' members or leaders 'entering the state' (an *institution* in the traditional sense of the term), becoming part of it and adopting its norms and modes of actions in order to influence its politics 'from within'. Secondly, it refers to the institutionalisation of the social movement itself: becoming an institution, a part of the formal organisation of the state, and possibly losing its soul (identity, cause, nature) in the shift. By accepting the electoral and the City Council's rules of the game, the leaders of social movements are likely to become 'governmentalised' (Roy 2009): they become governable subjects, renouncing their ability to be rebellious (Alexander 2010), or – an importance nuance – the likelihood of them using rebellion in their interaction with the state.

This is where the bulk of the existing literature of social movements has focused so far, assuming or suspecting, in line with Michels's 'iron law of oligarchy' (1911), that social movements' institutionalisation means their death: demobilisation, deradicalisation and co-optation (Meyer and Tarrow 1998; Barker 2001). Paradoxically, institutionalisation in the first sense (entering the state apparatus, as an official or an elected representative) seems relatively under-studied. This is perhaps because social movements are defined as essentially autonomous and antagonistic to the state, even if contemporary studies are more sensitive to the multiple interfaces developing between the two, in an era of rising globalisation, networked and identity politics (Castells 1996).

This chapter[1] examines the ways in which a former social movement based in Johannesburg (the Anti-Privatisation Forum, APF), through two of its local affiliates (Thembelihle Crisis Committee, TCC, and Soweto Electricity Crisis Committee, SEEC), strategically entered state institutions at the local level in the mid-2000s, having felt the limitations of the sole use of protests in driving social change, in particular in the face of increasingly violent state repression (Clark 2014). The movement entered local government institutions at two levels. Firstly, by setting up an electoral front, the Operation Khaniysa Movement (OKM), for the 2006 local elections in Johannesburg. The OKM has had one councillor standing in the City Council since 2006. Secondly, by having one member elected into the ward committee, chaired by the African National Congress (ANC) local councillor in Thembelihle, since 2012. The focus of this chapter is not the genealogy of the shift within the movements.

Rather, it concerns itself with activists' practices in this new setting (those elected as representatives of the movement in state institutions, and those in the executive committee of the movement), and what this institutionalisation has meant both for the movement and for the state.

After briefly presenting the case study, this chapter examines how TCC and SEEC have formalised mechanisms, norms and rules to regulate their political representatives' accountability, and to respond to the risks attached to their choice of entering the state apparatus: the rise of an oligarchy and the potential betrayal of the movement by leadership. The chapter then interrogates how the political front attempted to change the state, consciously framing their participation to increase the City Council's and councillors' visibility and accountability to the people. It finally enquires whether the movement has been able, through this new strategy, to pursue its goals, and whether these goals have been reshaped by the movement's institutionalisation.

The issues with social movements' institutionalisation

Based on the limited scope of this entry into the state,[2] we did not expect spectacular changes in the state or its policies, but were interested in paying attention to more subtle shifts, both in the movements itself and in the municipality, focusing on what the OKM attempted to do, and how it used this municipal platform in practice. When consolidating our theoretical framework, confronting and testing various positions on the institutionalisation of social movements, we were puzzled to find that institutionalisation, as in 'entering the state institution and playing by its rules', appeared an elusive, if not a non-object, in social sciences' literature at large. We struggled to find an operational definition of *institutionalisation* for our purposes, let alone case studies or theoreticisation of the matter, and found this terrain relatively unexplored, with the notable exception of the feminist (Staggenborg 1988; Katzenstein 1998; Revillard 2011) and environmentalist (Boucher and Villalba 1990; van der Heijden 1997; Seippel 2001) literatures. Redefining institutionalisation to analyse its effects on movements and activism, Katzenstein (1998) helps us further unpack what institutionalisation entails, without presupposing that engaging with, or entering, the state institutions *ipso facto* means the betrayal of the movement by activists:

> This presumed inconsistency between movement politics and institutional politics is based on a frequently drawn linkage *of location, form and content*. When social movement actors doing street politics (location) ... ally themselves with those who use conventional modes (form) of political activism such as lobbying or voting, a social movement is generally deemed to have crossed the threshold separating protest politics from institutional politics, and the result is presumed to be deradicalisation (content). ... It is too easy to presume that what occurs in the street is disruptive, and what occurs within institutional contexts is accommodative. But what does 'disruption' mean? ... Disruption needs to be distinguished from 'interruption'. Disruption is about challenges to power that has the potential of compelling change (Katzenstein 1998, 195–6, *our emphasis*).

For Katzenstein, institutionalisation encompasses a change in location, generally a change of form (not necessarily giving up repertoires of contention), and may or may not lead to a change in goals and objectives. In this chapter, we adopt Katzenstein's deconstruction of location-form-content of activism – and interrogate how entering a new location by partaking in the City Council does or does not change activists' and movements' forms of action, and to what extent it reshapes or not their goals.

The two meanings Katzenstein gives of institutionalisation, based on her study of feminist movements in two institutions (the church and the military) are also of relevance to our chapter (Katzenstein 1998, 198). The first meaning refers to a shift in movement's strategies, and in particular a shift in location; perhaps a shift in form (of mode of action), but not necessarily a shift in content. The second meaning describes the processes by which the movement's values or goals become integrated into an institution's cultures and behaviours (here, local government). While we will study the OKM as a 'shift in strategy', away from the sole reliance on street politics and protests, and unpack what this shift means for the movement (distinguishing forms or repertoire from content or goal) and also what opportunities it opens, we will also keep in mind how the OKM attempts to institutionalise its own values in the City Council.

The Anti-Privatisation Forum in Johannesburg: institutionalisation as a response to the new structure of political opportunities

The choice by the APF's affiliates to form an electoral front is best understood as the result of shifting structures of political opportunity (Hipsher 1998): in the spaces opened or closed by participatory local government within a dominant party system yet marked by growing electoral competition; in the increased cost for activists of violently repressed protests; and in the disappointingly limited policy influence of protest and litigation politics. Participating in local government, in spite of its shortcomings, has recently become an avenue, along with others, to influence the state.

Local government context: opportunities and constraints

One critical mechanism of the South African post-apartheid local democracy is the ward system. Every five years, in local government elections, voters cast two votes: one for their ward councillor, and one for a party councillor (PR – Proportional Representative, on party lists). Both the PR and ward councillor constitute the City Council.[3] The PR councillors are not attached to a ward, but they can be deployed by their party to one or several wards. The ward councillor has a direct representative role for their area. This dual system represents an opening up of the political system for minority voices and provides political opportunity for grassroots' movements to strategically position themselves within the local state.

In the City Council, councillors are distributed in committees with specific portfolios in the City of Johannesburg ('Section 79' Committees), for example, housing, economic development, safety and security, infrastructure. These committees have an advisory and oversight function to the member of the executive in charge of this portfolio (the Member of the Mayoral Committee, MMC) (Bénit-Gbaffou 2008). These committees are perhaps the main site of engagement, debate and deliberation between dominant and minority party representatives in the municipality. However, their purely oversight function mean that these committees have limited power: no decision-making and even limited capacity to decide on the agenda items to be discussed. Moreover, some committees are more important than others, corresponding to unequally strategic functions of the City, and unevenly budgeted departments.

At the ward level, ward councillors chair ward committees, consisting of 10 residents elected by the ward voters, each holding one specific portfolio (housing, infrastructure, etc.). The ward committee members support the councillor to reach out to the community, and help them assess their needs with respect to their specific portfolio. The limitations of the ward council and committee systems as a critical participatory mechanism have been amply explored, linked in particular to the structural lack of power of local councillors (Bénit-Gbaffou 2008) and the politicisation of ward committees (Piper and Deacon 2009) in a context where the ANC's domination at every level of government limited incentives to accountability and space for contradictory debate. The failure of institutional channels at municipal level to incorporate meaningful participation is arguably one of the key factors that lead residents to use protests to get heard. Despite the increasing number of mass protests since the late 1990s (Alexander 2010), these actions have had limited long-term impact on improving services, focusing in effect more on 'collective sustenance than on advocacy for policy change' (Friedman and McKaiser 2009,19). The lack of visible policy results from protest action is coupled with increasing violence against protesters by the South African police force.[4] Simultaneously, while several movements have used litigation to make their claims (encouraged by several occurrences where the Constitutional Court showed sympathy for the poor), this has also proved to have limited impact in state policy change (Rubin 2013). In this context, South African social movement organisations have increasingly debated their participation in elections – in particular, local elections where minority parties have a higher likelihood of winning seats, as a way to challenge the (declining) ANC hegemony and to enter more directly the space of policy-making. Such debates became central in a powerful social movement in Johannesburg, the Anti Privatisation Forum (APF).

An electoral front for the Anti Privatisation Forum – a contested move

The APF was created in Johannesburg in 2000, in response to shifts in national and local policies (McKinley 2012). Echoing the national shift to the Growth, Employment and Redistribution (GEAR) Plan, but also responding to internal political and financial challenges, the City of Johannesburg embarked in 2000 in what was termed a neoliberal restructuring, embodied in the strategic plan, Igoli 2002. The City Council was restructured along New Public Management lines, in particular, creating new entities, semi-autonomous from the City Council, expected to manage basic services and infrastructures along business principles, on a cost-recovery and sometimes on a profit-making basis. This movement crystallised the formation of the APF, in particular around the Soweto Electricity Crisis Committee (SECC), formed by a former struggle activist and former ANC councillor, Trevor Ngwane.

The APF was an umbrella structure for several area-based civic movements, which meant it held a multiplicity of ideological stances and interests. When the APF started debating how it could play a larger role in South African politics, and whether its members should engage in local elections, discussions were rife (McKinley 2010; 2012). Some wanted the APF to remain focused on its own campaigns and goals as a social movement, seeing competitive election as a distraction. Others were opposed in principle, believing as anarchists that the APF should not enter institutional politics. Most concerns were about leadership, betrayal and accountability. Some were reluctant to openly confront the ANC as a party.

Others were favourable to the APF entering the electoral race, believing that it was already operating as a political party and could unite the working class to gain electoral weight. Others argued for the creation of a broader party, separate from the APF. Among the latter group, some imagined a party that would be linked to community assemblies, an organ of popular expressions of collective power. Trevor Ngwane, and the Johannesburg branch of several APF affiliates, took the latter position, and in 2006 formed the Operation Khaniysa Movement (OKM).

The Operation Khaniysa Movement (OKM)

The name of the OKM ironically re-appropriates Eskom's[5] lead campaign against illegal electricity usage, launched in 2006 as 'Operation Khanyisa'. 'Khanyisa' means 'illumination' in IsiZulu. Eskom's campaign would throw light on electricity theft and allow for illumination through electricity provision. The name 'Operation Khanyisa Movement' spoke back to this criminalisation of the poor, arguing against the privatisation of electricity and for residents' re-connection to electricity as a basic need.

Members of the OKM describe both its status and its objectives consistently through the term 'electoral front' rather than 'political party'. It speaks of a particular way of engaging with the state through party politics: a strategic decision to utilise local participatory governance mechanisms with the long-term goal of impacting decision-making, and the more intermediate goals of being visible, gaining legitimacy, exposing wrong-doing, encouraging transparency and accountability and critically gaining insight and knowledge about the function of local government. It differentiates itself as an entity from the social movements it represents: the OKM does not have a separate ideology; rather it is a tool to advance the goals of the movements it represents. This does not mean that the OKM is not ambitious; it plans to expand representation in the City of Johannesburg through more PR councillors, and numerous OKM members have expressed the desire to contest elections at national level.[6] However, in the short term, the role of the OKM is to remain oppositional within local government structures to influence municipal decisions.

The OKM secured one single PR seat in the 2006 local elections, and maintained it in the 2011 local elections. The party that was initially supported by several organisations in the APF underwent internal challenges. Ngwane (personal communication, 2011) attributes this to tensions within the APF, crystallising around issues of funding for members to participate in meetings: OKM leadership, unlike APF, refused to fund the inflated transport costs put forward by members for attending meetings, leading several affiliates[7] to stop attending OKM meetings and withdraw from the electoral front. Therefore, by the 2011 local elections, only the Thembelihle Crisis Committee (TCC) and the Soweto Electricity Crisis Committee (SECC) were linked to the OKM. The TCC is a local community-based organisation in Thembelihle, an informal settlement in the south of Johannesburg, and primarily focusing on security of tenure and access to housing (Wilson, nd). The SECC has been specifically involved in the struggle to access electricity for residents in the wider Soweto area, with a particular stand against the privatisation of electricity (Egan and Wafer 2004). In this chapter, we will pay specific attention to Thembelihle's context, the way the TCC has mobilised around its issues and how the OKM sought to address them.

Thembelihle and the Thembelihle Crisis Committee (TCC)

Thembelihle is an informal settlement in the south of Johannesburg, in Region G, Johannesburg's poorest region, and forms part of a largely residential ward including a mix of suburban extensions in Lenasia (a former Indian township) and informal settlements (Thembelihle, Lawley and Precast) (**Figure 5.1**). The ward has elected ANC ward councillors since 1995.

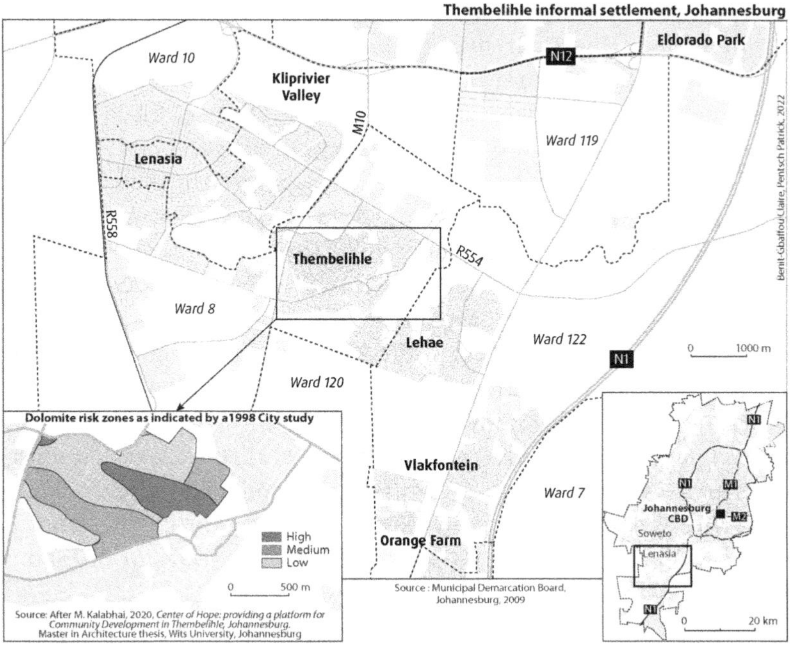

Figure 5.1 Location of Thembelihle informal settlement. Thembelihle is located southeast of the Indian township of Lenasia, in the south of Johannesburg. The proposed relocation area, Lehae, is further down to the southeast. The insert to the right maps the extent of dolomitic risks in the settlement, the technical argument used by the City of Johannesburg to justify the relocation of most residents.

Map: © Claire Bénit-Gbaffou and Patrick Pentsch, Aix Marseille University 2022

One of the biggest issues of contention with the state is around security of tenure and the development of public housing in Thembelihle, hindered by geo-technical conditions. Like many impoverished areas in Gauteng, Thembelihle is situated on dolomitic land, and its suitability for residential use has been contested from 1992. Two official studies, conducted for the City in 1992 and in 1998, concluded that people might continue to reside on 90 per cent of the site, provided water measures (better-secured drainage sites and larger foundations for top structures) are adhered to.[8] In 2001, however, the City started evicting Thembelihle's residents, on the grounds of unstable dolomitic conditions. A large protest erupted; Thembelihle Crisis Committee (TCC) was formed, and managed to stop the process.

In 2003, the City of Johannesburg filed an urgent interdict in the South Gauteng High Court to evict all the residents of Thembelihle. The TCC, with the help of the law firm Webber Wentzel, managed to suspend the eviction again (Wilson, nd, 14). In the meantime, the validity of geo-technical studies in the area was questioned: the issue was the completeness of the study, where the TCC supported by their technical team argued that 80 holes would need to be drilled in order to understand the geo-technical conditions for the full area. Despite these ongoing disputes, the City of Johannesburg resolved in 2008 that most of Thembelihle's residents would be relocated to public housing in Lehae (a greenfield development site 2 km south of Thembelihle). The TCC appealed the 2008 City resolution, requesting that the City conduct further geo-technical studies before resorting to relocation. The appeal was dismissed in the South Gauteng High Court in 2009, as such studies, estimated at R800,000, were considered financially unreasonable. Therefore, residents' relocation to Lehae is ongoing. Seeing the limits of protest and litigation, the TCC looked for other ways of engaging the state.

Entering the ward committee as an extension of the Operation Khaniysa Movement (OKM) strategy

After an OKM PR councillor from Thembelihle was elected in the 2011 local elections, the OKM and the Thembelihle Crisis Committee decided that they would put forward OKM candidates for the ward committee. The TCC, through the electoral front of the OKM, advanced eight candidates in the ward committee elections in February 2012.

The campaign needs to be understood as a TCC–OKM campaign, given that the ward committee delegation is community-, not party-based, but inspired by the OKM's local electoral strategy. Members of the TCC would not have entered the ward committee if they were not linked to the OKM and OKM's candidates would not have been elected without wide support from the TCC.

Due to several delays with the process, the election did not take place until June 2012, and only one of the TCC–OKM candidates was elected as ward committee member – Bhayiza Miya, in the housing portfolio. According to Miya, this limited victory was due to two factors. Internally, the TCC–OKM did not sufficiently mobilise, especially in the two other informal settlements in the ward; externally, there were complications in the ward election system (Bénit-Gbaffou 2012).

Impact of the Operation Khaniysa Movement (OKM) on the movement: changing tactics, inventing new modes of accountability

How did the social movement deal with the risks attached to institutionalisation – deradicalisation and leadership betrayal? To some extent, this was done by trial and error, but it was also an ongoing and explicit concern of activists that they responded to by creating specific norms, rules and practices to keep the OKM accountable to the movement.

Selecting leadership – avoiding personality cult, providing leadership opportunities

Specific leaders in the OKM clearly play critical roles, such as Trevor Ngwane, Bhayiza Miya, Siphiwe Segodi and Simphiwe Zwane, through their political experience, astuteness and charisma. However, the OKM ensures that formal positions of leadership rotate, and has set up specific mechanisms for leadership nomination, in order to avoid personality cults from consolidating.

Candidates are selected based on three criteria. They are selected alternatively from each of the two movements, SECC and TCC; they are women, so as to disrupt male dominance in the City Council and they need to demonstrate sufficient strength to manage the difficult position of minority councillor in the City Council. The first (2006) councillor was a woman from the SECC, Zodwa Madiba, and the current councillor (2011), Simphiwe Zwane, is a woman from the TCC.

The OKM also implements particular leadership structures to avoid the formation of a gap between the councillor and the movement, as well as grow organisational and leadership capacity beyond the councillor. The councillor has one role: to serve as the representative for the OKM and its constituency in the City's Council Chamber. She does not serve as the leader of the electoral front – unlike other parties such as the ANC and EFF,[9] where leadership of the party and leadership in Parliament are usually coupled. The OKM leader is elected from the two social movements (SECC and TCC) as well as the other members of the OKM's leadership structure, who have formed the Local Government Group (**Table 5.1**):

Table 5.1 Local Government Group: the Operation Khaniysa Movement (OKM) leadership structure

OKM Local Government Group	Thembelihle Crisis Committee (TCC)	Soweto Electricity Crisis Committee (SECC)
Party leader: S Nduthang (SECC)	**Chairperson:** G Gopane	**Chairperson:** J Kangedi
Secretary: J Rihlamfu (SECC)	**Deputy Chair:** B Thomo	**Deputy Chair:** M Mokhati
PR councillor: S Zwane (TCC)	**Secretary:** S Tswelekile	**Secretary:** F Pooe
PA to PR councillor: S Mbatha (TCC)	**Deputy Secretary:** M Mnguni	**Deputy Secretary:** T Maduma
Additional member: J Kangedi (SECC)	**Treasurer:** E Mbokazi	**Treasurer:** C Vezi
Additional member: M Mokhati (SECC)	**Organiser:** S Mbatha	**Organiser:** Z Madiba
Additional member: Z. Madiba (SECC)	**Public relations:** S Segodi	**Administrator:** S Toana
Additional member: T Ngwane (SECC)	**Member:** B Myia	**Member:** J Rihlamfu
Ward committee member: B Myia (TCC)	**Member:** S Zwane	**Member:** T Ngwane

Source: © Pingo 2012

The Local Government Group is carefully crafted to reach a balance between its two constituencies: the SECC and TCC. It is not chaired by the municipal councillor, but by a leader from the other constituency.

In the weekly meetings of the OKM (Local Government Group), it is not the councillor who chairs the meetings; she simply attends as the councillor. Members of the Local Government Group rotate. For instance, Bhayiza Miya previously sat on the Local Government Group, but no longer forms part of it, to allow for rotation of representation. It also corresponds to personal preferences – Miya prefers to be on the ground than in office meetings. This rotation ensures that numerous leaders experience different strategic positions, and that grassroots' linkages are maintained.

The question is then whether the leadership strategies employed by the OKM are efficient in meeting its goals as well as advancing the electoral front as a whole. Our personal observation of the previous OKM councillor highlights some of the challenges of this leadership approach:

> The City Council's budget meeting was running smoothly, with occasional outbursts from DA councillors, but the ANC majority meant that the budget would pass anyway. The OKM councillor, an old woman, stood up and shouted courageously, on her own, 'Amandla!' hardly answered, then yelled a series of 'Phansi! Privatisation! Phansi!' before addressing the City Council, and its ANC section in particular. She insisted it was winter, and councillors should think of the plight of the poor while voting budget – this was not a pro-poor budget. The Speaker ridiculed her: 'Let us ask our councillor to do her homework and read the City's policy documents. She might realise that there has been no privatisation of services in the City of Johannesburg.' There was no space for her to reply. I was shocked by this disrespect, even more so due to contrast in age and gender. I could not refrain from imagining what Trevor Ngwane would have made of the situation, and silently blamed OKM political choices of leadership, at the expense of political efficiency. And at the same time, it was strangely moving. She had stood firm, stated her beliefs and values on her own – and I started hoping that some of the principles she so sincerely expressed, and the disgrace of the Speaker's response, would touch the hearts of at least a few councillors (Bénit-Gbaffou, personal observation, City Council meeting, nd).

Consolidating accountability – the Operation Khaniysa Movement (OKM) pledge

Beyond the careful choice of leadership, original mechanisms of accountability were set up to ensure that councillors representing the electoral front remain loyal to the movement. The OKM councillor has to sign both a pledge and a contract binding her to the party's aims.

A key element of control focuses on the OKM councillor's salary, that is to be paid to the OKM, which will in turn give a portion of it to the councillor ('enough money to cover my basic needs and carry out my duties'), and keep the main part for the organisation. Councillors' salary (R17,000 net monthly in 2012) usually elevates their economic status in deprived communities. Few councillors move out of their communities as this would have a direct impact on their constituencies' support, but many purchase cars and are provided by the City with electronic equipment (tablets and smartphones). These resources differentiate councillors from their constituencies in impoverished areas. The OKM's structure ensures that councillors are not driven by personal enrichment motives – the OKM councillor receiving just R6,800, the rest of her salary sustaining the work of the OKM and to a smaller extent the TCC and SECC. These resources allow the organisation to canvass, to belong to and participate in wider umbrella movements such as the Democratic Left Front (DLF) and the Informal Settlement Network.[10]

A second key principle in terms of accountability is the right of recall stated in the contract signed by the councillor:

> It is solely in the discretion of the OKM to appoint a councillor, to end the position of a councillor, to limit the period of appointment of a councillor, and to rotate the service of a councillor with other councillors, to follow any criteria, orders or sequence or preference as to the order of appointment for its councillors, provided same is fair, just and reasonable, to the extent consistent with the provisions of the constitution, rules and regulations and directives of OKM (OKM contract 2012, 2.5, Pingo's personal archive).

This powerful tool was actually used: the first OKM PR councillor selected from the SECC, Joyce Mkhonza, was recalled in 2007. Zodwa Madiba, an activist in the SECC and the second OKM PR councillor elected by the OKM to replace her, describes what occurred:

> Unfortunately [former Councillor Mkhonza] never fulfilled the mandate of the people. She was trying to cross the floor to the DA.[11] She [announced her intention] before she went to register with the IEC [Independent Electoral Commission] for the other party. She was on radio, all over the media, that morning. Then we rushed to IEC to recall her and put in the letter saying that we recall that lady, so she is not an OKM member anymore. So we stopped her (Madiba 20 June 2012).

Strategising – how to best use the City Council platforms: Local Government Group pre-meetings

The Local Government Group, made up of selected members of the TCC and SECC, meets every Thursday in the City Council building. The team decides on how the councillor is to react to the agenda items put forward at the monthly City Council Chamber meetings, and strategises on her position in various municipal engagements.

Meetings of the Local Government Group provide the opportunity for activists to understand internal council dynamics, and develop concerted strategies in engaging with the state. The City Council Chamber is used as a classroom; being inside the City structures offers information usually not accessible to social movements. Practical knowledge of how decisions are made in local government is the first step in refining tactics to influence those decisions.

Some of the Local Government Group debates focused on the way the councillor dressed: given the limitations of having only one councillor, it is important that she remains visible in the City Council Chamber meetings. Initially, the OKM councillors wore T-shirts with socialist slogans. However, they were consistently expelled from the City Council Chamber for not being dressed properly. If the OKM had more councillors, they could have resisted such eviction and continued to use dress as a political statement.[12] Since this was not the case, both Zodwa Madiba (the previous councillor) and Simphiwe Zwane have finally conformed to dressing in the required semi-formal way.

Keeping grassroots mobilisation alive – visibility of a mass movement

Entering the City Council Chamber has not become the sole tactic of the movement, as the TCC has continued to resort to protest action. However, this street tactic is exerted more cautiously, as an element of a broader strategy, in moments where pressure and visibility are key.

In September 2011, Thembelihle's residents took to the streets in what community members call the largest march in the history of Thembelihle (Clark 2014). Residents had had enough of waiting, rumours of mass relocation, development and the dire impacts of dolomitic land filling their ears. For a protest of that size, formal procedures were followed weeks in advance, following the regulations of the 1996 Gatherings Act. Policeman lined the streets in Thembelihle in what was on most accounts a very peaceful march. The protest drew high-ranking City officials and the memorandum was handed over to the MMC for Housing and several representatives from the Gauteng Legislature.

There was no response so a second memorandum was drawn up, requesting a response from the City within the following three days. City officials indicated that they required seven days and the TCC reluctantly agreed. After more than two weeks passed, the residents' anger grew, prompting a week of 'illegal'[13] protest action in the settlement. Miya was arrested following the march and was detained for two months in jail. His case was then struck off the roll.[14] After Miya's release, on Friday 21 October 2011, the OKM Councillor Simphiwe Zwane, who participated in the march, was arrested on charges of intimidation and public violence. Councillor Zwane was held in a holding cell over the weekend. On Monday 24 October, she appeared in Protea South Magistrate court, where her case was also struck off the roll. Thirteen ordinary residents were also arrested in what became known as 'The Thembelihle 14'.

Actually, the participation of the councillor in the march had positive effects on its visibility, and gave the protest action a new meaning. The story of her participation and her arrest made headlines in some left-leaning media platforms,[15] and brought support from organisations such as the Socio-Economic Rights Institute (SERI). However, SERI advised that they now struggle to secure the release of protesters, especially if they have been arrested in previous marches.[16] As a result, neither the TCC as a social movement nor the OKM as a party have led a *large* mass protest in Thembelihle since the arrest of 'The Thembelihle 14'.[17] Therefore, the decreasing use of protests by OKM–TCC is not primarily linked to the institutionalisation of the movement – rather to the increasing state repression towards mass protests, confirming the need for a broader range of political repertoires.

Changing the state institution? Showcasing the Operation Khaniysa Movement's values in the City Council

Institutionalisation in the second sense highlighted by Katzenstein (1998); embedding the movement's values in the way the state works, is necessarily limited here. The OKM is too marginal and outnumbered in the City Council to be able to influence officials' practices on a broad scale. Furthermore, we have not documented officials' practices and their perceptions of the OKM to measure impact, if any. However, there are a number of occurrences in which the OKM was given, or has crafted, a platform to showcase its values, and set an example of how councillors should behave and how the City Council should work. This involves giving constant public reminders that the councillor's mandate is to represent its voters; concretely encouraging the public-ness of the City Council meetings and councillors' actions, and reminding councillors of their agency within their own party.

Reminding: councillors are representative of the people

The OKM councillor utilises the City Council Chamber as an arena to remind other councillors that their mandate is to represent the people. This representative role is one that ANC councillors tend to ignore or forget. In a dominant party context where one wants to be nominated again as councillor, it is more important to show loyalty to the party rather than to represent people's grievances in the City Council (Bénit-Gbaffou 2008).

The issue of the costs of basic services for the poor are constantly raised by the OKM councillors, and the need to reflect on this issue is shown in their decisions. Zwane, for instance, reported that when she raised issues of free basic services in the City Council Chamber, she was confronted by ANC councillors in the corridor, saying: 'You are saying the people mustn't pay for water for electricity. Would you be happy if you were not getting paid [for your work]?' She retorted that they are in the City Council as representatives of the people and not for their personal enrichment.

Another illustration of this practice is Zwane's response to the disciplinary hearing she was faced with following her participation in the 2011 protest. Zwane reported on the march and her arrest in the Section 79 Ethics Committee meeting, and her case was taken to the disciplinary committee. When she was told at the hearing that, given her status as a councillor and thus an employee of the City, she was not supposed to march against the City Council, she replied through a submission, written together with the Local Government Group:

> I told them [the Section 79 Ethics Committee] that I did lead the march to the Region G municipal offices, and they were laughing at me thinking that I didn't know that the councillor is not allowed to march. It was sad because they took me to the commissioner, the disciplinary committee. But when there I was very happy, I could tell them that what I think and what I thought the truth was that they should know. Because he was asking me, you [should not] lead the marches, but I did portray that the people asked me to lead the march. I am there because of the people: they are the ones that elected me. Unless I am not representing the very same ones who asked me. So they saw it, they read it, then they said that there is no case against me. And I am very happy with that (Zwane 16 July 2012).

It was subsequently announced in the City Council Chamber (8 December 2011) that Councillor Zwane was not guilty of disobeying the councillors' code of conduct. The rules around councillors leading mass protests are actually implicit rather than explicit in the City of Johannesburg's Ward Councillor's Code of Conduct. The lack of disciplinary sanction taken against Councillor Zwane acts as recognition of the values that she confidently asserted: that a councillor's mandate is primarily to represent her voters.

Developing publicness: City Council and councillor under the public gaze

The OKM also uses its position in the City Council to actively publicise the City Council's practices and modes of working and decisions. This is achieved by bringing the public to the City Council meetings and by publicising information on the City Council's and councillor's work in local community meetings.

The OKM uses its financial resources (derived from the councillor's salary) to transport members of the SECC and TCC to the City Council Chamber on a regular basis. The members sit in the public gallery and watch the political processes in action. This is important because, although these meetings are available to the general public, without insider's knowledge they are difficult to attend (starting with limited publicity around the date of the meeting). Ordinary residents are not actively encouraged to see the processes in practice. The OKM, therefore, provide an important educational space, allowing ordinary members to hold the OKM councillor accountable to her constituency; to learn about local government policies, practices and processes; and to view the behaviour of councillors from other parties.

Reflecting on councillors' agency in their party's policies

The OKM is further using the more secluded political spaces of Section 79 Committees, to challenge the norms that are shaping behaviour in the broader City Council Chamber, where councillors vote along party lines without being given or taking space for debate and reflection (beyond sparring with political opponents). Section 79 Committees, by being smaller in their scope, and closed to the public, provide potential spaces to escape political shows, and engage in genuine or content-related discussion across party lines. Despite the limitations of these committees – with an oversight role but no real sanction over policy decisions – they become a platform where the OKM councillor challenges other parties' policies and actions and encourage other councillors to change their approach:

> We keep on telling the truth to people. The councillor from OKM is not going to change anything, but she can say something. And maybe by doing so, things can change. I remember we were debating about the issue of hiring those with disabilities, then the other councillor says: 'But why can't we change this?' Then the other one says: 'No we cannot change this because this is our policy, as ANC councillors this is our policy.' Then she started saying, 'this means, it is useless for us to come and sit in the Section 79 Committee, whereas there is nothing we can change'. Then we started saying, the other councillors DA and me as OKM: 'Change the policy, from the ANC, go inside the conference where you are and tell them to change the policy. So that it will favour us, even you' (Zwane 16 July 2012).

In the same line of thought, even if perhaps less directly powerful, is the use that the OKM makes of the City Council meetings to voice concerns (such as the tariffs of basic services or the relocation of residents), even if these concerns are received with disbelief or contempt by the rest of the councillors:

> To tell you the truth it's stress, why I am saying so because I'm the only councillor from OKM there. Like ANC has got about 150 councillors, DA 90, 95 councillors. I cannot vote in the Chamber because it is only going to be my vote. And then, when I disagree with the item, the amendments that they put on the table, they howl at me. They say this one she's mad sort of thing. [... However] I am very proud because I can raise issues they don't want [to raise]. [Even when] they howl at me, I know that they hear what I am saying, and that they are going to write down everything: 'Councillor Zwane doesn't agree with that item.' That makes me more strong (Zwane 16 July 2012).

Pushing the movement's goals through new channels?

Obviously the OKM, with only one single councillor from a marginalised party in a City Council Chamber counting about 270 councillors, cannot significantly influence decision-making, in policies or in implementation.

Our enquiry is focused here on the OKM's specific pursuit of the Thembelihle issue. After the limitations of protests and litigation to push the case for in-situ upgrading and further geo-technical investigation, has entering the state opened new channels for advancing this specific goal? Or are these goals altered due to the institutionalisation of the movement – and to what extent?

Using informal networks within the state

The OKM councillor is exposed to a variety of state actors in the City of Johannesburg and beyond. Arguably, its position within the City Council allows the OKM to multiply its networks and develop informal interactions, beyond public antagonism, with key players, and find formal or informal arrangements. One such relationship is with the Member in the Mayoral Committee (MMC) for Housing, Dan Bovu. He was the first ward 8 councillor, and served two terms (1995–2006) before being promoted to MMC for Housing. The TCC has had a fraught relationship with him over the issue of housing with promises made and never fulfilled, as well as a number of antagonistic encounters framed by protests and repression, litigation and counter-litigation.

The regular interaction between the OKM councillor and the MMC, within the City, has, according to Zwane, yielded some results. Dan Bovu finally agreed, in 2012, to conduct the full geo-technical studies in Thembelihle:

> The person that has been changed there [in the City Council], it's the MMC of Housing, Dan Bovu. I know him, I can see him that he has gotten a little worried. The TCC played a major role in the City, things are changing we can see. We had a meeting with the MMC last month telling us that the City is prepared now to pay that R800,000 to drill the boreholes. That tells us that the TCC pushed the City to come to that decision. Earlier they didn't even want to hear about that, they said go and find money for the study (Zwane 16 July 2012).

Interestingly, Zwane mentions the TCC rather than the OKM in this (and many other) quotes. This might confirm the status of the OKM as a mere tool to fulfill the goals of the TCC, where deeper identities and identifications lie. It might also refer to the fact that the OKM is one tool among many (held together with protests and litigation as modes of action for the TCC), and that the ability to establish networks with the

MMC reflected both the presence of the OKM in the City Council (institutionalisation) but also the legacy of decades of confrontation and street politics based in Thembelihle.

The TCC was asked to assemble a team of technical assistants to meet with the municipal technical team and devise a way forward for the 80 boreholes to be drilled in Thembelihle. It is difficult to attribute the change to any specific action: no interviewee was able to isolate key events or achievements that resulted in the City of Johannesburg agreeing to conduct further dolomitic investigations. Siphiwe Segodi offers up a somewhat cynical explanation of why the MMC agreed to engage more extensively with the OKM and the TCC:

> Our [OKM] councillor has recently challenged the MMC for Housing in Council Chamber, around corruption, that we want [his] corrupt activity to be investigated. And that really puts him in a corner. He is not sure how far we know about what we are talking about. So he is cornered, but uncertain: 'How real are these people? How much of that evidence do they have at hand? What do they have?' So every time we say we should meet, he agrees maybe in the hope that we will spell out what we have on him (Segodi, 24 November 2012).

Being part of the City Council has provided the OKM with new and increased capacity to put pressure on the key decision-maker. This includes finding information that might compromise him, knowing the importance of such an accusation and taking the relevant public arena to publicise it, and having and using opportunities to engage and to talk – in threatening and non-threatening ways. Entering the state has not only taught the TCC how it formally works through committees, hierarchies and functions, but also how it informally works, and the politics that can be used to put pressure on decision-makers, and informally influence their decisions. However, even then, there are limitations: in 2015, despite an endless array of promises, the more extensive 80 borehole study has still not taken place, and residents of Thembelihle continued to be relocated to Lehae.

More generally, the TCC–OKM tries to pressurise the City to limit residents' relocation, and to engage instead with in-situ upgrading, using instruments such as the National Upgrading Support Programme (NUSP). Within the more cooperative political space created in the City Council, they have made an agreement with the MMC, Dan Bovu, in July 2012, according to which the TCC–OKM would commit to prevent new structures from being developed in the settlement on emptied stands (vacated by the relocation of some residents), with the understanding that the de-densification of the settlement may result in City investment in upgrading.

Possible shift in the movement's goal? Supporting residents relocating to Lehae

While some slow progress is made at City Council level, the process of relocation to Lehae is continuing on the ground, orchestrated by the ANC ward councillor and her ward committee. The challenge of maintaining the goals of the TCC–OKM is illustrated at this level of local government, at the coalface of the relationship with residents, through the involvement of Miya in the ward committee.

Despite the TCC's general stance against relocation, Miya found himself becoming part of the relocation process in 2012. The relocation process was fraught with inconsistencies and delays, errors on the housing and relocation list, which caused 46 angry residents to continually contact Miya, as the ward committee member charged with the housing portfolio and a well-known activist in Thembelihle. After months of tension and trying to resolve the matters in meetings with officials and councillors, Miya opted for direct action. At 5 a.m. on 1 November 2012, he walked with the 46 residents that had been allocated housing to Lehae to claim their allocated houses:

> That night I called all of them, I knew it was wrong, but, for the image of the City, I phoned them. I said OK let's meet on Monday. We have elderly citizens here. The first on the list is a woman born in 1930. We had to walk them. There was no money, there was no transport. I organised the media, the media was there. We walked, we walked to Lehae (Miya, 23 November 2012).

This event and its media attention forced the City to respond immediately and residents on the list were formally given their houses three days after the march. Miya was able to take this action for two reasons. Firstly, he was inside the state apparatus, so he had insight into the housing allocation system: he had become part of the process in a way he had never been privy to as an activist. Secondly, the type of institutionalisation promoted and supported by the OKM created a space where he could continue to act as an individual activist and utilise radical action in his role as ward committee member – making things happen for the benefit of people, shaking the rules and their inertia to solve issues. Here the political abstract principles (against relocation away from Thembelihle) gave way to the pragmatic solidarity with people in distress.

Beyond this contradiction between principle and practice, one might note that Miya could not vigorously challenge the relocation policy, as had been advocated by the TCC for decades, in his role as ward committee member responsible for housing. He needed to first understand the functioning of the ward committee, and secure his place in the committee. Although officially a ward committee member, if he did not conform, he would be excluded from ward committee meetings – even informally, as had happened to him early in his term. This might be seen as a form of deradicalisation of the movement's vision and goal – both as a compromise to be able to continue to participate in the state apparatus, but also as the rise of the 'ethics of responsibility' as opposed to an 'ethics of conviction' (Weber 1919). In charge of the housing portfolio, Miya could not ignore the residents asking for relocation and being mistreated, even if this goes against his own views on housing solutions for Thembelihle. How much these views have shifted with this experience can only be measured through a longer time span.

Conclusion

Roy, in her construction of the concept of 'civic governmentality' (2009), unpacks the complex strategy of an Indian organisation engaging with the state, using both empowering tactics (self-enumeration of pavement dwellers and visibilisation in the public realm), and forms of deradicalised negotiations (agreement to the relocation of informal dwellers in order to avoid violent dispossession of households' goods). While she states that this civic governmentality has indeed prevented mobilisation against the neoliberal principle that the poor should be relocated to urban peripheries (deradicalisation), she shares with the reader her own ambiguity towards this strategic choice. She suspends political judgment to examine what has been gained and lost in this specific context of violent repression; to question the concomitant empowerment and disciplining, leading us to ask ourselves what we would have done if we were the organisation's leaders, knowing that radical confrontation leads to state violence, imprisonment and death.

The difficulty, and inefficiency, of radical confrontation in the context of authoritarian regimes has also been thematised by Bayat (1997), for whom 'quiet encroachment' is often a more context-relevant form of resistance than open confrontation. Both authors open a space to think about mobilisation of the poor in various modes, forms and location, beyond a politics of protest, constantly adapting to situated constraints and opportunities.

In the case of the OKM in contemporary Johannesburg, there was limited scope in this chapter to examine the 'success' or 'failure' of institutionalisation for the movement – its impact being necessarily limited in terms of policy, institutional and cultural shifts, both because of our (short) timeframe of analysis, and of the limited scope of the party itself. This chapter has documented how a social movement has negotiated, internally and externally, institutionalisation as a deliberate shift in its strategy, in order to try and overcome Michels's 'iron law of oligarchy', and maintain party leadership's loyalty to the movement's principles and values. Of course, the OKM is quite specific, in its small scale, its grounding in a few specific areas, and in its lack of ideological autonomy vis-à-vis the social movement – elements that actually may be an obstacle to its growth as a party. Perhaps the solution to the 'iron law' it has developed can only work in such conditions. However, we believe that the movements' innovations are important directions for reflection on movements' institutionalisation, and are of relevance for broader social movement studies.

Firstly, the movement has developed innovative institutional settings for itself and the party, such as principles of leadership rotation, leadership training and mentoring, explicit deconstruction of personality cult, proactive distinction between several 'centres of power'; the councillor's pledge and right of recall; regular meetings between party representative and party/movement leadership. Secondly, the movement and party have taken specific stances in the public realm: not giving up protest politics; reflecting on other forms of disruption, in the City Council Chamber, that can be heard; emphasising the role of the councillor as the representative of the voters; highlighting the public-ness of council meetings and the agency of councillors.

Using Katzenstein's typology (1998), institutionalisation for the movement has meant a diversification (rather than a shift) of location (not leaving the township but entering the town hall); of form (not abandoning protests and marches; still resorting to disruption tactics, even in City Council; but also entering into dialogue with fellow councillors; better understanding of City Council's politics and being able to play with them), but not an abandonment of the movement's goals, values and principles. Arguably, the goals have been affected by institutionalisation, as illustrated by Miya's participation in the relocation of Thembelihle's residents to Lehae, that the movement is opposing in principle. The longer-term repercussions of this pragmatic choice (and of the lack of progress on the consolidation of the settlements in situ) on the movements' principled position remains to be studied.

What did we learn about the state? Studying the process of 'entering the state', from a movement's or activist's perspective, has alerted us to the importance of understanding its institutional settings and cultures, both formal and informal, to increase political efficiency and the possibility of being heard. The Local Government Group weekly meetings, consistent attendance to the (public) City Council meetings, show that movements' activists are acutely aware of this shortcoming of mobilisation, and the need to better understanding 'how it works', to more strategically pursue their goals and diversify their channels of action. As important as the formal institutional settings (the powers and functions of a Section 79 Committee; the scope and formalism of City Council Chamber's debates; the ways housing waiting lists function), are informal practices and tacit rules. Movements debate on which ones are worth challenging (the dress code; the formal registration of objections; councillors' agency in committees; councillors' right to protest; to whom are councillors accountable; etc.). A third realm of activists' understanding of state's practices (informal knowledge of corruption and clientelism) opens up the opportunity for new tactics and pressure that they can use to influence decision-making.

Notes

1 It is based on fieldwork (September 2011–November 2012) done by Nicolette Pingo for her Master's degree at the University of Witwatersrand (Pingo 2013), supervised by Claire Bénit-Gbaffou. It rests on in-depth interviews with the leadership of social movement (TCC) and political party (OKM), and participant observation both in the City Council and in Thembelihle informal settlement (in particular, OKM executive committee meetings, TCC public meetings and City Council meetings). Pingo also worked for PLANACT as project officer (August 2011–December 2013), an NGO focusing on community participation, which acted as a support technical committee for fostering TCC's interests in negotiations with the City of Johannesburg (Pingo 2012).

2 Local councillors (and their ward committee members) yield limited power in a centralised Johannesburg local government. This structural powerlessness is sometimes compensated by ANC networks (Bénit-Gbaffou 2008), but this cannot be the case for a single councillor from an opposition party.

3 In 2016, there were 135 PR and 135 ward councillors in Johannesburg's City Council, a total of 270 City councillors.

4 Duncan, J. and Royeppen, A. 2013. 'Death by a thousand pinpricks: South Africa's ever-vanishing right to protest', *Daily Maverick*, 8 March. Available at: https://www.dailymaverick.co.za/article/2013-03-08-death-by-a-thousand-pinpricks-south-africas-ever-vanishing-right-to-protest/. Accessed 19 July 2023.

5 The South African electricity supplier.

6 The birth of the Democratic Left Front (2010) following the demise of the APF, with an explicit electoral aim, and the rise of the Economic Freedom Fighters (EFF) since 2011, might significantly impact these debates.

7 The Alexandra Vukuzenzele Crisis Committee (AVCC), Wynberg Concerns Citizens, Motwaledi Concerned Citizens and the Kliptown Residents' Association.
8 Maryna Storie. 2012. 'Dolomite issues in the Gauteng City-Region: Preparing for community engagement'. Presentation to a community workshop, Protea South, 13 April.
9 The Economic Freedom Fighters (EFF) is a splinter group from the ANC, identifying itself as extreme left, advocating for a radical redistributive and nationalisation policy.
10 The Informal Settlement Network is a network of community-based organisations affiliated with Slum Dwellers International.
11 Democratic Alliance, the main opposition party to the ANC.
12 As did later the more numerous EFF party, wearing red overalls in Parliament, for instance.
13 The issue of the illegality of the march remains contentious. Community members maintain that the protests were a continuation of the protests before, so permission had already been granted.
14 Miya's case has been struck off the roll numerous times. This means that the court can give no judgement (often due to lack of evidence) and orders the case to be struck off the record. However, the police continually find 'new evidence' and Miya is continually called back to court to face the charges once again. The prosecutor has failed time and time again in over a year to build a substantive case against Miya.
15 Available at: http://abahlali.org/node/8441/; https://mg.co.za/article/2012-04-26-protesters-complain-of-intimidation/. Accessed 22 August 2023.
16 Communication with Kate Tissington, Senior Research and Advocacy Officer at SERI.
17 In February 2015, Thembelihle's residents again held mass protests resulting in the arrest of 33 residents. Trevor Ngwane and Nhlanipho Lukhele (youth representatives for the TCC) were among those arrested. Available at: http://www.seri-sa.org/images/Thembelihle_PressStatement_FINAL.pdf. Accessed 20 July 2023.

References

Alexander, P. 2010. 'Rebellion of the poor: South Africa's service delivery protests: A prelimenary analysis', *Review of African Political Economy* 37(123): 25–40.

Ballard, R., Habib, A., Valodia, I. and Zuern, E. 2006. 'Introduction: From anti-apartheid to post-apartheid social movements'. In *Voices of Protest: Social movements in post-apartheid South Africa*, edited by R. Ballard, A. Habib, I. Valodia and E. Zuern, 1–22. Pietermaritzburg: University of KwaZulu-Natal Press.

Barker, C. 2001. 'Robert Michels and the cruel game'. In *Leadership and Social Movements*, edited by C. Barker, A. Johnson and M. Lavallette, 24–43. Manchester: Manchester University Press.

Bayat, A. 1997. 'Un-civil society; The politics of informal people', *Third World Quartery* 18(1): 53–72.

Bénit-Gbaffou, C. 2008. 'Pratices of local participation in Johannesburg: Side-lining the institutional particpatory channels?', *Transformation: Critical perspectives on Southern Africa* 66–67: 1–34.

Bénit-Gbaffou, C. (ed), 2008. Special issue: 'Local government in South Africa', *Transformation: Critical perspectives on Southern Africa*, 66–67.

Bénit-Gbaffou, C. and Oldfield, S. 2011 (eds). 'Accessing the State: Everyday Practices and Politics in Cities of the South'.

Bénit-Gbaffou, C. 2012. 'Party politics, civil society and local democracy – Reflections from Johannesburg', *Geoforum* 43(2): 178–89.

Bénit-Gbaffou, C. and Piper, L. (eds), 2012, 'Party politics, the poor and the city: reflections from South Africa'. *Geoforum*: Special issue, 43(2).

Bénit-Gbaffou C. and Katsaura O. 2014. 'Community leaders and the construction of political legitimacy. Unpacking Bourdieu's political capital in post-apartheid Johannesburg', *International Journal of Urban and Regional Studies* 38(5): 1807–32.

Boucher, Y. and Villalba, B. 1990. 'Le militant, la compétence et l'éthique. Les conditions de l'investiture chez les verts', *Politix* 3(9): 37–43.

Castells, M. 1996. *The Rise of the Network Society*. Malden: Blackwell Publishing.

Clark, M. 2014. *An Anatomy of Dissent and Repression: The criminal justice system and the 2011 Thembelihle protest.* Johannesburg: Socio-economics Rights Institute of South Africa.

Dawson, H. 2014. 'Patronage from below: Political unrest in an informal settlement in South Africa', *African Affairs* 113(453): 518–39.

Dawson, M. and Sinwell, L. (eds). 2012. *Contesting Transformation: Popular resistance in twenty-first century South Africa.* London: Pluto Press.

Egan, A. and Wafer, A. 2004. *The Soweto Electricity Crisis Committee.* Case Study for the University of KwaZulu-Natal/Centre for Civil Society Project 'Globalisation, Marginalisation and New Social Movements in post-Apartheid South Africa', Durban.

Friedman, S. and McKaiser, E. 2009. *Civil Society and the Post-Polokwane South African State: Assessing civil society's prospects of improved policy engagement.* Research report, Johannesburg: Centre for the Study of Democracy.

Hipsher, P. 1998. 'Democratic Transitions as Protest Cycles: Social movements dynamics in democratising Latin America', In *The Social Movement Society: Contentious politics for a new century,* edited by D.S. Meyer and S. Tarrow, 153–72. Landham: Rowman and Littlefield.

Katzenstein, M. 1998. 'Stepsisters: Feminist movement activism in different institutional spaces'. In *The Social Movement Society: Contentious politics for a new century,* edited by D.S. Meyer and S. Tarrow, 195–216. Lanham, MD: Rowman and Littlefield.

McKinley, D. 2010. Transcript. Activists' interviews: Trevor Ngwane. Anti Privatisation Forum, 23 March 2010. South African History Archive Collection.

McKinley, D. 2012. *Transition's Child: The Anti-Privatisation Forum (APF).* Johannesburg: South African History Archive.

Meyer, D. and Tarrow, S. 1998. 'Introduction'. In *The Social Movement Society: Contentious politics for a new century,* edited by D.S. Meyer and S. Tarrow, 1–29. Lanham: Rowman and Littlefield Publishers.

Michels, R. 1966 [1911]. *Political Parties: A sociological study of the oligarchical tendencies of modern democracy.* New York: Free Press.

Oldfield, S. and Stokke, K. 2006. 'Building unity in diversity: Social movement activistm in the Western Cape anti-eviction campaign'. In *Voices of Protest: Social movements in post-apartheid South Africa,* edited by R. Ballard, A. Habib, I. Valodia and E. Zuern, 25–49. Pietermaritzburg and Durban: University of KwaZulu-Natal Press.

Pingo, N. 2012. *Report on Thembelihle.* Unpublished report. Johannesburg: PLANACT.

Pingo, N. 2013. 'Institutionalisation of a Social Movement: The case of Thembelihle, the Thembelihle Crisis Committee and the Operation Khanyisa Movement and the use of the brick, the ballot and the voice'. Unpublished Master's thesis, Development Planning, University of the Witwatersrand, Johannesburg.

Piper, L. and Deacon, R. 2009. 'Too dependent to participate: Ward committees and local democratisation in South Africa', *Local Government Studies* 35(4): 415–33.

Revillard, A. 2011. 'Le féminisme dans l'Etat', *Revue Francaise de Science Politique* 61(5): 956–9.

Roy, A. 2009. 'Civic governmentability: The politics of inclusion in Beirut and Mumbai', *Antipode* 42: 159–79.

Rubin, M. 2013. 'Courting Change: The role of apex courts and court cases in urban governance: A Delhi-Johannesburg comparison'. Unpublished Doctoral Dissertation, Planning, University of the Witwatersrand, Johannesburg.

Seippel, Ø. 2001. 'From mobilisation to institutionalisation? The case of Norwegian environmentalism', *Acta Sociologica* 44(2): 123–37.

Staggenborg, S. 1988. 'The consequences of professionalisation and formalisation in the pro-choice movement', *American Sociological Review* 53(4): 585–605.

van der Heijden, H. 1997. 'Political opportunity structure and the institutionalisation of the environmental movement', *Environmental Politics* 6(4): 25–50.

von Holdt, K., Langa, M., Molapo, S., Mogapi, N., Ngubeni, K., Dlamini, J. and Kirsten, A. 2011. *The Smoke That Calls: Insurgent citizenship, collective violence and the struggle for a place in the new South Africa.* Research report, Johannesburg: CSVR.

Weber, M. 2003 [1919]. *Le savant et le politique.* Paris: Edition La Découverte.

Wilson, S. nd. *Johannesburg's Informal Settlement Plan: A view from Mandlaville and Thembelihle.* Johannesburg: Centre for Applied Legal Studies.

Part II

Seeing the local state from its margins

6

Acting like the state? Leaders' participation in street trade management in Gauteng municipalities

Mamokete Modiba

Introduction

One of my initial interviews in Tshwane was with Mandla,*[1] one of the many street trader leaders in the inner city and we arranged to meet in Marabastad, the busiest street trading area in the municipality. I was picked up in a car driven by Lerato* and Tebogo,* who was introduced to me as a trader leader. Mandla said he needed a few minutes to do some work at Steve Biko Hospital and that the interview would take place after that. The two trader leaders were greeting Tshwane Metro Police officers along the way to the hospital and they seemed to know each other very well. When we arrived at the hospital, we started walking around and both Mandla and Tebogo were greeting some of the street traders on site and engaging in small talk. Lerato started pointing at different spots around the hospital while saying *'hona mo ho kaba shap'* [here would be fine]. I didn't really understand what was going on until Lerato told me they were trying to find a suitable spot to park her caravan where she would sell cooked food. Mandla seemed to be inspecting the site and later he, Tebogo and Lerato finally agreed on a spot. Mandla said *'oka beya caravan ya hao hona mo ene ha hona metro police etlo ho tshwenyang kele teng'* [You can put your caravan right here and no Metro Police officer will harass you as long as I am around]. While Mandla continued with his inspection, he indicated that he

> allocated most of the trading spaces in the vicinity. He then noticed one street trader he didn't know and threatened to remove him as he didn't allocate him the space and that, according Mandla, meant the street trader was unauthorised ... We left the site and went back to Marabastad where Lerato disappeared for a few minutes while I conducted the interview with both Mandla and Tebogo. When she returned, she called Mandla to the side (leaving Tebogo to keep me company) and gave him a folded black plastic bag. Immediately after that, they said their goodbyes with reassurance from Mandla that Lerato will not be harassed by anyone while trading in her newly allocated space (extract from fieldwork diary 8 April 2018).

The above encounter sheds some light on the role and influence of street trader leaders in the process of allocating spaces in the Gauteng City-Region.[2] This chapter explores the extent to which leaders participate in the everyday management of street trade, particularly waiting lists' administration and space allocation. It uncovers multiple and sometimes contradictory narratives of how these processes unfold: who are the street trader leaders with space allocation powers? What is the extent and the nature of their involvement in these processes? This chapter deepens the concept of 'twilight institutions' (Lund 2006) which captures the multitude of institutions and actors in the state–society interface that exercise public authority, by proposing a framework of two archetypes of such institutions along the fuzzy border of the state: there are street trader leaders who operate on the margins of the state and those that act as quasi-state officials. While these are two extremes on a continuum, the position of street trader leaders in relation to state power is constantly shifting depending on opportunities and agendas. This chapter shows how the position of trader governance structure in relation to state power profoundly affects the extent to which leaders participate in the everyday management of street trade. Where leaders operate on the margins of the state, they lack recognition from the state and are excluded from formal allocation processes. While formally excluded, leaders insert themselves in everyday management practices that run in parallel to formal processes, enabled by unorthodox arrangements with state officials. Where leaders act as quasi-state officials, as semi-institutionalised agents, they participate in allocation processes with certain duties partly delegated by authorities. This enmeshing of street trader leaders into the state apparatus effectively blurs and extends the fuzzy border of the state. The formal inclusion of street trader leaders in allocation processes creates opportunities for them to craft their own informal practices from below that can be integrated into formal state governance practices.

This chapter first presents the state–society interface literature and the participation of informal actors in urban governance, exploring the idea of 'informalisation of the state' vis-à-vis 'formalisation of society'. Then it presents the governance structures of street trader leaders in the case study areas to illustrate their positions in relation to state power, further analysing leaders' extent of participation in the everyday management of street trade. The final section of this chapter offers conclusions on the ways in which participation in the everyday management of street trade informalises the state and/or formalises society.

Informalisation of the state *vis à vis* formalisation of society

The state has the mandate to exercise public authority and provide public services, but this dynamic is changing, particularly in contexts where its capacity is weak (Brudney and England 1983; Joshi and Moore 2004; Mitlin and Bartlett 2018) or diminished (Büscher 2012). There exist 'multiple sites of urban governance' (Lindell 2008) where other stakeholders besides the state fulfil certain official mandates including the provision of public services. A variety of actors outside the state (conceptualised in various ways such as unorthodox organisations (Joshi and Moore 2004); twilight institutions (Lund 2006) and hybrid institutions (Büscher 2012) are exercising public authority and acting like the state in various ways.

There are various useful concepts that help unpack dynamics where non-state actors act like the state by fulfilling its core functions, especially in contexts of waning state capacity. One such concept is co-production which is used to understand ways in which citizens play an active role in providing public services in collaboration with the state (Brudney and England 1983; Joshi and Moore 2004; Mitlin and Bartlett 2018). A key underlying notion in co-production literature is that for collaboration to take place, an active, organised and empowered civil society is required to partner with the state. Recognition and support by the state determines the extent of rootedness of organised civil society in the state apparatus as well as their ability to deliver services. While the state might include non-state actors into governance processes to empower them, this inclusion can also be the state 'governing by discharge' (Hibou 2004). While co-production attributes partnerships between the state and non-state actors to a weak or absent state, governing by discharge sees this as expanding the realm of state power even when and where it does not have the capacity. In essence, the state works with non-state actors to find assistance to expand its reach and wield its influence indirectly.

With co-production legitimating the role played by non-state actors, concepts such as 'twilight institutions' (Lund 2006) and hybrid institutions (Büscher 2012) offer a slightly different dynamic where actors outside the state exercise public authority (roles and responsibilities traditionally assigned to the state) alongside the state. These organisations mainly operate independently from the state, sometimes challenging the state and its practices, as the relationship with officials is not formalised in any way even though state processes might be used to legitimate their existence. In most cases, these organisations adopt locally engineered parallel (informal) systems and networks that might also contradict official practices of the state.

The involvement of non-state actors in achieving a public mandate results in interpenetration that blurs and obscures boundaries between the state and society (Das and Poole 2004; Joshi and Moore 2004). This fuzzy line between the state and society is what constitutes a 'creation of the state at the margins' (Das and Poole 2004). The fact that public authority is exercised by stakeholders other than the state means that public institutions are constantly being produced and reproduced, requiring a reconceptualisation of what constitutes boundaries between the state and society, the centre and margins of the state. This creation and recreation of the state effectively renders the margins as spaces of power that constantly move in and out of the state. This shift in relative position to state power is what determines whether organisations are operating 'on the margins of the state' or 'on the inside borders of the state' thus acting as quasi-state officials.

Considering the latter in our case studies, these are street trader leaders who receive payment from the state, have some sort of contract in place to govern operations and utilise state resources. Considering the actors in this way opens up avenues to analyse their practices and how these produce and reproduce the state. While they act as quasi-state officials, they are able to flout official processes in search of practical ways to resolve issues. In turn, the state may adopt the informal practices used by these actors to resolve everyday issues on the ground. In this process, both the state and non-state actors are recreated and reconfigured such that formal and informal practices become entangled (Rubin 2018). This could be as a result of a realisation that formal processes are unable to address issues thus requiring flexibility, an element brought about by informal practices of non-state actors.

Yiftachel (2009) speaks of 'gray zones' as spaces that sit on the border between 'white' (legal) and 'black' (illegal) zones. This concept can also be extended to include informal systems and practices running parallel to formal ones which the state neither accepts nor denies, leaving them in a constant state of uncertainty. This state of uncertainty gives the state arbitrary power to legalise and incorporate them as their mode of operation or dispel (render them criminal, illegal and informal) and destroy them at its convenience (Roy 2009; Yiftachel 2009). By virtue of the state recognising, and in some cases adopting, informal practices of non-state actors, a process of informalisation of the state and formalisation of society takes place. With this theoretical framing in mind, we now turn to the relationship between trader governance structures and the state in our three case studies.

Street trader leaders and the state in the Gauteng City-Region (GCR): trader governance structures in relation to state power

The GCR is 'an integrated cluster of cities, towns and urban nodes that together make up the economic heartland of South Africa'.[3] It consists of three metropolitan municipalities of Ekurhuleni, Johannesburg and Tshwane (the economic engines) together with various other local municipalities and its footprint extends beyond the Gauteng province borders (Cheruiyot 2018). **Figure 6.1** is a set of maps showing the GCR in context. It is in this context that street trading is a feature of the urban landscape and an avenue through which various people, including the poor, unemployed, retrenched and marginalised sustain their livelihoods. In Johannesburg and Tshwane, street trading spaces are located mostly in the inner city, while in Ekurhuleni, a more fragmented municipality, there are several urban centres where street traders gather and organise.

The proliferation of street trading, especially in busy inner cities, has come with management challenges for local authorities. For instance, there are approximately 17,800 traders in Johannesburg,[4] 1,437 in Ekurhuleni and 15,000 in Tshwane[5]. This is in relation to an estimated population of 15 million in the whole of Gauteng.[6] Various forms of trader governance structures have emerged (organically or state engineered) to address issues associated with the everyday management of street trade. These structures are configured differently in each context and boast varying relationships with the state that either enables or constrains the extent to which leaders participate in the everyday management of street trade, particularly trading space allocation processes.

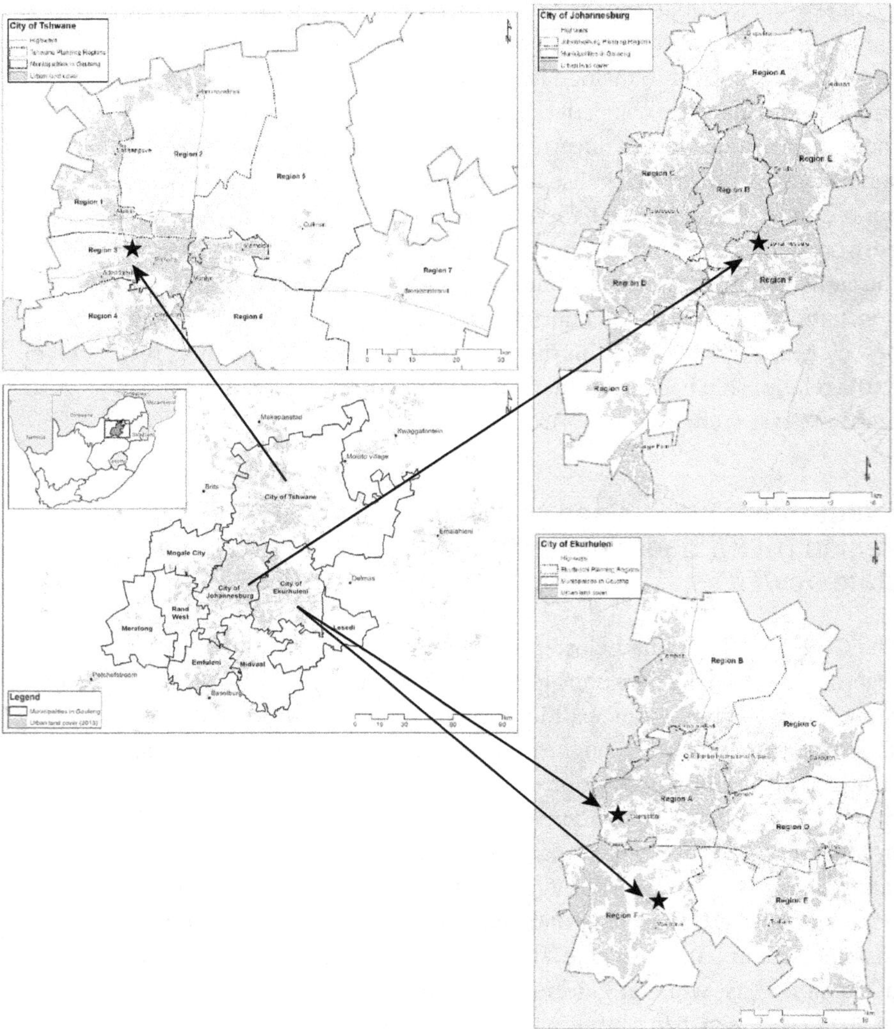

Figure 6.1 Location of the case study areas in the Gauteng City-Region (GCR). The politics of street trading management is examined in three different municipalities (Johannesburg, Tswhane and Ekurhuleni), all located in the urbanised area of the Gauteng Province.

Source: © Christian Hamann, Researcher at the GCRO 2022.

There are a range of trader governance structures in the case study areas which have varying positions in relation to the state. There are leaders who operate 'on the margins of the state' who tend to have unorthodox relations with authorities and mainly rely on confrontational politics resulting in strained relations with the state. There are also those leaders who are enmeshed in the state apparatus and operate as quasi-state officials, who generally cooperate with the state and have access to its resources. While these represent two extremes, the relationship between trader governance structures and the state are not fixed but are constantly shifting depending on opportunities.

Institutionalised area-based committees in Ekurhuleni

There appears to be no record of street trader mobilisation in Ekurhuleni over the years, giving a sense of harmony between traders and authorities. The seeming lack of collective mobilisation is explained by some leaders as being the result of a lack of history of massive clean-up campaigns and brutal attack of traders by authorities as is the case in Johannesburg and Tshwane. They argue that the only engagement between the state and traders was to resolve case-by-case issues brought forward in an atomised manner. This type of engagement created a problem over time as it became impractical for officials to engage individual traders. This culminated in officials facilitating a process to set up area-based committees in the various towns[7] of the municipality to represent traders. The area-based committees were created in early 2000s, particularly in towns where street trading was prevalent, to serve as a point of contact and engagement with officials.

The process of setting up committees was led by the municipal department of Local Economic Development (LED) which convened meetings in various towns over time for traders to elect their leadership. For instance, Germiston Traders Partnership (GEMTRAP) was constituted in the early 2000s in Germiston and Vosloorus Micro Traders Association in Vosloorus, as the area-based committees. The various committees in each town operate independently of each other with no coordination for the entire municipality and have a great deal of discretion in setting their own rules and regulations at the area level.

The elected leaders of these area-based committees are the only street trader representatives recognised by officials in Ekurhuleni, and as such have a monopoly over engagement with the state. There is an unwritten requirement which compels prospective traders to become members of the area-based committee in their locality, in order to become eligible to apply for a trading space. This requirement is not written in any institutional document, the committees are not visible on the City's website and the process of registering prospective traders is not incorporated in municipal guidelines on 'how to apply for a trading space'. This shows that the governance structure is recognised by officials but the partnership is only semi-institutionalised. Street traders who are members of these committees pay regular fees which guarantee them identification cards that act as proof of membership and access to the leaders. These cards are used by members to claim certain benefits, such as protection from Ekurhuleni Metro Police officers' raids and priority to access lucrative trading spaces.

Committee leaders seem to have a cooperative relationship with authorities, and there is no institutional platform of engagement to iron out broad issues. Engagements happen on an ad hoc basis to resolve urgent issues, such as expired permits. During fieldwork in Germiston, I witnessed that GEMTRAP leaders required permission from officials before engaging with an outsider. At our initial meeting to introduce the research and negotiate access,[8] the leaders dismissed my request. A few months later I secured an interview with one of the LED officials and I narrated my encounter with GEMTRAP.[9] The official indicated that I had to go through his office to gain access to the leaders. He called the leaders immediately and over the phone they agreed to meet with me the next day for an interview. And throughout the research process, the leaders largely aligned to officials' discourses in their responses to certain questions, such as the issue of 'illegal' traders.

Multiple street trader governance structures in Johannesburg

In contrast, Johannesburg's street traders have a long-standing history of collective organisation and mobilisation dating back to the late 1980s in a context of repressive municipal policies and practices (Rogerson 1988; Skinner 2007). At the time, organisations were advocating for authorities to allow more trading activity in the city. While many organisations have developed over time to amplify the voice of traders, their relationship with the state has often been characterised by antagonism. In recent years, the City has set up a second system of traders' representation in the form of elected block leaders, and this effectively created multiple forms of street trade governance structures.

Street trader organisation leaders and antagonistic encounters with the state

There exists a multitude of street trader organisations that operate in various parts of the city with most of their leaders having 'assumed representation' (Houtzager and Lavalle 2009) of grassroots traders. Officials' discourses regarding these organisations are negative and contribute 'directly or indirectly, to constructing or consolidating street trader organisations as marginal, inefficient, unrepresentative and therefore fundamentally irrelevant' (Bénit-Gbaffou 2016, 1, 106). Membership of some of these organisations is made up of both 'authorised'[10] and 'unauthorised'[11] traders, a fact that is also used by the state to denounce organisations.

The City has been reluctant to recognise and engage with independent organisation leaders over the years. The reluctance to engage, although still prevalent, has shifted somewhat in the aftermath of Operation Clean Sweep.[12] While lines of communication between the City and traders were limited and engagement mainly confrontational, these dynamics have tilted in favour of some trader organisations being given seats on the bargaining table. This is especially true for two of the organisations[13] that were instrumental in publicly challenging the City's clean-up campaign in court and claiming victory. The litigation victory gained the visibility and legitimacy for the organisations, some leverage on officials and a certain level of recognition and inclusion in engagement platforms (Bénit-Gbaffou 2016). This inclusion of trader organisations in engagements that they would previously have been excluded from can also be a strategy by the City to closely monitor the leaders and mitigate confrontation.

There are also clientelist organisations that have maintained close relations with some officials over time. These organisation leaders have always had a seat at the table and seldom publicly challenge any repressive practices of their allies. The clientelistic relations work in favour of both of the stakeholders where officials are able to push and realise their agenda through leaders, and they in turn access resources and certain powers from officials. One Voice of All Hawkers Association is alleged by other traders to be one such organisation that has close ties with the Department of Economic Development (DED) officials. Although this organisation has embarked on a number of marches over the years, they are seldom directly targeted at DED but divert blame to other parts of the City such as the Johannesburg Property Company and Johannesburg Metro Police Department (Matjomane 2013).

Block leaders as the main partners of the state

The block leader system was introduced by the City in the early 2000s to counteract the organisations which were largely confrontational. Block leaders are elected at the block or street level in the inner city to represent and manage traders in negotiation with the City (Bénit-Gbaffou 2014; Khwashaba 2016). This is the preferred and recognised system of trader leadership by authorities arguing that block leaders are the closest to grassroots traders and can therefore speak and act on their behalf, unlike organisation leaders.

Once elected, some block leaders are further elected into the block leader committee which is made up of 15 members that meet monthly with municipal programme officers to discuss trade related issues. It can be argued that the City engineered the block leader system so traders can be co-opted and pacified as they act as an extension of the state to traders. Block leaders received a stipend of an undisclosed amount on a monthly basis for their work. Authorities employ 'divide and rule' tactics that pit organisations and block leaders against each other. For instance, block leaders are invited to meetings where organisation leaders are excluded. Block leaders have a close collaborative relationship with officials who need them to act as their eyes and ears (Khwashaba 2016) as well as hands to get the work done on the ground. They are able to penetrate the state and operate as quasi-state officials due to the nature of their relationship with officials.

Attempt to reconcile the bifurcated street trade structure: constituting the Informal Traders' Forum and task teams

The engagement between the City and street traders was formalised through the Informal Traders' Forum which was initiated in 2009 by the municipality[14] and disbanded in 2014. The forum was supposed to be made up of street trade leaders (both independent organisations and block leaders) as well as officials from relevant departments within the City. The forum was meant to meet monthly to deliberate on issues, but in reality the meetings were irregular and in some instances traders had to request special meetings to address urgent matters.

While the intention of the forum was to create a platform for deliberation on issues pertaining to street trading in the City, it soon became a site for confrontation between traders and municipal officials (Matjomane 2013; Khwashaba 2019). Confrontations were almost exclusively by independent organisation leaders who would question certain decisions and practices by officials while block leaders and some clientelist organisation leaders would not openly challenge any decisions. Thus, forum meetings were in most cases a battleground where confrontational scenes were played out during engagements.

As part of the Informal Traders' Forum, three task teams (by-law enforcement, management and technical) were created to act as the implementation arm of the forum together with officials. Leaders were nominated into positions at a forum meeting in 2012 and constituted task teams. The Management Task Team's role was to advise and guide City officials on the allocation and management of trading spaces. The Technical Task Team provided guidance regarding policy review in ways that were developmental and conducive for traders. The By-law Enforcement Task Team provided oversight and advised enforcement officers on ways to enforce by-laws.[15]

Members of the task teams became the face of the state on the street as they worked together with officials. For instance, in an attempt to implement by-laws, traders would, together with officials, evict some traders in spaces which were deemed unsuitable for trading and this created conflict of interest for leaders. Officials would make decisions and use leaders to approve those decisions, and implement them without being given opportunities to deliberate. The task teams played a similar role to that played by block leaders: they acted as official partners of the state but without having a say in decisions.

Members of the task teams received a stipend of R2,000 per month for their positions which some traders argued made it difficult for those leaders to argue against the City, even in the face of repressive practices against street traders. Some argue that members of the task teams are representatives of traders on the ground but at the same time they get payment from the City to implement its plans which might cloud their judgement. Organisation leaders argue that payment of task team members is a 'divide and rule' tactic by the City which further fragments leaders and this is because not all members of the forum are members of the task teams.

From hostility to incorporation: phases of trader leaders' inclusion in Tshwane

In Tshwane, there seemed to be no relationship and engagement between traders and the state prior to 2012. This non-engagement led to violent encounters towards the end of 2012 during the implementation of 'Operation Reclaim', a renewal project including infrastructural development which largely resulted in the violent removal of traders from the inner city. This led to the city becoming a battle ground between street traders and local authorities, particularly the Tshwane Metro Police Department (TMPD). During this time, the inner city was characterised by a series of marches and pickets organised by various street trader leaders challenging the evictions while simultaneously demanding engagement with authorities.

Selective inclusion: constitution of the Mayoral Steering Committee

During this time, the City administration was under the African National Congress (ANC) with Kgosienthso Ramokgopa as the executive mayor. A meeting was secured between the City at the highest level, and trader leaders, to negotiate and forge a way forward, which eventually culminated in the signing of a memorandum of understanding (MoU) between the parties. The MoU with the City was signed with four street trader organisations[16] that were at the forefront of confrontation with the authorities during the evictions. Signing of the MoU facilitated the creation of the Tshwane Mayoral Steering Committee on Informal Trade made up of two representatives from each of the four trader organisations with officials from various departments including the Local Economic Development, City Planning and the Tshwane Metro Police department (TMPD).

The official objective of the MoU was to facilitate structured engagement between street traders and authorities in a context of hostility.[17] The definite objective was to contain the confrontational encounters between these stakeholders, negative stories in the media and to pacify traders. This is attested to in one of the City documents which states that 'setting up the committee has seen a reduction in informal trader marches and strikes against the City' (Business Support Operations, nd). It was not long until this objective of the agreement became clear to some of the leaders, a partial reason that led to them splintering away from the committee and creating a counter organisation known as the Tshwane Barekisi Forum in 2012. The organisation became popular among inner city traders for its challenge to City authorities, and continued struggle to change the status quo, resulting in growth in membership. While most traders in the inner city joined this organisation, authorities questioned the way it was formed and its modus operandi.

In 2012, the City published a report titled 'Setting the record straight'. The organisation was labelled a splinter organisation, which adopted disruptive repertoires of action leading to destabilisation of public order in the city, and was explicitly accused by authorities of playing on party politics, aligning itself to the Economic Freedom Fighters (EFF)[18] and using the street trading issue to fight partisan politics:

> Tshwane Barekisi Forum was formed and launched post the best practice tour [sic] and the organisation has brought new traders into some parts of the city, congesting the already overflowing pavement with traders.
>
> The Forum is a splinter organisation without a mandate of the traders in the city.
>
> This organisation does not offer meaningful solutions to the challenges posed by informal trade nor are they willing to offer reasonable and humane platform for engagement regarding contending market forces.
>
> Tshwane Barekisi Forum is an empty surrogate structure of the Economic Freedom Fighters (EFF) whose establishment is to render the city ungovernable and score sordid political goals at the expense of the vulnerable poor uneducated traders.
>
> This organisation has embarked on a series of illegal strikes to catapult the EFF brand within the trading space to attack the mayor with high octane profanities, discredit the city of Tshwane and to undermine the process underway.
>
> All these issues are irrelevant to the plight of the trader but more political, as a political action of the EFF, as could be seen throughout the country.
>
> Barekisi forum is a violent and confrontational organisation that employs criminal and 'nyaope' addicts to loot businesses to heighten their existence and build fear and victimisation within the inner city (extract from 'Setting the record straight' report, City of Tshwane 2012).

The extract above is a powerful depiction of how officials in the City conceived of the Tshwane Barekisi Forum during the early stages of its formation. Other street trader leaders, particularly those that were part of the 2012 Mayoral Steering Committee, were also publicly challenging the Tshwane Barekisi Forum in the same line as officials. While the Tshwane Barekisi Forum was continuously challenging the City through various means, it was also seeking inclusion into the inner city street trade governance structure. One of the major opportunities for the organisation came during 2014 when a street trader was shot dead during a TMPD raid in the inner city. Following the incident, the Tshwane Barekisi Forum, with the support from the ANC Youth League and South African Informal Traders Forum,[19] confronted the City and threatened to make the city ungovernable, through the organisation of violent marches and pickets in the streets of Tshwane.

Formal electoral processes as a mode of inclusion into trader governance structure

The hostile environment with constant confrontational encounters between traders and authorities eventually led to the disbanding of the Steering Committee in 2015 in favour of a more representative body through formal electoral processes. The mayor's office played a significant part to facilitate the process of trader elections into a Region 3 representative governance structure. Formal electoral processes of trader leadership were overseen by the national Independent Electoral Commission, and only authorised traders were allowed to participate as voters or candidates. June 2015 was the dawn of a new era when the Tshwane Informal Traders Representative Committee was constituted and all seats were won by the Tshwane Barekisi Forum leaders, to be in office until June 2018. The confrontational nature of engagement had gained the Tshwane Barekisi Forum a following from traders in the form of membership, as well as some sympathy with the public through the media, and eventually a level of recognition from the City particularly ANC Mayor Ramokgopa. It is alleged by other organisation leaders that the ANC co-opted the Tshwane Barekisi Forum to align itself with the administration, and cut its former ties with the EFF, in order to get a seat at the table.

The Tshwane Informal Traders Representative Committee is a platform where the Tshwane Barekisi Forum members had direct contact with the mayor and the broader leadership of the City of Tshwane. The committee is directly under the ambit of the LED's Business Support Unit, and elected leaders have direct access to and engagement with officials who deal with everyday management of street trade such as registration and allocation of spaces in the inner city. The elected leaders had monthly meetings with officials and were receiving a stipend of R2,000 per month with office space. The inclusion of the Tshwane Barekisi Forum into a Region 3 trader structure solidified the organisation as a main partner of the state with leaders leaning more towards cooperation with authorities.

The cooperative relationship between the Tshwane Barekisi Forum leaders and the state was disrupted by local government elections in 2016. During this time, City administration was taken over by the Democratic Alliance-Economic Freedom Fighters (DA-EFF)[20] coalition government which saw DA Mayor Solly Msimanga taking office. Relations between the DA mayor and the prevailing trader structure were strained. An instance of this occurred when a meeting to address traders in Marabastad by the mayor was boycotted by the Tshwane Barekisi Forum leaders, arguing that he did not call the meeting through them as Region 3 leaders. Confrontational dynamics were compounded by the Tshwane Barekisi Forum's term of office coming to an end in June 2018 without re-election processes being put into place to solicit new leaders to form part of the street trade governance structure. This meant that the Tshwane Informal Traders Representative Committee had vacant leadership positions. This period is characterised by heightened antagonism, with protests being organised and court cases being lodged against the City.

There are various configurations of street trader governance structures with varying forms of institutionalisation across the three metropolitan areas. In Ekurhuleni, there is recognition of specific area-based committees. This recognition of committees is not written in any official documents but is verbal. In Johannesburg, the institutionalisation of leaders is through payment of task teams and block leaders as well as exclusive meetings with block leaders. Members of the task teams were governed by a set of terms of references and block leaders by informal house rules that regulated their engagement with officials and grassroots traders. In Tshwane, leaders were initially institutionalised through the signing of a MoU between four trader organisations and the City. When the Region 3 Committee was elected into power, this arrangement was replaced by the signing of a three-year contract between the City and the elected trader leaders of the Tshwane Barekisi Forum. The relationship between leaders and the City was governed by terms of references which set out the rules of engagement. Furthermore, leaders were paid a stipend on a monthly basis and were given an office space to conduct official business.

Leaders' participation in everyday management of street trade: controlling waiting lists and allocating trading spaces

This section explores how these dynamics impact the extent of participation of leaders in the everyday management of street trade. Leaders operating as quasi-state officials have been included in allocation processes, with this power varying between the three case study areas. While some duties have been partially delegated by officials, leaders tend to subvert these processes in an effort to address everyday issues on the ground. Leaders operating on the margins of the state have not been officially included in allocation processes and find ways of inserting themselves with a level of support from some officials. These margins thus become spaces of creativity and power.

Space allocation with or through partners

In all case study areas, state-endorsed leaders are included in allocation processes to assess the availability and suitability of trading spaces and make recommendations to officials regarding whether those spaces can be allocated. According to officials, leaders do not have the mandate nor power to make the final allocation decision: this is a decision taken by officials in light of leaders' recommendations. In Ekurhuleni, area-based committees such as GEMTRAP and Vosloorus Micro Traders Association are included in allocation processes with duties specified by the LED office:

> In terms of people getting space, there is an organisation which is our eyes and ears in the Local Economic Development. They're the ones who will send people to us after looking and saying there is space. The organisations don't give you the space, they confirm first that what you want is available and refer you to us (Germiston Customer Care Relations manager 2018).

The trader leaders have a slightly different version of how allocation plays out. They argue that prospective traders can only be considered for allocation if they become members of the area-based committees. While this unwritten rule was confirmed by some grassroots traders in their testimonies of how they accessed space, it is dismissed by officials:

> Claims that to get a space one has to join an organisation is not true because that would be stepping on individuals' right or freedom of association (LED official 2018).

This contradiction could potentially result from the fact that the official does not want to admit the state's informal practices of governing street trading which involves civil society actors. The denial might also be motivated by fear of being sued for infringing on individual rights and freedom of association.

Area-based committees play an increasingly crucial role as they also have control over the management of waiting lists. While this aspect was not disclosed by GEMTRAP leaders, Vosloorus Micro Traders Association leaders claim that they draw and manage waiting list per street in their jurisdiction, which they use to allocate people. Street-based waiting lists are drafted by the committee and a person's name is put on the list once the suitability of space and its availability is confirmed by leaders and is kept by the leaders without sharing with the municipality:

> We have a list of people who want spaces. When a person wants space they come to us as leaders and we go with the person to the place they want. When we go to that space, we check if it's right for trading and if it's available and doesn't belong to another person. If it's unavailable, we put that person on a waiting list or we recommend that they find another space. The waiting list is another story because you have to wait until a space becomes available (Vosloorus Micro Traders Association leader 2018).

There are various waiting lists for each town and street or block in Ekurhuleni, particularly in areas where access to space is competitive. Each committee creates a waiting list per locality or street and in most instances this is done without the involvement of the municipality:

> The LED office has a database [waiting list] of people who are waiting for spaces in different towns of Ekurhuleni. You have a database for Germiston, one for Kempton Park, another for Springs, etc. and these are areas of high demand and congestion. If you can see the database, it's too long, because the demand is higher than the spaces that can accommodate trading. For example, in Plantation Street, there is space for less than 100 people but there are more applications (LED official 2018).

Apart from these databases which the officials seem to believe are rather inefficient, due to the limited number of authorised trading sites, there are informal processes of allocation that are condemned by officials but yet tolerated in reality:

> Some people think when elected as chairperson their word is final, so they do as they wish not thinking they are accountable to anyone. The issue is around money being gained illegally while they were supposed to represent their people. For instance they can ask money from a trader promising him or her that he or she will get space,

> there are always those individuals that engage in side dealings which are not legal (LED official 2018).

This talks to the real power that these area-based committees have on the ground where they are able to make decisions regarding sites and people to be allocated. This real power of allocation was confirmed by some traders in Germiston, who spoke of 'an organisation that controls the allocation of spaces' and the need to 'thank the leaders so they can arrange the trading space'; claims that are refuted by officials who insist leaders cannot make final decisions. There is a degree of denialism by officials of what is really happening on the ground, underplaying the actual power of area-based committees even though the partnership with them is recognised.

In Johannesburg, block leaders and task team members are included in the designation[21] process. During this process, officials go to the site together with members of the task teams (including block leaders) to assess the suitability of space for trading, and verify existing traders, if any. The task teams, however, were not allowed to go on site alone and had to be in the company of officials at all times.

While waiting lists were kept by municipal officials, block leaders managed waiting lists in streets or blocks that they were in charge of, by recommending those next in line for spaces. When a space became available, a block leader would indicate who was next on the list to be considered for allocation (endorsed by other block leaders in that block). The suggestion by one block leader would be seconded by other block leaders operating in the same street with approval from the programme officer (initial sign off) and the programme manager (final sign off). Khwashaba argues that:

> It can be hypothesised that programme officers are more focused on the administration part of the waiting list that is registering traders, licensing them and entering them into the waiting list. As block leaders are the ones who know who is next in the waiting list, it gives them power over traders (Khwashaba 2016, 62).

Municipal programme officers thus became dependent on block leaders to indicate where space was available and who on the list is next in line. The management of waiting lists also requires block leaders to constantly check and update the list. Block leaders indicate to officials when spaces in their area of jurisdiction become vacant and they negotiate with programme officers in terms of how the space should be filled:

> [The City] needs to explain that some streets have their own waiting list. In fact, almost all the streets have their waiting list, kept by the block leader. Programme officers, each allocated to a street, check the list and confirm with block leaders (organisation leader quoted in Bénit-Gbaffou 2015).

On the one hand, waiting list management provided block leaders with flexibility so that they can be responsive to local issues, while on the other, it was seen by other organisation leaders as being subject to corruption and manipulation owing to leaders' collusion with the state (Khwashaba 2016). Organisation leaders argued that block leaders manipulated the allocation process and ensured that their people jumped the queue even though some people had been waiting for years.

The Tshwane Barekisi Forum leaders are the official partners of the state institutionalised through formal elections into a Region 3 Representative Committee. These leaders have been included in allocation processes where they act as evaluators of suitability and availability of space and making recommendations to the City. Prospective traders like in Ekurhuleni and Johannesburg approach committee leaders as the first point of contact who facilitate the process. The decision to allocate is taken in consultation with officials whose main duty is to provide oversight. While these leaders have been formally included in the allocation process, they are accused of abusing their powers and exercising discretion in how they undertake their duties on the ground:

> Committee members are supposed to be the eyes and ears of the municipality on the ground. When someone wants to trade, they approach the committee members who then engage with the person and ask specific questions about where they want to trade, what goods and all of that. After that, the committee will put that person on a [waiting] list with the municipality, then allocate accordingly in consultation. But committee members are doing their own things, they are abusing their powers (LED official 2018).

The abuse of powers according to the LED official entails the committee members completely taking over the mandate of officials and issuing licenses to traders without the City's involvement while seeking financial compensation from traders:

> It's happening, they are doing it [allocating trading spaces] which becomes illegal because they take money from the people and they are not following the process (Business Support Unit official 2018).

Similar to officials' accounts, some traders on the ground narrate how they were allocated spaces by leaders. One trader indicated that a trader leader allocated his space for an undisclosed fee:

> You start by identifying where you want to sell and once that is done you call the chairperson of Barekisi Forum and set up a meeting and take it from there. That's how I got my space and obviously you will see how you thank him. When you agree then you get your license and trading space (grassroots trader 2018).

Once the space is identified, that sets the terms of engagement with the committee where negotiations regarding payment for access to space are made. When the above trader was probed regarding how he thanked the leader, he did not want to disclose the exact amount. This is similar to what I witnessed during initial fieldwork noted in the encounter in the beginning of the chapter. The leaders approved the site and immediately allocated the prospective trader space for a fee that she paid on the spot. The concerned leaders appeared to have discretion in allocating space without any involvement of officials. The leaders even went as far as promising the trader protection from municipal police who they seem to have established a good rapport with. One of the competing organisation leaders indicated that the Tshwane Barekisi Forum leaders would threaten to revoke traders' licenses if they refused to join their organisation:

> They would say if you don't join us we are going to cancel your license and you will lose your stall (organisation leader 2018).
>
> Leaders manage local area waiting lists which are paper-based as opposed to electronic and these become the basis through which space gets allocated. This means that leaders are able to influence and manipulate who gets placed on the waiting list, allocated or excluded, even though LED officials are said to be making the final decision. There was an instance during fieldwork where one of the committee leaders indicated that he had a waiting list in his pocket that he brought to a meeting to discuss who is next on the list to be allocated. I requested to see this waiting list but the leader refused, saying that it contained sensitive information such as people's identity numbers which could

> not be shared with an outsider. It was intriguing to understand how leaders have their own lists independent from officials which they use to allocate spaces, giving leaders real power on the ground.

Organised invasion of trading spaces through clientelist networks

While leaders who act as quasi-state officials have been included in allocation processes, some of the leaders operating on the margins of the state, who have been excluded from these processes, have found ways of inserting themselves. Some allocate spaces through organised invasion of trading sites, which is made possible by clientelist networks. In Johannesburg, there were instances where leaders were made aware of the possibility of a street being opened up for trading; they mobilised their members to occupy the street so that they could be legalised. In other instances, they invaded spaces and mobilised officials, with whom they had close relationships, to designate these as legal trading spaces. One Voice of All Hawkers Association is known for allocating spaces for its members in areas where trading is not (yet) allowed and lobbying the City for legalisation of the space:

> One Voice is one of the organisations that go against what officials propose as trading areas. One Voice gained popularity over the years because it came in as a response, saying: where there's restrictions we'll do it by force. They do indeed have members occupying restricted areas by force (ex official 2018).

The organisation has a reputation for getting its members trading spaces through organised invasions. This could be likened to what is currently happening in the country where the EFF is encouraging people to occupy prime land informally invoking slogans such as 'land expropriation without compensation'. In this instance, One Voice could be argued to be the EFF of traders as they allow their members to occupy any available space that is suitable for trading – and indeed the president of the organisation is identified by his red beret.[22]

There are instances where the president of the organisation approached the City with a list of existing traders in the inner city. He approached the City having evaluated the suitability of the street (wide pavements) and its availability, and lobbied officials to consider its designation as a trading space. Officials then do their own site inspection and make a decision regarding the space, which in most cases is in favour of the organisation's request. Besides accessing space through organised invasions, leaders of this organisation seem to be able to allocate spaces with the cooperation of certain officials. Other leaders argue that the organisation has been given the mandate to allocate spaces in certain parts of the city and they have the discretion to set conditions of that access:

> One Voice has been allocated spaces in President Street and Prichard Street by officials and they appear to be asking R200 for the stall from their members. If you're not a member of their organisation, you don't get a stall, or you pay exorbitant amounts. And if you're a member but your membership account is in arrears, you will lose the space. There was a case a couple of years ago in Hillbrow where One Voice was giving members accounts since 2009 and told them if they don't pay all their arrears they will lose their spaces (organisation leader 2017).

The organisation effectively rules in these parts because they can allocate or take away a trading space from a trader with the support of officials. The protection fees also ensure that traders do not get harassed by the municipal police. In an instance where a member does not pay these fees, their protection will not be guaranteed. Pezzano (2011, 6) talks about 'connivance between municipal authorities and association leaders' where the two benefit from favours from each other. Leaders who cooperate with officials are given the power to allocate spaces which they give to members and willing buyers. For officials, this is also a form of governability where the leaders effectively become allies of the state in instances where other leaders challenge and confront the City's repressive practices.

Conclusion

This chapter has shown the extent of leaders' participation in the everyday management of street trade and how this is enabled by the position of their governing structures in relation to state power. Traders who are recognised and institutionalised have resources at their disposal and have the capacity to manage street trade while those outside these formal systems find ways to insert themselves into these processes in parallel ways. In all cases, official processes give leaders the powers to evaluate and make recommendations to officials. For instance, officials in Johannesburg depend on block leaders and task teams to inform them when space is available and who is next in line to be allocated. While these leaders have been included in formal processes, they have devised their own informal practices from below which influence formal state practices.

The development of informal sub-systems by leaders means that the power of allocation is not the same in all cases. In Ekurhuleni, prospective traders have to join area-based committees before becoming eligible for a trading space. While this is not a rule written in any official document, leaders utilise this informal rule as a basis for allocation. This has created small bosses that have the power to decide who is included or excluded from accessing trading spaces by setting their own rules on the ground. In Johannesburg, block leaders are given ultimate powers of allocation while organisation leaders are pacified through inclusion in powerless task teams. Block leaders have the power to administer waiting lists and recommend those next in line for spaces. Some organisations that lie outside the formal processes of allocation have inserted themselves through collective invasion of spaces that have not yet been legalised by the state. In this way, they open an opportunity to lobby the state to legalise its members through official processes. In Tshwane, the Region 3 Committee has gained real power on the ground where they can allocate without officials, even though the official rule is that officials must be kept informed.

From these cases, it is clear that the state governs street trading with or through informal partners who are the state-endorsed leaders. At different times, officials adopt various practices such as turning a blind eye to the informal practices, letting things be because the leaders are providing a needed service and denialism of informal arrangements from officials, even if partnerships are well recognised. Officials' discourses underplay the actual power of leaders on the ground and they cannot publicly admit that leaders allocate spaces as they might be accused of nursing a mafia.

The involvement of non-state actors in the management of street trading in the above cases reveals how collaboration with the state strengthens its capacity to govern. The recognition of these informal partners by the state is important as it determines the extent of their participation in the everyday management of street trade. Leaders that are state-endorsed and act as quasi-state officials are included in allocation processes and this is done to varying degrees in the case study areas. This inclusion means that state practices are constantly influenced by non-state actors' practices, which often are informal, resulting in an entanglement of formal and informal practices. This effectively extends the realm of the state, resulting in constant production and reproduction of the fuzzy borders of the state.

Notes

1 *Pseudonym.
2 This chapter is based on my PhD thesis which investigates the role of traders in the governance of street trading in Ekurhuleni, Johannesburg and Tshwane metropolitan municipalities (Matjomane 2021).
3 The Gauteng City-Region Observatory (GCRO). nd. *The Gauteng City-Region*. Available at: https://www.gcro.ac.za/. Accessed 29 May 2019.
4 Metropolitan Trading company (MTC). 2008. Linear Markets for the Inner City of Johannesburg. Report, City of Johannesburg Archive. Tamilika Consulting Services, 2009. *Baseline Survey Report of Informal Street Trading in Six (6) Regions of the City of Johannesburg*. Report for the Metropolitan Trading Company. Inner City Library, City of Johannesburg Archive.
5 Gauteng Province Government Department of Economic Development. 2015. *Gauteng Informal Business Upliftment Strategy*. Policy memo. Johannesburg: Economic Development Department. These are estimated figures and do not capture the actual numbers on the ground.
6 StatsSA 2020. *2020 mid-year population estimates*. Available at: http://www.statssa.gov.za/?s=mid-year+population+estimates&sitem=publication. Accessed 13 July 2020.
7 Ekurhuleni is a metropolitan municipality without a single city centre but rather a fragmented collection of towns, corresponding to former segregated South African municipalities under apartheid, and which are now united under the metropolitan municipality.
8 12 September 2017.
9 Interview with Ekurhuleni LED officer, 15 February 2018.
10 Traders who have licenses or permits and operate in areas designated for trading.
11 Traders who do not have licenses or permits and/or operate in areas not designated for trading.
12 A clean-up campaign in Johannesburg in 2013 that resulted in thousands of traders being evicted off the streets in the inner city.
13 South African Informal Traders Forum and South African National Traders Retail Alliance, actively involved in fighting for the rights of traders.
14 City of Johannesburg. 2010. *Draft terms of reference for the sub-committees of the Johannesburg Informal Trading Forum*.
15 City of Johannesburg. 2010. *Draft terms of reference for the sub-committees of the Johannesburg Informal Trading Forum*.
16 Tshwane Informal Traders Forum, Tshwane Informal Traders Council, Tshwane Micro Entrepreneur League and Tshwane National African Federated Chamber of Commerce.
17 City of Tshwane. 2012. 'SA: Statement by the City of Tshwane on historic agreement reached with informal traders', *Polity*. 20 September.
18 A radical left-wing political party in South Africa which was founded by Julius Malema, a former ANC Youth League president, and allies in 2013.
19 One of the main street trader organisations in Johannesburg that was created in an effort to unify the sector, and has branches in Tshwane.
20 The DA (Democratic Alliance) is a centrist political party in South Africa and currently the official opposition to the ANC.
21 This refers to the process of opening up an area/street/block in line with what is prescribed in the by-laws to allow street trading to take place.
22 One symbolic element of the EFF 'uniform'.

References

Bénit-Gbaffou, C. (ed.) 2014. *A Political Landscape Of Street Trader Organisations In Inner City Johannesburg: Post Operation Clean Sweep*. Johannesburg: Centre for Urban and Built Environment Studies (CUBES).

Bénit-Gbaffou, C. 2015. *In Quest for Sustainable Models of Street Trading Management: Lessons for Johannesburg post Operation Clean Sweep*. Johannesburg: CUBES research report.

Bénit-Gbaffou, C. 2016. 'Do street traders have the 'right to the city'? The politics of street trader organisations in inner City Johannesburg, post-Operation Clean Sweep', *Third World Quarterly* 37(6): 1102–29.

Brudney, J.L. and England, R.E. 1983. 'Toward a Definition of the Coproduction Concept', *Public Administration Review* 43(1): 59–65.

Büscher, K. 2012. 'Urban governance beyond the state: Practices of informal urban regulation in the city of Goma, Eastern D.R. Congo', *Urban Forum* 23: 483–99.

Cheruiyot, K. 2018. 'City-regions and their changing space economies'. In *The Changing Space Economy of City-Regions*, edited by K. Cheruiyot, 1–24. Switzerland: Springer.

Das, V. and Poole, D. 2004. *Anthropology in the Margins of the State*. Santa Fe: School of America Research Press.

Hibou, B. 2004. 'From privatising the economy to privatising the state: An analysis of the continual formation of the state'. In *Privatising the State*, edited by B. Hibou, 1–47. India: Hurst & Co.

Houtzager, P.P. and Lavalle, A.G. 2009. 'Civil society's claims to political representation in Brazil', *Studies in Comparative International Development* 45(1): 1–29.

Joshi, A. and Moore, M. 2004. 'Institutionalised co-production: Unorthodox public service delivery in challenging environments', *The Journal of Development Studies* 40(4): 31–49.

Khwashaba, M. 2016. 'Street Trade Block Leaders and the Governance of Street Trade: Narrating untold stories in inner City Johannesburg'. Unpublished Research Report. Honours in Town and Regional Planning, University of the Witwatersrand, Johannesburg.

Khwashaba, M. 2019. 'The Role of Invited Spaces of Participation in the Governance of Street Trading: Lessons from Johannesburg's Informal Trading Forum (ITF) and City of Tshwane's Tshwane Informal Trading Committee (TITRC)'. Unpublished Research Report. Master in Town and Regional Planning, University of the Witwatersrand, Johannesburg.

Lindell, I. 2008. 'The multiple sites of urban governance: Insights from an African city', *Urban Studies* 45(9): 1879–1901.

Lund, C. 2006. 'Twilight Institutions: Public authority and local politics in Africa', *Development and Change* 37: 685–705.

Matjomane, M. 2013. 'Strategies Used By Street Traders Organisations To Influence Policy On Informal Trading'. Unpublished Master's thesis, University of the Witwatersrand, Johannesburg.

Matjomane, M. 2021. 'The Role and Influence of Street Trader Organisations in Urban Governance: The case of Gauteng metros'. Unpublished PhD thesis, Town and Regional Planning, University of the Witwatersrand, Johannesburg.

Mitlin, D. and Bartlett S. 2018. 'Co-production – key ideas', *Environment and Urbanisation* 30(2): 355–66.

Pezzano, A. 2011. 'Informal Traders and Informal Trading Policy'. Unpublished Report. Department of Asian, African and Mediterranean Studies, University of Naples, L'Orientale.

Rogerson, C.M. 1988. 'The underdevelopment of the informal sector: Street hawking in Johannesburg, South Africa', *Urban Geography* 9(8): 549–67.

Roy, A. 2009. 'Strangely familiar: Planning and the worlds of insurgence and informality', *Planning Theory* 8(1): 7–11.

Rubin, M. 2018. 'At the borderlands of informal practices of the state: Negotiability, porosity and exceptionality', *Journal of Development Studies* 54(12): 2227–42.

Skinner, C. 2007. 'The Struggle for the Streets: Processes of exclusion and inclusion of street traders in Durban, South Africa'. Paper presented at the *Living on the Margins Conference*, Stellenbosch, 26–28 March 2007.

Yiftachel, O. 2009. 'Theoretical notes on 'gray cities': The coming of urban apartheid?', *Planning Theory* 8(1): 88–100.

7

Crafting a xenophobic bureaucratic order after the May 2008 pogroms in Cape Town

Rodolphe Demeestère

Introduction

In March 2013, the South African Department of Trade and Industry (DTI) introduced the Licensing of Businesses Bill, which aimed at regaining control over the economy. The new bill affirmed a break away with the previous Businesses Act, a liberal law adopted in 1991 that precipitated the wholesale liberalisation of the economy (Lazar 1994) but also aimed at reverting historical economic repression, recognising small Black enterprises for the first time and imposing minimal bureaucratic control upon them (Bénit-Gbaffou 2018). In contrast, the new Licensing of Businesses Bill required all enterprises, big conglomerates and hawkers alike, to get registered on an up-to-date national registry, and licensed. Imposing substantial fines and even prison terms for unlicensed business people had two implications. Firstly, it drastically limited applications from international immigrants, applications for business licenses being strictly restricted to those possessing business visas. The bill thus excluded the most numerous and vulnerable segment of the foreign population – refugees. Secondly, the bill provided municipalities with a 'framework for cooperative governance',[1] suggesting they accredit and appoint chambers of commerce and business associations as 'business inspectors', who would be conferred the same discretionary power as police officers. Explicitly designed to protect South Africans' interests, the bill simultaneously downgraded refugees within the category of economic outsiders, and 'discharged' key administrative power to South African local chambers of business (Weber 1923; Hibou 1999), elevating the latter as the new 'street-level bureaucrats' of economic government (Lipsky 1980). This chapter interrogates the socio-political genesis of such transformation.

The Department of Trade and Industry (DTI) proposed the Licensing of Businesses Bill more than 30 years after the liberalisation of the South African economy, a period during which townships-based small retailers, locally known as *spaza* shopkeepers, had been confronted with increasing competition. This competition stemmed from big retailing chains that penetrated townships' economy as early as the 1990s (Crush and Frayne 2011), and competition from East African and South Asian diasporas who concentrated in the small retailing sector from the mid-2000s (Charman et al. 2012). Among them, Somali refugees quickly developed a particularly successful entrepreneurial model (Liedeman et al. 2013). Facing the degradation of the economic position they had secured in the townships during the last decade of the anti-apartheid struggle (Bonner and Segal 1998), South African *spaza* shopkeepers channelled their discontent against their foreign counterparts, increasingly affected by acts of collective violence but also targeted assassinations from 2006 onwards (Crush 2008; Piper and Charman 2012; Crush and Ramachandran 2015).

The rampant brutalisation of foreign small retailers was brought to the world's eyes in May 2008, when a two-week-long episode of xenophobic pogroms ravaged townships in South African main cities, costing at least 70 lives, severely injuring over 600 people and displacing around 100,000 refugees inside and outside the country (Landau 2011). The attacks targeted foreign *spaza* shopkeepers, their shops being systematically looted and burned to the ground (Hassim et al. 2008), and were recurrently orchestrated by South African business people who mobilised the residents of the township and hired unemployed youth to eliminate foreign competitors (Misago 2012).

Taking 'anti-foreign *spaza* shopkeepers' mobilisations seriously, this chapter aims at situating the place of South African small retailers – and notably local business associations and chambers of commerce – in (re)producing xenophobic violence, and, more importantly, in shaping bureaucratic norms and routines towards the systematic economic exclusion of refugees. This chapter retraces the sequences of the mobilisation in Cape Town townships, arguing that the proposed Licensing of Businesses Bill marked its political victory but also the 'consecration' (Bourdieu 1986) of a bureaucratisation cycle of the small retailing sector. This consecration emerged from the complex and ambivalent interactions between mobilised South African shopkeepers and governmental agencies between 2008 and 2015, resulting in the gradual legitimation of its xenophobic bedrock – what I call the 'bureaucratisation of xenophobia'.

Methodologically, this chapter adopts a synchronic approach, retracing the mobilisation's 'natural history' (Becker 1963) to shed light on the concatenation of sequences that led to the bureaucratisation of xenophobia. Grounded in the ethnographic observation of two Capetonian townships, Khayelitsha and Gugulethu,[2] this chapter analyses a set of documents produced by local business associations and chambers of commerce between 2008 and 2012. In the case of Khayelitsha, studied documents were published in a newspaper article.[3] Regarding Gugulethu, data was extracted from academic and grey literature, and notably from a report written by the Anti-Eviction Campaign, a social movement grounded in the Western Cape but also known nationally.[4] The analysis also includes national policy documents and working papers, published on the African National Congress (ANC) and the DTI's official websites. This set of documents is further illuminated by interviews and informal discussions conducted in the course of my Master's thesis and doctorate fieldwork (2013 and 2015–19) with Somali shopkeepers, representatives of the Western Cape office of the Somali Association of South Africa, employees from the Agency for Refugees Educational Skills Training and Advocacy (a Cape Town based non-profit organisation partnering with the United Nations High-Commissioner for Refugees, UNHCR), local councillors, leaders from various civic organisations, and Capetonian law-enforcement officers. This chapter also builds upon a set of newspaper articles. This composite methodological approach reconstructs the main sequences of the mobilisation under study.

This chapter starts with a discussion around bureaucratisation dynamics in contemporary South Africa. It is then structured into three sections. The first section starts in August 2008 when survivors of the May pogroms started returning to the townships. It explores the contested political process through which imposing a form of bureaucratic control over the small retail sector emerged as an *idea* to neutralise xenophobic violence displayed in Khayelitsha by one of the biggest South African chambers of business. The second section scrutinises the process through which this idea became technicised, transcending the townships scale to become a bureaucratic *system* that mobilised traders and urged the national government to recognise and adopt. The last section explores how the ruling party ANC and the DTI responded to increasing political pressure, proposing the Licensing of Businesses Bill and related institutional transformations, which marked the consecration of a xenophobic bureaucratic rationality.

State-formation and the contested construction of the dominant symbolic order

Pierre Bourdieu et al. defined the state as 'an X (to be determined) that successfully claims the monopolistic and legitimate use of the physical and symbolic violence over a definite territory and over the totality of the corresponding population' (Bourdieu et al. 1994, 3). Introducing the concept of symbolic violence, defined as a 'gentle, invisible form of violence, which is arbitrary but never recognised as such' (Bourdieu 1977, 192), Bourdieu enriched Max Weber's understanding of state bureaucracies. For Weber, domination in human groups requires a bureaucracy, that is, a system based on subjective *mis*representations of social issues, whose arbitrariness is encrypted and rendered invisible by the bureaucrats' ability to depict their practices as rational, politically neutral, scientifically efficient and oriented towards the common good (Weber 1978).

If governmental agencies often successfully claim the 'monopoly of the universal', the symbolic domination they impose always derives from a 'work of normalisation and codification' (Bourdieu 1986), whose most accomplished form is the power of adopting new pieces of legislation. Produced by 'authorised people' such as jurists and bureaucrats, this codification work 'institutes and inculcates common symbolic forms of thought, social frameworks of perception, understanding or memory, state forms of classification or, better, practical schemes of perception, appreciation and action' (Bourdieu 2000, 175). The official code is eventually imposed in a top-down movement, but such codification is only rendered possible because it aligns with pre-existing social norms and practices. Sectors of the social world are often already structured by (unofficial) codes and practices that are a posteriori (partially) recognised or (fully) 'consecrated' by governmental agencies and their experts of symbolic production (Bourdieu 1986, 43–44).

Acts of codification are not politically neutral, and the officialisation of a code is often the product of fierce 'symbolic struggles'. What therefore is important to study is less the official code itself than the power relations that led to its adoption (Bourdieu 2004). This constructivist conceptualisation of the dominant symbolic order echoes Berman and Lonsdale's thought of the state, distinguishing 'state construction' (a 'conscious effort at creating an apparatus of control') from 'state formation' ('a historical process whose outcome is a largely unconscious and contradictory process of conflicts, negotiations and compromises between diverse groups' – governmental agencies being only one of them). The state was then defined as emerging from 'storm-tossed relationships of power derived from the productive logic of any given social organisation and the conflicts of interest that threaten to disorganise it' (Berman and Lonsdale 1992, 5). Embracing such an approach, this chapter posits that 'bureaucratisation is first a social phenomenon, before being a mode of construction of the state' (Bayart 2013, 309). Because they emanate from social-political conflicts of interests, bureaucratic practices often emerge first as a socially approved *idea*, before being elevated as a governmentally sanctioned *system* (Abrams 1988).

Recent work has shown that the modalities of governmental intervention at the neoliberal era have contributed to the departure from a 'top-down' bureaucratic model to the gradual rooting of a 'bottom-up' model relying on negotiated agreements between governmental authorities and a variety of stakeholders, among which lobbies and private interest groups have increasingly gained importance (Hibou 2012). These authors have stressed the need to develop a reticular and de-centred approach of bureaucracy, which 'must not be understood as an administration, a hierarchised apparatus proper to the state, an institution, a structure', but rather 'as a mode of functioning through systematic formalisation, the use of norms, rules, procedures, and codes', which are collectively defined through a 'government-society' iterative relationship (Hibou 2012: 9–12).

Therefore, in this chapter, the bureaucratisation phenomenon will be explored as a set of practices that are not recognised as such and which are not necessarily incarnated by a clearly hierarchised structure. I will use the term 'proto-bureaucracy' to describe a series of rationalising practices that can be tacitly and partially recognised by governmental institutions but that remain out of the dominant symbolic order as those practices are not set out in the legislation. Conversely, a set of rationalising practices that are 'universally recognised' as they are sanctioned by law or, in other words, have received the 'indispensable officialdom', or consecration, from governmental agencies (Weber 1978, 991).

Symbolic struggle at the South African margins: toward the bureaucratisation of xenophobia?

Historically, colonial and apartheid governments, who never had the capacity to have full control over the national territory, developed racially and spatially differentiated ways of governing. The townships, and all areas where Blacks were confined, were subject to indirect rule: after redefining 'customary laws' at their own advantage, apartheid authorities implemented decentralised political control, inviting local chieftaincy systems' leaders to organise themselves as a so-termed 'native administration'. Such decentralised political control enabled apartheid authorities to 'govern from a distance' (Mamdani 1996), even if the customary law system remained systematically overruled by the colonial legal system in case of dispute (Seekings 2001, 76). This indirect ruling system increasingly eroded as the anti-apartheid struggle grew, the South African civic movement promoting a counter-hegemony symbolic order (Super 2016, 458–9). Defining new rules and norms, promoting new forms of justice in the townships, local residents' groups or 'civics' developed localised proto-bureaucratic practices that daily subverted the dominant symbolic order. From the late 1970's, they subverted the myriad of bureaucratic restrictions that systematically confined Black small retailers to illegality and clandestinity[5] (Dewar and Watson 1982), organising massive consumer boycotts that pushed many White-owned retailers to bankruptcy and largely re-channelled consumption towards Black-owned *spaza* shops in the townships (Bonner and Segal 1998, 122–4). Later, such symbolic struggle led by the civics contributed in rendering the country 'ungovernable', forcing apartheid authorities to negotiate a democratic transition: historically, 'symbolic orders [emerging] from below' (Burawoy and Von Holdt 2012, 72) have been engines for broader political change in South Africa.

Adopting a decentred approach of the bureaucracy seems even more appealing today given that democratic South Africa has developed decentralised participative structures, giving rise to vibrant local political scenes, and simultaneously embracing neoliberal reforms that tend to both reproduce apartheid spatial-political divide, and develop reticular forms of bureaucratic control (Bénit-Gbaffou 2008). This is the case when it comes to the administration of small businesses in Cape Town. Since the adoption of the Businesses Act of 1991, the municipality has developed a dual system. On the one hand, the Central Business District and its close periphery are actively regulated through by-laws that require aspiring traders (especially street-traders) to follow bureaucratic procedures and obtain formal authorisation to trade in the city centre. On the other hand, the city margins are not overseen by trading plans,[6] and by-laws are notoriously not applied, officials considering the townships as 'free trade areas'.[7] In this context of governmental laissez-faire, decisions related to businesses' distribution as well as trade conflicts' resolution are left to local civic and business organisations.[8]

The implication of business organisations in fomenting May 2008 pogroms is well established today. Yet, their role has mainly been studied from a micro-political perspective, the 'anti-foreign shopkeeper' mobilisations enabling local leaders to affirm and strengthen their political position (Misago 2012; von Holdt et al. 2011). Similarly, the myriad of local agreements that were signed between South African and foreign *spaza* shopkeepers after the 2008 pogroms have mainly been scrutinised from a local perspective (Gastrow and Amit 2015). Little is known about the impact of these power struggles and the localised proto-bureaucratic practices they led to on the broader redefinition of the South African contemporary dominant symbolic order, and more particularly on the ongoing diffusion of a hegemonic xenophobic discourse within governmental agencies (Neocosmos 2006). Indeed, what I term the 'bureaucratisation of xenophobia' in contemporary South Africa has mainly been explored (not from an iterative but) from a top-down perspective, authors emphasising the diffusion of exclusionary practices within official bureaucracies such as the Department of Home Affairs (Landau and Amit 2014), the South African Police Services (Demeestère 2016), hospitals (Crush and Tawodzera 2014), public schools (Bouyat, Chapter 9 in this book).

When the phenomena of bureaucratisation from below have been taken seriously, they have led to contrasted conclusions. Part of this literature has shown how the transition to democracy has participated in institutionalising the civics who had developed a counter hegemonic symbolic order during apartheid. These once counter-hegemonic groups are deemed to have increasingly pacified and bureaucratised their practices, a form of domestication that enabled them to access governmental financial resources and other symbolic rewards (Fourchard 2018, 208–15). And indeed, a number of government-accredited street-level organisations have emerged in the post-apartheid period – such as the South African National Civic Organisation, the Community Policing Fora and Neighbourhood Watches (Tshehla 2002; Super 2016) – who regularly meet and report to governmental agencies, and receive certificates officialising their nomination within official bureaucracies (Cooper-Knock and Owen 2015). The bureaucratic practices these street-level organisations develop epitomise their voluntary integration within the bureaucratic system and their subjugation under the dominant symbolic order.

Some authors have drawn a more conflictual picture, arguing that post-apartheid governmental agencies are unable to monopolise the legitimate use of both physical and symbolic violence, particularly in the townships. For these authors, the multiplication of protests – regularly involving collective destruction of governmental infrastructures and physical confrontations with police forces – marks a continuity in the ways township residents perceive(d) and act(ed) towards apartheid and democratic authorities. For them, subalterns through their constant confrontation with governmental agencies 'construct symbolic orders from below … to appropriate, disrupt and reshape dominant meanings' (Burawoy and von Holdt 2012, 71–2). Yet, what seems to be missing from these studies is a more systematic interrogation of the political productivity of this permanent confrontation with the dominant symbolic order. This chapter pays specific attention to the generative capacity of the symbolic crisis provoked by the South African small retailers' mobilisations in the townships, and its direct impact over the construction and legitimation of a xenophobic bureaucratic order; thus, attempting to contribute to the exploration of the intricated links between cycles of mobilisation and the specific trajectories of state-formation in contemporary Africa (Siméant 2013).

Xenophobic pogroms and the construction of a localised bureaucratic order in Khayelitsha

The wave of xenophobic violence started on 11 May 2008 in the Gauteng Province and reached Cape Town about 10 days later. The ANC-aligned Western Cape Province officials and the DA-aligned (Democratic Alliance) City of Cape Town officials fought over territorial and strategic dimensions, and collectively failed at preventing violence in the Mother City. It is not before 25 May that the City and the UNHCR opened six 'safety camps' to secure more than 20,000 displaced people around Cape Town. Municipal elections and spring season approaching, a so-called 'reintegration programme' was promptly launched (Steinberg 2014, 286). As early as August, Cape Town Mayor Helen Zille closed various camps, announcing an imminent general closure, which occurred in October. In some instances, reintegration took the form of forceful evictions; in others, the City simply cut off access to food, electricity, and water, leaving hundreds of people to their own devices, too scared to return to the townships (Mazibuko and Peberdy 2010).

A return under threat: Somali shopkeepers in Khayelitsha after the May 2008 pogroms

First returns in Capetonian townships were everything but appeased, cases of xenophobic violence still occurring around the city.[9] It is in this climate that, at the end of August 2008, Somali *spaza* shopkeepers returning to Khayelitsha received letters from a local business association named Zanokhanyo Retailers Association (ZRA) (**Figure 7.1**).[10]

The document ordered them to stay out of business for a three-week 'period of concern' during which 'business, political and community leadership' would be looking for 'a solution for the influx of [foreign]

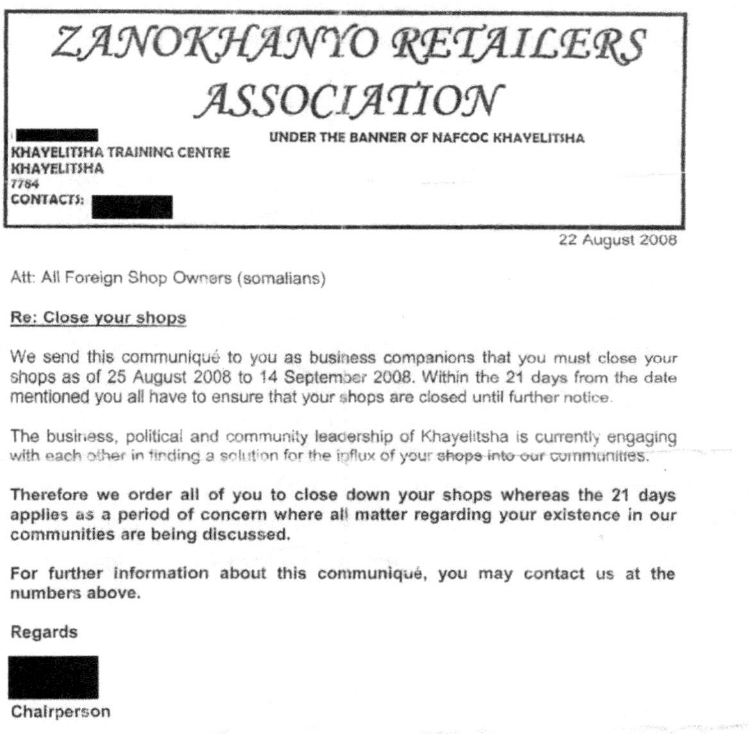

ZANOKHANYO RETAILERS ASSOCIATION

UNDER THE BANNER OF NAFCOC KHAYELITSHA

KHAYELITSHA TRAINING CENTRE
KHAYELITSHA
7784
CONTACTS:

22 August 2008

Att: All Foreign Shop Owners (somalians)

Re: Close your shops

We send this communiqué to you as business companions that you must close your shops as of 25 August 2008 to 14 September 2008. Within the 21 days from the date mentioned you all have to ensure that your shops are closed until further notice.

The business, political and community leadership of Khayelitsha is currently engaging with each other in finding a solution for the influx of your shops into our communities.

Therefore we order all of you to close down your shops whereas the 21 days applies as a period of concern where all matter regarding your existence in our communities are being discussed.

For further information about this communiqué, you may contact us at the numbers above.

Regards

Chairperson

Figure 7.1 Eviction letter from the Zanokhanyo Retailers Association in Khayelitsha, 22 August 2008. Submitted to the South African Competition Commission in 2016 as evidence of informal trade agreements that distort, prevent and restrict competition.

shops'. The letters further notified Somali shopkeepers of their potential irrevocable eviction from Khayelitsha. A final hyperbolic spurt stipulating 'all matter regarding your existence in our community are being discussed' seemed to announce more than economic banishment.[11] The performativity of the threatening message not only relied on semantic, as Khayelitsha-based foreign shopkeepers had received similar eviction letters a few days prior to May's violence outbreak. Inscribing themselves in Khayelitsha's emerging history of xenophobic violence, the August letters marked, in their material existence, a symbolic continuum between May pogroms and their survivors' return in the township. The letters were meant to stimulate post-pogrom terror, and they were understood by Somali shopkeepers as being a political signal announcing the resumption of violence. They provoked panic in Khayelitsha. Many shopkeepers immediately fled the township, unsuccessfully trying to reintegrate safety camps that were now being closed by the City. Others ran to local police stations seeking protection. No less than 48 cases of intimidation linked to the letters were opened against the ZRA. Warrants of arrests were issued against the letters' editors, senior officers promising 'harsh measures of policing'.[12]

Eviction threats multiplied in various Capetonian townships after the letters' circulation,[13] suggesting the influence of a bigger mobilising structure than the 50 Khayelitsha-based ZRA members. Since the eviction letter explicitly stipulated that the ZRA worked 'under the banner of the NAFCOC' – the National African Federated Chamber Of Commerce and Industry, the media's focus quickly shifted to the NAFCOC Western Cape provincial bureau. The NAFCOC's provincial secretary confirmed the chamber's involvement in editing and circulating 'more than 1,000 letters'[14] in Khayelitsha and beyond. Publicly threatening to 'start a civil war' to kick Somalis out of South Africa, he challenged police intervention and announced that the authors of the letters had been 'hidden at a safe space' to avoid arrest.[15] Meanwhile, NAFCOC members prevented the return of foreigners to the townships, molesting and violently threatening municipal and provincial officials in charge of supervising the 'reintegration programme'.[16]

The National African Federated Chamber Of Commerce and Industry is one of the oldest and biggest chambers of commerce in South Africa. It was founded in 1964 to defend Black traders and advocated for Blacks' full participation in the economy during apartheid. Self-proclaimed 'apolitical' (Maseko 2000, 125), the chamber developed an ambiguous positioning towards the White supremacist regime from the 1970's onwards, calling for the emancipation of Black traders but also 'pursu[ing] the class interests of African enterpreneurs within the framework of separate development' (Southall 1980, 64). In the 1980's, the NAFCOC played an administrative role within the municipal council system, which enabled its middle class aspiring leaders to consolidate their political position and obtain commercial concessions in the townships (Maseko 2000, 136). Such involvement led many anti-apartheid activists to dismiss its elite as political 'traitors' and 'errand boys' of White capitalists (Iheduru 2004, 5). Co-opted by ultra-liberal lobbies such as the Free Market Foundation and the South African Foundation, the NAFCOC stood for the rapid liberalisation of the South African economy during the democratic transition period (Handley 2005, 218). Rehabilitated politically after democratisation, the NAFCOC allied with the ANC. It has since become a central partner of post-apartheid governments, notably participating in the Black Economic Empowerment programmes deployed by the DTI (Southall 2004) – such partnerships extending across local, provincial and national spheres, in sectors as diverse as construction, transportation, industry, tourism, mining, agriculture, and retailing. These long-lasting partnerships have produced some of the most successful post-apartheid Black entrepreneurs. The NAFCOC also participated in South Africa's 'supermarket transition', some of its prominent leaders becoming the first Black owners of shopping malls in the country.[17]

The NAFCOC intervention did not come as a complete surprise. As early as 1998, human right organisations had pinpointed the NAFCOC's upcoming leaders as responsible for diffusing xenophobic feelings and practices,[18] notably after the multiplication of violent xenophobic campaigns forcing foreign traders to recurrently flee Johannesburg's inner-city (Bond 2000, 41). The disruptive capacity of the NAFCOC, an organisation consisting of hundreds of local offices across the country, gave the situation in Khayelitsha an extra-local dimension. Facing a potential resurgence of widespread xenophobic violence, municipal and provincial governments called for an urgent mediation with all parties, including the NAFCOC.

Khayelitsha's agreement: imagining a localised bureaucratic order to prevent pogroms

Alongside public threats that entrenched a climate of defiance and uncertainty, the media visibility that the NAFCOC received after the circulation of the eviction letters enabled its provincial secretary to vehiculate an interpretation of the recent events in Khayelitsha. The secretary diffused the representations of Somali shopkeepers benefiting from an 'unfair economic advantage', 'undercutting' and 'taking away the livelihood' of South African shopkeepers – in sum, 'eating the democracy' of those who had long fought for it.[19] Such a reframing of the situation, which insisted on Somali *spaza* shopkeepers' presupposed 'lack of commercial morality' (Zalc 2010, 217), indubitably displaced the latter within the category of economic transgressors, while depicting the NAFCOC's mobilisation as an attempt to remoralise business practices, euphemising its violence and authoritarianism. Such 'euphemising work' (Bourdieu 1977, 191) associated the South African retailers' economic marginalisation with the presence of Somali shopkeepers and eluded the impact of the broader 'supermarket transition' ongoing in the townships. This partial representation of the changing face of the township economy contributed to frame the debate of the yet-to-come mediation process, as shown by Cape Town's Mayor Helen Zille responding to the NAFCOC's pressing calls for state intervention by expressing her 'concern' about 'Somalis setting up their shops in front of local traders'.[20]

The first mediation meeting occurred a few days after the ZRA chairperson (who had officially signed the letters) was arrested, while Somali *spaza* shops were still being attacked and looted in Khayelitsha.[21] Chaired by the Mayoral Elected Committee for Economic Development and Tourism, it gathered members of the City Council and Provincial government, ANC and DA representatives, leaders of the ZRA and the NAFCOC, and a numerically under-represented group of Somali shopkeepers.[22] The meeting revealed a fierce factional battle within the NAFCOC's provincial leadership. Exposed to criminal sanctions and explicitly (and quite theatrically) disowned by its fellow leaders, the NAFCOC's provincial secretary eventually issued a public apology to the Somali shopkeepers and advocated for their safe return to Khayelitsha, claiming now that 'violence, blood shedding is not in our minds'.[23] This public renouncement to violence was rewarded with partial decriminalisation, the editors of the letters having their case for intimidation suspended pending further engagement with the Somali shopkeepers. The mayoral committee also stressed the need for re-regulating the townships' economy and called for the immediate gathering of a research team whose recommendations would pave the way for municipal reform. The spirit of the future reform was clarified when the committee suggestively announced the research would aim at 'ascertaining why certain communities are able to thrive in unregulated township conditions'.[24] Questioning the Somali shopkeepers' (presupposed lack of) commercial morality, the committee recognised the ZRA–NAFCOC's plea and elevated the 'influx of [foreign] shops', denounced by the ZRA, as a public issue to be added to the City's agenda – failing again to mention the broader economic transformation affecting the townships' retailing sector. Pending municipal policy reform and acknowledging the need for a quick regulatory intervention in Khayelitsha's *spaza* shop sector, the mayoral committee eventually invited the NAFCOC and its affiliate to further dialogue with the Somali shopkeepers for a memorandum of understanding to be agreed upon. This first mediation phase can be seen as an attempt from the mayoral committee to reaffirm the government's monopoly over physical violence, a monopoly that was bargained through allowing the ZRA–NAFCOC to participate in defining new rules and norms affecting the *spaza* shop sector. Sending the talks back to Khayelitsha, the committee then withdrew from the mediation process. The secretary of the NAFCOC's expressed his satisfaction for being acknowledged by the City.[25]

The second (and main) mediation phase spread from September to November 2008. It took place within the walls of the Khayelitsha Training Centre, the stronghold of the ZRA where the threatening letters had been produced and sent from. The mediation gathered the ZRA, the NAFCOC affiliated members and the (still) under-represented Somali shopkeepers organised under the name of Khayelitsha Somali Retailers Association (KSRA). The various meetings that ensued were monitored by Khayelitsha police officers and observed by local civic organisations. They led to the signature of two documents.

A temporary agreement (**Figure 7.2**) was signed by representatives of the KSRA at the end of October 2008 – at a time when all safety camps had been permanently closed and the Somali shopkeepers, who tried to make their way back to Khayelitsha and rebuild their shops, were still targeted by lootings and shootings.[26] In a document revealing the extreme vulnerability of the Somali shopkeepers and hence the weak leverage of their representatives, the KSRA endorsed the immediate closure of all Somali shops that had been (re)built since the return of the Somalis in Khayelitsha. In addition, the document compelled every aspirant Somali shopkeeper to obtain authorisation from the ZRA leadership before opening their business. These measures, suggesting that 'freezing' the effects of the May attacks was the prerequisite for discussions in Khayelitsha, insinuated the ZRA which, after having been apologetic during the first mediation phase, regained the upper hand in the debates as it came back on its political turf. The document's unilateral tenets, and the absence of compensation provided for KSRA for abiding to ZRA's initial claims, suggest that Somali representatives felt forced to sign the

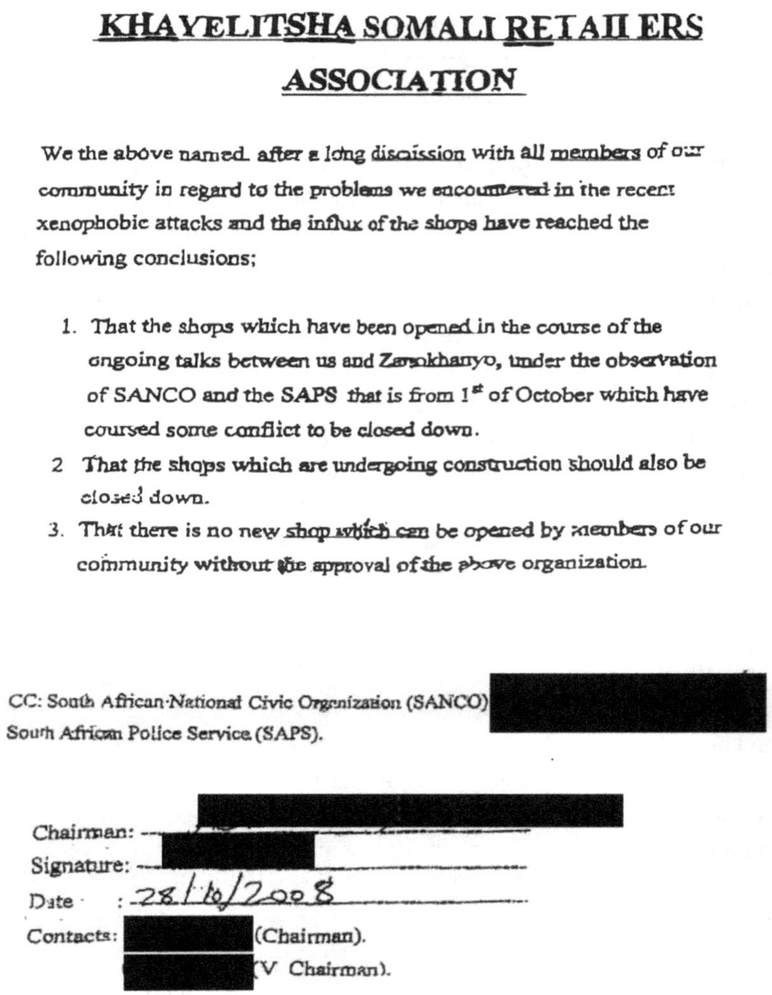

KHAYELITSHA SOMALI RETAILERS ASSOCIATION

We the above named. after a long discission with all members of our community in regard to the problems we encountered in the recent xenophobic attacks and the influx of the shops have reached the following conclusions;

1. That the shops which have been opened in the course of the ongoing talks between us and Zamokhanyo, under the observation of SANCO and the SAPS that is from 1st of October which have coursed some conflict to be closed down.
2. That the shops which are undergoing construction should also be closed down.
3. That there is no new shop which can be opened by members of our community without the approval of the above organization.

CC: South African National Civic Organization (SANCO)
South African Police Service (SAPS).

Chairman:
Signature:
Date : 28/10/2008
Contacts: (Chairman).
(V Chairman).

Figure 7.2 Letter signed by a representative of the Khayelitsha Somali Retailers Association (KSRA), 28 October 2008.

Source: © adapted from the image published in Washinyira 2012.

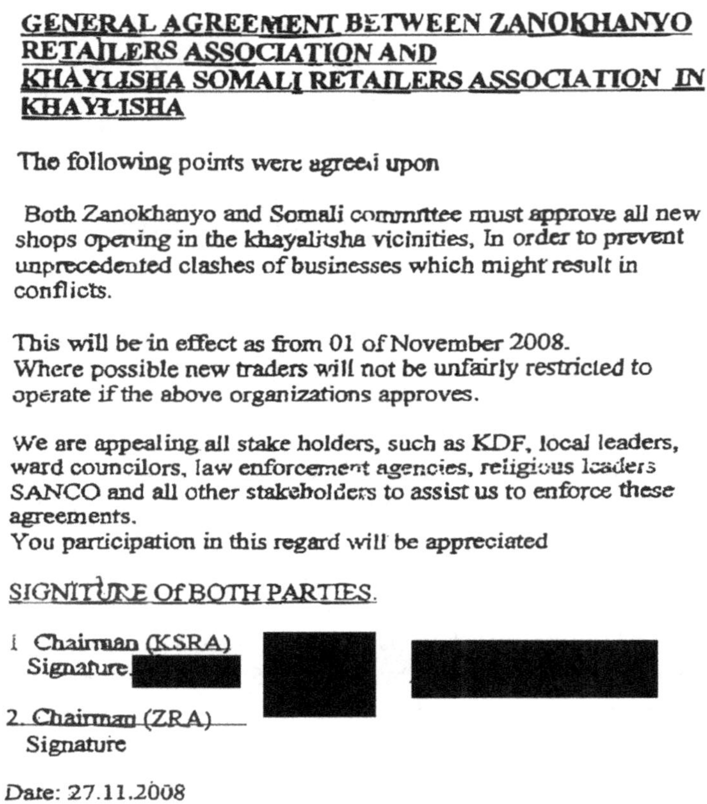

GENERAL AGREEMENT BETWEEN ZANOKHANYO RETAILERS ASSOCIATION AND KHAYLISHA SOMALI RETAILERS ASSOCIATION IN KHAYLISHA

The following points were agreed upon

Both Zanokhanyo and Somali committee must approve all new shops opening in the khayalitsha vicinities, In order to prevent unprecedented clashes of businesses which might result in conflicts.

This will be in effect as from 01 of November 2008.
Where possible new traders will not be unfairly restricted to operate if the above organizations approves.

We are appealing all stake holders, such as KDF, local leaders, ward councilors, law enforcement agencies, religious leaders SANCO and all other stakeholders to assist us to enforce these agreements.
You participation in this regard will be appreciated

SIGNITURE Of BOTH PARTIES.

1 Chairman (KSRA)
Signature

2. Chairman (ZRA)
Signature

Date: 27.11.2008

Figure 7.3 Khayelitsha General Agreement, signed under the supervision of the South African Police Service, 27 November 2008.

Source: © adapted from the image published in Washinyira 2012.

agreement. This is, at any rate, what the later claim today, arguing that both the volatile climate in Khayelitsha and the murder threats they received in the backstage of the mediation led them to sign the document against their wishes.[27]

The final memorandum of understanding was eventually produced at the end of November 2008. Signed under police observation, the 'Khayelitsha's General Agreement' was meant to be irrevocable, pending promised municipal reform (**Figure 7.3**). It can be understood as an attempt to put an end to the ongoing xenophobic aggressions in Khayelitsha through the collective edification of a localised administrative apparatus set to oversee and control the distribution of *spaza* shops. Firstly, the agreement recognised both the ZRA and the KSRA as the new 'proto-bureaucracies' of the *spaza* shop sector; aspiring shopkeepers having to obtain their mutual acceptance before opening their businesses in Khayelitsha. Secondly, restrictive measures previously imposed upon the Somali shopkeepers were now suspended, and the agreement applied to all new shopkeepers regardless of their nationality. Unlike the ZRA eviction letters and the KSRA concession letter, which were both marked by deep emotions (violent menace in the first, fearful reaction in the second), Khayelitsha's General Agreement presented xenophobic violence as a risk that could be prevented and controlled through the *rational* and *neutral* administration of *spaza* shops. This was expressed by the professed aims 'to prevent unprecedented clashes of business which might result in conflict' and ensure that 'where possible, new traders will not be unfairly restricted to operate'. Signed by both the South African and Somali leaders at the request of the mayoral committee and 'appealing all stakeholders' to 'assist to enforce' the future and concerted prerogatives of the ZRA and the KSRA, the agreement embraced a form of officialdom that was meant to be recognised by all within the borders of Khayelitsha.

However, Khayelitsha's General Agreement did not provide for the creation of a bureaucratic *system* in the Weberian sense. Aside from loosely recognising and placing both the ZRA and the KSRA in charge of governing the *spaza* shop sector in Khayelitsha, it did not define administrative norms to enable an effective and routinised bureaucratic control over the distribution of shops. Without proper applications protocols, standardised decision-making measures, and related resource allocation, the agreement seemed from its very inception doomed to operational failure. That said, Khayelitsha's General Agreement was imagined and formulated as an effective solution to put an end to a six-months-long episode of xenophobic violence that had torn the township apart, revealed the inability of the police to monopolise physical violence, and costed many lives. Formalising the ZRA–NAFCOC's earlier renouncement to physical violence, the agreement carried undeniable political weight. Subsequently, intimidation cases against the ZRA were fully withdrawn. Reminding us that bureaucratisation first penetrates imaginaries before becoming effective practices and structures (Bayart 2013, 296), it made the bureaucratisation of the *spaza* shop sector emerge as an *idea* to overcome xenophobic violence and foster durable peace. It is from this cognitive perspective – the agreement announcing that the small retailing sector would now be administered '*sine ira ac studio*' ('without hate and zealousness') (Weber 1978, 975) – that one can argue it participated in producing a 'localised (proto-) bureaucratic order' in Khayelitsha.

From the streets to the ministry: dis-enclosing localised bureaucratic orders (2009–12)

The recognition of the ZRA and the imagined proto-bureaucratic order were initially restricted to a clearly circumscribed geographic area: the township of Khayelitsha. But soon, the bureaucratisation of the *spaza* shop economy was systematised and started to transcend local boundaries. In this section, I explore how emerging localised bureaucratic orders got increasingly dis-enclosed. In Gugulethu, a bureaucratic toolkit was formalised in 2009 through a local agreement, and was replicated in other localities, in and outside Cape Town. In Khayelitsha, implementation was highly contentious, creating an inextricable political situation which led Khayelitsha's proto-bureaucrats to seek direct support from the national government.

Gugulethu's agreement (2009): standardising and dis-enclosing a bureaucratic system

The threat of collective violence formulated by the NAFCOC and the ZRA in the aftermath of the May 2008 xenophobic attacks was not an isolated case. Between 2009 and 2010, cases of collective violence against foreign shopkeepers were reported in six of the nine South African provinces – Western Cape and Gauteng Provinces being the most affected. During that period, no less than 12 localities within the Cape Town Municipality were shaken by these violent mobilisations (Crush and Ramachandran 2015, 38). The township of Gugulethu was one of them.

In June 2009, members of Gugulethu Business Forum circulated two series of letters in the Capetonian township. The first gave Somali shopkeepers one week to close their shops and leave. The second was addressed to South African shopkeepers, inviting them to mobilise with the Gugulethu Business Forum (GBF) and evict Somali *spaza* shopkeepers.[28] Alarmed by the risk of a xenophobic outburst, activists from the Anti-Eviction Campaign repeatedly alerted the local police, urging them to protect Somali shopkeepers and calling for a mediation to be held with the GBF. Such calls remained unanswered until two Somali shopkeepers were burnt alive in their *spaza* shops, a few days after the circulation of GBF's letters. Refusing to link the murder case to GBF mobilisation, local police nevertheless urgently called for a mediation between South African and Somali *spaza* shopkeepers.

Supervised by police, the meeting gathered Somali shopkeepers, members of the GBF, representatives of the Anti-Eviction Campaign (AEC), the Somali Association of South Africa and the UNHCR. Like the ZRA had done one year earlier in Khayelitsha, the GBF publicly withdrew its threats. A Committee of five South African shopkeepers and five Somali shopkeepers was established to find a local agreement.[29] Negotiations were immediately jeopardised by new acts of violence: a few hours after the meeting, a member of the newly nominated Somali Committee was assassinated in his *spaza* shop. An emergency meeting was organised, with the notable presence of the Minister for Community Safety who called for local police to act with neutrality, bring violence perpetrators to justice, and for the AEC to supervise future negotiations between South African and Somali shopkeepers.[30]

The AEC organised a follow-up meeting during which the Somali Committee received pamphlets informing them that four measures strictly discriminating Somali shops would now prevail in Gugulethu (Gastrow and Amit 2015, 23–24):

1. Somali shopkeepers had to respect a minimal 100 m distance from any South African shop.
2. Opening new Somali shops in the neighbourhood was prohibited.
3. Somali shops could not represent more than 30 per cent of the entire *spaza* shop market in Gugulethu.
4. Fixed prices were applied on basic items (bread, milk, meat, paraffin).

Unable to negotiate their content, Somali traders were given a month to make necessary adjustments to comply with these measures. The deadline reached, Somali shops had not conformed to all of the

Redrafting the 'agreements' – entrenching xenophobia in local planning rules

1. The Somalis agreed to the concept of 100 m distance between local and Somali shops. However, they claim that if Somali shops are found in a location not meeting the 100 m stipulation, and the shops must be shifted, a new location must be identified by the locals for the Somalis to open their shop.

2. The Somalis agree to the concept that no new shops must be opened by the Somalis. However, they requested to open new shops in the future if the opportunity arises. If any new shops are to be opened though, it should be done with the expressed permission from the community or the Committee.

3. The Somalis also agreed to the idea of uniform prices of basic commodities like paraffin, bread, milk, etc. But they would want emphasis to be placed on a range of prices on each item and not a specific price tag, as prices fluctuate depending on the demand and supply. …

4. The Somalis agreed to maintain the 30 per cent and the 70 per cent ratio for Somalis and the local traders respectively for shops allocation. However, this provision must not be applicable to the existing shops, but in the future. This is because, since Somalis are not allowed to open new shops and the locals have got no limitation, the Committee can only regulate that, in future the presence of Somali shops must not be more than 30 per cent and the locals must retain the 70 per cent.

5. Additionally, Somalis said they were ready to extend their expertise knowledge to the local traders on how to do trade. But again, they say they would like to know from local traders which areas are they really lacking so that the Somali traders can put emphasis there. They said the Government could also play a vital role by coming up with some guidelines on how the locals and the Somalis could cooperate in the areas of trade and commerce.

Source: Extracts from the *Draft mutual arrangement between local and Somali traders in Gugulethu and other communities in the Western Cape Province aimed at resolving trade conflict* 6 August 2009.

measures, the Somali Committee criticising both their severity and unilaterality. Facing renewed death threats, the Somali Committee urgently turned to the Cape Town's bureau of the UNHCR for help. Contested by the GBF at first, the involvement of the UNHCR led to redrafting the 'agreement'. Retroactivity of earlier measures was suspended. Relocation solutions for Somali shopkeepers to move their shops 100 m from South African shops were to be provided by South African shopkeepers. And some flexibility in price fixing was eventually accepted.[31] In sum, the UNHCR limited the draconian character of earlier measures, but did not dispute in principle an agreement that disregarded refugees' protection laws and limited Somalis' rights to freely trade in Gugulethu. In doing so, it participated in legitimising an anti-foreigner rationality.

In a context marked by collective violence and targeted killings, the UNHCR liaison officer described the agreement as an 'interim arrangement to extinguish fire', 'a deal which, if not implemented, could have led to a serious incident'. Yet, he added that '*for other communities, it could be used as a blueprint* but only if the implementation is correct' (my emphasis).[32] Despite the cautiousness and the reserves expressed, such declarations, largely covered by media, had a wide resonance, and it is perhaps no accident that similar agreements multiplied in Capetonian townships from 2009 onwards.[33] A few weeks after the signature of the Gugulethu agreement, the same '100 m exclusion zone' imposed on foreign *spaza* shopkeepers was adopted in the neighbouring township of Delft (Piper and Charman 2012, 92), while both the UNHCR representatives of the AEC leadership declared receiving calls from all around the country asking for help to replicate the agreement in other provinces (Gastrow and Amit 2015, 25–7). This suggests that Gugulethu's agreement set a pattern to be replicated elsewhere, instilling mutually reinforcing dynamics of (proto-) bureaucratic 'de-singularisation' (Boltanski et al. 1984, 19–23), and 'expansion' (Mather and Yngvesson 1980, 778–9).

Gugulethu's agreement participated in 'dis-enclosing' proto-bureaucratic practices notably because it thought to administer the small-retailing sector through the systematic use of calculable means. Introducing quotas, fixed prices, measured distances between shops, it framed future administrative routines, making them more un-subjectable to 'love, hatred, and all purely personal, irrational and emotional elements': the imposition of these standardised measures brought a supplementary degree of 'depersonalisation' (Weber 1978, 975) over the ongoing bureaucratisation of the *spaza* shop sector.

Khayelitsha's General Agreement had defined bureaucracy as an *idea* but only vaguely designated proto-bureaucrats whose administrative power would be limited to the borders of the township. Gugulethu's agreement delivered a technicised toolkit and turnkey measures – in other words, a proto-bureaucratic *system* – that could now be appropriated by anyone and adapted to any local requirements.

Implementing Khayelitsha's General Agreement: proto-bureaucrats in quest of political consecration

A few months after the signature of Gugulethu's agreement, the ZRA renewed their threats of a second wave of xenophobic violence in Khayelitsha,[34] in the face of the non-implementation of Khayelitsha's General Agreement. Indeed, South African Police Service (SAPS) had engaged in enforcing the agreement, but senior officers soon refrained their subordinates from engaging in the issue, notably after the Somali shopkeepers turned to lawyers and threatened SAPS with legal prosecution for infringing refugees' rights to freely trade in South Africa (Gastrow 2017, 130–1). In reaction to police disengagement, the ZRA forcefully closed Somali *spaza* shops on various occasions from 2009 onwards, entrenching a long-lasting political crisis from 2012.

In February 2012, members of the ZRA marched from *spazas* to *spazas*, giving Somali shopkeepers two days to close business, pack and leave.[35] The deadline reached, the ZRA closed by force, ransacked, and looted at least 25 Somali *spaza* shops.[36] When police intervened, members of the ZRA resisted arrests, claiming they were implementing an agreement that the police had committed to but failed to respect. Unable to arrest members of the ZRA, senior police officers publicly called for Somali shops to reopen. The decision enraged members of the ZRA who continued to evict foreign shopkeepers and started multiplying protests at Khayelitsha's police stations, urging the police to keep to their word.[37] Senior police officers then acknowledged that 'the problem [was] that the 2008 agreement was monitored by the police'.[38] Incapable of declaring the agreement null and void without bringing discredit to the police institution, officers limited themselves to expressing vague threats of arrest if the ZRA stuck to their violent actions.[39] Now brandished by the ZRA as the material evidence of their legitimacy to administer *spaza* shops' distribution in Khayelitsha, Khayelitsha's General Agreement became the unquestionable and 'stable point of reference' (Goody 2007, 81) and the evidence of the ZRA's 'objectified symbolic capital' (Bourdieu et al. 1994, 11) on which the association relied to affirm a form of 'state nobility' (Bourdieu 2004, 25), neutralise police repression and proceed with their eviction campaign in a (quasi-) state of legal limbo.

The de-legitimation of local police stations and the increasing brutalisation of Somali *spaza* shopkeepers in Khayelitsha's streets led to a new round of heated mediation meetings. When the City of Cape Town's law-enforcement senior officers ventured to distribute pamphlets reasserting refugees' rights to trade in the city, they received threats and, fearing for their security, eventually withdrew from the meeting.[40] Indeed, this period of contention is remembered today as 'an episode of total chaos'[41] during which both local councillors and police officers failed to contain ZRA members and called for outside stakeholders to intervene.

In early March 2012, the special advisor for the Minister of Police participated in one of the meetings, where he reasserted the validity of Khayelitsha's agreement, de facto overruling Khayelitsha's police officers. This decision was backed up by the Western Cape Provincial Commissioner of Police, who equally called for Khayelitsha's General Agreement to be effectively enforced (Gastrow 2017, 127). Playing on these obvious internal contradictions within the police, the ZRA carried out multiple brutal destructions of Somali (and now also Ethiopian) *spaza* shops over the following weeks. In some instances, police tried to intervene but, outnumbered, they had to flee the scenes, leaving foreign shopkeepers unprotected.[42] In other cases, police officers directly monitored forceful evictions undertaken by the ZRA.[43] In brief, the interventions of both provincial and national top-police hierarchy contributed to reverse power relations between local police agents and the ZRA in favour of the latter, as much as they constituted a signal for the association to look beyond local and municipal arenas to obtain political support.

The ZRA, backed by other local business organisations, soon addressed a memorandum to the Minister of Police: the 'Look-Out Hill communiqué' (**Figure 7.4**).[44] This marked the displacement of their political battle from municipal to national spheres. Lamenting 'sheer disregard' and 'lack of support from government structures to reinforce local initiatives', the communiqué called the Minister of Police to immediately deploy a so-called 'binding police' to ensure the implementation of Khayelitsha's General Agreement. Through the communiqué, the ZRA required the Minister of Police to provide the 'indispensable officialdom' that would enable the business association to

Look out Hill communiqué

Following a series of meetings that had been held in Khayelitsha, Lower Cross Road, Nyanga, Gugulethu, De noon and Delft since 2008 on the concern of the local community on the influx of foreign shop owners in the informal retail sector.

The local business community together with the Somali Retailers Association took the initiative to draft agreements in these various areas to regulate themselves in order to bring peace, mutual co-existence and co-hesion following the unfortunate and tragic event of 2008. A sample of the agreement made in Khayelitsha in 2008 is hereby attached for you attention.

These agreements have helped to foster peaceful co-existence between the local and foreign national business in the townships since 2008.

However given the lack of legal enforceability, sheer disregard by most concerned, lack of support from government structures to reinforce this local initiative we are once again witnessing the mushrooming of spaza shop owned by foreign nationals which is bound to breed social conflict within the community.

So we do hereby request you honourable minister of police to come to aid and assist the township in the following areas:

-Regulation of business in the informal retail business sector.

-Demographic representation within the sector.

-The 2008 agreement was an attempt at regulating our business environment. However we cannot enforce it ourselves. We are therefore requesting you honourable Minister for you office to assist the business community to implement our agreement or the government puts in place a binding police. Failure to do one of the above will breed anarchy in our community. This should be done without any further delay.

We count on your co-operation and action on the above.

Drafted and endorsed by representative of the local business communities, Sanco, USACO, MDC, foreign business community. On this day of 28 March 2012

Witnessed by: NGO representative, and the United Nations High Commission for Refugees in Cape Town.

Figure 7.4 The 'Look-Out Hill communiqué', 28 March 2012.

Source: © adapted from the image published in Washinyira 2012.

effectively enjoy the 'power position of a fully developed bureaucracy' (Weber 1978, 991), and more systematically dispose itself from the police's discretionary power. Calling directly upon the upper hierarchical level of the police institution for its local recognition to be universalised, the ZRA requested its political consecration as the official (and not solely the proto-) bureaucrats of the *spaza* shop sector.

National policymaking and the officialisation of a xenophobic rationality (2012–15)

In this last section, I interrogate the impact of the anti-foreign *spaza* shopkeeper mobilisation over national spheres of government, and more particularly over the DTI. Showing how the national ministry channelled its policy and regulatory efforts towards townships' economies from 2012 onward, I argue that such reconfiguration marked the political consecration of the ongoing anti-foreign shopkeepers' mobilisation, which materialised through the institutionalisation of xenophobic rationality and the co-optation of mobilised business associations and chambers of commerce within governmental bureaucracies.

Crafting a national policy for small businesses: uplifting South Africans, excluding refugees

The political crisis that led to the national government to intervene in Khayelitsha in March 2012, coincided with the preparation of the quinquennial conference of the ANC. Anticipating the event, the ANC published its Peace and Stability Policy Discussion Document[45] in March. The document marked the ANC's hardening of tone against refugees, recategorised as 'economic migrants'. The document asserted that '95 per cent of those claiming asylum in South Africa [were] not genuine asylum seekers but rather looking for work or business opportunities' and therefore represented 'both a security and economic threat to the country'. More than half of the document was devoted to strategies to tighten immigration control and strengthen the repressive capacity of a Department of Home Affairs the ANC now depicted as a 'highly strategic security department'.

The Peace and Stability Policy Document mirrored an undergoing securitisation trend within the Department of Home Affairs (DHA) (Landau and Amit 2014, 8), but ANC's proposals went further, calling for a broader revisiting of the Refugee Act of 1998, for it not to systematically recognise refugees' right to trade. The ANC also called for economic regulations to be tightened to limit refugees' (alleged) free-riding economic practices, stressing the need to specifically regulate the *spaza* shop sector. It urged for the tightening of municipal, provincial and national economic control for 'non-South Africans [would] not be allowed to buy or run *spaza* shops or larger businesses without having to comply with certain legislated prescripts'. Descended by human right

Together but unequal? The ANC calls for tightening control over non-South African *spaza* shops

One of the ways asylum seekers currently earn a living is to rent or manage retail outlets such as '*spaza*' shops. Strengthening and proper enforcement of municipal by-laws would control and regulate such activities. Ideally, municipalities should know who lives and works and runs businesses in their areas as well as their status.

In many townships ... some asylum seekers have been involved in informal trading – an activity that might contravene municipal by-laws and should not be legal under the Refugees Act given that asylum seekers are persons whose status has not been determined. This informal trading is mainly in the form of hiring *spaza* shops and houses from South African [sic]. Non-South Africans should not be allowed to buy or run *spaza* shops of larger businesses without having to comply with certain legislated prescripts. By-laws need to be strengthened in this regard. Should a regulatory framework for small and larger businesses be developed in terms of municipal by-laws and provincial and national legislation? This would have to be done in a way that does impact positively rather than negatively on the informal economic sector. Should by-laws apply equally to both asylum seekers and citizens?

(Extracts from the ANC's Peace and Stability Policy Document, March 2012).

organisations for both their unconstitutionality and anti-refugee bias, such proposals, which answered the requests of the 'Look-Out Hill Communiqué', was applauded by the ZRA.[46]

While the Peace and Stability Policy document was being discussed in preparation of the ANC's conference, the DTI announced a strategic reorientation of its policy towards what it called the 'informal economy'. The creation within the ministry of a new Directorate for Informal Business and Chamber Support during 2012 constituted the first step towards the recognition of the role of small and micro-businesses as a driver for economic growth (Rogerson 2016), the DTI acknowledging its past policies and development plans had largely overlooked the most disadvantaged and survivalist businesses in South Africa (Rogerson 2015). This reorientation went along with a spatial reconfiguration of the ministry's scope, the new directorate announcing specific interventions in townships, rural areas and other impoverished enclaves. After consultation with a variety of stakeholders (including business associations and chambers of commerce), the directorate eventually proposed its new action plan in October 2012: the National Informal Business Development Strategy (NIBDS).

The NIBDS marked the emergence of two rationalities within the DTI. On the one hand, it offered a developmental programme, aiming at creating an 'enabling policy, regulatory, and programming environment promoting and supporting a developmental continuum for the graduation of informal businesses into the mainstream of the formal economy' (DTI 2013, quoted by Rogerson 2015, 233). This developmental approach explicitly focalised on the 'enterprising poor' and materialised through the introduction of financial schemes and infrastructural supports services, as well as capacity building, skills and technological trainings. On the other hand, the NIBDS clearly marked the diffusion and the normalisation within the DTI of a xenophobic discourse (Rogerson 2015; Crush and Ramachandran 2015; Skinner 2019). The working documents of the NIBDS openly denounced a 'foreign traders' invasion' in the townships and lamented that 'no synergy between the DTI and [the Department of] Home Affairs [existed] in devising strategies and policies to control foreign business activities' (DTI 2013, quoted by Rogerson 2015, 239). Explicitly inspired by national preference policies that had excluded foreigners from street trading and other sectors of the economy in countries like Ghana, India or Malaysia (Skinner 2019), the DTI echoed the ANC's securitisation anxieties and called for the synchronisation and alignment of immigration laws and economic regulations, to effectively deal with a so-called 'foreign trader challenge' (DTI 2013, quoted by Rogerson 2015, 239). In sum, the NIBDS promoted 'a pro-development approach for South African informal entrepreneurs which [was] allied to an anti-developmental agenda towards migrant entrepreneurs' (Rogerson 2016, 184).

The Licensing of Businesses Bill: an attempt at removing refugees' right to trade

Introduced as the cornerstone of its strategic reorientation, the new regulatory environment the DTI had worked on from 2012 was approved by cabinet and opened to public comments in March 2013. As mentioned in the introduction, the Licensing of Business Bill marked the DTI's will to regain administrative control over the economy through the construction of an up-to-date national business registry.[47] The proposed bill required all businesses operating in South Africa, regardless of their sizes, to get registered and licensed. Enacting the Licensing of Business Bill implied repealing but also breaking away from the spirit of the Businesses Act of 1991, a legislation that had recognised Black enterprises, limited bureaucratic burden and allowed small businesses to operate without business licenses in townships (Bénit-Gbaffou 2018; Rogerson 2015). Indeed, the vast licensing operation the DTI sought to initiate was based upon a punitive approach, business people contravening the terms of the bill being exposed to administrative fines and even prison terms for up to 10 years.

The bill was criticised for both expanding bureaucratic red-taping and re-introducing apartheid-style punitive hints that would expose the most survivalist businesses to repression. However, the Minister of Trade and Industry Rob Davies defended the DTI's aggressive approach. He described the bill as a tool to 'know who is conducting business in our localities',[48] and argued that its objective was less to increase bureaucratic control for all entrepreneurs than to create a 'negative database',[49] which would work as 'a sanction to exclude big transgressors from business operations in South Africa'.[50] Somehow, qualifying the so-termed 'transgressors' the bill sought to repress, the Minister added that:

> the bill is not adding to red tape. It emanates from complaints we got from the townships [business people], which said they were facing unfair competition from businesses owned by foreigners. These were selling counterfeit goods and were also employing illegal immigrants.[51]

The bill stipulated that:

> if the applicant is a foreigner, such application [for a business license] must be accompanied by a valid business permit under the Immigration Act, 2002 and any other valid documentation required to verify the status of such a foreigner in the Republic issued under Immigration Act, 2002 or Refugee Act, 1998.

Requiring foreign aspiring traders to obtain a business permit (that is, a visa) from the DHA before being authorised to apply for a business license at the municipal desks directly jeopardised their ability to trade legally.

Applications for a business visa having to be lodged from the applicant's country of origin, the bill required any foreign applicant, and most notably refugees that had been recognised under the Refugee Act, to first return to their home countries and obtain a business visa. At the time the Licensing of Business Bill was proposed, the DHA required the applicants of business visas to have R2.5 million directly available for investment in South Africa (Skinner 2019) – a start-up capital that most township-based foreign business people would be unable to secure. Responding to both the ANC's and the DTI's earlier calls for synergy between the DTI and the DHA, the articulation of the bill's repressive tenets with the compulsory obtention of an immigration status restricted to wealthy entrepreneurs annihilated refugees' right to trade. Not dissimilar to the administrative rationality criminalising Black small retailers during apartheid, the Licensing of Businesses Bill sought to officialise a bureaucratic order within which refugees' economic activities would be unrecognisable and confined to economic clandestinity. Academics and human rights organisations descended the bill for 'scapegoating' foreign entrepreneurs,[52] and 'mak[ing] it so difficult for non-citizens to operate small businesses in the country that they [would] go back home'.[53] But the proposed legislation was also abundantly criticised for the administrative role it gave to local business associations and chambers of commerce – a role that was described as a 'suspicious attempt [from the DTI] to get South Africans onboard to assist the police in identifying and rooting out foreign traders'[54] and to which I turn now.

Consecrating South African business associations and chambers of commerce

From early 2012, the DTI consulted chambers of commerce and business associations to formulate its policies towards the 'informal economy'. To reach its developmental and regulatory objectives contained in the NIBDS, the DTI needed to 'strengthen the capacity of informal business sector organisations' (DTI 2012, quoted by Rogerson 2016, 177). Providing municipalities with a 'framework for cooperative governance', the Licensing of Businesses Bill confirmed the DTI's rapprochement with chambers of commerce and business associations. To build an 'efficient frontline agency' and proceed with the vast licensing and registration operations, the bill gave municipalities room to accredit 'community-based organisations, business associations or non-governmental associations', and appoint them as 'business inspectors'. This cooperative governance gave accredited organisations the authority to deliver business licenses, check traders' documentation (licenses, and business permits), conduct business inspections, deliver compliance notices, issue administrative fines, seize and remove goods, and even close business premises in the name of the bill. The latter thus paved the way for local business and civic associations to enjoy the same level of discretionary power as municipal and national law-enforcement agencies. In doing so, it removed the main local institutional barrier that had impeded local business associations to reach their political ends and systematically control the small retail sector in their localities. These elements in mind, one can read the proposed bill as the political consecration of the mobilisation – the DTI both officialising an 'anti-foreign shopkeepers' rationality and elevating the actors of such mobilisation as the new 'street-level bureaucrats' of the economy (Lipsky 1980).

The Licensing of Businesses Bill was nevertheless never enacted. Crawling under criticism, the DTI eventually withdrew it. In May 2013, it announced its redrafting, reinitiating a consultation process that ended in 2014. Yet, the DTI never proposed a revision of the bill and, by early 2015, it seemed clear that the ministry had dropped its regulatory reform plan. If the bill is remembered today as a political 'fiasco' from the DTI (Rogerson 2015, 236), the ministry eventually acknowledged the bill had clearly been motivated by a xenophobic logic (Rogerson 2016, 182–3). However, the DTI kept on advancing a 'South African only' developmental programme.

Business associations, and more particularly the NAFCOC which was part of the task teams that the Directorate for Informal Business and Chamber Support gathered from 2012 onwards, played a critical role in that regard. The leadership of the NAFCOC actively lobbied national government for the establishment of a ministry specifically dedicated to small, medium and micro-enterprises.[55] The calls of the NAFCOC were soon answered. In June 2014, the president of the Republic announced the creation of a new national ministry to specifically develop and regulate small and micro-enterprises: the Department of Small Business Development (DSBD). The new department was created 'to lead and coordinate the promotion of development of entrepreneurship, small businesses and cooperatives, and ensure an enabling legislative and policy environment to support their growth and sustainability'.[56] Applauding the announcement, the NAFCOC described the DSBD as its 'brainchild'. [57] The first DSBD Minister Lindiwe Zulu both acknowledged the NAFCOC's key contribution in creating the ministry and called for its deeper engagement with governmental agencies.[58] And, indeed, as soon as 2015, the NAFCOC was appointed by the DSBD to oversee hundreds of millions of rands' development programmes in several provinces of the country.[59] Strictly restricted to South Africans and designed to 'reignite small enterprises such as tuck shops [that] have been leased to foreign nationals', these programmes developed massive wholesalers around the country, who would in return offer preferential prices to locals for them to better 'compete with the foreigners who are believed to have flooded the market'.[60] Since then, the NAFCOC has been a central partner of the DSBD's national preference developing programmes affecting the *spaza* shop sector.

Conclusion

This chapter showed the direct linkages between a cycle of mobilisation against foreign small retailers operating in the townships, and the development of new forms of bureaucratic control oriented towards the systematic criminalisation of refugees' economic activities. The pervasiveness of xenophobia in contemporary South Africa has alternatively been analysed as emanating from society (the 'bottom') or produced by governmental authorities (the 'top'). The bureaucratisation of xenophobia has been constructed through an *iterative process* between the bottom and the top, which involved specific and identifiable segments of society but all levels of government, regardless of their partisan affiliations – both the ANC and the DA directly acting in the process. This chapter focused on a seven-year-period during which this iterative process was particularly observable, but one should always keep in mind that bureaucratisation is a perpetually dynamic process (Nuijten 2003).

The non-implementation of the Licensing of Businesses Bill of 2013 should thus not be seen as the ultimate rejection of a xenophobic bureaucratic rationality. The aims of the bill – and most notably the drastic limitation of refugees' rights to trade freely in the country – are being developed through other processes. The Refugee Act of 1998 was amended in 2017 and the refugees' right to work independently is not guaranteed anymore.[61] Moreover, as imagined by the bill, forms of public authority are being delegated to neighbourhood political and economic entrepreneurs. It is no accident that today South African municipalities all around the country (often officially) discharge the administration of street-trading activities and small enterprises to local business associations and chambers of commerce (Modiba, Chapter 6 in this book). It is not by chance that the administration of foreign *spaza* shops (specifically) has become a central activity for townships' politicians (Drivdal 2016). Even if not adopted, the Licensing of Businesses Bill had a tremendous effect in the townships, entrenching the idea that foreign *spaza* shops could not operate without being formally registered. In this context, the line between administration and economic predation gets thinner and blurred. For instance, after having participated in the Licensing of Businesses Bill's second round of consultation undertaken by the DTI between 2013 and 2014, one township-based chamber of commerce decided to implement the bill as a pilot project, requiring all foreign *spaza* shopkeepers to get registered or be expelled from its locality (Demeestère 2017). Far from pacifying the *spaza* shop sector, the ongoing entrenchment of a discharged administrative control is currently leading to fierce political battles between local notables and political dignitaries, who try to monopolise symbolic violence and build up bureaux to extract rents from increasingly vulnerable foreign shopkeepers. These forms of privatised and predatory bureaucratic control, building upon the exclusionary and xenophobic rationality I explored in this chapter, are yet another story.

Acknowledgements

Claire Bénit-Gbaffou, Emmanuelle Bouilly, Laurent Fourchard, Mehdi Labzaé, Johanna Siméant-Germanos and the Practices of the State in Urban Governance (PSUG) cohort commented on earlier versions and helped improving this chapter. I warmly thank them for their support.

Notes

1 Department of Trade and Industry, Licensing of Businesses Bill 2013. *Government Gazette*, 18 March 2013. Available at: https://www.gov.za/sites/default/files/gcis_document/201409/36265gen231.pdf. Accessed 15 July 2021.

2 The townships of Gugulethu and Khayelitsha were built as urban dormitories strictly reserved to Black workers during apartheid. Gugulethu was established in 1958 and is situated 20 km away from the Cape Town's city centre. Khayelitsha was erected in the late 1980s, situated between 30 and 40 km from the city centre and is one of the fastest growing townships in contemporary South Africa.

3 Washinyira, Tariro, 'Local businesses move against Somali shops in Khayelitsha', *GroundUp*, 7 November 2012.

4 Anti-Eviction Campaign, 'Draft mutual agreement between Somali and local traders in Gugulethu and other communities in the Western Cape Province aimed at resolving trade conflict', 6 August 2009, 4 pages published in Gastrow Vanya, 'Submission to the Competition Commission: Grocery retail sector inquiry', 14 August 2016. The full submission can be viewed at: https://bit.ly/45fd2jc.

5 The term '*spaza*', which means 'hidden' in Isi-Zulu, is testimony to this repressive climate.

6 Traders do not require a trading permit in townships (except in specific nodes such as train and taxi stations).

7 Interview with the head of the Department of Economic Development, Cape Town, 2 March 2015. Interview with the head of the law enforcement 'informal trading unit', Bellville, 11 March 2019.

8 Interview with the business support manager, Department of Economic Development, Cape Town, 19 November 2015.

9 McKune, Craig, 'Distress for Blue Waters residents', IOL, 31 October 2008; Hweshe, Francis. 'Refugees in danger', IOL, 5 December 2008.

10 'Zanokhanyo' means 'those who bring light' in isi-Xhosa.

11 Versions of the letters explicitly mention recourse to 'much higher actions that will include physically fighting' in case foreign traders refused to obey. Joubert, Pearlie, 'Nafcoc calls for Somali purge'. *Mail & Guardian*, 5 September 2008. https://mg.co.za/article/2008-09-05-nafcoc-calls-for-somali-purge/. Accessed 22 July 2023.

12 Phaliso, Sandiso, "Somali shopkeepers given 'ultimatum'", IOL, 9 September 2008.

13 Johns, Lynnette, 'Threats against shopkeepers spread', IOL, 6 September 2008.

14 Declaration of NAFCOC's provincial secretary, quoted by Dolley Caryn, 'Somali shopkeepers still uneasy', IOL, 11 September 2008.

15 Declaration of NAFCOC's provincial secretary, quoted by Phaliso, Sandiso, "Somali shopkeepers given 'ultimatum'", IOL, 9 September 2008.

16 Joubert, Pearlie, 'Nafcoc calls for Somali purge'. *Mail & Guardian*, 5 September 2008.

17 Perry, Alex, 'Retail Renegade: Richard Maponya'. *Time*, 29 August 2007. Available at: https://content.time.com/time/subscriber/article/0,33009,1657164,00.html. Accessed 22 July 2022.

18 Human Rights Watch. 1998. *'Prohibited Persons': Abuse of undocumented migrants, asylum seekers and refugees in South Africa.* Washington, 129.

19 Declarations of the NAFCOC's provincial secretary and the ZRA director, quoted by Joubert, Pearlie, 'Nafcoc calls for Somali purge'. *Mail & Guardian*, 5 September 2008.

20 Declaration of Zille, Helen quoted by Joubert Pearlie, 'Nafcoc calls for Somali purge'. *Mail & Guardian*, 5 September 2008.

21 Hweshe, Francis, 'Somalis to keep their businesses after threat', IOL, 12 September 2008.

22 Dolley, Caryn, 'Somali shopkeepers still uneasy', IOL, 11 September 2008.

23 The Provincial secretary declared: 'Violence, blood-shedding is not on our minds and we are sorry if you (Somali shopkeepers) felt intimidated. You are welcome in this country and in our communities and we should share our economy,' quoted in Hweshe, Francis', 'Somalis to keep their businesses after threat', IOL, 12 September 2008.

24 Declaration of Grindrod, Simon cited by Hweshe, Francis, 'Somalis to keep their businesses after threat', IOL, 12 September 2008.

25 Dolley, Caryn, 'Somali shopkeepers still uneasy', IOL, 11 September 2008.

26 On the day that followed the mediation meeting with the mayoral committee, a group of 11 rioters was arrested with illegal firearms after looting five Somali *spaza* shops in Khayelitsha: Witten, Jade, 'Fear stalks Somali business owners', IOL, 23 September 2008.

27 Interview with the Western Cape chairperson of the Somali Association of South Africa, Bellville, Cape Town, 12 March 2015. Interview with a Khayelitsha-based Somali shopkeeper involved in the 2008 mediation process, Khayelitsha, Cape Town, 26 March 2013.

28 Majavu, Mandisi. 'Xenophobia still smoulders in Cape Townships', *Mail & Guardian*, 19 June 2009. Available at: https://mg.co.za/article/2009-06-19-xenophobia-still-smoulders-in-cape-townships/. Accessed 22 July 2023.

29 Hweshe, Francis, 'Somali traders are welcome in Gugs, says community', *Cape Argus*, 16 June 2009. Available at: https://abahlali.org/node/5414/. Accessed 22 July 2022.

30 Anti-Eviction Campaign. 'Draft mutual agreement between Somali and local traders in Gugulethu and other communities in the Western Cape Province aimed at resolving trade conflict', 6 August 2009, p.1–2.

31 Quinton, Mtyala, 'Somali and local shopkeepers strike deal on peace', *Cape Times*, 20 August 2009.

32 Declarations of the UNHCR liaison officer, quoted in Quinton, Mtyala, 'Somali and local shopkeepers strike deal on peace', *Cape Times*, 20 August 2009.

33 Agreements were signed in the townships of Delft and Philippi (2009), in Philipi-East (2011) and in Kraaifontein (2012). For further details, see Gastrow and Amit, 2015.

34 Yazeed, Kamaldien, 'Cape tackles street traders' xenophobia', *Sunday Times*, 1 September 2009.

35 Unknown author, 'Somali shops closed, looted as 2008 trading agreement enforced in Khayelitsha', *West Cape News*, 27 February 2012.

36 Luthanga, Peter, 'Bribery accusations and local demand for Somali *spazas* puts paid to 2008 agreement', *West Cape News*, 12 March 2012.
37 Nombulelo, Damba, 'Somali shops re-open after local business owners' attempt to force them to close down', *West Cape News*, 1 March 2012.
38 Declaration of Lingelethu police station commander quoted in Nombulelo, Damba, 'Somali shops re-open after local business owners' attempt to force them to close down', *West Cape News*, 1 March 2012.
39 Declaration of a colonel from Lingelethu police station quoted in Nombulelo, Damba, 'Somali shops re-open after local business owners' attempt to force them to close down', *West Cape News*, 1 March 2012.
40 Interview with the head of the 'Informal Trading Unit' from the City of Cape Town law-enforcement, Bellville, Cape Town, 11 March 2019.
41 Interview with Anele Gabuza, ward councillor (ANC), Khayelitsha, Cape Town, 18 March 2019.
42 Maregele, Barbara, 'Storekeepers smash Somali shop in Khayelitsha', *Cape Times*, 23 May 2012.
43 Nombulelo, Damba, 'Somali-owned shops forced to close in Khayelitsha', *West Cape News*, 16 May 2012.
44 The Look-Out Hill Centre is a civic centre situated in Khayelitsha.
45 African National Congress, 'Peace and Stability Policy Discussion Document', March 2012.
46 Clayton, Barnes, 'Cut number of foreign *spaza* shops – ANC', IOL, 25 June 2012. Aziz, Hartley, 'Passop slams call to limit foreign shops', IOL, 25 June 2012.
47 Department of Trade and Industry, 'Licensing of Business Bill 2013', *Government Gazette*, 18 March 2013.
48 Declaration from Rob Davies quoted in: Unspecified author, 'Bill to crack down on illegal business', IOL, 20 March 2013.
49 Ensor, Linda, 'Licensing Bill to be redrafted after avalanche of disapproval', *Business Day,* 16 May 2013.
50 Declaration from Rob Davies quoted in: Unspecified author, 'Davies: Licensing bill to change', IOL, 1 May 2013.
51 Declaration from Rob Davies, quoted in: Wiseman, Khuzwayo, 'Davies defends draft bill for licensing of businesses', IOL, 4 July 2013.
52 Ségatti, Aurélia, 'Business Bill: Target trade policies not people', *The New Age*, 10 May 2013.
53 Crush, Jonathan, 'Proposed law will hammer informal economy', *Business Day*, 15 April 2013.
54 Crush, Jonathan, 'Proposed law will hammer informal economy', *Business Day*, 15 April 2013.
55 *Khwebo*, (a National African Federated Chamber of Commerce and Industry publication), Volume 2, December 2013, p.10; Buthelezi, Khaya, 'SMME is the real deal for jobs dilemma', IOL, 1 May 2014.
56 DSBD website. Available at: http://www.dsbd.gov.za. Accessed 15 July 2021.
57 Unknown author, 'Nafcoc takes credit', *City Press*, 3 August 2014.
58 South African Government, 'Minister Lindiwe Zulu: 50th anniversary of National African Federated Chamber of Commerce and Industry (Nafcoc) Conference', 1 October 2014.
59 Leshilo, Thabo, "Better ways to beat 'foreign invasion'", IOL, 1 February 2015. Boitumelo, Tshehle, 'North west premier supra Mahumapelo to bar foreign owned *spaza* shops', *The Sowetan*, 16 March 2016.
60 SABC Digital News report, 6 December 2016. SABC Digital News Report, 7 December 2016.
61 Department of Home Affairs, 'The Refugees Amendment Act 11 of 2017', *Government Gazette*, 18 December 2017. Available at: https://www.gov.za/documents/refugees-amendment-act-11-2017-english-afrikaans-18-dec-2017-0000. Accessed 25 August 2022.

References

Abrams, P. 1988. 'Notes on the difficulty of studying the State', *Journal of Historical Sociology* 1(1): 58–89.

Bayart, J-F. 2013. 'La cité bureaucratique en Afrique sub-saharienne'. In *La Bureaucratisation Néolibérale*, edited by B. Hibou, 291–313. Paris: La Découverte.

Becker, H. 1963. *Outsiders: Studies in the sociology of deviance*, New York: The Free Press of Glencoe.

Bénit-Gbaffou, C. 2008. 'Are practices of local participation sidelining the institutional participatory channels? Reflections from Johannesburg', *Transformation* 66/67: 1–33.

Bénit-Gbaffou, C. 2018. 'Beyond the policy-implementation gap: How the City of Johannesburg manufactured the ungovernability of street trading', *Journal of Development Studies* 54(12): 2149–67.

Berman, B. and Lonsdale J. 1992. *Unhappy Valley. Conflict in Kenya and Africa*, Book one: State and Class, London, Nairobi and Athens: Ohio University Press.

Boltanski, L., Darré, Y. and Schiltz, M-A. 1984. 'La dénonciation', *Actes de la Recherche en Sciences Sociales* 51: 3–40.

Bond, P. 2000. *Elite Transition: From apartheid to neoliberalism in South Africa*, London: Pluto Press.

Bonner, P. and Segal, L. 1998. *Soweto: A history*, Cape Town: Maskew Miller Longman.

Bourdieu, P. 1977. *Outline of a Theory of Practice*. Cambridge: Cambridge University Press.

Bourdieu, P. 1986. 'Habitus, code et codification', *Actes de la Recherche en Sciences Sociales* 64: 40–44.

Bourdieu, P. 2000. *Pascalian Meditations*. Stanford: Stanford University Press.

Bourdieu, P. 2004. 'From the king's house to the reason of state: A model of the genesis of bureaucratic field', *Constellations* 11(1): 16–36.

Bourdieu, P. and Wacquant L. and Farage S. 1994. 'Rethinking the state: Genesis and structure of the bureaucratic field', *Sociological theory* 12(1): 1–18.

Burawoy, M. and Von Holdt, K. 2012. *Conversations with Bourdieu. The Johannesburg moment*, Johannesburg: University of the Witwatersrand Press.

Charman, A., Petersen, L. and Piper, L. 2012. 'From local survivalism to foreign entrepreneurship: The transformation of the *spaza* shop sector in Delft, Cape Town', *Transformation* 78: 47–73.

Cooper-Knock, S. and Owen, O. 2015. 'Between vigilantism and bureaucracy: Improving our understanding of police work in Nigeria and South Africa', *Theoretical Criminology* 19(3): 355–75.

Crush, J. (ed.). 2008. *The Perfect Storm: The realities of xenophobic in contemporary South Africa*. Cape Town: South African Migration Programme.

Crush, J. and Frayne, B. 2011. 'Supermarket expansion and the informal food economy in Southern African cities: Implications for urban food security', *Journal of Southern African Studies* 37(4): 781––807.

Crush, J. and Ramachandran, S. 2015. 'Doing business with xenophobia'. In *Mean Streets: Migration, xenophobia and informality in South Africa*, edited by J. Crush, A. Chikanda and C. Skinner, 25–59. Southern African Migration Program, the African Centre for Cities and the International Development Research Centre.

Crush, J. and Tawodzera, G. 2014. 'Medical xenophobia and Zimbabwean migrant access to public health services in South Africa', *Journal of Ethnic and Migration Studies* 40(4): 655–70.

Demeestère, R. 2016. '"Même si tu as tes papiers, ils t'embarquent". Gestion policière de l'immigration africaine ou institutionalisation de la xénophobie dans l'Afrique du Sud postapartheid', *Politique Africaine* 142: 145–67.

Demeestère, R. 2017. 'Document Production and the Quest for Street-Level Political Legitimacy: Contested regulation of the spaza shop sector in a Capetonian township'. Paper presented at the research workshop *Materialities of Documentation: Negotiating statehood, rights and services in contemporary urban South Africa*, Johannesburg: French Institute of South Africa.

Dewar, D. and Watson, V. 1982. 'Urbanisation, unemployment and petty commodity production and trading: Comparative cases in Cape Town'. In *Living Under Apartheid*, edited by D. Smith, 124–42. London: Georges Allen & Unwin.

Drivdal, L. 2016. 'Community leadership in urban informal neighbourhoods: Micro-politics and micro-administration in informal settlements in Cape Town', *Urban Forum* 27: 275–95.

Fourchard, L. 2018. *Trier, exclure et policer. Vies urbaines en Afrique du Sud et au Nigéria*. Paris: Presses de Sciences Po.

Gastrow, V. 2017. 'Shop Gevaar: A socio-legal critique of the governance of foreign national *spaza* shopkeepers in South Africa'. PhD thesis. Johannesburg: University of the Witwatersrand.

Gastrow, V. and Amit, R. 2015. *Lawless Regulation: Government and civil society attempts at regulating Somali informal trade in Cape Town*. Research Report, African Center for Migration and Society, University of the Witwatersrand, Johannesburg.

Goody, J. 2007. *Pouvoirs et Savoirs de L'écrit*. Paris : La Dispute.

Handley, A. 2005. 'Business, government and economic policymaking in the New South Africa, 1990–2000', *Journal of Modern African Studies* 43(2): 211–39.

Hassim, S., Kupe, T. and Worby, E. (eds). 2008. *Go Home or Die Here: Violence, xenophobia and the reinvention of difference in South Africa*. Johannesburg: University of the Witwatersrand Press.

Hibou, B. 1999. 'La "décharge", nouvel interventionnisme', *Politique Africaine* 73: 6–15.

Hibou, B. 2012. *La Bureaucratisation du Monde à L'ère Néolibérale*. Paris : La Découverte.

von Holdt, K. Langa, M., Molapo, S., Mogapi, N., Ngubeni, K., Dlamini, J. and Kirsten, A. 2011. *The Smoke That Calls: Insurgent citizenship, collective violence and the struggle for a place in the new South Africa. Eight cases of community protests and xenophobic violence*. Research report. Johannesburg: Centre for the Study of Violence and Reconciliation.

Iheduru, O. 2004. 'Black economic power and nation-building in post-apartheid South Africa', *Journal of Modern African Studies* 42(1): 1–30.

Landau, L. (ed). 2011. *Exorcising the Demons Within: Xenophobia, violence and statecraft in contemporary South Africa*. Johannesburg: University of the Witwatersrand Press.

Landau, L. and Amit, R. 2014. 'Wither Policy? Southern African perspectives on understanding law, 'refugee' policy and protection', *Journal of Refugee Studies*, 534–52.

Lazar, D. 1994. 'South Africa: Privatisation and nationalisation in the post-apartheid economy'. In *International Privatisation: Strategy and practices*, edited by T. Clarke, 341–53. Berlin and New York: Walter de Gruyter.

Liedeman, R., Charman, A., Piper, L. and Petersen, L. 2013. 'Why are foreign-run *spaza* shops more successful? The rapidly changing *spaza* sector in South Africa', *Econ 3x3*.

Lipsky, M. 2010 [1980]. *Street-level Bureaucracy: Dilemmas of the individual in public services*. New York: Russel Sage Foundation.

Mamdani, M. 2018 [1996]. *Citizen and Subject: Contemporary Africa and the legacy of late colonialism*. Princeton: Princeton University Press.

Maseko, S. 2000. 'From Pavement Entrepreneurs to Stock Exchange Capitalists: The case of the South African Black business class'. PhD thesis, School of Government, Cape Town: University of the Western Cape.

Mather, L. and Yngvesson, B. 1980. 'Language, audience, and the transformation of dispute', *Law and Society Review* 15(3/4): 775–822.

Mazibuko, J. and Peberdy, S. 2010. 'Progressive humanitarian and social mobilisation in a neo-apartheid Cape Town: A report on civil society and the May 2008 xenophobic violence', *The Atlantic Philantropies* 7(2).

Misago, J-P. 2012. 'Disorder in a changing society: Authority and the micro-politics of violence'. In *Exorcising the Demons Within. Xenophobia, violence and statecraft in contemporary South Africa,* edited by L. Landau, 89–108. Johannesburg: University of Witwatersrand Press.

Neocosmos, M. 2006. *From 'foreign natives' to 'native foreigners': Explaining xenophobia in post-apartheid South Africa. Citizenship and nationalism, identity and politics*. Monograph series, Council for the Development of Social Science Research in Africa (CODESRIA), Dakar.

Nuijten, M. 2003. *Power, Community and the State: The political anthropology of organisation in Mexico*. London and Sterling: Pluto Press.

Piper, L. and Charman, A. 2012. 'Xenophobia, criminality and violent entrepreneurship: Violence against Somali shopkeepers in Deft, Cape Town, South Africa', *South African Review of Sociology* 43(3): 91–105.

Rogerson, C. 2015. 'Unpacking national policy towards the urban informal economy'. In *Mean Streets: Migration, xenophobia and informality in South Africa*, edited by J. Crush, A. Chikanda and C. Skinner, 229–48. Pretoria: The South African Migration Programme.

Rogerson, C. 2016. 'South Africa's informal economy: Reframing debates in national policy', *Local Economy* 31(1–2): 172–86.

Seekings, J. 2001. 'Social ordering and control in the African townships of South Africa: An historical overview of extra-state initiatives from the 1940s to the 1990s'. In *The Other Law: Non-state ordering in South Africa*, edited by W. Schärf and N. Daniel. Cape Town: Juta & Co.

Siméant, J. 2013. 'Protester/mobiliser/ne pas consentir. Sur quelques avatars de la sociologie des mobilisations appliquée au continent africain', *Revue Internationale de Politique Comparée* 2(20): 125–43.

Skinner, C. 2019. 'Informal sector policy and legislation in South Africa: Repression, omission, and ambiguity'. In *The South African Informal Sector: Creating jobs, reducing poverty*, edited by F. Fourie, 412–38. Pretoria: HSRC Press.

Southall, R. 1980. 'African capitalism in contemporary South Africa', *Journal of Southern African Studies* 7(1): 38–70.

Southall, R., 2004. 'The ANC and Black capitalism in South Africa', *Review of African Political Economy* 31: 313–28.

Steinberg, J. 2014. *A Man of Good Hope*. Johannesburg and Cape Town: Jonathan Ball Publishers.

Super, G. 2016. 'Volatile sovereignty: Governing crime through the community in Khayelitsha', *Law and Society Review* 50(2): 450–83.

Tshehla, B. 2002. 'Non-state justice in the post-apartheid South Africa: A scan of Khayelitsha', *African Sociological Review* 6(2): 47–70.

Weber, M. 1991 [1923]. *Histoire Économique. Esquisse d'une histoire universelle de l'économie de la société*. Paris : Gallimard.

Weber, M. 1978. 'Bureaucracy'. In *Economy and Society. An outline of interpretative sociology*, 956–1069. Berkeley: University of California Press.

Zalc, C. 2010. *Melting Shops: Une histoire des commerçants étrangers en France*. Paris: La Découverte.

8
The politics of formulating policy on housing evictions in post-apartheid Johannesburg

Neil Klug

Introduction

This chapter reflects on the process of formulating a potentially progressive local planning policy instrument in the City of Johannesburg, South Africa, in the post-apartheid period.

It was initiated in response to the Blue Moonlight case: a 2010 ruling of the Constitutional Court compelling the state to take responsibility for temporarily accommodating evictees, even if they were evicted by a private property owner. The case was that 86 people living in an inner city disused industrial building were sued in 2006 for eviction by the new owners of the site, Blue Moonlight Properties, having bought the property knowing that the building was occupied. The residents opposed the application on the grounds that they could not be evicted until the City of Johannesburg had provided them with alternative accommodation. The Southern Gauteng High Court granted the eviction but also ruled that the Johannesburg housing policy was unconstitutional; that the City of Johannesburg was to provide temporary accommodation or pay each resident R850 per month towards the cost of finding alternative accommodation. The City of Johannesburg appealed this ruling in the Supreme Court, lost the appeal, and appealed again to the Constitutional Court. In a unanimous judgment the Constitutional Court confirmed on 1 December 2011 that the City of Johannesburg has the same obligations to plan and budget around poor people evicted by private landlords as it has with those evicted from public lands (Dugard 2014).

Between 2011 and 2021, the City of Johannesburg had an opportunity to edict such policy – a process in which I was briefly involved as a consultant, and that started in 2011 with the formulation of the Special Process for the Relocation of Evictees (SPRE) and ended with the adoption of the Temporary Emergency Accommodation Provision Policy (TEAP) in 2021. This process, and my participation therein, seemed to open the possibility of contributing to a 'progressive' approach to deal with evictions at the municipal level.

By 'progressive', I draw on Campbell (2005), for whom 'progress' in planning 'takes concrete form through civic projects *[policy instruments]* that simultaneously improve individual utility, promote collective interests, and symbolise community values and identities' (Campbell 2005, 2). In South Africa, my understanding of the term 'progressive' derives from my early practices in the early post-apartheid years. The values of what was progressive then encompassed promoting strategies and policies that promoted non-racialism; non-sexism; pro-poor actions/ policies, incorporated in a general critique of free-market (or now neo-liberal) approaches to planning; non-violent approaches and community participation in decision-making.

The conditions for a 'progressive' approach to evictions from privately-owned buildings, leading to a more equitable balance of rights between property owners and occupiers (where the common law was, like in many countries in the world, largely in favour of highly protected property rights) appeared to be favourable. The post-apartheid context was marked by a public rhetoric filled with the need to rectify the imbalances of the apartheid inherited inequalities. This led in particular to the development of legislation prohibiting unlawful evictions, in reaction to apartheid legislation, such as the 1998 PIE Act[1] and 1997 EST Act,[2] and other Constitutional Court rulings limiting the powers of landowners, prioritising the needs of occupants and the homeless on a contested piece of land under certain circumstances. Examples include the 2017 Grootboom and Daniels v. Scribante Cases, where the Constitutional Court obligated a local municipality to grant emergency shelter to a group of informal settlers, as the alternative meant they would go homeless; and the private property owner to ensure that an occupier of their property lived under conditions that afforded them human dignity, respectively. Here, the state in the first instance and the private property owner in the second instance are obligated to provide alternative accommodation, proving that the courts can obligate both the state and private owner in certain circumstances.

However, the process and the final policy adopted by the City of Johannesburg proved disappointing – and no matter how subjective this appreciation might sound, I want here to reflect more broadly on the sense of progressive possibilities and why it was eventually not followed through, by analysing the policy-making process, the modalities, actors, and constraints that ultimately shaped it. Indeed, the final approved SPRE/TEAP Policy took a narrow interpretation of the Constitutional Court ruling, focusing on the one side of the equation between the landowners and homeless by only addressing alternative accommodation for evictees, to be provided by the state, effectively avoiding any challenge to the common law notion of absolute property rights of the landowner. By not bringing property owners' responsibility into the picture of providing shelter to the tenants they were evicting,[3] not only does the policy create the conditions for its own (financial and practical) failure, but it also could be seen even as encouraging developers to take over derelict buildings and promote further evictions of the occupiers, since the municipality would be solely responsible for relocating its residents.

This chapter undertakes a genealogical investigation of the process of formulating the above policies to illuminate the actors involved in the formulation, the various political pressures and interest groups, as well as the processes and tasks followed in a particular policy venue. It attempts to understand why a state with a strong rhetoric of pro-poor policy, in the redistributive and transformational political space opened by the post-apartheid era, and boosted by a progressive constitutional decision, ended up formulating non-progressive policies. Far from classic analysis in terms of policy-implementation gap (following here Bénit-Gbaffou 2018), this reflection scrutinises the process of policy formulation, which is argued has led to a non-transformative outcome. My embeddedness in this process, between April and August 2015, alerted me to the complexity of the policy-making process and gave me first-hand experience of the twists and turns that this policy instrument formulation took – which this chapter attempts at unpacking, based on the study of documents in their multiple drafts, and interviews with key players identified through my recollection of this process.

This research is based on reflections on an actual policy instrument formulation project that took place in 2015, outside of any research environment at the time. To this end, I have adopted a form of performance and reflexive auto-ethnography as advocated by Denzin (2006). There is a major debate between the various schools of auto-ethnography being adopted (Anderson 2006; Denzin 2006). On one end of the spectrum are those who advocate a more analytical form of auto-ethnography (Anderson 2006), combining evocative or emotional forms with traditional forms of enquiry. On the other end, there are those advocating a more creative, performance and personalised form of auto-ethnography (Denzin 2006). I have mixed the more conventional methods such as document analysis (which makes up the bulk of the empirical evidence), interviews and focused conversations with local actors, with information derived from personal recollections as an active participant, which provides an insider's view, acknowledges that we have our own political views and subjective impressions of interactions, and adds a nuanced quality to the empirical data if presented explicitly.

Practically, my data was acquired through critical document analysis, which includes analyses of the various iterations of the developing SPRE policy documents, beginning with the project brief. This included two iterations of the draft policy documents (June and July 2015) as they responded to discussions and comments from the client body. The process of redrafting the policy covered an intensive period of two months from appointment to final submission. I was part of a dual sector consulting team: Lawyers for Human Rights (LHR),[4] the lead consultant dealing with the legal aspects and myself, with sub-consulting colleagues responsible for the planning and housing aspects of the policy. During this consultancy, I attended some three information gathering meetings with various professional specialists, five internal LHR meetings and workshops; five work sessions with planning colleagues; and two meetings with City officials. Post-consultancy, I remained interested in the outcomes of the policy formulation process through informal discussions with officials in the City of Johannesburg and the monitoring of newspaper articles and city press briefings. In late 2019, I was personally involved in the academic team providing comments on the evolved versions of the policy, as part of the City of Johannesburg's stakeholder engagement process (CUBES 2019). The information from the above engagements were captured through meeting minutes, notes and personal recollections, data which I also cross-checked and consolidated through seven detailed interviews conducted with City officials and fellow consultants involved in the project.

My motivation in undertaking this research on the process was driven by a sense of disappointment, in that I felt, as engaged consultants (which had been selected for that purpose), we had not optimised the opportunity to make a progressive contribution. Possibly our efforts did not go far enough in achieving stronger rights for evictees in creating more robust, mitigating circumstances to avoid evictions in the first place, and increased role for evictors in providing relief for the evictees. This sense of disappointment derived from my recollections of the initial hopes I had in the policy's potential, not unlike the sentiments expressed by Moodley (2018) on the lack of achievements of the planning profession.

To analyse this massive archive of documents and memories archive, I have chosen to focus on three specific questions (or stakes), systematically sought throughout the multiple policy documents' iterations:

1. How is the central problem characterisation underpinning the policy document? Is it framed as a problem of housing, of poverty, of illegal invasion of private property?
2. How are evictees depicted by the State through the policy formulation process? Responses range in a continuum between evictees as culprits (suggesting a level of reluctance to address the court obligation), and evictees as victims (reflecting an empathy towards the obligation).
3. Whose responsibility is it to provide temporary accommodation to evictees? Is it the sole responsibility of the State, or is it also the responsibility of private property owners conducting the eviction?

After a short section presenting the theoretical framing of this chapter, and a brief presentation of the inner-city urban policy and political context, I analyse the genealogy of the policy, before tracking the three above-mentioned stakes more specifically, to understand when, how and possibly why the progressive potential of the policy-making was lost.

Tracing the urban policy-making process, unpacking officials' agency within 'wicked problems'

In accounting for this case study, as emblematic of processes of policy formulation in African cities, I have taken inspiration from the two following themes, running across planning and political studies: debates on policy design (around the notion of the policy circle and how it is researched), in its articulation with planning interrogations around 'wicked problems' particularly salient in urban settings (Rittel and Webber 1973); debates around policy instruments, between planning functional approaches and political studies' genealogical approaches.

Policy-making process and wicked problems

In analysing the above themes, two congruent theoretical conceptualisations of policy formulation processes come in useful.

The first has been to break down the policy-making process into a series of stages, such as agenda-setting, formulation, legitimisation, implementation, and evaluation (Cairney 2012). While acknowledging that policy-making is a never-ending process, is more circular than linear, and that the cycle cannot simply be divided into stages as they tend to overlap, it is useful as an organising framework for the study of the SPRE Policy.

The second approach, acknowledging that policy-making is a social and political process where actors compete against each other to attain goals (Howlett 2011), examines the main actors, processes, and venues of policy formulation, focusing on the stage of policy agenda-setting and formulation. The definition of the 'problem' that the policy intends to respond to (the problem characterisation, or framing), is not self-evident nor neutral: it is contested, subjective or socially constructed, and based on selected forms of evidence to support its characterisation. The way the issue is defined frames the way the objectives are defined, and to some extent the type of responses that will be provided by policy. The formulation phase generally involves many different actors interacting with each other often under intense political pressure from political and other interest groups. This specific phase 'is much more of a political netherworld, dominated by those with specialist knowledge, preferred access to decision-makers or a paid position in a government agency or department' (Jordan and Turnpenny 2015, 7).

These problem characterisations are exacerbated as many urban issues can be understood as 'wicked problems', defined as 'ill-defined, interlinked, and relying on political judgements rather than scientific certitudes' (Rittel and Webber 1973, 160 in Head 2008). Using the notion of 'wicked problems' provides additional insights concerning why many policies and programmes generate controversy, fail to achieve their stated goals, and cause unforeseen effects, while helping to generate a wider understanding of strategies available for managing them (Head 2008). The issues of evictions could be viewed as a wicked problem, as it lies within the contested terrain of individual property rights versus human rights. Is it a legal problem of interpretation of a constitutional clause, or is it a social and market problem (SERI 2016)? Two characteristics of a wicked problem as set out by Rittel and Webber (1973), are relevant to the issue of evictions. Firstly, there is no definitive formulation of a wicked problem and secondly, every wicked problem can be a symptom of another problem. Requirements for attempting to address wicked problems are better knowledge, better consultation, and better use of third-party partners; but frequently policy leaders choose to take safer, simpler routes rather than a problem-solving approach with its associated risks of failure (Head 2008).

Examining the process through the lens of policy instruments/instrumentation/instrumentality

The study of policy instruments is not new, it can be traced back to the 1500's in relation to the Enlightenment era in Europe. Renewed interest in policy instruments emerged around technologies of government, in Weber giving an autonomous role to the material technologies of government (Bevir 2010). Contemporary definitions of policy instruments vary from the broadest interpretations to more detailed breakdowns of their intentions and functions. A broad definition is of them being 'techniques of governance that, one way or another, involve the utilisation of state authority or its conscious limitations' (Howlett 2005, 30). A more detailed definition is that they have two interrelated elements, 'policy goals' and 'policy means' operating at different levels of abstraction (Howlett 2011). In the first instance, they are the aims set by government on what they wish to achieve, and the latter deals with the techniques they use (or not) to achieve those aims. These two elements consist, in turn, of a range of activities from abstract principles to concrete steps. The traditional approach of policy instruments focuses on the functional dimension of instruments, seen as a neutral, or at least a technical device reflecting the objectives of policy intervention, that is adapted to contexts, efficient, costly, easy to implement and leading to intended outcomes.

A more recent approach has been to focus on the instrumentation process – that is, the formulation and content of the instruments as well as the process of the choice of instruments (Lascoumes and Le Galès 2007; Bevir 2010). This approach differs from the functionalist approach in the following ways. Firstly, it views the power dimensions that underlie instrument choices as important, which explains that their effectiveness is not the only criteria, but only one of a range of aspects for their selected formulation and use (Bevir 2010). Policy instruments derive from conflicted or negotiated processes. By the same token, policy instruments contain meanings and have implications for social and political interactions: their use and implementation are not neutral, and they produce their own effects, independent of their stated objectives.

Secondly, it reconceptualises instruments as institutions that need to be constructed rather than being readily available objects (Linder and Peters 1990; Salamon 2002; Howlett 2005; Lascoumes and Le Galès 2007). To this end, Le Gales argues that instruments partly affect how actors behave in that they:

create uncertainties about the effects of the balance of power; they will eventually privilege certain actors and interests and exclude others; they constrain actors, while offering them possibilities; and they drive forward a certain representation of problems (Le Galès in Bevir 2010, 10).

Adopting the above framework helps making sense of the SPRE formulation process, as reflecting relationships between state and society. First, analysing the status of 'evictees' in the policy-making process: alternatively criminalised as responsible of their own situation, and sometimes salvaged as victims of structural poverty and housing crisis. Secondly, highlighting the place given to landlords in the legislation being drafted: partly responsible, including financially, for evictions and evictees; or made completely invisible in the actualisation of housing rights. Adopting such a genealogical approach to the policy process also makes visible power relations within the state, excavating which state entities or actors are the most influential in the process and the final policy.

Contextualising the issue – the governance of Johannesburg's inner city 1994–2019

Johannesburg's inner city is governed by a complex set of municipal departments, municipal agencies, and public–private partnership initiatives. Fundamentally, the inner city lies within Regional F of the metropolitan area and falls within the daily management of that regional administration. However, multiple municipal projects within the inner city are managed by a specific Inner-city Office, that falls under the direct management of the City Manager, and whose power and autonomy has fluctuated over the years. This office in turn deploys various municipal agencies (such as the Johannesburg Development Agency – JDA) and inter-departmental task teams to implement projects. The Inner-city Office also co-manages local districts as Public–Private Partnerships (PPPs) in the form of City Improvement Districts.

The inner city has been declining since the 1980s as a result of disinvestment by the major institutions, due to a range of push factors including congestion and parking problems and pull factors, the desire to reinvest liquid capital in new nodes, in particular suburban property markets (Goga 2003). This disinvestment took place relatively rapidly through what is described as a herd mentality among property managers (Beavon 2004). As a result, many buildings fell into disrepair due to the decline in mortgage and levy payments by owners and tenants alike. The late 1980s and 1990s also witnessed the rapid influx of poor and people of colour, who had been previously restricted from the inner city by apartheid legislation, moving into the inner city to be better located for work and other opportunities. Many of these people occupied the abandoned buildings left boarded up by the previous owners (Gardner 2011).

With local government in transition from 1995–2000, together with the financial crisis of 1997, the City of Johannesburg was unable to respond to the factors responsible for the decline, despite the call, push, and support from local business interests, gathered under the Central Johannesburg Partnership (CJP) (Beall et al. 2002). The CJP set up various business improvement zones covering Johannesburg's inner city. In 2000, the Johannesburg Development Agency, a municipal but autonomous institution, was set up by the City of Johannesburg to address run down areas in the inner city. However, it mainly focused on commercial development and later shifted its focus to public space upgrades to boost the City's tax base, as opposed to low-cost housing (Rubin 2015). Another initiative was the National Treasury's designation of the inner city as an Urban Development Zone in 2003, with its associated tax incentives for property developments. In 2007, the Inner-City Regeneration Charter was launched, bringing together various local stakeholders (state, local businesses, and civil society organisations) to work against urban decline in the inner city (City of Johannesburg 2007).

There were three initiatives concerning decayed occupied buildings that are significant in understanding the circumstances that led to the need to address evictions within the inner city. The first, as part of the CJP developed the Bad Buildings Programme, later renamed the Better Buildings programme (BPP). The second was the Inner-City Property Scheme developed by the Johannesburg Property Company (JPC). This was yet another municipal autonomous agency launched in 2011 along very similar lines to the BPP but with a strong empowerment component: trying to support the emergence of a new class of Black landlords. According to Rubin (2015), both of these schemes resulted in evictions and displacement of poor people. It was one of these evictions that spurred the Blue Moonlight case and the need to formulate the SPRE Policy in 2011.

Despite or in parallel to the SPRE process, a third initiative was launched in 2018, under a Democratic Alliance (DA)-led local government,[5] in which the City announced that it was offering 50-year leases on 71 properties across the inner city. This scheme again effectively ignored the issue of evictions in favour of another market-based approach to regeneration. While this programme is still underway with limited results to date (mainly because of the evictions dilemma), the private sector (mainly small-scale developers) and several housing trusts have been relatively successful at providing small lower-income accommodation units in the inner city (Turok et al. 2021). While it is acknowledged that these efforts have expanded the supply of affordable rental housing in the inner city, there remains a significant gap for 'entry level accommodation to meet the needs of displaced residence and other poor households keen to access urban jobs and livelihoods' (Turok et al. 2021, 15).

A former inner-city employee of the City of Johannesburg eloquently describes the state of the inner city from the City's perspective 'as a tussle between forces of fixity and flux, and between influx and flight' (Dinath 2014, 236). In this description, she outlined three interrelated systemic barriers to the municipal acceptance of informalisation and poverty in the inner city. The first is the political imperative to pursue global competitiveness and credibility and to demonstrate the ruling party's competence. The second is the institutional systems in the municipality that render support of any form of informality and participatory citizenship impossible due to the performance management system that focuses on short term tangible deliverables. The third is the institutional culture and its approaches to urbanity. She describes disparate ways that the inner city is viewed within the municipality, from those officials who believe the inner city is improving but requires a firm hand to pull it into shape through 'blitzes' and 'crack-downs', while other officials have a longer-term vision of regeneration through a 24-hour, inclusive and affordable city which tentatively incorporates informality.

It was these forces that over about three years (2003–6) evicted almost 25,000 people from their homes in the inner city (COHRE 2005, 19) and threatened a further 67,000 inner-city residents (Constitutional Court 2008 in Rubin 2015). Decayed buildings are an important component of the inner city as they accommodate most of the 8 per cent of the residents who live in the inner city of Johannesburg (Tomlinson et al. 2014). However, and meanwhile, a series of Constitutional Court rulings, including the 2010 Blue Moonlight case, made it clear that neither the City of Johannesburg, nor private landlords, were authorised to evict tenants if it meant making them homeless. The above residential development trends and their potential gentrification impacts emphasised how urgent it was for a policy instrument to be developed around the issue of evictions and accommodating those evicted – whether to accommodate and attract would-be property investors, or out of care for low-income residents, a tremendous majority of inner-city inhabitants.

Genealogy of the Special Process for the Relocation of Evictees (SPRE)/ Temporary Emergency Accommodation Provision (TEAP) policy document

In response to the Blue Moonlight Court ruling, the process of the formulation of the SPRE/TEAP Policy unfolded (**Figure 8.1**). It involved both internal City officials and external consultants, and it took over a decade to achieve an approved policy – which, for the purpose of analysis, I have broken into three periods. Firstly, the period leading up to the appointment of the LHR, which included the formulation (internal to the City) of the First Draft Policy. Secondly, the appointment of LHR and revision of the Draft SPRE Policy (in which I was personally involved). Thirdly, the post-appointment, which included several rounds of redrafting the policy internally through the Legal Department and its ultimate renaming and approval in City Council.

Preparation of the First Draft Policy and appointment of consultants

Within the municipality, the first response to the Blue Moonlight ruling was an assumption that it was a housing problem and therefore the responsibility of the Housing Department. In January 2011, the City of Johannesburg handed the matter over to the acting director of Management Support in the Housing Department to come up with a response. During 2012, this acting director consulted with legal specialists at the various levels of government for their interpretation of the ruling, to establish who was responsible for implementing it (that is, whose budget it should come from) and to try and establish exactly how many eviction orders were in progress throughout the city. After the Blue Moonlight ruling, the City of Johannesburg went from getting a few eviction notices in a year to approximately 10 to 12 a month, which also reinforced the need for a proactive programmatic policy (Housing official 1 2019).

A key debate ensued throughout 2012 about who was responsible for the cost of accommodating the evictees. Local government officials were of the dominant opinion that it was the Provincial government's responsibility, largely because municipalities had no allocated funds for such. The Provincial government felt that the national Human Settlements Department should foot the bill. Some of the leading advocates still interpreted the ruling as housing being a joint competence, that the

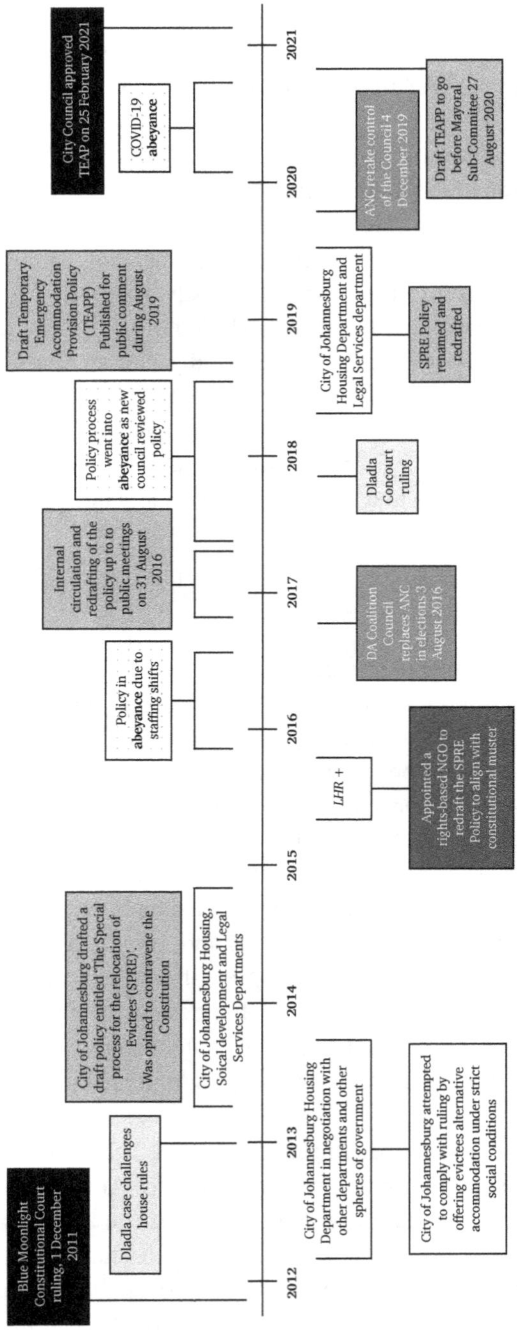

Figure 8.1 Timeline for the formulation of the housing eviction policy.

Source: © Neil Klug 2022

Provincial government was responsible for the funding, and the City for supplying the buildings. There was, however, broad agreement that there was a policy vacuum around this issue.

Officials of the City of Johannesburg then decided to prioritise the Blue Moonlight case itself, and therefore resolved to run a pilot project to house its evictees. This involved officials from the Housing and Social Development Departments practically trying to secure buildings within the inner city to be used as 'transitional residential accommodation' (TRA). In this process, they approached a range of programme managers within City entities and departments: Johannesburg Property Company (JPC),[6] Inner-City Property Scheme (ICPS),[7] Johannesburg Social Housing Company (JOSCHO)[8] and the JDA[9]. As they have their own mandates and priorities, all were reluctant to give their buildings to the TRA. The manager of the ICPS even requested them to 'back off trying to obtain buildings in the inner city, as it was putting pressure on the Inner-City Housing Scheme' (Housing official 1 2019). The only buildings offered were inappropriate: either office buildings or residential buildings in severe disrepair, requiring too much money to refurbish for TRAs. Housing officials even approached the national Department of Public Works to acquire buildings, to no avail. Eventually they did secure two buildings from JOSCHO, much to its CEO's dissatisfaction.

These practical considerations raised the debate around the temporary nature of the accommodation to be provided, and how it could be ensured that these residents moved on to permanent accommodation within a specified period. In the existing temporary accommodation facilities run by the City of Johannesburg, many residents never transitioned to permanent accommodation, thereby blocking the existing facilities to new evictees. In response, the City of Johannesburg developed the 'managed care model': they approached a Christian organisation called the Metropolitan Evangelical Services (MES), an NGO accommodating homeless people on a temporary basis, and contracted them to run a TRA facility. However, the MES's management approach was very constrictive, insisting that residents enter into a management agreement with them before taking occupation. This agreement involved personalised development plans that each resident would contract to, to ensure that they transitioned out of the temporary facility within a specified period and, in addition, they needed to agree to restrictive living arrangements involving access controls, limited visitors, etc. (Housing official 1 2019). Conditions imposed by the MES soon proved so unacceptable that residents approached SERI, a legal NGO, who took it to the Constitutional Court maintaining that the conditions contravened the constitutional clauses in relation to self-dignity. This was the Dladla case, submitted in August 2014, whose judgment was handed down on 22 August 2014. The judgment ruled against the City in that it declared the rules of the 'managed care model' to be an 'unjustifiable infringement of the applicant's constitutional rights to dignity, freedom and security of person and privacy in terms of Sections 10.12 and 14 of the Constitution' (Dladla Case 2012).

In a report submitted by the City of Johannesburg's Group Legal and Contracts Department to the Mayor on 13 November 2014, it was acknowledged that the City of Johannesburg did not have a plan to deal with Temporary Emergency Accommodation (TEA).[10] In the multiple proposals made in response, the Housing Department alluded to the need to prepare a systematic process for dealing with evictees and TEAs. Interestingly, one of the proposals was to relook at what by-laws could be used to hold landowners accountable for failing to secure their properties (Housing official 1 2019).

Meanwhile, with the challenge of the Dladla Case and the threat of personal liability of the mayor and senior officials, the City of Johannesburg's officials were prompted to draw up a systematic policy for the handling of evictees in Johannesburg (Wilson 2021). A Housing Department official formulated the first draft of the policy assisted by a Social Development Department official in early 2014. On completion of this draft policy, called Special Process for the Relocation of Evictees (SPRE), it was sent to the City of Johannesburg's Legal Department and a private law firm (the City of Johannesburg's lawyers) for comments (Housing official 1 2019).

Between May 2014 and March 2015, there appears to have been a hiatus in the development of the SPRE policy as the original author of the document left the City of Johannesburg in about June 2014. At about the same time, a newly appointed Housing official took up the role as the assistant director at JOSHCO, becoming the liaison person between the Housing Department and JOSCHO. According to him (Housing official 2 2019), the job had no clear description and the core task (the preparation of the annual review of JOSCHO for the Housing Department) only consumed about 20 per cent of their time. As an individual, they were passionate about issues of inequality and individually identified the Draft SPRE Policy as an urgent project to have it aligned with the constitutional order and to put in place the 'nitty gritty management tools for implementation'. Based on an internal City of Johannesburg workshop (COJ 2015a), they then took it upon themselves to get permission from their superior to obtain a budget and put a project in place. The budget was taken from an existing housing project to avoid a new open procurement process for service providers, as they had in mind a particular service provider (consultant) with human rights credentials and a 'sense of the realities on the ground', the LHR.

During this period, there was also a change in management within the Housing Department with a new executive director. Having been updated on the SPRE process, the new director insisted that a university professor in the Wits School of Governance be appointed to undertake the review, based on his affinity to the professor's work. This prompted debate among the Housing officials who maintained that the professor and his assistant were not specialists in the field. Furthermore, Housing official 2 indicated that he personally wanted a human-rights based approach and not just a compliance approach inserted into the policy, and therefore, an advocacy organisation to review the draft policy. It was suggested that the LHR be approached because, 'they were not connected to any other parties who had challenged the City in this respect' (Housing official 2 2019), unlike the Socio-Economic Rights Institute (SERI), who had great housing and inner-city expertise but was key in bringing the City to court in the Blue Moonlight and Dladla cases.

Brief to the consultants and process of external review of the Draft Policy

In early 2015, a brief and proposal call, (City of Johannesburg and WSG 2015a) was drawn up by the Johannesburg's Housing Department and the Wits School of Governance (WSG) and sent to the LHR for a proposal (LHR 2015a). The brief was to revise the SPRE Policy, to include findings from the Dladla judgement, to update it according to the current context. Importantly, the brief stipulated that the work was to also include a programme and implementation plan and that the programme was to form the bulk of the outputs, that is, the procedures, financing, and transitional housing options. As such, the brief focused on the implementation aspect of the policy rather than on the content of the policy itself (City of Johannesburg and WSG 2015a). What followed was the appointment of the LHR, contracted through the Wits School of Governance on behalf of the City, as an extension of an existing contract, to review and rewrite the policy in April 2015. This involved an intense three-month consultancy from the 1 May–31 July 2015, in which three iterations of the original policy draft (CoJ 2014), hereafter referred to as First (CoJ 2015b), Second (CoJ 2015c) and Third (CoJ 2015f) Drafts, and a policy guideline (CoJ 2015g) programme (CoJ 2015h) and implementation plan (CoJ 2015i) were prepared.

Inception phase

The terms of reference for the project were received on 1 April 2015, after a series of iterative engagements between the Housing Department and the LHR, as well as within the LHR, to arrive at a clear and agreed methodology for the project, in the form of an inception report (LHR 2015b). As such, the actual formulation of the policy process began in earnest on 5 May 2015, five weeks into a three-month deadline, leaving just seven weeks to formulate the revised policy. This began with meetings with the LHR to discuss the comments to our inception report (LHR 2015b), and a discussion on the existing Original Draft Policy document prepared by the City of Johannesburg's legal office with comments from its legal consultants (CoJ 2014) and the way forward.

The consultancy group was made up of human rights lawyers, urban planners and housing specialists. The lawyers would undertake the actual redrafting of the policy document ensuring that none of the clauses would be in contravention of the Constitution while also trying to balance the rights of the evictees against those of the City of Johannesburg and landowners. The planners (including myself) were to examine the TEA options and how they could be applied, and most importantly to identify a range of housing options into which the evictees could be transitioned (TRA). Given the tight timeframes, this involved a few joint workshops to align the housing options with the legal requirements.

Evaluation of the existing policy document

Our review (CoJ 2015b) of the original policy document (CoJ 2014), was assisted by prepared comments by the City of Johannesburg's legal service providers as well as officials from the Housing Department (our client). Overall, the legal members of the team agreed that certain aspects of the policy would be unconstitutional. My personal impressions were that the document was a relatively draconian instrument placing evictees into a 'managed care programme'. Wilson, the then director of SERI, argued that the practice of placing homeless people in a managed care programme 'posits the poor as patients with a sickness that can be cured with a short programmatic intervention'. Some of the onerous and perceived unconstitutional conditions included:

- The situational analysis to be undertaken of the pre-eviction circumstances were unspecified/not detailed.

- A list of conditions under which the 'evictees' would receive no or limited assistance, including whether they themselves caused their 'exceptional need' and whether they provided false information.
- The TEA could accommodate evictees only for 6 months with an option of staying for 12 months after which they had to leave. Should they not, their possessions would be removed and kept in an office off-site facility for collection.
- Every individual allocated a bed in a TEA would have to contract into a 'managed care programme' that included how they were going to access permanent accommodation, acquire additional skills and get access to government grants. Failure to comply or sign such a document would result in expulsion from any assistance.

Lawyers for Human Rights discussion document response

The LHR responded to the client through an internal discussion document (LHR 2015c). This document had a dual nature: it analysed jurisprudence relating to the relocation of evictees and identified some of the practical issues the City of Johannesburg would have to pay attention to 'if the policy was to be realistic and implementable while complying with the principles established by the courts' (LHR 2015c, 1). The document proposed that 'the City considers ways to decrease the number of evictions and share responsibility with building owners who acquire properties with the intention of evicting occupiers (LHR 2015c, 1 and Klug TRP SA 2015). The internal discussion document drafted by the consulting team also referred to two other documents relating to jurisprudence – minimum requirements and a fuller analysis of the SPRE draft identifying gaps and proposals (LHR 2015d).

A key issue relating to costs facing the City of Johannesburg, acknowledged in the discussion document, was that the City was stuck in what was referred to in the document as a 'cycle of evictions' – by providing alternative accommodation and then re-evicting people when they did not move on (referred to as 'non-transitioners') after the specified period of 12 months, then having to re-accommodate them in temporary accommodation. This essentially related to three key issues: the City's inability to enforce temporality; the missing housing rung for those only able to afford R500 per month; and the managed care model that could not be lifelong.

Dealing with evictions: planning and housing versus legal perspectives, a debate within the consultants' team

In our internal team preparation discussions of these documents, I remember debating with the lawyers the need to pre-empt evictions and to examine the pre-eviction circumstances with respect to the housing conditions that led up to the circumstances of the eviction (that is, reasons for the dereliction of maintenance of the 'occupied' buildings), as well as bringing into the picture the responsibilities of the landowners from a housing perspective. Evidence of some of these debates are reflected in our discussion document, in which I enquire whether the nature of the local authority's responsibility for alternative accommodation for private evictions could be expanded to also restricting private developers from acquiring such accommodation in the first place to avoid future evictions.

The legal members of the team tended to view these debates from the perspective of what the courts were likely or not to accept. There appeared to be a reluctance to impose legal rights' restrictions on private property owners: possibly from a legal perspective the policy was not an appropriate instrument to apply such imperatives. I recall the legal members of the team spending a lot of time with legal terminologies (that is, the meaning of the term meaningful engagement).

Source: © recollections from internal debates within the consultant team, Neil Klug 2020

First and Second Drafts of the special process for the relocation of evictees (SPRE) document – engaging with property owners

The responses by the Johannesburg Housing Department to the discussion document related to points of clarity rather than any objections to the two main innovations of decreasing the number of evictions and sharing responsibility with building owners who acquire properties with the intention of evicting occupiers.

The Original Draft Policy (CoJ 2014) had made no mention of 'meaningful engagement' with building occupiers. Therefore, the First Draft Policy (CoJ 2015b) inserted the requirement for 'meaningful engagement' as a jurisprudence requirement for practical implementation purposes introduced by the LHR. It suggested that it could also include engagement with the owners by the City to find alternatives to the evictions and more specifically to bring them into the picture.

Regarding the place of property owners within the whole process, the Second Draft Policy also included a section entitled: 'Negotiating with owners regarding alternatives to evictions', which just stipulated the positive reasons for doing so for the City, mostly saving costs. Generally, however, it only spoke of 'negotiating', rather than mentioning the responsibilities and obligations of property owners in the process leading to eviction.

Third Draft of the special process for the relocation of evictees (SPRE) policy document

The Third Draft iteration process commenced on 4 June 2015. There, the team appeared to only make minor technical adjustments, and restructured the sections. With respect to the issue with occupiers and the place of property owners in the policy, the notion of 'meaningful engagement' was now merely footnoted referring to a Constitutional Court ruling (and detailed in the accompanying Draft Policy Guidelines, CoJ 2015g). Engaging property owners was no longer included under 'meaningful engagement', limited to the occupiers. Instead, background information on the property owners and status of the building was included. But no mention was made of any financial obligations of the private property owners with respect to providing relief to evictees, although it maintained a section called 'Pro-active Steps' where negotiations with owners regarding alternatives to evictions were proposed.

Finally, the Third Draft of the SPRE Policy (CoJ 2015f) was submitted to the Johannesburg Housing Department on 25 July 2015. This was followed by the preparation of a Policy Guidelines document (CoJ 2015d and 2015g), and detailed programme (CoJ 2015e and 2015h) for implementing the policy, submitted end August 2015. These latter documents, in respect to funding and engagement, merely set out a brief list of funding options, of emergency funds and budgeting in the Medium-Term Budget, and detailed steps for meaningful engagement. Regarding alternative accommodation options, the team was only able, within the timeframes of the consultancy, to identify possible buildings for future feasibility research. This put an end to the consultant team's mandate.

Internal re-review of the Third Draft Policy

The internal redrafting and attempted approval process

The following months were spent by Housing official 2 consulting internally with other City of Johannesburg departments. However, in late 2015, Housing official 2's director was moved to the Manager's office along with Housing official 2. He requested that the SPRE project be taken with him but that was declined by his immediate line manager who said it had to remain in the Housing Department (Housing official 2 2019). As a result, no further work was done to finalise and approve the SPRE Policy until late 2016, when Housing official 2 returned with his original director to the Housing Department.

Through these internal consultations, changes were made to the Third Draft (CoJ 2015c) creating a Fourth Draft (CoJ 2016), probably through the City's own Legal Department. Housing official 2 circulated and presented the Fourth Draft to various departments within the City: while some departments gave written comments on the draft, agreements to support the draft policy were never put into writing. He then took the Fourth Draft through various technical committees and the Section 79 Housing Committee[11] and finally to the Mayoral Committee – the Mayoral Committee being the only committee where the report would be signed off by heads of departments and at which formal minutes and agreements would be recorded. Housing official 2 was informed at the Mayoral Committee that it had to go to public consultation before it could go to City Council for a vote.

Coinciding with this time was the ousting of the African National Congress (ANC) from the Johannesburg City Council in the local government elections in August 2016. Thereafter, Johannesburg was run by a fragile coalition government headed by the Democratic Alliance party (a liberal, pro-business party) with the Economic Freedom Fighters (EFF, a radical left party) as a junior partner. All draft policies were put on hold while they were reviewed by the new coalition government, with high levels of uncertainty.

With the Fourth Draft (CoJ 2016), the policy became even more legalistic and less human rights oriented. Firstly, the issue of meaningful engagement was reinterpreted again to include the owner only if they were willing to participate; and all clauses referring to 'negotiations with owners' regarding alternatives to evictions were removed from the policy. Secondly, it reintroduced relatively severe conditions on residence of temporary accommodation facilities. For example, 'Evictees who *inter alia*, refuse to conclude the necessary agreements, co-operate with the social workers, participate meaningfully in the self-betterment programmes, and abide by the house rules may be removed from the facility' (CoJ 2016, 14). Overall, the Fourth Draft of the policy (CoJ 2016) reflected a swing back to a more confrontational approach towards the evictees, confirming their criminalisation, explicitly spelling out that the policy was not intended to 'promote queue jumping under any circumstances whatsoever'. It also carried a more pro-property owner bias in that it limited even further landowner involvement and responsibility.

The retitling of the 'Special Process for the Relocation of Evictees' (SPRE) and emergence of the 'Temporary Emergency Accommodation Provision (TEAP): Draft Policy'

Between early 2018 and November 2019, the latest draft of the original SPRE Policy was further amended internally by the Housing Department's policy unit and retitled 'Temporary Emergency Accommodation Provision (TEAP): Draft Policy', then distributed for public comment (CoJ 2020). The TEAP (CoJ 2021) was also substantially revised from the final SPRE Policy (CoJ 2016): it focused even more on the emergency need for accommodation rather than the circumstances leading up to that 'emergency'. In so doing, as reflected in the renaming, the policy was reoriented to focus on the product rather than the subjects of the product.

Furthermore, the document largely extended the restrictive regulatory clauses on potential beneficiaries of the TEAP, included in new sections such as 'Qualifying criteria and exclusions', 'Application for TEA' (Section 13.2), justifying reasons for the City curtailing their obligations to potential beneficiaries. These restrictions were actually stated upfront, under 'Policy principles', where out of six principles, half referred to the limited, transitional, and temporary nature of the relief, and several caveats were mentioned about not encouraging queue jumping or illegal occupation of land, in other sections of the policy (CoJ 2019; Draft TEAP, 9).

The Temporary Emergency Accommodation Provision (TEAP): Draft Policy, was eventually approved by City Council on 25 February 2021. It can be assumed that the extended timeframe from comments to approval could have been due to the COVID-19 lockdown disruptions. What is noteworthy is the policy was approved without any guidelines, programme, or implementation plans.

Tracking three themes in the policy formulation process – problem framing, status of evictees and role of property owners

It was eloquently stated by SERI in their comments to the City of Johannesburg (SERI 2016 14), of the Fourth Draft Policy (CoJ 2016) document:

> The Policy and Guidelines should be amended to more appropriately reflect the legal principle around alternative accommodation that has been developed in the case law to ensure that the City's obligation is generally more positively framed.

Essentially, between the various iterations of the five drafts of the policy, the framing varies broadly from a rather progressive to a more regressive formulation of the issue: initially, relatively regulatory and positive in the LHR draft, towards a more regulatory and restrictive policy.

This section demonstrates this and traces these shifts, by tracking three specific threads throughout the formulation process. It starts by interrogating how the issue is framed and how this framing is or is not contested over time (1), continues by analysing how evictees are depicted and treated in the policy (victims or culprits) (2), and ends with a focused attention to the (diminishing) place and role of the property owner in the policy relating to evictions (3). Analysing the genealogy of these framings as results of negotiation and political choices, paying attention to the role of specific individual and institutions, assists us in understanding the final rather regressive document that has eventually become policy, in spite of seemingly potential progressive beginnings.

Problem characterisation underpinning the policy intent

From the City of Johannesburg's response throughout this process, the problem has been expressed as an 'emergency homelessness' issue that requires a 'temporary solution'. The problem for the City was also seen to be caused by the courts' ruling, making it an obligation of the City to provide temporary housing. So, it was seen by many of the state actors involved as a legal obligation to provide temporary accommodation, as opposed to a societal and market problem the City needed to take seriously. While some interviewees questioned whether it was an emergency issue, and while it was debated by the professional team, the analysis of documentation confirms that it was not actually contested by any of the role players.

The continued approach of viewing evictions as an emergency issue (equivalent to a natural disaster), perpetuates a mismatch between the ultimate objectives of the policy (that is, to provide evictees with alternative accommodation) and the potential policy instruments to achieve that. In treating evictions as an emergency, the priority remains to provide short-term emergency alternative accommodation. Eviction processes begin months before the tenants/occupiers are removed from the premises, which practically should provide ample time to negotiate and arrange longer term, more sustainable and integrated alternative options. Even in the case of 'unsafe buildings', the conditions of these buildings do not deteriorate into imminent danger overnight. In the public review of the TEAP (CoJ 2019), CUBES expressed the view that the issue of evictions is not purely a housing and legalistic issue, but a consequence of economic affordability and other social factors that are beyond the expertise and scope of housing officials and lawyers (CUBES 2019). Several reasons are posited to try and understand why the City adopted this problem characterisation.

A first argument around how responsibilities were initially allocated in response to the court ruling talks to a well-known proverb: 'If your only tool is a hammer, then every problem looks like a nail' (Maslow 1966), or, similarly in political sciences, what is known as 'the garbage can model of decision-making' (Cohen et al. 1972), uncoupling the perceived problem from the choices of responses to solve the problem, by adopting the set of policy instruments that already exists (what is within the 'garbage can'), and framing the issue so that the existing instruments might seem to respond to the issue – without considering other framings that might call for the creation or invention of new instruments.

In restricting the issue of evictions to a purely legal matter, linked to a temporary housing issue, of course the scope of this 'wicked problem' (Rittel and Webber 1973) is narrowed and seemingly possible to respond to by simple instruments. This would not be the case if the issue was characterised as being about poverty and inequality, as well as local economic development and the property market and speculation issue, which would be far more difficult to tackle. By attributing the responsibility of policy formulation to the Housing Department, by focusing the brief to consultants around finding housing alternatives for the evictees (the rapid and narrow response to the court requirements), only the tools of planning practitioners and lawyers were applied, which constrains the choices of policy instruments to be considered to solve the problem. On reflection, all role-players from the client to the various service providers could be apportioned some blame for assuming that, despite the awareness that the problem was multi-dimensional, their skill set could resolve the problem. This could, however, just reflect the growing dependence in South Africa on legal prescripts to get the state to deliver services and to mediate societal contestations.

To further complicate matters, according to the project manager of the LHR project team (LHR project manager, interview 2019), the 'senior management simply did not advocate for a human rights approach' when viewing the issues of evictions in the City, even though human rights' lawyers were pushed by one housing official to be appointed as consultants. More broadly, it can be argued that lawyers leading the policy drafting process from the City, as well as the consultants' perspective (in the context of litigation), are not equipped to formulate policies (Social Development official 2019). As evictions always involve a court order, the resolution of eviction issues through engagement mechanisms would negate the need for a legal process, which would not to be in the legal fraternity's interests. Several strong accusations were made by the interviewees in this respect, against lawyers on both sides: City of Johannesburg's attorneys and public interest lawyers. Claims that the City's lawyers had their own financial interests at heart with constant litigation, while the other accusation against the human rights' lawyers was that it was a 'shake-down' by building occupants supported by lawyers who are mainly set on winning legal precedents (Social Development official 2019). Tissington (2018) amply documented how more generally, ongoing, lengthy, and constant litigation makes it difficult to have an inclusive and constructive policy-making process, rigidifying relationships (internal to the City, and between City and civil society at large) in fear and antagonism and, on reflection, closing avenues for pragmatic resolutions of the policy issue.

A second important argument is that there also might be some benefit, or at least some policy interest, in framing the issue as 'an emergency' one rather than a structural policy issue. This relates to 'the elephant in the room' (Tissington 2018): the issue of funding for alternative or affordable accommodation in the inner city. Characterising its obligation to construct a plan for inner-city affordable housing as an emergency was an opening, for the City of Johannesburg, to tap into the national Emergency Housing Programme (EHP) funding. City officials repeatedly argued that it was the role of national and provincial government to provide funds for emergency housing (Housing official 1 2019 and Tissington 2018). This is in the context where all funding for affordable housing is allocated by the national Department of Human Settlements (via the provincial government to local governments), in response to applications made to the provincial government in terms of the various existing public housing programmes. The implication of this is that by restricting the problem to an emergency housing one, the City can apply for funding for TEA via the Emergency Housing Fund, one of the housing programmes in the Housing Code.

The depiction and treatment of evictees in the policy

An examination of the various iterations of the SPRE and TEAP draft policies exposes how the framing of the policies fluctuated from a relatively harsh position towards evictees in the initial draft (resulting in it being considered non-constitutional) to more evictee 'friendly' or empathetic in the LHR formulations in the Second and Third Drafts and back to even more regulatory and hostile vision in the last SPRE (CoJ 2016) and TEAP (CoJ 2020 and 2021) Drafts, amended and formulated internally by the City.

The Blue Moonlight constitutional ruling saw evictees as vulnerable people who needed state assistance, at least in the short to medium term, to be safely housed post-eviction. However, from the outset there were indications of hesitancy from the City about taking on the obligation which I argue implicitly demonstrated a mistrust and negative perception of evictees, by the City.

Firstly, the debates and attempts to avoid responsibility for the Constitutional Court stipulated obligation, centred around who should be responsible for funding the temporary accommodation. Even prior to establishing the need to formulate the SPRE Policy, the City attempted to redirect the responsibility for funding of alternative accommodation to other levels of government. While this reluctance to take responsibility centred around the financial implications for the City, it also indicated that such expenditure was low on their priority list despite the Concourt ruling.

Secondly, in the first draft (CoJ 2014), the mistrust of the evictees was expressed in the highly regulatory framing of the policy. These regulatory clauses would impose timeframes on the evictees to respond to terms and conditions, failing which the City would no longer be obligated to them. The LHR's Draft (CoJ 2015), reversed the emphasis on the evictees, by saying that the City had to prove that they had attempted to engage with the evictees rather than purely leaving it to the evictees to respond to a deadline. In the City's SPRE and TEAP final Drafts (CoJ 2016, 2020 and 2021 respectively), their policymakers reverted to imposing the obligation onto the evictees to respond and further specifying that the policy was not to 'promote queue jumping' of the municipal housing waiting lists – again, implying that evictees were purposely getting evicted to jump the housing subsidy allocation lists.

Councillors and senior officials were reluctant to support the SPRE Policy, afraid that they were 'rewarding bad behaviour' by providing temporary accommodation to residents occupying decayed buildings and that they were jumping the queue of people waiting for public housing (Housing officials 1 and 2 2019; Political Advisor 2020). This attitude worsened with the defeat of the ANC Council in the 2016 municipal elections, replaced by a coalition council led by the DA with the EFF being a major influencer on policies. According to the Political Advisor (2020), even after the last iteration of the policy renamed the TEAP in 2019, it 'was seen as a dirty sock which no-one wanted to touch'. Yet, it was the lack of a proper TEA solution that torpedoed Mayor Mashaba's inner city property release programme (Inner city specialist 2020). Essentially, the City's inability to relocate existing residents from the intended upgrade buildings resulted in the effective suspension of the implementation of the programme. Another impact at the time was the reluctance of the EFF to approve the draft SPRE Policy in early 2017 as they did not like the term 'evictees' in the title of the policy, as it suggested they condoned evictions.

The status and role of private or individual landlords in the process

The question of the private landlord's involvement in the eviction process in terms of sharing the obligations set out in the Constitutional Court ruling, arose in the early debates surrounding the preparation of the initial draft policy. 'Why not impose a fee to say: you've allowed a slum to evolve, you benefit commercially, if this changes, why can't we charge you for the cost of sorting this out?' (Social Development official 2019). These debates were corroborated by Housing official 2 when he was explaining how he took the Third Draft Policy (CoJ 2015f) through internal consultations within the City. He explained that one of the repeated concerns raised was why should the municipality have to provide accommodation in private-led evictions? As that was already stipulated by the Concourt as an obligation, he stated:

> So maybe yes, it is the municipality with the logistical responsibility; but musn't the private sector have to pay for eviction? If they bought a building like for one Rand, fully occupied illegally, then why is it that they can get away scott-free through the evictions process, not even covering the cost of relocation, let alone transitional housing? (Housing official 2 2019)

However, these interrogations did not seem to make it formally into the policy brief or drafts.

Yet, with regards to private landlords' involvement in the process, the LHR inserted a section under 'Proactive Steps' which referred to the need to discuss with owners alternatives to evictions but was watered down in the internal Fourth Draft (CoJ 2016) to giving the landlords an option of whether they 'wished to engage'. In the final TEAP version (CoJ 2021), there are only references to negotiations with landlords if they are 'willing'.

Based on my recollections and the interview transcripts, there was a reluctance from all legal actors, both on the City and the LHR side, to explicitly incorporate a shared obligation on the private landowners and landlords. Consternations at the LHR's reluctance was expressed by Housing official 2:

> I was wanting to test a lot more and I was feeling that they were a lot easier on the private sector than you needed to be. Because we could test this in court. And I think in the end it was just a blank spot there ... because they didn't want to test it legally. I don't remember if it actually made it into the policy or not, that the private sector should pay (Housing official 2 2019).

The discrepancy in expectations around including the private landowners in the obligations possibly stems from the disjuncture in the understanding between the legal and planning role players. By this, I mean the legal actors involved based their inputs on case law, that is, how the Constitution had been interpreted in various cases pertaining to the issue of evictions and on the wording of the Constitutional Court ruling; whereas the planners based their inputs on normative values and pragmatic proposals of how to address the issue of evictions and alternative accommodation. Human Rights' Lawyers tend to use 'strategic litigation': it is easier to argue in law that the state has obligations, particularly in relation to housing where the Constitution has already established that housing is a state obligation. In the case of the SPRE Fourth Draft (CoJ 2016), the LHR attempted, however, to extend the obligation horizontally to the landlords to find alternative solutions to the evictions prior to the actual eviction. These clauses, however, were changed to make the obligation voluntary on behalf of the landlords in the TEAP Fifth Draft (CoJ 2020 and 2021).

Moreover, according to the Social Development official (interview 2019), the Inner-City Property Scheme had considered the idea of a contributory trust to address this issue, involving property owners. This trust was never set up. While an appropriate instrument per se, he maintained that neither the scheme nor the policy was the right avenue to implement it:

> there's a lot of instruments that can resolve it, but you need a piece of joined-up government thinking to do it, and SPRE was designed to be that. But institutional problem goes back. It's still designed as a housing standard operating procedure (Social Development official, interview 2019).

This point alludes to the silo departmental structures between provincial and local government, both having housing mandates.

Ultimately, the exclusion of the private sector's obligations in the final policy is the result of converging logics, and avoidance of the huge political battle required to tax or constrain private property owners (a point also evident in the case studies presented by Krumholz and Clavel (1994). On the one hand, the City was afraid that private landlords would take them to court to fight the policy obligations, and those in favour of making them share responsibility were in a minority in the City. On the other hand, the City's lawyers and group legal were biased towards getting a quick win based on existing legislation and state housing obligations, rather than challenging the established practised case law property rights.

Conclusion

It took over a decade to respond to a Constitutional Court ruling and approve a policy that was intended to ameliorate the negative impacts of evictions on the most vulnerable members of our society. This time gap is testimony to the complexity of the issue (a wicked problem with competing framings), the absence of ready-made instruments, the reluctance of the municipality to address it: resource stricken, unable to mobilise other levels of government to fund alternative inner-city housing, and unable or unwilling to challenge the private property market to contribute. Evictions have been dealt with as a legal issue within the City despite it involving housing and stemming from social development issues. While all three departments were involved, with the Housing Department being responsible for overseeing the drafting process and ultimately providing alternative accommodation, the legal sector (in the form of Group Legal) appears to have had the final say as it was ultimately about legal compliance, with Social Development remaining marginal in the process.

When the approved TEAP policy instrument is operationalised, it will comply with the court order as it provides the court with a response to providing evictees with an institutional path to receive temporary accommodation after an eviction. The framing of the issue by policy is one-dimensional, as a legal compliance and housing solution, rather than a more multi-sectoral issue to be addressed through multiple inter-departmental and interlinked policy instruments. It is also framed as an 'emergency service' rather than as a structural issue: affordable housing provision in the inner city. On reflection of the consultancy, the tight timeframes for producing the policy limited the ability of the LHR team to focus on other aspects such as implementation strategies that could leverage a better balance of rights between landowners and occupiers. Ultimately, a pragmatic solution was sought. This involved identifying outside funding to cover the costs of 'emergency housing' and taking stock of the City's reluctance to address politically the issue of evictions as part of a long standing, structural housing policy issue.

In terms of the individual role players, despite the progressive attempts by some officials within the City and some of their consultants to produce a more rights-based policy instrument, there were definitive moments that altered the course of the formulation process when different stakeholders reviewed the policy drafts – finally returning to a regulatory and punitive approach to policy-making. The vagaries of the institutional structures (staff movements); the lack of inter-departmental protocols for addressing contested objectives; the divisive impacts of opposing outside consultants' advice and contributions, reflected the different power blocks within the City. Linked to this appears to be an animus towards evictees by some politicians and officials alike, while at the same time a fear or reluctance to confront the property owners/

evictors around the issues of joint responsibilities for evictions. All of these factors have played a role in undermining and delaying the policy formulation and adoption and possibly the implicit rejection of the Draft Policy and Guidelines produced by the LHR back in 2015.

This is essentially a narrative revealed through the analysis of a policy instrument formulation process of how a 'progressive state' has danced around the issue of evictions at the local level, as it sits as an anomaly between their humanist ideals and neoliberal practices. In theory, there was a unique opportunity to address the issue of evictions at the local level in a more comprehensive and multi-sectoral policy covering how to address the circumstances leading to evictions and the possible consequences, but the latter was chosen. It is difficult to surmise what could have been achieved. However, by defining the problem more broadly, taking a more humanistic approach to evictees and by sharing aspects of the obligation with the private sector, the policy document could have acted upon the legal instruction in a more progressive manner. In this way the 'passing of the legal instruction into the social world' (Wilson 2021), could have created opportunities to change individual or institutional behaviours or practices to further challenge the existing property rights' orthodoxies in South Africa.

Notes

1 Prevention of Illegal Eviction from and Unlawful Occupation of Land Act (PIE) (1998) – to provide for the prohibition of unlawful eviction; to provide for procedures for the eviction of unlawful occupiers; and to repeal the Prevention of Illegal Squatting Act 1951, and other obsolete laws; and to provide for matters incidental thereto.

2 Extension of Security of Tenure Act 62 of 1997, provides for measures with State assistance to facilitate long-term security of land tenure; to regulate the conditions of residence on certain land; to regulate the conditions on and circumstances under which the right of persons to reside on land may be terminated.

3 Through for instance making a financial contribution to their rehousing or developing some inclusionary housing as part of the building's redevelopment, for some of these former occupiers.

4 An independent, non-profit, non-governmental human rights organisation, started by a group of activist lawyers in 1979.

5 In 2016, Johannesburg shifted from being governed by the African National Congress (ANC), to being governed by the liberal Democratic Alliance (DA), the strongest opposition party in the country, in alliance with the radical left Economic Freedom Fighters movement (EFF).

6 The City of Johannesburg Property Company SOC Ltd (JPC), established in 2000, is a municipal company mandated to manage and develop the City of Johannesburg's property assets for the purpose of maximising both social and commercial opportunities for the Council.

7 The Inner-City Property Scheme (ICPS), replaced the Better Buildings Programme in 2011. It focuses on attracting investors to redevelop dilapidated, abandoned and illegally occupied or hijacked buildings in the inner city, through abandonment agreements with the property owners, sales in execution and expropriations, and will include the transfer of dilapidated buildings owned by the City.

8 The JOSHCO was established in March 2004 by the City of Johannesburg with a mandate to provide and manage social and affordable rental housing that services the income levels of various households.

9 The JDA is a municipal agency established in 2000 to lead urban redevelopment in the city of Johannesburg, with a specific (but not exclusive) focus on the inner city.

10 Temporary Emergency Accommodation (TEA): immediate and short-term relief preceding the medium-term Transitional Residential Accommodation (TRA).

11 Portfolio committees with an oversight role in the City, gathering elected councillors from all political parties.

Unpublished Primary Sources

Centre for the Built Environment Studies (CUBES). 2019. Submission on the City of Johannesburg – Temporary Emergency Accommodation Provision: Draft Policy, Submission by CUBES, School of Architecture and Planning, University of the Witwatersrand, Johannesburg.

City of Johannesburg (CoJ). 2007. Inner City Regeneration Charter, July 2007. Available at: https://www.gpma.co.za/files/inner_city_regeneration_charter.pdf . Accessed July 2017.

CoJ. 2014. 'Original Draft Policy. Special Process for the Relocation of Evictees (SPRE)'. Drafted by the City of Johannesburg's Housing Department, with comments by the City of Johannesburg's external legal advisors.

CoJ. 2015a. Minutes for the internal City of Johannesburg's Workshop on the Policy for the Special Process for the Relocation of Evictees (SPRE).

CoJ. 2015b. 'Draft Policy. Special Process for the Relocation of Evictees (SPRE)'. First Draft Policy submitted to the City of Johannesburg with comments from the City of Johannesburg's official managing the consultants, 3 June 2015.

CoJ. 2015c. 'Draft Policy. Special Process for the Relocation of Evictees (SPRE)'. Second Draft Policy submitted to the City of Johannesburg, 25 June 2015.

CoJ. 2015d. 'Draft Guidelines. Special Process for the Relocation of Evictees (SPRE)'. First Draft Guidelines submitted to the City of Johannesburg, 10 July 2015.

CoJ. 2015e. 'Draft Programme. Special Process for the Relocation of Evictees (SPRE)'. First Draft Programme submitted to the City of Johannesburg, 28 July 2015.

CoJ. 2015f. 'Draft Policy. Special Process for the Relocation of Evictees (SPRE)'. Third (and final) submission to the City of Johannesburg, 30 July 2015.

CoJ. 2015g. 'Draft Policy Guidelines. Special Process for the Relocation of Evictees (SPRE)'. Final submission to the City of Johannesburg, 30 July 2015.

CoJ. 2015h. 'Programme. Special Process for the Relocation of Evictees (SPRE)'. Final submission to the City of Johannesburg, 30 July 2015.

CoJ. 2015i. 'Implementation Plan. Special Process for the Relocation of Evictees (SPRE)'. Final submission to the City of Johannesburg, 30 July 2015.

CoJ. 2016. 'City of Johannesburg. Special Process for the Relocation of Evictees (SPRE)'. Final Draft of SPRE amended internally by City officials. Available at: https://www.gpma.co.za/news/special-process-for-the-relocation-of-evictees-policy-review/. Accessed 15 November 2018.

CoJ. 2019. 'City of Johannesburg Temporary Emergency Accommodation Provision (TEAP): Draft Policy. Policy, Planning and Research Directorate, Version number: 5.0, Working Document, presented by the City of Johannesburg for comment 30 October 2019.

CoJ. 2020. City of Johannesburg Temporary Emergency Accommodation Provision (TEAP). Draft Policy. Policy, Planning and Research Directorate, Version number: 7.0, Working Document, distributed for comment.

CoJ. 2021. City of Johannesburg Temporary Emergency Accommodation Provision (TEAP). Draft Policy. Policy, Planning and Research Directorate, Version number: 7.0, Working Document, approved by Council, 25 February 2021. Available at: https://joburg.org.za/departments_/Documents/Housing/TEAP%20Policy%20February%202021%20Approved.pdf . Accessed November 2021.

City of Johannesburg and Wits School of Governance (WSG). 2015. 'Development of special process for relocation of evictees: Policy, guidelines, programme and implementation plan'. Proposal call.
Klug, TRP SA. 2015. 'Discussion Document – Neil's Input'. Internal discussion document examining the background to evictions in the inner city and the housing situation, 18 May 2015.
Lawyers for Human Rights (LHR). 2015a. 'Development of Special Process for Relocation of Evictees. Policy, Guidelines, Programme, and Implementation'. Proposal, 17 April 2015.
LHR. 2015b. 'Development of Special Process for Relocation of Evictees. Policy, Guidelines, Programme, and Implementation'. Inception Report, 5 May 2015.
LHR. 2015c. 'Review of the SPRE Policy and Development of an SPRE Programme'. Discussion Document. Internal document looking at the jurisprudence related to the relocation of evictees and practical issues facing the City of Johannesburg, 20 May 2015.
LHR. 2015d. 'Analysis of the SPRE Policy. Issues, Gaps and Proposals'. Internal document, 20 May 2015.
Socio-Economic Rights Institute (SERI). 2016. 'Submission on the City of Johannesburg's Special Process for the Relocation of Evictees (SPRE)'. Johannesburg, October 2016.
Socio-Economic Rights Institute (SERI). 2019. 'Submission on the City of Johannesburg Temporary Emergency Accommodation Provision: Draft Policy'. Johannesburg, November 2019.

References

Anderson, L. 2006. 'Analytic auto-ethnography', *Journal of Contemporary Ethnography* 35(4): 373–95.
Beall, J., Crankshaw, O. and Parnell, S. 2002. *Uniting a Divided City: Governance and social exclusion in Johannesburg*. London: Earthscan Publications Ltd.
Beavon, K. 2004. *Johannesburg: The making and shaping of the City*. Pretoria: University of South Africa Press.
Bénit-Gbaffou, C. 2018. 'Beyond the policy-implementation gap: How the City of Johannesburg manufactured the ungovernability of street trading', *Journal of Development Studies* 54(12): 2149–67.
Bevir, M. 2010. *The SAGE Handbook of Governance*. London: Sage.
Cairney, P. 2012. *Understanding Public policy; theories and Issues*. Basingstoke: Palgrave Macmillan.
Campbell, S. 2005. 'Is "Progress" No longer Progressive? Reclaiming the ideology of progress in planning'. Unpublished manuscript. Available at: http://www-personal.umich.edu/~sdcamp/up540/Campbell,progress,draft.pdf. Accessed 25 March 2017.
Centre on Housing Rights and Evictions (COHRE). 2005. *Any Room for the Poor? Forced evictions in Johannesburg, South Africa*. Research report. Johannesburg.
Cohen, M.D., March, J.G. and Olsen, J.P. 1972. 'A garbage can model of organisational choice', *Administrative Science Quarterly* 17(1): 1–25.
Denzin, N. 2006. 'Analytic auto-ethnography, or déjà vu all over again', *Journal of Contemporary Ethnography* 35(4): 419–28.
Dinath, Y. 2014. 'Between fixity and flux: Grappling with transience and permanence in the inner city'. In *Changing Space, Changing City: Johannesburg after apartheid*, edited by P. Harrison, G. Gotz, A. Todes and C. Wray, 232–51. Johannesburg: University of the Witwatersrand Press.
Dladla and the Further Residents of Ekuthuleni Shelter v. City of Johannesburg and Another, South Gauteng High Court, Case No. 39502/2012.
Dugard, J. 2014. 'Beyond Blue Moonlight: The Implications of judicial avoidance in relation to the provision of alternative housing', *Constitutional Court Review* 5(1): 265–79.
Gardner, G. 2011. *Johannesburg – Ten Ahead: A decade of inner-city regeneration*. Johannesburg: Double G Media.

Goga, S. 2003. 'Property investors and decentralisation: A case of false competition?'. In *Emerging Johannesburg: Perspectives on the post-apartheid city*, edited by R. Tomlinson, R. Beauregard, L. Bremmer and X. Mangcu, 71–84. New York: Routledge.

Head, W.H. 2008. 'Wicked problems in public policy', *Public Policy* 3(2): 101–18.

Howlett, M. 2005. 'What is a policy instrument? Policy tools, policy mixes and policy implementation styles'. In *Designing Government: From instruments to governance*, edited by P. Eliadis, M. Hill and M. Howlett, 31–50. Montreal: McGill-Queen's University Press.

Howlett, M. 2011. *Designing Public Policies: Principles and instruments*. London: Routledge.

Jordan, A. and Turnpenny, J. 2015. *The Tools of Policy Formulation: Actors, capacities, venues and effects*. Cheltenham: Edward Elgar Publishing.

Krumholz, N. and Clavel, P. 1994. *Reinventing Cities: Equity planners tell their stories*. Philadelphia: Temple University Press.

Lascoumes, P. and Le. Galès, P. 2007. 'Introduction: Understanding public policy through its Instruments – From the nature of instruments to the sociology of public policy instrumentation and governance', *International Journal of Policy, Administration, and Institutions* 20(1): 1–21.

Linder, S. and Peters, G. 1990. 'The designs of instruments for public policy'. In *Policy Theory and Policy Evaluation*, edited by S. Nagel, 103–19. Westport: Greenwood Press.

Maslow, A.H. 1966. *The Psychology of Science*. New York: Harper and Row.

Moodley, S. 2018. 'Why Do Planners Think That Planning Has Failed Post-Apartheid? The Case of eThekwini Municipality, Durban, South Africa', *Urban Forum* 30: 307–23. Available at: https://doi.org/10.1007/s12132-018-9357-0. Accessed April 2019.

Rittel, H. and Webber, M. 1973. 'Dilemmas in a general theory of planning', *Policy Sciences* 4(2): 155–69.

Rubin, M. 2015. 'Johannesburg's bad buildings programme: The world class city hegemony at work?' In *Urban Governance in Post-apartheid Cities: Modes of engagement in South Africa's metropoles*, edited by C. Haferburg and M. Huchzermeyer, 211–30. Stuttgart and Pietermaritzburg: Borntraeger Science Publishers and UKZN Press.

Salamon, L.M. (ed.). 2002. *The Tools of Government: A guide to the new governance*. Oxford: Oxford University Press.

Socio-Economic Rights Institute (SERI). 2013. *Evictions and Alternative Accommodation in South Africa: An Analysis of the Jurisprudence and Implications for Local Government*, Johannesburg: SERI.

Socio-Economic Rights Institute (SERI). 2018. *Inner City Federation: Fighting for Decent Housing in Inner City Johannesburg*, Community Practice Notes, Social Movement Series. Johannesburg: SERI.

South African Local Government Association (SALGA). 2014. *Understanding and Planning for the Role of Municipalities in Evictions: Case Study of the City of Johannesburg*, Research report. Johannesburg.

Tissington, K. 2018. 'Responses of Municipal Officials to Litigation Around Inner-City Housing in Johannesburg: The Blue Moonlight case ten years on'. Draft paper presented at the international colloquium, *Practices of the State in Urban Governance*, University of the Witwatersrand, Johannesburg, 6–9 June 2018.

Tomlinson, R., Beauregard, R.A., Bremner, L. and Mangcu, X. 2014. *Emerging Johannesburg: Perspectives on the post-apartheid city*. London: Routledge.

Turok, I., Seeliger, L. and Visagie, J. 2021. 'Restoring the core? Central city decline and transformation in the South', *Progress in Planning*, 144.

Wilson, S. 2021. *Human Rights and the Transformation of Property*. Cape Town: Juta.

Part III

Seeing the local state through its policy instruments

9

Identifying learners in Johannesburg's schools: how state rationalities converge to construct institutional xenophobia

Jeanne Bouyat

Introduction

The increasing recurrence of episodes of xenophobic attacks in contemporary South Africa – notably in May 2008, April 2015, and September 2019, directed against African (and to a lesser extent Asian) immigrants confirms the exceptional intensity of xenophobia in this country. Besides these dramatic episodes, incidents of collective xenophobic violence have occurred on a continual basis in low-income[1] urban areas: more than three hundred people have died from it since 1994, thousands of shops have been looted, and more than a hundred thousand have been displaced or forced to leave the country (Mlilo and Misago 2019). Opinion surveys consistently find high levels of xenophobic attitudes among South Africans (Crush 2008; Gordon 2015) and xenophobic discourses are significantly present in the media (Nyamnjoh 2010) and social media (Oyedemi 2015).

The causes of this pervasiveness of xenophobia in South Africa are highly debated. Researchers dispute the relative importance of structural socio-economic factors and the 'relative deprivation' caused by competition for jobs, housing or public services; of psychological explanations such as 'scapegoating', 'isolation theory'; or the 'narcissism of small differences'; and of local factors including the political use of xenophobia by community leaders; how foreign-ness has been historically constructed through urban segregation; or the role of specific labour-related conflicts or criminal incidents (Landau 2011; Orkin 2019). In addition, most publications emphasise that the South African immigration laws are drastically restrictive and that officials from the Department of Home Affairs and of the South African Police Service systematically deny immigrants' fundamental rights, and often commit violence against them (Masuku 2006; Vigneswaran et al. 2010; Peberdy 2001). The role of the police during episodes of xenophobic attacks has indeed been ambivalent, to say the least. Officials often did not protect the immigrants despite warnings, and have conducted raids targeted at 'illegal migrants' during and in the aftermath of xenophobic attacks, in the very same areas.[2] More broadly, perpetrators of xenophobic attacks have hardly been prosecuted, while the displaced victims tend to be criminalised and deported (Monson and Misago 2009; Hayem 2013). These elements point towards the State's role in producing or amplifying xenophobia.

In this chapter I use a range of terminologies to underline the complexities of researching the State and highlight different aspects of this research object. In writing the word 'State' in singular with a capital letter, I try to acknowledge both the artificiality of its unity and the effectiveness of references to this unity and universality to seek authority, legitimacy and capacity to govern. As Bourdieu (2014, 31) puts it, it is a 'social fiction that is not fictitious but operative'. Through the expression 'state institutions', I attempt to highlight the partly independent 'institutional segments' (Biland 2010, 8) that form the State which officially perform distinct functions (such as the Department of Home Affairs and the Department of Basic Education) and the relationships between them and the agents who compose them. Finally, I use the Foucauldian notion of 'state apparatus' to apprehend the State as a set of devices, adopting a 'material approach to state practices' focused on 'instruments, procedures and the political rationalities that underpin them' (Lascoumes 2004, 3).

My doctoral research (Bouyat 2021), whose fieldwork was conducted from February 2016 to June 2018, which was an explorations of forms of xenophobia and anti-xenophobia in the schooling institution with a focus on high schools in low-income areas of Johannesburg, led me to explore this research direction. I had initially conceived xenophobia as a phenomenon that originates outside of the school. I tended to view it as a violent climate that recurrently escalates to crisis levels, which may occasionally ignite responses from the schooling institution, and that more strongly permeates schools located in specific areas where xenophobic attacks happen more frequently. My research methodology was geared at exploring how xenophobia was 'affecting' the school and how the school was 'responding' to xenophobia, through articulating two conceptualisations of the school. The first conceptualisation was as an ensemble of local institutions – schools anchored in neighbourhoods and serving localised communities of learners and parents; and the second conceptualisation was as a state institution – the schooling institution structured in a multilevel administration, regulated by legislations and procedures, and composed of officials who deliver education. I selected schools situated in various low-income neighbourhoods of Johannesburg, where attacks repeatedly occurred on a school's doorstep (in Alexandra and Soweto townships); where the school accommodated many immigrant learners (in the suburb of Yeoville); or when both conditions were combined (in the suburb of Denver). In parallel, I interviewed officials from the provincial and national Department of Basic Education to explore how immigrant learners and teachers were accommodated at school, and how the department's curricular and extra-curricular programmes assisted school staff in responding to xenophobia. Given that addressing racial discrimination has been one of the core drivers of post-apartheid educational policies, which have primarily been articulated around the notions of 'redress' and 'transformation' (Badat and Sayed 2014, 129–33), the schooling institution seemed a good research site to gain insights on the State's response to xenophobia.

However, as my research progressed, I came to reconsider xenophobia as being also specifically produced by and amplified within the schooling institution. The multiple testimonies of incidents of xenophobic discrimination experienced by immigrant learners, heightened in times of attacks, and the popularity of xenophobic stereotypes among learners could indeed be read as xenophobia 'affecting' the school. But this did not explain why immigrant learners faced tremendous difficulties in accessing and remaining at school due to documentary requirements (Bouyat 2021b), why immigrant teachers always had precarious working contracts, or why departmental programmes on anti-discrimination education systematically avoided the term 'xenophobia'. These implied a specific contribution of state institutional mechanisms and of state agents' professional practices to the production of xenophobia – which I call 'institutional xenophobia'[3]. Yet, this contribution is not as straightforward as that of the Department of Home Affairs or the Police. It is more mediated, more indirect. Unpacking it calls for an exploration of the inner complexities and tensions of state institutions, to look for their multiple rationalities. In particular, it led me to explore the forms and the effects of the partnerships between the Department of Basic Education (DBE) and the Department of Home Affairs (DHA) to co-produce immigration control at school. In this chapter, I submit that institutional xenophobia is being constructed through a plural process of 'Home Affair-isation of the school' by looking at the co-development of learners' identification devices by the two departments.

I conceptualise the 'Home Affair-isation' of the school as the process of alignment of the DBE's administration and of schools on the DHA's mandate. The DHA has a dual mandate: immigration control – including the management of asylum – and civic services, which entails the recording of births and deaths, the maintenance of the National Population Register and the issuance of identification documents (ID) to citizens. Hence, I distinguish a *policing* and a *delivering* 'Home Affair-isation'. This dual mandate echoes the department's institutional history, which emerged from the fusion of the apartheid's Chief Directorates for Migration and Civic affairs (Vigneswaran 2011,107).

The 'Home Affair-isation' of the school takes both material and symbolic forms. It refers to an abstract diffusion of ideas within the DBE – its laws, instruments, officials' practices – that mimic Home Affairs' discourses. It also describes the simultaneous adoption of practices of regulation in the DBE that use or indirectly depend on devices produced by the DHA. These processes are not linear nor stable, and are informed by broader processes of nation- and state-building through official identification (Breckenridge 2014), elite and citizenship formation through a political discourse of xenophobia (Neocosmos 2006) and a worldwide drive to tighten borders (Fassin 2011). The concept of 'Home Affair-isation' specifically highlights the institutional contribution of the DHA in producing the routinisation and normalisation of practices beyond its department, in the state apparatus and through its agents.

I empirically track these processes through learners' identification practices and argue that the 'Home Affair-isation' of the school is effective as it does not simply amount to xenophobic surveillance. Rather, it is underpinned by the convergence of managerial, socio-historical justice, and national preference rationalities. Identification devices are primarily presented as tools for socio-historical justice and managerial efficiency in education policies, and by the DBE's officials, and less explicitly for immigration control enforcement at school. Yet, national preference is mainstreamed as immigration control at school is inscribed in the state apparatus through identification devices. This modifies the professional ethos of officials and school staff as they incorporate this participation to immigration control as a new professional norm through a mix of constrain and consent: they contribute to the systematic exclusion of immigrant learners, even if it may subvert their individual intentions.

Immigration control highly permeates South African schools and is enforced through direct and indirect means. Direct practices refer to 'identification and permit checks' (SAHRC 2019, 14). It includes requesting immigrant permits at admission or to register for national examinations, which is systematically practiced in South African schools. It also refers to arrestations, detentions or deportations of deemed illegal immigrant learners while they attend school or are on their way to school. These practices are emerging in South Africa. In Edenvale, in 2017,[4] and in Pretoria in 2018,[5] school administrators have issued letters to immigrant parents which contains a threat that their children will be sent to the police if the parents failed to submit their immigration permits to the school.

Indirect practices entail 'reporting obligations or the sharing of personal information' (SAHRC 2019, 15) by school staff or DBE officials to detect immigrant families staying irregularly. In South Africa, these practices are institutionalised via an inter-departmental collaboration between the DBE and the DHA, notably supported by the Immigration Act of 2002 (Section 44). These indirect practices create a 'general atmosphere of fear' which deters immigrants without permits to access schooling (SAHRC 2019, 15). This calls for an exploration of the inner workings of the state apparatus and how state institutions act through their agents. Here, I submit that Foucault's concept of 'political rationality' is relevant to research counterintuitive processes of institutional convergence which reveal purposefulness. I discuss how it can be operationalised beyond discourse analysis through looking at the materiality and utilisation of policy instruments. This inscription in the state apparatus consolidates a direction for how policies are devised and implemented, and produces a powerful subjectivation of state agents.

I first set my conceptual framework to research the convergence of state rationalities. Then, I describe how it materialises in policy instruments supporting the inter-departmental collaboration that mainstreams immigration control at school. Finally, I emphasise how the professional ethos of the DBE's officials and of school staff is shifted through this collaboration, along hierarchical lines.

The 'Home Affair-isation' of the school as a convergence of state rationalities

This section discusses the concept of 'state rationalities' and how it can be operationalised, conceptually and methodologically, to study my research object. It then identifies three sets of rationalities underpinning the development of learners' identification in South Africa and submit that the 'Home Affair-isation' of the school is supported by their convergence.

Researching state rationalities: showing consistency in policies, instruments, and in the subjectivation of state agents

Researching the purposefulness of the State from the inside considering its internal fragmentation and contradictions is a theoretical and methodological challenge. Policy objectives are often unclear as policies are formulated and implemented by multiple actors and state institutions are highly heterogenous (Bénit-Gbaffou 2018a, 7). Using Clarence Stones' conceptualisation of governing as an activity of selection of matters, populations and areas to be governed at a particular time through 'deliberate efforts to bring about or actively prevent policy changes' (Stone 2013, 4, quoted in Bénit-Gbaffou 2018a), the State might be seen as 'a system of strategic selectivity' and the political struggle as 'a field of competing strategies for hegemony' (Jessop 1994, 221). Researchers interested in the State must explore 'how past processes and strategies have shaped the selectivity of the [S]tate' in privileging 'some strategies over others' (Uitermark 2005, 139). Hence, exploring the State's purposiveness might be reframed as an examination of its motivations to regulate selectively.

As Claire Bénit-Gbaffou (2018b) submits, multiple terms have been coined by different research traditions to make sense of this selection according to 'interests' for neo-marxists, 'preferences' for liberals or 'policy objectives' and 'agenda' in public administration studies. While these approaches shed complementary lights, they tend to adopt a rather static and functional approach to the State. In contrast, the Foucauldian notion of 'rationality' apprehends power and governing practices as fluid and allows to conceptualise the State as a system made of institutions and actors.

By looking for 'state rationalities', I am trying to apply the theoretical and methodological approaches initially developed by Foucault (2008) in researching 'political rationalities' to the narrower domain of state institutions. This might seem an unconventional use of Foucault's concept for at least two reasons. Firstly, Foucault was more interested in the historical constitution of the relationship between the State and other authorities (religious, familial, economic, etc.) and between those who govern and the governed, than in the inner workings of the State. However, even if he did not take the State as his main research object, he was analysing processes of the constitution of the State ('statisation'), of delimitation of its domain of direct and indirect intervention, within the broader 'art of governing'. Hence, his ways of analysing political power in terms of 'problematics of government' can be fruitfully applied to the study of the State, as Rose and Miller (1992) and Lascoumes (2004) have emphasised. Secondly, Foucault coined the term 'political rationality' to make sense of macro-level evolutions in the ways in which the rules to govern are conceived. In his work on the genealogy of the 'arts of governing', Foucault describes the ruptures between the political rationalities that underpin the 'Reason of State' in the seventeenth century, liberalism in the eighteenth century, and various forms of neo-liberalism since the mid-twentieth century. The scale of his analysis and the historical approach may not seem suited to investigate the practices of contemporary state institutions. Yet, as Tikly (2003, 162) underlines, Foucault's work may also be read as an investigation of the 'changing nature of the state as being a function of changing rationalities of government'. Thus, focusing on the contemporary state institutions leads us to analyse how a 'plurality of rationalities of government' (Tikly 2003, 165) articulate with one another, their conflicts or indeed their convergence, and how they 'play out' (Tikly 2003, 171).

In their theoretical elaboration on the 'problematics of government' applied to state power, Rose and Miller (1992, 178) define political discourse as 'a domain for the formulation and justification of idealised schemata for representing reality, analysing it, and rectifying it', and political rationalities correspond to those political discourses that have more 'regularity', are more 'stable'. Hence, the political rationalities of state institutions – which I call state rationalities – are not just rhetorical or contemplative; they are constructed as 'intellectual machineries' to make reality 'amenable' to political programming. They call for and justify the intervention of the State. They are more than a set of ideals or principles; they carry particular conceptions of the objects or subjects to be governed, they produce processes of subjectivation. What is more, these state rationalities are 'translated' into what Rose and Miller (1992, 175) call 'government technologies', which correspond to 'the complex of mundane programmes, calculations, techniques, apparatuses, documents and procedures through which authorities seek to embody and give effect to governmental ambitions'. This does not simply correspond to an 'implementation' of ideas, but rather to the codification and the association between a vocabulary and conducts that are consistent with a particular rationality'. This translation is not solely material, but also cognitive, as Rose and Miller insist:

> actors come to understand their situation according to a similar language and logic ... shared interests are constructed ... common modes of perception are formed ... particular and local issues become tied to much larger ones. What starts out as a claim comes to be transformed into a matter of fact (Rose and Miller 1992, 184).

Hence, researching state rationalities entails investigating these governmental technologies, to identify the plural rationalities (Tikly, 2003) that underpin them.

However, the concept of political rationality has mainly been operationalised through policy discourse analysis only, especially in education policy studies (Tikly 2003; Fimyar 2008). Yet, given Foucault's attention to the 'anatomy of details' (Hibou 2017, xv), the architecture of the state apparatus and the materiality of devices, state rationalities might more adequately be researched through a multilevel analysis of governing practices from strategic planning to microlevel implementation, rather derived empirically from the 'texts of rule', the 'micro-technologies of the everyday' or 'mundane practices' of governing (O'Malley et al. 1997) than from 'abstract principles of rule' (MacKinnon 2000, 295). The production of governable subjects by state institutions entails more than formalising policies and justifying them in policy documents. It requires the inscription of this programming in materiality in order to influence state agents' professional practices and representations. Hence, state rationalities can be excavated from the consistency in policy formulation, technical instrumentation and the subjectivation of state agents. State rationalities underpin policy discourses, are activated through technologies of government and enacted by state agents.

Top-down and bottom-up methodologies may be combined to research state rationalities. Bénit-Gbaffou calls for an investigation of the role of leadership in promoting and diffusing state rationalities to go beyond an analysis of 'public rhetoric' and of the 'ideological vagueness' contained in policy discourses. She contends that 'publicly accessible documents' often mask 'the reality of state practices and objectives' (Bénit-Gbaffou 2018c, 8). This echoes Max Weber's remarks on the tendency of the bureaucracy to 'keep secret its knowledge and intentions' in order to reinforce its power and prevent criticism (1978, 992). Hence, less visible and more informal practices of leadership deserve more attention, which might best be researched through ethnographic methods. Interviews with officials might also be informative: those in higher positions do not always adopt a 'politically correct' language in interviews when they feel that they cannot be held accountable, while middle-rank officials might take it as an opportunity to express their frustration in navigating the discrepancy between the rhetoric of strategic documents and the constrains of implementation. Yet, opportunities to conduct meaningful observations and interviews are rare for researchers who are not embedded in the state institutions they study, as current or former employee, intern, or consultant. Alternatively, internally circulated documents can help to trace practices of leadership. As an outsider to the state institutions under study, I adopted this method to analyse the formalisation of the inter-departmental collaboration between the DHA and the DBE. Noteworthy, the internally circulated documents discussed below were included in annexure of court papers (CCL 2018). Only one (GDE and DHA 2017) was transmitted by an official, with whom I had developed a relationship of trust – after obtaining a research permit, conducting interviews with her and her colleagues, and sending multiple emails. Thus, internal documents can, in specific situations, be accessible from outside.

Complementarily, a sociology of public policy instrumentation is useful to unpack the complex finalities of governing. Alongside Pierre Lascoumes and Patrick Le Galès (2007, 5), policy instruments may usefully be conceptualised as an institution 'carrying a concrete concept of the politics-society relationship'. Warning against a too functional approach to instruments, they emphasise that they can act independently of the initial and remodelled objectives at which their designers aimed. This does not mean that instruments bear no rationalities. Rather, through mapping trajectories of their materiality, stabilised forms may be identified which consolidate techniques of government and specific utilisations, from which may be derived state rationalities. This is most relevant to analyse technical 'tools' (Lascoumes and Le Galès 2005, 15). Bénit-Gbaffou (2018c) further recommends to analyse instruments as 'a system' and pay attention to guidelines and tools maintaining consistency when rhetoric fluctuates. She differentiates instruments that significantly constrain action, assorted with sanctions, from the 'toothless' ones. While exploring state rationalities tends to highlight contradictions and variations of purposiveness within the state, special attention should be given to efforts to build coherence across this fragmented reality. As Gilles Deleuze (1988, 188) in his seminal discussion of Foucault's notion of device: there is a need to 'explain universalities' within the State as they are actively constructed.

Following these methodological considerations, the set of policy instruments analysed in this chapter consistently support immigration control at school from strategic to operational level. Focusing on a tool that 'has teeth' – the South African School Administration and

Management Software – I combine an analysis of its materiality, of associated implementation guidelines given to schools, and of its actual utilisation by school staff.

As state institutions act through their agents, this last aspect is methodologically crucial. Analysing how agents perform their professional duties and how the values or meanings they associate to them – in other words, their 'professional ethos' (Jorro 2013) – are shifted to be aligned on policy formulation and instrumentation is key to empirically evidence state rationalities. Hence, I also focus on processes of 'subjectivation' – broadly conceptualised as 'the formation of governable subjects' (Fimyar 2008, 4) – experienced by officials working in the national and provincial administrations of the DBE and by school staff produced by the inter-departmental collaboration. At this stage, it is useful to differentiate the agents' individual 'intentions' from the 'rationality' of the state institutions where they work, especially when it comes to institutional discrimination (Sala Pala 2010). Indeed, agents may act in line with a state rationality while only partly adhering to the direction inscribed in the state apparatus; the subjectivation of agents may only require minimal consent. Their intentions may clash with the state rationality they reinforce through their professional practices, as they act under constraint. This is the case of school administrators who participate in immigration control as they fear sanctions. Even more, the agents may act in tension with their (stated) intentions without coercion as they are caught in a complex system in which the exclusionary effects of their actions are not immediately visible from the positions they occupy. The agents in higher hierarchical positions, remote from 'street-level' implementation (Lipsky 2010), may be blind to the exclusionary effects of the policies they implement. They are less likely to experience moral dilemmas as they negotiate the tensions between multiple rationalities in state institutions. It facilitates their adherence to the dominant discursive markers of an institutional culture (Biland 2010).

Before tracking state rationalities in instruments and professional ethos, I briefly characterise multiple state rationalities underpinning the development of learners' identification in South Africa.

Managerial, socio-historical justice and national preference rationalities in developing learners' identification

Schematically, official identification may be used for three main purposes: the surveillance and control of the population and of individual 'persons' made 'legible' (Scott 1998; Caplan and Torpey 2001; Lyon 2001), the

Table 9.1 Three State rationalities underpinning identification at school

School's practices of identification	**Function of identification**	**Associated political rationality**	**Post-apartheid trend in state- and nation-building**	
Resource allocation through databases of learners. *Example*: South African School Administration and Management System *(SASAMS)*	Tracking	Managerial	1) Build capacity in State administration for public service delivery	'Delivering Home-Affair-isation'
Facilitate registration and documentation. *Example: Birth registration at school*	Recognition	Socio-historical justice	2) Build equal citizenship to redress the past	
Restrict immigrant's schooling rights. *Example: Visa checked at school admission*	Control	National preference	3) Nationalistic nation-building in context of scarcity	'Policing Home-Affair-isation'

recognition of rights associated with citizenship (Breckenridge and Szreter 2012; Dhupelia-Mesthrie 2014) or counting and tracking for purposes of management and public service delivery (Clarke 1994; Otjacques et al. 2007). These functions are intertwined, as Amit and Kriger underline (2014) through studying the management of asylum and permits' dispensation for Zimbabwean immigrants in South Africa. Yet, they may be conceptually distinguished as they are underpinned by different rationalities. Tracking serves a managerial rationality; recognition is linked to the acknowledgement of citizenship and the redistribution of resources to redress inequalities, and implies a drive towards socio-historical justice and democracy, while control may be associated to sorting out practices underpinned by national preference. These three functions of identification and associated state rationalities embody different post-apartheid state- and nation-building processes, respectively associated with building capacity for public service delivery, constructing an equal citizenship to redress inequalities and injustices of the past, and a chauvinistic form of nation-building in a context of scarcity of resources. The former two are associated with 'delivering' 'Home Affair-isation', while the latter articulates to 'policing' 'Home Affair-isation' of the school (**Table 9.1**).

I argue that the 'Home Affair-isation' of the school is underpinned by the convergence of these three rationalities. Focusing on its policing side – immigration control – I stress that national preference is mainstreamed as it is inscribed in the state apparatus and increasingly informs professional practices and representation of state agents, even in schools.

The inscription of national preference in the state apparatus through instruments facilitating immigration control

I track the inscription of state rationalities in the state apparatus through three types of instruments. Firstly, two strategic instruments are examined: a national inter-departmental protocol signed in 2010 between the DBE and the DHA and a provincial Memorandum of Understanding between the Gauteng Department of Education (GDE) and the DHA signed in 2017. Then, I consider meta-instruments, used to frame the utilisation of tools, to examine the articulation between policy formulation and its instrumentation. I look at letters and circulars sent by a provincial Department of Education giving guidelines to schools on the utilisation of the national software managing learners' identification. Lastly, I scrutinise the South African School Administration and Management Software's component on learners' identification, which I identify as a tool that 'has teeth', and analyse how materiality disciplines school staff's practices of identification of learners.

The Inter-departmental agreements: an infrastructure for 'Home Affair-isation'

Policy instruments consolidating partnerships are useful in tracking rationalities as they formulate a (partly) common purpose for fragmented institutions and official motivations to collaborate. I submit that they both reflect and structure the top-down 'Home Affairs-isation' of schools. This echoes the conceptualisation of device by Deleuze (1988, 191) as both an 'archive' and a 'future'. The national protocol is from its inception rather geared towards policing than delivering 'Home Affair-isation' but remains elusive, while the provincial Memorandum of Understanding more explicitly plans immigration control at school.

The national protocol signed in March 2010 (DBE and DHA 2010) deals with information sharing about learners. It is presented as a way to improve the DBE's internal management, strengthening the accuracy of statistics 'for review of the registers and administrative records of the DBE' and enhancing its 'monitoring and evaluation system'. The DHA must 'track' and 'sort out' 'duplicates' and identify 'ghost learners' (those allegedly over-reported to access more resources, as subsidies and educators are allocated to schools based on the number of learners) and conduct school visits to 'investigate' suspicious cases. Moreover, the protocol plans to roll-out campaigns of birth registration in the schools concentrating learners without birth certificates, identified through the information sharing. Hence, delivering the 'Home Affair-isation' of the school is emphasised in the protocol. Yet, policing 'Home Affair-isation' is present: the protocol mentions that the DHA must 'investigate a mechanism of tracking non-South African learners' (paragraph 4.1). This wording does not specify that this tracking of 'non-South Africans' serves immigration control. Thus, the protocol depoliticises the collaboration as a form of technical progress mainly beneficiating the DBE, while planning the dependency of the DBE's internal software on the DHA's instruments.

The integration of the identification infrastructure of the two departments developed in the following years, incrementally constructing capacity to conduct immigration control at school. This evolution is well perceptible in the provincial Memorandum of Understanding signed in

May 2017 (Gauteng DE and DHA 2017). It officially serves the 'enforcement of relevant provisions of the immigration legislation pertaining to learners enrolled in Gauteng public schools'. Birth registration or management improvement are no longer listed. Schools must provide the DHA with learners' 'identity numbers' for 'verification of names and surnames' and with 'copies of temporary residence visas, permanent residence permits or asylum or refugee permits for verification' of 'foreign' learners. The Memorandum of Understanding compels principals to provide the DHA with a proof of registration and deregistration for learners on study permits, to report the details of immigrant learners who do not have a permit, or 'any discrepancies' occurring during identity verifications. Signed seven years after the national protocol, the Memorandum of Understanding gives an institutional solidity to immigration control at school.[6] Its effectiveness relies on the use of a tool that has 'teeth': the South African School Administration and Management System (SASAMS).

The South African School Administration and Management System (SASAMS): a tool with teeth to enforce immigration control at school

Introduced in 2005, the purpose of SASAMS was 'to provide schools with a cost effective, easy to use and fully integrated computer solution containing all aspects of school administration and reporting requirements' (DBE 2017). Since December 2012, schools must report to provincial education departments using SASAMS. Resources are then allocated based on the numbers of learners recorded on the software. I argue that it serves, among multiple purposes, the mainstreaming of immigration control at school.

I focus on a series of internally-circulated documents giving instructions to schools on the use of SASAMS in the Eastern Cape. Similar to the national protocol, they primarily emphasise managerial rationalities to develop learners' identification, but are also geared towards immigration control.

In November 2015, a circular entitled 'academic year program of submission of SASAMS databases' (ECDOE 2015) is transmitted by the Eastern Cape Department of Education (ECDOE) to schools. In the 10 pages of general guidelines on the software, five points concern learners' identification. They emphasise that schools must respect the admission policy and provide accurate details of learners for purposes of management and planning. Identification or passport numbers 'if the learner is an immigrant' must be 'updated' and learners without numbers must be given a 'provisional status' and schools must put 'timely interventions in place' to assist learners to obtain a birth certificate or ID, which can be achieved through the collaboration 'between the DBE and the DHA'. Thus, it stresses the need to build accurate data and presents the protocol as a tool to assist learners with documentation.

Some months later, in March 2016, a second circular (ECDOE 2016a) is sent with far reaching consequences. Authoritatively entitled 'Schools to update SASAMS with identity or passport numbers of learners', it announces a new funding model: only learners whose identity numbers have been successfully captured on SASAMS will be counted for the allocation of subsidies and educators' posts, including for the nutrition programme. This applies to the most deprived no-fees schools, solely relying on subsidies. This decision is justified to consolidate data reliability for financial reporting; as it is used to allocate resources, SASAMS 'cannot be compromised'. Supported by detailed charts, the circular stresses that 420,000 learners have no ID numbers in Eastern Cape schools, including 93,000 duplicates, which leads to 'over-payment' that schools must refund – it echoes the 'ghost learners' wording of the protocol.

A letter sent in May 2016 (ECDOE 2016b) emphasises the need to enter 'study permit' numbers in SASAMS, and another one sent in June 2016 (ECDOE 2016c) mentions that 'undocumented' learners' details are communicated to the DHA. Lastly, a letter sent in September 2016 (ECDOE 2016d) announces the appointment of a firm to conduct 'verification of learner profile data, including their identity document numbers'.

Thus, the guidelines insist on improving tracking for management purposes, but also for immigration control. They give flesh to the 'Home Affair-isation' of the school consistent with the strategic planning of the protocol, using the biting 'teeth' of resource allocation. Similar funding models have also been introduced in KwaZulu-Natal in 2017 (KZNDOE 2017) and in Limpopo in 2018 (Limpopo DOE 2018).

The materiality of SASAMS further supports immigration control at school. The software component dedicated to recording learners' identification contains two boxes. The 'registration information' box contains all the necessary details to monitor the schooling journey of the learner: the date and Grade when the learner entered the schooling system, the learners' names, and most importantly the 'Learner Tracking Number'. It is derived from the national learners' database maintained by the DBE, and enables learners to be followed individually as they change schools. It is also used for planning and budgeting purposes. On the other hand, the 'identification details' box contains information used to code and verify learners' identities based on age, gender, and race[7] criteria, and a photograph. Most significantly, SASAMS' identification section contains items for learner's 'citizenship' and 'Identity Number' or passport and study permit numbers for non-South Africans, issued by the DHA. Thus, it makes SASAMS dependent on DHA's identification devices. The software even requests reasons for an absence of ID/passport/study numbers.

Learners' details are usually entered by secretaries. One of them, based in a private low-fees school in Yeoville which accommodated learners of more than 14 African countries, showed me how she did it. The interaction illustrates how SASAMS creates the impression that it can authenticate identification numbers:

> I ask, 'Can you not put any identification numbers in those boxes?' And she responds that 'the system is aligned with the DHA's records' and would detect fraudulent or random numbers. The software 'can even identify the expiry dates of immigration permits', she adds. As I look incredulous, she opens the software to show me. She clicks on the sub-module on learners' information. Two windows pop up. The first one indicates that it is a learner's birthday while the second presents three rows: the first two (in light red) contain the details of learners whose permits are about to expire, and the last one (in dark red) those of a learner who no longer has valid documentation (Fieldnotes, Yeoville, 30 October 2017).

Through intimidating pop-up windows and red colours, SASAMS automatically generates warnings to remind the secretary that she must check learners' permits, and it seems to send this information to the district and to the DHA. In fact, the screen only recalls the information entered by the secretary herself, which is not integrated with the National Population Register and immigration registers.[8] Nevertheless, the software's design is persuasive enough to discipline the secretary, who believes she is under institutional surveillance. She participates in immigration control, even though she is individually reluctant to do so. She indeed emphasised that 'it is not the school's role to check fraudulent documents' but still reported data serving immigration control. Thus, SASAMS works as a low-cost governmentality device, partly for immigration control.

The DBE uses SASAMS among other tools to track the identification and documentation of immigrant learners. The online admission gate in Gauteng, used by parents to apply for a school, also differentiates the submission of 'South Africans' and 'Non-South Africans' and requires ID numbers. Since 2018, the system is integrated with the National Population Register and conducts real-time verifications of ID numbers for South Africans while permits' numbers are retrieved and manually verified by DHA officials.[9] Most significantly, immigration control intensifies at the end of high school national exams, the Matric. According to principals, immigrant learners and lawyers, it is very difficult to obtain Matric results and certificates without an ID number, and learners on asylum seeker permits also struggle to obtain them. These certificates, which have no ID numbers, do not enable access to university or formal jobs.

Thus, this set of policy instruments consistently inscribes immigration control at school in the state apparatus. This disciplines the practices of agents using them, and shifts their professional ethos.

The subjectivation of the Department of Basic Education's (DBE) officials and school staff to enforce immigration control through constraint and consent

The mainstreaming of the rationality of national preference in the development of learners' identification is most strongly evidenced through the participation of school staff and DBE's officials in the enforcement of immigration control at school. The shift in the professional ethos of the school staff operates through a fear of sanction, while it takes a more persuasive form for the DBE officials.

The fear of sanction limits school staff's ability to attenuate immigration control

The interactions between officials of the DHA and school staff are mainly structured around late birth registration and the issuance of identity documents – the delivering form of 'Home Affair-isation' of the school, geared towards the recognition of rights for learners. However, this assistance does not benefit immigrant learners, even when school staff or NGO members explicitly push for them to obtain documentation. Only a few temporal arrangements occur between schools hosting immigrant learners (in Yeoville in particular) and specific DHA offices. School administrators tend to be encouraged and even put under pressure to participate in immigration control, as acknowledged by a DHA regional centre manager:

> *'Can school staff be arrested if they admit learners without proper documentation?'*

'Principals can be charged – arrested is a big word! We go out for warnings, we go and inform about the danger, they must know what is wrong' (Interview with the manager of a regional centre of the DHA in Soweto, 19 April 2016).

This threat of sanctions is at times directly communicated by DHA's officials during school visits or professional trainings at the Education district level. In addition, education district officials transmit similar messages, as the deputy principal of a school in Soweto explained:

> There was a time where Home Affairs was saying they will raid schools. To find foreigners there. I think this was three or four years ago. But they never did. ... At the education district, they told us: Home Affairs can come in and have you arrested as a principal, because you have learners who don't have study permits (Interview with a deputy principal of a school in Soweto, 12 June 2018).

When the source of knowledge is DHA's officials, as appears to be the case in the township schools under study, threats of sanctions are highly effective. School staff associate hosting undocumented learners with 'breaching the policy'. They still seem to host them but feel they have to 'bury it':

> 'After three months of admission, some learners still do not have the documentation, but the policy requires it. We don't expel anyone. We actually are breaching the policy. ... We end up allowing them to go through until Grade 12 and sit for examination' (Interview with the principal of a public school in Soweto, 14 September 2017).
>
> 'If we take them without the study permit, passport, asylum permit, we have broken the rules of admission. ... Look, we bury it.'
>
> *'You cannot straightforwardly admit them and then assist them with papers?'*
>
> 'Then it is disciplinary hearing. You see why I was saying xenophobia is also institutionalised' (Interview with the deputy principal of another public school in Soweto, 12 April 2016).

The school staff highlighted the sanctions they risk with a striking consistency: losing their job, getting arrested or being fined. The fines were standardly indicated: 'R5,000 per undocumented learners'. The principal quoted above even witnessed a member of staff getting fined:

> 'I only interacted once with [the DHA] on this matter. It was about five years ago. They came to do an inspection. [A clerk at the school] gave a proof of attendance to a learner who was from Mozambique and he was fined R5,000' (Interview with the deputy principal of a public school in Soweto, 12 April 2016).

Moreover, school staff testified of their difficult experiences in attempting to assist immigrant learners with documentation. One former teacher explained that it took her four years to help an orphan learner from Mozambique to obtain a birth certificate. She went to three DHA offices before she resorted to her personal connection with a high rank official:

> 'His mom and dad passed away, he was in a shelter. He was part of my mentoring team. He was a very profound learner, well spoken... That is how I got involved. When I started with him, we tried to get information. Home Affairs would send and say: this is what you need to do. I did everything. But it took me four years, until he was in Matric to get this child documented. Home Affairs has always been reluctant to assist: I have been to three different offices! Three different places: same problems. That prompted me. I knew the director of Home Affairs, but I didn't want to go to him. It is like you ask for a favour. But eventually I went. And he assisted. If they could do it for this learner, I don't see why they couldn't do it for another learner!' (Interview with a previous teacher in Eldorado Park, 13 June 2018).

Another testimony suggests that the reluctance to assist immigrant learners is reinforced by threats. A deputy principal of a school in Soweto explained that he was discouraged to help a Zimbabwean learner to obtain documentation as he was told he would be suspected of child trafficking:

> 'We only assist with advice. Because you know, one runs a risk. If I am actively involved, I may be charged for human trafficking. Because I am facilitating that.'
> *'Really, but who says so?'*
> 'The Home Affairs people.'
> *'Did you actually try and got told this?'*
> 'Yes, here in Soweto. It was a kid from Zimbabwe. I was told: look, don't interfere, let the parents do it' (Interview with the deputy principal of a school in Soweto, 12 June 2018).

In Yeoville, where legal advocacy groups and migrant organisations interact with schools, the school staff can insist that 'they are not the DHA' and give advice for regularisation. However, they are also forced to implement strict documentation requirements for Matric.

Hence, school staff take part in immigration control and enact the rationality of national preference as they are constrained by a fear of sanction and computerised systems of identification. For the DBE's officials who work in the bureaucracy, the participation in immigration control is more consented.

Towards a normalisation of immigration control at school among the Department of Basic Education's (DBE) officials?

Indeed, the institutional culture within the DBE seems to be shifted through inter-departmental collaboration. The notion of institutional culture helps to conceptualise how an institution creates a 'stimulation to act' (Biland 2010) and 'gives a collective meaning to actions' (Lagroye 2006, 259). It foregrounds the capacity of institutional devices to produce 'subjectivation' among its agents. It refers to a form of collective habitus that is unevenly incorporated according to the agents' positions and reconfigured by the internal tensions and circulations within an institution, and by processes of convergence and divergence between institutions.

Hence, the 'Home Affair-isation' of the school may be conceptualised as a convergence of the DBE and the DHA's institutional cultures. Indeed, the DHA and the DBE emblematically give shape to the right (policing) hand and the left (redistributing) hand of the State (Bourdieu 1993). As officials themselves synthetise, in the DBE 'we must place the child at the centre' while in the DHA 'we protect our citizenship':

> 'We cannot deny a child's education. I did a diploma in teaching, and the things that were drilled into our heads at the college, it is like we were indoctrinated: we must place the child at the centre. I have taught for 15 years, at a high school. I still think it is our role to place every single child. And I think all of us (in the DBE) work with that understanding' (Interview with a middle-rank official managing admission at the GDE, 10 November 2017).

> 'The responsibility of the DHA is to make sure that we protect our citizenship and ensure that we provide security to *our* people' (Interview with a senior official at the DHA in Gauteng, *emphasis mine* 19 July 2016).

The quotes illustrate the different 'desires for the state' (Hibou 2017, 328) and how learners' identification is understood in line with the institutional culture of each department. However, through the inter-departmental collaboration, the officials within the DBE experience a transformation of their professional ethos towards a normalisation of the enforcement of immigration control at school. It affects officials in strategic positions more than those who regularly interact with schools and families.

All the DBE officials that were interviewed primarily looked at identification devices in a managerial sense, as tools facilitating planning and accountability. Officials in higher rank positions are more likely to minimise their exclusionary effects. As a senior official in charge of partnerships between schools and NGOs at national level puts it: his focus is on 'policy'. From this 'broad' level, he considers that the intergovernmental collaboration is 'non-discriminatory'. For him, the right to education must be 'looked at within the context of the papers', and pressure should be put on parents to regularise their children. When asked about the exclusionary effects of strict documentary requirements and immigration control at school, he acknowledged that there are 'misinformation' and 'incoherence' between the DBE's and the DHA's positions, but maintained that the DHA tries to assist learners:

> '[When the DHA does interventions in schools] it is non-discriminatory. We intend to assist. But fears do arise, misinformation ... We speak to the level of the policy, but what you see happening on the ground could be a different thing.'
>
> *'But do policies of the Home Affairs challenge the right to education? Since schools have to check papers, and can be inspected by the DHA and principals can be fined ...'*
>
> 'There could be an incoherence between the position of Home Affairs and the position of our Department. The Department will speak to its mandate: we must provide education and Home Affairs will stick to its mandate: to ensure that everyone in the country is legitimate. ... Some principals are not aware of that and have a lot of fear' (Interview with a senior official of the social mobilisation branch of the DBE, 29 March 2016).

Two years later,[10] I interviewed the same official again and he confirmed his position. He approached the inter-departmental collaboration 'from a programmatic perspective', whereby it formally fosters the right to education. The official is so used to designing programmes without questioning the principles of the policies implemented that he tends to depoliticise them: 'You could either say that this law is clearly exclusive of those who do not have papers or say that this law promotes access to papers.' His reflections are bound by the duties associated with his position.

Officials in strategic positions at the GDE tend to adopt a similar perspective. An official in charge of the financial relations and governance of schools stressed that schools cannot discriminate based on nationality or documentary status as every learner must be funded equally. Yet, he believed that 'a minimal recognition criteria' is needed at school and added 'you will not be registered unless you have a certain type of document'. For him, there is no problem of discrimination if 'undocumented' learners are 'ticked off' during the admission phase, and are not discriminated through his actions:

> 'We are using the online registration, and you cannot apply online if you don't input your ID or your permit. That eliminates a lot of challenges. We don't discriminate against a learner coming through. We put the online registration where we automatically have a database that links with our Home Affairs database. So in that way, it puts the barrier on the DHA, not on the schools. By the time it goes to the schools, it's already been ticked off' (Interview with a senior official in the GDE finance branch, Johannesburg, 19 June 2018).

Similarly, an official managing education statistics explained that he communicates information about the documentary status of immigrant learners to the DHA issued from SASAMS. He did not consider it problematic to share these details serving immigration control, but was concerned by the 'inaccuracy' of the statistics 'self-reported' by schools, as he is mandated to ensure data accuracy. I was puzzled by the contrast between his lack of critical perspective on data production and use and his inclusive stance towards immigrant learners and his commitment to education as a tool for emancipation:

> 'You are speaking to an educationalist. I don't care where learners come from. If I am a principal, I will open the doors. From a schooling perspective, the principal cannot simply chase learners. This is an educationalist principle. Education is more than a right, it is a weapon to liberate people' (Interview with a senior official in charge of EMIS at the GDE, 20 June 2018).

Overall, the officials in strategic positions tend to overlook how the institutional production of discrimination works through an accumulation of procedures which join together, as links in a 'chain' (Dhume 2014). Situated at the level of policies, programmes or statistics, they fulfil their professional duties in a segmented fashion, contributing to immigration control. They overlook the exclusionary consequences of their actions, while abiding to principles of non-discrimination.

Officials working at more operational levels tend to be more aware of the exclusionary consequences of their professional practices and express moral dilemmas. They insist that they and school staff do not directly participate in immigration control, but nonetheless justify the information sharing for inclusionary and managerial purposes, and tend to approve the enforcement of immigration control at school. For an official managing admission at the Gauteng Department of Education (GDE), principals are caught in a conundrum, as they are accused of breaching immigration regulations but cannot expel learners:

> 'When a principal enrols an undocumented learner] Home Affairs has the right to fine him because he has breached the law. Now the principal has to expel. But he can't do it! That is the Catch-22. So we issued letters to schools: if the parents show good cause, the district can extend the period up to six weeks. …The school must submit records of undocumented non-South African learners to the district, forwarded to the DHA, so that principals can show evidence that they are not harbouring illegal immigrants' (Interview with a middle-rank official managing admission at the GDE, 10 November 2017).

For this GDE official, the participation of principals and district officials in immigration control through information sharing is part of their professional mandate and guards from legal sanctions. Interestingly, she also justifies it as preventing 'child trafficking' – echoing stereotypical responses to child and women migration in Southern Africa (Palmary 2010):

> 'We have a responsibility towards all the children in South Africa. However, we also have the responsibility to check that we are dealing with the legitimate parents of a child because child trafficking exists! Part of us is that will to protect better. Something harsher needs to be done to abide people to follow the rules. It needs to be done for a purpose. We want the fees exemption and the

> Matric to benefit to all, but you need documentation for that' (Interview with a middle-rank official managing admission at the GDE, 10 November 2017).

The following year, I conducted a follow-up interview with this GDE official and her colleagues specialised in procedures of regularisation for school admission. They all acknowledged that they participate in immigration control, but only indirectly, through information sharing:

> A colleague: 'What we are doing is just compiling the databases and send it to the Home Affairs, but the documents remain with the schools. Should Home Affairs decide to visit a certain school, then they can go check the documents there, upon request.'
>
> *'So it enables both the delivery of documents and immigration control…'.*
>
> The official: 'Yes, indeed. But what is key for us is that we are the DBE. We don't control the borders. That is the role of the DHA. Allow the DHA to do their work, and we will do ours. The school will keep the learners as long as they have submitted the database and declared them, so to speak, to the Home Affairs as undocumented. The Home Affairs has the task to do the policing.' (Focus group with officials of the admission branch of the GDE, 15 June 2018).

I then explicitly asked if they considered it normal to be tasked to facilitate immigration control. They did not welcome the enlargement of their mandate, but approved the enforcement of immigration control at school:

> The official: 'I don't see it as normal, because I feel there is a distinction between the DBE and the DHA. There is so much I have to do, why do I also have to do that?'
>
> Colleague: 'I agree. Our country is not saying no to legal immigrants, but obviously there is a problem with illegal ones. We are undergoing these processes, so that we can assist Home Affairs to assist those who are illegal to be documented. Our intention is to help those learners! But why as a country can't we stand together to do migration control?' (Focus group with officials of the admission branch of the GDE, 15 June 2018).

Another official managing IT development shared a similar view, emphasising inclusionary and managerial aspects while minimising the exclusionary effects of imposing stricter regulations on documentation at school. She considered that 'regulatory rules', including documentary requirements, have to be 'built up' in the digital management systems to improve the 'department's performance' and make them 'fair'. She worked on the online admission gate. For her, the automatisation of identification avoids parents having to queue for long hours at school to negotiate a position and ensures that the only criteria is 'first come, first served'. She wishes to develop an integrated system linked to learners' IDs:

> 'My wish is to have interlinked databases with education, health and social development that would allow for the country to manage its systems technically. You deal with one learner with one ID. It is all about ensuring the quality of the data' (Interview with an official managing IT development at the GDE, 27 November 2017).

She did not acknowledge that the gate filters applicants according to their documentary status. With regard to immigration control, she insisted that the DBE should align itself with the DHA:

> 'If there are challenges with [a non-South African] learner, we should have one unique response as the government. We are aligning ourselves with the Home Affairs. We register the learners but they need to know who is in the country. We will not deny anyone access. But if we allow someone that has no documentation, we are caught in a Catch-22 situation! We want to ensure that we don't have contradiction with the Home Affairs' policies' (Interview with an official managing IT development at the GDE, 27 November 2017).

Thus, the distance from the daily reality of schools and professional duties significantly influences how officials consider their collaboration with the DHA and immigration control at school.

A similar stratification of institutional culture within the French Department of Education is described by Colette Le Petitcorps (2019). She compares the professional ethos of teachers facilitating the schooling of newly arrived immigrant learners with that of 'inspectors' higher up in the hierarchy. She shows that teachers, who are in daily contact with immigrant families, are mainly concerned with providing access to school near to the immigrant learners' place of residence to facilitate their local integration, while inspectors prioritise the effective allocation of teaching posts within budgetary limits, as the integration of immigrant learners is only one mission among the 'package' of duties managed by inspectors. Her analysis converges with mine in revealing that officials in higher hierarchical positions are more likely to incorporate managerial rationalities and to support immigration control than those in operational positions. Thus, the subjectivation of officials is stratified along hierarchical lines.

Conclusion

Learners' identification devices at school are co-developed by the DBE and the DHA and are underpinned by a convergence of managerial, socio-historical justice and national preference rationalities. The mainstreaming of the rationality of national preference results in a stricter enforcement of immigration control at schools. This mainstreamning is evidenced because it is consistently formulated in policies of inter-departmental collaboration and materially inscribed in the state apparatus. It impacts the allocation of resources and disciplines the practices of agents in state institutions – albeit unevenly according to their professional position and the specificities of the local context where they operate.

The dominantly rural provincial departments of the Eastern Cape, Limpopo and Kwa-Zulu Natal appear to rely more on the devices of the DHA to control the 'overreporting' of learners than dominantly urban ones, such as Gauteng or the Western Cape. It can be hypothesised that the automatisation of resources allocation based on ID numbers is cheaper than conducting headcounts in remote schools and that it enables the provincial departments to present clean budgets, which is especially crucial for the Eastern Cape and Limpopo departments who have previously been put under the oversight of the Treasury. This might explain their strictness on documentary requirements. Conversely, the school staff in the private schools in Yeoville are less picky on documentation than in the public schools in Soweto as immigrant learners constitute a significant part of their customer base. This suggests that the processes of subjectivation of agents in state institutions are locally differentiated. This echoes the importance of 'site effects' on the accommodation of immigrant learners at schools and on school staff's abilities to circumvent the institutional production of xenophobia (Bouyat 2019).

In addition, processes of 'Home Affair-isation' are not specific to the schooling institution in South Africa. Hospitals (Kaplan 2011; Crush and Tawodzera 2014), social services (Ncumisa and Mfubu 2016) and police services (Demeestère 2016) also undergo similar transformations that support immigration control. Nevertheless, there seems to be a particular capacity for resistance to the 'Home Affair-isation' of the school from outside the schooling institution. Indeed, in December 2019, after three years of litigation, the identity documentation requirements for school admission were declared unconstitutional and the Eastern Cape's DOE was forced to abandon its funding models derived from the SASAMS's data.[11] It remains uncertain whether this court ruling will be sufficient to dismantle the deep inscription of immigration control at school in the state apparatus and to revert its normalisation among officials of the DBE. The fact that the court ruling has not declared immigration control at school unconstitutional makes this unlikely.

Looking for state rationalities, through their inscription in the state apparatus and in the subjectivation of state agents, and showing paradoxical processes of convergence between and within state institutions, helps to conceptualise the construction of institutional xenophobia, beyond the 'right hand' of the State. Indeed, institutional xenophobia stretches beyond the harassment of immigrants by the Police and Home Affairs' officials or the adoption and enforcement of stringent border control or asylum policies. The participation of a wide range of state institutions in immigration, often in collaboration with private firms, necessitates the investigation of a more diffused and mediated form of institutional xenophobia, including by the 'left' hand of the State, such as the schooling institution.[12] Identifying multiple state rationalities shows how institutional xenophobia is never 'pure' but is always supported by or hidden behind other more laudable political ends such as allocating resources more efficiently, registering citizens to grant them rights, fighting corruption, or preventing crime. In paying attention to the materiality of state practices underpinned by these multiple state rationalities, it is possible to tangibly identify the concrete steps that incrementally (through signing Memorandum of Understandings, interacting with the DHA's officials at school) or abruptly (through new funding rules based on automatic software such as SASAMS) construct institutional xenophobia. In parallel, investigating the subjectivation of state agents highlights the unevenness of the construction of institutional xenophobia, and how it works through both consent and constraint. Lastly, studying the forms of institutional xenophobia produced by the 'left hand' can also renew analyses of institutional xenophobia produced by the 'right hand', in paying more attention to the frightening effectiveness of managerial practices in exacerbating the exclusion and stigmatisation of those deemed foreign.

Notes

1 I use the term 'low income' to describe neighbourhoods or schools which exclusively host both working class and unemployed households with little income.
2 Bornman, J. 2019. 'Xenophobic mob rampages through Joburg', *New Frame*, 8 September 2019.
3 I further elaborate on my conceptualisation of institutional xenophobia as being both in filiation and distinct from the concept of 'institutional racism' and identify three core dimensions of institutional xenophobia at school elsewhere (Bouyat 2024)
4 Gaum, A. 2017. 'Xenophobia's shameful assault on schoolchildren', *Mail and Guardian*, 10 March 2017.
5 Unspecified author. 2018. 'Pretoria school threatens to remove children of 'foreign parents', *Sowetan Live,* 23 February 2018.
6 Similar provincial agreements have since been passed with similar content in other provinces including the Eastern and Northern Cape, Mpumalanga and Kwa-Zulu Natal.
7 The 'Population Group' or 'Race' boxes remain common administrative categories in post-apartheid state institutions and, as they are often used for purposes of affirmative action, they are routinely asked.
8 The integration was in project. Interview with a GDE official in charge of IT development, 27 November 2017.
9 Focus group with officials from the admission branch of the GDE, 15 June 2018.
10 Follow-up interview with the official, 4 June 2018.
11 Allsop, G. 2020. 'Court decision is major victory for Eastern Cape learners', *Ground Up,* 20 January 2020.
12 I further discuss how the 'Home-Affairs-isation' of the School in South Africa may be analysed as a process of 'righticisation of the left hand of the State' elsewhere, see Bouyat (forthcoming).

I would like to thank Claire Bénit-Gbaffou, Sarah Charlton, Laurent Fourchard, as well as the members of the PSUG research group for their helpful comments on earlier versions of this chapter.

Official documents

Centre for Child Law (CCL). 2018. *Joinder Application for 37 Children and Minister of Home Affairs in the Matter Centre for Child Law and School Governing Body of Phakamisa High school v. Minister of Basic Education et al.* Case 2480/17, Grahamstown High Court, submitted 12 December 2018.
Department of Basic Education (DBE). 2017. 'Note on SASAMS' in *Answering affidavit. Centre for Child Law and School Governing Body of Phakamisa High School v. Minister of Basic Education et al.* Case Number 2480/17, Grahamstown High Court, submitted 31 August 2017.
Department of Basic Education and Department of Home Affairs (DBE and DHA). 2010. *Implementation Protocol of the Intergovernmental Relations Framework Act 2005 Between the Department of Basic Education and the Department of Home Affairs*, signed 1 March 2010.
Gauteng Department of Education and Department of Home Affairs (GDE and DHA). 2017. *Memorandum of Understanding Entered into Between the Department of Home Affairs and the Gauteng Department of Education on Verification of Information in Respect of Admission and Registration of Learners in Gauteng Schools*, signed 5 May 2017.
Eastern Cape Department of Education (ECDOE). 2015. *Circular 7 of 2015*, 16 November 2015.
Eastern Cape Department of Education (ECDOE). 2016a. *Circular 6 of 2016*, 17 March 2016.
Eastern Cape Department of Education (ECDOE). 2016b. *Letter from the National Department of Basic Education to Eastern Cape Superintendent in Education*, 30 May 2016.
Eastern Cape Department of Education (ECDOE). 2016c. *Letter from the Superintendent General*, 6 June 2016.
Eastern Cape Department of Education (ECDOE). 2016d. *Letter from the Superintendent General*, 20 September 2016.
KwaZulu Natal Department of Education (KZNDOE). 2017. *Circular 40 of 2017*, 24 March 2017.
Limpopo Department of Education (Limpopo DOE). 2018. *Circular 109 of 2018*, 18 July 2018.
South African Human Rights Commission (SAHRC). 2019. *Position paper Access to a Basic Education for Undocumented Learners in South Africa*. 12 September 2019.

References

Amit, R. and Kriger, N. 2014. 'Making migrants "il-legible": The policies and practices of documentation in post-apartheid South Africa', *Kronos* 40(1): 269–90.

Badat, S. and Sayed, Y. 2014. 'Post-1994 South African education: The challenge of social justice', *The ANNALS of the American Academy of Political and Social Science* 652(1): 127–48.

Bénit-Gbaffou, C. 2018a. 'Beyond the policy-implementation gap: How the City of Johannesburg manufactured the ungovernability of street trading', *Journal of Development Studies* 54(12): 2149–67.

Bénit-Gbaffou, C. 2018b. 'Unpacking State practices in city-making, in conversations with Ananya Roy', *Journal of Development Studies* 54(12): 2139–48.

Bénit-Gbaffou, C. 2018c. 'Governing street trading in contemporary cities: Anatomy of the policy instruments used by the City of Johannesburg in the post-apartheid era', *Urban Research and Practice* 11(4): 396–425.

Biland, E. 2010. 'Les cultures d'institution'. In *Sociologie des Institutions*, edited by J. Lagroye and M. Offerlé, 177–92. Paris: Belin.

Bourdieu, P. 1993. 'La démission de l'Etat'. In *La Misère du Monde*, edited by P. Bourdieu, 219–32. Paris: Le Seuil.

Bourdieu, P. 2014. *On the state: Lectures at the Collège de France, 1989–1992*. (English edition) Cambridge: Polity Press.

Bouyat, J. 2019. 'Ancrage local et (dé)construction scolaire de la xénophobie: Les effets de lieu sur les représentations de l'étranger chez les lycéens de quartiers populaires à Johannesburg', *Hérodote* 3(174): 65–84.

Bouyat, J. 2021. 'Digitalised paper barriers. Identity verifications and exclusion of immigrant learners in Johannesburg's low-income high schools'. In *Identification and Citizenship in Africa. Biometrics, the documentary state and bureaucratic writings of the self*, edited by S. Awenengo-Dalberto and R. Banégas, 81–100. New York: Routledge.

Bouyat, J. (forthcoming) *'Droitisation de la main gauche' de l'État en Afrique du Sud. Home Affairs-isation de l'École et batailles juridiques autour de la scolarité des Sans Documents*. In Dounies, Thomas, Laborde, Vanille and Silhol, Guillaume (dir.) Fabrique politique de l'École, fabrique scolaire du politique. Villeneuve-d'Ascq, Presses universitaires du septentrion.

Bouyat, J. 2024. 'Gatekeeping the school against foreign Others. Three dimensions of institutional xenophobia at school in South Africa'. In Bouyat, J, *Le Bellec, Amandine and Puygrenier, Lucas (dir.). States and the Making of Others: Perspectives on Social State Institutions and Othering in Southern Africa and Western Europe*. New York: Palgrave Macmillan.

Bouyat, J. 2021. *The school boundaries of the national community: institutional xenophobia, site effects and counter-hegemonic education in high schools of low-income areas of Johannesburg*. Thèse de doctorat. Sciences Po Paris.

Breckenridge, K. 2014. *Biometric State: The global politics of identification and surveillance in South Africa, 1850 to the present*. Cambridge: Cambridge University Press.

Breckenridge, K. and Szreter, S. 2012. *Registration and Recognition: Documenting the person in world history*. Oxford: Oxford University Press.

Caplan, J. and Torpey, J. 2001. *Documenting Individual Identity: The development of State practices in the modern world*. Princeton: Princeton University Press.

Clarke, R. 1994. 'Human identification in information systems: Management challenges and public policy issues', *Information Technology and People* 7(4): 6–37.

Crush, J. (ed.). 2008. *The Perfect Storm: The realities of xenophobic in contemporary South Africa*. Cape Town: South African Migration Programme.

Crush, J. and Tawodzera, G. 2014. 'Medical xenophobia and Zimbabwean migrant access to public health services in South Africa', *Journal of Ethnic and Migration Studies* 40(4): 655–70.

Deleuze, G. 1988. 'Qu'est-ce qu'un dispositif ?'. In *Michel Foucault Philosophe: Rencontre internationale Paris, 9, 10, 11 Janvier 1988*, 185–95. Paris: Le Seuil.

Demeestère, R. 2016. 'Même si tu as tes papiers, ils t'embarquent': Gestion policière de l'immigration Africaine ou institutionnalisation de la xénophobie dans l'Afrique du Sud post-apartheid', *Politique Africaine* 142(2): 145–67.

Dhume, F. 2014. *Entre L'école et L'entreprise, la Discrimination en Stage: Une sociologie publique de l'ethnicisation des frontières scolaires*. Aix-en-provence: Presses Universitaires de Provence.

Dhupellia-Mesthrie, U. 2014. 'Paper regimes', *Kronos* 40: 10–22.

Fassin, D. 2011. 'Policing borders, producing boundaries. The governmentality of immigration in dark times', *Annual Review of Anthropology* 40: 213–26.

Fimyar, O. 2008. 'Using governmentality as a conceptual tool in education policy research', *Educate: the Journal of Doctoral Research on Education,* 3–18.

Foucault, M. 2008. *The Birth of Biopolitics: Lectures at the Collège de France, 1978–1979.* (English edition) London: Palgrave.

Geron, T. and Levinson, M. 2018. Intentional collaboration, predictable complicity, and proactive prevention: U.S. schools' ethical responsibilities in slowing the school-to-deportation pipeline. *Journal of Global Ethics.* 14/1: 23-33.

Gordon, S. 2015. 'Xenophobia across the class divide: South African attitudes towards foreigners 2003–2012', *Journal of Contemporary African Studies* 33(5): 494–509.

Hayem, J. 2013. 'From May 2008 to 2011: Xenophobic violence and national subjectivity in South Africa', *Journal of Southern African Studies* 39(1): 77–97.

Hibou, B. 2017. *The Political Anatomy of Domination.* New York: Palgrave.

Jessop, B. 1994. 'Post-Fordism and the state'. In *Post-Fordism: A reader,* edited by A. Amin, 253–79. Oxford: Blackwell.

Jorro, A. 2013. 'Ethos professionnel'. In *Dictionnaire des Concepts de la Professionnalisation,* edited by A. Jorro, 109–12. Paris: De Boeck Supérieur.

Kaplan, C. 2011. *Migration, Vulnerability and Xenophobia: Central African refugee and asylum seekers' access to health services in Durban, South Africa.* Unpublished paper, Independent Study Project Collection 1112. Available at: https://digitalcollections.sit.edu/isp_collection/1112. Accessed 29 July 2023.

Lagroye, J. 2006. *La Vérité dans L'église Catholique. Contestations et restauration d'un régime d'autorité.* Paris: Belin.

Landau, L. (ed.). 2011. *Exorcising the Demons Within: Xenophobia, violence and statecraft in contemporary South Africa.* Johannesburg: University of the Witwatersrand Press.

Lascoumes, P. 2004. 'La gouvernementalité: De la critique de l'État aux technologies du pouvoir', *Le Portique* (online), 13–14.

Lascoumes, P. and Le Galès, P. 2005. 'Introduction: L'action publique saisie par ses instruments'. In *Gouverner par les Instruments,* edited by P. Lascoumes, P. Le Galès and J. Halpern, 11–44. Paris: Presses de Sciences Po.

Lascoumes, P. and Le Galès, P. 2007. 'Understanding public policy through its instruments: From the nature of instruments to the sociology of public policy instrumentation', *Governance* 20(1): 1–21.

Le Petitcorps, C. 2019. 'L'inclusion des enfants primo-arrivants à l'école: l'institution scolaire à l'épreuve', *Migrations Société* 176(2): 65–78.

Lipsky, M. 2010. *Street-level Bureaucracy: Dilemmas of the individual in public service.* New York: Russell Sage Foundation (30th Anniversary Expanded Edition).

Lyon, D. 2001 'Under my skin: from identification papers to body surveillance'. In *Documenting Individual Identity: The development of state practices in the modern world,* edited by J. Caplan and J. Torpey, 291–310. Princeton: Princeton University Press.

Mackinnon, D. 2000. 'Managerialism, governmentality and the state : A neo-Foucauldian approach to local economic governance', *Political Geography* 19(3): 293–314.

Masuku, T. 2006. 'Targeting foreigners: Xenophobia among Johannesburg's police', *South African Crime Quarterly* 15: 19–24.

Mlilo, S. and Misago, J-P. 2019. *Xenophobic Violence in South Africa: 1994–2018. An Overview.* Xenowatch Report. Johannesburg: African Centre for Migration and Society.

Monson, T. and Misago, J-P. 2009. 'Why history has repeated itself. The security risks of structural xenophobia', *South African Crime Quarterly* 29: 25–34.

Ncumisa, W. and Mfubu, P. 2016. 'No future for our children: Challenges faced by foreign minors living in South Africa', *African Human Mobility Review* 2(1): 423–42.

Neocosmos, M. 2006. *From 'Foreign Natives' to 'Native Foreigners': Explaining xenophobia in post-apartheid South Africa.* Dakar: Codesria.

Nyamnjoh, F. 2010. 'Racism, ethnicity and the media in Africa: Reflections inspired by studies of xenophobia in Cameroon and South Africa', *Africa Spectrum* 45(1): 57–93.

O'Malley, P., Weir, L. and Shearing, C. 1997. 'Governmentality, criticism, politics', *Economy and Society* 26(4): 501–17.

Orkin, M. 2019. *Predicting Xenophobic Attitudes: Statistical path models of objective and subjective factors.* Johannesburg: Gauteng City Region Observatory.

Otjacques, B. Hitzelberger, P. and Feltz, F. 2007. 'Interoperability of e-government information systems: Issues of identification and data sharing', *Journal of Management Information Systems* 23(4): 29–51.

Oyedemi, T. 2015. 'Digital xenophobia: The bullying of 'self' and the cultural caricature of a criminal Nigerian 'other', *South African Review of Sociology* 46(2): 60–76.

Palmary, I. 2010. 'Sex, choice and exploitation: Reflections on anti-trafficking discourse'. In *Gender and Migration: Feminist interventions*, edited by I. Palmary, E. Burman, K. Chantler and P. Kaguwa, 50–63. London: Zed Books.

Peberdy, S. 2001. 'Imagining immigration: Inclusive identities and exclusive policies in post-1994 South Africa', *Africa Today* 48(3): 15–32.

Rose, N. and Miller, P. 1992. 'Political power beyond the state: Problematics of government', *British Journal of Sociology* 43: 173–205.

Sala Pala, V. 2010. 'Faut-il en finir avec le concept de racisme institutionnel ?', *Regards Sociologiques* 39: 31–47.

Scott, J. 1998. *Seeing Like a State: How certain schemes to improve the human condition have failed*. New Haven: Yale University Press.

Tikly, L. 2003. 'Governmentality and the study of education policy in South Africa', *Journal of Education Policy* 18(2), 161–74.

Uitermark, J. 2005. 'The genesis and evolution of urban policy: A confrontation of regulationist and governmentality approaches', *Political Geography* 24: 137–63.

Vigneswaran, D. 2011. 'Migration control, documentation and state transformation'. In *Contemporary Migration to South Africa: A regional development issue,* edited by A. Segatti and L. Landau, 105–119. Paris: Agence Française du Développement.

Vigneswaran, D., Araia, T., Hoag, C. and Tshabalala, X. 2010. 'Criminality or monopoly? Informal immigration enforcement in South Africa', *Journal of Southern African Studies* 36(2): 465–81.

Weber, M. 1978. *Economy and Society: An outline of interpretive sociology.* (English edition) Berkeley: University of California Press.

10
Seeing and unseeing: housing, poverty and privilege on Johannesburg's Corridors of Freedom

Sarah Charlton

Introduction

For more than 20 years Diane lived in a rented room in the backyard of a building on Louis Botha Avenue in Orange Grove, Johannesburg. This is a long-established, predominantly residential suburb flanking the prominent avenue which connects the city's central business district with the northern hub of the township of Alexandra, not far from the high-income suburb of Sandton. In the middle of October 2017, without warning, without any notice period and in contravention of the law, Diane was issued, along with everyone else living in the property, a notice to vacate the premises 'immediately'. The reason given by the notice was 'renevations' (sic). Near to this building, up and down the main arterial it faced onto and along its side street, there was construction activity: refurbishment of buildings, demolition of old houses and building of new ones, much of it with a strong residential component. The main arterial road was itself a hive of construction work: within a stone's throw of Diane's building, a new passenger station was being built for the forthcoming rapid bus system.

The notice to vacate that was issued to Diane and others in the building was blatantly illegal in pronouncing a cancellation of residents' leases,[1] in failing to provide a reasonable notice period, and in its lack of basic information, such as an address for the building (see **Figure 10.1**). But rather than fight the notification, Diane's long-standing dissatisfaction with her shoddy room and the constant change of building owners and managing

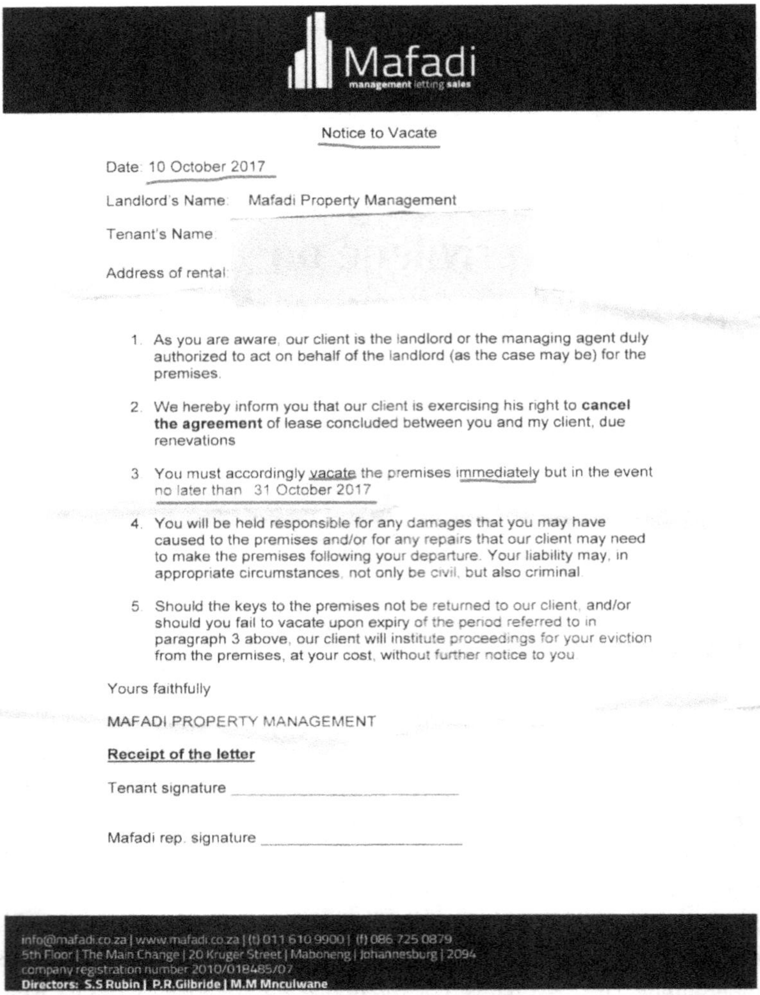

Mafadi
management letting sales

Notice to Vacate

Date: 10 October 2017

Landlord's Name: Mafadi Property Management

Tenant's Name:

Address of rental:

1. As you are aware, our client is the landlord or the managing agent duly authorized to act on behalf of the landlord (as the case may be) for the premises.
2. We hereby inform you that our client is exercising his right to **cancel the agreement** of lease concluded between you and my client, due renevations
3. You must accordingly vacate the premises immediately but in the event no later than 31 October 2017
4. You will be held responsible for any damages that you may have caused to the premises and/or for any repairs that our client may need to make the premises following your departure. Your liability may, in appropriate circumstances, not only be civil, but also criminal.
5. Should the keys to the premises not be returned to our client, and/or should you fail to vacate upon expiry of the period referred to in paragraph 3 above, our client will institute proceedings for your eviction from the premises, at your cost, without further notice to you.

Yours faithfully

MAFADI PROPERTY MANAGEMENT

Receipt of the letter

Tenant signature ______________________

Mafadi rep. signature ______________________

info@mafadi.co.za | www.mafadi.co.za | (t) 011 610 9900 | (f) 086 725 0879
5th Floor | The Main Change | 20 Kruger Street | Maboneng | Johannesburg | 2094
company registration number 2010/018485/07
Directors: S.S Rubin | P.R.Gilbride | M.M Mnculwane

Figure 10.1 'Notice to vacate' issued to Diane. *Emphasis* on the document is mine, stressing the very short notice that Diane was given to vacate her accommodation. Diane's name and contact details have been hidden for confidentiality reasons. Source: © Sarah Charlton 2017

agents, each with new rules and new requirements, led her to look for an alternative place to stay in the neighbourhood. She contacted the author for help. But our search encountered significantly higher prices. The lowest cost room (with shared ablutions) that she found near her building was more than double the price of her current premises, and in addition, required water and electricity charges to be paid over and above the rental amount.

In addition, for many potential leases it was impossible for Diane to meet eligibility requirements. Despite her being a legal citizen, being employed twice a week on a domestic worker's salary and having a bank account with fairly substantial savings, she simply did not earn enough to be considered a viable tenant. Clearly, Diane was falling victim to a form of property boom in the area.

So far, this is a common story of the squeezing-out of poor residents that happens when an area gentrifies (Lees 2014). Property decline, recycling and renewal is a recurring part of Johannesburg's history. However, in this key area for post-apartheid public intervention, the displacement of low-income Black African residents as the result of this intervention was both puzzling and alarming. Indeed, the area formed part of the flagship municipal initiative known evocatively as the 'Corridors of Freedom', a major City of Johannesburg transport-linked development initiated in 2013. The Corridors of Freedom initiative underpinned Johannesburg's bus rapid transit (BRT) system. It constituted a programme of City-guided transformation of the built form and occupancy density along BRT routes to support the functioning and viability of the new transport. Crucially, the Corridors of Freedom initiative aspired to mitigate persistent apartheid geographies, aiming to counter the notorious spatial legacy of apartheid still shaping the lives of many poor people living in less favourable localities. Among its multiple aims were to have 'rich and poor, Black and White living side by side' (CoJ nd(a), 6) along strategic routes in the city.

Herein lies the conundrum: how could it be that such an initiative – with its much-touted ideals of class and race transformation – was implicated in displacing long-standing poor residents? Furthermore, how was it that the intervention was failing to increase low-cost housing options for poor people in these areas, and were shrinking these options instead? How could this be, given also the significant recent history of high-profile litigation in the nearby inner city of Johannesburg, specifically and successfully contesting the displacement of poorer people from well-located buildings as part of urban renewal? In this chapter, I try to explain this anomaly – of the uneven and contradictory housing dimensions of the Corridors of Freedom initiative in Orange Grove – and I make a case for the explanatory power of the notion of a 'politics of invisibility'. Through this, very poor people's specific housing needs along the Corridors of Freedom routes were rendered unseen and therefore unaddressed, including by City officials, and I unpack the factors that enabled this.

Lack of intent, no mechanism, or invisibility?

I start with a brief outline of three possible explanations for the puzzle outlined above, including the invisibility argument, and I use these later in the chapter to frame the empirical discussion.

The first potential explanation is the contention that the Corridors of Freedom was never intended to be a *pro-poor* initiative, in the sense of including *very* poor people (as opposed to less poor, or relatively poor) among its targets and objectives. From this perspective, reading pro-poor aspirations and intentions into the Corridors of Freedom statements and terminology is stretching the project beyond its objectives. While the initiative was indeed intended to shift demographics, this was not to the extent of incorporating those in the very low-income strata but rather those with some funds. I respond to this in two ways. Firstly, by showing later in the chapter terminology from the Corridors of Freedom documents and public pronouncements that clearly include very poor people in its vision. Secondly, I argue that the local conditions along the Orange Grove section of the Corridors of Freedom, coupled with the known desperate need for very low-income accommodation in Johannesburg, the right to housing enshrined in the Constitution and South Africa's well-known mass low-income housing programme, raised reasonable expectations that ultra-low-income housing initiatives were to be included in this flagship undertaking.

A second and related potential explanation for the inadvertent displacement and the lack of pro-poor housing in the Corridors of Freedom initiative could be that there were no mechanisms available to deliver such accommodation, and that the absence of such instruments indicates also the absence of intention or clear policy objective (Bénit-Gbaffou 2018). In other words, if supporting or delivering such accommodation was a real public objective, the necessary programmes and tools to achieve this would have been found and implementation would have occurred. However, I advance a different argument here – not that such mechanisms do exist, but that key officials assumed them to be in place. The means to effect pro-poor housing were assumed to be part of the large national housing programme, and low-income housing delivery was also thought to be possible through private sector initiatives. This was a misconception fostered by blurred terminology and misunderstanding of the notion of 'affordable housing', a phrase widely used, including in the Corridors of Freedom policy documents. Through the vagueness with which such terminology was used, there was not a specific attempt to develop housing interventions for very low-income people, but rather an assumption that affordable housing projects would meet their needs.

A third explanation that is developed in this chapter is the prevalence of a form of 'politics of invisibility' (Razon 2017): very poor people already living in the area, or as a potential incoming target population, are effectively made 'unseen' or only selectively seen by the state and others actors shaping this space. Through this unseeing, a loose grouping of poor people who are not institutionally connected, coordinated or mobilised become vulnerable to displacement or having their circumstances worsened. I try to understand the construction of this 'invisibility'. Despite the state being the key driver of the Corridors of Freedom initiative, I see the problem emanating from a more interstitial space, part of a broader failure of society where the state is one significant protagonist. Thus, I extend the discussion of visibility or selective visibility beyond the state to include that of organised middle-income residents and others, in a situation where the vision of the future for the neighbourhood but also of its status quo, rested on the combined efforts of multiple state and non-state actors. Through these processes, the place of very poor people was largely glossed over. While some of this was to do with literally not recognising the extent and depth of low-income housing need, it was also about not seeing the gaps and omissions in responses assumed to be meeting this need, nor recognising the diverting power of other imperatives that clamoured for attention. Ultimately, the chapter points to the fragility of the transformation efforts by local governments with seemingly progressive objectives, at the complex and multi-faceted interface between policy, strategy, and implementation. The chapter aims, as with Razon (2017, 56), to contribute to 'a more complex understanding of the role of visibility in state practices', and in the next section I briefly conceptualise the construction of invisibility.

Constructing invisibility

Razon (2017, 57) analyses 'the *making* of invisibility', arguing how this is used to avoid addressing some problems and populations in favour of addressing others, with the avoidance concealed through omissions, silences and rendering people or issues unseen. Thus, he argues in the Israeli context that 'it is through the production of invisibility that neglect and exclusion come to be justified and obscured, and themes of inclusion and democracy can be highlighted'. In a different context, Roy's (2009) concept of 'unmapping' has resonance, referring to the sometimes fine-grained detail of different land conditions and claims that are literally not mapped and recorded by authority, thereby opening the way for the state to exploit the uncertainty and ambiguity it has itself created through its lack of recognition and documentation.

Razon calls for 'attending to how state officials make particular individuals, communities and histories invisible', as this helps to explain contradictions within an institution, such as advocating an 'ideology of equality despite a hierarchy of privilege' (Razon 2017, 55). In Razon's discussion, the hierarchy of privilege is a tangible one, inscribed into the complex duality of citizen versus national in Israel, and the production of invisibility is deliberate and nefarious, for political ends. While inspired by this notion of the production of invisibility, I use it differently in the Corridors of Freedom housing issue discussed here, intrigued by how a population comes to be overlooked despite what I see as progressive intentions rather than deliberate attempts at exclusion. Therefore, the 'politics' in the situation is a different one, to do with how local participatory processes play out, how roles and responsibilities are understood, and what assumptions are made.

A transitioning neighbourhood

To understand the type of transformation envisaged by the Corridors of Freedom initiative and the opportunities it presented, I briefly describe the neighbourhood of Orange Grove, a particular sub-section of the Louis Botha Avenue portion of the Corridors of Freedom initiative. The area is a former middle-class White suburb (largely immigrant working class in the 1930s and 40s), and is described at the start of the Corridors of Freedom initiative as having 'a fine grain of historical houses tightly packed on small erven[2] arranged along narrow streets' (CoJ 2016, 19). The City noted that 'in recent years the character of the neighbourhood has changed with residents erecting high walls and fences as a response to the high crime rate experienced' (CoJ 2016, 19).

Louis Botha Avenue is a key arterial road running through the area, lined with a mix of four or five storey buildings, generally with retail on the ground floor and residential above, and some low-rise, single-story houses. Most of the rest of the area has single-story detached housing, many in tree-lined streets with a suburban feel. Louis Botha Avenue itself has become somewhat degraded in recent times, with several buildings showing poor maintenance and upkeep, and the retail showing signs of economic struggle and awkward adaptions to crafting smaller lettable spaces.

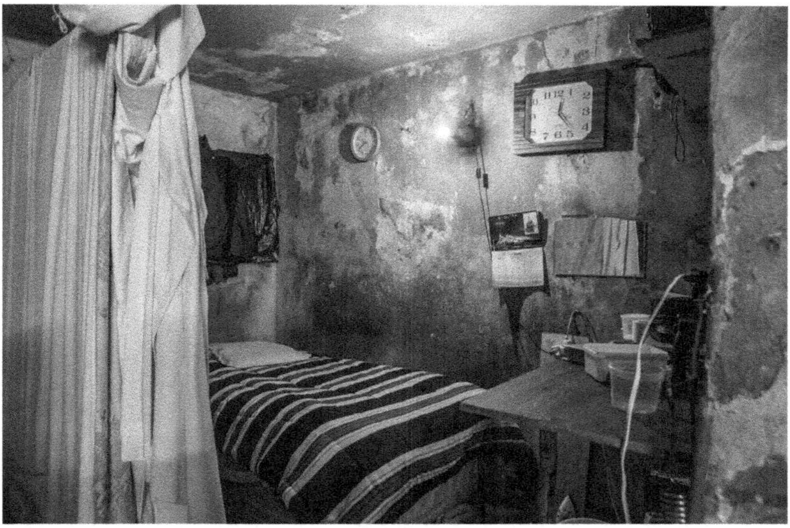

Figure 10.2 Small subdivided living space, Louis Botha Avenue.

Source: © Mark Lewis

The detached suburban houses would traditionally have been owned freehold, typical across the suburbs of Johannesburg, and in the Corridors of Freedom processes it seems the City recognised most residents of the area in their role as property owners. However, in an interview, a senior City of Johannesburg Planning official noted that among the residential typologies are also backyard rooms, though these are not easy to see behind garden walls and houses (CoJ senior Planning official A interview, May 2017). These are small rooms for rent, generally with shared ablutions, often part of generally poor-quality staff quarters built at the time of constructing the main house. In addition, personal observation as well as key informants confirm many 'rooms and spaces' (Mayson and Charlton 2015) in the area – referring to small, low-cost lettable spaces created through informal sub-divisions in houses and apartments (see also Appelbaum 2016). Notices on specific walls along Louis Botha Avenue advertise these spaces and rental amounts, echoing a similar market and 'churn' or turnover of very low-income rental accommodation in nearby central city areas in Johannesburg (Rebelgroup 2016; Mayson 2019). Interior photographs of living arrangements taken in 2016 and 2017[3] starkly illustrate how basic and inadequate some of the living conditions are in the area (**Figure 10.2**). Together, these existing and generally non-conforming typologies in Orange Grove – yard dwellings, subdivided houses and multiple-occupancy flats – signal the presence of many tenants in addition to owners, and of a significantly lower-income population within the suburb than typically reflected among property owners. Drawing partly on a small survey[4] done in 2016, Appelbaum notes not only significant population growth in recent decades[5] but changes in the demographic and racial mix of the area, and that:

> While very few households earn no income or less than R1,500 per month, 20 per cent of residents surveyed live in households earning between R2,500 and R4,500, putting them in a relatively low-income bracket (Appelbaum 2016).

There is no clear information on how many people living in the area are in these very low-income cohorts, or how many are living relatively hidden within the building envelopes of the various typologies mentioned above. It is also not clear how much displacement of the kind described at the beginning of the chapter through Diane's experience, is actually occurring. What is not in dispute, however, is the dire need for accommodation in this area for people with highly constrained incomes who are looking to pay around R1,800 and below for a combined shelter and services package. This would require an income of approximately R5,400 per month. The evidence for this need can be seen in the adverts seeking and offering cheap accommodation, in the work done for the City of Johannesburg's Inner City Housing Implementation Plan (Rebelgroup 2016), and in the personal observations and experiences of key people involved in the Corridors of Freedom initiative or in analysing it (Appelbaum personal communication; CoJ official B interview, April 2016).

Exploring explanations

So how was it that people in these basic housing circumstances and very low-income ranges were not the subject of specific housing interventions as part of the Corridors of Freedom work in the area? I return to the three possible explanations introduced earlier in the chapter, starting with refuting the idea that this demographic was not included in the intended target group of the Corridors of Freedom initiative.

Intended target demographic

As noted earlier, the Corridors of Freedom was an initiative in support of the city's new BRT system, and was intended to shape the land use and intensity of development on either side of the transport routes. But from a spatial perspective, these interventions did not only aim at a localised impact in the immediate vicinity of the bus routes; they had city-wide aspirations of spatial transformation. Mayor Parks Tau boldly stated that:

> When we launched the Corridors of Freedom last year, we emphasised that our intention is to address what the National Development Plan refers to as 'the challenge of apartheid geography' (Tau 2014).

The Corridors of Freedom initiative was articulated as a key way to 'transform entrenched settlement patterns that have kept many marginalised communities at the outskirts of the City, away from economic opportunities and access to jobs and growth' (CoJ nd(b), 9). The reference to settlement patterns signalled that the initiative was not only about facilitating better commuting and mobility from outlying areas, but also about shifting typical and historic arrangements of who lived where in the city.

Thus, included in the envisioned changes were shifts in the racial and economic profiles of residents living along the Corridors of Freedom routes. The text used to describe the Corridors of Freedom initiative indicates that people previously living in far-out parts of the city and relying on long hours travelling in public transport were among those who would not have to travel so much in the future, through finding a convenient place to live along the Corridors of Freedom routes. As **Figure 10.3** shows, publicity documents reference 'the majority of South Africans' as experiencing the inconvenience and injustice of spatial apartheid that the Corridors of Freedom will help change; this notion of 'the majority' would necessarily encompass large numbers of very poor people, thus linking them here to the target demographic.

The long hours of travel in the above text references people living in apartheid-era townships and similar localities, and references Black residents historically confined to these areas. Not all Black African households in townships are poor by any means, but many are, and speeches and documents on the Corridors of Freedom initiative signalled that poor households were included in its vision, through using wording such as 'marginalised communities' (CoJ nd(b), 9) in

Hearing the voices of people

For the average Joburger the option to live in close proximity to public transport facilities with easy access to the City and to make use of an improved transport system will be a life-changing experience.

Gone will be the days of being forced to rise at dawn to catch a train, bus or taxi to a place of work. Gone will be the days of days of returning to your home late in the evening, unable to share a family meal together or spending quality time with your spouse and children.

The Corridors of Freedom will usher a new era of access to opportunity and a choice for residents to work, stay and play within the same space without the inconvenience and high costs of travelling over long distances every day.

The majority of South Africans have been forced by apartheid social engineering to live on the outskirts of cities and towns. In terms of these policies they were temporary sojourners, fit only to provide cheap labour to industry and commerce, unable to share in the fruit of their production.

Although the transition to democracy in 1994 brought fundamental changes in political freedom to the majority of South Africans many of the racially-based settlement patterns remained in place.

All this will change through the development of the corridors of freedom based on an effective public transport system and high-density neighbourhoods closer to the places of economic opportunity giving rise to sustainable human settlements.

Figure 10.3 Extract from *Corridors of Freedom: Re-stitching our City to Create a New Future*. This extract from an official presentation of the Corridors of Freedom initiative, aimed at the broader public, explicitly refers to linking the peripheral areas of the city (the townships where Black residents were previously segregated) to areas of job opportunities.
Source: © Group Communication and Tourism Department (CoJ nd(a))

describing current problems that the Corridors of Freedom initiative would address, and in extending its vision to 'residents and citizens of Johannesburg from *all* walks of life' (CoJ 2014, *emphasis* added). Poverty-stricken residents were specifically referenced at times. As noted at the beginning of the chapter, in the Corridors of Freedom promotional material, one of the specific features of the Corridors of Freedom initiative was identified as 'rich and poor, Black and White living side by side' (CoJ nd(a), 6). And in his state of the city speech in 2015, Mayor Parks Tau stated that the Corridor of Freedom initiative along with the transport intervention:

> … is the leading edge of an approach that will alter the spatial destiny of the City. Left to the forces of the market alone, the poor would be cast to the edges of the City, huddled together in crowded shacks, trapped there by the cost of mobility. This is exactly what we seek to disrupt and transform when we speak of confronting apartheid spatial patterns (Tau 2015).

The creation of housing along the Corridors of Freedom routes was seen as one of the key tools to achieve this transformation (Tau 2014). Diverse housing options and typologies were envisaged (CoJ nd(a), 6) and specific budget at local authority level was set aside to assist with this. In 2014, the City's promise was that 'R225 million will be spent over the next three years on housing projects within the Corridors' (CoJ 2014). As Mayor Tau summarised it:

> The corridors programme, as we have outlined in the last two State of the City speeches, uses public transport as the backbone of new kind of mixed-use, mixed-class development, and focuses on location and affordability of housing as an enabler to embrace economic vitality and diversity of Joburg (Tau 2015).

It is clear therefore that among the multiple objectives of the Corridors of Freedom initiative was the inclusion of poor people in the adjacent developments and neighbourhoods – or at the absolute minimum, the wording of publicity and promotional material can certainly be interpreted this way. However, there was lack of clarity both within and outside of the state as to how this 'inclusion of poor people' would be achieved, and the vagueness, obfuscation and confusion around this is something I turn to in the next section. Before doing so, however, I return to the specific context of the Orange Grove section of the Corridors of Freedom, to argue that there was a lack of clear understanding that 'poor people' similar to those identified to benefit from the Corridors of Freedom initiative, were already living in the area as described above. There was therefore little done to protect their existing foothold, leaving them relatively invisible and vulnerable to the forces of change that were unfolding.

Certainly, the presence of poorer people along the Corridors of Freedom routes *more generally* is acknowledged by the City. For example example, the Louis Botha Strategic Area Framework (which covers a much wider stretch of the route than Orange Grove) notes under the heading of 'Conversion and regeneration of buildings for affordable housing':

> There are numerous buildings along the Louis Botha spine that have fallen into disrepair, are over-crowded and have become 'slum' housing facilities. Many of these buildings have 100–20 m flats occupied by as many as six families. There is a strong indication that the services are no longer paid, and that the building is in default with the City. These buildings should be mapped in the next stage

of the study, and the full assessment done of the suitability of the building as a regenerated affordable housing development. This will assist the city or designated housing agencies to target these as potential investments (CoJ nd(b), 43).

However, it is not apparent that this situation of multiple-occupancy or 'slum-housing' was understood to also occur in the Orange Grove portion of Louis Botha Avenue (as opposed to the Wynberg or Marlboro end of Louis Botha Avenue, near Alexandra). Several times a key official directly involved in the Orange Grove development commented that that City officials don't seem to know who is renting what space in the area and what rental amounts are people paying (CoJ official B interview, April 2016). Pointedly, this official noted that he 'doesn't know who (which officials in the City) goes *into* buildings' to find out what is going on within them. Instead they are 'read as external fabric': in other words, what the buildings' exteriors indicate at face value about occupancy and land use (**Figure 10.4**), rather than what the de facto situation within occupied or subdivided building envelope might be (CoJ official B interview, July 2016. In this way, the extent and depth of cheap living and low incomes remained unconfronted.

Urban planning officials within the City did try and get a better understanding of many aspects and characteristics of the Corridors of Freedom initiative, partnering with Agence Française de Développement (AFD) and the University of Witwatersrand's researchers in a substantial project[6] which aimed to 'provide operational support to, and empirical evidence for, the City of Johannesburg's Transit-Oriented Development (TOD) programme' (Appelbaum 2016, iii). Appelbaum noted that it became clear in the course of investigation 'that some planners are reliant on the overarching spatial plans – such as the Louis Botha Strategic Area Framework – and have little local knowledge of Orange Grove' (Appelbaum 2016, 54). Significantly, 'there was confusion among some planners as to whether anyone living in Orange Grove would fall into the qualifying income bracket for social housing' (Appelbaum 2016, 54). Social housing – in South Africa, a term for a specific rental programme within national housing policy – targets people with incomes significantly higher than those of poor residents being referred to here, accommodating working and salaried relatively low-income people, not the very poor.

However, in the City–AFD–Wits project, the need for this very low-income housing and strategy around it is also not flagged, though the potential for displacement in Orange Grove through increased rentals is recognised, mainly in relation to migrants (Appelbaum 2016, 57).

Figure 10.4 Typical retail and residential building along Louis Botha Avenue. The external fabric of the neighbourhood, made up of low-rise brick buildings with retail activities on the ground floor, does not tell us much about their internal subdivisions and the pockets of poverty they may host. Source: © Sarah Charlton 2018

More generally across Johannesburg, there are large numbers of people unable to afford formal housing models in well-located areas. Approximately half of all households in the city earn less than R3,500, for many years the cut-off point for qualifying for full state housing assistance. Of these households, 25 per cent are extremely poor, with incomes between R0–R1,730 per month (adapted from Lembede 2016, 79). Affordability is thus highly constrained, a result of high levels of unemployment and joblessness as well as low-paying casual work, leading some to argue that the shelter problem is economic rather than housing in nature (ICHIP 2016). It is well understood among Housing and Planning officials that there is a need for very low-income housing in the city, though the form and location this should take is not universally shared.

Lack of appropriate instruments signals lack of intention

Moving from the intended target demographic and the evident need for low-income housing, the second potential argument to explain the lack of these initiatives in the Orange Grove area is that there were not appropriate instruments to deliver pro-poor housing. Could the absence of these instruments indicate a lack of clear policy objective, as Bénit-Gbaffou (2018) argues in relation to the mis-management of street trading in Johannesburg? I argue here somewhat differently: that it is rather the misconception that there *were* appropriate endeavours underway that helps explain the omission. In part, this relates to the diverse actors and initiatives envisaged to fulfil the objectives of the Corridors of Freedom initiative.

A key grouping were private sector developers, wooed to invest, build, and find development opportunities along the bus route – most significantly for residential accommodation, much of it rental. Todes and Robinson note that by 2017, the Corridors of Freedom initiative was becoming:

> a space for experimentation, where new forms of private property development focused on the affordable rental housing market are being attempted, in a context where this sector is being 'discovered' as a new source of profitability both internationally and in South Africa (Todes and Robinson 2017, 1).

The provision of 'affordable' housing had become a growth area both in South Africa and internationally, with developers noting 'how large this market is and how undersupplied – with demand seen as almost unlimited' (Todes and Robinson 2017, 6). But, crucially for this chapter, this notion of 'affordable' housing targets *relatively* low-income households but by no means the very poor (see also Butcher 2016). Referring to the bottom end of mortgage housing, it is by no means synonymous with pro-poor accommodation. Sometimes this was shown, though the point not highlighted, in the Corridors of Freedom documents. For example, noting that the 'demand for housing at the affordable housing level is very high' (CoJ nd(b), 45), the Strategic Area Framework for the Louis Botha part of the Corridors of Freedom gives a rental amount of R3,000 per month in an example of an affordable housing development. The document does not discuss this, but this rental amount would imply a minimum income of R9,000[7] (even higher than this if payment for utilities is factored in), which is way about the *maximum* income of about R5,000 per month of the demographic that I am flagging in this chapter.

Further, rental amounts are typically cited exclusive of services/ utilities,[8] and these costs of water, electricity and refuse removal add up to very significant amounts. When added to rental charges, they make the overall cost of living in such apartments beyond the reach of many people. In addition, many potential tenants whose incomes are derived from informal or irregular work cannot meet the entry requirements stipulated by developer-run rental housing – the 'barriers to entry' presented by the need for deposits, formal pay-slips and bank statements, as well as sometimes the requirement to show a South African identify document.

In terms of building typology, achieving rental amounts low enough for poor people would generally require rooms with shared ablutions. In this neighbourhood, Todes and Robinson note reluctance by developers to do this due to concerns about future profitability, as '... dormitory style accommodation and more shared facilities ... could not be easily converted or sold on within real estate markets' (Todes and Robinson 2017, 10). Also, developers argued that the conditions in which they were operating were unsupportive of efforts to create budget accommodation. This is not only because more intensive management would be needed but, more critically, because the uncertainties and inefficiencies of City supply, management and billing of utilities was a major financial risk, constituting 'the single biggest threat for landlords' and causing developers to shift towards more profitable, higher rentals (developer A interview 2017). Ultimately, the vast majority of developer-provided housing in this area is not going 'down market' enough to be affordable to very poor people – and developers argue it is not able to. In their discussion of the Corridors of Freedom initiative more generally (not specifically Orange Grove), Todes and Robinson give examples of very small units being built by developers for prices starting at R1,650 per month, saying these units 'might be occupied by domestic workers, shop workers, nurses, students' (Todes and Robinson 2017, 6) but it is not evident that these prices are being achieved, inclusive of services in the Orange Grove area. With services added of say R800 per month, a rental of R2,450 would require an income of R7,350, perhaps feasible for two domestic workers sharing but not for one – and not accessible for many others in the area.

While officials in the Corridor of Freedom initiative worked hard to attract private sector developers and investors, the introduction of new rental accommodation was not to be left entirely to developers. The Strategic Area Framework for Louis Botha emphasised both social housing and affordable housing obligations for the City:

> To realise the objective of inclusivity, both the public and private sector must deliver on a range of housing typologies that can cater for all the City's residents. The City's role is therefore ... also to extend its own delivery models to create more social and affordable housing within these well located areas (CoJ nd(b), 138).

In the Orange Grove area of Louis Botha Avenue, City officials did indeed promote some lower-income options. The largest and most significant was the City plan to build social housing in Paterson Park, a public open space between Orange Grove and the suburb of Norwood to its west. 'Social housing' in this context refers to rental flats, at least some of which will financed through state subsidies and will be allocated to qualifying households earning between R3,501 and R7,500 per month, or above, (crudely, 'relatively poor households' but not the 'very poor'). However, this development, even though not targeting very poor people, was resisted by the Norwood Residents Association (NORA) in particular, which mobilised over 600 objections (Appelbaum 2016). The articulated concerns were about the height of the proposed buildings, traffic congestion, loss of environmental amenity and insufficient social facilities, among other things. The concerns of the residents' association about densities and about the socio-economic status of incoming residents remained, however, couched in queries about insufficient 'quality public transport' for non-car-owners.[9] These objections were directed against a perceived low-income development, although ultimately through City tribunal processes the development was adjudicated to proceed. While the socio-economic profile of potential residents of the Paterson Park development remains relatively unclear, the housing typology mix does not enable very low-income residents to be accommodated. At the City's subsequent tribunal hearing in 2017,[10] City officials referred to the 1,400 units (revised downwards from initial estimates) as being composed of a specific mix, still to be determined, of home-ownership linked to state-supported mortgages (termed 'FLISP' or Finance Linked Individual Subsidy Programme housing), bonded and social housing.

Investigations into the potential for additional social housing by Johannesburg Social Housing Company (JOSHCO), the municipal housing entity, found that it was difficult to do, requiring the consolidation of small land parcels and dealing with heritage protection (CoJ ex-official C interview, August 2018). Further, to make the low-cost 'rooms for rent' model of the nearby inner city work, one needed high volumes (a critical mass of numbers of rooms) but it was argued that the private sector had been quicker off the mark in seizing development opportunities: 'it didn't take very long for private investors, once it was clear that Louis Botha was going to get a BRT, ... to go and snap [properties] all like this. It was very quick' (CoJ ex-official C interview, August 2018). My own attendance at one of the neighbourhood consultation meetings in 2017 left me unsure about how best to advise Diane about supporting the City's densification proposals.[11] Professionally, I absolutely supported the proposals but at the consultation meeting it was very clear that people like Diane were absent from the process, and it seemed evident that if the area became attractive to developers as intended, it was likely to push up costs and make poorer residents potentially vulnerable to displacement. Options for people like Diane – who had never heard of the Paterson Park development and are unlikely to afford accommodation there – were unclear.

There was thus little appetite by JOSHCO to pursue very cheap accommodation in this area. Nevertheless, the Paterson Park development and any attempt to explore social housing in the area represent important City initiatives to introduce a more diverse and in part, lower-income demographic to the area.

There were a few other attempts to engage with low-income housing issues. Noteworthy was an individual effort driven by one key official facilitating private sector development in the Corridor of Freedom initiative, in response to the displacement of homeless people or rough sleepers from Paterson Park as a result of infrastructure and environmental improvements. However, this attempt to create a city-run overnight shelter failed, partly due to procedural problems and inter-departmental protocol tensions within the City.[12] In another development, the Johannesburg Property Company (JPC) acquired property in Orange Grove potentially for social housing purposes among other things as well as social facility schemes, the detail of which is not clear.[13] However, newspaper reports in 2018 point to considerable tensions around the usage and plans for these JPC properties, and astonishingly 'hijacking' (occupation) of them by a disgruntled 'Orange Grove community group'[14]. One of the occupiers interviewed, Angie Nyatyoba, explained the occupation was 'because the City of Johannesburg is overlooking homeless South Africans in favour of foreigners', claiming that the JPC is corruptly leasing these properties to 'foreigners'. She explained that her attitude was not one of xenophobia but that foreigners should be renting from private property owners not from the City as 'we have rights as local South Africans to live in houses owned by the City' – this property is for the people. The properties appear to have been subsequently sold by the City and no known low-income housing initiative resulted.

In a final example of City efforts, City planners initially recognised the backyarding prototype as something that could be extended in Orange Grove, and their consultants Osmond Lange Architects & Master Planners proposed guidelines of what would be acceptable if developers mimicked:

> an existing trend known as 'Ma Lines' or Shack Farming. These are very basic and cheaply constructed rooms or shacks arranged right-up against the boundary walls ... ablution is normally shared, sub-standard and under provided (Osmond Lange Architects and Master Planners' poster on housing typologies, displayed at a City of Johannesburg public meeting on the Louis Botha Special Development Zone, Spark Gallery, February 2017).

However, at a public meeting where this proposal was on display, consultants noted that this was to be removed from the suite of options because of the City's concerns about perceived difficulty in properly managing facilities with communal ablutions (City of Johannesburg public meeting on the proposed Louis Botha Special Development Zone, Spark Gallery, February 2017).

These few City initiatives[15] around low-income housing in the Orange Grove area are symbolically very important, but practically negligible, and it remains the case that very low-income housing options do not appear to be on the delivery agenda. In mid-2017, deep into the Corridors of Freedom initiative, a key City official confirmed that in the area 'there are very few projects targeting the "very poor" at the moment'. Another official said bluntly that on Louis Botha Avenue itself: 'Not one cent has been allocated [by the state] for housing ... – if you want to make housing work there you must work with developers' (Planning official, personal communication). However, as seen above, developers did not find low-income housing a viable market to venture into.

I return here to the point that the terminology and discourse around low-income accommodation along the Corridors of Freedom routes served to muddy the waters and helped conceal the fact that a critical need remained unmet. For people not steeped in the intricacies of low-income housing provision and affordability, the introduction of 'social housing' into the area was likely to signal housing options for poor and very poor people, and further, that the 'affordable housing' being built by developers in various places along the Corridor of Freedom routes would also meet a range of low-income needs. This assumption, I argue, was not only among property owners but also officials in planning and other non-housing departments of the City, and it helps explain the lack of a coherent housing strategy specifically for very poor people. Herein lies part of the construction of invisibility: in the realm of terminology and the instruments that attach to it.

The politics of invisibility

Three key points were made in the previous two sections. Firstly, that discourse and publicity surrounding the Corridors of Freedom initiative signalled that poor and very poor people would be accommodated along the Corridors of Freedom routes. Secondly, the presence and needs of very poor people already living in the Orange Grove area were not well acknowledged and therefore not advocated for. Thirdly, the blurriness of terminology in the housing terrain and assumptions that 'low-income housing' would be achieved under the umbrella of 'affordable housing', meant that specific pro-poor housing initiatives hardly existed in this portion of the Corridors of Freedom initiative. In this section, I identify a further set of processes, relationships and responsibilities, within and outside of the municipality, that worked to overlook specific attention being given to housing for very poor people and leaving them vulnerable.

I start with the voices which dominated the public participation processes in the area. Tenants living in different kinds of cheap rental accommodation were not organised, nor represented by a particular organisation or movement. By contrast, there were two residents' associations representing overwhelmingly property owners in the wider area. A broader vision of the Corridors of Freedom initiative that included lower-income housing development thus landed in a context where immediately adjacent to Orange Grove and impacted by proposals including for social housing, the established and organised middle-class property-owning neighbourhood of Norwood was able to mobilise. Similar to that described by Purcell in the USA, they acted to 'defend and proactively realize their spatial vision in the material space of their neighbourhoods' (Purcell 2001, 178). Purcell argues that North American suburban homeowners' engagement in neighbourhood issues is motivated by lessening the difference between the place their suburb is and the place they would like it to be – or, by extension in this Orange Grove and Norwood case, by defending a perceived threat to the status quo of the place. Norwood's residents were thinking of their area becoming increasingly up-market and fashionable, not as accommodating 'the other' that the Corridors of Freedom vision and social housing project suggested to them (Appelbaum 2017 personal communication).

Norwood's residents argued that their objections to the proposed social housing in Patterson Park were about 'process'. This was not an inclusive participatory process but rather an imposed one, while the City saw their objections as 'NIMBY' resistance (Appelbaum 2017 personal communication). Appelbaum makes a compelling argument that these residents were taken aback by an unexpected City intervention in their neighbourhood, in contrast to decades of not being interfered with, except when they needed the City to attend to maintenance of public infrastructure and services. Although the social housing, in a somewhat modified form, was ultimately planned to proceed, the mobilising of resistance to spatial transformation served to further obstruct the City officials' view of a latent and patent need for very low-income housing. Just trying to land the Paterson Park social housing development consumed enormous resources and energy, in a thinly resourced local authority: 'high-level officials in the City's Department of Development Planning have had to devote countless hours trying to ameliorate the situation in Paterson Park' (Appelbaum 2016, 36).

Thus, arguably, a hierarchy of privilege (Razon 2017) is evident in the processes that unfolded in the Corridors of Freedom, even if inadvertently from the City officials' perspectives – signalling the strength of participation and the voice of suburban property owners relative to the tenants of micro-spaces, for example. In other cases, it is noted that land ownership similarly confers this status. In the case of Chinatown in Bangkok, density privileges awarded in a similar Transit Oriented Development initiative favoured property owners, overlooking 'fraught housing tenure relationships' and serving to 'justify eviction' (Rugkhapan 2016, 619). Here, the instrument of planning tools is added to that of participatory processes often favouring property owners. Rugkhapan criticises tools such as land use categorisation and zoning declarations for ignoring local land and cultural histories, 'unseeing' inherent characteristics of a place beyond its function and potential role in the city, and arguing that 'such difference is actively unseen under the banner of technical science urban improvement' (Rugkhapan 2016, 619). In his case, the concern is about long-standing residents in an old and historic neighbourhood. In Orange Grove, neighbourhood changes over the last few decades, subtle, not easily seen and recognised, had led to an increased number of poor people living in a former relatively middle-class area, many of them as tenants (Appelbaum 2016), who were largely overlooked.

Moving from outside the municipality to within the institution itself, an important factor in the construction of invisibility was the apparent disconnects between City entities involved in the Corridors of Freedom initiative in the Orange Grove area. City planners were driving the overall Corridors of Freedom process and anticipated that the City's Housing Department and the Johannesburg Property Company would take forward the specific housing aspects of the initiative. Detailed proposals were needed for new typologies for housing; a management strategy was needed 'for the high-density public housing stock', and a social housing strategy was needed. It was envisaged that 'The Department of Housing will take the lead in unpacking the City's delivery strategy within the Corridors of Freedom' (CoJ nd(b), 140), with the Johannesburg Property Company envisaged to take a lead in the land strategy (CoJ nd (b) 141).

However, by May 2017, a senior planner indicted that 'no one from [the Department of] Housing is really involved' (CoJ senior planning official A interview, May 2017). A year before this – already deep into the Corridors of Freedom initiative, another official was more outspoken: 'Housing [Department] is nowhere – they are not present – they are focused on mega projects' (CoJ official B interview, April 2016). Admittedly, the announcements and discourse around mega projects or mega human settlements – large scale, new, usually urban edge-location developments of mixed income housing – from national and provincial government demanded huge attention for their direct implications for cities. At the same time, some crucial inner-city work on housing was also coming to fruition, in the completion of the Inner City Housing Implementation Plan (ICHIP). Combined with other key issues such as attempting to respond to informal settlements, there were thus multiple other strategic imperatives confronting housing officials, which might go some way to accounting for their attention not being on the Corridors of Freedom initiative despite its status as a flagship City project. Ultimately, it seems there was no champion to develop and push *a strategy* for very low-income housing, and so it did not materialise despite sporadic efforts by planners and other City officials.

I have argued that various factors fed into a situation where the issue of very low-income housing need was not properly acknowledged, including a lack of explicit recognition of the presence of poor residents such as Diane, whose story started this chapter. Together these factors fed 'invisibility' or perhaps 'selective seeing' by the state and others involved. While this is not Razon's notion of a politics of invisibility – in his case, an explicit playing and manipulation of the situation as part of broader politics of difference (Razon 2017) – the term is useful to the extent that it helps articulate different dimensions of the silences and omissions in the Corridors of Freedom initiative.

What is being pointed to is perhaps quite a subtle issue: it is not a straightforward story of ignoring, dismissing, or discriminating against a poorer cohort of residents. On the contrary, several City initiatives attempted to introduce accommodation for a lower-income demographic, and to use state resources to assist with this. Other City efforts encouraged private sector providers to include relatively poorer tenants in their offerings. To do this required enormous energy on the part of City officials to drive forward the project, to enthuse sceptical developers, and to overcome the resistances of property owners. During the process, an official wearily commented that it is 'miraculous to have achieved some concrete projects on the ground by now' (CoJ official D personal communication, January 2016), with another noting just how small the team was that was trying to drive this major flagship initiative.

Yet within this scenario, there are surprising oversights. Firstly, in the lack of depth of understanding of the socio-economic and housing status quo of Orange Grove and thus a lack of acknowledgement of those very low-income residents in cheap, poor quality accommodation, their legitimacy in the area, their contribution to the area and their potential vulnerability to the very developer interest the City was working hard to attract. Secondly, in the lack of understanding of the target market of proposed social housing and its limited reach 'down-market', and perhaps a misplaced optimism in the ability of private sector initiatives to reach down-market. Thirdly, is the lack of strategising on how the Corridors of Freedom initiative with spatial transformation ambitions in a former White suburb should advocate for local opportunities for Johannesburg's marginalised households.

Conclusion

The protagonist I began the article with, Diane, falls into the category of overlooked in-situ residents. As Razon points out (Razon 2017, 57), exploring Scott's notion of 'seeing like a state' (Scott 1998) 'also requires understanding of what remains unseen' – comparatively little explored (Razon 2017, 76). Although included by way of a general invitation to everyone in the area to participate in public consultation sessions, Diane was not aware of them, and her actual ability to participate would have been highly constrained, given the format, dominance by property owners and lack of an organised peer cohort able to articulate positions. Through this and in other ways, her accommodation situation remained partially hidden and her situation was not elevated by state officials in the Corridors of Freedom processes into what Razon terms as 'what and who counts as legible and recognisable' (Razon 2017, 57).

Yet in Diane's case even this notion of being 'seen' or lack thereof is complex, if the gaze moves beyond the Corridors of Freedom initiative. In a number of ways, she *is* 'seen' by the state: she is in receipt of a state grant, she has an ID document, and has a recognised address for voting purposes. She should also be visible to organisations in the area, such as the residents' association, and she is also firmly embedded in the neighbourhood in her two decades of residence: a faithful at the local Catholic church, a long-standing patient of the local GP's practice, and a well-known client in the local Congolese and Bangladeshi-run convenience stores.

At a personal level and in relation to different components and spheres of the state, Diane thus reflects something of an 'interplay between visibility and invisibility, seeing and unseeing' (Razon 2017, 57). More generally, between local state and poor people's housing circumstances in Johannesburg, there is considerable 'visibility', with very poor people's housing needs and issues very clearly on the City's agenda as a whole. However, by and large, these seem to be recognised only in some geographies[16] – in the inner city where poor people's unauthorised ways of occupying inner-city buildings has been an intense, long-standing concern, the subject of litigation and Constitutional Court judgments;[17] and similarly in the terrain of informal settlements in various parts of the city, and some high-profile informal settlements in particular; also in the increasing phenomenon of backyard dwellings, recognised in some townships and new housing settlements. This is not to say the issue – decent affordable accommodation in these localities – has been resolved there, but there is activism, and some policy attention. One could argue 'the poor are everywhere in discourse and policy', and they are in some places evident geographically or spatially, but in this case, they are largely not visible in 'the suburb', resonating, in a way, with the fictional story entitled *The City and the City* (Miéville 2009), where two city-states:

> ... occupy broadly the same space, but remain separated by the inhabitants' mutual and conscious practice of 'unseeing' people, spaces and objects considered to be present in the other city (Wilcock 2020, 2).

Beyond the individual impacts of displacement and the significant irony of this occurring within an area guided by embracing inclusive pro-poor vision, this chapter draws attention to the historical intransigence in adequately addressing very low-income accommodation in Johannesburg, pointing to the need to innovate and demonstrate in this sector and in these sorts of localities. The discussion illuminates the fragility of pro-poor initiatives by the state, particularly in the relatively un-tested terrain of 'the suburbs'. In particular, it flags how progressive intentions can be undermined by the construction of invisibility, even if inadvertent by many of those involved – the layering of factors that worked to conceal, mask and downplay the needs of those who should otherwise be at the forefront of government priorities.

Acknowledgements

The author draws material from interviews she participated in which were part of the project 'Governing the Future City: A comparative analysis of governance innovations in large scale urban developments in Shanghai, London, Johannesburg' funded by the Economic and Social Research Council (Swindon, GB) (ES/N006070/1) (PI: Jennifer Robison).

Notes

1 Rather than 'termination', which can happen legally under certain circumstances.

2 Erf (plural erven) means 'lot', 'land parcel'.

3 Photos taken for the Corridors of Freedom project funded by the Agence Française de Développement (AFD) and run by the South African Research Chair in Spatial Analysis and City Planning at the University of the Witwatersrand, for the City of Johannesburg.

4 Survey undertaken for the project as above.

5 Sixty per cent growth in population between 2001 and 2011 (Appelbaum 2016, 16).

6 A project undertaken between the Agence Française de Développement, the City of Johannesburg and the South African Research Chair in Spatial Analysis and City Planning at the University of the Witwatersrand. The project aimed to provide operational support to, and empirical evidence for, the City of Johannesburg's Transit-Oriented Development (TOD) programme – at the time known as the Corridors of Freedom.

7 Using the rule of thumb of rental amounts being no more than about one-third of income.

8 Johannesburg Development Agency (JDA) Workshop. 2017. 'Developing affordable urban neighbourhoods', Finance and development facilitation session, Johannesburg, 28 September 2017.

9 Norward Orchards Residents Association (NORA). 2016. *Comment on the Paterson Park Development Application Amendments*. Letter submitted to Liana Strydom, Development Planning: City of Johannesburg, 22 December.

10 City of Johannesburg Municipal Planning Tribunal Hearing 3, Thursday 13 July 2017.

11 City of Johannesburg public meeting on Special Development Zones, February 2017.

12 See Bénit-Gbaffou (this book, Chapter 3).

13 Seemingly, 80 properties in the wider Orange Grove, Highlands North, Upper Houghton areas, acquired for community facilities as well as 'higher-rise buildings to increase densification' (*The Star* 15 March 2018).

14 Cox, A. 2018. 'Why we highjack houses' by Anna Cox. *The Star*, 15 March. Available at: https://www.pressreader.com/south-africa/the-star-south-africa-late-edition/20180315/282553018763709. Accessed 23/08/2023.

15 In addition to the above, in Lembede (2016), there is reference to some ideas from the Department of Housing such as container developments for transitional housing along the Corridors of Freedom routes, but no specific localities were yet identified.
16 Thanks to Appelbaum for discussion on this point.
17 See Klug (this book, Chapter 8).

Interviews and meetings

Senior Planning Official A, May 2017, Johannesburg.
Official B, 2016, Johannesburg.
Developer A interview, September 2017, Johannesburg.
Ex official C, August 2018, Johannesburg.
Official D, January 2016, Johannesburg

Official documents

City of Johannesburg (CoJ). nd(b). *Strategic Area Framework for the Louis Botha Avenue Development Corridor.*

CoJ. nd(a). *Corridors of Freedom Re-stitching our City to Create a New Future.* Group Communication and Tourism Department. Available at: https://www.joburg.org.za/Campaigns/Documents/2014%20Documents/corridors%20of%20freedom_s.pdf. Accessed 23 July 2020.

CoJ. 2011. *Joburg 2040: Growth and Development Strategy.* Available at: https://www.joburg.org.za/documents_/Documents/Joburg%20GDS%202040/Joburg%202040%20GDS%20Low%20Res.pdf. Accessed 23 July 2020.

CoJ. 2014. 'Corridors of Freedom, a vision of a city that works for its people.' Advertorial. 26 June 2014, *Mail and Guardian*, 26 June 2014. Available at: https://mg.co.za/article/2014-06-26-corridors-of-freedom-a-vision-of-a-city-that-works-for-its-people/. Accessed 22 July 2020.

CoJ. 2016. *Special Development Zones.* Unpublished report produced for the City of Johannesburg's Corridors of Freedom project by Osmond Lang Architects and Planners, Gibb Engineering and Architecture, and Amara Quantity Surveyors.

Tau, P. 2014. *2014 State of the City Address by the Executive Mayor of Johannesburg.* Available at: https://www.gov.za/2014-state-city-address-executive-mayor-johannesburg-clr-mpho-parks-tau. Accessed 23 July 2020.

Tau, P. 2015. *2015/16 City of Johannesburg State of the City Address.* Available at: https://www.gov.za/speeches/mayor-parks-tau-city-johannesburg-state-city-address-6-may-2015-0000. Accessed 23 July 2020.

References

Appelbaum, A. 2016. 'Contestation, transformation and competing visions: A study of Orange Grove and Norwood'. *Spatial Transformation through Transit-Oriented Development in Johannesburg Research Report Series*, 7. Johannesburg: University of Witwatersrand.

Bénit-Gbaffou, C. 2018. 'Beyond the policy-implementation gap: How the City of Johannesburg manufactured the ungovernability of street trading', *Journal of Development Studies* 54(12): 2149–67.

Butcher, S. 2016. 'Infrastructures of Property and Debt: Making affordable housing, race and place in Johannesburg'. PhD thesis, University of Minnesota.

Lees, L. 2014. 'Gentrification in the Global South?' In *The Routledge Handbook on Cities of the Global South*, edited by S. Parnell and S. Oldfield, 506–21. London: Routledge.

Lembede, M. 2016. *Johannesburg City Officials' Visions for Low Income Housing Typologies Along the Corridors of Freedom*. Research report produced in partial fulfilment of a BSc Urban and Regional Planning degree at the University of the Witwatersrand.

Mayson, S. 2019. 'Sharing a flat in Yeoville: Trajectories, experiences, relationships'. In *Politics and Community-Based Research – Perspectives from Yeoville Studio, Johannesburg* edited by C. Bénit-Gbaffou, S. Charlton, S. Didier, and K. Doerman, 233–48. Johannesburg: Wits University Press.

Mayson, S. and Charlton, S. 2015. 'Accommodation and Tenuous Livelihoods in Johannesburg's Inner City: The 'Rooms' and 'Spaces' Typologies', *Urban Forum* 26: 343–72.

Miéville, C. 2009. *The City and the City*. London: Macmillan.

Purcell, M. 2001. 'Neighborhood activism among homeowners as a politics of space', *The Professional Geographer* 53(2): 178–94.

Razon, N.A. 2017. 'Seeing and unseeing like a state: House demolitions, healthcare, and the politics of invisibility in Southern Israel', *Anthropological Quarterly* 90(1): 55–82.

Rebelgroup. 2015. *Johannesburg Inner City Housing Strategy and Implementation Plan 2014–2021. Strategy and Programmes*. Report produced for the Johannesburg Development Agency/City of Johannesburg Department of Housing.

Roy, A. 2009. 'Why India Cannot Plan Its Cities: Informality, Insurgence, and the Idiom of Urbanization', *Planning Theory* 8(1): 76-87.

Rugkhapan, N.T. 2016. 'Unseeing Chinatown: Universal zoning, planning abstraction and space of difference', *International Journal of Urban and Regional Research* 40(3): 601–20.

Scott, J. 1998. *Seeing Like a State: How certain schemes to improve the human condition have failed*. New Haven: Yale University Press.

Todes, A. and Robinson, J. 2017. 'Reshaping the City? Developers and Johannesburg's Corridors of Freedom'. Paper Presented at the Transit-Oriented Development Colloquium. Johannesburg: University of the Witwatersrand.

Wilcock, S. 2020. 'Seeing is believing: Perception and liminality in China Miéville's *The City and The City*', *Critique: Studies in Contemporary Fiction* 61(5): 534–44.

11
Deceptive lenses: officials' and activists' visions of water issues in eThekwini

Mary Galvin

Introduction

Rapid densification is transforming the rural periphery of South Africa's cities. One of the main ways in which the local state extends its reach into these newly urbanising areas, to make them legible and to assert its governance, is through the delivery of services. This is far more than a straightforward technical exercise implemented by officials. Officials' plans interact with the political interests of elected councillors and traditional authorities, the expectation of local residents, and the position of activists.

In areas of the Global South where the state is pressured to provide for poor, marginalised areas, they have deliberately although informally adopted a 'will not to know' (Bénit-Gbaffou 2018a, 2142). Certainly, the concept of invisibility applies to a wide swathe of the poor population in India, China, Brazil or South Africa, and reflects simplification of reality, not primarily to render society readable and intervention possible (Scott 1998), but in some cases to make certain groups invisible so that the scope of demands on the state is narrowed. Informal practices of the state have been explored at large by Bénit-Gbaffou, one of which relates to this 'will not to know' (Bénit-Gbaffou 2018a). The theme is also developed by Charlton analysing housing officials who are 'confounded' (by the complexity of social dynamics and housing needs they witness) 'but complacent' (not able nor willing to adapt public intervention to this complexity) (Charlton 2018). Similarly to Bénit-Gbaffou (2018b) in the field of street trading, to Charlton (2018) in the field of public housing,

Samson and Razon (Samson 2020; Razon 2017) thematise this common practice of the state in the cities, in the fields of waste collection and informal housing respectively: 'unseeing', so as to escape its obligation to deliver when it is perceived as not possible to fulfill.

The case that I explore here differs: neither officials not activists aim to exclude or exhibit a 'will not to know'. Instead, they struggle to extend the same treatment to all areas through what I will call a 'will not to show'. Through an in-depth study of specific urban policy sector and spatial configuration, this chapter explores what has led officials and activists to adopt a deceptive lens (without sinister intention) and how this can make local realities invisible, in the field of water and sanitation services.

James Scott's (1990) examination of the everyday politics of power, between what he refers to as the dominant and their subordinates, is particularly useful here. Most readers focus on Scott's portrayal of how subordinates use a 'hidden transcript', which is the discourse used to resist repression, 'offstage' or beyond what can be directly observed. What is often overlooked is his important discussion of powerholders, and how they are burdened by maintaining a dominant 'public transcript' in their discourse to openly (but not always with conscious intent) assert power in their interactions with subordinates.

While Scott (1998) developed his work on 'transcripts' to apply to repressive and often brutal regimes, I use it here in a democratic context: a post-apartheid South African city, but one in which local *hydropolitics* between social movements and academic–activists and officials are fierce. Their ideological position on the issue of payment for water is radically different, but this chapter shows how they share a public transcript, which in turn negates the local reality of poor residents and scuppers the possibility of addressing very real issues.

Given the worsening impacts of climate change, increasing water scarcity, and deepening inequality – and the fact that water is critical to life and, in many cases, to livelihoods – water services are an ideal lens through which to consider these dynamics. This chapter focuses on water services in what is considered by most water sector leaders to be a success case: eThekwini Water and Sanitation (EWS). After being featured in *National Geographic* as a leading institution in 2002, in 2014 it won the prestigious Stockholm Industry Water Award as the 'most progressive water utility in Africa and a forerunner in the world of utility-run service' and 'for its transformative and inclusive approach to providing water and sanitation services' (EWS nd). How such an accomplished municipality addresses complexities of delivery at a local level is instructive for understanding other municipalities.

A complex governance context

eThekwini is an important context in which to consider the push and pull of traditional authorities and the formal administrative apparatus. Two seemingly contradictory demarcations have had a defining impact on the lives of people on the outskirts of Durban: the formation of the Ingonyama Trust in 1994, and the formation of eThekwini Municipality in 2000, each governing a part of the urban agglomeration (**Figure 11.1**). While the former reinforced the power of the traditional leaders, the latter extended the reach of the state into rural areas on the periphery of the metro.

Prior to the country's first democratic elections in 1994, the National Party[1] reached a deal with the Inkatha Freedom Party,[2] placing the 2.8 million hectares of land owned by the government of the so-called homeland[3] of KwaZulu, into a Trust. This comprises 32 per cent of all land in KwaZulu-Natal and is inhabited by about 5 million people.[4] With King Zwelethini[5] as its sole trustee, the Ingonyama Trust is to be administered for the 'benefit, material welfare and social well-being of the members of the tribes and communities' living on the land (KwaZulu Ingonyama Trust Act No 3KZ of 1994). Six years later, eThekwini Municipality or 'Unicity' was formed by amalgamating seven former municipal areas and incorporating some 'tribal land' into one metro, swelling to 2,297 km^2. This extension to mostly rural areas with little infrastructure increased the Durban Metropolitan area by 68 per cent (although the population increased only by 9 per cent, to 3.09 million residents in 2001 (StatsSA 2001; eThekwini Municipality 2011). The municipality faced the challenge of extending services[6] to dispersed households located on 1,500 km of hilly, rugged terrain northwest and southwest of Durban, as well as in peri-urban areas alongside the N2 and N3 corridors (eThekwini Municipality 2012).

This chapter asks: beneath the surface of intended water services delivery, how do the interests, identities and ideologies of stakeholders intersect and interact? It argues that the interests of officials and activists, alongside their identities and ideologies, leads them to misrepresent payment of water services, making invisible the local struggles of residents to gain attention to their challenges in accessing water.

I first examine the narratives of municipal officials responsible for water services, and then the narratives of activists, exploring how officials' and activists' interests converge to create and maintain a deception about payment for water. I then consider a second level of deception, which

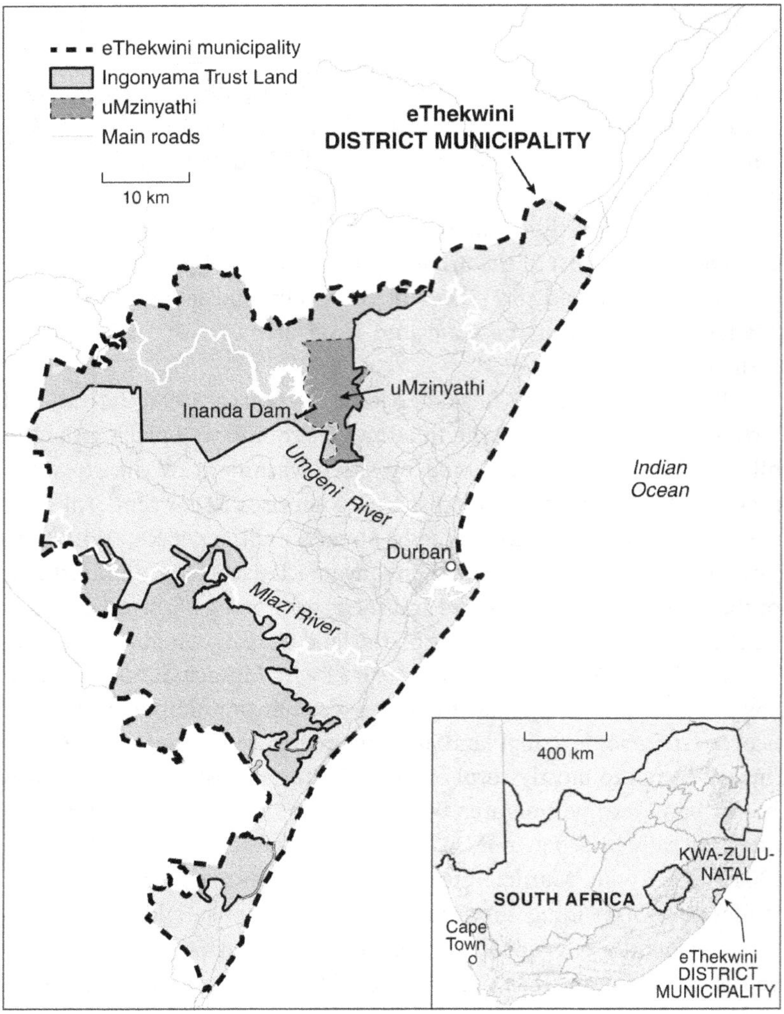

Figure 11.1 Governing the City? eThekwini Municipality and Ingonyama Trust land. The Trust governs large tracks of the eThekwini municipal area. On this land, the municipal land registration and the local taxation system do not apply.

Source: © Mary Galvin 2021

appears in the gap between these narratives and the issues that arise when local residents engage with their local councillor. Finally, I analyse the relationship between officials, local politicians, activists, and local residents, and their impact on municipal functioning.

A long-standing and multi-pronged familiarity with the issue

This chapter is based on over 10 semi-structured interviews and focus groups, observation while conducting action-research in the area over the past 10 years, and a review of documents and secondary sources.

In the 1990s, I gained extensive experience in rural KwaZulu-Natal, as the director of a membership-based NGO focused on water and land, and through PhD fieldwork involving traditional leadership and the new democratically-elected councillors. In the late 2000s, I facilitated the Water Dialogues-South Africa, a multi-stakeholder process that drew together senior government officials, private sector and civil society leaders over a four-year period, to engage with findings from primary research I managed in five municipalities around South Africa. We got to know each other's ideas and values, we debated and questioned, and we grew together as leaders.

One participant in the Water Dialogues was Neil Macleod, Head of eThekwini Water and Sanitation (EWS). He was invaluable in his insights from running a utility and was widely respected by all stakeholders. He describes how repeated challenges – and the provision of data – from civil society representatives in the Water Dialogues were critical to his extension of the free basic water policy from 6 kl to 9 kl per month in eThekwini. While sitting on airplanes from Durban to Johannesburg or driving to areas like Harrismith, we developed a close collegial relationship.

During this period, I also developed a relationship with an academic–activist, Patrick Bond. One of our common interests was water issues, and we debated all aspects of provision, particularly in eThekwini where we each lived. While he was particularly involved in the Constitutional Court case against water privatisation in Johannesburg, I remained as distant as possible since this court case threatened to tear The Water Dialogues apart.

After the Water Dialogues ended in 2008, I conducted action-research related to water, sanitation and climate change in the newly urbanising areas of eThekwini, through an NGO I formed called *Umphilo waManzi* ('Water is Life'). Neil granted me interviews because I had done my background research, was asking informed questions and would use his answers and data with integrity. He was adamant that he would not entertain researchers who twisted his replies to make their argument against the City. This did not mean that he blocked critique: while at the

University of Johannesburg, I published on eThekwini and, while he confirmed the accuracy of his interview, he disagreed with the overall argument.

Neil retired from EWS in 2014, but over time he had built bridges for me within EWS, referring me to Teddy Gounden for interviews and data. A highly capable, senior civil servant who is thoroughly dedicated to his work, Teddy is at the forefront of innovation within EWS, particularly the Urine Diversion toilets, and provided longitudinal interviews over a 10-year period. He described the difficulty EWS had in providing water services in Ingonyama Trust areas, both around infrastructure and billing. One the places we discussed was uMzinyathi – the focus of the second section of this chapter – where MaDudu Khumalo, a fieldworker with Umphilo, comes from and where I have continued to do research.

While at the University of Johannesburg, I sought data on water payments in eThekwini, and was supported by a consultant who specialises in quantitative research and water issues. Neil referred me to his Geographic Information System (GIS) manager Steve Pieterson to access information. After a late-night discussion with the new Head, Ednick Msweli, about whether to give me access to EWS data, Steve explained to us how the GIS system worked, moving from a view of individual household provision and payment to an increasingly aggregated view of wider areas. He explained that there is no payment in Ingonyama Trust areas. He left us with an understanding of what information the GIS system could provide, and it was up to us to ask for specific data, which they would then consider providing.

Once we had established the pattern around Ingonyama Trust – that people are not paying there – we did not ask EWS to access specific data. Not only was it not needed, but we also realised that doing so would be using our access for reasons that would or could harm EWS' functioning (not just reputation) and place our integrity as researchers in question. In the meantime, allegations of corruption in the municipality as a whole means that EWS has become less open to researchers.

My understanding of the water sector, and the idea for this research, developed out of two decades of work ranging from the Water Dialogues, the South African Water Caucus as well as multi-stakeholder and government fora, and ongoing NGO work in uMzinyathi. I gained a deeper understanding of issues and context by knowing people who I write about and engaging with them with as much integrity and rigour as I could.

Deception 1: 'People are paying for water'

Activists and municipal officials in the water sector rarely agree in any context, and eThekwini is no exception. Yet in eThekwini their approaches to water, which are otherwise in direct contention, are surprisingly both based on the claim that all poor people pay (or are forced to pay) for water.

Water services are provided by the public sector in almost all South African municipalities, alongside ongoing pressures to carve out a role for the private sector and to corporatise public utilities. Committed to providing an acceptable level of water service, as Head of EWS for 22 years, Neil Macleod developed a commercial approach to running the utility. He focused his efforts on building a partially ring-fenced utility that worked, in terms of financial sustainability and delivery of services, which depended on its ability to obtain and utilise revenue from its customers for operations and maintenance, in addition to funds provided by National Treasury.

In the early 2000s, activists and academics confronted the extremes of this approach. Throughout the country, municipalities focused on 'cost-recovery' and began cut offs to force people to pay. In eThekwini, for instance, the municipality cut off people's water or blocked taps by welding a coin-sized device with a small hole over the tap, which became known as a 'trickler'. A national study estimated the number of cut offs due to non-payment at 10 million between 1994 and 2001, which the minister contested on methodological grounds (Galvin 2016). However, no one questioned that poor people struggled to pay for water. The effect of this policy was painfully visible in KwaZulu-Natal where poor residents reverted to rivers and streams, which resulted in a cholera epidemic in August 2000 that killed 265 people and infected 117,000 (Hemson et al. 2006).

Both EWS' decision to use a commercial approach to water services and the role of activists in fighting the devastating impacts of cost-recovery approaches are clear. However, the claim of both officials and activists that 'all eThekwini residents are forced to pay for water' constitutes what we call a deceptive lens: in reality, people are not billed, and revenue is not collected, in vast areas of the municipality. This chapter argues that this deception has arisen from a coincidence of interests between activists and municipal officials around a deliberate will to 'leave unnamed' or a 'will not to show'.

Officials

Recognising that poor people are unable to pay for water, EWS developed and introduced Free Basic Water (FBW) in 1998, a policy that provides all households with 6 kl of free water per month and was adopted as a national approach following the cholera epidemic in 2000. In 2008, as a result of community participation in focus groups and user platforms introduced in response to civil society demands (Macleod communication, 16 November 20221), EWS increased the amount of FBW to 9 kl, which was then adopted in many municipalities. EWS also moved away from universal free basic water, simply billing households with property prices over R250,000 for all of their water (Galvin 2010, 2016; Bond and Galvin 2018). Over and above this free allocation, Macleod claimed success: all households were billed and paid for water. He drew public attention to the exceptions: the nearly 70,000 households and businesses (out of 956,713 households, according to 2011 StatsSA) that he explained were stealing water, benefiting from the system but contributing nothing (see **Table 11.1**). They are not paying their bills or have bypassed the meters, and remain the focus of EWS, which is at pains to show that it has taken punitive measures and legal steps to ensure that all households must pay:

> There are 70,000 households and businesses who make illegal connections and steal water – many are not poor. They bypass the meter, we reconnect and they continue to bypass. After they bypass three times, we make what is called a ferule disconnection. They are cut off completely. They will be forced to pay huge fines or will be taken to court. We will achieve wall to wall payment (Macleod workshop presentation, 16 April 2013).
>
> Our collection rate is 100 per cent. Of 910,000 customers, 280,000 do not pay. This is legal because they use less than the FBW amount. That comprises about 10 per cent of EWS' water. But households and businesses who make illegal connections consume 2–3 times as much as the FBW amount, so the 70,000 households also use 10 per cent of the water (Macleod interview, January 2015).

This official perspective reflects a business need to collect revenue alongside an attempt to do so in a difficult socio-economic reality. In addition to revenue management, Macleod said EWS focused on four other areas to be successful: human resources management, customer

Table 11.1 Water consumption and payment in eThekwini, 2010.

Number of households as water customers (rounded), depending on water payment	Percentage of water consumed	Payment?
560,000	80	Yes
280,000	10	No – Free Basic Water
70,000	10	No – illegal
Total 910,000	100	

Source: © Mary Galvin 2022, based on data summary provided by Macleod in late 2000s

management, new services delivery and asset management. He developed policies to enable poor families to deal with services debt, including water amnesty, debt relief and illegal connections policies (EWS nd; Pollution Research Group 2014, 26). He explained:

> Households must pay for consumption over the FBW amount of 6 kl per month (now 9 kl in eThekwini). We help households with their debt through water amnesty and the installation of flow limiters while they pay off their bill (Macleod workshop presentation, 16 April 2013).

A powerful GIS system of data collection has been developed by EWS over the last 20 years. The entirety of eThekwini is on the GPS system, the payment (and arrears) of each metered household is recorded and houses without meters are also on the system. This data can be viewed at any level, from individual households up to ward level, and the areas of payment and non-payment are visually clear. Even a cursory look at the high-level GIS map of payment, one sees payment stop along clear lines. Steve Pieterson, GIS Manager, explained that these boundaries delineate communal land that is part of the Ingonyama Trust (Pieterson interview, 18 April 2016). A rough calculation shows that 35 per cent of the land in eThekwini Municipality is part of the Ingonyama Trust.

Ingonyama Trust land is communally-owned, with no individual title deeds and therefore no cadastral or postal addresses. Without cadastral or postal addresses, EWS is technically unable to bill households in these areas, much to officials' frustration. They clearly recognise it as a problem, going to lengths to describe how they are piloting a way around this in Adams Mission, a settlement under the Ingonyama Trust, where EWS will replace all the pipes with larger ones, install meters to large households and install flow limiters (with meters that cut off water after the free basic amount is met) to other households. They will use a special machine to go household to household and pick up the reading and deliver bills to the household on the spot. The reading that is taken can be checked against the meter reading on the municipal office system. But this is still to be done (Gounden interview, 9 July 2015). It seems likely that the process has been stymied by political interests of elites who live in these areas and receive free services. Macleod has indeed written a number of reports to the City Council to address this problem, but councillors were reluctant to allow him to act to regularise these illegal connections and the plans he proposed collapsed (Macleod correspondence, 17 November 2021).

Despite knowing that all of these households are not charged for water and do not pay (how many of the 70,000 are on Ingonyama Trust land is unclear), and although they respond to questions about the Ingonyama Trust land, the replies and statements of top officials about payment in eThekwini do not acknowledge this. In semi-structured and open longitudinal interviews conducted between 2008 and 2020 on water and sanitation in eThekwini, both Macleod and Gounden focused on a broad range of technical issues that they were seeking to overcome to ensure water access and on promising innovations to deal with water scarcity and affordability issues. Non-payment in Ingonyma Trust areas never arose, until I asked specifically about developments in one community. In short, officials know that people are not paying in Trust areas, but their main focus is on ensuring water access.

Pieterson showed me that he had the level of detail to show which areas were paying or not, but that I would need to get permission from the Head of EWS to get more information. The sector expert who accompanied me thought it indicated a 'nervousness to expose things that may not want to be known' (sector expert interview, 8 August 2020) Although not formally confirmed by EWS, there is one clear explanation for Ingonyama Trust areas remaining 'invisible' in the narrative expounded publicly by EWS.

Community interviews that I conducted in poor areas in the north, west and south of eThekwini found areas of overall non-payment directly adjoining areas that are charged and do pay. 'Paying residents' were furious about the situation and threatened to stop payment. There are also areas where meters are not working and/or are completely disregarded by residents. Residents report that they receive bills that are unrelated to their broken meters and that they do not pay these bills (Khumalo interview, 6 October 2016). It is likely that these areas fall under the 70,000 households referred to above. Sector experts have highlighted the danger of EWS acknowledging that entire areas do not pay: the neighbouring areas may slowly stop paying, sparking a wave of non-payment:

> EWS knows that word would spread like contagion if people found out. They are naturally concerned that, should people learn that their neighbours are not paying for water, they will refuse to as well. This would undermine the entire income basis of the utility and would change its break-even point (sector expert interview, 8 August 2020).

This logic has been articulated more generally by the Ingonyama Trust's acting chairman, former judge Jerome Ngwenya, in regard to the issue of 5 million people on the Ingonyama Trust land not paying rates (property taxes) to the municipality. Over a 14-year period (1998–2012) this totalled a reported R278.3 million, and the municipality took the treatment of the Ingonyama Trust as a state institution to the court for its consideration. Exhibiting his understanding of the issue and his reasonableness in the face of litigation against the Trust, he stated: 'We need to sit and sort this [situation of people not paying rates] out. My concern is that if we don't, other ratepayers will balk at paying their rates.'[7] The same holds for water tariffs not paid on Ingonyama Trust land.

Activists

Many activists engage with EWS as a sinister arm of the state that is forcing poor people to pay for water and disconnecting them when they cannot pay. Understanding this deception requires a consideration of activists as a set of different actors at the global, national and local levels who are interacting with each other within a changing context.

In the context of the early 2000s, the global voice of academic–activists, the national voice of social movements, and the local voice of community organisations moved in the same direction: they reinforced one another. This only changed in the late 2000s when the weakening and demise of social movements meant that they no longer coordinated the wider position of activists. Power differentials and differences in ideology then affected the overall 'activist' register, which became a disjointed mixture of local struggles and well-established narratives of academic–activists.

Early 2000s: activists with mutually reinforcing positions against payment and meters – and eThekwini Water and Sanitation (EWS)

In the 2000s, the united struggle of activists from the global to the local level was against the privatisation of water utilities and full cost-recovery. In South Africa, insensitive revenue collection and credit control measures meant that people who could not afford to pay for water were disconnected. This was one of the key issues that led to the rise of social movements, beginning in 2000 with the Anti-Privatisation Forum (APF) as an umbrella organisation of community activist organisations. The APF campaigned against privatisation, the commodification of water as an economic good and the full cost-recovery, which makes water unaffordable for the poor. They affected and were affected by global discourse and organising around privatisation. Then, 40 water organisations (community-based and NGOs) came together to form the South African Water Caucus, in preparation for the World Summit on Sustainable Development in 2002, with its founding principles as fighting against privatisation and for the human right to water (Bond 2004).

Two interrelated activist groups were active around the payment for water in Durban. Firstly, formed in 1999, the Concerned Citizen's Forum (CCF) was a loose network with its main roots in working class areas of Chatsworth, with the active involvement of veteran activist Fatima Meer. One participant described the CCF as growing out of 'problems in the community, people are unemployed, people don't have water, people don't have electricity, people have AIDS' (interview cited in Dwyer 2004). Participants came from other areas and the CCF grew from a defensive, survivalist network to be part of wider national and international groups, events and ideologies through its links with the Social Movements Indaba, which started in 2002.

Secondly, the Westcliff Flats Residents Association (WFRA) was formed in 1998 around housing evictions, electricity disconnections, and water cut offs. Westcliff's residents faced extensive water cut offs in the 2000s:

> The bill is very high, it's always escalating. They give 300 L per day but it's insufficient, we always pay on top (interview as cited in Rogoll 2017, 44).

The WFRA was at the forefront of not only challenging eThekwini Municipality's approach to water provision, but also its 'ignorance towards the poor' (Rogoll 2017, 1). Its tactics included technically restoring (reconnecting) or destroying (bypassing) municipal devices and, importantly, through court action. In 2002, Christina Manqele took the Durban Metro to court for denying her socio-economic right to water due to non-payment. The applicants lost on the grounds that there was no guidance from the legislature or executive, or the lack of national legislation clarifying the basic requirements of the right to water (Loftus 2005a). Macleod, who was personally involved in this court case, summarises the verdict as recognising that 'the right to water is not unlimited and that water can be disconnected if customers exceed the free basic amount and do not pay for the excess or tamper with the connection to access water illegally'. (Macleod correspondence, 17 November 2021).

Although the court case was lost, Desai explains how: 'Litigation consumes the energies of the other side, ripping aside the mask of political rhetoric and forcing the council to reveal in sworn affidavits the brutality of its anti-poor policies' (Desai 2002, 73). To illustrate, he quotes Deputy Mayor Bonhomme in 2000: 'As much as water is a basic human right, there is a cost to recover. The Metro Council insists on payment and if no payment is made the Metro Council disconnects' (Desai 2002, 67).

Litigation was also the main approach used by activists nationally, focusing on technology around disconnections (von Schnitzler 2016). Activists' historical moment was the Constitutional Court case Mazibuko et al. v. the City of Johannesburg, in which the legality of pre-payment meters in Soweto (and the adequacy of the amount of water provided by the City) was challenged. Although the case was ultimately lost at the Constitutional Court, a hugely important result of this struggle was the mass mobilisation of the Coalition Against Water Privatisation in 2003, when community activists, trade unions, NGOs and academics came together against the violation of a basic human right (McKinley 2016; Coalition Against Water Privatisation 2004). Local activists were mobilised to fight payment for water, with popular action using slogans like 'Destroy the meter, enjoy the water' (Bond 2014, 152). Not only was the court case evidence of the power of activists standing up to the state, demanding that it fulfil their human right to water, but it also fed the energy of activists throughout the country.

What is important here is how national developments articulated with ones in eThekwini. Social movement activists took a position against payment overall. Payment became the main focus, even though the main limitation in most municipalities is people's lack of basic infrastructure and interruptions in the supply of water (Sahle et al. 2019). This focus is evident in statements by eThekwini activist and community scholar (Centre for Civil Society, University of KwaZulu-Natal), Gcina Makoba, against payment and meters:

> Most of the people who are living in Inanda's RDP houses,[8] which do have individual water taps, have a problem with the high billing costs. If they impose these (water meters), we will make sure that they are removed from each and every house.[9]

Even discussing the area where she comes from, she focuses on payment instead of the reality that this is not the challenge of most households. To get water to their household, most households divert water from the pipe feeding a communal tap, making their 'own' connection, and do not pay.

The injustice of what poor people must pay for water in eThekwini was part of Bond's affidavit in support of Mazibuko et al. In particular, referring to the 'bureaucratic sabotage of free water', he focused on what poor people were charged after consuming the 6 kl free basic water allocation:

> Their pricing system is biased in favour of wealthy, high-volume consumers – a reflection of the insensitivity of some in government to the plight their poor compatriots face in even as simple a task as collecting and paying for water.[10]

Bond uses a study by Bailey and Buckley to argue that the convex tariff curve forced poor people to curtail their water use in response to a steep rise in cost as their usage increased (Bailey and Buckley 2004). Although EWS used this study to evaluate the fairness of the tariff structure and then restructured the tariff to include additional blocks and increase the free basic amount, this study continues to be used by Bond to make the overall point that EWS tariffs are unjust and disproportionately hurt the poor.

Other academic–activists focused on EWS' revenue collection. Allence explains that the free basic water policy relieved municipalities from recovering the cost of 6 kl from consumers, but it 'intensified pressures to secure payments from those consuming more than basic services' (Allence 2002 in Harvey 2007, 116). Loftus argued that the 'right to water is thus accompanied with a clampdown on many households' access to water' (Loftus 2005b), referring to EWS as 'inhumane' (Sahle et al. 2019).

Late 2000s: local and national activists' state engagement diverges from academic–activist protest

By the late 2000s, within the context of the court case and protest, EWS engaged with civil society through focus groups and user platforms and sought research to assess the impact of its tariffs and revenue collection on poor households and consider changes. Macleod explained how this activism had affected positive change over time in increasing the FBW amount to 9 kl and changing the tariff structure to be more welfare maximising. It also reformed its revenue collection policies, including amnesty and negotiation of payment of arrears with residents (Galvin 2016). These changes in EWS' approach made the WFRA more receptive and dialogue ensued. Given local residents' need to access affordable water, it was in the interest of the WFRA to engage with EWS. The WFRA moved from protest to engagement, doing what they could to obtain the most consistent and affordable supply of water possible (Galvin 2016).

However, this was not the view of activists nationally. Due to its (partial) cost-recovery measures, EWS had already been established in their minds with distrust. Engaging with EWS 'implied an acceptance of the commercialisation of basic services, minus its harshest impact' (Waetjen and Vahed 2012, 266). Bond adds:

> By the time that [FBW] mandate was finally honoured by Kasrils [then Minister of Water and Sanitation], the commercialisation instinct was already thoroughly accepted by municipalities. As a result, the right to water ended up either being sabotaged or delivered in a tokenistic way (Bond 2019, 59).

Bond describes this 'tokenism' as the national policy of allowing a regressive block tariff in which municipalities provide 6 kl free water per month but then:

> charge extremely high rates for subsequent consumption, which results in people using far less water than needed. It represents a strategy for 'talking left' while 'walking right' – or more precisely, 'turning the tap right', disconnecting those unable to pay (Bond 2019, 49).

While this is based on data from the early 2000s and on a 'faultlines' report by the Centre for Applied Legal Studies (Tissington et al. 2014) considering the complexities of this policy, he explains that the neoliberal trend that reinforces class apartheid has not changed. Similarly, Nash applies a Gramscian analysis, pointing to each progressive or pro-poor change undertaken by EWS or promoted by civil society as an assertion of EWS' hegemonic neoliberal approach (Nash 2013). What is absent from these analyses is the reality behind the lack of water experienced by poor people around the country today: StatsSA[11] reports this to be a long period of disrupted supply, which is well recognised as a result of dysfunctional municipalities who do not maintain infrastructure at the same time that these systems are exhausted by 'own' (illegal) connections and do not collect necessary revenue from business and households who are able to pay.

Bond drove the main hub of activism and academic–activists around water at the Centre for Civil Society (CCS) at the University of KwaZulu-Natal. Here he created a position of 'community scholars', a mirror image of 'academic–activist'. Orlean Naidoo from the WFRA and MaDudu Khumalo from uMzinyathi community were selected as scholars. When publicly sharing their stories in activist events and in co-authored publications with the Director of CCS (Mottiar et al. 2011),[12] the focus of academic–activists was selective, around two general themes: payment and disconnections resulting in poor access to water (unfair tariffs and ruthless collection are underlying issues) and sub-par sanitation services provided to the poor, due to neoliberalism. During my engagement and participation with activist groups, information that was inconsistent with this narrative, such as non-payment on IT land, was not discussed.

Yet the voice of the CCS was not uncontested. Growing community resentment of 'middle class leftists who set the agenda without consulting them' or asserted undue influence on strategy, alongside personal and political infighting, reached a boiling point at the Fourth Annual National Social Movements Indaba meeting in Durban in 2006, which fell apart when activists who began to *toyi-toyi* (protest 'dance') and sing outside the venue moved inside to disrupt the meeting (Harris 2006, 12; author observation).

National organising distorts local specificities

Although social movements appeared strong in this instance, particularly the shackdweller's movement, Abahlali BaseMjondolo, social movements focusing on water (Anti Privatisation Forum, Coalition Against Water Privatisation, and Concerned Citizen Forum) folded during this period. This left the national South African Water Caucus (SAWC) as the main water activist structure, which depends on poorly resourced community members to organise voluntarily. It also moved from its founding, fervent focus on payment and privatisation to more pragmatic and local concerns that could be taken up with national and municipal government. Its strategy of engagement was influenced by the expertise and limited administrative support of NGOs (Environmental Monitoring Group – EMG – Geosphere, Umphilo waManzi and other committed resource people). Its provincial caucuses are comprised of members from specific communities whose messages are not necessarily representative but inform SAWC's national positions.[13] For example, although some members from the KwaZulu-Natal provincial caucus live on Ingonyama Trust land themselves and certainly know that people in their area are not billed and do not pay for water, they focused on issues related to the Inanda Dam. Alongside dam affected communities, one of SAWC's main issues has remained water metering and payment, driven primarily by members from its Western Cape caucus who experience water management devices in Khayelitsha and work closely with the EMG.

Academic–activists and national activists took up the struggles of specific areas, with the effect of selectively covering issues facing communities in eThekwini, as observed first-hand by a foreign academic:

> Debates that take national prominence tend to apply only to highly specific cases [around payment for water] that resonate in national and international networks. Actors at this level simultaneously claim to speak to strategic and pragmatic issues alive at the local, municipal and catchment levels across the country, but our research indicates this is rarely the case. Rather, taking one's political cues from national movements, in the South African case, will result in a highly distorted perception of water politics, which for historical and contemporary – as well as ecological – reasons tend to be overwhelmingly local (Wilson 2007, 407).

So the SAWC did not attend to water access in rural areas on Ingonyama Trust land. If community members from Ingonyama Trust areas participated in wider activist gatherings, their issues were subsumed into a wider analysis. More cynical activists may have chosen to ignore these complexities, since they would muddy clear activist positions.

Although growing exponentially throughout the country (Galvin 2023), activism in the form of local service delivery protests around water has been very concentrated and limited on the ground in eThekwini (Galvin 2016), and very loud and public in popular and academic accounts. A globalising narrative of academic–activists sometimes seems to disregard the 'messy' experiences of local residents who focus on and are driven by their immediate circumstances. This can lead academic–activists to redefine movements to fit predetermined theoretical constructs (Choudry 2015, 55), resulting in scholarly interpretations of local dynamics that are 'out of tune with reality on the ground' because they rely 'on definitions of transformation imposed from the outside rather than those generated by activists themselves' (Dawson and Sinwell 2012, in Choudry 2015, 61).

Because their area of concern is an ideological power struggle against neoliberalism, many academic analyses are rooted in the 2000s and continue to focus on payment as the key issue, relying on fieldwork or secondary sources from nearly two decades ago (Bond 2019; Loftus 2005a; Hellberg 2014; Nash 2013). Instead of engaging with the turn around on the part of one of South Africa's successful public utilities with capable and committed officials, and asking how to improve public utilities, EWS continued to be heavily critiqued by academic–activists who maintained a narrative around payment and celebrated bypassing as a strategy. They do not acknowledge that that there are extensive areas where people are not being billed or forced to pay – all the households on Ingonyama Trust land and households whose meters are not working due to technical reasons. They choose to reiterate, reinforce and respond to the municipality's false claim that all people are being forced to pay for water.

Reasons for officials' and activists' deceptive lens

It is clear that actors perceive their water world differently depending on where they sit. This has led to a curious coincidence of positions, which can be referred to as a 'hologram'. The same object is seen in different way by officials and activists, who respond differently. They purposely ignore key factors that would affect their perception of the water reality. Each have self-protective and self-interested reasons to 'not see' the reality of people not paying for water.

There are three interrelated factors (**Table 11.2**) that result in officials ignoring the reality of people not paying for water: protecting the billing system (interest), considering the issue technically and pragmatically (ideology), and maintaining their prizewinning profile (image). The first factor was described earlier; officials' interest in protecting EWS' billing system is the driving force behind their deception.

Table 11.2 Interest, image and ideology: factors behind the deceptive lenses, for officials and activists

Actor	Interest	Image (desired) identity	Ideology
Officials (senior leaders): employed by the EWS, responsible for ensuring delivery.	Ensuring financial viability through revenue collection. Finding new solutions so that it can extend and maintain water and sanitation services. Protect high level of autonomy.	Efficient public entity able to deliver to all 'customers' using a commercialised approach. Award-winning for using advanced, innovative approaches to meet the needs of the poor. Apolitical.	Pragmatist: acceptance of global neoliberalism. Technicist: commodification of water (partial cost recovery and revenue collection measures). Commercial business principles. Strategic: innovation as a solution to address the needs of the poor, within the financial constraints of the municipality.
Activists: assert positions/ plan actions on water and sanitation.	Positioned to challenge neoliberal government and corporates from a position of global and national strategy but local tactics and action.	Politically cutting edge (not party political), acting in interest of the poorest. Radical: not compromising and not compromised.	Anti-neoliberal, non-commodification. Seeking systemic change (anti-hegemonic, anti-capitalist).

Not forcing people to pay due to a calculation of their interest has been the focus of studies in other African countries. For example, in Mizes and Cirolia's study, officials know that demanding payment may lead to people rebelling against the whole neoliberal system and demanding redistribution (Mizes and Cirolia 2018). In Uganda, Tutusaus and Schwartz explain that small-town utilities may not support a commodified approach, and officials report to donors that they are implementing cost-recovery when they are actually turning a blind eye to non-payment (Tutusaus and Schwartz 2020). Neither of these is applicable to eThekwini where officials are advocates of a commercialised approach to water services and there is ample evidence of forcing people to pay outside of Ingonyama Trust.

In contrast, interest operated as one factor alongside identity and ideologies in eThekwini. In terms of the second factor, they do not consider their claim that everyone pays for water as a deception as their approach is technicist, in line with their ideology. Only through payment for water are they able to make the system work and provide water to customers. They are pragmatic about what they can do, and are in the process of piloting an 'innovative way of billing' that may allow them a means of doing so on Ingonyama Trust land. They also point to their ongoing action against illegal connections. Although the situation has not changed for years, they are always anticipating their success. This relates to the third key factor driving officials' self-deception. As a utility, EWS is a prizewinner, and this image must be maintained. Its efficiency and ability to overcome problems is part of its self-image, which has also been adopted by individual officials.

Image is also a factor for activists: that they act in the interest of the poor against unjust treatment by the municipality. They are most effective in doing so if they avoid anything that would place the municipality in a positive light. If it were known that poor people in large parts of eThekwini are not billed or pay for water, it would become difficult to project it as a clear enemy. In order to do so, it is in the interest of activists to mobilise around a clear position, not muddied by complexities that make it less effective for advocacy. Their ideological position against the commodification of water is a global one advocated by water warriors in many developing countries, in this case against the tariff structure and forcing poor people to pay for water.

In the case of both officials and activists, it is senior people who set the agenda. Using a deceptive lens promotes and supports the development of their own work and position. In addition, it feeds into the protection and assertion of their identities.

What is particularly interesting is the relationship between interests, identity and ideology. James Scott's *Domination and the Arts of Resistance: Hidden transcripts* (Scott 1990) provides a useful analysis of domination that is relevant here. The structural settings he discusses are ones of extreme repression, such as slavery, caste and serfdom – while the dynamics in the context of eThekwini are not extreme, I argue that concepts of dominance can be applied. What is ordinarily observed in terms of power relations are the 'public transcripts' of the dominant. In eThekwini, it is apparent from this research that the public transcript 'everyone pays for water' is a creation of top officials and of activists who are (perhaps unduly) influenced by academics.

According to Scott:

> a sceptic might well ask at this point how we can presume to know, on the basis of the public transcript alone, whether this performance is genuine or not. What warrant have we to call it a performance at all, thereby impugning its authenticity? The answer is, surely, that we cannot know how contrived or imposed the performance is unless we can speak, as it were, to the performer offstage, out of this particular power-laden context, or unless the performer suddenly declares openly, on stage, that the performances we have previously observed were just a pose (Scott 1990, 4).

In applying these concepts to eThekwini, the research was able to access the hidden transcripts of officials and activists, due to my particular positionality in this field. The concept of the public transcript ('everyone pays for water') versus the hidden transcript ('not on Ingonyama Trust land', a sizeable proportion of the poor in eThekwini) is straightforward in the case of officials.

It is interesting to consider how public transcripts might apply to the relationships among types of activists. Academic–activists play a dominant role in developing activist discourse about fighting eThekwini on the ground and winning global and national media attention, while local community activists may have differing priorities or even interpretations of the water challenges that they confront. Such intra-group dynamics are described by Scott:

> Domination, as we have seen, produces an official transcript that provides convincing evidence of willing, even enthusiastic complicity. In ordinary circumstances, subordinates have a vested interest in avoiding any explicit display of insubordination (Scott 1990, 56).

As academic–activists engage in broader debates about power, they assert and insert their own power within communities and social movements. Their position is bolstered by their public profile, academic status and/or access to resources as well as their typically privileged position in terms of class, race and/or gender. Some academic–activists drown out or manipulate the voices of those whom they seek to reflect; this is done in a variety of ways, enumerated by Bond in a 2015 PowerPoint presentation as the 'Ten Sins of Scholar-Activists'. The complex interplay between academic–activists and social movements has been the source of much debate (Walsh 2008). In this case, academic–activists argue that the poor are suffering under eThekwini's policies, and that people at the grassroots level are fighting in this water war, or power struggle. This is a structural argument that fails to 'see' the state and its ability to adjust its approach in response to people's experiences. So while 'insubordination' may not appear fitting in the activist context, this description shows how community priorities can remain invisible.

Deception 2: 'we are tackling issues impeding local water access'

By focusing on payment for water, activists and officials share a second deception: that their work is engaging with the realities of local people's struggle to access water. At the local level, people's access is contingent on the favour of local leaders, typically their local councillor. The failure of officials and activists to engage with this reality impedes people's ability to access water. This section uses the case of one local area under the Ingonyama Trust to show that residents are not forced to pay for water; instead, their access to water is mediated and can be controlled by the councillor.

The challenges of water access in uMzinyathi

About a 30-minute drive northwest of Durban city centre, uMzinyathi is quickly becoming peri-urban with rapid densification and growth. In the early 2000s, uMzinyathi was sparsely populated by poor households. Their FBW daily water allocation into a 200 L tank next to their homes was filled early each morning through an automatic valve. Eight years later, in 2008, EWS increased the amount of FBW to 9 kl or 300 L per day[14] and replaced tanks with flow limiters that allowed water to flow from the tap until the daily allocation was used. As in many other areas, some people have hired their own plumbers to access unlimited water by connecting directly to the main water line ('self-connection') or illegally bypassing the flow limiter.

Over the last 20 years, there has been an influx of households into uMzinyathi. The area is highly attractive due to its proximity to Durban and because, as Ingonyama Trust land, rates (property taxes) and service charges cannot be levied. The only way that the municipality can limit the amount of water used by households is through flow limiters. Yet new residents have built large homes and hired local plumbers (who were trained by EWS to install the initial reticulation system) to connect to their water supply independently (and illegally). Without a flow limiter or meter, they access unlimited, free supply and have no incentive to limit their water usage (Neil Macleod, email conversation, 17 March 2020). Unlike poor households using dry sanitation, new homes have flush toilets with septic tanks that use 8 to 10 L of water per flush, a relatively large quantity. Their overall usage greatly exceeds the FBW limit of 9 kl per month that other households confront. They have even buffered themselves against water interruptions affecting the entire area by installing and storing water in tanks of up to 10,000 L (Galvin 2022).

Many large homes are being built above the roadside with unmetered, unlimited water. Such high water consumption affects supply to the entire area. The water systems – the size of pipes and pumps, and the source of water that feeds them – do not have the capacity to cope with the demand from a dramatically increased number of households consuming large quantities of water; they were designed to provide a basic amount of water to a much smaller population. It is not simply the influx of people into the area, but their use of excess water through these illegal routes that puts additional pressure on the water system.

With limited water supply and growing demand, distribution has become the problem. In uMzinyathi, a household's ability to access water depends on local topography. After providing water to wealthy households raised above the roadside, water pipes run alongside the road and across a small river, and then the pipe dips before going up a steep hill. The technical limitation of small pipes coping with high use by households along this route makes water pressure inadequate. Water does not reach the poor households on the hill. Some households experience interruptions, but others have been without piped water for over four years. They rely solely on water tankers hired by the municipality to fill containers twice a week.

Some residents allege that even if the pipe system works, the water tanker operators 'get hungry' and ask the councillors to close the water, and then they receive a percentage of profit. Or that tankers prolong the issue, sitting in the municipal offices, so that they are paid overtime. While the politics of water tankers may seem extreme, it is similar to an allegation made in the Pietermaritzburg area prior to the 2016 local government elections: that the African National Congress (ANC) cut off water so that people depended on water tankers, and then the ANC could be the ones to remedy the situation.[15] The manipulation of water tankers for profit by officials is also recognised elsewhere (Galvin 2023).

Officials are in a no-win financial situation in uMzinyathi. Throughout the country, officials complain that illegal connections do not generate revenue to put toward the treatment of water, the maintenance of the system or its extension. In uMzinyathi, this situation is extreme – no households pay for water because the land belongs to the Trust. Since unlimited access for some means a lack of access for others, EWS must provide costly tankered water, which is financially unsustainable for EWS.

For years EWS has continued to search for ways, legally, technically and administratively, to bill households living in Ingonyama Trust areas, with no success (interview with EWS official, 22 October 2020). The Trust seems impenetrable. Since its formation, its existence has remained under regular challenge politically, but decades later it remains in place. Still, seeking to meet its constitutional obligation to provide access to all households, EWS has developed technical plans to install new water systems. It has sought approvals and budgets, put out tenders to increase the capacity of the water system in uMzinyathi, installed some meters, presently unused, in hopeful anticipation of being able to collect revenue in the future.

Paradoxically, some residents who I interviewed from poor households, frustrated that their lack of water is not being addressed or even acknowledged by local leaders, expressed a willingness to pay for water as long as it is available without interruption. One resident explained:

> Without a doubt everybody says that if they are supplied with water, they're happy to pay for it. All people want is a secure supply of water. The councillor favoured people with big houses and everyone else got nothing (Khumalo interview, 20 September 2019).

What people expect is water that is running for 24 hours. Some poor residents show interest in engaging with the state and using a pragmatic approach to improve their water supply. Their focus in on survival, perhaps development, and advocacy is not a priority (Galvin 2010).

Local councillor: un-representative of the people?

Power configurations at the local level undermine the possibility of change. Clearly, new, wealthier households do not want meters that would limit the amount of water that they can access, and that would make them pay for it. The politicians and business leaders who live there have significant clout in the area. Local residents said that when the municipality attempted to install meters in these new homes, they were chased away by Councillor Chili (uMzinyathi focus group, 3 October 2016). It seems he is fearful of losing the support of wealthy residents and works only through his patronage network: the ANC branch executive. While a designated representative from his office referred to 'community meetings', some local residents explain that this refers to ANC Branch Executive Committee (BEC) meetings. Indeed, his representative also explained that the ward committee (intended as a vehicle for communication between councillor and community members) is comprised completely of ANC members and affiliates. The councillor participates in the BEC and meets with his ward committee as his means of consultation. The councillor's representative said he convenes meetings in all 17 voting districts every three months: 'the meetings are well attended because people are happy that the councillor delivers houses, water pipes, toilets, paved and tarred roads and speed humps' (Ndlovu interview, 2 July 2015). Yet residents who were interviewed say that no one communicates with them and that they have no information (uMzinyathi focus group, 3 October 2016).

While one's first impression is of a responsive councillor who works closely with his constituency, this does not apply to his non-supporters or residents who make demands. Residents who are not part of this 'scene' or are suspected of belonging to another faction of the ANC, or supporting anyone other than the councillor, are 'stuck'. Some residents reported that they took their water and sanitation issues to EWS, but were asked whether they have taken their issue to the councillor (uMzinyathi focus group, 3 October 2016). They were told that this is the route they must follow and that they could not be assisted without doing this first. Similarly, EWS introduced a 'Citizens Voice' project in the late 2000s (Galvin 2016; Smith 2011) that aimed to educate and involve residents in engaging with the municipality directly around their water and sanitation issues. However, those involved from uMzinyathi say that this did not help, as they were still required to go through the councillor, who retained his position through patronage and ANC support and was only replaced after his death (Khumalo interview, 20 September 2019).

Any alternative route, through NGOs or residents seeking to install their own systems are seen by the councillor as being 'too clever or important' and as a challenge that threatens to undermine him. Although the Inkosi (chief) is well-respected and wields significant power in the area, particularly as the manager of communal land, even he has chosen not to get involved. The relationship between amakhosi and councillors differs per ward; some work together, others delineate roles that do not overlap, and others are in open conflict (Beall et al. 2004). In uMzinyathi, the Inkosi restricts his involvement to land issues and 'keeps his head down' when it comes to engaging with the councillor. One local resident explains that Inkosi does not want to get involved in water issues since his dignity is at stake (Khumalo interview, 20 September 2019).

Some residents alleged that the councillor will 'work behind the scenes' to co-opt members of a community organisation with a job; since members are volunteers, having an income often makes this irresistible (uMzinyathi focus group, 3 October 2016). Some residents allege more sinister interactions. One resident claims that, when he complained that there was no water in his tank, the Councillor told him not to worry – he would come and urinate in the tank. Similarly, the threat that the tanker driver may not return to their area results in residents not raising issues, worrying that their situation will worsen. A local group of citizens committed to development in the area said that they do not take up water and sanitation issues because they are scared: 'When we complained about road humps, guns were pulled and people were stabbed at the protest.' They say that there are people who have been shot and even killed in the area because the councillor perceived that his power was being challenged (uMzinyathi focus group, 3 October 2016; Galvin 2022).

The Councillor's representative asserted that there were no service delivery protests in uMzinyathi since the Councillor is 'more consultative and delivers services to all people compared to his predecessors' (Ndlovu interview, 2 July 2015). This is inconsistent with the accounts of some residents, who explained that dissatisfaction with the Councillor was ultimately raised through political channels. Although protest was not in direct relation to water services, it is not possible to divorce governance issues from service delivery.[16] One focus group of residents explained: 'We are all ANC but are against how the ANC is working.' They recounted that they had been part of a large march in September 2016 after the local government elections, in which over 4,000 people rejected the councillors who they claimed were elected unfairly.

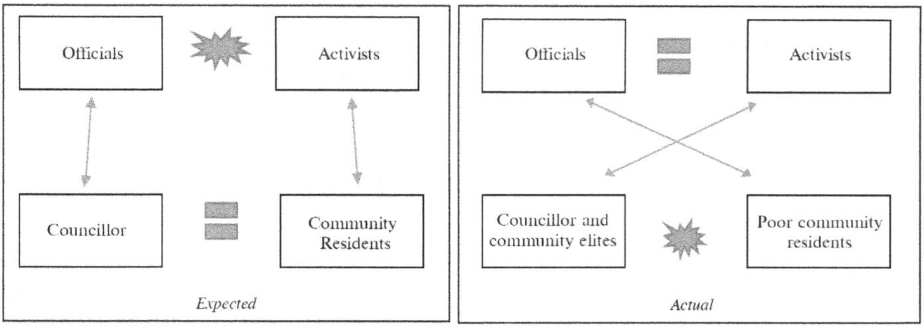

Figure 11.2 Expected versus actual alignment of interests and positions of water stakeholders. Source: © Mary Galvin 2021

So officials and activists not only share a deceptive lens that all people are paying for water, but by focusing on payment they are missing (or not seeing) what is actually happening at the grassroots level between councillors and local residents around the delivery of water. Like Ferguson's *Anti-Politics Machine* (Ferguson 1994), this account shows how seemingly a-political, technical projects feed into and are used by local political processes. The interesting factor here is that it is not the use of donor resource that provides leverage to the locally powerful, but the non-implementation of policies that would force the elite to pay that bolsters the councillor's power. This has resulted in an unexpected alignment of interests and positions among stakeholders.

Councillors' interests diverge from officials', and activists align to local elite's interests

Given the combative relationship between officials and activists, one might expect the interest and position of officials at the municipal level to align with councillors at the local level, and for the interests and position of activists at a municipal (and national and global) level to coincide with that of residents (**Figure 11.2**).

Ethekwini Water and Sanitation stands in contrast to many municipalities in South Africa where the divide between councillors and officials has collapsed, where decision-making and the running of the municipality are subject to the assertion of political or party interests. In EWS, the divide between officials and councillors/politicians has been maintained, in large part due to the former Head of EWS. Macleod considers his insulation to be a result of his tactics, and describes his success in insulating its officials and politicians from interference by politicians:

> Many councillors from a deprived background think they've got five years to make the most money they can. Corruption is endemic in most municipalities, through collusion between officials and councillors. Oversight is blurred with execution. Officials do what councillors tell them, including who to hire and not to fire. People are appointed so long as they're in the club. At EWS we said 'you hold us to account, but let us run business'. If politicians told me who to appoint, I would ask them to put it in writing, otherwise I would say 'I haven't heard you'. When I was pushed to sign certain contracts, I would table them at committee meetings. I protected my management and staff from political interference (Macleod interview, 4 October 2016).

Bénit-Gbaffou (2008) and Hart (2013) note that ward councillors are often at odds with council policies and policy directions. However, the reasons for this in uMzinyathi are very different to those in Johannesburg, Ladysmith or Newcastle. Instead of feeling the pressure of discontent or of popular democracy, or possibly sympathising with needs in the ward, ward councillors in uMzinyathi are positioning themselves within the ANC. To some extent, ward councillors are becoming a petit bourgeoisie, seeking to win the battle over local government resources through class contestation and exclusion/inclusion (Hart 2013).

Coming from a completely different ideological angle, of standing up against commodification of water, activists paradoxically align with this petit bourgeoisie and higher-income residents, in their opposition to payment for water. Instead of activists defending the interests of the poorer residents on Ingonyama Trust land, it is finally the City officials' position that aligns with these residents around immediate delivery of water. This is not only by advocating that high-income residents actually pay for the water their use, but also by lower-income residents indicating their willingness to pay if the service were working and improved.

While the interests of officials and residents converge in the short term – people want water services – their longer-term interests may diverge. As explained earlier, EWS focuses on the technical challenges of delivering water, set upon a foundation of inequality and lack of services and now facing the challenge of rapid urbanisation. In this context, low levels of service have been described as linked to cost-recovery in other words, 'the guiding principle had become one of "you get what you can pay for"'(McDonald and Pape 2002, 5 in Harvey 2007, 161). In this interpretation, its ideology can be labelled as neoliberal, since it does not challenge pervasive neoliberalism, but is more accurately portrayed as pragmatic.

The Ingonyama Trust areas are located behind EWS' 'urban development line', which is used in planning as a boundary within which the City has the capacity to provide higher service levels (Sutherland et al. 2014). Whether residents are relegated to second-class citizens through what has been termed class apartheid or are in a queue for improved services is open to interpretation. Ruiters (2005) explains that:

> An active lowering of standards and consumption levels by municipalities re-inscribe racial aspects of inferiority associated with 'third world services' and Black townships. This has important consequences for reinforcing powerlessness and knowing one's place (Ruiters 2005, 12).

Hellberg argues that the unevenness of infrastructure provision in eThekwini means that people see themselves as second-class citizens (Hellberg 2018). Whether EWS can reach the stage of delivery and implement plans to extend the urban development line and improve the level of services in these areas is critical to its evidencing that it is not just a commercialised utility with a technical focus, but one concerned with social transformation through its services.

Conclusion

Officials and activists need to dispose of their deceptive lenses if they are to address the lack of water access by those who live on Ingonyama Trust land. Instead of asserting that all people pay for water, they can see and engage with local realities and dynamics of water access. With greater organising around local issues, with academic–activists supporting local activists and being held accountable to them, there is scope for agency. In areas such as uMzinyathi, academic–activists could support poor residents and local groups to communicate directly with officials, bracketing their own ideological view. Doing so would allow officials to do the same. Together, challenging councillors to expand their calculation of their interests to include poor residents, they can formulate practical plans to achieve an important and immediate win of water access.

Instead of explicitly seeking long-term systemic change, past experience has shown that civil society can create an opening for systemic change through a mixture of protest and participation that pressures EWS to move past surface reforms within its commercialised approach (Galvin 2016). This approach acknowledges a complex reality of uneven development, and engages with it. It means demanding that EWS formulate a transparent plan to improve its service levels to areas outside the urban development line, particularly for the poorest on Ingonyama Trust land (eThekwini Municipality 2019), so that its approach to provision does not reinforce or create differentiated groups (Hellberg 2014; 2018). Of course, activists will need to assert ongoing pressure for a more progressive rising block tariff or a concave tariff curve, since integrating these areas into the overall approach of eThekwini means that EWS will install meters (flow limiters) while replacing and laying water pipes.

However, it is only possible if activists embrace a political strategy that refuses the reification of the state 'as either the principal locus of struggle, or as its supreme villain' (Angel and Loftus 2019, no page). As argued by Levenson, how residents and activists see the state impacts on their organising, which in turn affects how they are seen – and treated – by the state (Levenson 2021). Winning water wars through systemic change requires activists to replace their purely ideological long-term view to see local realities, and to consider the complexities and opportunities within the state. Achieving small, immediate successes has the potential not only to improve poor people's water access today, but also to act as the key to wider systemic change needed for our tomorrows.

Notes

1 The National Party, which governed South Africa from 1948 until the country's first democratic elections in 1994, was responsible for apartheid policies.

2 Inkatha was launched in 1975 as a Zulu nationalist movement by Chief Gatsha Buthelezi, and was later transformed into a political party, the Inkatha Freedom Party (IFP). From mid-1980s into the 1990s, the IFP remained in fierce political conflict with the ANC, which resulted in localised violence.

3 Pursuing the ideal of 'separate development', the apartheid regime created what it termed bantustans or homelands, specific geographical areas designated for each ethnic group to live. KwaZulu, or the place of Zulus, was comprised of less desirable, segmented land spread around the province of Natal and was semi-independent.

4 Broughton, T. (2012). 'Ingonyama Trust ruling scrutinised.' Available at: https://www.iol.co.za/news/south-africa/kwazulu-natal/ingonyama-trust-ruling-scrutinised-1312570. Accessed June 2018. Harrisberg, K. (2020). 'Rural South Africans fight for Zulu King to return

their land.' *Reuters Emerging Markets*, 10 December 2020. Available at: https://www.reuters.com/article/us-safrica-landrights-court-trfn-idUSKBN28K00K. Accessed 10 September 2021.

5 King Zwelithini, a descendant of Shaka Zulu, was monarch of the Zulu nation from 1971 until his death in 2021. Although his role was ceremonial, he was an important cultural figurehead with significant political influence.

6 In the newly incorporated areas, 80 per cent of households lacked appropriate water or sanitation services (Gounden conference presentation, 2006).

7 Broughton, T. 2012. 'Ingonyama Trust ruling scrutinised'. Available at: https://www.iol.co.za/news/south-africa/kwazulu-natal/ingonyama-trust-ruling-scrutinised-1312570. Accessed 1 June 2018.

8 RDP (sanding for Reconstruction and Development Programme) houses are the public houses built massively by the post-apartheid regime to fullfil the ANC promise that 'there shall be houses for all'.

9 Makoba, G. 2014. 'Water Award Mocks Our Suffering', *The Mercury*, 2 September. Available at: www.academia.edu/8251756/Water_award_that_mocked_suffering_of_the_communities. Accessed 4 January 2023.

10 Bond, P. 2006. Affadavit and Responding Affadavit, High Court of South Africa (Witwatersrand local division), Case no 06/13865, p.28.

11 2016. Stats SA. General Household Survey. Available at: https://www.statssa.gov.za/publications/P0318/P03182016.pdf. Accessed 20 February 2019.

12 Naidoo, O., Khumalo, D. and Bond, P. 2007. 'eThekwini: Drought hits the poors', *The Mercury*, Eye on Civil Society column, 3 July. Available at: eThekwini: drought hits the poors « WESTCLIFF FLATS RESIDENTS ASSOCIATION (wordpress.com). Accessed 20 June 2020. Bond, P. 2008. 'The Neoliberal Loo'. *Znet Commentaries*, 19 February. Available at: https://znetwork.org/zcommentary/the-neoliberal-loo-by-patrick-bond/. Accessed 23 August 2023.

13 I have been active in the SAWC from 2008, first in the KwaZulu-Natal provincial caucus, as a representative of a water advocacy NGO Umphilo waManzi, and then as a 'support person' assisting in providing contextual information, facilitating meetings, and representing SAWC in national multi-stakeholder fora. Within the SAWC, I have lobbied for a strategy in which the SAWC chooses representative local struggles and uses them for wider policy advocacy with EWS and municipalities, in order to address people's tangible local issues while affecting policy for all areas.

14 In 2017, with a new Head, EWS took a retrogressive step that decreased the FBW amount back to 6 kl or 200 L per day.

15 Olifant, N. and Skiti, S. 2016. 'ANC Captures State Taps in Water-for-votes Move'. *Times Live*, 12 June. Available at: https://www.timeslive.co.za/sunday-times/news/2016-06-12-anc-captures-state-taps-in-water-for-votes-move/. Accessed 2 May 2021.

16 Residents stated: 'Democracy is the councillor drinking expensive liquor.' And: 'We experienced what democracy had to offer, and it's not working for us.'

Official documents

eThekwini Municipality. 2019. *Municipal Spatial Development Framework 2019/20*. Available at: https://parks.durban.gov.za/storage/Documents/DPEM/Documents%20%20Notices/Strategic%20Spatial%20Planning/SDF/SDF%202019%20-%202020/Report/SDF%202019%20-%202020%20Report.pdf. Accessed 3 October 2019.

eThekwini Municipality. 2011. *Water Service Development Plan*. eThekwini Water and Sanitation Unit, eThekwini Municipality, Durban.

eThekwini Municipality. 2012. *Spatial Development Framework Report 2012–2013*. eThekwini Municipality, Durban.

eThekwini Municipality. nd. The Rural Area Based Management: An Introduction. Available at: https://roads.durban.gov.za/storage/Documents/Integrated%20Development%20Plans%20IDP/Annual%20Reviews/Reviews/IDP_2004_05%20Annual%20Review.pdf. Accessed 20 January 2020.

eThekwini Water and Sanitation (EWS). nd. *Most Innovative and Progressive Utility in Africa: Selected highlights*. eThekwini Municipality. Available at: http://prg.ukzn.ac.za/docs/

default-source/default-document-library/stockholm-water-week-brochure.pdf?sfvrsn=0. Accessed 27 July 2023.

Pollution Research Group. 2014. *City Partnerships for Urban Sanitation Services in eThekwini Municipality, South Africa: Institutional analysis of the eThekwini Municipality*, draft V1.4. Durban: University of KwaZulu-Natal, Pollution Research Group. Available at: http://prg.ukzn.ac.za/docs/default-source/projects/institutional-analysis.pdf?sfvrsn=2. Accessed 10 March 2020.

References

Allence, R. 2002. 'Sources of successful cost recovery for water: evidence from a national survey of South African municipalities', *Development Southern Africa* 19(5): 619–717.

Angel, J. and Loftus, A. 2019. 'With-against-and-beyond the human right to water', *Geoforum* 98: 206–13.

Bailey, R. and Buckley C. 2004. 'Modelling Domestic Water Tariffs.' *Proceedings of the 2004 Water Institute of Southern Africa (WISA) Biennial Conference*. eThekwini: University of KwaZulu-Natal.

Beall, J., Mkhize, S. and Vawda, S. 2004. 'Traditional Authority, Institutional Multiplicity and Political Transition in KwaZulu-Natal, South Africa', LSE Development Research Centre, Crisis States Programme. Working paper 48(1).

Bénit-Gbaffou, C. 2008. 'Are practices of local participation sidelining the institutional participatory channels? Reflections from Johannesburg', *Transformation: Critical Perspectives on Southern Africa*, 66–67: 1–33.

Bénit-Gbaffou, C. 2018a. 'Unpacking state practices in city-making, in conversations with Ananya Roy', *Journal of Development Studies* 54(12): 2139–48.

Bénit-Gbaffou, C. 2018b. 'Beyond the policy-implementation gap: How the City of Johannesburg manufactured the ungovernability of street trading', *Journal of Development Studies* 54(12): 2149–67.

Bond, P. 2004. *Talk Left, Walk Right: South Africa's frustrated global reforms*. London: Zed Press.

Bond, P. 2014. 'Tokenism in South African social policy', *Transformation* 86(1): 48–77.

Bond, P. 2019. 'Tokenistic water and neoliberal sanitation in post-apartheid Durban', *Journal of Contemporary African Studies* 37(4): 275–93.

Bond, P. and Galvin, M. 2018. 'Water, food and climate commoning in South African cities'. In *Routledge Handbook of Food as a Commons*, edited by J.L. Vivero-Pol, T. Ferrando, O. De Schutter, and U. Mattei, 231–48. Abingdon: Routledge.

Charlton, S. 2018. 'Confounded but complacent: Accounting for how the state sees responses to its housing intervention in Johannesburg', *Journal of Development Studies* 54(12): 2168–85.

Choudry, A. 2015. *Learning Activism: The intellectual life of contemporary social movements*. Toronto: University of Toronto Press.

Coalition against Water Privatisation, Anti-Privatisation Forum, and Public Citizen. 2004. *'Nothing for Mahala'. The forced installation of prepaid water meters in Stretford, Extension 4, Orange Farm, Johannesburg, South Africa*. Durban: Centre for Civil Society.

Dawson, M. and Sinwell, L. (eds). 2012. *Contesting Transformation: Popular resistance in twenty-first century South Africa*. London: Pluto Press.

Desai, A. 2002. *We Are the Poors: Community struggles in post-apartheid South Africa*. New York: Monthly Review Press.

Dwyer, P. 2004. 'The contentious politics of the Concerned Citizens Forum (CCF)'. A case study for the UKZN project *Marginalisation and New Social Movements in Post-Apartheid South Africa*. eThekwini: University of Kwazulu Natal.

Ferguson, J. 1994. *The Anti-Politics Machine*. Minneapolis: University of Minnesota Press.

Galvin, M. 2010. 'Rural survival, development or advocacy?' In *Zuma's Own Goal: Losing South Africa's 'war on poverty'*, edited by B. Maharaj and P. Bond, 335–58. Pietermaritzburg: University of KwaZulu-Natal Press.

Galvin, M. 2016. 'Leaving boxes behind: Civil society and water and sanitation struggles in Durban, South Africa', *Transformation* 92: 111–34.

Galvin, M. 2022. 'Water and sanitation woes, community despondency and empty democracy in South Africa'. In *Environment, Power and Justice in Southern Africa*, edited by J. Carruthers, N. Jacobs, and G. Wynn. Athens, OH: Ohio University Press.

Galvin, M. 2023. 'Dying to Drink: Water tenderpreneurs, community agency and protest in Mothutlung, North West'. In *Protest in South Africa: Rejection, reassertion, reclamation*, edited by H. Brooks, R. Chikane, and S. Mottiar. Johannesburg: MISTRA.

Harris, J. 2006. 'Towards a Poor People's Movement? A survey of Durban activists views on struggle, unity and the future'. Blogpost, Abahlali baseMjondolo, November 2006. Available at: https://abahlali.org/node/848/. Accessed 7 August 2020.

Hart, G. 2013. *Rethinking the South African Crisis: Nationalism, populism, hegemony*. Pietermaritzburg: University of KwaZulu-Natal Press.

Harvey, E. 2007. 'The Commodification of Water in Soweto and its Implications for Social Justice.' Unpublished PhD thesis. University of the Witwatersrand, Johannesburg.

Hellberg, S. 2014. 'Water, life and politics: Exploring the contested case of eThekwini Municipality through a governmentality lens', *Geoforum* 56: 226–36.

Hellberg, S. 2018. *The Biopolitics of Water: Governance, scarcity and populations*. London: Earthscan.

Hemson, D., Dube, B., Mbele, T., Nnadozie, R. and Ngcobo D. 2006. *Still Paying the Price: Revisiting the Cholera Epidemic of 2000–2001 in South Africa*. Municipal Services Project Occasional Paper number 10.

Levenson, Z. 2021. 'Becoming a population: Seeing the state, being seen by the state, and the politics of eviction in Cape Town', *Qualitative Sociology* 44: 367–83.

Loftus, A. 2005a. 'A Political Ecology of Water Struggles in Durban, South Africa.' Unpublished PhD thesis. University of Oxford.

Loftus, A. 2005b. '"Free water" as Commodity: The Paradoxes of Durban's water service transformations'. In *The Age of Commodity: Water privatisation in Southern Africa,* edited by D. McDonald and G. Ruiters, 189–203. London: Earthscan.

McDonald, D. and Pape, J. 2002. *Cost Recovery and the Crisis of Service Delivery in South Africa*, London: Zed Books.

McKinley, D. 2016. 'Lessons in community-based resistance? South Africa's Anti-Privatisation Forum', *Journal of Contemporary African Studies* 34(2): 268–81.

Mizes, J.C. and Cirolia, L.R. 2018. 'Bypass: Informal exceptions to urban land taxation in M'Bour and Kisumu', *African Policy* 151(3): 17–37.

Mottiar, S., Naidoo, O. and Khumalo, D. 2011. 'Women's organisations and the struggle for water and sanitation services in Chatsworth and Inanda, Durban: The Westcliff Flats Residents' Association and the Didiyela Women's Group', *Agenda* 25(2): 122–30.

Nash, F. 2013. 'Participation and passive revolution: The reproduction of neoliberal water governance mechanisms in Durban, South Africa', *Antipode* 45(1): 101–20.

Razon, N. 2017. 'Seeing and unseeing like a state: House demolitions, healthcare, and the politics of invisibility in Southern Israel', *Anthropological Quarterly* 90(11): 55–82.

Rogoll, J. 2017. 'Shaping Hydropolitics in Durban: Community activist strategies in Chatsworth.' Unpublished Master's dissertation. eThekwini: University of KwaZulu-Natal.

Ruiters, G. 2005. 'Knowing your place: Urban services and new modes of governability in South African cities'. Paper for Centre for Civil Society Seminar. eThekwini: University of KwaZulu Natal.

Sahle, E., Galvin, M., Pierce, B. and Todd, K. 2019. 'The UN's human right to water in the context of new water governance regimes in South Africa and Tanzania'. In *Human Rights in Africa*, edited by E. Sahle, 285–319. New York: Palgrave Macmillan.

Samson, M. 2020. 'The political work of wastepicker integration'. In *The Informal Economy Revisited: Examining the past, envisioning the future,* edited by M. Chen and F. Carre, 195–200. London: Routledge.

von Schnitzler, A. 2016. *Democracy's Infrastructure: Techno-politics and protest after apartheid*. Princeton: Princeton University Press.

Scott, J. 1990. *Domination and the Arts of Resistance: Hidden transcripts*. New Haven: Yale University Press.

Scott, J. 1998. *Seeing Like a State: How certain schemes to improve the human condition have failed*. New Haven: Yale University Press.

Smith, L. 2011. 'The limits to public participation in strengthening public accountability: A reflection on the 'citizens' voice' initiative in South Africa', *Journal of Asian and African Studies* 46(5): 504–17.

Sutherland, C., Hordijk, M., Lewis, B., Meyer, C. and Buthelezi, S. 2014. 'Water and sanitation provision in eThekwini Municipality: A spatially differentiated approach', *Environment and Urbanisation* 26(2): 469–88.

Tissington, K., Dettmann, M., Langford, M. and Dugard, J. 2008. *Water Services Fault Lines: An assessment of South Africa's water and sanitation provision across 15 municipalities.* Johannesburg: Centre for Applied Legal Studies (CALS), Norwegian Centre for Human Rights (NCHR) and Centre on Housing Rights and Evictions (COHRE).

Tutusaus, M. and Schwartz, K. 2020. 'Commercialisation as organised hypocrisy: The divergence of talk and action in water services in small towns in Uganda', *Water Alternatives* 13(2): 248-265.

Waetjen, T. and Vahed G. 2012. 'Gender, citizenship and power: The Westcliff Flats Residents' Association', *The Oriental Anthropologist* 12(2): 249–68.

Walsh, S. 2008. 'Uncomfortable collaborations': Contesting constructions of the 'poor' in South Africa', *Review of African Political Economy* 35(116): 255–79.

Wilson, Z. 2007. 'South Africa Case Study.' In *Technical Report: Second order water scarcity in Southern Africa*, edited by in J. Trottier, 224–395. London: Department for International Development.

12

Lost in translation: the elusive equity objective in Johannesburg's water policy

Darlington Mushongera

Introduction

'Working hard to know who is who in the zoo, in order to get things done in the City of Johannesburg.' This is what a senior official working in the City of Johannesburg told me when I started my research on water governance in the City and enquired about her job. Firstly, this suggests the vastness of the City's governance structure; secondly the multiplicity of actors and their opacity; and thirdly the strategies and tactics officials routinely deploy in their daily work in order to get things done. This chapter seeks to uncover the governance of water services in the City of Johannesburg, and explore further who the key players are, and what role they play in the determination, execution and monitoring of water policy in the City.

In post-apartheid South Africa, water access and delivery are at the core of what City government is supposed to be delivering, in a difficult balance between equity and efficiency, and where numerous so-termed 'service delivery protests' constantly remind local governments of strong expectations from citizens (Alexander 2010). This chapter asks how, within the complex existing governance structure of water services in Johannesburg, this balance is decided upon. In the City of Johannesburg, contestations over access to water have been rife, in particular around the use of prepayment water meters (Bond and Dugard 2008; Tissington et al. 2008), culminating in a famous court case: the Mazibuko and other v. City of Johannesburg (2010). The contention was on the sufficiency of the prescribed 6 kl free water per household per month and the constitutionality of the prepayment meters that were being rolled out by the City in low-income areas (Maphela and Cloete 2020; von Schnitzler 2008). It took the Constitutional Court to settle the matter, after passing through the High Court and the Supreme Court (Smith and Rubin 2015).

This chapter draws on ethnographic research conducted in the City of Johannesburg between November 2016 and June 2018 (Mushongera 2021). Data was collected by means of participant observation, over 30 in-depth interviews, analysis of documents and actual involvement in some of the officials' work activities. I conducted most of my research in the Environment, Infrastructure and Service Delivery Department (EISD)[1] assuming it was where water governance occurred centrally in the City. It turned out that I was wrong to assume that this was a function of a single department, and my study turned into a quest to identify who was involved in water governance.

For this reason, I decided on an Actor-Network Theory (ANT) approach, inspired by the work of Bruno Latour, to make the terrain more legible by identifying who was involved, how they were connected, and what key policy instruments and processes were used. The ANT is an analytical tool for understanding complex scenarios and socio-technical processes, emphasising relationships and the agency of both human and non-human actors (Bilodeau and Potvin 2016), referred to as 'actants' (in contrast with 'actors' that generally refers to human agents). Its basic premise is that objects, entities or phenomena are a result of the assemblies, associations, connections and interactions of diverse or heterogeneous actors (Zawawi 2018). The ANT postulates that to achieve a particular objective, both humans and non-humans must be 'enrolled' as actors through a process of 'translation' to form a socio-technical network (McLean and Hassard 2004). Given its premise of symmetry between human and non-human, the ANT assists in understanding complex or muddled social situations (Braga and Suarez 2018), by articulating their relationships and entanglements, which together form a unified and stable actor-network. An essential element of the ANT is the concept of 'translation', which is a process of enrolling various actors into a network in a way that brings all their divergent views into alignment (Zawawi 2018). For action to occur or a network to function, translation is indispensable because of its power to connect disparate entities, lock them into a network and amass their effort to achieve the objective of the main actor (Callon 1986; Fenwick and Edwards 2011).

This approach has led me to look at City structures and processes; actively looking not only for the main actors, but also the concrete and material documents (the 'intermediaries') that connect and bind them together, that 'enrol' these actors into forms of coordinated practices.

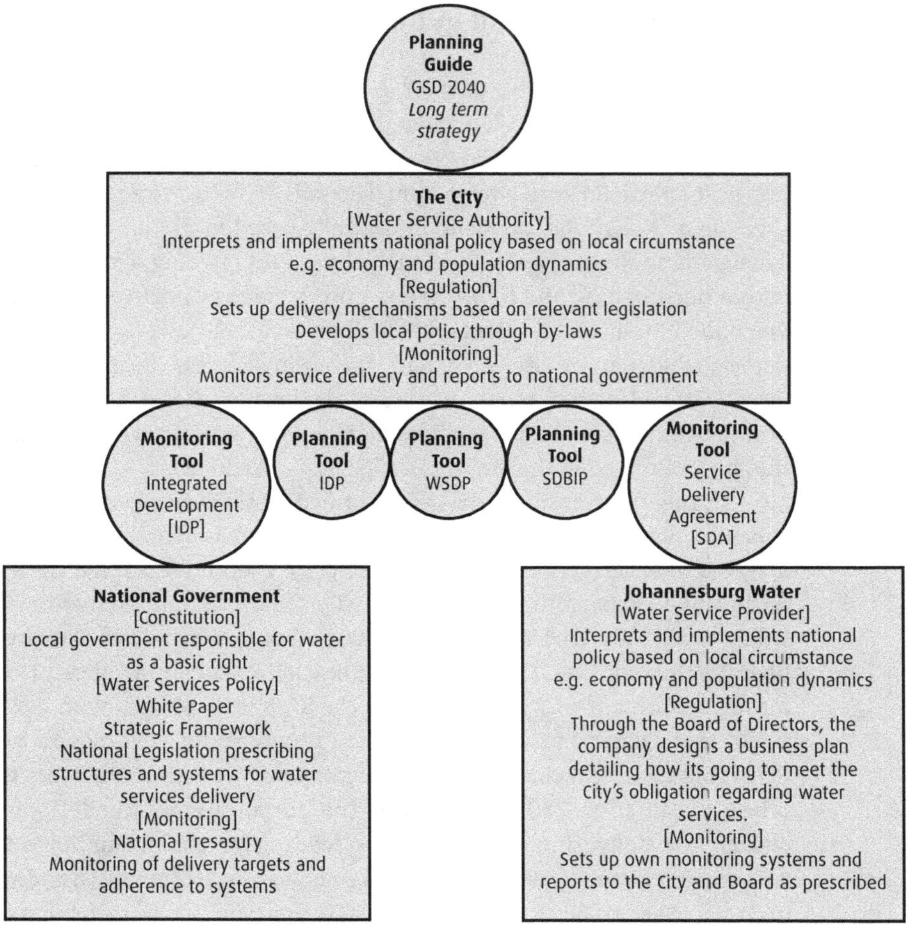

Figure 12.1 Main actants and the respective intermediaries.

Source: © Darlington Mushongera 2021

I scrutinised the complex ways these policy documents are aligned (or not) with one another (the 'translation' they operate), in particular in respect to the way issues of equity are framed by the different actants (**Figure 12.1**).

This chapter first provides historical perspective in the way water and service delivery has been framed in post-apartheid Johannesburg. It then interrogates which actants define Johannesburg's water policy, and what this policy states about the place of equity issues in water strategy. This is followed by an analysis of how various actants in the City oversee and regulate the implementation of this policy.

Service delivery reform in the City of Johannesburg

The administrative history of the City of Johannesburg from the early 1990s to the present is well documented (Allan et al. 2001; CoJ 2006). The establishment of a unified metropolitan municipality followed the first post-apartheid local government elections of 2000. Prior to that, the City comprised 13 independent and racially-based local municipalities. Amalgamating these separate municipalities and building a single City with a one tax-base and to institute a universal service delivery system demanded immediate attention (Beall et al. 2003). It was key in deracialising service delivery and increasing access to previously disadvantaged communities, in line with the new Constitution. The process was not a one-off event but an on ongoing process of adjustment that has continued to the present (CoJ 2012a; CoJ 2002).

During this transition, the newly formed local government (Greater Johannesburg Metropolitan Council – GJMC)[2] found itself in the middle of a severe financial crisis in 1997, triggered by a loose legal framework, uncontrolled expenditures, political tensions and lack of accountability (Allan et al. 2001; CoJ 2006; Smith 2006). In order to confront the dire financial situation, the GJMC introduced the iGoli 2002 Plan, a radical plan for restructuring the City's institutions. The iGoli Plan, aligned with new public management principles, contained proposals for new models of delivering services including water, electricity and waste removal among others (Allan et al. 2001; CoJ 2006). The 'corporatisation model' was chosen for delivering water services leading to the formation of Johannesburg Water (JW) as a municipal wholly-owned corporatised entity in 2001 (Seedat 2001; Smith 2006). The rationale was to have an independent entity, JW that would operate 'efficiently', improve service delivery, and generate much needed revenue for the City (Magdhal 2012; Allan et al. 2001). However, both the revenue generating objective, and the corporatisation of water delivery through a relatively autonomous entity following business rules (JW), reflected an inherent tension with this model which made it problematic for the City to achieve efficiency and equity in service delivery simultaneously (Smith 2006; Smith and Morris 2008).

Constitutionally, the City is responsible for service delivery: having water services delivered by an independent third party meant that City's mandate could be compromised due to a fragmentary administration, loosely defined roles and weak instruments for holding the corporatised entity to account (Eales 2006). Hence, an appropriate governance model was needed not only to design water policy but also to oversee the implementation (by JW) of that policy (Seedat 2001; Smith 2006).

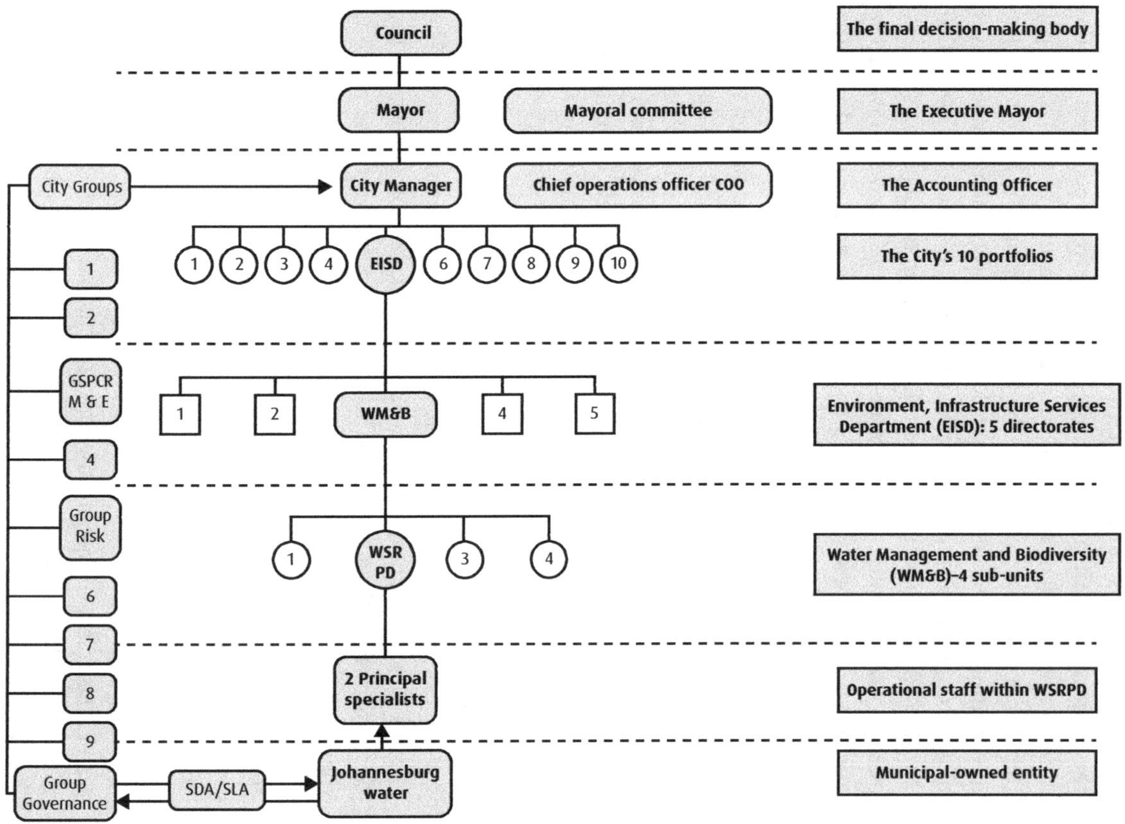

Figure 12.2 Environment and Infrastructure Services Department (EISD) – organogram. Source: © Darlington Mushongera 2021

After its formation in 2001, JW operated under a five-year management contract where its primary task was to establish the water utility, set up operational systems and place it on a sound financial footing (Allan et al. 2001). The City administered the contract with the JW (as contractor) using a small but powerful unit within the City administration: the Contracts Management Unit (CMU). After the lapse of the management contract in 2006, the Infrastructure and Services Department (ISD) was set up in the City administration to serve as the new centre for service delivery and associated infrastructure, taking over most of the functions that were performed by the CMU (CoJ 2008; CoJ 2012a). The primary function of the ISD was to translate the strategic agenda of the executive management into a comprehensive infrastructure and services plan with policies, strategies, objectives, aligned with the City's long-term goals.

After 2011 local government elections, the City undertook another restructuring of the entire administration. The ISD was merged with the Environment department to form the Environment and Infrastructure Services Department (EISD). The EISD was mandated to manage and oversee the three service delivery entities: JW, City Power, and Pikitup (CoJ 2012a). Furthermore, the City introduced a new administrative layer known as the 'Group' approach, involving the formation of separate units whose function was to ensure alignment and consistency between the City's strategic goals and their actual implementation (CoJ 2012b). The Groups were meant to deal with transversal issues such as finance, governance, strategic planning, marketing and communications. The Groups that matter most in terms of water services governance are the Group Strategy (GSPCR), Group Risk, and Group Governance which is the City's shareholder representative (**Figure 12.2**).

However, rather than creating a lean administration, these 2011 reforms introduced a more expanded and complex City administration and further fragmented its oversight function of its entities. While there was a change in the political leadership in August of 2016, the City's administrative structure remained the same. The EISD continued to play an oversight and regulatory role over JW, City Power, and Pikitup (CoJ 2016). With respect to water, the role was specifically assigned to the Water Resources and Biodiversity (WR&B) unit of the EISD and handled by a sub-unit known as Water Services Regulation and Policy Development (WSR&PD). However, in a closer analysis of this oversight and regulatory function, it was evident that the function was spread across multiple but loosely connected units within the City.

Johannesburg Water (JW) is the agent through which the City of Johannesburg delivers water and sanitation services to its residents. In terms of the Water Services Act, the City is the water services authority while JW is the water services provider. A private limited company, JW is wholly owned by the City of Johannesburg. It officially commenced business on 1 January 2001. At the time of research, the company employed 2,655 people and operated a network of 10 water depots and 6 wastewater treatment plants across Johannesburg (CoJ 2017).

As a private company, JW has a board of directors as its highest governing body. However, since it is its sole shareholder, the City Council appoints the board members to which the board reports directly. On one hand, the City expects the company to operate efficiently in order to generate revenue, while on the other, the company is expected to provide water equitably in ways that take into account past injustices in delivery. To ensure that this happens, the City and JW enter into a Service Delivery Agreement (SDA) in which both parties bind themselves to make everything possible to ensure that both the financial and social objectives of the City are met. Within the City structure, Group Governance is the custodian of all the SDAs entered into between the City and its entities, and its officials regularly attend JW quarterly board meetings to assess the performance of the company.

A key official in JW is the Managing Director (MD). The MD is the main link between JW and the City, reporting the everyday running of the company as well as responding to all the reporting requirements on operational issues based on agreed performance areas. As a result, the MD is part of the City Manager's executive management team, accountable to the City Manager. On the other hand, running a private company, he is also accountable to JW Board, which will check that the company is run according to sound business principles. It is therefore clear that although JW is constituted as a private company, it has dual accountabilities – theoretically a business-oriented one to the JW Board, and a policy-targeted one to the City. My next step is therefore to determine what this policy is, how it is framed and who decides on Johannesburg's water policy.

Identifying who decides on Johannesburg's water policy

According to national legislation, the City as the Water Service Authority has the task of developing a water services strategy. This strategy is informed by national policy legislation, population size, and the financial resources at the City's disposal.

National government – a key role in framing social equity in access to water

While the research focus was on the City, it was evident that the national government is a key player in the determination of water policy and exerts considerable influence on local municipalities through various departments and policy instruments. Through the Constitution, water was elevated to the status of basic right resulting in the promulgation of several pieces of national legislation designed to implement this right, including the 1994 White Paper on Water and Sanitation.

The 1994 White Paper recommended that access to affordable water be included in the Bill of Rights as part of the new Constitution, in order to reverse the skewed pattern of access that existed at the time due to apartheid (Goldin 2010). The White Paper contained a set of key recommendations related to water services policy such as demand-driven approach; basic services, human rights; 'some for all' rather than 'all for some'; equitable regional allocation of development resources; economic value of water; and the 'user pays' principle. The White Paper mandates local government to develop service provision, while national government ensures that all citizens have access to adequate basic services by providing national policy, guidelines and standards, and to monitor and audit progress (DWAF 2002). Notable recommendations of the White Paper that eventually became effective were allocation (for free) of a minimum of 25 l per person per day (translating to 6 kl per household), communal access not more than 200 m from dwelling, a flow rate of water not less than 10 l a minute and that the water should be available on a regular daily basis (DWAF 2002). This was to be implemented via the national Department of Water and Sanitation, which sets up the minimum standards to be met in terms of water supply and sanitation to residents. The Norms and Standards for Domestic Water and Sanitation Services gazetted on the 8 September 2017 illustrates how legislation provides for a 'water ladder' in terms of quality of water services provided, in order to cater in particular to informal settlements and to provide minimum basic services for free to poorer households.

Though the Department of Water and Sanitation (DWS) sets norms and standards (DWS 2017), it is within the municipality's hands to progressively realise the right of access in terms of the Constitution (Chenwi 2013). It was clear from discussions with City officials that defining a minimum level of standard was a contentious issue. Once set into the City's Services Development Plan, residents had a right to lodge a complaint to court if this right was not realised. A senior official noted that there were changes to how the setting of minimum standards was done, and certain cultures and debates over what was considered minimum was slowly fading away:

> National Department of Water Affairs reduced the requirements for that Water Services Delivery Plan into something like an Excel sheet and it is now a mere numbers game. When I first did the Water Services Development Plan for the City, it was a very fat document and it had a lot of policy issues and that's where we had all these debates about stand pipes, affordability, and it's like a ticking time bomb now, issue of affordability. [In parallel however], Joburg Water has gone on to define their own level of sanitation for the last 10 years, before, we were trying to jointly decide whether your sanitation approach is the correct one. We used to have these debates but now I do not see them, these debates were definitely part of our mandate at the time (Deputy Director of Open Space Planning interview WR&B – EISD, 2017).

National government also exerts pressure on the local government water sector by requiring municipalities to publish an annual report showing progress made towards meeting water service delivery that the City (captured through documents called Integrated Development Plans – IDP). The Annual Report is a legislated required report that is strictly monitored by the National Treasury and is one of the conditions that municipalities must meet in order to receive the municipal grants from national government.

Other mechanisms of accountability specific to the water sector are administered through the national Department of Water and Sanitation (DWS) to ensure that municipalities have put in place water services development plans and tools for ensuring service delivery as per standards. There are DWS guidelines for Compulsory National Standards Regulations and guidelines for Norms and Standards for Water Services Tariffs regulations published in 2002 in terms of the Water Services Act of 1997. This document states that

> The norms and standards are aimed at promoting socially equitable, financially viable and environmentally sustainable tariffs. The departure point in compiling these norms and standards was to provide the responsible water services institution with a framework that reflects best practice while allowing it discretion on how it actually sets and quantifies the tariffs' (DWS 2017, 30).

A major component of tariffing which had bearing on equality and affordability was the introduction of the rising block system which included at least three tariff blocks. The basic idea of the Rising Block Tariff System was to ensure that those who consume more water will pay more, based on the notion that those who use water luxuriously can afford to pay and hence should pay more to subsidise those who cannot afford to pay. A household consuming 5 kl per month will pay nothing ('free basic water'), whereas the household consuming beyond 6 kl per month will pay.

In addition to the issue of access to a minimum quantity of water, national government through the DWS also came up with the Blue Drop and Green Drop Assessments for drinking water quality and waste water quality respectively. These tools are meant to ensure that residents are not only supplied with potable but that the water is clean and of a high standard and that disposal of waste water is done properly. While these tools help the City plan and monitor its performance and account to national government, they are essentially tools for national government of ensuring that constitutional obligation and right of access to water for citizens is achieved. It is obvious that national government cannot execute this mandate solely and directly; it has had to enrol local government into its network through these instruments.

City of Johannesburg – water services planning at local level

The City of Johannesburg is a 'Water Services Authority', meaning it is constitutionally responsible for delivering water services in the city, and does so by setting up structure and systems as required by law, interpreting and implementing national water policy while taking account of local circumstances such as the nature and size of the economy, population size, water sources, poverty and inequality. Within the City, the critical players in the City can be found both in the political arm and in the executive arm. The political arm of the City comprises Council, which through two key policy documents, the Growth and Development Strategy (GDS) and the Integrated Development Plan (IDP) set the tenor of the policy, agree and approve the targets suggested by the entities. The City Council overall acts as a monitoring institution to hold the executive to account. Sub-committees of the Council, known as Section 79 Committees, oversee in more detail the functions of the executive and the municipal entities (such as JW).

The executive arm, on the other hand, is the City administration, headed by the mayor, who executes his office with the help of a Mayoral Committee. Below the mayor is the City Manager and the members of the

Executive Management which are essentially heads of line Departments and Groups. The mayor is very much controlled by the political party manifesto and he sets the strategic agenda of the City for his or her electoral term, while the City manager is guided by the IDP in terms of the agreed service delivery targets required by the National Treasury, and the City objective of ensuring financial sustainability.

Lower down, the Executive Management Team (Section 57 managers), focus on service delivery itself using the Business Plans, the SDA and the Service Delivery Budget Implementation Plan (SDBIP).[3] In order to hold them accountable, Section 57 managers are tied to a 'performance contract' with the City, with the incentive of a performance bonus. The following quotes from officials demonstrate these aspects.

> We also have Oversight Portfolio Committees, which are made up of councillors, almost like mini councils. The different political parties are represented and they oversee your department. From time to time, they request us to come and present to them what we are doing on illegal dumping or on water services' (Acting ED interview EISD, 2018).
>
> The City manager implements the contract that the mayor has got with the public, which is the IDP. It is detailed in his scorecard which he signs with the mayor, and one of the areas is the financial sustainability of the City: there must be money in the City. Also, when you read the Municipal Systems Act, it tells you that the City shall produce an Annual Report. That is the sole responsibility of the City manager. If the City fails to produce the Annual Report, the National Treasury won't be talking to me, they will talk to the City manager and he will crack the whip! (Deputy Director of Monitoring and Evaluation interview GSPCR, 2017).

From an ANT perspective, the executive mayor is the focal actor in this network given his role in setting service delivery priorities. Although these are informed by an agreed strategy (the Growth Development Strategy, GDS), the mayor usually decides on areas to be prioritised during his term of office. The mayor, through the Mayoral Lekotla meetings,[4] enrols all City departments into his network by obliging them to design explicit plans whose object is to fulfil the mayoral plans. When departmental plans are approved at the Mayoral Lekgotla meetings, a budget is allocated and the plans are ready for implementation through the Service Delivery Budget Implementation Plan.

This makes the Budget Office of the City an important actant in deciding how much is allocated to each department. However, as one official expressed, the Planning Office of the City and the Spatial Development Framework (SDF) that is developed were viewed as the most important office and document for determining budget. The SDF shows where current and future developments in the city will occur, and departments must be seen to align to the SDF, otherwise they risk losing their budget. One official captured as follows:

> I was in the Department of Development Planning, in a sub-unit responsible for capital planning within the city. Our main aim was to align the budget to the spatial plans of the city. In other words, trying to *ensure that more money went towards marginalised areas* and towards nodal areas within the city. Therefore, we would work very closely with the Budget Office and the Finance Department. We would then get all of the departments and all of the Municipal Owned Entities to submit their bids. So, our key ally is Budget Office because they've got very strict reporting requirements, boxes to tick. Our other ally was EISD because they are responsible for the [Municipally Owned Entities] which generate income: Joburg Water and City Power (ex-official interview, City of Johannesburg Spatial Planning, 2018, *my emphasis*).

There is a fairly large number of actors involved at the City level for ensuring that service delivery occurs – and that equity targets in the delivery of water are partly ensured spatially, at least in terms of capital budget, where public investment is targeting previously disadvantaged areas.

The Environment and Infrastructure Services Department (EISD) – policy planning

The EISD is the department responsible for developing policy relating to water services through research and monitoring. This is how its mandate is framed, away from implementation:

> The Department's main function is policy development, regulatory and monitoring rather than being an implementation agent or a service delivery agent. The mandate of the Department … is reflected in the following key performance areas:
>
> - **Urban water management** is meant to ensure security of supply and … the quality of river health.
> - **Biodiversity protection** … is concerned with ensuring protection of eco-systems and biodiversity …
> - **Infrastructure planning and coordination** is … meant to ensure adequate and resilient infrastructure to support the City's spatial vision. The tool that is used is commonly referred to as the Consolidated Infrastructure Plan.
> - **Environment education and awareness** is aimed at behavioural change on environmental sustainability (EISD *Business Plan*, 2016/17, City of Johanneburg, 6–7).

Interestingly, the EISD's mandate explicitly focuses on water supply management, whereas the issue of access and water delivery is not formulated. It is important to follow that lead by interrogating the key documents that the EISD produces in order to achieve its targets: the GDS and the IDP (which set out the vision and short-term target respectively), as well as the SDA (as the legally binding document with JW). In ANT terms, these actants 'enrols' actors into a network and 'locks' them into delivering particular amounts of services, at specific times within available resources.

Non-human actants in water governance: Growth and Development Strategy (GDS) and Integrated Development Plan (IDP)

With respect to water, two main documents outline the strategic intent of the City: the GDS and the IDP.[5] The GDS sets out the overall aspiration of the City over a long-term period while the IDP breaks that down into a five-year plan of what can be achieved over that period as a contribution to the long-term vision.

The Growth and Development Strategy (GDS)

At the City level, the GDS 2040 document is the main document that guided planning across departments and entities in the long term. Officials called this their 'Bible', and all planning by all departments, units and entities must be explicitly linked to the objectives emphasised in the GDS:

> Whatever is in the IDP must be aligned to what we have said must happen in the GDS. And our departmental business plans must say how are we are actually addressing the issues in the IDP and in the GDS. You find, if you look at the Business Plan, it says what objective in the IDP and in the GDS it is addressing. This is how we do our planning, ensuring that the Departments are addressing the City's priorities (ex-director interview WR&B – EISD 2014).

The GDS states in its introduction its resolve to respond to the apartheid injustices still shaping the present city, but without explicit reference to service delivery:

> The strategy restates the City's resolve in confronting the past injustices created during Apartheid, working towards a democratic, non-racial, non-sexist and just City while simultaneously confronting present and future challenges as they emerge (CoJ 2011, 8)

The GDS makes several proclamations specifically about water. Its Outcome 2 states that the City aims to 'provide a resilient, liveable, sustainable urban environment – underpinned by infrastructure supportive of a low-carbon economy' (GDS 2040, 8). The first major principle guiding the GDS is the eradication of poverty:

> City of Johannesburg will continually assist the poor to build capacity, thereby supporting them in accessing the city and stepping onto the ladder of prosperity [... by targeting] new households, internal and circular migrants, those in hostels, informal settlements and historical ghettoes, the unemployed youth, refugees and others who are vulnerable *to access urban services* (CoJ 2011, 8, my emphasis).

More precisely, the GDS states that the City will contribute towards its constitutional duty to provide basic needs for community by 'ensuring the affordability of municipal services, public transport and social facilities, through progressive tariff structures, creative cross-subsidisation and targeted social packages' (GDS 2040, 33).

A challenge facing the City is the large number of informal settlements.[6] The GDS takes cogniscence of the spatial role that informal settlements play as representing 'the means by which the most socially and economically disconnected queue for access' (GDS 2040, 47). However, there is no particular statement in the GDS regarding their status and the provision of basic services to these specific spaces. The dominant statements with regards to water provision in the GDS relate to the issue of responding to the water resource scarcity (to provide for the whole of Johannesburg) and the need to ensure sustainable and quality water provision, through strategies such as reducing consumption and water losses. Hence, the proposed indicators identified to measure progress against Outcome 2 focus on resource conservation rather than the issue of access and equity: 'Indicator 8: Per cent of unaccounted for water' and 'Indicator 9: Per cent of water reclaimed' (GDS 2040, 96). Actually:

> Water conservation can be achieved through multiple strategies: technical losses through effective asset management and maintenance can achieve considerable savings – as noted above. Effective billing based on accurate meter readings and precise consumption is vitally important, to ensure water supplied is not unaccounted for or lost. Improving the billing system and making sure everyone contributes to payments for water will go a long way. This means the City must work to ensure water is valued and priced correctly. Demand can be reduced through changing behaviour, with this necessitating a programme of collaboration and engagement with residents (GDS 2040; 2011, 58).

While there are hints in the strategy towards the acceptation of the in situ upgrading of informal settlements, there is no explicit mention of any policy direction towards infrastructure provision of water in these areas in particular. The general discourse rather points to classic neoliberal rationalities: cost-recovery and behavioural change through 'engagement with residents', linked to public investment to fix and upgrade infrastructure using smart technologies.

The Integrated Development Plan (IDP)

Directions related to service delivery are more explicit in the Integrated Development Plan (IDP) document, a five-year plan claiming to materialise all the strategies contained in the GDS, based on the mayoral priorities for specific mayoral terms. The 2015 IDP dedicates an entire chapter to service delivery. This chapter provides an overview of the City's service delivery

Table 12.1 Water service standards in the City of Johannesburg 2015 Integrated Development Plan.

Core services	Service standard
Burst water pipes	Response within an hour and repair within 12 hours of logged call
Restoration of sewer system post overflow	Response within an hour and repair within 12 hours of logged call
Compliance with SANS 241 water standards	100% compliance – uninterrupted Blue Drop Score>98%
Water meter readings	98–100% currently read meters monthly
New water connections	Installation within 7 days and 100% functional and correctly read within 24 hours of installation
Clearance/repair of sewer blockages	Within 24 hours of logging call
Call Centre billing queries	Acknowledgement within 24 hours and resolution within 3 days of logged call
Reduction in water losses	>10% reduction: Quarterly (Target 36.8% non-revenue water losses)
Service interruptions	Communications sent to citizens. Planned: 7 days before interruption. Unplanned: immediately

Source: © After CoJ 2015a, 162

Table 12.2 City scorecard on specific Integrated Development Plan (IDP) programmes related to water.

IDP programme	Key Performance Indicator	Target 2013–14	Base line	Target 2014–15	Target 2014–16	Intervention	Implementing department	Lead cluster
Customer Service Charter	Percentage achievement in service level standards	70% achievement of service level standards	41.07%	80%	90%	Area based service standards turnaround time improvement	Group Governance All departments and municipally owned entities (MoEs)	Good governance
Urban Water Management Programme	Demand side management percentage reduction in water loss (non-revenue)	Non-revenue water loss at 27% (target revised downwards)	Non-revenue water losses at 35%	Non-revenue water losses at 29%	Non-revenue water losses at 35%	Interventions to reduce non-revenue water Blue Economy projects	Johannesburg Water (JW)	Sustainable services

Source: © After CoJ 2015a, 163

programme, in which 'equitable access, quality basic service provision, and the extension of services to cater for demand and growth pressures' are key objectives (CoJ 2015a, 162). In particular, the City believes that 'to get basic services right', it must commit to the 'progressive and systematic reduction of service delivery breakdowns and backlogs across all regions' and provide for a minimum service level standard for all (CoJ 2015a). These service level standards are illustrated in **Table 12.1** below.

Interestingly, there is no specific attention paid in these standards to the issue of access (or lack thereof). This omission is confirmed by the City's 'scorecard' which specifies the indicators along which the City will measure its performance and the achievement of its set targets (**Table 12.2**).

While it is clear under the 'Urban Water Management programme' that the target is to reduce water losses,[7] the target remains quite vague under the 'Customer Service Charter'. By looking at the implementing department, one can infer that the document refers to all services that the City provides. This is problematic, in that the City cannot set the same level of standard for all services given the difference in the nature of services. This leaves one wondering as to the where exactly the service standards and quantities for water services are specified.

Key but impenetrable actants for water provision – Johannesburg Water and the Service Delivery Agreement (SDA) that enrols it

The primary task of JW, a municipally-owned entity formed in 2001, is to provide water services to residents of Johannesburg on behalf of the City (Allan et al. 2001), following the policy directions inscribed in its strategic documents, such as universal and uninterrupted access to water and sanitation services. Johannesburg Water is 'locked' into the water service network by means of the SDA, a legal document binding the Municipally Owned Entities (MoE) to deliver services on behalf of the City. In terms of the ANT, the SDA acts as 'intermediary', in the form of text inscribed on paper transporting meaning and force to the entity and prescribing how it should act. The SDA between the City and JW says that JW will provide water in accordance with City strategy:

> **Principal objective of the SDA and link to the budgeting process:** The SDA is entered into between the Parties with the principal objective of providing a framework within which detailed service delivery plans can be developed and implemented by JOHANNESBURG WATER in a manner which is consistent with and which plays a part in giving effect to the City's strategic planning process (Extract from the CoJ 2015b, 22).

The vagueness of the agreement, referring to imprecise municipal strategic documents and not stating the key objectives of Johannesburg's water policy, in a brief section of a very bureaucratic type of document, is reflective of the limited oversight capacity of the City over its water utility.

An analysis of the SDA document shows that it is mostly a process document that guides JW in terms of the requirement relating to planning, implementing and reporting and what documentations must by produced. As such, the statement above is not really binding as it needs to be read with a host of other, unspecified documents.

The blurriness of the SDA in terms of what JW needs to achieve might lead us to think that JW is a largely independent entity. In fact, many other elements link JW to the City, not stated in the SDA, in particular, the fact that City Council is responsible for appointing the board of directors:

> These companies are independent up to a point. On one hand, they feel accountable to their Board of directors, and on the other hand, supposedly accountable to the City through the service delivery agreement, but everyone knows that JW operate according to a budget allocation that is determined at the City level. Hence, they are not really an independent company that can go off and negotiate their own contracts. They are still bound to the rules of the Municipal Finance Management Act. They are still bound to a large degree by the City's procurement rules and these Municipal Acts (Deputy Director of Open Space Planning interview WR&B–EISD, 2017).

What transpires in this quote, however, is that JW accountability is mostly framed in financial and legal terms – nowhere are equity targets explicitly formulated, or the need to strike a balance between universal access and profitability or cost-recovery. However, JW has multiple reporting lines to Council, the mayor and the City manager as well through line departments and units such as the EISD, Group Governance, Group Strategy and Group Risk and Audit. Therefore, we now turn to this more opaque and fuzzy way of 'enrolling' JW, which sits in the oversight and monitoring functions of the City, interrogating its actants – actors and their policy instruments.

Table 12.3 Oversight bodies for water in the City of Johannesburg.

Council	Executive	Environment and Infrastructure Services Department (EISD)	Johannesburg Water (JW)
Council (*final approval body*) Section 79 Committee (*oversight body*)	Mayor (*priority setting*) Mayoral Committee (*priority setting*) City Manager (*accounting officer*) Group Governance (*compliance monitoring*) Group Strategy (*service target monitoring: IDP*) Group Risk and Audit (*MFMA compliance*)	MMC (*political head – policy*) Executive Director (*accounting office: department level*) Director (*water services – planning*) Deputy Director (*regulation and policy development*)	Board of Directors (*financial sustainability*) Managing Director (*operational efficiency*)

The multiplicity of oversight bodies at different levels of the City administration is illustrative of a political fragmentation that is ultimately disempowering municipal officials and councillors.

Source: © Mushongera 2021

Overseeing water delivery and management in the City of Johannesburg

Given the relative vagueness of equity targets in terms of water delivery in the overall policy, it is important to track what officials do when they oversee Johannesburg's water and service delivery, in particular, to the poorest households or areas in Johannesburg.

Identifying actants in water delivery oversight

There are numerous bodies within the City that perform oversight functions: the elected Council, the administration (the Executive), the EISD (**Table 12.3**). Even within each of these bodies, oversight might be spread between various sub-units – for example, within EISD alone, Water Services Regulation and Policy Development (WSR&PD), Open Space Planning, and Catchment Management Unit. Or, within the executive, there is Group Governance, GSPCR's Monitoring and Evaluation Unit, Group Risk and Audit, The Mayoral Committee through the mayor, the Executive Management Committee (EMT) through the City Manager. Even within JW, there are several bodies involved in management and forms of oversight, with its board of directors, and its managing director as the key actants.

The oversight function of the City over JW is performed at multiple levels with a high level of overlap occurring in some cases. The EISD demands data from JW on performance targets, and checks whether the company is operating according to City policy and by-laws related to water services, for reporting to the ED and the Members of the Mayoral Committee (MMC). Group Strategy (GSPCR) checks on progress towards the IDP, on which it must report to National Treasury. Group Governance, as the shareholder representative, checks on the SDA and demands performance data to be reported to the City Manager. Reporting is not done just to City departments and units but specific individuals such as the mayor, the City Manager and the MMC for the EISD who also undertakes oversight from a political standpoint. Johannesburg Water actually complained about the fact that they are being called to upon to provide the same data to all these parties, as some officials said:

> There is a whole lot of duplication in terms of reporting. We report quarterly to the Group Strategy because they do monitoring and evaluation: they will send us spreadsheets for us to complete on our

achievements for that particular quarter. Group Risk Audit also will want us to report to them, with supporting documents for them to do their verification. So we spend a lot of time reporting to the City over one thing. In any case we give them a report every quarter, it is mandatory. We also provide a report to Group Governance because they are responsible for managing the entities. Over and above that we get asked by different units and divisions within the City for the very same information that actually has already been submitted as part of the quarterly report (ex- official JW interview – Innovation 2017).

The Section 79 Committee (or portfolio committee) is made up of councillors of various parties. They are supposed to scrutinise quarterly reports from the entities and make recommendations to Council. However, they are not decision-making bodies, and their recommendation may not take effect if the ruling party decides so. It was made clear by officials that the Mayoral Committee could by-pass these committees and only submit reports to them when decisions had already been taken:

> Most of the reports come to the Sections 79 after the decisions have already been taken. Yet, the reports are supposed to go up through the portfolio committees, then go to the mayoral committee. That is how the DA didn't understand they were being cut out of power because the ANC would send all their reports straight to mayoral committee. These Sections 79 think that they are very important and I am saying the decisions are already taken, guys: at the mayoral committee! (Deputy Director of Open Space Planning interview, WR&B–EISD, 2017, CoJ)

This multiplicity of oversight bodies, often working in silos, and some of which with limited capacity to act (such as the Section 79 Committees) or a narrow and specialised overview of JW operations, obviously reduces the City's oversight capacity over JW. However, one official described how this diffuses responsibility within the City:

> What has happened is that, because the number of people who are doing a form of oversight has expanded, we end up with three parties all involved in a way in the same issue and it sort of muddies the waters as to who is taking charge now. There is us as Open Space Planning, there is Water Services Regulation and there is Group Governance (Deputy Director of Open Space Planning interview WR&B–EISD, 2017).

However, it is worth going deeper in terms of analysing the way the EISD performs its oversight function as it can be safely argued that the greater part of the oversight function relating to water happens through the EISD as the provision of water has environment and infrastructure aspects attached to it such as pollution and conveyance infrastructure – that is, pipes, tanks, and taps.

Oversight of Johannesburg water within the Environment and Infrastructure Services Department (EISD)

The water sector is vast, comprising various aspects such as water quality, catchment management, storm water management, biodiversity, groundwater and provision of basic services to informal settlement, that is water and sanitation.

The main parties involved here are the Executive Director (ED) for EISD and the Deputy Director for Water Services Regulation and Biodiversity sub-unit. There are several intermediaries between the City and JW. These intermediaries are various instruments and processes designed to provide some form of monitoring from various angles such as drinking water quality (as in the case of the Blue Drop Assessment) and business plans which are designed to give structure to the planning process.

Line departments in the City (see **Figure 12.2**) are headed by EDs. These are senior managers who have dual accountability, one to the City manager through the 'balanced scorecard', and the other to the MMC, the political head of the department. This scenario places the ED in a difficult position because these two immediate superiors pursue different and contrasting objectives. The MMC wants to see issues of equity addressed, particularly in poor, high-density areas, while the City manager is more concerned about financial sustainability and prefers strict collection of revenues for use of water services. This is how one official described the expectations of the MMC for the EISD:

> So how do we balance political needs versus the technical requirements? Politically, the focus is on service delivery and our MMC is responsible for water, electricity which is your Joburg Water, City Power and Pikitup, the three main entities for which within this Department we have oversight role over. And those three main entities are basically your service delivery arm of the City. So our MMC, which is our political head, she reports to the Mayor. She normally says that when we have our quarterly meetings that, you

Table 12.4 Compared Key Performance Areas for various senior City officials in charge of water (2017–18)

Key performance areas **Executive Director: Environment and Infrastructure Services Department (EISD)**	Key performance areas **Group Head : Group Governance**	Key performance areas **Group Head : Group Strategy (GSPCR)**
To reduce greenhouse gas emissions to reduce risk of climate change To improve water quality by managing and protecting water resources for utilisation and ecological integrity To manage and protect critical biodiversity To accelerate sustainable waste management practices for a healthier and cleaner living environment To support job creation To coordinate and plan infrastructure for the City To ensure a financially prudent City with clean audits by the Auditor General	To enhance tracking of the implementation of committee and council decisions To enhance group committee systems and processes *To ensure ongoing improvement in service delivery and promote sound governance* To promote sound governance, improve overall City of Johannesburg and municipally owned entities (MoE) performance and evaluation of the committees, ensure ongoing improvement in business management governance	To strengthen intergovernmental relations to ensure alignment to municipal, provincial and national strategic priorities and plans. *To ensure continuous improvement in service delivery to the residents of the City of Johannesburg* To ensure evidence-based decision-making To leverage opportunities from key city-to-city engagements for deriving mutual benefits to ensure that Johannesburg retains its global, regional, and local competitive advantage

	To ensure a financially prudent City with clean audits by the Auditor General	To ensure responsiveness of the City of Johannesburg to meet developmental and economic goals To bridge the digital divide through automation of systems and enhanced interfacing for improved service delivery To oversee the development of the City's central knowledge repository to promote effective knowledge management, sharing and learning practices To ensure a financially prudent City with clean audits from the Auditor General

Water provision and its expanded and improved delivery sit almost nowhere in the objectives of the most senior City officials in charge of water.

Source: © Mushongera, based on various City of Johannesburg official documents posted on the website (www.coj.org) 2019

> know, service delivery depends upon people seated around the table, so if we fail as EISD, we fail the City. So there is a lot of pressure on service delivery (ex-Director interview WR&B –EISD, 2014).

Ultimately, however, the City manager generally wins the day, given that the ED's performance contract is negotiated with the City manager: the EDs are expected to meet specific standards and achieve certain targets measured in quantitative terms, in line with the principles of New Public Management. The City's choice on achieving accountability and efficiency is based on the close monitoring of senior managers, done at strategic level rather than as part of normal human resources as one senior official mentioned:

> The City believes that the monitoring of the City's executive management – the bosses of the City, is strongly linked to strategic performance. The assumption is that if the top three managers perform, the City can achieve its strategic objectives. So, we want the managers to focus on the outcomes. As a result, they are monitored by us here at GSPCR, and not by the Human Resources Department (Director of Monitoring and Evaluation interview GSPCR, M&E, 2017).

Unpacking officials' priorities through scorecards – no explicit role in monitoring water service delivery

In spite of this strategic affirmation, looking at the actual items being monitored in senior officials' practices shows that little direct attention is being paid to social or equity issues, as far as the EISD is concerned.

Table 12.4 shows the Key Performance Areas (KPA) of the three principals in the City to which JW reports in part: the Director of EISD (where issues of water services policy are developed and monitored), the Head of Group Governance (who prefects the Service Delivery Agreement) and the Group Head for GSPCR (who is responsible for reporting on the IDP to National Treasury).

Two elements are striking when analysing the EISD's Key Performance Areas, in comparison with other senior City officials (Group Heads). Firstly, while on the official organogram JW falls under the EISD, it is surprising that the EISD's executive director's scorecard contained nothing relating to service delivery provision. Although the EISD's official role is to perform a regulatory and oversight function relating to water service, this is not set as a Key Performance Indicator (KPI). However, officials in the EISD revealed that their role was to 'develop policy related to water services'. As a result, they would be interested in the progress of water services provision in as far as the information assists them in developing policy, and not as a performance target charged on them. An official in the WSR&PD sub-unit said:

> There is no way I can have performance targets of JW in my scorecard! I can't be held responsible for something that I have no control of (ex-official interview Innovation, JW 2017).

By creating an external agent to deliver water services, it is now very difficult to hold officials accountable in the City for poor delivery of water to citizens. Johannesburg Water undertakes the actual delivery but is governed by its own leadership of which City officials are unable to influence. What is surprising is how defensive the City official becomes: how even monitoring (reporting if JW is or is not delivering on targets) is excluded from her sense of her mandate or mission.

Secondly, there are no explicit Key Performance Areas associated with provision of water services to informal settlements, neither in the EISD, Group Governance nor the GSPCR executive level. It is not very surprising, given that as shown above, it is not explicitly mentioned either in the City strategic documents (GDS nor IDP). Officials also explain that they would not want a policy around this issue:

> It's not like when this [informal settlement] comes, you are ready to go and provide. It will take some time, maybe they can be there for a year or two without services, and then they are provided. If you put a policy that if there is any squatter camp we must service it within three months, you will be inviting trouble for yourself, because the same people will just come and put up a squatter camp and they will take you to court. You know there are always these civil society organisations, they will take you to court and then that will be a problem for the City. So ideally, I don't think the City commits itself to saying 'we will provide', at this time (Principal Specialist interview WSR&PD, WR&B – EISD, 2017).

As a result, the ED for the EISD could not be held responsible for the water service delivery in informal areas, neither Group Governance nor the GSPCR, hence representing a gap in terms of social equity. According

Table 12.5 Elements of water service regulation in the City of Johannesburg.

Elements of water service regulation to be overseen by the Environment and Infrastructure Services Department (EISD) and the Water Services Regulation and Policy Development (WSR&PD) sub-unit
1. *Access to basic water services (water and sanitation)* 2. Drinking water quality 3. Impact on the environment • license status of waste water works requirement and this includes wastewater meeting the license compliance of 97% (efficient quality) 4. Strategic asset management • to ensure that Johannesburg's Water Asset Management Plan is in place • monitoring 5. Water use efficiency • water demand management • meter reading performance • unaccounted for water 6. Customer service standards • continuity of water supply: number of interruptions of greater than 6 hrs, 24 hrs, and 48 hrs per incident (response time) • continuity of water supply: pipe burst per annum per 100 kl of water and sewer networks

Source: © After EISD Internal document, nd.

While access to basic water for all is a primary municipal objective, it is not qualified nor detailed, in particular vis à vis water delivery to the poorest.

to one official, it is those communities that make a lot of noise by striking that will get prioritised in terms of service provision:

> From what I have heard, there isn't necessarily a policy that I know that dictates which informal settlements are prioritised. It is the ones that make the most noise, those that protest and what not, and then the councillor of that ward lobbies with the Mayoral Committee and with Council (Principal Specialist interview WSR&PD, WR&B – EISD, 2017).

Informal settlements in Johannesburg are developing in unexpected ways, making it difficult to plan for them as the City does not know when and where another informal settlement will be established. However, once established, the City is required by law to make provision for basic services.

Looking further down in the administrative hierarchy (Figure 12.2), I've investigated the mandate and the scorecards of the Water Resources and Biodiversity (WR&B) unit, and more particularly one of its sub-units interacting with JW: the Water Service Regulation and Policy Development (WSR&PD) sub-unit. It consisted of a deputy director and two officials who described their task as regulating and overseeing the activities of JW. An interview with the official could not clarify how this regulatory process happened as the statement below indicates:

> Now, how do we then regulate? So we put out the KPIs, and from that, we monitor Joburg Water based on those KPIs. Why do we have those KPIs? We are expected to comply with the national department. So we have got this, and from that, we've got the KPIs, basic services, we have got water demand, we have got response time, we have got asset management and all the business of Joburg Water that you need to regulate. How do we do it? From a strategic point of view when they plan, when they do business plans we are part of it, so that at least we are informed, and every quarter we report to the MMC. (Deputy Director interview WSR&PD, WR&B – EISD, 2016).

In order to reconcile what the official was attempting to explain, I consulted the EISD's Business Plan document to find out how this regulatory function was to be performed. **Table 12.5** lists the regulatory elements of the EISD relating to water services and hence to be performed by the WSR&PD sub-unit.

The department drew its regulatory role over JW from the Water Service Act, as administered by the national DWS, and stating that one of the roles of the Water Services Authority (here, City of Johannesburg) was to 'ensure access to basic water services'. According to officials, this means in particular services to informal settlements. In the City, it is the deputy director for WSR&PD who was responsible for 'Access to Basic Services' and 'Water and Water Use Efficiency'. There were no corresponding equivalents upon which senior managers could be held responsible. It is strange that these KPIs were found at this (rather low) level of the bureaucracy. Whether this was deliberate or an oversight, it could not be established, but it was clear such were other instances of policy gaps, where the policy objective of equity was underplayed.

Table 12.6 Assessing progress in water delivery to Johannesburg's informal settlements.

Measurement	Annual target	Quarterly target	Actual		Comments
Access to services: basic water provision to informal settlements	83.89% coverage (2,290 households)	Q1=82.64% Q2= Q3= Q4=	0		**Performance:** In this quarter, no households were provided with basic water. Johannesburg Water reported that the procurement process is underway. The tender is anticipated to be advertised in October 2017. **Regulatory standard compliance:** SFWS requires everyone to have access to basic water supply by 2008. This City did not achieve this target. **Evidence:** Report on site visit that was undertaken.

Access to services: basic sanitation to informal settlements	39.27% coverage (2,240 households)		0		**Performance:** In this quarter, no households were provided with access to basic sanitation as per plan. Again, this is due to the procurement process which is not concluded yet. It is reported that the tender is anticipated to be advertised in October 2017. **Regulatory standard compliance:** The DWS requires 100% provision of basic services which is impossible to achieve. While the Ventilated Pit Latrines must have air ventilation and be sealed inside the pit if built in high water table. Johannesburg water conformed to this standard. **Evidence:** Site visits undertaken.
Overall assessment No households were provided with basic water and sanitation in the quarter under review.					

No progress on water delivery to informal settlements, and no action taken, which seems to mean that none is expected.

Source: © After EISD, 2017, Assessment report submitted by WSR&PD to the City hierarchy (2017 first quarter), City of Johannesburg.

Continuing to track how the City of Johannesburg monitors the equity objective of water provision through the regulation of JW, I looked for the Deputy Director's instruments to perform her task. In performing her regulatory function, the deputy director relied on JW's quarterly reports from which she prepared an assessment report for the ED. **Table 12.6** below shows part of the assessment report that is produced by the WSR&PD deputy director, and submitted to the ED: EISD.

The overall assessment, in this particular 2017 report, was that no additional households living in informal settlements were provided with basic water and sanitation in the quarter under review. There was no evidence to show that officials at this lower level had an obligation to ensure that JW delivered or could be held responsible for the low performance of the entity in this area.

One reason was the performance management system used for seniors was not effectively implemented on lower-level officials. In fact, the performance management system collapsed at this level after the City decided to remove monetary rewards for good performance. As a result, the deputy was not concerned about how JW performed: she could not be held responsible, and she was not going to be rewarded nor sanctioned if things did not change. However, it seems that the situation was not so in the past and the approach of the person occupying this office mattered, as shown from these quotes from officials that have held this position previously:

> When I am acting, I don't just take the report as given. I scrutinise the report and ask hard questions on why performance is at a certain level. For example, JW can report 95 per cent performance in sanitation and yet we know that there are sewer spills that are happening. So let's say there is a breakdown of the pump station in the north and we are getting sewer spills. In the old days, we would just go ourselves to Joburg Water and say you are polluting the environment. This has to be remedied. What are you doing? We would go and sit with their CAPEX [capital expenditure] department; we would go and harass their Operations department (Deputy Director of Open Space Planning interview WR&B – EISD, 2017).

The role of the deputy director has been reduced to one of mere administration and pushing papers. If these issues are not picked up by the portfolio committees, the challenges with the provision of basic services will continue unresolved. The discussion on the deputy director seemed to sum up what looked like a gloomy picture of water services regulation. Indeed, the City regulatory and oversight role performed in various ways by various actors is not effective as it should be. The very weak way of addressing services delivery problems in the most precarious areas – the informal settlements – is only indicative of the limited importance of equity targets as a driving objective of official performance.

Conclusion

This analysis showed that the model split the City's role as Water Service Authority into two. The City was responsible for planning and policy development, while the entity (JW) would implement. However, the operation distance between the two created problems of oversight. The City, which had been reforming its structure over the past two decades, had made a number of institutional changes. The effect of these changes resulted in a dispersion of the City's role of oversight and regulation. The task was split and spread across many different actors operating independently of each other in the City to such an extent that it was difficult to locate where decision lay. This was manifested in the way these City divisions interacted with JW with each trying to extract information to help its mandate.

These kinds of complexity are often present at local government level because this is a sphere of practice and the situation is usually fuzzy and unpredictable. While water services get delivered, it is very clear that one cannot clearly pinpoint who in the City is responsible and accountable for non-delivery. A scan through the scorecards of top- and lower-level officials show that their KPIs are not binding in terms of assigning responsibility. Thus, the City relies on statutory oversight structures, in particular, the Section 79 Committees, to act as watchdogs by scrutinising reports and pointing out where failures are happening – committees that are formally and in practice largely disempowered, with recommendation functions and often by-passed by the Mayoral Committee.

The resultant complex actor-network is linked together with rather weak intermediaries in the form of regulatory instruments, legislation and planning documents that assign roles and shape relationships. Because they are poorly inscribed, the actor-network created is not strong enough to hold the entity to account. Additionally, the City's interests of ensuring access to water by all remain in direct tension with the profit motive of the entity, with more attention given to financial balance sheets and audits than to equity objectives. This is quite obvious when one takes the time to actually track equity targets in the various strategic and operational documents produced by the City on the issue of water. This might result from two elements. First, from a conscious reluctance to inscribe in official documents standards and procedures that will be binding, and may constitute a possible political instrument from civil society to fight for access to water. And secondly, importantly, this results from a degree of disempowerment and sedation of officials, under the vast and duplicated amount of reporting they are required to do, on sometimes meaningless indicators – or at least indicators that have little to do with equity objectives – and upon which they have limited instruments for action anyway.

Accounting procedures administered on municipalities by National Treasury through the Municipal Finance Management Act (MFMA) are effective in instilling (financial) accountability in municipalities. The MFMA is a powerful piece of legislation with very strict compliance requirements and municipalities face severe consequences for breaching its provisions, but they focus on financial efficiency objectives rather than on social equity targets. On the other hand, the Department of Water and Sanitation (DWS) is notorious for introducing a whole range of instruments for regulating and assessing equitable water delivery, but most of its instruments are only 'nice-to-have', adding to the burden of bureaucracy due to the large number of indicators that have to be repeatedly reported.

Hence, the multiplicity of planning documents and regulatory instruments, the vagueness of equity objectives, the multiplicity of units with overlapping mandates within the City, the split between monitoring and operation (delegated to JW) are responsible for creating a complex and amorphous governance landscape for the City's water sector. This scenario in Johannesburg only serves to show the limits of New Public Management (both within the City and between City and national government), where the attempt to separate efficiency principles (embodied in JW, and monitored by the National Treasury) and equity objectives (driven by strategic City policies, supported by the Department of Water and Sanitation) have led to the blurring of the latter. Rather an opaque governance framework emerges, where no one is actually responsible for carefully balancing these two necessary requirements.

Notes

1 City administration uses a huge number of acronyms: an everyday language on its own. I have had to adopt quite a few in this chapter, providing a list at the end of this chapter for the ease of reading.

2 The GJMC was the outcome of the initial attempt to amalgamate the many independent municipalities that made up Johannesburg. The GJMC was at the apex of a two-tier system of administration, including four sub-councils. It was responsible for policy and monitoring. The GJMC ceased to exist following the 2000 elections when the City of Johannesburg Metropolitan Municipality was established as a single-tier administration.

3 The SDBIP is a document and management tool for linking service delivery outputs to the budget of the municipality. It provides a credible and detailed plan on how the municipality will provide services including the inputs and financial resources to be used.

4 Mayoral Lekgotla meetings are special strategic meetings called by the executive mayor to discuss and approve annual plans for the various departments. Departments and entities present their proposed programme and these should in line with what the executive mayor hopes to achieve during his term.

5 A third key document, the Water Service Development Plan goes into detail in terms of programmes and projects pertaining to the water sector over a five-year period. It was beyond the scope of this paper to examine it here.

6 At the time of research, officials estimated the number of informal settlements to be over 200.

7 Water losses are referred to in the City as 'non-Revenue water': water that gets lost through leaks, illegal connections, burst pipes, where no revenue accrues to the City. It is part of the City's mandate to reduce non-revenue water.

Official documents

City of Johannesburg (CoJ). 2002. *Joburg 2030. Growth and Development Strategy.*

CoJ. 2006. *Reflecting on a Solid Foundation. Building developmental local government, 2000–2005.* Research Report, City of Johannesburg.

CoJ. 2008. *A Message of Progress.* City of Johannesburg Mid-term Report, September 2008.

CoJ. 2011. *A promising Future. Joburg 2040: Growth and Development Strategy.*

CoJ. 2012a. *Committing to a Promising Future: A world class African city that is resilient.* City of Johannesburg, Integrated Development Plan, 2012–2016.

CoJ. 2012b. *The City of Johannesburg's Monitoring and Evaluation Framework.* Annexure 3 Final.

CoJ. 2015a. *Turning Challenges into Opportunities.* 2012–2016 Integrated Development Plan: 2015–2016 review.

CoJ. 2015b. *Service Delivery Agreement entered between the City of Johannesburg Metropolitan Government and Johannesburg Water.*

CoJ. 2016. *Business plan, 2016/2017.* Environment and Infrastructure Services Department (EISD).

CoJ. 2017. Group Risk Management Framework.

Department of Water and Forestry (DWAF). 2002. Guidelines For Compulsory National Standards Regulations Under Section 9 Of The Water Services Act (Act 108 Of 1997)) And Norms And Standards For Water Services Tariffs Regulations Under Section 10 Of The Water Services Act (Act 108 Of 1997) April 2002.

Department for Water and Sanitation (DWS). 2017. *National Norms and Standards for Domestic Water and Sanitation Services.* Version 3-Final 41100. Department of Water and Sanitation, September 2017.

Eales, K. 2006. 'Sector 4 – Infrastructure and Services.' City Power, Pikitup and Johannesburg Water. PowerPoint presentation received from author, Kathy Eales, a former employee of the City of Johannesburg.

References

Alexander, P. 2010. 'Rebellion of the poor: South Africa's service delivery protests: A prelimenary analysis', *Review of African Political Economy* 37(123): 25–40.

Allan, K., Gotz, G. and Joseph, C. (eds). 2001. *Johannesburg: An African city in change*. Cape Town: Zebra Press.

Beall, J., Cranshaw, O. and Parnell, S. 2003. 'Uniting a divided city; Governance and social exclusion in Johannesburg', *Review of African Political Economy* 30(95): 171–76.

Bilodeau, A. and Potvin, L. 2016. 'Unpacking complexity in public health interventions with the Actor-Network Theory', *Health Promotion International* 33(1): 1–9.

Bond, P. and Dugard, J. 2008. 'The case of Johannesburg water: What really happened at the pre-paid 'Parish pump'?', *Law Democracy and Development* 12(1): 1–28.

Braga, C. and Suarez, M. 2018. 'Actor-Network Theory: New perspectives and contributions to consumption studies', *Cadernos EBAPE.BR* 16(2): 218–31.

Callon, M. 1986. 'The sociology of an actor-network: The case of the electric vehicle'. In *Mapping the Dynamics of Science and Technology*, edited by M. Callon, J. Law and A. Rip, 19–34. Basingstoke: Macmillan.

Chenwi, L. 2013. 'Unpacking "progressive realisation", its relation to resources, minimum core and reasonableness, and some methodological considerations for assessing compliance', *De Jure* 46(3): 742–69.

Fenwick, T. and Edwards, R. 2011. 'Introduction: Reclaiming and renewing Actor-Network Theory for educational research', *Educational Philosophy and Theory* 43(1): 1–14.

Goldin, J.A. 2010. 'Water policy in South Africa: Trust and knowledge as obstacles to Reform', *Review of radical political economics* 42(2): 195–212.

Magdahl, J.E. 2012. *From Privatisation to Corporatisation: Exploring the strategic shift in neoliberal policy on urban water services*. Oslo: FIVAS, Association for International Water Studies.

Maphela, B. and Cloete F. 2020. 'Johannesburg's implementation of the National Water Act, 1998 in Soweto, South Africa', *Development Southern Africa* 37(4): 535–52.

McLean, C. and Hassard, J. 2004. 'Symmetrical absence/symmetrical absurdity: Critical notes on the production of Actor-Network Theory', *Journal of Management Studies* 41: 493–519.

Mushongera, D. 2021. 'Who governs Johannesburg water? An actor-network reading of water services governance in the City of Johannesburg.' Unpublished PhD dissertation. Johannesburg: University of the Witwatersrand.

von Schnitzler, A. 2008. 'Citizenship prepaid: Water, calculability, and techno-politics in South Africa', *Journal of Southern African Studies* 34(4): 899–917.

Seedat, R. 2001. 'Regulation of the Johannesburg Water and Sanitation Utility.' Unpublished Master's thesis. Johannesburg: University of the Witwatersrand.

Smith, L. 2006. *Neither Public nor Private: Unpacking the Johannesburg water corporatization model*. Social Policy and Development Programme Paper No 27. Geneva: United Nations Research Institute for Social Development.

Smith, L. and Morris, N. 2008. 'Municipal entities: A panacea for service delivery constraints?' In *Consolidating Developmental Local Government: Lessons from the South African experience*, edited by M. van Donk and E. Pieterse, 423–44. Cape Town: UCT Press.

Smith, L. and Rubin, M. 2015. 'Beyond invented and invited spaces of participation. The Phiri and Olivia Road court cases and their outcome'. In *Popular Politics in South African Cities: Unpacking community participation*, edited by C. Bénit-Gbaffou, 248–81. Pretoria: HSRC Press.

Tissington, K., Dettmann, M., Langford, M., Dugard, J. and Conteh, S. 2008. *Water Services Fault Lines. An assessment of South Africa's water and sanitation provision across 15 municipalities*. Research report. Centre for Applied Legal Studies (CALS), Norwegian Centre for Human Rights (NCHR) and Centre on Housing Rights and Evictions (COHRE).

Zawawi, N.H.M. 2018. 'Actor-Network Theory and inter-organisational management control', *International Journal of Business and Society* 19(2): 219–34.

13
'Doing things right' or 'doing the right thing'? Limits to evaluative thinking in Johannesburg

Laila Smith

> Because this is such a large and complex organisation, the left hand doesn't know what the right hand is doing (key informant responsible for Monitoring and Evaluation] from the City of Johannesburg, 2017).

Introduction

This chapter is about how a municipal institution that generates and uses information for reporting and monitoring skews the incentives influencing how it produces that information, preventing itself from learning from its own practices to improve its capacity to govern. The cultural shift from using data for monitoring for compliance to using knowledge to spur evaluative thinking to learn from mistakes for improvement requires a combination of leadership and systematic embeddedness of evaluation processes. Drawing on an engagement with senior officials in the City of Johannesburg, I examine how challenging such a cultural shift has been by reflecting on two oversight bodies designed to improve the City's capacity to govern. This chapter reflects on the meanings and challenges of institutionalising an evaluative culture as an effort to improve the performance management of a large city.

This chapter focuses on monitoring and evaluation (M&E) as a management instrument for wielding the empirical data that tracks progress in moving the machinery of Johannesburg's bureaucracy forward, when trying to realise the objectives laid out in its strategic planning frameworks. It does so by analysing how City officials work within two sites of M&E within the City organisation. Each of these sites is mandated to exercise a degree of oversight on the City's activities, and that involves contestations between locally grounded politicians trying to ensure responsiveness to community pressures and often upsetting the planned implementation conducted by administration, and officials trying to demonstrate 'progress' through reporting on the implementation of strategic plans as laid out across various departments.

The first site of research is the primary oversight body located within the executive section of the City: the central coordinating unit of the City's M&E reporting called the Group Strategy, Policy, Communications and Research unit (GSPCR, hereafter called the Group Strategy Unit). The Group Strategy Unit is meant to track the degree to which officials are moving their departmental objectives forward in the implementation of the City's long-term development strategy: the Growth and Development Strategy 2040 (GDS).

The second site of research is the Section 79 Committees, a set of oversight bodies located within the municipal legislature. Section 79 Committees are portfolio committees made up of local councillors of all political parties, along with City officials. Their role is to monitor the quality of services being delivered and in doing so, to hold the executive, City officials and Mayoral Committee Members (MMCs) accountable for the executive decisions regarding planning, spending, and service delivery. The City executive has to submit quarterly and annual reports to the Council on their Key Performance Areas (KPAs). It is the role of the Section 79 Committees in each portfolio to review these reports and make recommendations to the Council. The councillors' oversight role in these committees is in trying to reconcile evidence provided by City officials with what they observed on the ground through site visits.

Methodology and positionality

This chapter was written when I was the Director of the Centre for Learning on Evaluation and Results for Anglophone Africa (CLEAR-AA), an evaluation capacity development centre based at the School of Governance at the University of Witwatersrand.[1] I wanted to write this chapter to grapple with various pieces of a puzzle related to urban governance, wondering why it is so hard for cities in general, and Johannesburg in particular, to put evaluation systems in place

– considering evaluations as a tool that can strengthen governance structures to encourage an organisational culture that moves away from fearing admission of mistakes to identifying why mistakes and problems are recurring, and what can be done to resolve and/or improve the organisational performance needed to address complex urban challenges.

From 2014 to 2016, CLEAR-AA and the City of Johannesburg were in discussion about developing a medium- to long-term capacity development intervention to support organisational change by establishing a City-wide evaluation system. The City's choice of CLEAR-AA as a service provider to support its capacity development was by virtue of the longstanding and close working relationship between the City and Wits University's School of Governance, which was a training ground in public administration for City Officials. As CLEAR-AA was hosted within the School of Governance from 2011, it was deemed only appropriate that the CLEAR-AA take forward the conversation and implementation of the evaluation capacity building request from the Group Strategy Unit. It also helped that I had worked for the City nearly a decade earlier in the Contract Management Unit within the City manager's office and had a good sense of the engagements between senior management and political councillors in the City.

From the moment I stepped into the contract negotiations, the leadership of the Group Strategy Unit in the City was in flux. Its deputy, or second in command, wanted to see an evaluation system evolve from the City's existing, but largely still unimplemented, M&E framework. The deputy had been fighting for an opportunity to bring about organisational change by transforming the City's endless reporting requirements into a more reflective and cohesive evaluation system. He seized the moment when a charismatic leader of the Group Strategy Unit was appointed, with a strong background in participatory urban planning and democratic praxis. The Head of the Group Strategy Unit became the champion in moving the City to adopt a City-wide evaluation system and had the authority to get a contract in place, a feat that had been three years in the making.

The research driven by the CLEAR-AA, conducted in 2016–17, drew on an extensive desktop review of grey literature relating to planning, reporting and monitoring in the City of Johannesburg. It organised 32 key informant interviews with senior officials, a survey with 54 M&E officers, and three workshops with selected interviewees and survey participants who were designated for receiving training, as a second step of the process in building a City-wide evaluation system. Inclusive in the contract was indeed repairing what was deemed at the time by many officials as a 'broken monitoring system'.

In 2016, CLEAR-AA began the first phase of this intervention by carrying out a situational analysis of the City's M&E practice. The situational analysis entailed access to heads of departments in an effort to understand what the status quo was in the officials' understanding of the City's M&E system and how useful or not it was in their planning function. The design of the assessment phase consisted of three capacity-building workshops in which group heads and front-line M&E staff came together to learn the basic components of how to carry out a programme evaluation. Key to the success of the team's efforts was that a member of CLEAR-AA evaluation capacity development team was a former senior staff person of the Group Strategic Unit. His deep understanding of the institutional weaknesses as well as his good networks with City officials made a significant difference in the quality of the information the consultant team was able to tease out of the three workshops. The opening presentation delivered by this former Group Strategy Unit staff person gave the evaluation team credibility that created an openness and frankness in the key informant interviews that were interspersed between the three capacity development workshops.

During the conduct of the study, local government elections occurred (2017), the African National Congress (ANC) lost its historical hold on the City and the Democratic Alliance (DA), one of South Africa's opposition parties, swept into power. A significant portion of senior managers with more than a decade of institutional memory then left the City administration. This considerably weakened the City's strategic capability to resolve problems through reflective praxis, as it had been anchored in understanding the history and evolution of the institution. As a result, the second phase of CLEAR-AA intervention, which was set up to put in place the architecture for a City-wide evaluation system, subsequently never happened.

This chapter evaluates, beyond the change in political regimes and in leadership commissioning the work (an instability which is not an insignificant piece of the puzzle), what the key structural variables were in constraining the City in moving from an organisation that uses monitoring mechanisms to cover up mistakes and poor performance, to an organisation that wants to improve by gaining a deeper understanding about how to resolve these issues by developing an evaluative culture through the setting up of a City-wide evaluation system.

The genesis of monitoring and evaluation in South Africa

Before proceeding, it is important to clarify the difference between monitoring and evaluation. Monitoring 'asks whether the things we planned are being done right, while evaluation is asking are we doing the right things: are we effective, efficient, and providing value for money, and how can we do it better' (DPME 2013, 3). Monitoring activities involves a continuous process of collecting and analysing data in real time to understand how well an intervention, programme or organisation is performing against expected results (Kusek and Risk 2004, 227). Evaluations support accountability in resource allocation by focusing on understanding the worth of what has been accomplished. This involves a process that provides data for larger, longer-term, strategic feedback processes (Nielson and Hunter 2013,17). I outline some key definitions below which are helpful to readers from other disciplines who may not be familiar with basic M&E terms:

- **Outputs** tell the story of what you produced, and relates to an organisation's activities. Output measures do not address the value or impact of a service for beneficiaries.
- **Outcomes** look at the level of achievement that occurred because of the activities that an organisation provided and can often be a pathway towards assessing the impact of a service for beneficiaries.
- **Key Performance Areas** (KPAs) relate to the area of responsibility that is assigned to an individual or unit.
- **Key Performance Indicators** (KPIs) are qualitative or quantitative measures used to assess the measure of progress of an organisation in meeting pre-defined outcomes.

The field of M&E has evolved since the 1950s in the Global North to determine how policies, projects and programme interventions were performing. These methods of social science and statistical research were mainstreamed throughout the USA and UK governments in the years after World War II. The growth of this method of inquiry in the disciplines of public administration and management, education and public health, led to a proliferation of capacity and practice through the evolution of evaluation departments within the state, and of evaluation firms outside of the state. The main value of M&E, ascribed by academics in these disciplines, is the proposed process provided to effect long-term improvements in institutional performance (Ledger and Meny-Gibert 2018, 31)

New Public Management (NPM) rose as a dominant paradigm in the 1980s to overcome the shortcomings of public administration through the adoption of private-sector values, market-based operations and techniques of management. Key features of this approach were efforts to streamline state bureaucracy by outsourcing non-essential functions and in-sourcing private sector principles – both of which were deemed to contribute to greater efficiency and effectiveness (Hood 1990; Dunleavy and Hood 1994; Pollitt and Bouckaert 2017). A further selling card by the proponents of the NPM was that it offered the management technique of monitoring and evaluation as a key tool to improve the measurements for assessing public sector performance (Alonso et al. 2015).

Detractors of the NPM have seen this adoption of market principles as a 'roll-out' of neoliberalism by instilling a competitive logic into public services through rewards and penalties and in doing so entrenching 'market-like' techniques of management in the public sector as a substitute for more direct marketisation (Jessop 2019; Harvey 2007; Amable 2011). Monitoring and evaluation as a tool for the NPM laid out the techniques for the quantification of the public sector and use of performance indicators to reflect a form of social engineering aimed at embedding the norms of competition and for ordering society along market-based lines (Davies 2014, 160). The neoliberal signature of policy-making was to ensure greater accountability of bureaucrats to the public by reducing the cost of public services. Critiques of this approach have documented how such cost-recovery efforts have been at the expense of social outcomes (Peck and Tickel 2002).

Dutta et al., however, see the NPM as an actual departure from the logic of neoliberalism by empowering managerial forces through 'managerial governance' (Dutta et al. 2022). They posit that the spread of managerial planning, oversight and audit under the NPM 'necessitated the establishment of a vast bureaucratic infrastructure the neoliberals had long resented' (Dutta et al. 2022, 8). Key within this ascent of managerialism was the consolidation of hierarchies that were fed and supported by systems of data collection to assess the performance of the cogs in the wheel of government.

Yet, the managers using the data from these systems were often not the designers nor drivers of analysing their meaning as they often did not have the expertise to do so. This helps explain why mid-level bureaucrats feeding data into monitoring systems, without the ability to engage in sense-making, have often found the process to be meaningless. The notion of a decentred conception of power (Foucault 1979; Donzelot 1979) is useful for explaining how the benign intent of M&E as a tool of the NPM can have unintended outcomes. Ferguson uses the theory of a decentred conception of power (Ferguson 1990) in a 'development' context whereby the outcomes of planned social interventions can end up as an apparatus of control that was never intended, and in the case of the City of Johannesburg was never even recognised. This constellation of control is, according to Ferguson, effective by being 'subjectless' (Ferguson 1990, 19). This resonates conceptually with the subject of this chapter where the embedding of an M&E system in a local government bureaucracy is experienced by mid-level officials as one that commands 'compliance' in inputting the data, but where the custodians of the system have no idea how to fix it.

The use of the NPM instrument has had a different genealogy in the Global South. While evaluation practices have existed in many developing countries as part of the mid-term review or closing step to a programme, the learning from this instrument has had little impact on policy and management decisions due to the lack of demand (Dabelstein 2003). From the 1970s onwards, M&E became a standard accountability bearer for international donor communities wanting to assess the degree to which their contributions were having the intended impacts across the Global South. The demand from donors stimulated the development of M&E practice across the Global South, in the absence of national government demand (Basheka and Byamagisha 2015). As a result, M&E grew in popularity in the Global South to determine how policies, projects, programmes and interventions were or were not working (Goldman et al. 2020; Ledger and Meny-Gibert 2018). With increasing wealth and expectations from its citizens for development results, there have been increasing demands placed on African governments for accountability (Porter and Goldman 2013; Eresia-Eke and Boadu 2019). Since the early 2000s, there has been a growth in demand from African governments for the integration of M&E functions across major programmes, such as in South Africa, Benin and Uganda (Goldman et al. 2018). Such centralised systems only began to filter down to other spheres of government a decade later.

The way in which M&E systems have emerged through central government agencies within South Africa has influenced how it has been approached at the local government level. Government-wide Monitoring and Evaluation Systems (GWM&E) emerged in 2006 with a distinct purpose of focusing on monitoring in order to strengthen coordination and alignment across different sectors and between local, provincial and national governments (Engela and Ajam 2010, 23). With the GWM&E systems, government departments and municipalities tended to focus on results in terms of outputs and activities. This was partially due to the regulatory frameworks for planning, which have emphasised the setting of targets for KPIs in annual performance plans at national and provincial levels and annual service delivery and budget implementation plans (SDBIP) at the municipal level (CLEAR-AA 2017a). With its introduction, the National Treasury influenced a programme logic where monitoring was related to a financial management perspective driven by the Public Finance Management Act 1999 (PFMA). This prioritised financial reporting to assess programme performance.

In 2009, when Jacob Zuma came to power as President of the ANC, the government response to growing levels of service delivery protests across the country (Alexander 2010) was a concern from national government to achieve results and make them visible to the public. Within the national government, there was an increasing appreciation of evaluations as a distinct instrument for improving policy-making, planning and implementation. The Department of Monitoring and Evaluation (later to become the Department of Planning, Monitoring and Evaluation (DPME) when it incorporated a planning function) emerged in 2011 to take forward the government's adoption of an outcomes-based approach. The goal was to centrally coordinate, within the Presidency, an evaluation function in order to develop the tools and systems that could better demonstrate outcomes and impact to the Cabinet. The DPME became the custodian for establishing a National Evaluation System and did so by drafting a National Evaluation Framework (2011), a National Evaluation Policy (2012), Guidelines for different evaluation methods (2012–14), quality-assurance approaches, establishing an Evaluation Technical Working Group for selecting which evaluations were national priorities and so forth. This helped to transition the national government away from the sporadic use of evaluations to a more systematic and planned approach of assessing national departments' ability to deliver on their programmes. The aim was to ensure large programmes with substantial budgets, such as early-childhood education, or programmes that were highly sensitive to the public, such as social housing, were evaluated in order to spur programmatic improvements. The DPME's custodianship and construction of the National Evaluation System also helped de-link M&E from budget programme management with more emphasis on reviewing implementation (CLEAR-AA 2017b).

The National Evaluation System was, for a brief moment, successful in the policy-making space around evaluations at the national and provincial levels. The DPME can be credited with playing a key role in supporting this expansion, which resulted in spreading planning, learning and capacity for evaluations across line departments within both national and provincial governments (Goldman et. al. 2020). This has not, however, been extended to local government.

The legislation governing performance of local government is largely driven through the PFMA 1999, followed by the Municipal Systems Act 32 of 2000, requiring metropolitan governments (Metros) to establish a performance management system, of which M&E was envisioned as an operational tool. This was followed by the Municipal Finance Management Act 2003 (MFMA) putting more emphasis on financial accountability, and in more recent years, greater emphasis on linking budgeting and planning processes to foster policy implementation. Efforts to implement these various pieces of legislation at the local government level have resulted in M&E being conflated with performance management – the monitoring of officials by their hierarchy (CLEAR-AA 2017a).

Specific clauses within the above legislation have contributed to a short-term reporting structure, which has contributed to the local government's monitoring processes largely being about 'compliance'. For instance, the MFMA requirements for the SDBIP focuses on quarterly and annual reporting. Yet, it is difficult to measure progress with outcome and with impact indicators on a quarterly or annual basis, as achieving behaviour change (outcome), performance change (impact), and change at an organisational level takes years. Metros have followed suit with their reporting requirements and focused on monitoring output and activity indicators. These legislative requirements have therefore influenced the monitoring culture of local government to be largely compliance-driven and have neglected the development of an evaluation culture that focuses on thinking about longer-term outcome and impact indicators. The latter would create the capacity to begin tracking organisational behaviour in the efforts to improve performance (CLEAR-AA 2017b, 12) of a programme or policy. This is corroborated by the findings of a 2013 DPME national survey, where 54 per cent of the 96 departments surveyed indicated a general deficiency of a strong M&E culture in national, provincial and local governments, and where more than half of the respondents identified the fact that problems were not treated as opportunities for learning and improvement as being a significant barrier (DPME 2013).

One of the key differences in the legislation guiding national and local level reporting is the Municipal Systems Act (2003) requirement to ensure community involvement in its planning, as is currently affected through Integrated Development Plans (IDPs)[2] and review processes (that is, the M&E space). In fulfilling their M&E function, municipalities are required to involve communities in the process of monitoring and evaluating service delivery programmes, such as consulting on what indicators might be appropriate from a user perspective, so that the reporting upward on whether the service in question is working effectively or not means something to those who are using the service.

Unfortunately, the practice of this public consultation in defining what is important to monitor from the public's perspective has been lost, mostly due to the tedious reporting requirements from local to national government. Local governments are extremely burdened with national level reporting requirements where there are simply too many indicators that Metros need to report to national government (Phillips et al. 2014). Dlamini and Migiro argue that 'local government finds itself delivering too many indicators that are not in line with its budget and this creates a local government that always fail to deliver in terms of its mandate' (Dlamini and Migiro 2016, 381). These reporting processes to national government are furthermore directed to numerous central government agencies like the National Treasury, the Cooperative Governance and Traditional Affairs (COGTA), the DPME and the Department of Public Service and Administration (DPSA) as well as line ministries. Each have their own frameworks and often do not align to one another. This has created significant duplication of efforts, leaving limited scope left for processing what the data from this monitoring means for City managers wanting to understand municipal performance, or to engage with communities on its meaning or its framing. Mushongera's chapter in this book takes this point further by highlighting how the lack of sense-making with such reporting demotivates the officials involved in this monitoring process.

Some Metros are, however, taking a growing interest in moving beyond monitoring towards evaluation in order to better assess the impact of key policies, programmes and projects, but there are not yet any systems in place to manage this objective. In 2017, the CLEAR-AA and the DPME collaborated with the aim of trying to institutionalise the function of evaluations in Metros, as the DPMEs experienced increasing requests from metropolitan governments for capacity development. It was found that there is limited support from Central Agencies with an explicit function to build evaluation capacity at the Metro level. In the three Metros of eThekwini, Tshwane and Ekurhuleni, there was hardly any budget allocated to evaluations within the Treasury budgets of these Metros (CLEAR-AA 2017a). The M&E frameworks existed but their implementation was uneven; the implementation of the monitoring component of these frameworks was well developed and the evaluation element weakly conceptualised in the framework, and not implemented in practice. Furthermore, the study found that there were no standard operating procedures for evaluations in Metros. While Metros are developing M&E units to institutionalise this function, such units are not adequately staffed and evaluation expertise remains a challenge to recruit for carrying out evaluations. All three Metros in the DPME/CLEAR-AA study indicated they are overburdened with compliance reporting, be it externally and internally (CLEAR-AA 2017a, 59).

All of the above resonates with the experience of the City of Johannesburg. The 'City of Gold' has been the leader among Metros in trying to move forward in this space by establishing an M&E framework as far back as 2012. This was driven by the Corporate Strategy Unit in the second term of the ANC Amos Masondo's Mayorship tenure (2006–11), which understood that there was a disconnect between the plethora of reporting on SDBIPs, IDPs, national government reporting requirements and what was needed to really track progress in achieving its long-term development plan: Joburg 2040. A finding from the CLEAR-AA/DPME study (CLEAR-AA 2017a) was that the City of Johannesburg framework was stronger than other Metros in trying to address the internal processes that needed to be established to strengthen the City's monitoring, but was thin in framing the institutional reforms for driving evaluations more systematically across the City. At the time (2016–18), evaluations occurred sporadically and only on capital expenditure projects related to the mayoral priorities. The M&E framework, largely a declaration of intention, did not speak to how to address the fact that no formal system was in place to guide how evaluations should be commissioned and managed or how the findings should be used to influence programme reform. It is in recognising these challenges that the City of Johannesburg approached CLEAR-AA to assess how the City could move forward in implementing this M&E framework, with a view to strengthening the evaluation component and eventually establish a City-wide evaluation system.

The two case studies below present an analysis of the contestations between two sets of actors in the City of Johannesburg: politicians trying to ensure responsiveness to community pressures versus officials trying to demonstrate 'progress' through reporting on the implementation of strategic plans as laid out across various departments. The former often upsets the planned implementation of the latter. The case studies delve into two oversight bodies of the City that oversee how effectively politicians are representing the voice of communities on how planned projects are unfolding on the ground.

Learning from practice (1): the Group Strategy Unit – dominated by auditing and compliance dynamics

The Group Strategy Unit is located directly under the City manager. As part of the executive management team, it is meant to coordinate strategic knowledge for the City of Johannesburg. Every line department has an annual business plan and produces quarterly reports against it, which is the main source of monitoring data in the City. The Group Strategy Unit (which was reframed under Mayor Tau, after Mayor Masondo's former Corporate Strategic Unit) is responsible for integrating and analysing the quarterly reports and in this way is performing a monitoring function for the City of Johannesburg. **Figure 13.1** illustrates the City's organogram in relation to the strategic layer at the executive level, which is comprised of Group heads. Departments are led by executive directors who manage the day-to-day operations. Executive directors account to Group heads for the performance of their departments. Group heads account to the Members of the Mayoral Committee (MCC) who govern the politics of the City.

Data was collected through three focus-group meetings, which included both Group heads driving strategic functions of the City as well as representatives of the M&E units. The M&E staff tended to be junior with limited M&E experience – even though there had been a steady growth of M&E staff in the City. These positions require compiling data across various City divisions/departments to provide the evidence of whether inputs have been spent and whether the required outputs have been met, but the junior status of this position has often caused barriers in M&E staff gaining access to the data needed in order to complete a report, particularly for data unobtainable through online systems.

One respondent from Group Finance spoke about how the compliance orientation of reporting inhibited the evaluative thinking among the Group heads of line departments, which drives decisions that affect financial allocations across the City. The existing regulation 'drives people to tick lists' and has created a compliance culture. 'Evaluation is a foreign concept because in a public organisation you don't question things, as this is insubordination'. Such a statement is characteristic of a culture of fear and intimidation for discussing problems more openly in an effort to learn from mistakes. The unwillingness to question or interrogate the data and what it is saying is compounded by a disproportionate amount of time spent by staff on reporting. The survey with 54 M&E officers across line departments in

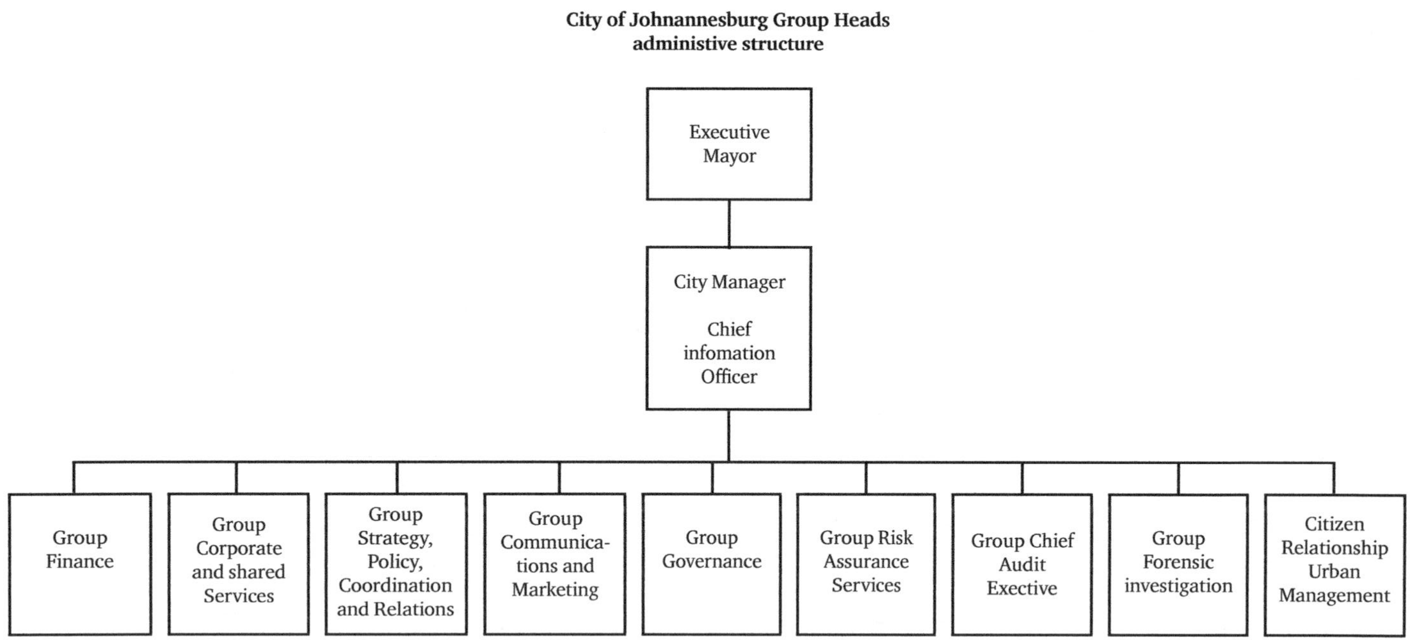

Figure 13.1 City of Johannesburg Group Heads administrative structure.

Source: © City of Johannesburg's Annual Report 2017–18, 41

the City, conducted by CLEAR-AA, concluded that 41 per cent of the respondents spent 75 per cent of their time on internal finance and audit reporting, usually required for legislative compliance, leaving little time for processing information on non-quantitative indicators that could reveal deeper dimensions of service delivery problems (CLEAR-AA 2017b, 18). There were also fears of raising questions on the quality of the quantitative data submitted.

During the period under review, the bulk of the City's monitoring process was manually collected rather than being submitted into a centralised online database, accessible to all. This meant that the ability to verify the data provided for the monitoring system was onerous as it required officials having to call several different departments to verify whether the information provided was correct or not, often with limited levels of responsiveness. As such, the verification process for data compiled for departmental scorecards was uneven. The limited rigour in verifying the data provided for what results had been achieved ended up diminishing the credibility of the monitoring system.

The vast amounts of human resources concentrated on compliance reporting was what most officials interviewed referred to as 'malicious compliance'[3] and was perhaps the largest inhibitor to encouraging evaluative thinking at middle management levels of the civil service. The respondent from Group Finance referred to how selected indicators dictated how data collection occurred and that the process of manual upward reporting on these indicators made validation of the information nearly impossible:

> We rely heavily on what the unit heads are reporting through the Service Delivery Budget Implementation Plans (SDBIP), which is rolled out to unit heads. In their reports, they can write anything regarding what the indicator is, what the deviation is, making Group Finance a glorified data collector. We can't interrogate the quality of what they are getting from unit heads.

The inability to engage with the quality of the data being collected inevitably leads to disengagement with what the data is revealing, thus undermining the monitoring value associated with this reporting. A good example of this is the growing trend of linking departmental performance management to performance-management scorecards that are tied to individual bonuses of the executive driving the line department. This practice has created an incentive system whereby as the above respondent put it: 'The impact of this on M&E is that it dictates to staff what to report on and it gives reasons as to why these things deviate.' Therefore, the level of analysis occurring with the above reporting is on why there was a deviation from the target in order to justify why the target should be seen as met, in order to ensure the performance bonus incentives kick in, rather than analysing the underlying causes of the deviance in the target and what larger problems this might be pointing to. This same employee from Group Finance relates to how data being put forward to meet targets undermines the analytical dimensions of trying to understand what the data is saying in relation to financial management problems in the City. The respondent spoke to the degree to which monitoring information underscores accountability in relation to how Group Finance responds to the Auditor General's report. His unit, when confronting the threat of a disqualification from the Auditor General, tries to address damage control but:

> the underlying problems don't really get addressed because people don't know what the real underlying problem is. No one knows where the problems start in terms of why particular outcomes are not reached ... Instead of monitoring to try to fix things, we retrospectively look at what the Auditor General will look for and pre-audit these things and try to step into smoothing these items to prevent a negative look from the AG. This not the way to work.

The above quote underscores the real meaning of 'malicious compliance' where reporting is done to meet predefined targets linked to regulatory requirements but is done in such a rote manner that the process ends up trying to cover up problems by masking them (von Holdt and Murphey 2007) rather than using the data to raise red flags when problems arise.

Another senior official within Planning spoke about the difficulties in tracking City performance relative to outcomes. She stated that 'there is a broken loop between activities, outputs and inputs and this links to outcomes'. Her key question was whether it was the responsibility of departments to fix these broken loops, or of the Group Strategy Unit. This issue was compounded by the identification of another yet larger problem related to the lack of measurement discipline in the City. The same official gave an example of this problem by stating:

> If we look at the Bus Rapid Transit system (BRT) we are measuring passenger trips per year. How does this tell us whether we are achieving a modal shift? This is an output measure. To get an outcome measure, we need to look at the contribution or uptake

of passengers on BRT in relation to the total portion share of public transit. This means that we need to draw the correlation between an increase in passenger numbers and a percentage increase in public transport. If there is a strong correlation then we are achieving an impact. The ability to measure the relationship between an output and an outcome is not a working practice in the City.

Seeing the logical flow of how City projects are contributing towards broader changes depends on how the indicators are defined. This same correspondent spoke of the problem of a lack of measurement discipline in the City resulting from a limited capacity to understand what indicators were important for tracking activities (output level) versus bringing about broader behavioural or performance change (outcome level) at immediate (three year) or intermediate (five year) timeframes. The inability to do this makes it difficult for a department to assess how their quarterly and annual reporting frameworks are contributing towards larger societal changes that relate to tracking the City-wide performance in meeting the objectives of Johannesburg's 2040 long-term City development plan.

Yet cities, such as Johannesburg, are not isolated and operate within a larger network of cities that are looking at similar issues, and in doing so, sharing approaches on how to do this. Unless the foundational capacity of getting measurement and log frames right is in place, adhering to a global practice of indicators could be cause for even further confusion. The same Planning department respondent noted that the requirement to use global indicators for cities is becoming standardised, which has been difficult to address given the human and technical capacity needed to track these indicators; first and foremost, in a local context, before assessing how to improve these indicators to align with an international benchmarking process. The respondent raised the issue that Planning officials at times do not find these global indicators as relevant and would prefer aligning indicators with their City strategies so as to incorporate local contexts, as these are seen as more useful as progress markers. The Group Strategy Unit was the central coordinating body in the City meant to be addressing the kind of issues outlined above by line departments.

Unfortunately, the Group Strategy Unit was significantly under-resourced to perform these tasks. The Group heads noted that it was a far cry from what the Group Strategy Unit had once been under Mayor Masondo (2001–11). The then Corporate Strategy Unit (CSU) had been established with significant powers in the City for collecting data from communities and line departments, and synthesising this into levels of analysis that fed the City's various strategies and supported the decision-making of the City manager and mayor. Under the mandate of Parks Tau (2011–16), the CSU was transformed into the Group Strategy Unit and in the process, the strategic weight diminished significantly. It had been relegated to a post-box role in terms of sending out templates to various departments, requesting departments to provide relevant indicators and to report on these, collating this information, and then selectively drawing from these quarterly reports and packaging it to present to the City manager and the mayor (CLEAR-AA 2017b). Yet, one of the key complaints expressed in the focus group was that when information was packaged to assess performance, there was insufficient feedback to a given line department, to ensure the accuracy of the analysis or to discuss what the performance issues were. The need was expressed for greater data analytics within the Group Strategy Unit in order to provide feedback on the information provided, as well as for the Group Strategy Unit to play a greater capacity development role on M&E across departments.

Clearly, the M&E system's ability to inform strategic decisions and how these are taken on by the various line departments was dysfunctional for a variety of reasons. These reasons include evidence drawn from an assessment of short-term outputs as opposed to longer-term outcomes; onerous national reporting requirements leaving limited time for officials to conduct their own analyses; and skewed incentive systems encouraging a 'malicious compliance' rather than proactive learning.

Learning from practice (2): the municipal legislature – disempowered councillors

The political oversight function in the City of Johannesburg is also carried out by the City's legislature through various committee structures, such as Section 79 committees (comprising councillors from different political parties) and ward committees (comprising members of civil society elected at the ward level to work with, and monitor, the ward councillor). The separation between the executive and legislature, while in place theoretically since 2000, changed considerably in 2011 as an outcome of a major institutional review of the City. The review concluded that the role of councillors in these committees needed to be formalised and elevated, but it actually considerably weakened the power of the

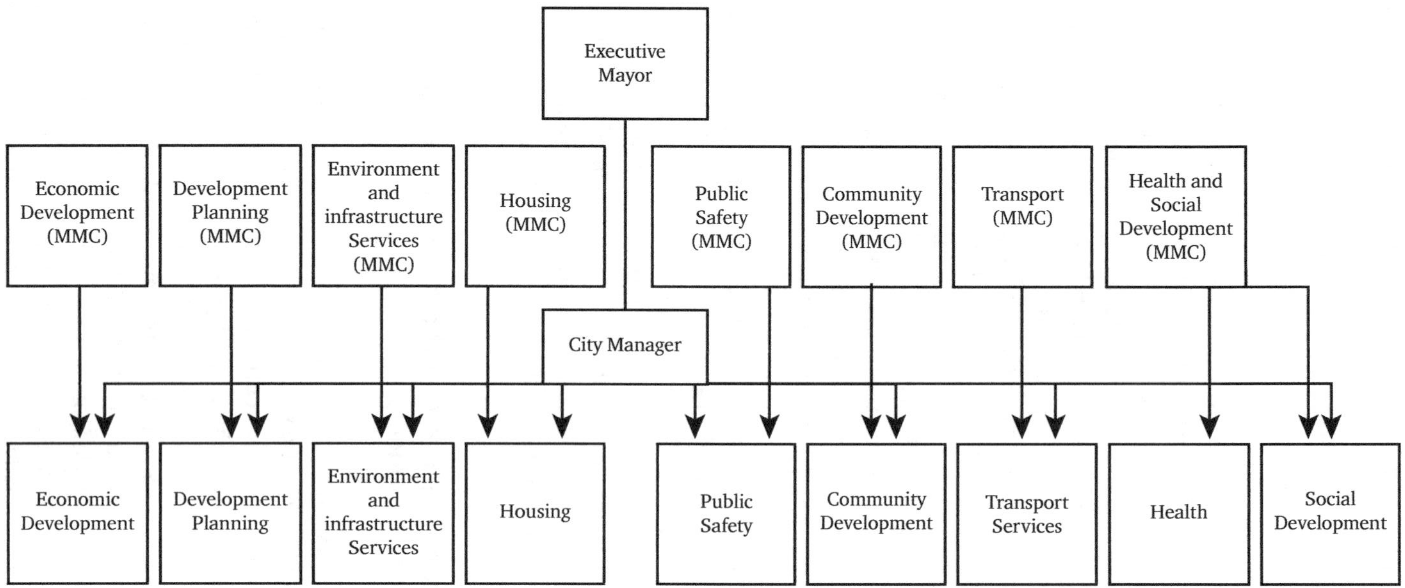

Figure 13.2 City of Johannesburg line functions reporting to the City manager and relevant political portfolios.

Source: © Laila Smith

Section 79 committee structure, by suppressing their chairing by the MMC, who had brought clout and influence to the committee structure.

According to the Municipal Structures Act (1999), the intention of the political oversight function of Section 79 committees is to ensure accountability in driving capital spending over a five-year political term of office, which makes members of this committee responsible for monitoring the plans, programmes and projects of City departments. These committees consist of councillors who carry out site visits to inspect projects in communities. They use these observations, combined with the reports they get from their officials from line departments, to make recommendations to the City manager's office on service delivery progress in relation to capital spending. Ndlovu et al. (2017) have noted the levels of mistrust between officials and councillors regarding the degree to which site visit findings can often use political channels to escalate key community issues that were not budgeted for. This can cause tensions with officials that are tracking performance against pre-existing plans (Ndlovu et al. 2017).

By the same token, evidence brought to bear by councillors during these site visits can often be discounted because they do not have the technical language to frame their findings in a way that is deemed by officials as factual (CLEAR-AA 2017b). Moreover, as noted above, the whole monitoring system incentivises the achievement of department scorecards, whereby the departments' executive directors are rewarded through a bonus for such achievements. This skews the incentive structure for feeding its monitoring tools. As one key informant in the Legislature indicated: 'Executive Directors jippo the stats because they want to get a bonus.' If an executive gets 80 per cent of their target, they will get R1 million bonus. This has a knock-on effect to the councillors of Section 79 committees that are relying on these reports to inform their site visits. The councillors would look at business plans and come up with a report that shows shortfalls against the minimum that the department is meant to achieve. Apart from skewing the data that goes into the main source of monitoring via the quarterly reports, a second challenge confronting the councillors is the lack of technical expertise in M&E. An interview with the former Chief Whip of the Legislature noted the importance of politicians needing to be trained to ask the right questions.

When it comes to evaluation, a senior respondent confessed that the legislature plays no role in outcomes-based reporting, as most of their site visits are related to monitoring activities (outputs). Furthermore, when there are strategic meetings within the Executive Manager Forum, which is where all the Heads of Department (HoDs) meet on a regular basis to discuss the City's performance against the GDS 2040,[4] the respondent noted that there is no consultation with the legislature regarding the outcomes of these high-level strategic discussions. Furthermore, the ability to see the big picture through an evaluative lens is thwarted by the piecemeal approach taken by departments in their reporting in relation to the City's strategic plan, the GDS. The flaw in this design is that no single unit, such as the Group Strategy Unit, can provide an overview of how the City is performing as a whole against these medium- to long-term outcomes.

Beyond capacity challenges, there are fundamental governance challenges in the City's legislature that relate to the degree to which the evidence it provides has clout in swaying decision-making. One challenge is the bottlenecks in the journey the evidence from councillors' site visits has to go through as it trickles its way upwards for discussion in Council. The second challenge is whether the clout of councillors is sufficient to influence decision-making when their recommendations pertain to disciplinary action associated with consequences for poor performance by the administration. In optimal terms, the result of site visits gets channelled into reports where recommendations can be put forward; then these reports are discussed in Section 79 committee meetings and then in Council. Ultimately, for the City legislature, the highest point of authority is the Chief Whip. For officials in Council, the highest point of uthority is the City manager who, along with the accountable officer on all governance decisions affecting the City, holds the discretion on whether to discipline poor performance. As a senior political representative of the City stated:

> In terms of the Labour Relations Act, Council can't recommend sanctions against an official. I can ask the City Manager to investigate and it is up to him to take what necessary steps need to be done. It is up to the City Manager. There are hundreds of disciplinary cases against officials that are suspended, most often on pay. Council cannot suspend an official or a councillor. Reward is getting your scorecard; discipline for non-performance [can only come from] a recommendation to Council.

The delving into the positions of councillors in this case study reveals that politicians are in the end subservient to the administration of the City bureaucracy. At best, a Section 79 committee can make recommendations to the City manager, but the ultimate decision lies with the latter. This finding reveals the flaws in legislation in vesting real power in politicians, as representatives of the people holding officials to account.

The highest levels of power in the City lies with the authority of the mayor and the mayoral committee (a committee of 10 councillors nominated by the mayor within the mayor's political party, that jointly holds the executive authority). This authority is legislatively delegated to local politicians through Section 79 committees to be the 'eyes and ears' of the mayor at the community level. Ironically, the behaviour of politicians, through Section 79 committees, who raise 'unplanned' issues related to planned infrastructure, often upsets the planned implementation of the City strategy as they demand that the ad hoc concerns of their constituencies should have priority over what was planned. This is particularly the case when community expectations are not met in relation to the quality of services delivered in their neighbourhoods. Such articulations of poor-quality delivery and delayed 'achievements' of set targets disturbs reporting against planned budgets, which threatens to undermine the implementation of plans on which bureaucrats' performance scorecards are based. These tensions between administrators and politicians are resolved through the recommendations of Section 79 committees that are presented to the City manager requesting where and when they should intervene on service delivery matters. The City manager has the discretion to ignore such recommendations, particularly if there is evidence from officials to counter observational evidence from site visits led by councillors.

This example raises larger questions about what kind of evidence in monitoring systems gets used and what gets ignored. The case study examples speak to a broader point of how systematised routine monitoring may provide regular data for planned infrastructure provision, but the quality of delivery, the actual outcome, may be thwarted if this data is not quality assured by live processes, which in this case is the role of local councillors that have been largely disempowered from playing this role (Bénit-Gbaffou 2008).

Conclusion: reintroducing 'the public' in co-defining what matters?

This chapter has provided a case study of a decentred conception of power where the original intention of implementing a City-wide evaluation system to support greater learning and accountability failed to materialise. The efforts to improve organisational performance were undermined by the incentive structures that took root within the City bureaucracy. The monitoring system that took hold was seemingly 'subjectless': devoid of the sense-making features that enable officials to analyse whether the data being provided could shed light on whether organisational performance was progressing or whether the data was only addressing activities completed, regardless of whether they contributed to the intended service delivery outcomes.

Through the study of two oversight bodies, this lack of evaluative culture was explained by a number of factors. The flaw in the City's current institutional design is that no single unit, let alone the Group Strategy Unit, was able to provide an overview of how the City was performing as a whole against its medium- to long-term outcomes. The intent in making the Group Strategy Unit the centre of power by virtue of its coordination function across line departments failed to come to fruition because it did not have the capacity to analyse and synthesise the spotty 'evidence' it was getting from line departments.

The reporting processes, internal and external, local and national, were too numerous and cumbersome to leave time for officials to reflect, debate and interrogate. The nature of this reporting did not seem adapted to the needs of improving policies and practices. Most reporting processes were linked to the fear of sanction – bad audit or loss of bonus – and disconnected from actual incentives to learn from mistakes or adapt complex policies and implementation practices to their actual effects on the city. The quality of the data gathered was thus uneven and difficult to validate, all the more that no central database system was set up. As such, the Group Strategy Unit was a site of decentred power that had lost its influence to play an effective oversight role. The second oversight structure was also unable to live up to the intentions of its design. When information 'from the ground' was accessed by local councillors reporting on the expression of residents' claims, it was seen as a disturbance and seldom had influence on assessments on municipal actions, due to limited credit, power and capacity allocated to local councillors and their Section 79 committees. As such, the data collection process did not succeed in providing the evidence as to whether a given department's activities have contributed toward achieving their organisational outcomes. The lack of community-level nor front-line worker input into the definitions of these KPIs certainly contributed to a lack of ground-truthing of the indicators being used to assess service delivery outcomes.

The M&E systems, despite the challenges outlined in this chapter, have become a permanent fixture of modern bureaucracies. The challenge is how to design them and run them in order to enable a City, inclusive of its various stakeholders, to see how its day-to-day operations are moving towards achieving its medium- to long-term objectives. One of the lost dimensions in the original set up of the City of Johannesburg's oversight system was the involvement of the public in mechanisms of accountability, such as through the design of the measures used to track progress in the city's service delivery outcomes. Such accountability measures were not designed for public involvement in M&E to be a single event but rather to inaugurate an ongoing process to sustain public engagement. Resurrecting these mechanisms of public input is essential for drawing in the public's insight as to where the causes of the structural flaws in service delivery lie. The ability to see these structural flaws are blurred in the siloed approaches of individual departmental review mechanisms.

A second step forward for the City of Johannesburg to improve its monitoring system would be to address the malfunctioning culture within the bureaucracy by re-coding the incentive structures to reward learning and the sharing of learning. This could involve setting up sense-making sessions among officials, between officials and councillors and among officials, councillors and community representatives. Triangulating these sense-making sessions with the data collected could help build greater analytical capacity and in doing so restore some credibility to the monitoring systems that feed how the City understands its performance. These steps would go a long way towards building an evaluative culture.

Notes

1 CLEAR-AA was one of six centres of excellence located across the Global South, all based in universities with the intent of building M&E markets through the capacity development on both the demand for and supply of M&E services. The Centres were funded by a multi-donor trust fund hosted by the Independent Evaluation Unit of the World Bank. The six university centres operated as think tanks with a primary aim of capacity development. CLEAR-AA, based at the University of the Witwatersrand, had a strong focus on knowledge generation through research and publications.

2 Every municipality in South Africa is required to produce plans through a consultative process that considers short-, medium- and long-term issues such as spatial planning, disaster management, finances, performance targets and economic development.

3 This term refers to reporting according to the letter of the law, without using the reporting to bring any greater meaning to the query at hand.

4 The City's strategic long-term plan at the time in which research for this chapter was conducted.

References

Alexander, P. 2010. 'Rebellion of the poor: South Africa's service delivery protests – a preliminary analysis', *Review of African Political Economy* 37(123): 25–40.

Alonso, J.M., Clifton, J. and Díaz-Fuentes, D. 2015. 'The impact of New Public Management on efficiency: An analysis of Madrid's hospitals', *Health Policy* 119(3): 333–40.

Amable, B. 2011. 'Morals and politics in the ideology of neoliberalism', *Socio-Economic Review* 9(1): 3–30.

Basheka, B. and Byamugisha, A. 2015. 'The state of monitoring and evaluation (M&E) as a discipline in Africa: From infancy to adulthood?', *African Journal of Public Affairs* 8(3): 75–95.

Bénit-Gbaffou, C. 2008. 'Are practices of local participation side-lining the institutional participatory channels? Reflections from Johannesburg', *Transformation* 66–67: 1–33.

CLEAR-AA 2017a. *Situational Analysis of the Role of DPME and other National and Provincial Organisations in Institutionalising Evaluation in Metropolitan Municipalities.* Report commissioned by DPME, South Africa.

CLEAR-AA 2017b. *Developing and Implementing a Comprehensive Capacity: City building programme for monitoring and evaluation in the City of Johannesburg.* Report commissioned by the City of Johannesburg.

Dabelstein, N. 2003. 'Evaluation capacity development: Lessons learned', *Evaluation* 9(3): 365–69.

Davies, W. 2014. *The Limits of Neoliberalism.* Los Angeles: Sage.

Dlamini, P. and Migiro, S. 2016. 'Performance monitoring and evaluation systems in the South African local government', *Journal of Public Administration* 51(3): 376–90.

Donzelot, J. 1979. *The Policing of Families.* Baltimore: Pantheon Books

DPME. 2013. *A Diagnostic Study on M&E Human Resource Capacity and Training Provision.* Pretoria: Department of Performance M&E.

Dunleavy, P. and Hood, C. 1994. 'From old public administration to new public management', *Public Money and Management* 14(3): 9–16.

Dutta, S.J., Knafo, S. and Lovering, I.A. 2022. 'Neoliberal failures and the managerial takeover of governance', *Review of International Studies* 48(3): 484–502.

Engela, R. and Ajam, T. 2010. *Implementing a Government-wide Monitoring and Evaluation System in South Africa.* ECD Working Paper Series, 21. Washington: World Bank.

Eresia-Eke, C. and Boadu, E. 2019. 'Monitoring and evaluation preparedness of public sector institutions in South Africa', *Journal of Reviews on Global Economics* 8: 532–42.

Ferguson, J. 1990. *The Anti-politics Machine: 'Development' depoliticization, and bureaucratic power in Lesotho.* Cambridge: Cambridge University Press.

Foucault, M. 1979. *Discipline and Punish: The birth of the prison.* Chicago: Vintage Books.

Goldman, I., Byamugisha., A., Gounou, A., Smith, L., Ntakumba, S., Lubanga, T., Sossou, D. and Rot-Munstermann, K. 2018. 'The emergence of government evaluation systems in Africa: The case of Benin, Uganda and South Africa', *African Evaluation Journal* 6(1): online. Available at: https://aejonline.org/index.php/aej/article/view/253. Accessed 29 July 2023.

Goldman, I., Olaleye, W., Ntakumba, S. and Waller, C. 2020. 'Mere compliance or learning: M&E culture in the public service of Benin, Uganda and South Africa'. In *Using Evidence in Policy and Practice,* edited by I. Goldman and M. Pabari, 54–74. London: Taylor and Francis.

Harvey, D. 2007. *A Brief History of Neoliberalism.* Oxford: Oxford University Press.

von Holdt, K., Murphey, M. 2007. 'Stressed institutions, disempowered management'. In *State of the Nation: South Africa* 2007, edited by S. Buhlungu, J. Daniel, R. Southall and J. Lutchman, 312–41. Cape Town: HSRC Press. Hood, C. 1990. 'A public Management for all seasons?', *Public Administration* 69: 3–19.

Hood, C. 1990. 'A public Management for all seasons?', *Public Administration* 69: 3–19.

Jessop, B. 2019. 'Ordoliberalism and neoliberalization: Governing through order or disorder', *Critical Sociology* 45(7–8): 967–81.

Kusek, J. and Rist, R. 2004. *Ten Steps to a Results-based Monitoring and Evaluation System.* Washington, DC.: The World Bank.

Ledger, T. and Meny-Gibert, S. 2018. *The Challenge of Prioritisation and Alignment in Public Sector Planning and Implementation: A literature review.* Report commissioned by Twende Mbele. Johannesburg: Public Affairs Research Institute.

Ndlovu, L. Smith, L. and Narsoo, S. 2017. 'Searching for the right methodology to unpack urban complexity: A case study of the City of Johannesburg, South Africa', *African Evaluation Journal* 5(1), 1–11.

Nielson, S. and Hunter, D. (eds). 2013. *Performance Management and Evaluation.* New York: Wiley.

Peck, J. and Tickell, A. 2002. 'Neoliberalizing space', *Antipode* 34(3): 380–404.

Phillips, S., Goldman, I., Gasa, N., Akhalwaya, I. and Leon, B. 2014. 'A focus on M&E of results: An example from the presidency, South Africa', *Journal of Development Effectiveness* 6(4): 392–406.

Pollitt, C. and Bouckaert, G. 2017. *Public Management Reform: A comparative analysis into the age of austerity.* Oxford: Oxford University Press.

Porter, S. and Goldman, I. 2013. 'Growing demand for monitoring and evaluation in Africa', *African Evaluation Journal* 1(1): 1–9.

Part IV
International perspectives on the art of progressive city government

14

Is there a 'left art' of city government? A view from post-apartheid South Africa

Claire Bénit-Gbaffou

Preamble: Sobering realities – South African municipalities in crisis

At the time of finalising this book (late 2022), South African state and municipalities were in a state of severe crisis, marked by dysfunctionalities generally attributed to significant if not massive corruption. Several national infrastructures such as the national electricity company (Eskom) and airline (South African Airways) had collapsed, while others (such as the South African Revenue Service) had significantly weakened, emptied out of their human, financial and material resources by rent-seeking state and party elites. 'Two-thirds of municipalities appear to be in financial distress or dysfunctional in differing degrees.'[1] The 2018 water crisis in Cape Town, the recurrent lived experience of daily power cuts ('load-sheddings') in Johannesburg, the catastrophic management of the 2022 major water floodings in eThewkini, alert us to the fact that major metropolises, even if marked by a certain political and functional autonomy, are not immune to such crises, aggravated by global environmental change.

Beyond popular and general denunciation of elite corruption and greed, this process has been widely analysed as 'state capture' (Chipkin and Swilling 2018): a system of nepotistic appointments in the state and civil service, put in a position to effect wide resource-plundering and develop rent-seeking practices, set up under the auspices of President Jacob Zuma (2009–18). Behind this largely malevolent and destructive behaviour also lies the effect of more structural dynamics, some of which may be related to the generalisation of the 'contract-state' (Brunette et al. 2019).

Procurement, at national but also local level, has become an essential part of the state's developmental and redistributive policies (Swilling 2017), and awarded contracts and jobs a major lever for the upward mobility of an aspiring Black middle class (von Holdt 2010). It is, however, a key site of clientelism, corruption, sometimes violence, and destabilisation of state capacity to govern, in spite of many attempts for regulatory reform (Brunette et al. 2019). Some authors, observing directly the workings of municipal government at a local level, add how the conjunction of an opaque political party funding system and a large confusion between the African National Congress (ANC) and local government networks and hierarchies have led to municipal maladministration (Reddy 2018), 'perpetual instability' (Phadi et al. 2018), wide use of violence (von Holdt 2013), and sometimes municipal collapse (Olver 2017) – at least in the smaller and less resourced municipalities.

There are reasons to believe that large cities are less prone to such capture and instability. Not only are they more autonomous financially and politically, through a larger tax base and a wider and more professional administration, they also cannot be allowed to collapse for the national economy, and when they encounter a deep crisis (such as the financial crisis having shaken the City of Johannesburg in the late 1990s), State remediation is quick but also under international scrutiny, far more so than in small, remote, peripheral, often voiceless municipalities. It does not mean, however, that large cities are not marked, too, by corruption and maladministration.

This book is not blind to such dynamics, but does not take them as its primary object. It focuses about a moment in the life of cities and Cities: a 'progressive moment'. In South Africa, this moment is gone, and the 'dark side' that could be considered then an element of context (among others) in which officials deployed their action, has now grown in significance, probably disabling possibilities for progressive change. Some institutional activists may have remained in the state, but they are less visible, and their tactics may have shifted from proactive pursuit of progressive goals, to more covert resistance. But this moment has existed, definitely opening a sense of possibility and a degree of agency in City administrative and political circles. This is what this chapter proposes to reflect upon, interrogating and framing what 'a left art of government' (Ferguson 2011) may mean, at City level, from the South African post-apartheid urban experience. It examines successively the key role of intermediary bureaucrats in driving change; what 'activism' in an institution requires and entails; taking 'porous bureaucracies' seriously by asking the question of space and scale of municipal action; how to decipher where political choice lies within a complex process and institution; knowledge, meaning and capacity to act; and the challenges of institutionalisation.

The role of intermediary bureaucrats in driving change: key interface between policy and implementation with relative autonomy

A large part of this book explores officials' agency, adopting an emic perspective seeking to understand officials' point of view (Hahonou and Martin 2019). But, differing from classic anthropologies of bureaucracy, most of this book focuses on intermediary officials in City bureaucratic hierarchy. These officials remain accountable to higher-level officials, but also manage an administrative staff. They are sometimes in contact with user groups and civil society (as project managers for instance), but not as the bulk of their jobs, and their mandate and tasks are to a large degree to drive their teams and construct resources, respond to crises, to implement policies and projects that are generally reshaped in the course of their implementation.

Thus, the discretionary power described by Lipsky (2010) for street-level bureaucrats in applying or not applying certain regulations or classifying people in a category or another, the petty everyday corruption and other arrangements analysed by Anjaria (2011), the selective sensitivity to individual cases observed by Auyero (2012), the gate-keeping power and invented statistics illustrated by Gupta (2012), the coping mechanisms to face the double-binds presented by Bierschenk (2014), constitute only a part of the initiatives and puzzle-assembling work that those middle-rank bureaucrats do. Their level of autonomy, even if under constraints, appears higher, with a space for innovation and creativity that does not fit neatly in descriptions of bureaucrats' routines, even if subverted and appropriated. So, rather than focusing mostly on these routines in order to find regular patterns in bureaucratic behaviour that would indicate the various norms (official, practical, professional, moral, etc.) shaping their practices (Olivier de Sardan 2015), we have focused on individual officials and their navigation of rules, in order to 'act': to perform an intervention that may be part of their job, but requires creativity, networks, lobby and battles.

Interestingly, the use of multi-tasking, flexible understanding of the job as service to users, the ability to respond to citizens' issues and to unexpected requests and situations even if outside of officials' direct mandate, is also what Judith Tendler (1997) emphasises as key to 'good government'. Another of these key elements is, she adds, a deep public awareness of what public service is supposed to provide, which replaces Key Performance Indicators (KPIs) as a bottom-up (rather than top-down) and qualitative (rather than quantified) way of exerting oversight over bureaucracies.

An understanding of routines, rules, structures, procedures and processes are part of the job: how and when to follow them or not points to the gap between official and practical norms. But another part is intermediary officials' exploration of multiple institutions, and how, through attempting to act, they become aware of what these rules and norms are, and how they really work. If multiple constraints and norms exist, the 'rules of the game' (Olivier de Sardan 2015) do not fully pre-exist intermediary officials' actions – they are shaped, framed, negotiated as the officials test their limits when solving a problem in the city.

Whether the multiplicity of norms they work under and with lead to officials' paralysis or create windows of opportunity depends on the political local and national contexts. Meny-Gibert (2017) has shown how, in the Department of Education of the Eastern Cape (a peripheral and impoverished South African province), such multiplicity of norms, in a climate of political uncertainty and instability as well as scarce resources and high corruption, led officials to inaction and paralysis. Others, in areas of state intervention seen as sensitive and politically strategic such as immigration policies, have exposed how the intense and minute hierarchical control compels even senior officials to act contrary to their own common sense and humanity, confining their autonomous agency to small cracks in the rules (Laurens 2008). In Johannesburg and in eThekwini, where contributors to this book were able to partly observe City officials' agency, empirical evidence showed high degrees of tactical and strategic autonomy from intermediary and senior officials, under the broad umbrella of explicit (even if not always dominant in the City politics) progressive political support.

This intermediary level of bureaucracy is said by an emerging literature to be vested with some potential to drive change (Chiha 2006; Cosson 2015), not limited to the work of operationalisation and translation of strategic directions into practical rules (Barrier et al. 2015). A French critical academic tradition tends to read this autonomy as partly if not fully illusory, pointing to the weight of broader structures within various 'fields' (Bourdieu and Cristin 1990) in which their individual agency is extremely limited. Other work in the same school of thought (Bourdieu 1991; Jeannot and Goodchild 2011) empirically examines the work of those who are said to have 'fuzzy jobs': local development officers, project managers. These constitute specific types of intermediary bureaucrats – probably more junior than intermediary, but who have a team that they lead, and report to higher-ranked bureaucrats and politicians, vesting them with the conduct of a project. This work highlights the 'impossible mission' they are to carry, the contradictory imperatives combined with limited resources, the precarious nature of their work often bounded in time, that contain in these authors' view the impossibility of success, and creates high levels of 'suffering at work'. While this structural analysis should be kept in mind, other work rather highlights their ability to initiate change, their 'constrained autonomy' (Cosson 2015). What this book adds, beyond their relative access to strategic players in the City (senior officials, members of the City executive) and in the city (business organisations, housing associations, private developers, social movements), and their ability to drive implementation by directing operational staff, is the importance of their practical understanding of urban societies, that keeps them aware often quite directly of the effects of policies and implementation on local communities.

This intermediary position allows officials to build strategic or policy proposals based on a deep knowledge of operational conditions within City administration and of urban societies where policies and projects are to be implemented. This grounding of policy instruments building in social, operational and practical experience is precious and probably specific. This is the case of Ayanda, a senior manager in City parks, who was able to construct, together with peers from other City departments, a pilot project for participatory park design and management in Johannesburg's inner city, and use this pilot to both engage with and train regional park managers about how to operationalise participatory park management (Bénit-Gbaffou, Chapter 3, this book). Another example is Nikki, first a project facilitator then promoted in the Johannesburg Development Agency, who, based on her first-hand experience of being confronted by poor residents claiming decent and affordable housing, identifies public sites for housing, has them earmarked in planning documents, and contributes centrally to a progressive housing policy proposal with an implementation plan. Rubin (Chapter 4, this book) also narrates how Planning officials are able to operationally delay the attribution of building permits in the inner city to private developers refusing to contribute to inclusionary housing, and to strategically contribute to setting up a high-profile forum with a coalition of inner-city businesses to jointly deal with urban decay, before crafting a whole new policy.

The second element to be stressed is the creative character of those intermediary officials attempting to drive progressive change. Their pragmatic quest for overcoming obstacles, finding resources, building allies, keeping enemies in check through a carefully crafted politics of 'carrots and sticks' (Vedung 1998), has been illustrated by Krumholz and Clavel (1994) for North American cities of the 1970s. Some of the tactics found are very similar to the North American ones in the 1970s; other are specific to the place and time – where New Public Management and Public–Private Partnerships (PPPs) are commonplace, where public capacity is limited and poverty and informality are massive. This book sheds light on the transversal nature of this work – how these intermediary officials, thanks to their position, navigate their own institution to find solutions literally 'outside of the box', discovered outside of their own unit or department – with peers but also with more junior and sometimes more senior officials. A City Park official will build a partnership with City Safety and City Planning to deal with inner-city parks management; planners will need to find ways to work with reluctant Housing officials, income-generating focused Property Department and under-resourced Community Services to build an inclusive housing complex in a suburb.

The degree of creativity might be enhanced in our particular case (post-apartheid South African cities). Officials are not only part of an administrative hierarchy in the making (where administrative control might not be as rigid as in more consolidated administrations), but where they are also, often, benefiting from party (ANC) networks that give them access to other sites of power, intersecting the City's (Bénit-Gbaffou 2008). The 'post-apartheid moment' gave innovative individuals a place and a space to act within local government; City administration was then not only 'business as usual'. In such a context, another concept has been useful to analyse intermediary officials' practices – institutional activism.

The heuristic value of 'institutional activism'

Encounters with Brazilian academia were crucial in this respect. Although this literature revolved mostly around national rather than urban processes in their focus, it took seriously the issue of officials' practice in the conduct of progressive change, inspired by a particular moment in Brazilian history: the Lula and Rousseff presidencies, where a number of social movement activists became state officials.

What echoed from this body of work in our South African cities debates was first the conclusion that for state officials conducting progressive reform requires relying on and maintaining a network of allies and institutions in civil society: not only through social movement mobilisation, but also through constantly engaging with professional bodies (*sanitaristas* in the health sector and civil management bodies in the water sector) (Dowbor and Houtzager 2014; Abers and Keck 2013). This is necessary to take into account the long temporality of policy reform, including its implementation and institutionalisation: maintaining popular pressure on politicians tempted to favour quick fixes as electoral gains, and building the conditions for a successful implementation and institutionalisation of reform within society.

A second illuminating idea was the conceptual difference developed, as empirical work progressed, between 'institutional' and 'bureaucratic' activism. While we continue to talk about 'institutional activism' at large (and did not adopt the term 'bureaucratic activism'), this distinction is illuminating. In this literature, 'institutional activism' was initially focused on movements' activists entering the state and the normative, cultural and political change this entailed, to the point of creating tensions between former fellow activists having remained in social movements, and the activist-in-the-state whose pragmatic compromises towards progressive reforms were often misunderstood (Abers and Tatagiba 2015). 'Bureaucratic activism' then framed forms of activism in the institution that were disconnected from any formal relation or previous experience of any existing social movements (Abers 2019): officials in loose networks proactively promoting self-defined contentious causes. Both configurations coexist in bureaucracies, but the latter, disconnecting institutional activism at large from social movements, opens new avenues for analysis. This book takes stock of what has been produced in a Brazilian context, interrogating what it does to use this concept at the local, urban scale and in a South African context, but perhaps more centrally, continuing the work of exploring the richness of the concept of 'activism' to study institutional practice and ways of governing societies.

What do City institutional activists do compared with street activists?

What is specific, what differs, when one engages in activism in the state rather than in the street? Or, to cite Verhoeven and Duyvendak (2017): what is it that institutional activists 'know and do best'? This book proposes several elements of response.

Firstly, and foremost, what City institutional activists do is to create new policy instruments – technically, administratively, financially and politically. Changing categories and norms of action or control (a KPI, for instance), challenging a rule overtly or quietly (defending councillors' right to protest alongside constituencies, wearing a workers' uniform in City Council, using portfolio committees to have discussions with councillors from other political parties), creating or altering planning documents and spatial frameworks to render visible or start addressing specific issues, negotiating and lobbying for a line in budget, initiating agreements, contracts or partnerships with other institutions, drafting new policies and having them passed, etc. That is what institutional activists are equipped to do, and can seize opportunities to do, from their position in the administrative hierarchy and in a specific portfolio or sector.

This differs radically from social movement or street activism, generally crystallised in opposition to broad policy change, with open ends regarding what alternative policy would or could be advocated. When street activists develop positive demands, these seldom fit neatly into administrative, political, scalar or sectoral categories of the state apparatus – this is where the work of institutional activists may start. Institutional activists are compelled to be constructive – constructing instruments that will produce a different city and a different way of responding to urban issues. They are compelled to be pragmatic: constructing instruments that will work in practice, relatively simple and as liberating as possible, as Ferguson (2013) would argue in uncertain and dependant societies and complex state administration; constructing instruments that will pass in City Council, through a work of balance and trade-offs, without losing the core of the initial objective. Institutional activists create policy instruments, and when possible a set of policy instruments – whether they start from policy drafts and then need to grant resources (budget, institutions, staff, guidelines, data) to implement it; or they begin with practical tools (mapping, planning practices, staff training) and move up to policy reform. Sometimes, they even (re)create their own mandate, within their official position – either informally (as 'their' cause, sometimes publicly displayed and sometimes not), or officially (Ayanda held for instance a unique title in Johannesburg City administration: 'head of knowledge and partnership management', within City Parks – Chapter 3, this book). A position that allows and entitles them to work transversally, and not be encapsulated in a single portfolio, unit or department – this transversality being often key to their project and their work (Needleman and Needleman 1977).

When one reflects further on which networks and alliances City institutional activists build and how, and interrogates what the conditions are for institutional activism to be successful, there are cases in which stars seem to align – when sufficient bureaucratic support (the departments key to the specific intervention), political support (from the mayor and executive committee, or from a majority of councillors), and social support (visible constituency or media campaign), has been gathered. While this might appear as a tautology, or an impossible alignment to attain, most institutional activists in the City have worked on at least two, and often three, of what we can call 'fields' (as each has its own rules, positions and battles for position, even if they may intersect). It is classic to describe how institutional activists need to mobilise administrations: their own department (their boss higher up, as well as their operational staff), but also other departments whose portfolio is relevant or required to conduct the project or policy, and to overcome resistance, or find ways of side-lining those who might obstruct. It is also quite expected, although less easily described, that institutional activists need support from politicians: mayor and the executive committee, councillors or parties. Generally, intermediary officials are not likely to be directly in touch with councillors. In post-apartheid South African cities, it was however often the case, through prior ANC networks. Lastly, the importance of the link to civil society has been emphasised by the work of Dowbor and Houtzager (2014) on the Brazilian health sector. They demonstrate how social mobilisation matters to keep motivating politicians to go for the 'difficult dive' (Stone 1995) so that they keep trying to conduct progressive reforms which require a difficult and politically costly confrontation with market forces, that only a mobilised constituency might assist in compensating. Observing various City activists' practices in post-apartheid South African cities, it is striking to see how their work generally straddles the three fields – with different balances depending on position, ability, skill and appetite. Generally, when one of these fields is insufficiently invested, it is where the obstacles (and likely failure) emerge even though, as in Bourdieu's notion of capital convertibility, mobilisation in one field may compensate for the lack of mobilisation in another (civil society mobilisation becoming the condition for political support; political support a way to avoid administrative obstruction).

So, in response to the question about what *institutional* activists do, we can answer that institutional activists build policy instruments, and build capital in two or three of the political, bureaucratic or civil society fields. Two specificities need to be highlighted.

Firstly, this form of institutional activism may be specific to these short progressive moments in the lives of cities. Other modes of institutional activism exist in other contexts, such as covert resistance to policy, especially when there is radical change in national government, and municipalities attempt to keep some autonomy. Analyses of officials' practices in 'sanctuary cities' or 'cities network for climate' in North American cities opposing the national policy of ex-president Donald Trump, and inventing instruments to resist or circumvent national directions, would probably lead to other features for institutional activism. These features would echo the 'guerrillas in the bureaucracy', described by O'Leary (2014) in the form of covert, individual resistance against administrative or political order, and by Needleman and Needleman (1974) analysing collective, sectoral battles within the bureaucracy.

A second specificity is that this book is focused on institutional activism at the City level, with the specificity we highlighted earlier: a close proximity to societies to be governed, allowing intermediary officials in particular to see rather immediately the effects of the policies promulgated and crafted. At this scale, the 'policy and implementation gap' is probably narrower than elsewhere, and officials' discretionary power, due to their position, might be higher.

Why are institutional activists, activists? Intensity and the (in) ability to last in position

These conclusions help us to reflect on further heuristic dimensions of the concept of institutional activism. What does considering activist officials as 'activists' help us see and understand? Here, we can only indicate directions for reflection. We have mostly looked at what activist officials 'do', not centrally on who activist officials 'are' (their biographies, their training, their professional trajectories), which seems to coincide with dominant approaches to activism in the studies of social movements seeking to explain why, how, and when people enter or leave social movements or political parties (Sawicki and Siméant 2009). These directions are two-fold: the blurred boundary between work and life experienced by institutional activists, and the opportunistic and blurred framing of 'the cause'.

The reference to 'activism' to describe some officials' practices first allows us to understand the intensity of their life at work, and the blurry boundary between their life and their work, where their work becomes an important part of how they see and define themselves. This lived intensity, the sense of a mission carried by many officials in intermediary or high positions, is both exhilarating and exhausting. Our understanding of institutional activism (playing simultaneously on three different fields of action – bureaucratic, political and social – alongside the transversality of activist officials' actions, not confined to their own unit or department) does explain this intensity practically. It requires the constant and regular engagement of activist officials with a number of departments, officials, sectoral issues and regulations, civil society activists, politicians and media. This produces new understandings, opportunities and instruments for action but is also extremely time- and energy-consuming.

Bourdieu analyses this 'suffering at work' (Bourdieu 1991), but possibly underplays the exhilaration generated by the felt possibility of change and creative responses to issues, the sense of meaning and contribution, the collegiality created by a jointly constructed ethos of public service and social justice. However, the toll taken by the demands of activism and the many failures for few victories generally lead officials to not last very long in their position, which also limits the possibility for consolidating and institutionalising change. As fundamentally, for institutional activists, political reform requires longevity in the institution – the incremental building of technical capacity, of institutional knowledge, of various political, technical, administrative, media and social networks, that may be mobilised when an opportunity emerges. This book does not go further on what makes institutional activists stay, nor on what makes them leave the institution: retributions of activism, activism fatigue, moments of biographical disposition to activism or retreat thereof, dismissal or marginalisation by the institution, gendered dimensions of institutional activism, are directions for complementary research.

Why are institutional activists, activists? The usefully blurred framing of 'the cause'

A second direction emerging empirically from our collective study and striking stimulating parallels with the literature of social movements, is interrogating the framing of 'the cause'. Following Abers, we define a cause as 'ideas that, from the perspective of believers, need to be defended against powerful forces of stability or change' (Abers 2019, 24). Empirically, for activist officials, cause framing seems far more blurry, opportunistic, fluid and self-constructed than for social movement collectives. A number of factors may explain this. Firstly, the 'cause' in institutional activism is less in need of being explicitly formulated than in social movements, because the adoption of a new policy or norm or instrument precisely requires flexibility in the way it is framed, a degree of discretion if not of secrecy in subtle and multi-institutional tactical and strategic moves, so as to garner wide and diverse support, building compromises without losing too much content. Publicity might be needed at times, but carefully framed at specific moments of the process. A second reason for this blurry framing might be the effect that operationalisation (constructing a concrete public intervention in its broad and minute practicalities) has on causes – that, in social movements, can be built in broad and principled, oppositional and confrontational ways. The 'institutionalisation' of the cause, that some have called 'domestication' (Neveu 2011) but that Katzenstein (1998) has distinguished from its 'de-radicalisation', transforms it substantially, as illustrated by Abers and Tatagiba (2015), and in this book by Pingo and Bénit-Gbaffou (Chapter 5).

In municipal activism, the framing of the cause is generally profoundly grounded in specific urban contexts – perhaps even more than for street activism – and is possibly far more individual than collective. If institutional activists are likely to be driven by a broad sense of justice and wanting to contribute to better societies, the specific cause they are pushing in the institution generally emerges opportunistically. It does so as officials encounter opportunities or are stricken by issues arising with urban policy processes and their local implementation. For the Planning officials described by Rubin (Chapter 4), the broad 'cause' (a conception of justice where the poor should access the city) was opportunistically embodied and framed in a specific inclusive housing policy process they had the opportunity to push, without being mandated explicitly by their political boss. Likewise, a project facilitator portrayed by Bénit-Gbaffou discovered the world of homelessness and developed his intervention around it: it could have remained a marginal issue in his project, but a polite but radical criticism by academic consultants tasked to follow the project made him brutally realise its exclusionary dynamics. While this sudden realisation or crystallisation might be similar for activists joining social movements (not specific to institutional activists), the difference lies in the fact that the latter are able to join a collective process framing 'the cause' and exploring different directions and repertoires of action – while institutional activists will also, and perhaps mostly, frame the cause according to the opportunities provided by their position in administration, and by the policy instruments they are able to construct.

Here we come back to Clavel's (2010) fundamental idea that progressive cities are built through pushing boundaries in both participatory and redistributive dimensions of justice. While some officials analysed in this book (generally those at more senior positions) have built their cause and politics through an acute and principled sense of the need for redistribution, and the necessity for planning to protect the most deprived (and majority) sections of the city and residents, many officials at more intermediate levels have experienced participatory engagements first-hand. From there, they have worked their way up in strategic policy-making, incrementally becoming aware of the shortcomings of policy and instruments, ill-adaptation or blindness to the social dynamics on the ground, but also on the possibilities of reform, instruments and resource mobilisation. This dimension of participatory planning, 'behind the scene' type of work – where the moment of encounter with local communities might bring new understandings to officials, some of which might take it further and work with it in multiple realms – is largely understated by literature on urban politics, democracy and participation.

As explained earlier, we have not delved into the biographies, political and personal trajectories of those activists. As a consequence, we are not able to analyse why specific officials would be predisposed to become institutional activists, in their own life path and in this particular moment of South African history; this remains a direction for future research. But we can see empirically how the 'cause' itself is generally not external nor independent of officials' practice and position. It is not as a force shaping and channelling those practices, as a collective movement with a collective framing process defining boundaries, principles and identity. It is often tacit, at least for officials who are not expected nor in a position to directly hold public discourses. It is constructed and framed by the specific institutional position and context in which officials are located, crystallising around a window of opportunity (at large, the post-apartheid moment, and specific – a crisis, a public issue, a moment in the political or electoral cycle), and incrementally refined as those officials engage in conceptualising, resourcing, implementing and institutionalising the policy instrument that is key to their intervention.

Taking 'porous bureaucracies' seriously – understanding the making of policy instruments in space and scale

On the nature of officials' constrained autonomy, beyond the discretion of street-level bureaucrats, we were continuously inspired by the work of Indian scholar Solomon Benjamin (2004), who proposed the concept of 'porous bureaucracies'. By this, he did not just mean that the state is not autonomous from society and is always subjected to its influence; he highlighted that local administrations were particularly permeable to the societies they were meant to administer because of their social and spatial proximity. In his view, not all bureaucracies are equally porous, and not in the same ways or to the same social groups. Paying attention to the local level of policy-making (below the scale of metropolitan or State authorities whose plans and officials are the most famous and prestigious), he looked at how local councillors and bureaucrats ended up being open to their local constituencies' claims and needs, even if in contradiction with master plans or other existing broader legislation. A 'politics by stealth', he did not term it a 'progressive politics' (the term might be too strong), but illuminated how these practices contributed substantially to the inclusion or even upliftment of the poor, sometimes in contrast to grand claims by NGO or social movements' discourses of rights, which ended up having large exclusionary effects. He explained this porosity as a result of the social proximity of those councillors and bureaucrats, originating from backgrounds similar to that of their constituencies; by direct interest as well, local councillors owing their position to their ability to attract local votes (the democratic, albeit not rosy, dimension of clientelism: Chatterjee 2004) and (generally at least)[2] to avoid social unrest, an objective that might be shared by local administrations.

This reflection emerged in a long international tradition of studying the state and deconstructing the idea of its autonomy, through observing state–society encounters (as moments) or the fuzzy framing of the borders between state and society (as institutions), classic but important ways of studying the state, 'from the outside'. Seeing the 'state from its margins' that reflects its core (Das and Poole 2004); from the 'street-level' (Lipsky 2010); from its 'interfaces' (Dubois 2017; Gupta 2012); from its spaces of 'engagement' (Wafer and Oldfield 2014); or its 'institutional surface area' (Heller 2019) where categories of public action meet reality of society; observing the movements and mutual influences ('state-in-society' and 'society-in-state') (Migdal 2001), to cite only a few.

A number of these authors use this interface to interrogate how civil society dynamics shape both policies and practices of (local) officials. That is how Tendler (1997), moving away from a normative participatory agenda, sees the improvement of local officials' practices both through a higher public awareness of citizens' rights and what the state is supposed to deliver, and through an enhanced central intervention that, far from relinquishing power to decentralised authorities, continues to provide a shield and a recourse (alongside increased public awareness) against clientelistic practices and pressures, often paramount at the local level (Olver 2017). Tendler's shift away from state–society binary, towards a tryptic (central state, local authorities and the public) is illuminating. It is also what Benjamin investigates, grounding his critique of broad-brushed analyses of state practices in cities (identified as neoliberal or clientelistic or both) in a constant attention to differences between scales of government. In his case studies, metropolitan authorities, not only because of specific objectives and mandates but also because of their relative social, spatial and electoral remoteness from their poorer constituencies, have historically developed regressive Master plans and urban policies that are disconnected from 'the majority of the people' (Chatterjee 2004). In reverse, local councillors and administrators, be it by electoral interest, fear of social unrest, pragmatism or sympathy with residents, more often ended up being de facto, informally, more progressive. This experience of local public institutions in practice more progressive than higher levels of government contrasts with Tendler's conclusions, as well as Gupta's (2012) and Dasgupta and Williams' (2022), whose work on Indian rural development argues that the more progressive directions driven by the Indian national government are lost in the transmission to the lower levels of administration, where social and caste prejudice, locally-embedded norms, clientelist practices generally lead to the reproduction of the status quo. While similar clientelist interests may drive local councillors in cities to pay attention to the demands of their constituencies and to confront (at least in practice) Master planning, one can only conclude that context does matter – one scale of government not being inherently more progressive than another (Purcell 2006). Looking at the interplay and contradiction between scales of public intervention is crucial in grasping elements of progressiveness in politics.

Benjamin's work can also be placed in a rich Indian scholarship inviting reflection on, and from, the state's ordinary, mundane, 'everyday' practices, in a way that may have become banal but was then novel (Fuller and Benei 2000; Das and Poole 2004; Corbridge et al. 2005; Gupta 2012). Benjamin is one of the first scholars to have developed this examination of state everyday practices in urban, rather than rural, settings in India. His study of 'porous bureaucracies' is strongly grounded in various local urban settings, with their specific issues, configurations and stakes: in areas of informal settlements, 'porous bureaucracy' is about inventing new, ad hoc ways of regularising tenure (Benjamin 2005). In areas of industrial-residential areas (Benjamin 2004), where mixed-land use generates a degree of social cohesion and upliftment, 'porous bureaucracy' is about finding semi-official ways to provide electricity to small informal businesses. This regulatory creativity is not studied from the bureaucrats' perspective – difficult to reach especially as they work in grey zones, but from the various documents (internal, officials, informal) provided by local administrations to individual residents or entrepreneurs, that have a degree of 'officialness' (as they generally parallel existing regulations).

Studying the urban policy-making process not only in time (such as those inspired by Foucauldian, genealogic approaches to policy instruments), but also in grounded and specific spaces; paying attention to policy instruments' circulation across government scales; and actively looking for documents with different degrees of 'officialness' reflecting the policy-making process between state and society (as advised by Hull 2012), are the three directions we have followed in this book, inspired by Indian scholarship. I want to illustrate this with two specific examples.

The grounded contexts in which urban policies originate, be it through a specific local mobilisation calling for public attention or a situated modality of regulation and city making set up locally, and their lasting influence on the final policy framing, are often understudied in the analysis of urban policy-making. This is at the core of Modiba's contribution (Chapter 6), interrogating how urban street trading is governed in three South African municipalities. The governance arrangements she found depended centrally on two main (interrelated) factors: the way street traders' organisations were structured, and the local history of contention between the City and the traders. Indeed, from a local bureaucracy's point of view, in order to delegate managing power to street traders' organisations (necessitated by the incapacity of bureaucracies to manage street trading on their own), street traders needed to be sufficiently organised to have some management capacity, but not to the point of becoming antagonist and making too contentious claims towards the municipality. In parallel, where the history of street trading regulation was marked by deep violence, the fear of triggering civil unrest had often led local administration to concede more power to street traders' organisations. Here, an institutional governing arrangement, and the specific urban policies deriving from this arrangement, are directly framed by local historical configurations.

Interrogating policy-making not only in time and space but also across scales, is even more telling. Demeestère (Chapter 7) studied the framing of regulation of neighbourhood shops from local to national policy (and back), from a letter of threat issued at the local level by business organisations, to its various iterations in documents of different nature and scale, up to a national bill endorsed by the ANC. The nature of the initial document (a letter) produced by the business owners, their insistence on having agreements (mediated by the police, then local authorities assisted by the United Nation High Commissioner for

Refugees) written down and signed – as a mark of officialness – played a key role in framing the issue and policy. Even if the direct xenophobic threats were incrementally removed as regulatory documents became more official, the letter's initial xenophobic framing remained, became the object to be negotiated, amended and rephrased but not structurally questioned. The traders' lobby accepted the policing of xenophobia against the promise of its institutionalisation, in a form of trade-off. Such porosity here between state and society, where society becomes bureaucratised and the state informalised, is in this occurrence deeply regressive. This shows the limits of pragmatic politics, where populist framings of problems and policies are no longer mediated, transformed and challenged by an open, public, programmatic or principled politics, but negotiated as close as possible to local communities. A politics by stealth, porous or open to popular claims, is not necessarily progressive, especially in times marked by populist dynamics, nurtured by social deprivation as well as narrow political ambition.

Deciphering public political choices: officials' intentions, public transcripts, and state rationalities

A constant and productive tension throughout the research programme and in this book is what to make, how to conceptualise, how to operationally grasp and observe, and how to analyse, 'strategic choices' made by 'the state' to govern cities. These strategic choices were collectively constructed and contested, blurry, messy, collective, iterative, with a part of arbitrariness and informality that keeps escaping an observer's grasp; but strategic choices nevertheless were made, had an existence, had effects, and we believed it mattered to look for such choices as they were key to our ability to reflect on democracy at large, to raise issues of public accountability and of political alternatives.

The variety of disciplines that made up our research team, the fact that political scientists and sociologists were a minority compared to the planners who often assumed functionalist understandings of 'the state' and its urban policies led to naïve yet fresh and meaningful discussions on how to conceptualise issues of 'intention', 'policy objective', 'political choice', 'urban strategy' that are consubstantial to the act of governing. On our way, we found many theoretical framings of the state – many leaving the researcher disempowered and lost, due to their highly abstract nature and their disconnection from the materiality of city spaces and societies, from the practicalities of officials' action, and their silence or blurriness on empirical methods for researchers attached to ethnography. If our book provides methodological guidance, and if this guidance opens to epistemological reflections, then we will have produced useful work.

Most contributors interrogating officials' agency and working in ethnographic ways (Part I in this book), used the term 'objectives', not attributed to a specific agent or even institution but generally to a policy or a policy instrument. The use of this term avoided the challenging question of individual or collective agency, the personification of the state, and the psychological approach of officials. Officials' constrained autonomy was then grasped through the concepts of 'tactics and strategies', at the intersection of individual agency, power position and situated contexts. Even if the issue of alliance building (and among these, political and institutional support) were key, they were observed as processes and interplay of positions, rather than described as a definite City direction or clear political strategic choice.

Parts II and III this book, which generally did not adopt ethnographic approaches of City institutions and could not observe practices, reflected more directly on how Cities frame strategic choices and how policy decisions might be made in one direction or another, using different conceptual frames.

One way of doing so has been to use the notion of officials' or politicians' 'intentions'. The notion of intentionality has been defined in psychology, but also in economics, management and anthropology, to analyse how agents imagine and effect voluntary actions as a means to an end (Blackler and Regan 2009). Debates are mostly about what factors frame intentions, between beliefs, desires, but also awareness (of the context, the possibilities for change, what it would take) and skills (mastering the tools, garnering the resources needed to effect change) (Malle and Knobe 1997). Charlton (Chapter 10), for instance, uses the notion of 'intention', in a layman's way, to frame the paradox at the core of her chapter, echoing Murray Li's (2007) and Gupta's (2012) central questions – how come good-willed, well-intentioned, policies and agents end up increasing rather than challenging, or even mitigating inequality and injustice in the city? One of her conclusions is that too few good-intentioned (planning) officials ended up exhausting their capacity by confronting oppositional middle-class residents' groups around a new middle-income housing project, diverted from the other, key battle of protecting existing affordable housing for the poorest. A second factor of failure was their false belief that existing policy instruments were sufficient for doing so, without strongly engaging with City housing officials, who worked in other directions. What an approach in terms of officials' 'intentions' might show is that the intention failed to achieve the desired change due to lack of 'awareness' (of the real possibilities for change) and to the lack of 'skills' (inattention to housing instruments).

The idea of objectives driving practice is also analysed using Scott's (1990) concept of 'public versus hidden transcripts', where the analysis of what different actors choose to show and to hide is used to reveal the situated interests, objectives or directions of different parties. Galvin (Chapter 11) does so to study water politics in eThewkini, where City objectives are particularly muddled, as state officials and social movement leaders paradoxically use the same 'deceptive lens' in their public discourse to describe access to water in eThekwini (pretending that the poor do pay for water, while they both know it is not the case). Galvin explains the deception by differentiating between what she calls actors' 'interests'; the 'image' each actor wishes to project of themselves and their institution; and their 'ideology' or worldview – useful notions operationalising several levels of explanations. Here, 'hidden transcripts', the resistance of social life to state policies, are potentially taken up by the City official who, by stealth, keeps fighting for water resources' distribution to the poor. The study thus operationalises the study of 'public' and 'hidden' transcripts in original ways to understand City officials' objectives that are not immediately observable, leading to unsettled assumptions that public transcripts are borne by a modernist and oppressive state, versus hidden ones borne by civil society (organised or not) in resistance.

A third family of approaches, dominant in this book, has been to use a Foucauldian lens that conceptualises political choices not as individual leadership and agent's making but as the result of diverse and competing 'state rationalities', reflected and revealed in the genealogy and framing of 'policy instruments' (Lascoumes and Legales 2004). This book contributes to operationalise such an approach, following previous work (Halpern et al. 2014), taking it one step further. Not focusing on the contested genealogy of one single instrument (a particular policy or a given institution), but a set of various policy instruments used by different public actors on a site or sector of public interventions, the study of their divergence, intersections or convergence assists in identifying competing state rationalities (Bénit-Gbaffou 2018a). Bouyat (Chapter 9), tracking the construction of 'foreignness' in Johannesburg's low-income schools through the study of policy instruments used at national, regional and micro-local levels is thus able to follow the distributive, the managerial and the xenophobic rationalities of school registration, where she sees how the latter is growing in prominence. Beyond her documentation of the rise of xenophobia in South African society and state, investigating policy instruments in that way (as a set, transversal to several units and scales of the state), within a sector and with a specific question in mind, is a novel way of deciphering state competing rationalities as they are actually implemented and lived by citizens.

In this framing, however, the issue of political choice is often left unresolved, policy effects being conceptualised as the result of competing rationalities, not necessarily intentionally designed. However, their persistence in time, especially when they are contested by civil society groups attempting to put the issue on the public agenda, gives an indication of their functionality in the eyes of political leadership, and hence reveal a form of political choice.

New Public Management, knowledge on municipal action, and the loss of meaning

The link between state knowledge and public action rests on a long academic tradition questioning the categories used by the state to make society legible in order to act (Scott 1998). It has been renewed by contemporary reflections on state ignorance, where the illegibility of society is partly functional to government. Breckenridge (2012) has coined the idea of 'no will to know', where no effort is made by the state to gather data on a specific phenomenon, area or community – reflecting a lack of interest for issues not framed as 'public problems'. Roy (2009) has proposed the 'politics of unmapping', where large portions of space or society remain out of sight of public maps, registers and databases, an opacity that may well serve the interests of the state, sinister or not. Aguilera (2017) has shown how gathering and displaying data, constructing instruments and categories to measure a phenomenon, compel the state to intervene – thus, not gathering specific data, conversely, allows the state to overlook the need for intervention. Elsewhere, I have termed this feature, paraphrasing Breckenridge, 'the will to not know' (Bénit-Gbaffou 2018b): not the absence of effort or resources to gather knowledge, but the active refusal of ways of knowing, of publicising existing knowledge, or even the denial that such knowledge exists. In an urban context of poverty, informality and social fluidity (Simone 2004), gathering data does require resources, that are often lacking especially in areas that are not identified as public problems or political priorities. Yet, simultaneously, in the age of New Public Management in urban governance, a plethora of data is produced and circulated within and between various public and semi-public institutions, to monitor and evaluate public action and bureaucratic practice. What to make of this paradox, and how to understand the production of data as both reflecting and potentially guiding municipal intervention?

A cross-cutting result in this book is the loss of meaning experienced by many officials at low, middle and even sometimes high levels of the City, when it comes to their own or municipal action. Much has been written about how New Public Management and its quantification of everything constitutes, like many forms of technicisation of political action, an 'anti-politics machine' (Ferguson 2004), a way of invisibilising the political choices encapsulated in what is presented as undecipherable technical decisions (Hibou 2012). This loss of meaning and capacity for strategic action in officials' experience is anchored in the type of data they are gathering and working from – as if their lenses were ill-adapted and they were conscious of this ill-adaptation without however being able to change them. Charlton (Chapter 10) explains how well-intentioned officials, genuinely working towards including lower-income households in a flagship urban project, fail to 'see' both the social groups they are aiming at protecting (the poor in a middle-class suburb, a non-issue and a non-group), and the ill-adaptation of the policy instruments advanced to protect, maintain or develop affordable housing. Galvin (Chapter 11) presents how deceptive lenses, used by both officials and activists to frame and literally map (based on precise GIS data) the problem with water provision to the poor in the eThewkini metropolitan area, are used as functional political tools by each party but ultimately deprives them of instruments of action in their respective field to expand water access to the poor. Bouyat (Chapter 9) analyses how education professionals (school staff and Provincial bureaucrats), trained in an ethos of care, education and humanism, become complicit in tracking and excluding undocumented learners from access to education, in spite of themselves: trapped in a computerised registration system supposed to facilitate public action and allocation of resources. Mushongera (Chapter 12) presents how middle-rank City officials, having delegated the operation of water services to a para-municipal and autonomous agency which they are supposed to oversee and give strategic direction to, end up disempowered, having lost track of urban realities, filling their time with compiling meaningless figures to respond both to their own Key Performance Indicators and to the requested audits from various other services and public institutions. Smith (Chapter 13) focuses on high ranking officials on the one hand, and local councillors on the other, mandated to provide oversight on the City's strategic action – the former being lost in meaningless quantitative data failing to measure and interrogate the 'outcomes' of public action (focusing rather on easier to measure and to perform 'outputs'), the latter being utterly disempowered in the face of an increasingly complex, overlapping and sedimented administration whose reports bear little relation to material realities of the city and their local constituencies.

This loss of meaning could be one effect of 'governing by numbers', generally described as a feature of the governance of mass societies marked by large scale and high complexity (Desrosières 2008), where statistics are one means of rendering society legible to the state in order to act upon it (Scott 1998). In a number of cases described in this book, the collection of data seems to have lost this function of governing society, instead becoming a bureaucratic exercise that may be used to control officials' practices, but in quite pointless ways – disconnected from officials' meaningful activities as much as from existing social dynamics. In Mushongera's and Smith's chapters (Chapters 12 and 13 respectively), numbers seem to have become a mode of governing by apathy, or by sideration, with officials trapped in endlessly compiling meaningless quantitative data on which they have no power, limited understanding, nor mandate neither real motivation, to act. Sometimes, however, 'reality' strikes back, surging in violent ways through protest action or litigation, and leading political leaders to suddenly ask for the compilation of meaningful data – data that can contribute to knowledge of social dynamics and needs.

Here the spatialisation of analyses provides an original dimension to understanding the way urban materiality sometimes resist the ill-adapted categories and measurements. Scattered, decayed and over-occupied flats in the dense urban fabric of a suburban, formerly White, middle-class area in Johannesburg (Charlton, Chapter 10), partly explains the political invisibility of poor Black residents. The hilly topography of vast peri-urban land owned and managed by the opaque Ingonyama Trust in eThewkini, poses specific water pressure problems where overuse, non-payment, absence of mapping and coordination of land construction aggravate the topographic factor to explain poor water delivery. This issue may ultimately shift the power balance towards the City administration (Galvin, Chapter 11). The location of low-income schools in Johannesburg, in migrant-friendly or xenophobic townships, strongly influences how their staff responds (through compliance or resistance) to institutionalised xenophobia embedded in the computerised school registration systems (Bouyat, Chapter 9). Perceived 'mushrooming' informal settlements whose spatial and political marginality renders City-wide mobilisation difficult, allow officials to justify and not bother too much about the lack of progress on residents' access to water and sanitation services (Mushongera, Chapter 12).

To make sense of this decreasing sense of meaning of public action for City officials, linked to a probable diminished capacity to act, this book offers several hypotheses. Firstly, increasing neoliberal rationalities incrementally hollows out the post-apartheid rhetoric of redistribution, without discarding it as it remains a key feature of public discourses, thus rendered meaningless and disjointed. Secondly, this increasing meaninglessness can be seen as one outcome of the adoption of New Public Management's principles – not only in the way quantification of all action prevents assessing key dimensions of public intervention, or how it constitutes a way of depoliticising and invisibilising actual policy choices (Hibou 2012), preventing from asking 'the right questions' (Smith, Chapter 13), but perhaps mostly through the disconnection between oversight and operation, depriving local officials from their key power: their intermediary position between situated, local knowledge ('the field') and knowledge on the political and bureaucratic apparatus. Nowhere is it more visible than in Mushongera's chapter (Chapter 12), where water delivery is thrust upon an opaque para-municipal agency, and City officials in a skeleton water department supposed to exercise oversight (but incapable of doing so) express their disempowerment, explicitly or through high levels of absenteeism and job vacancies. Besides the divorce between strategic and operational capacity (straddling both constituted the strength of intermediary officials), it is also the contradiction between revenue generation and basic rights' provision, two core and contradictory drives of local government, which becomes disarticulated. As long as this tension is held by a single entity, department, municipal agent, the drive to find a balance between these two essential needs remains paramount. When revenue generation becomes encapsulated in a water autonomous agency (business-like and responding to an independent board checking the financial balance) while the objectives of redistribution, or mere public service delivery to the poorest is only defended by officials disconnected from operational capacity and odd politicians in times of protests or elections, the essential requirement of local government to balance the two contradictory objectives (providing basic services in both efficient and equitable way) collapses.

Lastly, this loss of meaning in bureaucratic public office might derive from what Bierschenk (2014) calls bureaucratic 'sedimentation' – where new institutions are created to respond to dysfunctional ones, without suppressing the latter nor fixing the former, leading to duplication, overlapping and competition, opacity and confusion in mandates and responsibilities. This sedimentation is the result of usual dynamics in complex organisations, but it is aggravated by at least three factors. The first factor, post-apartheid local government underwent a series of successive and repeated institutional reforms (a story recalled in Mushongera and Smith, Chapters 12 and 13 respectively), to incrementally move from apartheid local government to complex democratic institutions. A second, both contextual and global factor, is the sometimes uncritical adoption of New Public Management principles, pushing for the creation of parallel agencies and the use of private contractors, fenced-off from political 'interference' seen as corrupt or inefficient, while the state institution with similar functions cannot be suppressed, to maintain at least the illusion of democratic accountability in the form of political oversight over this parallel agency. A third, intersecting factor relates to 'pockets of excellence', temporarily set up as responses to crises or innovative pilot projects, or linked to specific grand mayoral urban projects that ephemerally attract political and administrative attention and resources (Pinson 2009). These administrative 'pockets' are only superficially inscribed in the state apparatus and therefore have low ability to institutionalise the innovations they might be developing.

Progressive change as incomplete policies: the never-ending work of institutionalisation

In retrospect, it is striking to see how in the South African case studies we observed, many of the attempts to construct progressive legislation ended up incomplete. Benjamin's (2005) case studies on multiple, albeit fragmented, parallel local legislations giving informal settlements' residents a form of security of tenure, which seems widely developed in Indian cities, contrasts starkly with the challenges narrated by Harrison (Chapter 2) in creating policy instruments recognising incremental regularisation of Johannesburg informal settlements, an ambition actually inspired by the municipal planner's trip to Brazil. Klug (Chapter 8) analyses his deception when what he saw as an opportunity for progressive inner-city housing policy led to a meaningless policy document that failed to engage with the real issues. Charlton (Chapter 10) is puzzled by the eviction of the working poor in the Corridors of Freedom, which was aimed at offering better life conditions for this social group, and her whole chapter investigates this contradiction. The three activists portrayed by Bénit-Gbaffou (Chapter 3) multiplied attempts at reforming policies and institutions for social justice – if they won small victories, they encountered large defeats and two eventually left the City.

This does not mean that progressive legislation was not passed in post-apartheid cities. Progressive strategic decisions were made at municipal level, complementing an imperfect but existing national welfare system – for instance, firmly and systematically redirecting the bulk of municipal investment towards townships and disadvantaged communities, massively developing basic municipal services in under-equipped areas and promulgating a decent living package (free basic services for the poorest). This book did not target specifically these policy champions (as did Krumholz and Clavel (1994) in collecting purposeful and edited interviews of equity planners retrospectively reflecting on their action)[3] looking at the work of officials and institutions to understand the way they worked, and following the process that they crafted towards conducting progressive change. What we were able to observe doing so is possibly less spectacular, but perhaps there is something to learn there too. As a matter of fact, Krumholz and Clavel's (1994) collection of narratives from policy champions, although entailing inspiring stories of political astuteness and technical progressive instruments, innovative processes and courageous tricks, also testifies to the huge difficulties these progressive planners, even in high positions and with major political backing, experienced in institutionalising their practices and consolidating change.

This requires further reflection, structured here around the two understandings of 'institutionalisation'. Firstly, as officialisation of intermediary officials' practices that remain informal and fragile as long as they are not acknowledged and endorsed by the institution. Such a movement of institutionalisation of progressive practices, from the bottom-up, may be key to their continuation in time. Secondly, as the wide naturalisation of a practice or a policy, its grounding in everyday administration, across its different levels. This movement of institutionalisation, from the top-down, from a policy objective to its appropriation by mundane administrative practices, is key to its implementation, today as much as tomorrow. Institutional activists engage in both movements of institutionalisation, with different stakes and degrees (towards the top – passing a new policy; towards the bottom – training staff and reframing institutional structures and incentives) depending on their position in the administrative hierarchy, their resources and their capacity.

Institutionalisation from the bottom-up, from intermediary officials' practice to municipal strategic policy, is costly, challenging and scarce. City officials' battles to pass progressive municipal policies, based on innovative practice and progressive reform, grounded in pilot projects, responses to participatory claims and international best practices were more often than not lost. The experience of success (narrated in Rubin's Chapter 4) and the many stories of failure seem to indicate that passing progressive policies in City Council is not to be understood primarily as a beginning (setting up a new instrument for progressive municipal action). It is rather to be analysed as an end – the conclusion, or at least the reflection, of a political battle that has already taken place. In many cases, this battle was held (and lost) with property developers, the land-based elite and its political allies described long ago by Logan and Molotch (1987), and still central in contemporary urban politics. This battle was won (Rubin, Chapter 4) first in practice, by Planning officials using practical incentives and sanctions with individual developers and their coalitions (delaying building permits, opening up an inner-city forum and partnerships), but also with other City departments, agencies and politicians having other linkages and agreements with private developer groups (blocking the public projects they were driving, if they did not bring their support to the inclusive housing policy). This resulted in a new inclusive housing policy being passed. This battle with the land-based elite was avoided in the making of a policy around inner-city evictions and relocation (analysed by Klug, Chapter 8), which left property owners off the hook even though they were largely responsible for inner-city decay and slumlording. This was a battle neither the City Housing Department nor the human rights lawyers saw fit to start – the former not wanting to embark on a such a large battle about which the mayor was not very keen, the latter finding it easier to win the case by attacking the state than making property owners accountable. Many other stories show the difficulty in consolidating, within official urban policies or through clear political directions, what intermediary officials have tried to build through a series of informal practices and technical instruments explorations.

The second story illustrates what institutionalisation from the top-down might mean. A senior official, working in a strategic City unit advisory to the Johannesburg mayor, had lobbied the mayor for a long time to have the 2006 Growth and Development Strategy (GDS) (a strategic document guiding City planning for five years) include, as part of its five driving principles, 'the proactive absorption of the poor', and succeeded, due to both his persistence, his credibility, and contextual elements opening an opportunity. This official did not stop there: he took upon himself to workshop each and every City department, to present the GDS principles and content, and consolidate collectively how each department could and would contribute practically to this 'proactive absorption of the poor'. Department-specific translations of this strategic objective were formalised and encapsulated in a set of Key Performance Indicators, annually checked and discussed. Aligning strategic priorities (worked upon at a political level), and basic administrative duties, is hard work, invisible work. Few officials understand the importance of embedding and translating so practically, in coordinated and systematic ways, the key strategic policy directions and political priorities into the actual work and objectives of lower levels of administration. Actually, the following version of the Growth Development Strategy (GDS), conducted by another official in the same position, did not follow that track. This lack of alignment, this loss in translation, is the object of Mushongera's chapter (Chapter 12): how a specific indicator or a progressive water policy (improving water provision to informal settlements), mentioned in the GDS, is in fact nobody's responsibility, and disappears, or becomes meaningless, in City Water officials' Key Performance Indicators. Similarly, Charlton (Chapter 10) shows how a flagship project such as the Corridors of Freedom, with strong political backing and a large budget, fails in programming relevant housing policy instruments to construct socially integrated neighbourhoods. This lack of deep inscription of a policy in administration is telling of a lack of political priority, the hollowing out of strategic documents, or competing state rationalities, where the progressive one lost the battle. It also indicates, in reverse, the work required by officials to have a policy progressive objective (that requires going against the market flow) pursued, fought for and followed through.

What to make of these two different but complementary stories of the challenging work of institutionalisation? These challenges do not mean that progressive practices were not developed. They testify to the difficulties of a 'left art of government', and indicate the type of work in which institutional activists are immersed. If the dominant condition is of incomplete and partial institutionalisation of municipal progressive policies, what does it mean for institutional activists in the City? Many continue to work at their own, intermediary level – building informal but concrete practices, shared with lower-level bureaucrats; training their staff and their peers to alternative, more participatory or inclusive ways of performing their jobs; building joint actions and projects with fellow officials and external partners, with a short time span and a limited scale, but that can be elevated to the status of pilot projects and be expanded, should a window of opportunity open. The work of institutionalisation, in the sense of formalisation on the one hand, grounding as normal practices on the other, is still at play, even if at a modest level. This is not to downplay the importance of strong redistributive policies and instruments, or ambitious democratic reforms – but to come back to the context in which (even in exceptional circumstances such as in the post-apartheid moment) most officials work, which still allow some progressive practices to continue under the radar, as a 'politics by stealth' (Benjamin 2004), building resources and waiting for opportunities to come into the open.

Notes

1 National Treasury. 2022. *System of Capacity Building for Local Government: Diagnostic Review*. Public Affairs Resarch Institute Report, Johannesburg (p. iii).

2 Recent populist and fundamentalist politics in India, at national and local levels, constitute an important change in this respect.

3 Such a set of interviews was conducted by Claire Bénit-Gbaffou and Rachid Seedat in parallel, but has not been included in this book but is part of another publication project.

References

Abers, R. 2019. 'Bureaucratic Activism: Pursuing environmentalism inside the Brazilian State', *Latin American Politics and Society* 61(2): 21–44.

Abers, R. and Keck, M. 2013. *Practical Authority: Agency and institutional change in Brazilian water politics*. New York: Oxford University Press.

Abers, R. and Tatagiba, L. 2015. 'Institutional activism: Mobilising for women's health from inside the Brazilian bureaucracy'. In *Social Movement Dynamics: New perspectives on theory and research from Latin America*, edited by F. Rossi and M. von Bülow, 73–101. London: Ashgate.

Aguilera, T. 2017. *Gouverner les Illégalismes Urbains: Les politiques publiques face aux squats et aux bidonvilles dans les régions de Paris et de Madrid*. Paris: Dalloz.

Anjaria, S. 2011. 'Ordinary State: Everyday corruption and the politics of space in Mumbai', *American Ethnologist* 38(1): 58–72.

Auyero, J. 2012. *Patients of the State*. Durham: Duke University Press.

Barrier, J., Pillon, J.M. and Quéré, O. 2015. 'Les cadres intermédiaires de la fonction publique. Travail administratif et recompositions managériales de l'État', *Gouvernement et Action Publique* 4(4): 9–32.

Bénit-Gbaffou, C. 2008. 'Practices of local participation in Johannesburg – side-lining the institutional participatory channels?', *Transformation: Critical Perspectives on Southern Africa* 66–67: 1–34.

Bénit-Gbaffou, C. 2018a. 'Beyond the policy-implementation gap: How the City of Johannesburg manufactured the ungovernability of street trading', *Journal of Development Studies* 54(12): 2149–67.

Bénit-Gbaffou, C. 2018b. 'Unpacking state practices in city-making, in conversations with Ananya Roy', *Journal of Development Studies* 54(12): 2139–48.

Benjamin, S. 2004. 'Urban land transformation for pro-poor economies', *Geoforum* 35: 177–187.

Benjamin, S. 2005. 'Touts, pirates and ghosts', *Sarai Reader* 5: 242–54.

Bierschenk, T. 2014. 'Sedimentation, fragmentation and normative double-bind in (West) African public services'. In *States at Work: Dynamics of African bureaucracies*, edited by T. Bierschenk and J-P. Olivier de Sardan, 221–45. Leiden: Brill.
Blackler, F. and Regan, S. 2009. 'Intentionality, agency, change: Practice theory and management', *Management Learning* 40(2): 161–76.
Bourdieu, P. 1991. 'Une mission impossible. Entretien avec Pascale Raymon, chef de projet dans le Nord de la France', *Actes de la Recherche en Sciences Sociales* 90: 84–94.
Bourdieu, P. and Christin, R. 1990. 'La construction du marché. Le champ administratif et la production de la 'politique du logement', *Actes de la Recherche en Sciences Sociales* 81–82: 65-85.
Breckenridge, K. 2012. 'No Will to Know: The rise and fall of African civil registration in twentieth-century South Africa'. In *Registration and Recognition: Documenting the person in world history*, edited by K. Breckenridge and S. Szreter, 1–38. Oxford: Oxford University Press.
Brunette, R., Klaaren, J. and Nqaba, P. 2019. 'Reform in the contract state: Embedded directions in public procurement regulation in South Africa', *Development Southern Africa* 36(4): 537–54.
Chatterjee, P. 2004. *The Politics of the Governed. Reflections on popular politics in most of the world*. New York: Columbia University Press.
Chiha, G. 2006. 'Les cadres intermédiaires, leviers du changement radical', *Revue des Sciences de Gestion* 4(220–21): 177–82.
Chipkin, I. and Swilling, M. 2018. *Shadow State: The politics of state capture*. Johannesburg: University of Witwatersrand Press.
Clavel, P. 2010. *Activists in City Hall. The progressive response to the Reagan era in Boston and Chicago*. New York: University of Cornell Press.
Corbridge, S., Williams, G., Srivastava, M. and Véron, R. (eds). 2005. *Seeing the State: Governance and governmentality in India*. Cambridge: Cambridge University Press.
Cosson, A. 2015. 'Construire son autonomie sous contrainte. Les directeurs de parcs nationaux entre desserrement et resserrement du verrou de l'État', *Gouvernement et Action Publique* 4(4): 153–71.
Das, V. and Poole, D. (eds). 2004. *Anthropology in the Margins of the State*. London: James Currey.
Dasgupta, D. and Williams, G. 2022. 'The Creation and Withdrawal of Spaces for Participatory Governance: The case of village development committees in West Bengal, India', *Politics and Society*, pre-published online. Available at: https://doi.org/10.1177/00323292221102133. Accessed 23 August 2023.
Desrosières, A. 2008. *L'Argument Statistique (Tome II). Gouverner par les nombres*. Paris: Presses de l'Ecole des Mines.
Dowbor, M. and Houtzager, P.P. 2014. 'The role of professionals in policy reform: Cases from the city level, São Paulo', *Latin American Politics and Society*, 56(3): 141–62.
Dubois, V. 2017. 'Policy Ethnography as a Combat Sport. Analysing the welfare state against the grain'. In *If Truth be Told. The politics of public ethnography*, edited by D. Fassin, 184–202. Durham: Duke University Press.
Ferguson, J. 2004. *The Anti-Politics Machine: Development, depoliticisation, and Bureaucratic power in Lesotho*. Minneapolis: University of Minnesota Press.
Ferguson, J. 2011. 'Toward a left art of government: From 'Foucauldian critique' to Foucauldian politics', *History of the Human Sciences* 24(4): 61–68.
Ferguson, J. 2013. 'Declarations of dependence: Labour, personhood, and welfare in Southern Africa', *Journal of the Royal Anthropological Institute* 19: 223–42.
Fuller, C.J. and Benei, V. (eds). 2000. *The Everyday State in Modern India*. New Delhi: Social Science Press.
Gupta, A. 2012. *Red Tape: Bureaucracy, structural violence, and poverty in India*. Durham: Duke University Press.
Hahonou, E. and Martin, T. 2019. 'Immersion in the bureaucratic field: Methodological pathways', *Critique in Anthropology* 39(2): 122–38.
Halpern, C., Lascoumes, P. and Le Galès, P. (eds). 2014. *L'instrumentation de L'action Publique. Controverses, résistance, effets*. Paris: Presses de Sciences Po.
Heller, P. 2019. 'Trajectories of democratic deepening: Brazil, India and South Africa compared', *Theory and Society* 48(3): 351–82.

Hibou, B. 2015 [2012]. *The Bureaucratisation of the World in the Neoliberal Era: An international and comparative perspective*. New York: Palgrave Macmillan.

von Holdt, K. 2010. 'Nationalism, bureaucracy and the developmental State: The South African case', *South African Review of Sociology* 41(1): 4–27.

von Holdt, K. 2013. 'South Africa: The transition to violent democracy', *Review of African Political Economy* 40(138): 589–604.

Hull, M. 2012. 'Documents and bureaucracy', *Annual Review of Anthropology* 41: 251–67.

Jeannot, G. and Goodchild, B. 2011. 'Fuzzy jobs in local partnerships: Case studies of urban and rural regeneration in France and England', *Public Administration* 89(3): 1110–27.

Katzenstein, M. 1998. 'Stepsisters: Feminist movement activism in different institutional spaces'. In *The Social Movement Society: Contentious politics for a new century*, edited by D.S. Meyer and S. Tarrow, 195–216. Lanham, MD: Rowman and Littlefield.

Krumholz, N. and Clavel, P. 1994. *Reinventing Cities: Equity planners tell their stories*. Philadelphia: Temple University Press.

Lascoumes, P. and Le Galès, P. (eds). 2004. *Gouverner par les Instruments*. Paris: Presses de Sciences Po.

Laurens, S. 2008. 'Les agents de l'Etat face à leur propre pouvoir. Éléments pour une micro-analyse des mots griffonnés en marge des décisions officielles', *Genèses* 3(72): 26–41.

Lipsky, M. 2010. *Street-Level Bureaucracy: Dilemmas of the individual in public service*. (30th Anniversary Expanded Edition). New York: Russell Sage Foundation.

Logan, J. and Molotch, H. 1987. *Urban Fortunes: The political economy of place*. Los Angeles: University of California Press.

Malle, B. and Knobe, J. 1997. 'The folk concept of intentionality', *Journal of Experimental Social Psychology* 33: 101–21.

Meny-Gibert, S. 2017. 'Shifting Power, Shifting Rule in the South African State'. Working paper 1, presented at the European Conference on African Studies, Basel.

Migdal, J. 2001. *State in Society: Studying how states and societies transform and constitute one another*. Cambridge: Cambridge University Press.

Murray Li, T. 2007. *The Will to Improve. Governmentality, development and the practice of politics*. Durham: Duke University Press.

Needleman, M. and Needleman, C. 1974. *Guerrillas in the Bureaucracy: The community planning experiment in the United States*. New York: John Wiley.

Neveu, C. 2011. 'Démocratie participative et mouvements sociaux: Entre domestication et ensauvagement?', *Participations* 1(1): 186–209.

O'Leary, R. 2014 [2006]. *The Ethics of Dissent: Managing guerrilla government*. Los Angeles: Sage Publications (second edition).

Olivier de Sardan, J-P. 2015. 'Practical norms. Informal regulations within public bureaucracies (in Africa and beyond)'. In *Real Governance and Practical Norms in Sub-Saharan Africa*, edited by T. de Herdt and J-P. Olivier de Sardan, 365–98. Abingdon: Routledge.

Olver, C. 2017. *How to Steal a City: The battle for Nelson Mandela Bay*. Cape Town: Jonathan Ball Publishers.

Phadi, M., Pearson, J. and Lesaffre, T. 2018. 'The seeds of perpetual instability: The case of Mogalakwena local municipality in South Africa', *Journal of Southern African Studies* 44(4): 593–611.

Pinson, G. 2009. *Gouverner la Ville par Projet. Urbanisme et gouvernance des villes européennes*. Paris: Presses de Sciences Po.

Purcell, M. 2006. 'Urban democracy and the local trap', *Urban Studies* 43(11): 1921–41.

Reddy, P. 2018. 'Evolving local government in post conflict South Africa: Where to?', *Local Economy* 33(7): 710–25.

Roy, A. 2009. 'Why India cannot plan its cities: Informality, insurgence, and the idiom of urbanisation', *Planning Theory* 8(1): 76–87.

Sawicki, F. and Siméant, J. 2009. 'Décloisonner la sociologie de l'engagement militant. Note critique sur quelques tendances récentes des travaux français', *Sociologie du Travail* 51(1): 95–125.

Scott, J.C. 1990. *Domination and the Arts of Resistance: Hidden transcripts*. New Haven and London: Yale University Press.

Scott, J.C. 1998. *Seeing Like a State: How certain schemes to improve the human condition have failed*. New Haven: Yale University Press.

Simone, A. 2004. 'People as infrastructure: Intersecting fragments in Johannesburg', *Public Cultures* 16: 407–29.

Stone, C. 1995. 'Political leadership in urban politics'. In *Theories of Urban Politics*, edited by D. Judge, G. Stoker, and H. Wolman, 96–116. London: Sage.

Swilling, M. (ed). 2017. *Betrayal of the Promise: How South Africa is being stolen*. Johannesburg: Public Affairs Research Institute (PARI): Research Report.

Tendler, J. 1997. *Good Governance in the Tropics*. Baltimore: John Hopkins University Press.

Vedung, E. 1998. 'Policy instruments: Typologies and theories'. In *Carrots, Sticks, and Sermons: Policy instruments and their evaluation*, edited by M.L. Bemelmans-Videc, R. Rist, and E. Vedung, 21–58. New Brunswick and London: Transaction Publishers.

Verhoeven, I. and Duyvendak, J. 2017. 'Understanding governmental activism', *Social Movement Studies* 16(5): 564–77.

Wafer, A. and Oldfield, S. 2014. 'Contesting the participatory sphere: Encountering the state in Johannesburg and Cape Town'. In *Popular Politics in South African Cities: Unpacking community participation*, edited by C. Bénit-Gbaffou, 232–47. Pretoria: HSRC Press.

15

Preserving the progressive City: a North American perspective

Pierre Clavel

Introduction

I began thinking about the 'progressive city' in about 1980. I had started out doing plans for small towns and parts of cities, then did a doctorate to see how this practice connected to the needs and ideals of Americans in actual cities and regions.

This would not be easy. Once, having given a talk to a group of city officials and businessmen, I was at the bar with one of them, anxious to hear his thoughts. 'Your ideas were exciting (he exaggerated), but your schemes are "planners' dreams" and will never happen.' While I thought that over, he continued: 'Remember, the planner proposes, the politician disposes.'

By the end of the 1970s, most cities did not support 'planners' dreams'. The most they would look for was 'growth'. The usual strategy was to adopt 'incrementalism' – accept small gains, because they would frighten people less.

To this my response was: 'What's the point?' As Alan Altshuler (1965) had shown in a Minneapolis case study, City planners could seldom out-argue highway engineers or other specialists. Their only advantage was to speak to an ideal future – often a civic design argument, sometimes simply a Rousseauian 'general interest'. Focus on this, I would argue. At least, keep it in mind.

The 'progressive city' was one way to do that. In the 1970s, there had been some cases, places where, beyond 'growth', planners and politicians took an expansive view of their city's possibilities. They reacted against highway projects or expansion plans that would have crowded out places to live. They worried about the needs of the city's poorer neighbourhoods. In Berkeley, a group of graduate students bonded with City Council member Loni Hancock and then produced *The Cities Wealth* (Bach et al. 1975) adapting the British 'New Town' idea that had begun as a land ownership scheme giving citizens a share of control over City administration and even public utilities. In Santa Monica, the city's largely renter population, facing rent increases, voted in a rent control ordinance that redistributed wealth in the heretofore owner-dominated city. In Cleveland, Mayor Dennis Kucinich fought a proposal to merge the city's public power company into a private utility that would raise rates. In Hartford, a new City Council leadership took control of downtown redevelopment projects and, using City-owned land as leverage, provided new spaces and jobs for residents of the city (Bach et al. 1975; Bach et al. 1982; Gilderbloom and Capek 1992; Krumholz 1982).

What to do?

After this first phase of progressive cities, I published *The Progressive City* (Clavel 1986), summarising what I had learned. But then what? One option was to delve deeper into neighbourhood issues, which would encompass a large number of cases and where the emergence of Community Development Corporations (CDCs) created new interest. Another was to continue with a deeper look at what happened after progressives had 'captured City Hall', perhaps in larger places. This was attractive because larger cities meant a larger role for minorities, particularly African Americans, recently mobilised in the civil rights movement.

Either way, one could see an impending shift in activity. After the 1970s, things were calming down. There was a tendency towards incorporation within or instead of established organisational forms. There would be organisations like CDCs, but also notable efforts to take control of city government. I had a 'head of steam' in both venues, city governments and neighbourhood projects. I made serious beginnings with several months of residence doing interviews in Chicago and then in Boston in 1988 and 1992, but then I concentrated on CDCs through the 1990s. As it happened, the large city cases took up more time over a longer period.

Neighbourhood planning

I managed several neighbourhood-scale initiatives starting in the 1970s. The 'studio' class format was most immediately feasible. City planning had begun to experiment with 'advocacy planning' in the 1960s and I found a niche focusing on economic development. I found 'clients' and taught classes doing 'economic development' studies and proposals in Ithaca, Binghamton, Utica, Rochester and Syracuse. These continued sporadically into the 2000s.

In the late 1990s, I broke away from the class project format to undertake deeper efforts with publishable output for CDCs in Youngstown, Ohio and Coastal Enterprises, Inc. (CEI) in Wiscasset, Maine (Clavel 1999; Clavel and Westmont 1998). All these had to be financed out of my pocket. I had managed the class efforts because they were nearby and students could visit these places on their own dime. The Youngstown project was possible because a former Cornell colleague, Jim Converse, had settled there at the end of the 1970s, and was willing to talk about his organisation, Commonwealth, Inc. at length, while giving us access to local contacts: his wife Pat Rosenthal, co-workers and allies like Brian Corbin who had been hired by the Catholic Diocese and on one occasion Alice and Staughton Lynd, distinguished scholars and activists who entertained my students on a visit in the 1990s.

The Coastal Enterprises piece came when one of our students, Valerie Rutstein, had an internship with them and invited me to come by. This was in the summer of 1995. I met CEI's executive director Ron Phillips, who invited me to come in residence and learn what they were doing. I followed up in the spring of 1996. I was on sabbatical leave for a semester and wrote on an interesting series of projects they were doing. These were convenient to family visits. My mother had been living in Maine, and when her house passed to me, I continued the arrangement with CEI and contacts with community development activities here.

Progressive mayors in larger places

The Boston and Chicago experiences built on my earlier work on smaller cities in the 1980s, but over a longer period. As I learned through the experience, one can get a sense of history and a more compressed time in a smaller place in as little as a month's residence – though I had often done repeated additional trips. But, in larger places, I found significant gaps – topics I was simply unable to understand with just a few interviews. The events were also more complicated: often the players had opposing views that I could not easily rectify. In the end, I simply postponed final writing on Boston and Chicago. I spent a sabbatical year in Chicago in 1988–89 collaborating with Wim Wiewel on a retrospective volume called *Harold Washington and the Neighbourhoods* (Clavel and Wiewel 1991), written by several authors – I had interviewed them first – with Wiewel and I as editors, each writing a chapter. There was also a video based on interviews, mainly produced by Wiewel with funds from local foundations (Wiewel and Clavel 1992). I was hugely supported in Chicago by Wiewel and the University of Illinois at Chicago Centre for Economic Development, leaning on others for most of my sources.

Boston was a similar challenge. In the spring of 1992, I managed a semester's residence there, in which I did perhaps 40 interviews. I had less of a backup in Boston than in Chicago. It is a smaller city, and perhaps I covered a larger part of the city case. Raymond Flynn was mayor there from 1983 until 1993, 11 years to Washington's four and one-half. Later I managed two chapters on Boston, did three on Chicago, thus the bulk of *Activists in City Hall* (Clavel 2010). I thought I had captured the essence of both efforts and of progressivism, particularly on the part of the City planners involved. But neither provided a complete story, and unfortunately this was over two decades, too long for the book to get much attention.

Theory

Looking at small cities, then neighbourhoods, then larger cities, I found myself writing – and teaching – descriptively. Having picked progressive cases, it was impressed on me that theory got in the way of simply indicating that progressive organisation existed. Political culture – and theoretical work in the USA – tended to deny the existence of collective efforts. I satisfied myself with a simple description that I thought captured the difference between 'progressive' and otherwise 'normal' cities: they tended toward redistributive policies (rent control in Santa Monica), and participatory innovations (a 'Fair Representation Ordinance' in Berkeley, and such simple innovations as putting City Council meetings on the radio). But I did not elaborate these attributes, I simply described them.

It was somewhat ingenuous. While protesting my innocence of causal factors, I was aware what I was doing. After all, I had gone rather deeply into certain aspects of social theory in the past, so it was in my head somewhere. I left theorising the progressive city to others, or until later, hoping to make the description clear (Clavel 1986).[1] The 'Progressive City' was the dependent variable, the 'thing to be explained'. It seemed reasonable to describe it, to be thorough, and leave it at that.

Later, I thought it would be important to theorise about what I was seeing. I did start to posit the existence of a social movement alongside of the 'redistribution' and 'participation' of the book that appeared in 1986. More appeared later, but not with great effect.[2] What did the more intensive issues of race suggest as we looked at larger cities? Could we see this at the neighborhood level as we looked at CDCs in the 1990s?

Preservation

While this was going on, there had been an effort at preservation of City planners' documents in the Cornell University Library. It had begun with the arrival of Herbert Finch as a librarian attached to and later directing the Library's Division of Rare and Manuscript Collections (RMC) in 1966, soon before I joined the Cornell faculty in 1967. I had met Finch, and colleagues at Cornell like Barclay Jones and Kermit Parsons had a great interest in Finch's project, which was to collect as many papers of older City planners as he could. I was polite but disinterested in the beginning. I think I exaggerated this, but my idea of city planning was different from those of older colleagues; the whole idea of 'progressive cities' went against the grain of what Finch appeared to be doing. But the potential of the larger collections – which mounted to several hundred names by the time I was collecting things in Boston and Chicago – was beginning to interest me. Why not add 'progressive planners' to the collection? I would not have to mention 'diversity' – just present my collection. What I had by 2005 was 10 file drawers and a large office, just finishing a three-year term as department chair. It was never completely clear that these 'progressive city' papers were simply the deposit of a professor's own work as he neared retirement, or as I characterised it – the record of an innovative city planning approach, per se – and then began adding to it.

Then by about 2012, Cornell Library was geared up to create a digital collection with 'e-commons', an innovative operation done in concert with Stanford, Yale Columbia, and other large schools that would make possible several things: one was online publications as an alternative to the more cumbersome and expensive publications in academic journals, increasingly taken over by large international publishers. These were burdensome particularly in the sciences, and there were hopes for an easier path for many producers of written work.

Another main feature was the attempt to counter the deterioration of web-based work, just becoming known in the 1990s.[3] The associated universities creating e-commons created new software to counter the 'broken links' problem, and this gave an added reason to put material on this facility. In 2012, I succeeded in placing a number of items from the Conference on Alternative State and Local Policies on E-commons. This was made possible by a library staff – perhaps a dozen at the time – knowledgeable in the nuances of the appropriate software. We were able to follow this with many more items in following years, so that now there are perhaps 200 separate papers and reports preserved in this manner.

Preservation – elaborated

I come back to the 'what to do' question. I think it was a good idea to study and write about 'progressive cities' in the 1980s. At that time, the fate of progressivism in places like Berkeley, Santa Monica and Burlington was unknown and it seemed opportune to create a record if others wanted to follow. Hartford and Cleveland had rejected progressives at the polls, though survivals would continue to emerge.

Of major importance to scholars looking at the progressive city cases was the emergence of the Conference on Alternative State and Local Policies, begun by Lee Webb and Derek Shearer in 1975. Webb, who had been Secretary of the Students for a Democratic Society (SDS) was by 1974 teaching at Goddard College in Vermont and found interest in that state's legislature in several pieces of legislation proposed with redistributive intent. One was to support dental work for poor people who otherwise would routinely have their teeth pulled. Contacting advocates in other states with these ideas, Webb found a lively interest in the collection of information on such initiatives. He soon found foundation support and set up an office in Washington. He and Shearer went to a number of states and by 1975 held a conference in Madison, where some 300 activists constituted the organisation. Subsequent national meetings occurred in 1976–80 in Austin and Pittsburgh; and there were several smaller regional conferences. After that, the earliest 'progressive city' cases declined in intensity, though some survived. Webb left for other work in the 1980s, and there was less call for the kinds of interchange he had envisioned. Any sense of a national movement to 'capture' City Hall died.[4]

For two more decades, these kinds of City government almost ceased to appear in the USA, though one could mention elements here and there. In 2013, there was a revival, partly visible because of changes in the economy, partly because of social movements' interest particularly focused on larger issues like inequality. The DeBlasio mayoralty in New York was the most dramatic; but journalists and advocates pointed to Los

Angeles, San Jose, Seattle along with northeastern and rustbelt developments like Minneapolis, Pittsburgh and Boston. Marc Doussard and Greg Schrock (2022) made an argument that the new resurgence of central cities set up mayoralties to take progressive innovations like the living wage. It did not seem that change was over.

My question now goes back to the 1970s and 1980s, and how the world has changed: what features of those progressive cities led to their disappearance and what is it now that brings at least some elements back to life? Robert Kraushaar and I, now retired, had been presenting papers at conferences, and in 2018 decided to organise a roundtable on 'progressive cities' at the Association of Collegiate Schools of Planning, in Buffalo. We invited several speakers and wrote to dozens to invite attendance. The hour allotted did not make for much discussion. The Buffalo session pointed out the evolution of the metropolitan venue since the 1980s. Certain features, and in some cases whole regimes, seemed to disappear without a trace. Disinvestment and plant closings, the dominant feature of the earlier decades, was replaced by reinvestment and issues of equality, including gentrification. Above all, perhaps, was Marc Doussard and Gregg Schrock's argument ostensibly against 'capturing City Hall', advocating for paying attention rather to social movements like the 'Fight for 15'.[5] As many private corporations departed from cities, downsized and started shedding the services they managed, cities had to fill the vacuum and take over the responsibility – either by providing the services themselves, or by setting up incentives to the small firms that arose to fill the gaps. The cities and social movements' activists, in turn, could then demand corporate support in various ways – starting having more 'leverage'. To this, Susan Fainstein, however, responded, 'Don't forget City Hall!' The research problems facing urbanists were being restructured, but I could now see a larger role for the more 'activist' cities. In their 2022 book, *Justice at Work,* Doussard and Shrock (2022) did not focus on this, interrogating instead underlying factors that made the social movements' activists – 'urban policy entrepreneurs' – effective.

What remains today of the 1970s and 1980s 'progressive cities'?

I cannot be sure, but Carbone's Hartford initiatives seemed to disappear with his 1979 electoral defeat. It is true that within less than a decade a new progressive mayor, or with progressive ambitions, was elected and her council faction remained in the majority or at least maintained importance for two election cycles (Simmons 1994). But a 'linkage' idea similar to Boston's failed, and a new Latino-based regime soon established itself, and nothing like what Carbone had put together re-emerged.

Something similar happened in Chicago after Washington's death in office in 1987. Eugene Sawyer maintained the Washington coalition administrative constituency for 18 months but when Richard M. Daley, the son of the long-time City boss (1950s–70s) took office and maintained it for 22 years, few thought the Washington forces would be able to reconstitute, and they did not. They did, however, maintain some things and for some time – notably the attempt to slow the loss of manufacturing jobs, done partly with foundation help and the persistence of university outreach resources mobilised by community development elements who had been part of the Washington regime. The most recognisable instrument for saving manufacturing jobs was 'planned manufacturing districts' (PMDs), devised by community organiser and planner Donna Ducharme, who prevailed on the Washington administration to initiate it as a zoning device, and finally succeeded prior to Richard M. Daley's election in 1989. Daley had opposed PMDs as a candidate, but reversed and hired Ducharme as Deputy Planning Commissioner in the early 1990s. She not only oversaw the creation of additional PMDs, but supported manufacturing through 'industrial corridor studies' that pointed to needed infrastructure improvements. Ducharme's tenure ended after several years and this story is largely untold.[6]

Other places maintained progressive outposts and some even remained in power: Santa Monica remained a progressive government; and Burlington's progressives maintained control of the mayoralty for all but two years from Sanders' initial victory in 1981 until a more definitive defeat in 2012. Berkeley's progressives, like Burlington's, maintained a City Council presence periodically.

Theory, and the Doussard and Schrock contribution

What accounted for these successes, and for their failures?

1. National social movements. Civil rights, university and college-based student movements in the 1960s triggered most that has been reported of the 1970s and 1980s progressive city initiatives. These were certainly evident in Chicago when Washington won in 1983, and when university and foundation initiatives saved some elements after 1987.

2. But with some limited similarity, an overall backlash also emerged after the 1980s, eventually expressed as 'neoliberalism', putting a damper on and also co-opting progressive city initiatives and community development generally. Thus, the social movement energy made itself apparent in both directions, if at different times.
3. I noted Doussard and Schrock's *Justice at Work* earlier. Their innovation borders on the theory of all this: neoliberalism, until the 1990s, offered the cold shower of budget cuts to established social programmes, co-optation to others. Meanwhile, Cities remained essential as corporate entities downsized, by shedding associated services – personnel, legal services, many functions that were still needed, often offered up to recently 'remaindered' corporate functions. Corporate entities asked cities to offer these at cut rates, which they did, while non-profits and smaller enterprises took up the slack, forcing City Hall to support them. Doussard and Schrock (2022) saw in this, by the 1990s, a larger potential for social change rooted in the needs of urban populations and networked social movements.

In the face of these changes, what is the prospect for cities now? I do not know, but my thoughts turn to 'preservation' in the archival sense.[7] I have not discussed the 'theory' here. Is there a social movement comparable in scale to the collective surges of the 1960s and 1970s, in the aftermaths of the neoliberal cutbacks and retreats of later decades? Doussard and Schrock are noteworthy for suggesting it, but time will tell as to the evidence. What I know universities can do is description, case studies – more like 'preservation'. What we had done was 'preserve' the record of what seemed heroic, if doomed, prospects to keep a valued set of activities alive, or partly alive. What may now be in prospect is the documentation of new initiatives again – possibly leavened by reflection on earlier events.

Notes

1 When I published *The Progressive City* in 1986, I had just recently published *Opposition Planning in Wales and Appalachia* (1983) – also descriptive, but burdened by a rather extended effort to preface the story of two sub-national regional cases with a type of social theory, and in hindsight, I thought I had gone too far. In *The Progressive City*, parallel in some ways, was a reaction to the apparent lack of interest in my earlier topic. I thought the section on theory had smothered the cases. One comment, I think tongue in cheek, was 'I did not realise there were whales in Appalachia.'

2 I made a number of paper presentations, most never published. I created a website with blog posts, sometimes noted by others, for example, P. Clavel, 'What's the Progressive City?' Available at: http:// progressivecities.org/what's-the-progressive-city-3. Accessed 31 July 2023. In the course of these, my concept of the 'progressive city' began to include larger portions of civil society, in addition to the features of City Hall that were the focus of the 1986 book.

3 Lepore, J. 2015. 'The Cobweb. Can the internet be archived?', *The New Yorker*, 26 January.

4 For documentation, see: http://progressivecities.org and the 'Lee Webb Collection' available at: https://hdl.handle.net/1813/41473. Accessed 31 July 2023.

5 A social movement advocating the minimum living wage of $15 an hour, which was adopted in dozens of cities from the mid-2010s (see Doussard and Lesniewski 2017).

6 However, see Ducharme 1991, and Rast 1999.

7 South Africa, to its credit, made a start. Xolela Mangcu (2011) argued for preserving the archive of its institutions and their transformation including the transition after apartheid. I argue there needs to be an urban policy category, so that recent events are put into context, as evolution rather than a single 'moment' in history.

References

Altshuler, A. 1965. *The City Planning Process*. Ithaca, NY: Cornell University Press.

Bach, E., Brom, T., Estrella, J., Goldberg, L. and Kirshner, E. 1975. 'The Cities Wealth: Programmes for community economic control in Berkeley, California.' In *Alternative State and Local Public Policies*, National Conference on Alternative State and Local Public Policies. Washington: Institute for Policy Studies.

Bach, E., Carbone, N. and Clavel, P. 1982. 'Running the city for the people', *Social Policy* 12(3): 15–23.

Clavel, P. 1986. *The Progressive City: Planning and participation 1969–84*. New Brunswick, New Jersey: Rutgers University Press.

Clavel, P. 1999. *Rustbelt Community Development: Common Wealth, Inc. in Youngstown, Ohio*. Unpublished research report. Available at: https://hdl.handle.net/1813/45771. Accessed 31 July 2023.

Clavel, P. 2010. *Activists in City Hall*. Ithaca, New York: Cornell University Press.

Clavel, P. and Westmont, K. 1998. 'The Politics of jobs in Maine'. In *Jobs and Economic Development: Strategies and practices*, edited by R. Giloth, 195–213. New York: Sage.

Clavel, P. and Wiewel, W. (eds). 1991. *Harold Washington and the Neighbourhoods: Progressive city government in Chicago, 1983–87*. New York: Rutgers University Press.

Doussard, M. and Lesniewski, J. 2017. 'Fortune favours the organised: How Chicago activists won equity goals under austerity', *Journal of Urban Affairs* 39(5): 618–34.

Doussard, M. and Schrock, G. 2022. *Justice at Work*. Minneapolis: University of Minnesota Press.

Ducharme, D. 1991. 'Planned Manufacturing Districts: How a Community Initiative Became City Policy'. In *Harold Washington and the Neighborhoods*, edited by P. Clavel, 221–37. New York: Rudgers University Press.

Gilderbloom, J. and Capek, S. 1992. 'Santa Monica a decade later: Urban progressives in office', *National Civic Review* 81(2): 115–31.

Krumholz, N. 1982. 'A retrospective view of equity planning: Cleveland 1969–1979', *Journal of the American Planning Association* 48(2): 163–78.

Mangcu, X. (ed). 2011. *Becoming Worthy Ancestors: Archive, public deliberation and identity in South Africa*. Johannesburg: University of Witwatersrand Press.

Rast, J. 1999. *Remaking Chicago: The political origins of urban industrial change*. DeKalb, Illinois: Northern Illinois University Press.

Simmons, L.B. 1994. *Organising in Hard Times: Labour and neighbourhoods in Hartford*. Philadelphia: Temple University Press.

Wiewel, W. and Clavel, P. 1992. *Harold Washington and the Neighbourhoods*. Video available through E-Commons at: https://ecommons.cornell.edu/handle/1813/41480. Accessed 21 July 2023.

16

Porous bureaucracies, land and urban inclusion: a perspective from Indian cities

Varun Patil and Solomon Benjamin

Introduction

The concept of 'porous bureaucracy', introduced by Benjamin (1996; 2004), unpacks how majority groups seeking land and infrastructures shape democratic politics, reformulate state intervention while building agency in Indian cities. This chapter seeks to expand this concept, empirically and conceptually, through seven propositions tested through two case studies, in North Bangalore and East Delhi. These interlock the particularities of land settings of shelter, economy, large infrastructure and territorial interventions into specific and general official procedures, directives, court orders and policy. Such an approach allows for a nuanced consideration of working state spaces by a very large political constituency of majority groups, seeking not just shelter but also economic activities, based on a small firm economy that is central to the politics of land premised on infrastructure and services. Concepts from legal pluralism enlighten territory as 'practised tenure' around varied state spaces, which reflect historical traces and deeper foundations in diverse colonial and pre-colonial histories (Razzaz 1994; von Benda-Beckmann 2006; de Souza Santos 2020). This includes incrementally developed, mundane procedures that evolve as more explicit policy (Banerjee 2002; Buch 1984).

Dominant analyses of Indian urban politics miss the reality of a 'left art of government'

This complexity, missed by many analyses of Indian cities' politics, talks to Ferguson's argument towards a 'Left Art of Governance' (Ferguson 2011). Usual assumptions see local bureaucracy as robbed of any real political agency through metro-politics dominated by large private developers with global connections, state developmental agencies with non-elected CEOs and higher-level professional policy consultants, and corrupt urban planning and judicial system favouring urban elites. Those assumptions dominate South Asian post-colonial urban scholarship, where a unipolar global capital reveals local bureaucratic spaces as deviant and dysfunctional (Leitner and Sheppard 2020). Here, the 'marginalised poor' devoid of citizenship remain victims of brokers and local politicians corrupting bureaucracy via 'mafia'-like clientelism (Baliga and Weinstein 2022; Sud 2020). Real estate surpluses further fuel and fracture the promise of planning, churning city frontiers for accumulation (Balakrishnan and Pani 2020; Nair 2005).

The 'porous bureaucracy' remains discordant to these accounts, just as the complexity of land tenure is flattened of political texture and possibility, when considered only as a good soon to be commodified from its 'customary' past once accessed as a utopic 'commons'. An exception is Leitner et al.'s 'Everyday Speculation' (Leitner et al. 2022) that challenges Goldman's broad-brushed 'Speculative Urbanism' (Goldman 2020): however, this remains superficial as they treat land, as in early marxism, within simplistic rentier logic, thus reduced to pseudo-concrete materiality. Instead, porous bureaucracy analyses state mediated spacialities around tenurial nuanced complexities of rentiership. Here political agency lies outside the usual frames of social movements premised in the constitutional rights (Mehta 2010). Like Ferguson's critique of traditional 'left' politics, porous bureaucracy fundamentally questions planning and participation via 'rights-based housing', seen in equivalence to 'reforms' against clientelism.

Porous bureaucracies, a way of situating state practices in space, time, and scale

The porous bureaucracy's attention on mundane administrative procedures at city and regional level remains an important breakaway to emphasise complex politics, usually viewed as a contaminant of policy. It problematises the reluctance to accept and view the politics of the poor and their agency lying both within and outside of social movement and ideologically driven party politics. The porous bureaucracy's different and more everyday dimension of urban politics reiterates the importance of the material understanding of how majority groups access land and infrastructures is facilitated by the 'actually existing' bureaucratic–administrative practices. Our approach to land regularisation and complexity of local state refers to the work of Ananya Roy (Roy 2016, 816) who emphasised the urban question to be a land one, where land remains rooted in socio-materiality. In critiquing the functioning of state spaces and practices governing land to larger encompassing planetary logics, she argued for foregrounding the particularities. It is these where the category of urban and its territorial politics remain enacted at a space and time. In similar sensibility, we argue that the complexity of land politics, embedded in public administration in the subcontinent, requires an epistemological and ontological equivalence and thus to build theory from these situated histories and practices.

Thinking through the porous bureaucracy, we reiterate analysing urban state practices in its particularities beyond the placeholders of gentrification/neoliberalism and clientelism/vote bank narratives. It focuses instead on state spaces and practices centred on land. By state spaces and practices, we mean the plural institutional landscape which is more useful than the abstract and misleading term 'state'. It is thus possible to engage with the embedding of market mechanisms in state in the city and the evictions they engender, without necessarily the meta-framing of gentrification and neoliberalism. And it is possible and useful to describe the often unequal relationship of engaging the state without the framing of clientelism, counter-hegemony and corruption. Finally, we believe it is possible to problematise and focus attention to support the local government space as a scalar, without the framing of it as a space siting 'local resistance'.

We argue that the public administrative realms and practises governing cities (be it local, regional and national) remain un-spatialised and analysed as a place bounded in by larger governmentalities or encompassing logics. Spatialising the bureaucracy reveals how entangled the land and infrastructure politics of majority groups is within the state. We enter the debate on the institutional complexity of the state in post-colony and the mainstream and redistributive nature of porous bureaucracy. The analytic argues for centering land's materiality and embeddedness, engaging with the legal pluralism situation, recognising the multiple modes of democratic engagements with state and the radical nature of generating rent surplus from land regularisation.

Seven propositions towards a 'left art of government'

Starting from these critiques of South Asian postcolonial contemporary literatures, we make seven propositions towards a 'left art of government'.

1. **Proposition 1:** The state is porous and socially embedded in majority groups. Porosity is not just the ability by officials to bend the policy through ad hoc creative practice or appropriation of existing master-plan procedures. Porosity is also the ability of majority groups in complex constellations with bureaucrats and politicians to produce various kinds of instruments continuously mainstreamed, integrated and entangled in regional plan and policy. Yet they remain fluid, posing a spatial politics at lower municipal levels but also at other scales, across all state fields including parastatals, shaped by space and time, class and caste dynamics.
2. **Proposition 2:** The spatiality of porous bureaucracy implies practices crystallised as 'pro-poor' land policy. The porous bureaucracy remains fluid, to be appropriated, morphed and evolved, subverted, negotiated and lobbied. Thus, policy instruments remain continuously evolving and appropriated in ways and by actors that its full richness, as a space, cannot be read off the internet as a policy text published by that institution, and instead calls for against-the-grain ethnography.
3. **Proposition 3:** Land-focused policy instruments and directives are durable, meaning they have a long history, despite all its twists and turns, even if seemingly 'ad hoc' and 'provisional incorporation to proper policy' (Oldenburg 1976; Buch 1984; Banerjee 2002; Benjamin 1996). Such longevity of land regularisation policies impact vast constellations of groups on both shelter and economy and should thus be taken seriously and considered a mainstreamed form of progressive politics.
4. **Proposition 4:** Politics of land regularisation through porous bureaucracy are radical – in democratising access to housing and importantly expanding jobs enhancing economies by linking both use value and exchange value. Access to real estate surpluses for majority groups, erronously termed 'speculation' fuels economies, cements political alliance into social mobility (Banerjee 2002; Benjamin 1996; 2004). Its political spatiality as a core aspect of the 'left art of government' reflects the complexity of democracy in immediate and material terms, where land and economy manufactured through porous bureaucracy are central in creating socio-spatial equalities.

5. **Proposition 5:** The porous bureaucracy is decidedly a critical site of political learning. Dalit groups and women enter political life as workers, councillors at times into higher positions, are fuelled experientially. Often, they are termed 'social workers' after they mobilise fellow residents to lobby for infrastructure and services, and engage with the administration. Being noticed by more experienced politicians, they are mentored but such political leaning constituting the porous bureaucracy, can be viewed as a core aspect of the 'left art of government'.
6. **Proposition 6:** Democratisation of access to land is created by complex constellations with complex interests, and does not depend on well-intentioned state officers nor progressive politicians. The structure of political claim-making is central to facilitate this space, rather than only progressive constitutional courts. 'Presumptive' titles account for relatively open-ended claims of the majority groups, built via bureaucratic documentary practices (electricity and water bills, voter ID, certificates, and school report cards). Often innocuous and mundane, these are upheld in the lower courts, or, under mass political pressures, accepted by parastatal service providers to extend basic services. Such actions, establishing claims to 'fragment' territory into small plots, or then entangling multiple tenures, unsettle the fixity of private property that works in favour of large powerful players like private real estate pushing gated complexes, or then elite focused state planning schemes that acquire land often occupied by poorer groups.
7. **Proposition 7:** The porous bureaucracy reveals the politics of how implementing 'progressive' constitutional law (as in state-provided public housing) leads paradoxically, in its current iterations, to the displacement of majority groups. It exposes modernist social planning housing schemes 'targeted for the general population', and often reproduce class inequality. This is when territories and settlements already containing dense economies developed by the urban poor have their land re-categorised as 'public' within planning schemes. Here, court-mandated 'rehabilitation' measures focusing on 'housing the poor', allow administrators to displace the urban poor from the city centre to the periphery destroying them socially and economically, where massive vertical towers remain of poor quality stock and do not take into consideration the cultural and economic needs of the urban poor (Raman 2015).

We illustrate and consolidate these propositions with two case studies exploring various contexts of the porous bureaucracy: the first in north Bangalore, on claims to land, infrastructure and services for shelter upgrading, and the second in east Delhi, on the establishment and upgrading of small manufacturing and trading firms.

Case study one – porous bureaucracies in North Bangalore: constructing land tenure for 'squatters' in urban peripheries

This case study forms part of Patil's larger study on land and building regularisation schemes, known as Akrama Sakrama schemes, in Bangalore. This case study focuses on the settlement on Uru commons land that took shape in two waves of occupation. The first wave of Uru settlement began in the 1980's when Dalit[1] and other poorer families staying in cramped households in the central 'village land' looked at the village grazing commons at the edge of the village as a possible site for occupation (**Figure 16.1**). The election of the popular Dalit leader, Basavalingappa, who became Member of Legislative Assembly (MLA) as part of the welfarist Indian National Congress government, provided hope, since Uru was under his electoral constituency. A leader of Dalit Sangharsh Samiti (DSS), a regional organisation fighting for rights of poor and lower caste groups, told us that, after many petitions and requests, Basavalingappa directed the land revenue department to earmark part of Uru commons for housing Dalit and poor groups, which came to be known as the Uru Layout. In October 1979, around 500 Dalit and poor people were awarded *hakku patra* (title deeds) with a 25-year ban on re-selling the allotted sites. Four other such master-planned housing layouts for urban poor and Dalits were set on grazing lands in nearby villages.

As the population of the peri-urban region again grew, backward caste groups looked for further spaces within the grazing lands of Uru 'village' to occupy. In the 1990's, the second wave of occupancy began on the remaining part of the grazing land which was earmarked as a civic amenity site and a *Rajakaluve* (storm water drain connecting lake systems in Bangalore) for Uru layout. Apart from the caste networks of DSS, political party networks were crucial in consolidating occupation. Informants also told us that the newly elected member of regional state parliament from Congress encouraged their squatting on the remaining common land.

Figure 16.1 The squatter settlement at Uru on Gowmala land. The interstitial location of this settlement and its high density on a small track of land show its integration in the urban fabric of the city.

Source: © Varun Patil 2018

As the second wave of squatters were opening up spaces to claim infrastructure, they encountered many attempts to close down. A local elected representative allotted their land to a school trust run by his family after his election in 1994. The squatters opposed the trust's claims on land; the DSS and Congress networks helped the squatters to stall the eviction threat. There was also a legally mandated green belt planned around the city to prevent urban sprawl and protect the environment – where only farming activities would be allowed. The squatters, however, accessed infrastructures and property tax papers, documents materialising the various schemes and procedures of the city municipal councils which governed peri-urban areas as well as existing rural village institutions (Panchayat). This wealth of documentation became the basis on which they claimed occupation.

To bolster their occupations, the second-wave squatters started politicising the state, especially the Karnataka Land Revenue Department, to get the *hakku patra* land titles which had been given to the first wave squatters in 1980. In 1999, the Karnataka government, after a long period of agitation by Dalit groups state-wide, inserted an amendment to the Karnataka Land Revenue Act, allowing for regularisation of encroachment of government land for housing purposes in rural and peri-urban areas, popularly known as 'Section 94c'. According to many Uru residents, the DSS/Congress networks of the settlement helped pool the applications of squatters, submitted the applications and even got in the surveyors. Overall, under Section 94c, the Land Revenue Department received 600,000 applications for regularisation across the state, of which 145,000 were approved (see **Figure 16.2**).[2]

The political space opened up by politicising the land revenue department for occupation by squatters was, however, disrupted by the announcement of the master-planned Arkavathy layout in Uru and the surrounding 16 'villages' by the Bangalore Development Authority (BDA). The BDA abruptly modified the green belt zone pushing it further away in order to enact its ambitious scheme. For the layout, the BDA planned to take (apart from over 3,000 acres of private farm lands) close to 500 acres of government land such as Gowmala (grazing) and Gundthopu (tree groves) in these 'villages', including Uru. The BDA, however, was unable to take the remaining Gowmala land in Uru as it was already occupied by squatters and the BDA had to write it off as 'encroachment' in their records, a common practice it employs since its inception in 1976. **Figure 16.3** shows a map drawn by Benjamin (2023) which is based on the BDA's map (2014) of Uru and its surroundings, North Bangalore District. The 2014 map was given to Varun Patil by a farmer activist who acquired it due to his good links with state officials. Theoretically, it is a public document but it is generally hidden from the general public. Firstly, this is because it constantly evolves over time,

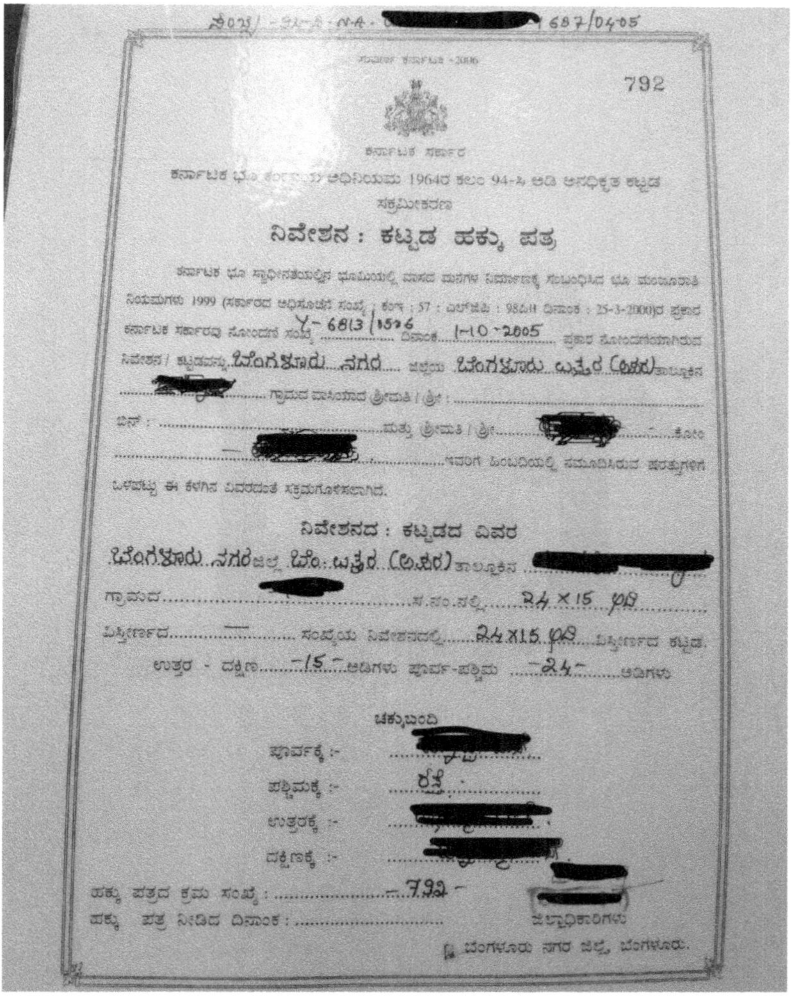

Figure 16.2 The title deed of a squatter in Uru. The document known as *hakku patra* was issued by Karnataka's Land Revenue Department under Section 94c, dated 2005. It says that 24 ft x15 ft of land belonging to a squatter in Gowmala land, Survey Number 100, is being regularised.
Source: © Varun Patil 2018

with land being acquired or included into the master planning schemes. Secondly, it is because information of whose land is being acquired (in yellow on the original map) is used discretely by state officials to negotiate with landowners. The diversity of land statuses demonstrates

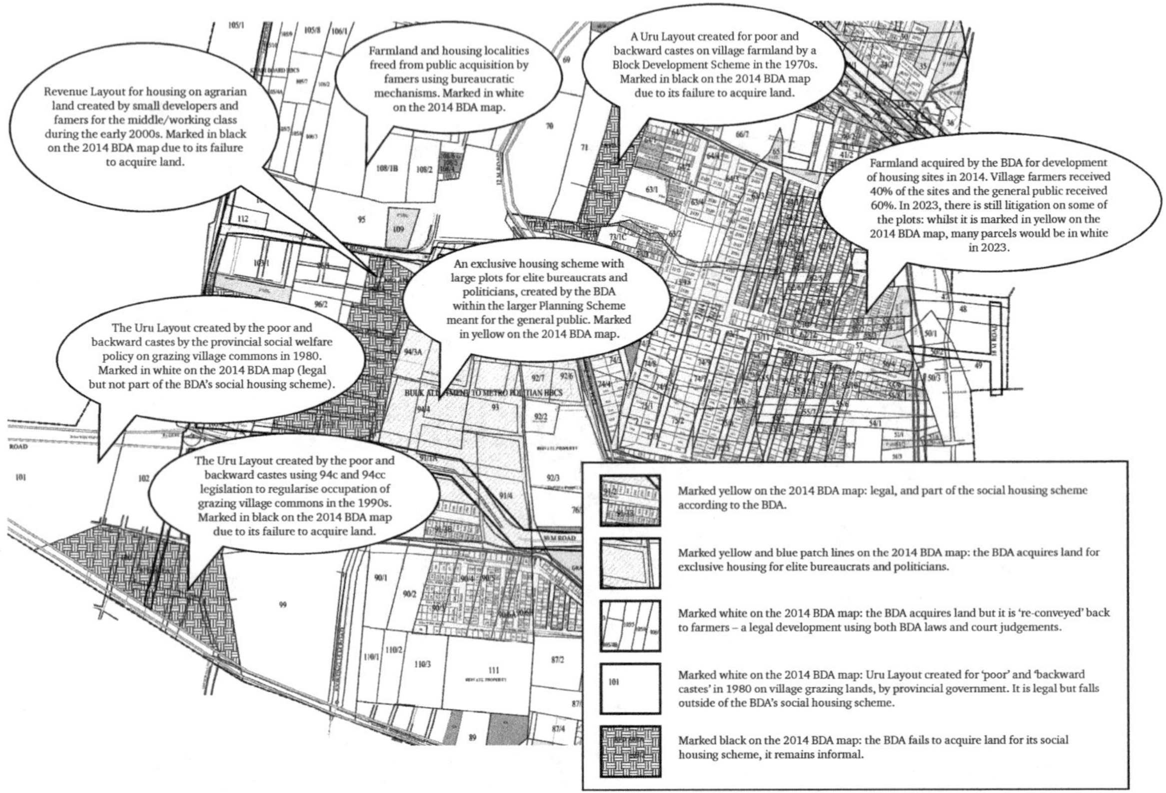

Figure 16.3 Regularising informal settlements through a variety of land statuses – Uru and its surroundings.

Source: © Benjamin's drawing (2023), based on the Bangalore Development Authority's (BDA) 2014 map of Uru and its surroundings, North Bangalore District.

the continued negotiations and entanglements between multiple levels of the state and various social groups.

The political space opened up by politicising the rural and peri-urban state institutions, such as the land revenue department (with the creation of the policy instrument 'Section 94c') and City municipal councils, was threatened with the absorption of Uru into Bangalore's metropolitan municipal limits in 2007–8. Land values were rapidly increasing and the regional state was pushed by the Information Technology and large real estate companies to aid them in assembling land. Given the intense litigations and difficulties in assembling private farmlands, state-controlled lands became a target for acquisition by many of these powerful actors who mobilised state entities like the Karnataka Industrial Areas Development Board (KIADB), which had powerful land acquisition powers. A part of the Uru Gowmala land was auctioned by the municipality to a real estate group which has built a housing complex for middle and upper classes. Similar auctioning of parts of grazing lands began in some of the nearby villages affecting squatting strategies.[3]

The politicised state spaces opened by the squatter settlements and other occupancies across Bangalore were also seriously threatened by the counter-mobilising of elite civil society groups, such as the 'Save Karnataka Campaign' over the issue of 'public land encroachment' and 'land mafia', who lumped under these abstract categories all types of occupations by various groups on public land: large capital, small developers and squatters alike. As a result of these mobilisations, various task forces were set up by the regional governments which carried out extensive public land encroachment surveys, especially in peri-urban areas, and succeeded in temporarily stopping the municipality from issuing any house property tax papers. The metropolitan jurisdiction also opened up newer avenues as the squatters became eligible to avail the metropolitan municipal housing scheme to upgrade their existing houses, which many residents are using to improve their shelters.

Newer occupations were continuously occurring on the Uru grazing land, which brought forth the question of getting land titles from the Land Revenue Department again. Since 2010, there were state-wide agitations by squatter groups across the state to pressurise the governments to amend the Karnataka Land Revenue Act and insert a new section to allow for regularisation of unauthorised constructions in public land which had now come under urban/metropolitan areas. Uru's DSS leader Krishnanna said that they intensely lobbied with the Revenue ministry offices and held protests for implementation of *hakku patras*. They also met Kagodu Thimappa, Revenue Minister and pressured him to fast-track the

Table 16.1 The various state institutions mobilised by residents to produce the Uru settlement over the years (Bangalore).

Practice or instrument aiding eviction	Type of state space	Practice or instrument aiding regularisation
Occasionally sells public land to raise revenue	Village Council	Plans infrastructure schemes
		Issues fines used as proof of residence
Occasionally sells public land to raise revenue	City municipal Council (Bangalore rural)	Plans infrastructure schemes
		Issues house property tax papers (Khata)
Auction of land	Bruhat Bengaluru Mahanagara Palike (Bangalore urban municipality)	Plans infrastructure schemes
		Issues house property tax papers (Khata) used as de facto ownership
Land acquisition of village commons and farmlands Bangalore Development Authority (BDA)	Para Statal entities: Bangalore Water and Sanitation Services (BWSSB), Bangalore Development Authority (BDA), Bangalore Electricity Company (BESCOM)	Provides basic services without checking ownership – water BWSSB
		Provides basic services – electricity without checking ownership BESCOM
Legislative Commissions on land grab (example –Ramaswamy Commission)	Regional State Legislature/Chief Minister	Passes legislation expanding eligibility criteria of title deeds (94c and 94cc)
	Land Revenue Department/Revenue Minister/Tahsildar	Issues title deeds (94c and 94cc)

	Food and Civil Supply Department	Issues ration cards which boosts squatting claims
	Education Department	Issues proof of address which boosts squatting claims
Issues orders to evict residents on storm water drains	High Courts	Issues stay orders to prevent eviction without rehabilitation
Auctions land	Area Legislator	Facilitates issue of house property tax papers (Khata) and infrastructure schemes
	Sub-Registrar Office	Registers transfer of ownership by general power of attorney method, without checking with land owning agencies, boosting squatting on public land

Not only are squatters able to mobilise a multiplicity of public institutions and authorities, and not only are various policy documents created that feed a legal pluralist situation, but a single same state space can both aid and undermine occupation, depending on the politics at that space and time.

Source: © Varun Patil 2022

amendment process. In 2013, the newly elected state government passed the new amendment called '94cc' to the Karnataka Land Revenue Department, which included (under certain conditions) regularisation of houses built within City limits. According to a case worker at the local Land Revenue Department, 183 temporary title deeds were issued in Uru alone and the permanent land titles are slowly being issued in small batches. Overall, in Uru at the time of research in 2018, we were told that around 350 squatters had received the land titles.

However, despite the opening up of political space in the Land Revenue Department again (through the Section 94cc), the second wave occupations continued to face threats, due to mobilisations by elite groups and NGOs over the 'ecological' issue of *rajakaluve* or storm water drains connecting the lake system of Bangalore.[4] As a result, according to a DSS leader, the Land Revenue Department has issued only temporary *hakku patras* to around 40–60 houses which are on the Kaluve.

The story of Uru settlement and its two phases of occupation reveals both the institutional complexity of public administration in a globalising city such as Bangalore and the possible route to construct a 'left art of the government' (see **Table 16.1**).

Firstly, it reveals the porosity of bureaucracy at work. Porosity is not just the ability to bend the policy through ad hoc creative practice, like Uru residents using *panchayat* fines and property tax papers as property claims. Porosity is the ability to produce the policy instrument 'Section 94c and 94cc' and keep it going. Porosity is across scalars of state as residents may at that time find regional state much easier to channelise than the field bureaucrat or municipal commissioner. For example, in the DSS office, the researcher witnessed the celebration of a Dalit deputy chief minister being elected and the talk of the route finally opening up to lobby for the extension of Section 94cc eligibility.

Secondly, it reveals the spatiality of the bureaucratic spaces. The same state space could be mobilised differently by different groups contributing to unevenness in support for the urban poor. The high courts have both issued stay orders against eviction by a local representative wanting the trust land and yet in a different time issued eviction orders against Uru (and many city) residents for occupying storm water drain public areas.

Thirdly, it reveals the durability of policy instruments evolved by porous bureaucracy. Land regularisation instrument Section 94c, dating pre-globalisation Bangalore, continues in the post-globalisation era (in the 2000s) through newer iterations.

Fourthly, it reveals the importance of seeing progressive policy instruments as an outcome of complex group constellations with complex interests, and not privilege actions of well-intentioned state officers or progressive politicians driven by social welfare. In Uru, in the first phase of occupation, the presence of radical pro-poor politicians in the ministry was important. Though residents remarked that even the first phase was a result of lobbying: power did not yield until it was forced to. In the second phase post 1990's, where so-called real estate driven politicians and bureaucrats took over the state, policy instruments continued as local democracy space remained competitive in addressing the needs of the urban poor.

Fifthly, the politics of Section 94cc reveals the complementarity between the progressive plan policy of land redistribution and public housing (the classic social welfare state) which aided the first phase of occupation and the porous bureaucracy-led land regularisation politics in the cities of the subcontinent which aided the second phase of occupation in Uru. The Uru settlement was not just about creating housing; it was host to small tailoring and other rental economies contributing to the creation of social mobility for the urban poor. The centrality of land as infrastructure and not just as a housing issue was stressed by a local urban poor resident–activist of the area, Sidappa, who told us, '*Akki kododu beda, bhoomi koodi. Yellaru dudithive* [Don't give us rice. Give us land instead and we will grow and feed ourselves].'

Finally, the Uru case reveals the need to exercise caution over the solutions to democratising housing through implementing 'progressive' constitutional law. As we saw in the Uru case, modernist master planning seen in the BDA's Arkavathy scheme aiming for the general population may lead paradoxically, in its current iterations, to the possible displacement of majority groups.

Case study two – porous bureaucracies as 'left art of government': energising East Delhi's majority economies

The 'Neighborhood as Factory' (NAF) pertains to terrains of mixed land use with inter-connected firms usually in specialised manufacturing and associated commerce set within residential areas. The output of one firm would be the input of another who then would connect to the third forming the NAF as an integrated system, just as a large factory may have different departments. Their development was incremental, on the private subdivision of agricultural land or 'urbanised' villages

Incremental regularisation of industrial activities in Viswas Nagar, East Delhi – porous bureaucracies in practice

We are in East Delhi Viswas Nagar (VN), which in 1995, was Asia's largest cluster manufacturing copper and aluminium wire cables and conductors (Benjamin 1996). We look at the practices of Deoki Aggrawal, who at 82 in 1993, was a patriarch energising a larger constellation of his fellow residents. His daughter and son-in-law living 1 km away in western VN's Block 28–29. In 1991, this area was still to be upgraded, often flooded in its low-lying ground. By 1987, Aggrawal had his legendary experience of being a 'mover and shaker' in Shahdara's DESU zonal office, well experienced in the 'Household industry category' (Layer B). Aggrawal's daughter's post-marriage home housed two buffalo calves, but like others, started off life on almost bare plots of land. Her rudimentary two-roomed structure left space for a third small street-fronting room, a lease for a future factory like many others. Aggrawal's political lobbying was rewarded with basic electricity for the home after they got street lights to ward away the wild pack of pigs and dogs. Aggrawal moved his politics 'up the game' towards a 'household' connection (Layer B, between 1–3 KV), allowing machines of 15–20 HP in the front room to attract youth tenants to start a small sub-manufacturing unit. Such upgrading in Block 28–29 established them as a powerful vote bank to push regularisation via their main patron, Ajit Chowdari, heading the local Youth Congress. Soon well-publicised posters, celebrating the successful installation of the new electricity transformer, had Chowdari's photo with the customary folded hands as the chief guest to the inauguration of the unit – a build-up to forthcoming elections. As is common, Chowdari's brother, Ashok Dabas, was in the dominant opposition party Bharatiya Janata Party (BJP). Dabbas owned one the earliest and largest copper wire drawing factory, while their cousin, was the local leader of the Janata Dal party's youth wing, the third and less dominant opposition party. Almost always, the three sat together sipping tea in Dabas's small air-conditionned office set off in the main factory hall. Chowdari's other main job was as a property agent and, with his business partners, he had invested heavily in empty plots in Block 28–29. As they helped people settle in, often offering cheap loans to 'facilitate' electrical connections, their 'unsold' plots would reap huge profits with the increase of land value. It was this emerging voting block that helped push the DA, the MCD, and the DESU to get in services and infrastructure. Soon, within months, as in the case of Aggrawal's daughter's front room lease, rental advances and their 'partnership' would pay for housing upgrades into industrial units as workers and foreman would settle here to start off on their own factories, helped by their earlier employers. In a few years, this western extension of the VN extended the NAF. Such lease, entangled in real estate market logic, inflected the valuation of the factory's share. Political and social connections helped get the electricity, and in turn, these developments consolidated a larger political voting clout, by way of the family's social and caste connections, and also by its marriage alliances into lower and middle bureaucracy.

In similar social dynamics, an incremental precursor would pave the way for Layer C1, heating loads by the DESU–Municipal Council and much later, if possible, Layer C2: Ad hoc Registration schemes under the DA. These C1 and C2 regularisation schemes, requiring larger political clout at national-level election time, would involve a key role played by Chaudari and other relatively political heavyweights and a much larger political constituency of VN. Here, this path included a Chowdary's 'hunger strike' sent as a notice to the local DESU manager. Aggrawal's letter petition cajoled his main contact, the same bureaucrat and specifically his underling officer to provide access to the DESU's exact work order details and cost estimates. These were mentioned in his letter, and explicitly indicated the support and backing of a political heavyweight – the DESU ex-chairperson of the Works Committee and senior counsellor for Shahdara, Abjit Singh Gulati. Gulati at the time of the letter was the elected head of the Municipal Corporation of Delhi's water supply agency. A side-politics, but a key part of the 'implementation deal' was to mobilise the Block 28–29 residents as a vote bank to Chowdary, to trade his empty plots to house the new transformer, a political move which would also offset the 'development charges' they would otherwise have to pay to the DESU.

Table 16.2 Varied electrical loads as land tenures schemes for 'unplanned' activities in Delhi.

Applicants	**A** **Urban village**	**B** **Household industry**	**C1** **Heating and cooling loads**	**C2** ***Ad hoc* registration**	**D** **Local commercial area**
For what	Villages to be in urban areas	Entrepreneur operating from planning unit	Main road enterprises	Units in non-conforming areas, functioning in unauthorised ways without any licence	'Light industrial areas' as identified periodically by the Delhi Development Authority/Municipal Corporation Delhi/Ministry of Rehabilitation
Power load allowed	Up to 20 HP	Up to 1 KWH (3 KV), raised to 15–20 HP	Up to 11 KV	Up to 40 HP, increased to 80 HP in 1982–83 then to 120 HP under ad hoc certificate policy of 1991	Up to 7,5 HP
Granted to	Trading services such as dal, rice, wheat, flour, mill, kutti cutting, cotton carding	Listed 38 trade groups of Delhi Financial Corporation (DFC) List	Showrooms, restaurants, clinics, auto maintenance shops	Units having come up before 31 December 1989 (proof of date to be submitted)	Includes light industry, light mechanical workshop, repair shops, cooling and refrigeration plants and service trades

Granted by		DESU (Delhi Electrical Supply Unit)	DESU – Municipal Council	Delhi Administration	Delhi Development Authority/Municipal Corporation Delhi/Ministry of Rehabilitation
Specific conditions	No licence needed inside the village settled area (*lal dora*) if power load is under 20 HP			Unauthorised constructions after 10 June1992 shall be kept pending until further instructions	
		On all floors except basement		Only on ground floor	Not adjacent to any medical clinic
	Expandable licence			Licence is non-expandable and non-renewable	Licence is expandable and renewable
	Maximum of 10 workers	Maximum of 4 workers		Polluting/obnoxious/ hazardous units not to be registered	
		Surface not more than 300 sq ft		No change of trade allowed, no transmission to entrepreneurs' heirs	

The table shows that for each type of 'unplanned' industrial activities, depending on their location, size, age, their place and visibility in buildings, but mostly the type of electrical load they require, there are different sets of (conditional) regulations granted by various public administrations, that de facto constitute different forms of land tenure, which we may then call 'electrified tenures'.

Source: © Benjamin 1996

Layers B: Household industry 1–3 KV (view from the outside).

Layers B: Household industry 1–3 KV (view from the inside)

Layers C1 and C2: Heating and cooling loads' and 'ad hoc registration' (11 KV)

Changing tenurial 'claims' from Layer C2 (ad hoc registration) to Layer D (Local Commercial area): 40 HP in 1970s to 70–80 HP in 1982–83, and 100–120 HP in 1990–91

Figure 16.4 'Electrified tenures' shape urban landscapes. The integrated nature of small-scale industrial activity and residence is visible everywhere in the urban landscape, from rooms in existing buildings to small makeshift extensions, to full workshops. Beneath this urban integration, a variety of politicised processes have led to a wide diversity of land tenures, mostly shaped around the electrical load needed by each activity. Source: © Solomon Benjamin (incorporating the city's expanding boundary) interlocking both political access and economic consolidation (Benjamin and Bengani 1998; Benjamin 2004). In 1995, the NAFs accounted for 95 per cent of Delhi's 220,000 micro-'tiny' manufacturing clusters, where only 11,500 were located in the Master Plan's designated small-scale industrial ('SSI') plots ranging from one half to one quarter of an acre. Almost all others were in plots sized 30 ft x 60 ft, many smaller, and usually with a residence on the upper floors with factories leased out on the ground floor, or a part of it.

The porous bureaucracy is a fundamental keystone to regularise these dense mixed-land uses. It is part of the re-distribution process of real estate surpluses in peri-urban terrains, which fuels shelter upgrading and capital investments in small firms manufacturing, through leased plots to factory owners as tenants but also 'partnership' with the land owner, at low entry cost. Crucially, such tenurial practices set within a 'presumptive' land claiming system also cements the local economy into a substantive politics across diverse constituencies. Factory owners and tenants in partnership with foremen form a jointed 'occupancy claim' and thus share a substantial stake in the politics of regularisation. Capital investments are deeply entangled in a variety of local 'jointed' saving-investments such as 'Committees – Lucky Draw' (Benjamin 1996). These groups include a foreman, but also other residents in these neighbourhoods, and lower- and middle-end bureaucrats from the local regulatory or service provider agencies such as electricity suppliers, who would invest part of their salary (and 'bribes') to co-share business partnerships. The tenant factory owner and foreman mobilise political clout to expand their field of influence via their workers staying in close proximity. The presumptive based land titles shape tenurial practices via 'security deposits and pugree' (Benjamin and Bengani 1998), and distribute negotiated surpluses between tenants and landowners into joint lobbying where upgraded electricity supply via a new transformer raises real estate surpluses. Another binding link between owners, tenants, and various bureaucratic and technical workers, is their close social connections of similar class and caste, shaping political access into relevant administrative realms building the idea of 'the porous bureaucracy' (Benjamin and Bengani 1998).

While the NAF's incremental settlements' morphology reveals the unaffordability of areas in the Master Plan, popular politics is also about confronting elite groups. The latter mobilised 'their' porous bureaucracy shaping the Master Plan's high regulatory policy in their favour – claims also routed via the courts. Elite stake in corporate finance also sought to tap financialised real estate surpluses, leading in the mid-1990s to the framing of an 'environmental problem of air pollution' (Benjamin and Bengani

1998). Thus, it was vital for popular groups that their economic interests remained bounded into politically expansive voting constituencies that included workers in low-end rentals forming a 'vote block', rallying with factory owners and managers in relatively better housing and plot owners, all to lobby for land regularisation shaping shelter and economy.

If the porous bureaucracy is also an inter-class and caste conflict, it is important to look at the combination of the 'NAF' and the porous bureaucracy as being one of deep, life-long learning to engender political agency, autonomous of NGOs, social movement, or ideologically shaped party politics. Learning the porous bureaucracy would start when 10-year-old children listen into daily dinner conversations discussing municipal councillors who have helped to get basic services, or 'turned a blind eye'. Many young people, workers in units or children of plot owners, often barely 16 years old, would assist in property 'deals' affected by the latest round of regularisation. And for children of plot owners, who leased out their plot to a factory on the lower floor, political learning is built around the manufacturing process where its upgrading of product lines is premised on better electricity connections.

We shall now consider a vignette from Viswas Nagar which deals with the complexity of its spaces as an NAF. This is presented in **Table 16.2** where various categories of electricity provision evolve into tenure status, and in **Figure 16.4**, where we show how different forms of tenure status shape and transform urban landscapes.

The vignette presented in the box on pages 444–45 senses the porous bureaucracy's spatiality where the synchronous composite of electricity regulations entangled in everyday life's concerns of rental income, 'partnership' with tenants, manufacturing as an affective craft, connect the complexity of land: plots for children and their favourite buffalo, and of course jobs and shelters. This is sensed in Li (2014, 591): 'land supports every aspect of human and non-human life, so complete exclusion from its affordances is not possible'.

The land regularisation shaped by porous bureaucracy could be viewed as a 'pro-poor' land policy that consolidates and expands access to shelter with a substantive economy, works with real value addition via real estate surpluses shared with tenants, incentivises skilling, and fosters experiential political learning and agency. Such entanglement of land tenurial practices via 'working the porous bureaucracy' underpins the rapid consolidation of the NAF into a powerful political machine. It poses the porous bureaucracy's spatiality via the elected wing of municipal body expanding into the DESU, which, rather than a techno-managerial agency, is 'popular politicised'.

Reflecting the 'art of left government'

Ferguson (Ferguson 2011, 64) notes, in his call for the theorisation of a 'left art of government': '...our inability to conceive of forms of politics that would give (the majority of the population) a central place' and the problem with '...the old left strategy of dismissing such people as a residual and degenerate fringe can hardly suffice.' By continuing to construct land regularisation as a marginal, clientistic state space, many of the progressive groups have failed to see resistance and construct a politically appropriate right to the city space for majority groups.

As is very common, such groups move into political careers through 'local' politics at village and City councils, building a constituency of poor groups around land and access to infrastructure by their ways of 'working the bureaucracy'. Through this work, they promote the extension of infrastructure and services and, as in this particular case, stall and subvert acquisition. The figuration of the 'rowdy' or 'lumpen' present not just a 'law and order' problem for the state, it also:

> feeds into the everyday discourse of the ideologues of the middle-class, from Left to Left-liberal to liberal-Right, who invoke 'lumpenisation of politics' as an explanation of all that they find disturbing in the social and political life of the nation (Dhareshwar and Srivatsan 1996, 249).

The eminent political theorist Mehta (2010) emphasises this point, and the need to consider democracy as a deeply negotiated practised space around everyday materialities: to see law as process rather than only constitutionally derived aimed at equal citizenship. Drawing from Rancière, a 'left art of government' could include a reconfiguration where:

> Political activity is whatever shifts a body from the place assigned to it or changes a place's destination. It makes visible what had no business being seen, and makes heard a discourse where once there was only place for noise (Rancière 1999, 29–30).

In this framing, land regularisation can be seen as a reconfiguration of the consensus. While much of the literature boxes the poor's concern with land as 'housing', it misses the intent of them making land as an 'asset' whereby to tap its speculative potential to fund economy too, and thus, in Rancières' terms, to be understood as a politics of dissensus, outside of ideological logic but through complex everyday practice. Considering Ferguson's (2011), Rancière's (1999), and Mehta's (2010) point, we could argue that the contemporary right to the city is already being articulated in the form of porous bureaucratic politics, in the existing everyday mundane administrative procedures, evolved sometimes visibly and often clandestinely. A 'left art of government' might well take root in these practices rather than waiting for a progressive, top-down constitutional law pushed by visible social movement and delivered through deliberative democracy.

Finally, we see porous bureaucracy and our seven propositions aim to contribute to building a methodological tool to analyse the complex governance of cities. Rather than reading a state policy via initial iterations of the Master Plan's documents and high profile court judgments, we advocate reading it diachronically (over time) and how they are materialised on the ground in a complex way. It is not uncommon that land acquisition notices of state planning agencies are often used by majority groups to argue in courts that the state has recognised their occupation! We stress reading the state simultaneously through its multiple bureaucratic inscriptions dismissed often as corrupt and informal practices but which turn out to be legally entangled and durable.

Methodologically, we argue for constructing state practices through a range of everyday archives: petitions, letters and notes, administrative orders, newspaper and digital media, consultant reports, in order to recover the institutional complexity of city administration. No document is small in the game of playing with and in reading the state. We also stress reading the state from the echoes of multiple inscriptions of state in society via the story form (de Souza Santos 2020). As researchers, we are already familiar with these mundane stories like applying for a driver's licence with an agent or working on a balcony extension using kinship links in the local state. The often incomplete, contradictory narratives of state expressed as interesting stories by residents and the wide range of bureaucratic inscriptions give a density to the state which gets missed in the straightforward formal interviews with state officials and textual reading of policy texts.

We want to stress that struggles about conceptualising the state are not benign acts by academics in conferences and lecture halls leading to loss of institutional complexity. Analytical narratives of state practices and the accompanying policy prescriptions to reform the state often end up having tangible material effects on the politics of occupation by popular groups, but also their dispossession. We argue that the institutional complexity of the urban state seen in the durability, often redistributive and mainstream nature of porous bureaucratic practices asks us to then re-draft our epistemological apparatus of the 'left art of government'.

Acknowledgements

We remain deeply indebted to Claire Bénit-Gbaffou whose hard work through several iterations of this chapter, with wise comments, giving space to ethnographic details, and careful editing have played a huge role sharpening our arguments. All mistakes remain ours. Varun Patil's study was undertaken from April 2018 to November 2018 as part of the Urban Land Commons project with the Centre National de la Recherche Scientifique and the Indian Institute of Human Settlements.

Notes

1 A term preferred by Backward caste members to describe themselves.

2 Bangaluru, DHNS. 2020. 'Revenue department to regularise 60k urban houses on govt land.' *Deccan Herald*, 24 January. Available at: https://www.deccanherald.com/state/top-karnataka-stories/revenue-dept-to-regularise-60k-urban-houses-on-govt-land-797632.html. Accessed 2 August 2023.

3 Although, according to residents, Panchayats and City municipal councils have also over the years sold public land off to various buyers to raise finances occasionally.

4 Bangaluru, DHNS. 2016. 'BBMP uploads 1,923 rajakaluve maps on its website.' *Deccan Herald*, 14 August. Available at: https://www.deccanherald.com/content/564340/bbmp-uploads-1923-rajakaluve-maps.html. Accessed 2 August 2023.

References

Balakrishnan, S. and Pani, N. 2020. 'Real estate politicians in India', *Urban Studies* 58(10): 1–16.

Baliga, A. and Weinstein, L. 2022. 'Grounding urban production: Resident claims-making as financialisation in Mumbai's 'slum' lands', *Economy and Society* 51(2): 283–306.

Banerjee, B. 2002. 'Security of tenure in Indian cities: An overview of policy and practice'. In *Holding Their Ground: Secure Tenure for the urban poor in developing countries,* edited by A. Durand-Lasserve and L. Royston, 37–58. London: Routledge.

von Benda-Beckmann, F.K. and Wiber, M. (eds). 2006. *The Properties of Property*. London: Berghahn.

Benjamin, S. 1996. 'Neighbourhood as factory: The influence of land development and civic politics on an industrial cluster in Delhi, India.' PhD thesis. Massachusetts Institute of Technology. Available at: https://dspace.mit.edu/handle/1721.1/11045. Accessed 1 August 2023.

Benjamin, S. 2004. 'Urban land transformation for pro-poor economies', *Geoforum* 35: 177–87.

Benjamin, S. and Bengani, N. 1998. 'The civic politics of industrial districts'. In *Decentralised Production in India: Industrial districts, flexible specialisation, and employment*, edited by M. Holmstrom and P. Cardene, 376–92. New Delhi: French Institute and Sage.

Buch, M. 1984. 'Land policy and the urban poor', *Nagarlok* 16(4): 1–10.

Dhareshwar, V. and Srivatsan, R. 1996. 'Rowdysheeters: An essay on subalternity and politics'. In *Subaltern Studies* IX, edited by S. Amin and D. Chakrabarty, 201–31. New Delhi: Oxford University Press.

Ferguson, J. 2011. 'Toward a left art of government: From 'Foucauldian critique' to Foucauldian politics', *History of the Human Sciences* 24(4): 61–68.

Goldman, M. 2020. 'Dispossession by financialisation: The end(s) of rurality in the making of a speculative land market', *Journal of Peasant Studies* 47(6): 1251–77.

Leitner, H. and Sheppard, E. 2020. 'Towards an epistemology for conjunctural inter-urban comparison', *Cambridge Journal of Regions, Economy and Society* 13(3): 491–508.

Leitner, H., Nowak, S. and Sheppard, E. 2022. 'Everyday speculation in the remaking of peri-urban livelihoods and landscapes', *Environment and Planning A: Economy and Space* 55(2): online.

Li, T. 2014. 'What is land? Assembling a resource for global investment', *Transactions of the Institute of British Geographers* 39(4): 589–602.

Mehta, P.B. 2010. 'Citizenship As A Claim Or Stories Of Dwelling And Belonging Among The Urban Poor.' Second Ambedkar Memorial Lecture by Professor Veena Das, 23 August 2010. YouTube video. Available at: https://www.youtube.com/watch?v=dUjf79z9Yog. Accessed 10 February 2023.

Nair, J. 2005. *The promise of the metropolis: Bangalore's twentieth century*. New Delhi: Oxford University Press.

Oldenburg, P. 1976. *Big City Government in India: Councillor, administrator, and citizen in Delhi*. Tucson: University of Arizona Press, Association for Asian Studies.

Raman, B. 2015 'The politics of property in land: New planning instruments, law and popular groups in Delhi', *Journal of South Asian Development* 10(3): 369–95.

Rancière, J. 1999. *Disagreement: Politics and philosophy* (translated Julie Rose). Minneapolis: University of Minnesota Press.

Razzaz, O. 1994. 'Contestation and mutual adjustment: The process of controlling land in Yajouz, Jorden', *Law and Society Review* 28(1): 1–74.

Roy, A. 2016. 'What is urban about critical urban theory?', *Urban Geography* 37:6: 810–23.

de Souza Santos, B. 2020. 'The law of the oppressed: The construction and reproduction of legality in Pasargada'. In *Towards a New Legal Common Sense: Law, globalisation and emancipation*, 121–95. Cambridge: Cambridge University Press.

Sud, N. 2020. 'The unfixed state of unfixed land. Development and change', *Development and Change* 51(5): 1175–98.

17

Blurred boundaries and institutional activism: reflections from Brazil

Rebecca Neaera Abers

Introduction

Over the last few decades, a vibrant literature has emerged in Brazil exploring the blurred boundaries between social movements and the state. Although movements themselves had long been dabbling in institution building, academic interest in how they could influence state action began to develop in the 1990s, when Brazil gained renown for local government experimentation in participatory governance. In the 2000s, with the left running the federal government, activists from a variety of movements got involved in efforts to scale-up those experiments into national policies. As these changes occurred, social movement scholars increasingly felt the need to study the inner workings of the state. The result has been a broad-based network studying how social movements influence policy-making and democratic institutions more broadly in Brazil.[1] The network brings together perspectives ranging from the study of how formal mechanisms (such as participatory institutions) give movements access to the policy process to exploring how movement actors devise strategies to influence policy through less formal channels. These concerns are held together by a common understanding that movements and the state should not be understood as wholly separate spheres of action. Political institutions – participatory councils, bureaucracies, legislatures, parties, and so on – are potential arenas of struggle that social movements sometimes occupy in the effort to advance their causes.

I have often asked myself whether the propension of Brazilian social movement scholars to see the relation between movements and the state this way is the reflection of a particular political ontology characteristic only of that country or if it is an intellectual trend that could be transferred to other realities. Were we simply following the activists themselves, who joined progressive political parties in the 1980s, and helped them win local elections in the 1990s and the presidency from 2003–16? Is there something about the Brazilian state that makes it particularly porous to these incursions? Or should we always be looking at the state as a potential space for activism, even when 'political opportunities' are absent and institutions seem less permeable?

In 2019, I visited Johannesburg to participate in a 'Practices of the (Local) State in Urban Governance' workshop organised by Claire Bénit-Gbaffou and found myself among kindred spirits. Many participants had experienced the state 'on the inside', by working in local government jobs. After spending time inside its offices and corridors, the state could no longer be bracketed as a 'black box' for these scholar–practitioners. They spoke of it as neither a positive nor a negative ideal, but rather as a heterogeneous, internally contradictory terrain for action. An organisational space inhabited (Hallett and Ventresca 2006) by humans with variegated interests, struggles, resources, powers and beliefs, including, in some cases, themselves. In this chapter, my intention is to speak briefly to the sense of intellectual kinship while also identifying some key differences between the way the authors of this book talk about activism inside the state and the focuses and tone of the Brazilian literature.

State and movement actors in Brazil

In the late 1970s, a wave of civil society mobilisation against the dictatorship convulsed Brazil. The authoritarian regime had begun in 1964 and intensified after 1968, violently suppressing all forms of activism. Mobilisations re-emerged with the gradual liberalisation of the regime, led by a new, radicalised unionism and by a broad array of progressive movements. This early phase of organising typically posed the state as the primary adversary and affirmed the need for movements to establish autonomy – a response in part to the fact that labour unions had long been nearly totally controlled by the government. Yet, new social movements and the (pro-autonomy) 'new unionism' did not entirely turn their backs on politics. On the contrary, they were active participants in the creation of the Workers' Party (*Partido dos Trabalhadores* – PT), founded in 1980. Led by labour leader Luis Inácio Lula da Silva, the PT identified itself as a new kind of left-wing party, radically participatory and critical of the authoritarian tendencies of the traditional socialist left. Social movements found space inside the party to debate what kind of state the PT should work to create (Keck 1992).

Over time, these debates coalesced into Brazil's version of what Bénit-Gbaffou (Chapter 14, this book) calls a 'left art of city government'. It was actually transcribed into a much-read manual, *O Modo Petista de Governar* (The PT Mode of Governing) by Jorge Bittar (Bittar 1992). Dagnino et al.'s term for the emerging vision was the 'participatory democratic project' (Dagnino et al. 2006). The central idea was to associate distributive justice with the effort to build civil society. A strong state was required, not to replace society, but to help strengthen it.

The operationalisation of the vague ideas comprising the participatory democratic project initially occurred through policy experimentation in cities governed by the PT.[2] The 1990s were a period of progressive innovation in multiple policy areas in city government, including local infrastructure, housing, recycling, food, security, health care, human rights, informal economic activities, environmental protection and many other policy areas. Cities – especially those run by the Workers' Party – were thus the landscape for democratic experimentation in the 1990s. The Participatory Budget, first implemented in Porto Alegre, governed by the PT from 1989–2004, was perhaps the most renowned such experiment (Abers 2000; Baiocchi 2005). But participation was also central to many other alternative policy models invented by movements and initially implemented in progressive local governments: recycling cooperative programmes for trash pickers (Brandão 2021); participatory housing initiatives (Viana 2021); efforts to involve family farm cooperatives in food security initiatives (Amaral 2021); and so on. These programmes had in common the idea that combatting inequality required organising the poor and giving them control over the policies that were supposed to benefit them (Tatagiba and Teixeira 2021).

Brazil thus seems to contrast the South African experience in the sense that the construction of its 'left art of governing' favoured the city level in the early period. Unlike the African National Congress (ANC), the Workers' party had little national presence between 1989 and 2003, when the nation was governed by centre-right, neoliberal coalitions. Social movements did try to deepen the democratisation process at the national level, even in this less auspicious context. This began with efforts to influence the design of the 1988 Federal Constitution, with some success. Beyond re-instituting representative democracy and basic liberal rights, the Constitution expanded social rights – at least on paper – and called for participatory decision-making in various policy areas, especially health care. The health care movement then led the way in creating a nation-wide participatory system. Health activists devised a multi-scalar system of participatory institutions (from the community health post to municipal, state and national councils) that was enshrined in national legislation in the early 1990s (Dowbor 2012; Mayka 2019). This model was emulated by other movements over the course of that decade to create similar decentralised, participatory systems for social welfare, child and adolescent policies, protected area management, river basin management, and other policy areas. Yet, the struggle for effective implementation occurred largely through local initiatives.

In 2003, PT leader Lula won the presidential election. It was a moment of euphoria among progressive activists who hoped that his government would strengthen participatory institutions and adopt many other progressive ideas until then only tested locally. During Lula's first administration, innumerable activists, most of whom had experience in local government, joined the federal administration – a new Ministry of the City brought in urban reform and housing activists (Serafim 2013; Lizandra 2013), environmentalists joined the Ministry of Environment (Abers and Oliveira 2015), feminists moved into a new Secretariat for Women's Policy and anti-racist activists joined a new Secretariat for the Promotion of Racial Equality (Rodrigues 2020). The government strengthened national policy councils (Alencar et al. 2013) and national conferences, a form of short-term mass participation that involved millions in discussions of specific policy areas (Avritzer and de Souza 2013).

Over the course of this period, social movement scholars began to look ever more closely at the state. The initial focus was on participatory institutions such as participatory budgeting, policy councils, and conferences. Although some believed that they represented the advent of radical democracy, the majority explored the limitations and contradictions of these attempts to involve civil society in government decision-making. Scholars also began to focus on civil society involvement in state building beyond those institutions. Dagnino et al. described the state as a heterogenous arena in which networks of actors moved between civil society and state agencies, some defending not only the participatory democratic project, while others defended a neoliberal one (Dagnino et al. 2006). Hochstetler and Keck's study of Brazilian environmentalism similarly argued that environmental movements had been working within state structures as early as the 1970s (Hochstetler and Keck 2007).

As the heady years of the early Lula administration faded and 'real politik' prevailed, it became clear that progressive movements were minority actors in the government. They had space to defend alternative policy models, but it would always be an uphill struggle. Key events made this clear, such as when Lula farmed out the Ministry of the City to a conservative politician in an effort to placate opposition during a corruption scandal (Serafim 2013). Lula's successor, Dilma Rousseff, was more 'technocratic' than Lula and held a more fragile congressional majority, further shrinking the space for movements' influence. These changes did not, however, dampen enthusiasm for the research agenda. Indeed, they only confirmed the importance of viewing the state as a variegated organisational terrain ridden with cracks and ambiguities.

In this context, the prevailing tone of debate refused traditional caricatures and presuppositions about movements and institutions. Rather than presuming that proximity to the state automatically implied co-optation, research explored the *experience* of activism inside the state as an empirical problem, trying to identify the challenges that actors face within the constrained boundaries of government organisations. For example, in a chapter I wrote with Luciana Tatagiba (Abers and Tatagiba 2015), we examine the struggles by feminists in the Ministry of Health to protect women's rights to abortion by fine-tuning a protocol for administering pregnancy tests. Their main concern was to inform women who might discover that they were pregnant that they had certain rights, even in a country that outlawed abortion in most situations. The chapter tells the saga of this apparently minor document as it was censured by superiors and re-written over several drafts. In the end, far from an explicit pro-abortion statement, the final version instructed health care workers to guarantee women's privacy and to inform them about their rights to legal abortion in the case of rape and to health care should they suffer from complications caused by an illegal abortion. For many pro-choice feminists this would be far from a success story, but for those we interviewed in the women's health department, the tiny changes in wording could affect the lives of millions of women. Who are we to say that this kind of work is not radical?

Even as the PT came under fire and Rousseff was impeached in 2016 on fragile legal grounds in a wave of populist anger against the status quo, research into the state as an (increasingly difficult) arena of struggle continued. Two recent edited volumes published in Portuguese give a sense of how Brazilian social movement scholars have developed sophisticated theoretical frameworks for thinking about the relationship between states and movements. *Movimentos Sociais e Institucionalização* (Social movements and Institutionalisation), organised by Lavalle et al. (2019) proposes a theory of institution building through which movements create 'institutional fits' within the state: long-lasting mechanisms of influence such as new agencies, politically appointed positions or seats on participatory councils.

A central question here was how such points of access can survive the vicissitudes of electoral politics. Dowbor, for example, explores how a sub-group within the health movement struggled to promote municipal public health services (Dowbor 2019). This effort started during the military regime, and to a large extent occurred through the work of movement members who took jobs in municipal health departments or in the federal government agency responsible for health care. From multiple points of access, they built models of municipal health care services that provided preventative care on city peripheries, found ways to disseminate those models and eventually to institutionalise their own role in the health care system. This involved guaranteeing movement participation in the policy area by democratising the historic National Health Council through a 1990 law. Those defending municipal health care went further by getting written into law a permanent seat for their organisation, the National Council of Municipal Health Secretaries. Such institutionalisation efforts have paid off in recent years as the right-wing government of Jair Bolsonaro (2019–22) dismantled many participatory institutions, but was unable to shut down the participatory health councils. The Council became an important site of resistance to Bolsonaro during the COVID-19 pandemic (Almeida 2020).

Another recent anthology, *Movimentos Sociais e Políticas Públicas* (Social Movements and Public Policy), organised by Tatagiba and Teixeira (Tatagiba and Teixeira 2021), brings together a broader set of theoretical approaches, with some authors emphasising more agentic and relational approaches. There, I look at the promotion of alternative policy models for solid waste management, housing and food security as a form of 'creative action in complex ecologies' (Abers 2021a). Rather than describing the arena for action as inside the state, my work zooms out to the broader terrain for action that these actors navigated, populated by 'different powers, capacities, normative orientations, that interact both through organisational relations and through interpersonal networks' (Abers 2021a, 125). Those actors defended alternative policy models by migrating from opportunity to opportunity, from local to national agencies, from civil society organisations to international agencies, and so on. Without denying the importance of institutionalising policies and participatory institutions, the focus here is more on how actors navigate a fluctuating terrain where, over time, political shifts cause some spaces to open while others are closed.

Since 2019, when extreme right-wing President Jair Bolsonaro took office, the conditions for activism inside the federal executive branch severely contracted. Recent research has focused on government efforts to dismantle the structure of participatory decision-making that took decades to build (Bezerra et al. 2022) and on resistance to this dismantlement (Almeida 2020). Zaremberg and de Almeida´s study shows how feminists in Brazil concentrated on blocking efforts to reduce abortion rights in the Brazilian legislature and the judiciary (Zaremberg and de Almeida 2022). As progressive movements have thus been shut out of federal government policy processes, they have sought out other arenas for action, in both state and society. At the same time, institutional activists (as well as many bureaucrats simply attempting to do their job) within the national executive branch suffered systematic persecution under Bolsonaro. Recent scholarship has shown that in this context they have devised new strategies, better described as subversion and resistance (Lotta et al. 2023).

Blurred boundaries and inhabited institutions

Local officials and the Struggle to Transform the City presents a dynamic perspective on cities and urban planning that resonates deeply with the Brazilian literature on social movements and the state. The chapters in this book lay out a vision of the state as a terrain constructed of heterogeneous configurations of people, rules and relations. It is neither abstract and monolithic, nor exactly contextual, in the sense that the chapters view human actors as both constrained by and creators of that terrain. As could only be the case when people who have worked inside the state go on to write about their experiences, the book hardly describes government programmes as a magic bullet. Indeed, working inside the state is described as arduous, as the title to Philip Harrison's chapter (Chapter 2 in this book), 'Welcome to Alcatraz' aptly suggests. The task for the activist inside the grey halls of government institutions is not to commandeer grandiose change, but to chisel at giant boulders, hoping to open cracks and set off waves of tiny vibrations.

This book evokes a resistance to binaries that also pervades the Brazilian state–society literature. The choice often posed by the literature between radical action outside and submission to the status quo inside institutions is hard to find in this book. Instead, actors and the authors writing about them question the very boundary between state-ness and society-ness, exploring the 'formalisation of society and informalisation of the state' (Bénit-Gbaffou, Introduction). Awareness that the state is a hostile terrain controlled by powerful forces does not lead to the automatic presumption that insiders must submit to those forces. When Pingo and Bénit-Gbaffou (Chapter 5) 'interrogate how entering a new location by partaking in the City Council does or does not change activists and movements' forms of action, and to what extent it reshapes or not their goals', they suggest that 'deradicalisation' may result from institutional activism, but as an empirical finding, rather than a foundational assumption. Moreover, they suggest that lowering the heat of demands on the state may be a strategic decision that, in itself, requires courage. Inversely, when Demeestère (Chapter 7) and Modiba (Chapter 6) explore how societal groups 'act like the state', and also influence the state, they seem to question the very distinction between state-ness and society-ness. This rejection of binaries does not result from conceptual confusion – we know that the state exists and operates as a structure of domination – but from an awareness of fuzzy borders and significant overlaps that mean that any ideal form of the state (whatever your theory for it is) will be rarely encountered in practice.

Another idea that this book has in common with the Brazilian literature is a refusal of the 'black box' approach to the state. This book seeks to explore the inner workings of the 'instruments' of local state action understood not as 'anonymous forces', but rather creations and tools of human actors – in both state and society. Lighting up the state's interior includes exploring how even state actors find it difficult to navigate the opaqueness of the multi-layered and historically sedimented state apparatus within which they work (Mushongera's and Smith's Chapters 12 and 13 respectively). Knowledge instruments constructed by actors in different agencies and branches of the state constitute practical compromises that construct and reveal dominant rationalities. Smith's chapter (Chapter 13) analyses similar contradictions between different instruments for monitoring and evaluating municipal workers, that ultimately hamper policy oversight.

How rules and roles become institutionalised, in the sense that they are routinely reproduced and hence difficult to change, is of course a central question in political sociology and political science. Often, however, the question becomes (again) an assumption, and scholars forget that institutions are human constructs. In Brazil, the constructed nature of institutions has been cruelly demonstrated by the ease with which the Bolsonaro administration has dismantled wholesale what we blithely called 'participatory institutions', carefully set in place over the course of decades and so easily toppled. The extent to which they are 'resilient' (Almeida 2020) is, of course, affected by their institutional status – Bolsonaro has been unable to gut participatory councils that were enacted by congress. Such resilience, however, is not an anonymous force: what stays when politics cannot dismantle institutions are people. As Hallett and Ventresca put it, institutions are inhabited (Hallett and Ventresca 2006). Their desks and offices are occupied by humans with worries, interests, capacities and beliefs, and those things affect not just what the people do but how the institutions work. So much so that one of the main tasks of the government employee is simply to understand 'who is who in the zoo', as Mushongera puts it in this book (Chapter 12). The next step is to identify potential allies and collaborators, a task discussed in several chapters in this book (Bénit-Gbaffou, Chapter 3; Rubin, Chapter 4; Charlton, Chapter 10).

On agency and intentionality

A final set of ideas that I found refreshingly familiar in this book is the way the authors talk about agency. Sociology has largely offered us (once more) a binary choice between the view of society as the result of infinite individual actions and one in which individuals are nothing more than cogs in structural wheels that they, at best, help reproduce. In practice, neither of these approaches provides much space for creativity: if actors in structural approaches are but victims of social forces, the rational actor approach basically preordains what an individual should do based on rational calculation (Hay 2008, 61).

I have found the work of pragmatist author Hans Joas to be a helpful escape from the binary (Joas 1996). Joas proposes that action is not just sometimes, but rather normally, 'creative', the term he applies to action simultaneously situated in context and intelligent/reflexive. Key to Joas's thought is the idea that creative acts do not represent the actor's ability to free themselves from cultural norms, social roles, political rules or material distributions of resources. Instead, context produces the raw material on which actors rely through what Rubin calls 'taking advantage of context' (Chapter 4). Following Dewey (1922), Joas makes no clear distinction between the moment of routine or habit and the use of intelligence or the will. Practical experimentation occurs only because the actor has predispositions and values acquired in social contexts and life stories. Reflexive capacities can only be used on the basis of pre-existing resources and skills. Joas's approach allows us to avoid the tendency to think of agency as a sort of superhuman escape from structures. Though they do not cite Joas, the chapters in this book similarly suggest that creativity is an everyday struggle that includes frustration and failure (as in Klug's Chapter 8) and even burnout (Bénit-Gbaffou, Introduction).

Joas also disrupts the understanding of action as an application of 'means' to previously defined ends. He argues that goals are more often defined in the process of action. In my own work on institutional activism, I have applied this idea to the notion of the 'contentious cause'. Activism is distinguished from other forms of action in that it is guided by contentious causes, defined as 'a collection of ideas that propose some kind of social, political or cultural transformation or that questions perceived undesirable transformations' (Abers 2021b, 333). Joas's pragmatist approach to action would suggest, however, that causes do not predate action, but rather are constructed in the process of acting. In my research on institutional activists in Brazil, I show, for example, how bureaucrats initially critical of a policy later come to defend it as it comes under threat (Abers 2021b).

Bénit-Gbaffou´s (Chapter 14) discussion of causes goes further in this direction by noting that causes can be defined 'opportunistically', that is, as activists operating inside bureaucracies often encounter opportunities to address specific issues that cohere with their broader policy agendas, but which they may not have formulated as part of their causes until the opportunity appears. Another interesting twist that Bénit-Gbaffou brings to the table when discussing the construction of causes by institutional activists is the suggestion that they often present their causes as less radical than they actually are. This strategy seeks to avoid alerting superiors or other authorities to the destabilising potential of their activism.

Joas's criticism of the means–ends view of social action is also coherent with various discussions in this book about unintended consequences. If actors are always re-defining their ends as they experiment with means, they can also lose control of the results of their actions. Various chapters in this book emphasise this darker side of unintended consequences. Bouyat's analysis (Chapter 9) of the contested production of state registration systems for school learners, for example, shows how well-intentioned efforts of public servants ultimately produced 'foreignness' and institutionalised xenophobia. Acts of 'seeing and unseeing' (Charlton, Chapter 10) by state officials can have violent consequences, as strikingly described in Demeestère's account of 'the bureaucratisation of xenophobia' (Chapter 7).

Beyond exploring how individuals engage in tiny acts of creativity in their everyday 'institutional work' (Lawrence et al. 2009), the chapters emphasise that agency is not something people do alone. Although sometimes it might feel lonely, activism is never really effective except when it involves others. This makes it important to understand not just the strategies of individuals, but the process through which alliances and coalitions are formed (Bénit-Gbaffou, Introduction). Some networks act intentionally, with a clear goal in mind, as when groups linked to the Anti Privatisation Forum decided to field a movement member in a local election (Pingo and Bénit-Gbaffou, Chapter 5). Other times, outcomes 'emerge' through relational processes themselves, as when 'complex and ambivalent interactions between local mobilised South African shopkeepers and governmental agencies between 2008 and 2013' resulted in the construction of xenophobic legislation to regulate the informal economy (Demeestère, Chapter 7). The case told by Demeestère, it should be noted, also reminds us that creative action does not necessarily promote inclusion and social justice. The protagonists of the stories progressive planners tell confront human adversaries who also creatively form networks and mobilise resources available to them to promote their goals.

Brazil/South Africa

The synchrony between the approach presented in this book and the Brazilian literature on state and society is suggestive of a fruitful research agenda. Despite profoundly different histories, certain parallels between the two countries make for intriguing comparison. The end of apartheid in South Africa and the end of the military era in Brazil occurred more or less at the same global moment of political repositioning. While in the north, left-wing models of government were deeply shaken by the fall of the Berlin Wall, in the 1990s both South Africa and Brazil became international symbols of the possibilities for inclusive political change. These efforts, in both cases, were led by mass-based political parties and charismatic leaders identified with pro-democracy struggles. Despite substantial advances, progressive actors and projects associated with those struggles ended up implementing conservative economic policies and were tainted by corruption. Certainly, the waves of hope and despair in the two countries follow different rhythms and intensities, and are propelled by different causes, but those differences also would make for fascinating comparative analysis.

One point of comparison has to do with how the 'left art of governing' was built through interactions between state and non-state actors. As suggested earlier, in the Brazilian case, the advances of the PT national governments (2003–16) were largely the fruit of decades of experimentation in local level governments during a period of neoliberal and conservative national administrations. Observing these initiatives, social scientists engaged an intellectual conversation that included and compared multiple policy areas. Urban planning, housing, health, social assistance, children's rights, women's rights, the rights of the elderly, human rights, and the environment are just some of the policy areas that have been framed in terms of relationships between social movements and states. This may explain why the Brazilian literature has given substantial attention to policy subsystems or networks that bring together state actors, academics, social movements, and other organisations around particular policy areas. The literature has shown that while movement actors may move in and out of state positions (and between local, state and national levels), they usually remain members of these policy subsystems, in which they seek to defend their particular policy models. Those subsystems are thus also arenas for struggle in the long term (Abers et al. 2018).

As both countries undergo rocky post-transition periods, marked by huge corruption scandals and dramatic austerity politics, the strength and multiplicity of Brazilian policy subsystems may signal greater state capacity to withstand political crisis. Despite the dramatic scale of corruption in Brazil revealed by the Car Wash investigation, those practices did not seem to have the devastating effect on the Brazilian state that has occurred in South Africa. Writing before the Car Wash scandal, Evans and Heller argued that that although Brazil and South Africa had 'similar political trajectories' (Evans and Heller 2015), Brazil was better at 'delivering wellbeing during recent decades of democratic rule' (Evans and Heller 2015, 689). They explain the difference as likely resulting from a stronger relationship between state and civil society actors in Brazil – precisely the relationships that I have been describing throughout this chapter. Few studies compare the two countries from the perspective of state capacity[3] so it is hard to say whether this stronger starting point helped prevent the hollowing out of the state that has occurred in South Africa. Nonetheless, it does seem fair to say that despite the dramatic economic crisis in Brazil, key areas of notable state capacity – such as the universal health system – have continued to supply crucial support to citizens.

On the other hand, it is worth noting that recent events remind us of another difference between the two countries that may affect the future of the progressive state agenda: the capacity to dismantle pre-transition authoritarian structures. While South Africa engaged in a major effort at transitional justice, Brazil's slow transition failed to enact a clear rupture with the past. The 1988 Constitution did not establish clear limits on military participation in politics and in practice, efforts to put the military under civil control have been fragile. Although for decades, most observers believed that the armed forces had accepted democracy, the Bolsonaro period changed that perception. Bolsonaro, whose administration nominated thousands of military personnel to policy positions, expressed great nostalgia for the authoritarian period. The atavistic notion that his government was elected to combat communist tendencies was a central force in his effort to dismantle participatory institutions along with all policies and programmes that empowered civil society organisations. For most of his administration, it seemed that he did not have enough support from the military to conduct a self-coup, as he often implied to desire. Nonetheless, key military personnel supported his effort to undermine the 2022 elections and possibly conspired to overthrow Lula's presidency. Although under Lula's third administration, activists are returning to the nation's capital in throngs to participate in the new government, Bolsonaro's continued popularity and the quasi-coup attempt of 8 January 2023 put a shadow over efforts to restart the long process of democratising the Brazilian state.

Although the historical and political differences between the two countries are thus significant, Brazilian and South African scholars share the experience of both hope and despair about the possibilities for social movements to transform the state. This shared legacy may, in the end, help explain the affinity between our work. We know that activism inside the state is possible, but it is rough terrain and success, if it comes, will likely be fragile, potentially undone by the creativity of adversaries. That is why it is so important that people keep doing it.

Notes

1 The Democracy and Participation network now brings together dozens of researchers and has organised five editions of the Participation, Democracy and Public Policy Conference.

2 Brazil's political system is federative, composed of municipalities, states and the union. Each has an elected executive and a legislative branch, uni-cameral at the municipal and state level, and bi-cameral at the national level.

3 But see Hochstetler (2020).

References

Abers, R.N. 2000. *Inventing Local Democracy: Grassroots politics in Brazil*. Boulder: Lynne Rienner Pub.

Abers, R.N. 2021a. 'Ação Criativa em ecologias complexas: A construção da autoridade prática de políticas associativas'. In *Movimentos Sociais e Políticas Públicas*, edited by L. Tatagiba and A.C. Chaves Teixeira, 121–42. São Paulo: UNESP.

Abers, R.N. 2021b. 'Institutions, networks and activism inside the state: Women's health and environmental policy in Brazil', *Critical Policy Studies* 15(3): 330–49.

Abers, R.N. and Oliveira, M.S. 2015. 'Nomeações políticas no ministério do meio ambiente (2003–2013): Interconexões entre ONGs, partidos e governos', *Opinião Pública* 21(2): 336–64.

Abers, R.N. and Tatagiba, L. 2015. 'Institutional activism: Mobilising for women's health from inside the Brazilian bureaucracy'. In *Social Movement Dynamics: New perspectives on theory and research from Latin America*, edited by F.M. Rossi and M. von Bülow, 73–101. London: Ashgate.

Abers, R.N., Silva, M.K. and Tatagiba, L. 2018. 'Movimentos sociais e políticas públicas: repensando atores e oportunidades políticas', *Lua Nova* 105: 15–46.

Alencar, J., Cruxên, I., Fonseca, I., Pires, R. and Ribeiro, U. 2013. 'Participação social e desigualdades nos conselhos nacionais', *Sociologias* 15 (32). Available at: http://seer.ufrgs.br/sociologias/article/view/38674. Accessed 2 August 2023.

Almeida, D.C.R. 2020. 'Resiliência institucional: Para onde vai a participação nos conselhos nacionais de saúde e dos direitos da mulher?', *Caderno CRH*. Available at: https://www.scielo.br/scielo.php?script=sci_arttext&pid=S0103-49792020000100502. Accessed 3 August 2023.

Amaral, L.A. 2021. 'Entre enquadramentos e agências: Gestão do programa de aquisição de alimentos pela ótica do ativismo institucional'. In *Movimentos Sociais e Políticas Públicas*, edited by L. Tatagiba and A.C. Chaves Teixeira, 237–360. São Paulo: UNESP.

Avritzer, L. and de Souza, C.H.L. (eds). 2013. *Conferências Nacionais: Atores, dinâmicas participativas e efetividade*. Brasília: IPEA.

Baiocchi, G. 2005. *Militants and citizens: The politics of participatory democracy in Porto Alegre*. San Francisco: Stanford University Press.

Bezerra, C.P., Rodrigues, M. and de Melo Romão, W. 2022. 'Conselhos de políticas públicas no governo bolsonaro: Impactos do decreto 9.759/2019 dobre a participação da sociedade civil.' In *Participação e Ativismos: Entre retrocessos e resistências*, edited by L. Tatagiba, D.C.R. de Almeida, A.G. Lavalle and M.K. Silva, 37–64. Porto Alegre: Editora Zouk.

Bittar, J. 1992. *O Modo Petista de Governar*. São Paulo: Teoria e Debate.

Brandão, I.R. 2021. 'Efeito ricochete: Trajetórias técnicopolíticas e a criação de novos modelos de políticas públicas'. In *Ativismo Institucional: Criatividade e luta na burocracia Brasileira*, edited by R.N. Abers, 89–122. Brasilia: Editora UnB. Available at: https://books.scielo.org/id/y9zwc. Accessed 2 August 2023.

Dagnino, E., Olvera, A.J. and Panfichi, A. 2006. 'Para uma outra leitura da disputa pela construção democrática na América Latina'. In *A Disputa Pela Construção Democrática Na América Latina*, edited by E. Dagnino, J.A. Olvera and A. Panfichi, 13–92. São Paulo: Paz e Terra.

Dewey, J. 1922. *Human Nature and Conduct*. New York: The Modern Library.

Dowbor, M. 2012. 'Arte Da Institucionalização: Estratégias de mobilização dos sanitaristas (1974–2006)'. PhD Dissertation. São Paulo: Universidade de São Paulo.

Dowbor, M. 2019. 'Escapando das incertezas do jogo eleitoral: A construção de encaixes e domínio de agência do movimento municipalista de saúde'. In *Movimentos Sociais e Institucionalização: Políticas sociais, raça e gênero no Brasil pós-transição*, edited by A.G. Lavalle, E. Carlos, M. Dowbor and J. Szwako, 89–118. Rio de Janeiro: Eduerj.

Evans, P. and Heller, P. 2015. 'Human development, state transformation, and the politics of the developmental state'. In *The Oxford Handbook of Transformations of the State*, edited by S. Leibfried, E. Huber, M. Lange, J.D. Levy and J.D. Stephens, 679–701. Oxford: Oxford University Press.

Hallett, T. and Ventresca, M.J. 2006. 'Inhabited institutions: Social interactions and organisational forms in Gouldner's Patterns of Industrial Bureaucracy', *Theory and Society* 35: 213–36.

Hay, C. 2008. 'Constructivist institutionalism'. In *The Oxford Handbook of Political Institutions*, edited by R.A.W. Rhodes, S.A. Binder and B.A. Rockman, 56–74. Oxford: Oxford Handbooks Online.

Hochstetler, K. 2020. *Political Economies of Energy Transition: Wind and solar power in Brazil and South Africa*. Cambridge: Cambridge University Press.

Hochstetler, K. and Keck, M.E. 2007. *Greening Brazil: Environmental activism in state and society*. Durham and London: Duke University Press.

Joas, H. 1996. *The Creativity of Action*. Chicago: University of Chicago Press.

Keck, M.E. 1992. *The Workers' Party and Democratisation in Brazil*. New Haven: Yale University Press.

Lavalle, A.G., Carlos, E., Dowbor, M. and Szwako, J. (eds). 2019. *Movimentos Sociais e Institucionalização: Políticas sociais, raça e gênero no Brasil pós-transição*. Rio de Janeiro: Eduerj.

Lawrence, T.B., Suddaby, R. and Leca, B. 2009. 'Introduction: Theorising and studying institutional work'. In *Institutional Work: Actors and agency in institutional studies of organisations*, edited by T.B. Lawrence, R. Suddaby and B. Leca, 1–27. Cambridge: Cambridge University Press.

Lizandra, S. 2013. 'Participação No Governo Lula: As pautas da reforma urbana no Ministério das Cidades (2003–2010)'. Unpublished PhD thesis. Brazil: State University of Campinas.

Lotta, G.S., de Lima, I.A., Fernandez, M.V., Silveira, M.C., Pedote, J. and Guaranha, O.L.C. 2023. 'A resposta da burocracia ao contexto de retrocesso democrático: Uma análise da atuação de servidores federais durante o Governo Bolsonaro', *Revista Brasileira de Ciência Política*, forthcoming.

Mayka, L. 2019. *Building Participatory Institutions in Latin America: Reform coalitions and institutional change*. Cambridge and New York: Cambridge University Press.

Rodrigues, C. 2020. *Afro-Latinos em Movimento: Protesto negro e ativismo institucional no Brasil e na Colômbia*. Curitiba: Editora Appris.

Serafim, L. 2013. 'Participação No Governo Lula: As pautas da reforma urbana no Ministério das Cidades (2003–2010)'. PhD Dissertation. Campinas: Universidade Estadual de Campinas.

Tatagiba, L. and Chaves Teixeira, A.C. 2021. 'Movimentos sociais e políticas públicas no cíclo dos governos petistas: A controversa novidade dos programas associativos'. In *Movimentos Sociais e Políticas Públicas*, edited by L. Tatagiba and A.C. Chaves Teixeira, 23–48. São Paulo: UNESP.

Viana, R.R. 2021. 'Programa minha casa minha vida: Entidades ativismo institucional no acesso à terra urbanizada'. In *Ativismo Institucional: Criatividade e luta na burocracia Brasileira*, edited by R.N. Abers, 255–86. Brasilia: Editora UnB. Available at: https://books.scielo.org/id/y9zwc. Accessed 2 August 2023.

Zaremberg, G. and de Almeida, D.C.R. 2022. *Feminisms in Latin American: Pro-choice nested networks in Mexico and Brazil*. Cambridge and New York: Cambridge University Press.

Index

Abers, R. 51–2
abortion rights 461
academic-activists 295, 301, 304, 306, 307–8, 311–12
academic studies 3–4
activism
  academic-activists 295, 301, 304, 306, 307–8, 311–12
  bureaucratic activism 51, 81–103, 393
  civil society networks and 53–4
  definition 51–2
  engagement with eThekwini Water and Sanitation (EWS) 301–6, 317–19
  governmental activism 51
  location of 54
  see also activists in the State; institutional activism
activists in the State 49–80
  community engagement in City Parks 64–71
  framing 50–6
  homeless shelter provision 57–64, 281
  networks 70
  policy instruments 55–6, 69, 71–4, 75–6
  suspicion of 49–50
  what they know and do best 54–5
  see also institutional activism
Actor-Network Theory (ANT) 326
administrative hierarchy 43
advocacy 60–2, 67–8
affordable housing 71–4, 268–9, 278, 279, 282
African National Congress (ANC) 30, 86, 184
agency 20, 45, 69, 84, 122–3, 201–4, 463–5
agents of the state, subjectification 238–42, 249–58
Aggrawal, Deoki 444, 445
Alexandra Renewal Project (ARP) 36, 37
alternative policies (alterpolicies) 6
Anti-Eviction Campaign 163, 178
Anti-Privatisation Forum (APF) 106, 109–14, 302
Appelbaum, A. 272, 276, 283–4
auto-ethnography 28, 199–200

backyarding housing prototype 281–2
Bad Buildings Programme 205
Bangalore Development Authority (BDA) 436
Bangkok, Chinatown 284
bargaining tools 61
Basavalingappa 434
Baskin, Julian 37
Bayat, A. 127
Bénit-Gbaffou, C. 238, 240, 241
Benjamin, S. 399, 401, 410
Better Buildings Programme 205
Bizos, George 39
Black Economic Empowerment programmes 171
Blame Game: Spin, bureaucracy, and self-preservation in government (Hood) 45
blitz-style operations 36
Blue Drop Assessment 334
Blue Moonlight evictions 197
Bolsonaro, Jair 460, 461, 463, 467
Bond, P. 295, 303, 304, 305, 306
Borraz, O. 9
Bourdieu, P. 16–17, 162, 164, 395, 397
Bovu, Dan 124
Brazilian social movements 455–69
  abortion rights 461
  agency 463–5
  healthcare system 53–4, 457–8, 459, 460
  intentionality 463–5
  participatory institutions 456–61, 462
  Workers' Party (*Partidos dos Trabalhadores*) 456–8
Breckenridge, K. 406
budgets 41–2, 44, 75, 92, 117, 275, 335–6
bureaucracy/bureaucrats
  bureaucratic activism 51, 81–103, 393
  bureaucratic identity 97–8
  bureaucratic sedimentation 409–410
  bureaucratisation of xenophobia 163, 165–8
  construction of a localised bureaucratic order 168–77
  decentred approach 166
  dis-enclosing localised bureaucratic orders 177–83
  field of action 28, 42–5, 395
  fuzzy jobs 391
  guerrillas in 396
  interface with politics 42–5
  intermediary level 11, 389–92
  proto-bureaucracy 165, 166, 176, 177, 181–3
  tactical repertoires 28–9, 45
  top-down/bottom-up model 165
  see also porous bureaucracies

business associations 188–90
business inspectors 188–9

cause
contentious 52, 464
definition 51–2
framing 397–9
Central Johannesburg Partnership (CJP) 57, 205
Centre for Civil Society (CCS) 306
Centre for Learning on Evaluation and Results for Anglophone Africa (CLEAR-AA) 362–4, 370, 371
Centre for Urbanism and the Built Environment Studies (CUBES) 200, 219
chambers of commerce 188–90
Chinatown, Bangkok 284
Chowdari, Ajit 444–5
Citizens Voice project 315
City Transformation Unit 81, 82, 89, 92, 94, 95, 96
civic governmentality 127
civil rights movement 3
civil society networks 53–4
Clavel, P. 1–2, 52–3
clientelist organisations 143, 155–6
Coalition Against Water Privatisation 303
Coastal Enterprises, Inc. (CEI) 421
colonialism 15, 429
committee system *see* Section 79 Committees
community
community development corporations (CDCs) 420, 421
Community Policing Fora 167
community scholars 306
park management 64–71
compliance 369, 372, 374–5
Concerned Citizen's Forum 302
Conference on Alternative State and Local Policies 424
contentious cause 52, 464
contextual issues
evictions 204–6
homeless shelters 58–60
inclusionary housing 85–7, 95–7
parks as social objects 65–6
Contracts Management Unit (CMU) 330
contract-state 387–8
Converse, Jim 421
co-production 65, 137–8
Corbin, Brian 421
Corporate Strategy Unit 376–7
corporatisation model 328
Corridors of Freedom 265–90
affordable housing 268–9, 278, 279, 282
backyarding prototype 281–2
hierarchy of privilege 284
homeless shelters 57–64, 281
inclusionary housing 86, 87–8
invisibility 268–70, 283–6
Louis Botha Avenue 270–2, 279–80
private sector developers 278, 279, 280, 281
pro-poor policy 268, 277–82
social housing 276, 279, 280–1, 283–4
target demographic 273–7
transitioning neighbourhood 270–2
corruption 82, 318, 389–90, 466
creative acts 460, 463–4
creative power 91, 92
critical document analysis 200
CUBES 200, 219

Dabas, Ashok 444
Daley, Richard M. 426
Dalit Sangharsh Samiti (DSS) 434, 436
Davies, Rob 187
decentred conception of power 366–7
deceptive lens 297, 308–12, 317, 405, 407
delivering state 12
democracy, demand for 14
Democratic Alliance–Economic Freedom Fighters coalition 96–7, 148, 216, 222
Department of Basic Education (DBE) 235–6, 241, 245, 249–58
Department of Home Affairs (DHA) 235–6, 241, 245, 252–3
Department of Human Settlements 85, 86, 91, 93
Department of Planning, Monitoring and Evaluation (DPME) 368–9, 370, 371
Department of Small Business Development (DSBD) 189–90
Department of Trade and Industry (DTI)
Black Economic Empowerment programmes 171
informal economy policy 185–6, 188
Licensing of Businesses Bill 2013 161–2, 186–8, 189
Department of Water and Sanitation (DWS) 332–3
de-radicalisation 398
Desai, A. 303
developmental state 14
Development Facilitation Act 1995 35
Development Planning and Urban Management (DPUM) 27, 32–7
domestication 398
domination 164–5, 168, 292, 311
Doussard, Marc 425, 427
Dowbor, M. 83, 100–1
Ducharme, Donna 426
Dutta, S.J. 366
Duyvendak, J.W. 54

Economic Freedom Fighters (EFF) 146–7
Democratic Alliance–Economic Freedom Fighters coalition 96–7, 148, 216, 222
economic migrants 184
efficiency 14, 15, 328, 358, 366
embeddedness 84, 431
environmental studies 51
Environment and Infrastructure and Services Department (EISD) 330–1, 337, 347–8, 352
equity planners 84
eThekwini Water and Sanitation (EWS) 291–324
activist engagement 301–6, 317–19
billing system 308, 310
Citizens Voice project 315

deceptive lens 297, 308–12, 317, 405, 407
Free Basic Water (FBW) provision 298
Geographic Information System (GIS) 296, 299
Ingonyama Trust 293, 299–301, 314, 319
interest, ideology and image 308–12
ethics of responsibility/conviction 127
Everyday Speculation 430
evictions 197–229
Anti-Eviction Campaign 163, 178
bad buildings 30, 37–8, 205
Blue Moonlight case 197
contextualising the issue 204–6
cycle of evictions 213
decayed occupied buildings 205, 206
depiction and treatment of evictees 221–2
genealogy of policy documents 207–17
Grootboom and Daniels v. Scribante cases 198
managed care model 209, 213
notice to vacate 265–7
private and individual landlords 222–4
problem characterisation 218–21
progressive approach 198
Special Process for the Relocation of Evictees (SPRE) 198, 199, 204, 207–17, 222, 224
Temporary Emergency Accommodation Provision (TEAP) policy 198, 199, 207–17, 222, 223, 224, 225
Thembelihle 112–14, 125, 126–7
transitional residential accommodation 209
as a wicked problem 202, 219
exchanges 93–4

Fainstein, Susan 425
feminist issues 51, 459
Ferguson, J. 367, 429, 451, 453
field of action 28, 42–5, 397
Finance Linked Individual Subsidy Programme (FLISP) housing 280
Finch, Herbert 423
Flynn, Raymond 422
formalisation of society 137–9
Foucault, M. 237, 238–9
framing issues 50–6, 92, 202, 218–24, 225, 332–4, 397–9, 402–3
fuzzy jobs 391

Geographic Information System (GIS) 296, 299
Germiston Traders Partnership (GEMTRAP) 141, 142, 150
Gounden, Teddy 296, 300
governance, urban 7–10, 50–6, 137, 204–6 *see also* street trader governance structures
governing
by discharge 137
by numbers 408
government
governmental activism 51
left art of 5, 387–417, 429–30, 432–4, 443–50, 451–3, 457, 465–6
monitoring and evaluation systems 367–8
problematics of 239
role in water policy 332–3
technologies 239–30
urban governance and 7–10
gray zones 139
Greater Johannesburg Metropolitan Council (GJMC) 328
Green Drop Assessment 334
Grootboom and Daniels v. Scribante cases 198
'Group' approach 329, 330
Group Strategy, Policy, Communication and Research (GSPCR) unit 330, 362, 363, 372–7
Growth and Development Strategy (GDS) 30, 334–5, 337–9, 362, 412
Growth Management Strategy 34
Gugulethu Business Forum (GBF) 178
Gulati, Abjit Singh 445
Gupta, A. 8

Hancock, Loni 419
Hartford, Carbone 425
healthcare system 53–4, 457–8, 459, 460
hidden transcript 292, 311, 405
hierarchy
administrative 43
of privilege 270, 284
Home Affair-isation of school 236, 237–44, 245–6, 247, 252–3, 258–9
homeless shelters 57–64, 281
Hood, C. 45
housing
affordable housing 71–4, 268–9, 278, 279, 282
backyarding prototype 281–2
Finance Linked Individual Subsidy Programme (FLISP) housing 280
inclusionary housing 81–103
Inner City Housing Implementation Plan (ICHIP) 72–3, 285
invisibility 268–70, 283–6
private sector developers 278, 281
pro-poor housing 268, 277–82
public (state) sector 88, 91
purchase of land 73, 74
social housing 276, 279, 280–1, 283–4
transitioning neighbourhood 270–2
see also evictions
Houtzager, P.P. 83, 100–1
humanity 97–100
hybrid institutions 138

identity
bureaucratic 97–8
politics 52
racialised 99–100
iGoli 2002 Plan 328
immigration control, school-based 237, 244–58
incentives 94, 374–5, 379, 382
inclusionary housing 81–103
Indian porous bureaucracies 399–400, 401, 429–54
constructing land tenure for squatters' 434–43
left art of government 429–30, 432–4, 443–50, 451–3

Neighbourhood as Factory (NAF) 443–50
situating state practices in space, time, and scale 430–1
informal conversations 94–5
informal economy 185–6, 188
informalisation, the state 137–9
informal networks 124–6
informal settlements 38, 39–41
Thembelihle 112–14
water services 339, 352, 354
Informal Traders' Forum 144–5
Infrastructure and Services Department (ISD) 330–1
Ingonyama Trust 293, 299–301, 314, 319
Inner City Discussion and Monitoring Forum Meeting 38
Inner City Housing Implementation Plan (ICHIP) 72–3, 285
Inner-City Property Scheme (ICPS) 205, 209
Inner-City Regeneration Charter 37–8, 205
inside activism 50–6
institutional activism 3, 20, 50–6, 63–4, 69–71, 84
agency and structure interaction 69
compared to street activism 393–6
covert resistance to policy 395–6
fields 28, 42–5, 395
framing the cause 397–9
heuristic value 392–9
intensity of life at work 396–7
networks 50, 51, 53, 70, 74
policy instruments 393–4
suspicion of 49–50
see also activists in the State
institutional culture 252–3
institutional ethnography 28
institutional fits 459–500
institutionalisation
bottom-down and top-down understandings 411–13
of the cause 398
definition 56
progressive change 410–14
response to political opportunities 109–14
social movements 106, 107–8, 120, 128–9
institutional xenophobia *see* school-based institutional xenophobia
Integrated Development Plan (IDP) 334, 338, 340–2
Integrated Urban Development Framework 87
intentions/intentionality 242, 403–6, 463–5
invisibility 268–70, 283–6, 291–2
iron law of oligarchy 106, 128

Jackson, Matt 57–64
Joas, Hans 463–4
Jo'burg 2030 strategy 29
Johannesburg City Parks and Zoo (JCPZ) 64–71
Johannesburg Development Agency (JDA) 39, 57, 205, 209
Development Facilitation Unit (DFU) 58, 71
Johannesburg Property Company (JPC) 35, 205, 209, 281
Johannesburg Roads Agency (JRA) 67
Johannesburg Social Housing Committee (JOSHCO) 91–2, 209, 280–1
Johannesburg Strategic Infrastructure Platform (JSIP) 92
Johannesburg Water (JW) 328, 331, 340, 342, 353
'jointed' saving-investments 449
Jones, B. 16, 17, 423
justice
in cities 6
participatory and redistributive dimensions 398–9
socio-historical 242–4

Katzenstein, M. 107–8
Key Performance Areas (KPAs) 350–3, 365
Key Performance Indicators (KPIs) 91, 93, 351, 352, 356, 365, 390, 407, 413
Khayelitsha General Agreement 176–7, 181–3
Khayelitsha Somali Retailers Association (KSRA) 173–7
Khumalo, MaDudu 296, 306
Kraushaar, Robert 425
Krishnanna 439
Krumholz, N. 1–2
Kucinich, Dennis 420

land banks 93
Lascoumes, P. 55
Lawyers for Human Rights (LHR) 200, 211, 212, 213, 220, 222, 223, 224
leadership
selection 115–17
state rationalities 240–1
see also street trader governance structures
left art of government 5, 387–417, 429–30, 432–4, 443–50, 451–3, 457, 465–6
Le Galès, P. 9, 55, 203
Lehman Brothers collapse 30–1
Le Petitcorps, C. 257
Licensing of Businesses Bill 2013 161–2, 186–8, 189
Local Economic Development (LED) 141
Local Government Group 118–19
Look-Out Hill communiqué 182–3
Lula da Silva, Luis Inácio 456, 458–9, 467
Lynd, Alice and Staughton 421

MacLeod, Neil 295–6, 297, 298, 300, 303, 305, 317–18
Madiba, Zodwa 115, 118, 119
Madikizela-Mandela, Winnie 36–7
Makoba, Gcina 304
malicious compliance 374–5
managed care model 209, 213
managerialism 366
Manqele, Christina 303
Mashaba, Herman 73, 96, 222
Mashatile, Paul 37
Masondo, Amos 30–1, 37, 38, 40, 371
Mayoral Steering Committee on Informal Trade 146–7, 148
Mazibuko et al. v. the City of Johannesburg 303
Mbeki, Thabo 30
measurement discipline 375–6

Meer, Fatima 302
Mehta, P.B. 451, 452
Memorandum of Understanding 146, 245–6
Meny-Gibert, S. 390
Metcalfe, Mary 39
Metropolitan Evangelical Services (MES) 209
Miller, P. 239–40
Mistra Urban Futures Programme 28
Miya, Bhayiza 114, 115, 116, 119–20, 126–7
Mkhonza, Joyce 118
Mokonyane, Nomvula 40
monitoring and evaluation (M&E) 361–85
  Centre for Learning on Evaluation and Results for Anglophone Africa (CLEAR-AA) 362–4, 370, 371
  compliance culture 369, 372, 374–5
  Corporate Strategy Unit 376–7
  decentred conception of power 366–7
  Department of Planning, Monitoring and Evaluation (DPME) 368–9, 370, 371
  difference between monitoring and evaluation 365
  Government-wide (GWM&E) systems 367–8
  Group Strategy Unit 362, 363, 372–7
  incentives 374–5, 379, 382
  measurement discipline 375–6
  municipal legislature 377–81
  National Evaluation System 368–9
  New Public Management (NPM) 366–7
  scorecards 44, 347–56, 374, 379
  Section 79 Committees 362, 377, 379, 380–1
  terminology 365
Msimanga, Solly 148
Msweli, Ednick 296
Mthethwa, Nathi 38
Municipal Finance Management Act 2003 44, 369
Municipal Structures Act 1999 379
Municipal Systems Act 2003 369

Naidoo, Orlean 306
National African Federated Chamber of Commerce and Industry (NAFCOC) 170–3, 189–90
National Development Plan 87
National Evaluation System 368–9
National Informal Business Development Strategy (NIBDS) 186
National Upgrading Support Programme (NUSP) 125
native administration 166
Neighbourhood as Factory (NAF) 443–50
Neighbourhood Watches 167
networks
  Actor-Network Theory (ANT) 326
  clientelist networks 155–6
  informal networks within the state 124–6
  inside/institutional activism 50, 51, 53, 70, 74
New Public Management (NPM) 21, 110–11, 366–7
  loss of meaning 406–10
Ngwane, Trevor 111, 112, 115
Ngwenya, Jerome 301
'no one will know' 406
Nyatyoba, Angie 281

officials
  agency 20, 45, 69, 84, 122–3, 201–4, 463–5
  intentions/intentionality 242, 403–6, 463–5
  practices 10–11
  see also bureaucracy/bureaucrats
Olivier de Sardan, J-P. 12, 13
One Voice of All Hawkers Association 143, 155–6
operationalisation 398
Operation Clean Sweep 2, 143
Operation Khaniysa Movement (OKM) 106, 111–12, 115–27
  accountability 117–18
  institutionalisation 106, 107–8, 120, 128–9
  leadership selection 115–17
  new channels 123–7
  protest action 119–20, 121–2
  strategy 118–19
  values 120–3
  ward committees 114
Operation Reclaim 145
Osmond Lange Architects & Master Planners 282

park management 64–71
Parsons, Kermit 423
participatory institutions 456–61, 462
party (PR) councillors 109, 114, 118
Patil, Varun 436
Peace and Stability Policy Discussion Document 184–5
performance management 44
  Key Performance Areas (KPAs) 350–3, 365
  Key Performance Indicators (KPIs) 91, 93, 351, 352, 356, 365, 368, 413
  see also monitoring and evaluation
Phillips, Ron 421
Pieterson, Steve 296, 299, 300
Pingo, Nicolette 71–4
planned manufacturing districts 426
planning discipline 52–3
pockets of excellence 410
police action 39, 145, 181–2, 234
policy change, progressive 4–6, 410–4
policy goals 203
policy implementation 8, 389–92
policy instruments 20–1
  activists in the State 55–6, 69, 71–4, 75–6
  institutional activists 393–4
  instrumentation process/instrumentality 203–4
  policy-making and 203–4
  porous bureaucracies 399–403
  state rationalities 238–42, 405–6
policy-making
  genealogy of housing eviction policy 207–17
  policy instruments and 203–4
  social and political process 202
  stages 201–2
policy means 203

political instrument 69
political rationality 237, 238–9, 240
politics
deciphering public political choices 403–6
identity 52
inclusionary housing 86
interface with bureaucracy 42–5
invisibility 283–6
of unmapping 269–70, 406
porous bureaucracies 429–53
constructing land tenure for squatters 434–43
left art of government 429–30, 432–4, 443–50, 451–3
Neighbourhood as Factory (NAF) 443–50
policy instruments 399–403
situating state practices in space, time, and scale 430–1
post-apartheid moment 3, 5, 392
post-colonialism 15
power
creative power 91, 92
decentred conception of 366–7
inclusionary housing 91–4
Practices of the State in Urban Governance (PSUG) 19–20
private sector 39, 86, 95, 222–4, 278, 279, 280, 281
problematics of government 239
problem characterisation 202, 218–21
professional ethos 242
progressive change 4–6, 410–4
progressive cities 3, 53, 398–9, 419–28
progressive policies 6, 53, 198
pro-poor policies 32, 268, 277–82
protest action 110, 119–20, 121–2
proto-bureaucracy 165, 166, 176, 177, 181–3
public (state) housing 88, 91
public transcript 292, 311, 403–6
Purcell, M. 283

racialised identity 99–100
Ramokgopa, Kgosienthso 146, 148
Rancière, J. 451–2
Razon, N.A. 269, 270, 286
realistic management 61
reconstruction 5
refugees 38, 161, 162, 184, 186–8
regeneration, inner-city 37–9, 205, 206
reintegration programme 168
Reinventing Cities: Equity Planners Tell Their Stories (Krumholz and Clavel) 1–2
Rising Block Tariff System 333
Robinson, J. 278, 279
Roji, Ayanda 64–71
Rose, N. 239–40
Rosenthal, Pat 421
Rousseff, Dilma 459
Roy, A. 127, 269–70, 406, 431
Rugkhapan, N.T. 284
Ruiters, G. 319
Rutstein, Valerie 421

school-based institutional xenophobia 233–63
Department of Basic Education (DBE) 235–6, 241, 245, 249–58
Department of Home Affairs (DHA) 235–6, 241, 245, 252–3
Home Affair-isation of school 236, 237–44, 245–6, 247, 252–3, 258–9
immigration control 237, 244–58
institutional culture 252–3
learner identification 242–4
Memorandum of Understanding 245–6
South African School Administration and Management System (SASAMS) 246–9
subjectivation of officials and school staff 249–58
Schrock, Gregg 425, 427
scorecards 44, 347–56, 374, 379
Scott, J. 292, 311
Section 79 Committees 109, 110, 122–3, 334, 346, 362, 377, 379, 380–1
Segodi, Siphiwe 115, 125
Service Delivery Agreement (SDA) 330, 342
Shearer, Derek 424
Sidappa 443
social housing 276, 279, 280–1, 283–4
social movements
governmentalised 106
institutionalisation 106, 107–8, 120, 128–9
Social Movements Indaba 302, 306
see also Brazilian social movements
Socio-Economic Rights Institute (SERI) 120, 209–10, 211, 212, 218
Somali Association of South Africa 178
Somali shopkeepers 162, 169–71, 172–7, 178–80, 181–2
South African National Civic Organisation 167
South African Property Owners Association (SAPOA) 85, 86, 95
South African School Administration and Management System (SASAMS) 246–9
South African Water Caucus (SAWC) 302, 306–7
Soweto, politics of 36–7
Soweto Electricity Crisis Committee (SECC) 106, 111, 112
spaces of hope 5
Spatial Development Framework (SDF) 87, 88
Spatial Planning and Land Use Management Act (SPLUMA) 2013 87, 89
spatial transformation 87–8
spaza shopkeepers 162, 166, 169–71, 172–7, 178–80, 181–2, 184–5
Special Process for the Relocation of Evictees (SPRE) 198, 199, 204, 207–17, 222, 224
squatters, securing land tenure 434–43
state
anti-apartheid activists entering 3
bifurcated nature 15
City as local state 12–17
conceptualised in unified terms 2–3
construction 164
contract-state 387–8
creation of the state at the margins 138
delivering state 12
developmental state 14
formation 164–5
heterogeneity 15–16
informalisation 137–9

informal networks 124–6
post-colonialism 15
rationalities 237–44, 403–6
right and left hand 16–17
state capture 387
state housing 88, 91
state in/from the City 17–19
state-society binary/tryptic 400–1
subjectivation of state agents 238–42, 249–52
Stone, C. 9, 52
street activists, compared to institutional activists 393–6
street trader governance structures 2, 139–49, 402
area-based committees 141–2, 150–2
block leader system 143–4, 152–3
clientelist organisations 143, 155–6
formal electoral processes 148–9
Informal Traders' Forum 144–5
leaders' participation in everyday management of trade 149–56
Mayoral Steering Committee on Informal Trade 146–7, 148
Memorandum of Understanding 146
One Voice of All Hawkers Association 143, 155–6
Operation Clean Sweep 2, 143
organisation leaders 142–3
organised invasion of trading sites 155–6
space allocation 135–6, 150–4
task teams 144–5, 152–3
Tshwane Barekisi Forum 146–7, 148–9, 153–4
subjectivation, state agents 238–42, 249–58
subordinates 292
suffering at work 397
symbolic violence 164, 165–8

tactical repertoires 28–9, 45
task teams 144–5, 152–3
Tatagiba, L. 51
Tau, Parks 58, 95–6, 273, 274–5, 377
Temporary Emergency Accommodation Provision (TEAP) policy 198, 199, 207–17, 222, 223, 224, 225
tendering process 44–5
Tendler, Judith 390, 400
'Thembelihle 14' 120
Thembelihle Crisis Committee (TCC) 106, 112–14, 119–20, 124–5, 126
Thimappa, Kagodu 439
Tikly, L. 239
Tissington, K. 220
Todes, A. 278, 279
transcripts 292, 311, 403–6
transformation
of citizenship 105
City Transformation Unit 81, 82, 89, 92, 94, 95, 96
contentious cause 464
education policies 235
left art of government 5
spatial transformation 87–8, 267
transformative policies 6
Transient Oriented Development (ToD) 88
transitional residential accommodation 209
transitioning neighbourhood 270–2
Tshwane Barekisi Forum 146–7, 148–9, 153–4
Tshwane Informal Traders Representative Committee 148–9
twilight institutions 136, 138

Umphilo waManzi 295
uMzinyathi, water access 296, 312–14
Un-Habitat 88
United Nations High-Commission for Refugees (UNHCR) 39, 178, 180
unmapping 269–70, 406
Urban Development Boundary 35
Urban Development Framework (UDF) 71
Urban Development Zone 205
urban governance 7–10, 50–6, 137, 204–6
urban management 36, 38, 63
Urban Morphology Institute 88

van Wyk, J. 89
Verhoeven, I. 54
Verryn, Bishop Paul 39
Viswas Nagar 444–5, 450
Vosloorus Micro Traders Association 150

ward councillors 109, 110, 114, 318
Washington, Harold 433, 426
water services 325–59
academic-activists 306, 311–12
activist engagement 301–6, 317–19
Blue Drop and Green Drop Assessments 334
Coalition Against Water Privatisation 303
corporatisation model 328
cutting off water 297
deceptive lens 308–12
Department of Water and Sanitation (DWS) 332–3
Environment and Infrastructure and Services Department (EISD) 330–1, 337, 347–8, 352
in eThekwini *see* eThekwini Water and Sanitation (EWS)
Growth and Development Strategy (GDS) 334–5, 337–9, 362
hydropolitics 292
informal settlements 339, 352, 354
Integrated Development Plan (IDP) 334, 338, 340–2
Johannesburg Water (JW) 328, 331, 340, 342, 353
local councillor involvement 315–17
local level planning 334–6
national government role 332–5
non-human actants 337–40
oversight of water delivery 345–58
paying for water 297–312
prepayment meters 325–6
Rising Block Tariff System 334
Service Delivery Agreement 330, 342
service delivery reform 328–31
South African Water Caucus (SAWC) 302, 306–7
tackling water access 312–19
water conservation 339

Water Dialogues-South Africa 295
Water Resources and Biodiversity (WR&B) 330
Water Services Regulation and Policy Development (WSR&PD) 330
water tankers 313–14
weapons of the weak 91
Webb, Lee 424
Wentzel, Webber 114
Westcliff Flats Residents Association (WFRA) 302–3, 305
wicked problems 202, 219
Wiewel, Wim 421–2
Wilson, Z. 307
Witts School of Architecture and Planning 2, 19–20, 66
Workers' Party (*Partidos dos Trabalhadores*) 456–7
xenophobia
bureaucratisation of 162, 165–8
causes of 233–4
officialisation of a xenophobic rationality 184–90
police involvement 181–2, 234
xenophobic pogroms 2008 30, 162, 167, 168–83
see also school-based institutional xenophobia

Zanokhanyo Retailers Association (ZRA) 169–70, 172–3, 176, 181–2
Zille, Helen 168, 172
zones of exception 33
Zulu, Lindiwe 189
Zuma, Jacob 368
Zwane, Simphiwe 115, 119, 120, 121–2, 123, 124

www.ingramcontent.com/pod-product-compliance
Lightning Source LLC
LaVergne TN
LVHW010731020926
846742LV00029B/36
* 9 7 8 1 8 0 0 0 8 5 4 7 3 *